The European Union and Its Eastern Neighbourhood

This edited volume brings together some of the most important scholarly perspectives – in the form of both journal article reprints and original contributions – on the structure and dynamics of the EU's multi-layered relations with its Eastern neighbours within the Eastern Partnership (EaP) framework and beyond.

In May 2019, the EU's EaP – an ambitious and sophisticated policy framework, conjoining elements of cooperation and integration, with the EU's six Eastern neighbours, i.e. Ukraine, Belarus, Moldova, Georgia, Armenia and Azerbaijan – turned ten years. This anniversary, in conjunction with repeatedly voiced critique by scholars and policy-makers alike regarding the framework's effectiveness and utility, led the EU to submit the EaP to a fundamental auditing and revision.

Structured around both enduring and emerging issues in the broader EU–Eastern neighbourhood framework, this book provides a retrospective analysis of key structural and relational challenges, unfolding regional dynamics, distinctive forms of bilateral/multilateral engagement, whilst also offering a critical perspective on the contested future relations between the EU and its Eastern neighbours. Looking backwards and providing a critical and thorough assessment of the first ten years of the EaP in practice, this book thinks forward and gauges its many potential future avenues. This comes at a crucial moment, as the EU and its six Eastern neighbours are in search of new and mutually acceptable forms of association.

Andriy Tyushka is Senior Research Fellow in the European Neighbourhood Policy Chair at the College of Europe in Natolin, Poland. He published widely on IR theory, European security and EU foreign policy. His latest book publication is the co-edited volume *States, International Organizations and Strategic Partnerships* (2019).

Tobias Schumacher is Professor of International Relations and Chairholder of the European Neighbourhood Policy Chair at the College of Europe, Natolin campus (Warsaw) and Associate Professor in European Studies at the Department of Historical and Classical Studies (IHK) at the Norwegian University of Science and Technology (NTNU), Trondheim. He is the lead editor of *The Routledge Handbook on the European Neighbourhood Policy* (2018), and his articles have appeared in journals such as *Journal of Common Market Studies*, *Geopolitics*, *Democratization*, *Mediterranean Politics*, *European Security*, *Contemporary Politics*, *Global Discourse* and others.

The European Union and Its Eastern Neighbourhood

Whither 'Eastern Partnership'?

Edited by
Andriy Tyushka and Tobias Schumacher

LONDON AND NEW YORK

First published 2022
by Routledge
2 Park Square, Milton Park, Abingdon, Oxon, OX14 4RN

and by Routledge
605 Third Avenue, New York, NY 10158

Routledge is an imprint of the Taylor & Francis Group, an informa business

Introduction © 2022 Tobias Schumacher
Chapters 1 and 12 © 2022 University of Glasgow
Chapters 2-4 6, 7 and 9-11 © 2022 Taylor & Francis
Chapter 5 © 2022 Istituto Affari Internazionali
Chapter 8 © 2022 European International Studies Association
Chapter 13 © 2022 Andriy Tyushka and Tobias Schumacher
Conclusion © 2022 Andriy Tyushka

All rights reserved. No part of this book may be reprinted or reproduced or utilised in any form or by any electronic, mechanical, or other means, now known or hereafter invented, including photocopying and recording, or in any information storage or retrieval system, without permission in writing from the publishers.

Trademark notice: Product or corporate names may be trademarks or registered trademarks, and are used only for identification and explanation without intent to infringe.

British Library Cataloguing in Publication Data
A catalogue record for this book is available from the British Library

ISBN: 978-0-367-53895-8 (hbk)
ISBN: 978-0-367-53898-9 (pbk)
ISBN: 978-1-003-08363-4 (ebk)

DOI: 10.4324/9781003083634

Typeset in Bembo
by codeMantra

Publisher's Note
The publisher accepts responsibility for any inconsistencies that may have arisen during the conversion of this book from journal articles to book chapters, namely the inclusion of journal terminology.

Disclaimer
Every effort has been made to contact copyright holders for their permission to reprint material in this book. The publishers would be grateful to hear from any copyright holder who is not here acknowledged and will undertake to rectify any errors or omissions in future editions of this book.

Contents

List of tables, chart and figures	ix
Citation information	xiii
Notes on contributors	xv
Acknowledgements	xvii
Foreword	xix
KATHARINÁ MATHERNOVÁ	

Introduction: The European Union, its Eastern Neighbourhood and an Evolving Structured Engagement within and beyond the Eastern Partnership Framework   1
TOBIAS SCHUMACHER

PART I
The EU's Eastern Partnership and Regional Dynamics: Enduring Issues and Contending Perspectives   17

1 The European Union's 'Ideal Self' in the Post-Soviet Space   19
CRISTIAN NITOIU

2 Between the Eastern Partnership and Eurasian Integration: Explaining Post-Soviet Countries' Engagement in (Competing) Region-Building Projects   39
LAURE DELCOUR

3 "The transformative power of Europe" beyond enlargement: the EU's performance in promoting democracy in its neighbourhood   58
TANJA A. BÖRZEL AND BIDZINA LEBANIDZE

4 The Geopoliticisation of the EU's Eastern Partnership   77
DAVID CADIER

5 The Unintended Consequences of a European Neighbourhood
   Policy without Russia 100
   TOM CASIER

6 Bringing "the political" back into European security:
   challenges to the EU's ordering of the Eastern Partnership 113
   LICÍNIA SIMÃO

PART II
The EU's Bilateral Engagement with Eastern Neighbours:
A Growing Menu of Choice 129

7 State building and European integration in Ukraine 131
   KATARYNA WOLCZUK

8 When Goliath meets Goliath: how Russia and the EU
   created a vicious circle of instability in Moldova 147
   RYHOR NIZHNIKAU

9 The Politics of Flexibility: Exploring the Contested
   Statehood–EU Actorness Nexus in Georgia 163
   MADALINA DOBRESCU AND TOBIAS SCHUMACHER

10 Armenia and Belarus: caught between the EU's and Russia's
   conditionalities? 180
   ALENA VIEIRA AND SYUZANNA VASILYAN

11 The European Union and Belarus: democracy promotion by
   technocratic means? 198
   ELENA A. KOROSTELEVA

12 From 'Unilateral' to 'Dialogical': Determinants of EU–Azerbaijan
   Negotiations 216
   ESKE VAN GILS

PART III
Looking Backward: The EU, the Eastern Neighbours and the
'Eastern Partnership' a Decade Past 239

13 Looking Backward: Deliverables and Drawbacks of the Eastern
   Partnership during 2009–2020 241
   ANDRIY TYUSHKA AND TOBIAS SCHUMACHER

Conclusion: The EU and its Eastern Neighbourhood – whither 'Eastern Partnership'? 265
ANDRIY TYUSHKA

Annexes 279
Annex 1 Content Analysing the Joint Declarations of the Eastern Partnership Summits in 2009–2017 281
Annex 2 Studying EU-Eastern Neighbours Relations Within and Beyond the Eastern Partnership in 2009–2020: A Bibliometric Perspective 291
Index 339

Tables, chart and figures

Tables

1.1	The presence of role expectation and legitimacy in the EU's ideal Self and post-Soviet states' perceptions of the EU	27
3.1	Consistency and effectiveness of democratic conditionality	62
3.2	The groups of ENP states	69
13.1	Interlocking dimensions of EU–Eastern neighbours relations (2009–2019)	247
13.2	'20 Deliverables for 2020': Monitoring and implementation progress (February 2020)	255
A1.1	Co-occurrences of policy clauses and partnership principles vis-à-vis EaP countries in EaP Joint Declarations 2009–2017	285
A1.2	EaP countries co-occurrences in EaP Joint Declarations 2009–2017	285
A1.3	Co-occurrences of policy issues vis-à-vis EaP countries in EaP Joint Declarations 2009–2017	285
A1.4	Distribution dynamics of policy issues in EaP Joint Declarations throughout 2009–2017 (no. of occurrences and relative shares, %)	288
A2.1	Co-occurrences of clustered topics vis-à-vis EaP countries in the EaP scholarship 2009–2020	317
A2.2	Correlations of clustered topics vis-à-vis EaP countries in the EaP scholarship 2009–2020	319

Chart

I.1	The structure of the EaP framework	7

Figures

3.1	Decision tree for EU consistency and effectiveness in the ENP countries	70
5.1	Summary of the 'unintended consequences' model and its application to the case of EU decoupling of its East European policies	103
13.1	(a&b). The state of EU-EaP countries' linkage and approximation in 2011–2017	250
A1.1	Occurrences of countries in EaP Joint Declarations 2009–2017	284
A1.2	Co-occurrences of 'gradual rapprochement' and 'differentiation' clauses vis-à-vis EaP countries in EaP Joint Declarations 2009–2017	284

A1.3	Distribution dynamics of policy issues in EaP Joint Declarations throughout 2009–2017 (no. of occurrences)	284
A1.4	Distribution of policy issues in EaP Joint Declaration 2009	287
A1.5	Distribution of policy issues in EaP Joint Declaration 2017	287
A2.1	Semantic map of the EaP scholarship 2009–2020: a clustered term networks view	294
A2.2	The EaP scholarship 2009–2020: publication performance	294
A2.3	Publishing 'homes' of the EaP scholarship 2009–2020: journal outlets and productivity	295
A2.4	Locating the research objects of the EaP scholarship 2009–2020: EaP countries in focus (occurrences)	296
A2.5	The EaP scholarship 2009–2020: disciplinary diversity and main research approaches	297
A2.6	The EaP scholarship 2009–2020: main research approaches and research designs	298
A2.7	The EaP scholarship 2009–2020: main research approaches and research methods	298
A2.8	The EaP scholarship 2009–2020: main research approaches and research methods (focus on unspecified research methods)	299
A2.9	The EaP scholarship 2009–2020: research methods development (focus on unspecified research methods)	300
A2.10	The EaP scholarship 2009–2020: research methods development (focus on qualitative research methods)	301
A2.11	The EaP scholarship 2009–2020: research methods development (focus on quantitative research methods)	302
A2.12	The EaP scholarship 2009–2020: research methods development (focus on mixed research methods)	303
A2.13	The spatial dimension of the EaP: Occurrences of space designations in the EaP scholarship 2009–2020	303
A2.14	Occurrences of space designations in the EaP scholarship 2009–2020 (focus on non-specified regionality of the EaP)	304
A2.15	Occurrences of space designations in the EaP scholarship 2009–2020 (focus on the EaP space as the 'EU's Eastern neighbourhood region')	305
A2.16	Occurrences of space designations in the EaP scholarship 2009–2020 (focus on the EaP space as the 'post-Soviet region/space')	306
A2.17	Co-occurrences of space designations and EaP countries in the EaP scholarship 2009–2020	307
A2.18	Co-occurrences of the EaP countries as objects of comparative analyses in the EaP scholarship 2009–2020	308
A2.19	Georgia in a comparative outlook of the EaP scholarship 2009–2020	309
A2.20	Armenia in a comparative outlook of the EaP scholarship 2009–2020	310
A2.21	Azerbaijan in a comparative outlook of the EaP scholarship 2009–2020	311
A2.22	Ukraine in a comparative outlook of the EaP scholarship 2009–2020	312
A2.23	Moldova in a comparative outlook of the EaP scholarship 2009–2020	313
A2.24	Belarus in a comparative outlook of the EaP scholarship 2009–2020	314
A2.25	Analytical connections: co-occurrences of external actors and EaP countries in the EaP scholarship 2009–2020	314

A2.26 Analytical connections: co-occurrences of external actors and EaP
countries in the EaP scholarship 2009–2020 (focus on non-EU,
EUMS, EUINST and Russia)   315
A2.27 Issue areas and topical diversity of the EaP scholarship 2009–2020:
a comprehensive outlook   316
A2.28 Issue areas and topical diversity of the EaP scholarship 2009–2020:
a clustered topics outlook   316

Citation information

The chapters 1 to 12 in this book were originally published between 2015 and 2020 in the following journals: *Democratization, East European Politics, Eurasian Geography and Economics, Europe-Asia Studies, European Politics and Society, Geopolitics, Global Affairs, Problems of Post-Communism* and *The International Spectator: Italian Journal of International Affairs*. When citing this material, please use the original page numbering for each article, as follows:

Chapter 1

Nitoiu, C. (2018). The European Union's 'Ideal Self' in the Post-Soviet Space. *Europe-Asia Studies, 70*(5), 692–710.

Chapter 2

Delcour L. (2015). Between the Eastern Partnership and Eurasian Integration: Explaining Post-Soviet Countries' Engagement in (Competing) Region-Building Projects. *Problems of Post-Communism, 62*(6), 316–327.

Chapter 3

Börzel, T. A., & Lebanidze, B. (2017). "The transformative power of Europe" beyond enlargement: the EU's performance in promoting democracy in its neighbourhood. *East European Politics, 33*(1), 17–35.

Chapter 4

Cadier, D. (2019). The Geopoliticisation of the EU's Eastern Partnership. *Geopolitics, 24*(1), 71–99.

Chapter 5

Casier, T. (2019). The Unintended Consequences of a European Neighbourhood Policy without Russia. *The International Spectator, 54*(1), 76–88.

Chapter 6

Simão, L. (2017). Bringing "the political" back into European security: challenges to the EU's ordering of the Eastern Partnership. *East European Politics, 33*(3), 338–354.

Chapter 7

Wolczuk, K. (2019). State Building and European Integration in Ukraine. *Eurasian Geography and Economics, 60*(6), 736–754.

Chapter 8

Nizhnikau, R. (2016). When Goliath meets Goliath: how Russia and the EU created a vicious circle of instability in Moldova. *Global Affairs, 2*(2), 203–216.

Chapter 9

Dobrescu, M., & Schumacher, T. (2020). The Politics of Flexibility: Exploring the Contested Statehood–EU Actorness Nexus in Georgia. *Geopolitics, 25*(2), 407–427.

Chapter 10

Vieira, A., & Vasilyan, S. (2018). Armenia and Belarus: Caught between the EU's and Russia's conditionalities? *European Politics and Society, 19*(4), 471–489.

Chapter 11

Korosteleva, E. (2016). The European Union and Belarus: democracy promotion by technocratic means? *Democratization, 23*(4), 678–698.

Chapter 12

van Gils, E. (2018). From 'Unilateral' to 'Dialogical': Determinants of EU–Azerbaijan Negotiations. *Europe-Asia Studies, 70*(10), 1572–1596.

For any permission-related enquiries please visit:
http://www.tandfonline.com/page/help/permissions

Notes on contributors

Tanja A. Börzel is Professor of Political Science and holds the Chair for European Integration at the Otto-Suhr-Institute for Political Science, Freie Universität Berlin, Germany.

David Cadier is Researcher at the Center for International Studies (CERI), Sciences Po, Paris, France. He is also Adjunct Lecturer at Sciences Po's School of International Affairs (PSIA) and Associate at LSE IDEAS, the foreign policy think-tank of the London School of Economics (LSE).

Tom Casier is Jean Monnet Chair and Reader in International Relations at the University of Kent's 'Brussels School of International Studies' (BSIS). He is currently Director of the Global Europe Centre (GEC) at the University of Kent, UK.

Laure Delcour is Associate Professor in International Relations and EU Studies in the Institute of European Studies at the University Sorbonne Nouvelle, Paris, France.

Madalina Dobrescu is Postdoctoral Research Fellow in International Relations at the Vienna School of International Studies, Vienna, Austria.

Elena A. Korosteleva is Professor of International Politics, and Jean Monnet Chair of European Politics at the School of Politics and International Relations at the University of Kent, UK. She is Principal Investigator of the UK Government-sponsored (Global Challenges Research Fund) COMPASS project (2017–21).

Bidzina Lebanidze is Postdoctoral Fellow and Lecturer at the Institute for Slavic and Caucasus Studies at Friedrich Schiller University Jena, Germany. He is also Associate Professor of International Relations at Ilia State University in Tbilisi, Georgia, and an analyst with the Georgian Institute of Politics (GIP).

Cristian Nitoiu is Lecturer in Diplomacy and International Governance at the Institute for Diplomacy and International Governance at Loughborough University London, UK. He is also Co-Founder and Deputy Director of the Craiova-based Center for Foreign Policy and Security Studies (CFPSS).

Ryhor Nizhnikau is Senior Research Fellow at the Finnish Institute of International Affairs (FIIA) in Helsinki and member of FIIA's 'EU's Eastern Neighbourhood and Russia' Research Programme.

Tobias Schumacher is Associate Professor in European Studies at the Department of Historical and Classical Studies (IHK) at the Norwegian University of Science and

Technology (NTNU), Trondheim, Norway. He is also Professor of International Relations and Chairholder of the European Neighbourhood Policy Chair at the College of Europe, Natolin campus, Warsaw, Poland.

Licínia Simão is Assistant Professor at the School of Economics and Senior Researcher at the Centre for Social Studies at the University of Coimbra, Portugal.

Andriy Tyushka is Senior Research Fellow in the European Neighbourhood Policy Chair at the College of Europe, Natolin, Poland.

Eske van Gils is Assistant Professor at the Faculty of Arts at the University of Groningen, the Netherlands.

Syuzanna Vasilyan is Research Fellow at the Université Libre de Bruxelles (ULB) and scientific collaborator at the University's Institute for European Studies (IEE-ULB).

Alena Vieira is Assistant Professor of Political Science and International Relations at the *Research Center in Political Science (CICP)* at the University of Minho, Braga, Portugal.

Kataryna Wolczuk is Professor of East European Politics at the Centre for Russian, European and Eurasian Studies (CREES) at the University of Birmingham, UK. She is also Associate Fellow at the Russia and Eurasian Programme of Chatham House at The Royal Institute of International Affairs in London, UK.

Acknowledgements

On the occasion of the recent tenth anniversary of the EU's Eastern Partnership, this edited volume brings together a set of curated articles, published in recent years by influential Taylor & Francis journals, as well as new material, exclusively written for this volume. Addressing the European Union's Eastern Partnership and relations between the EU and its Eastern neighbours during the period 2009–2020, this volume provides the select articles with a platform to speak to one another and be complemented by hitherto unpublished analysis and data.

We are grateful to Routledge for granting us the right to reuse the select articles that have been already published in the following Taylor & Francis journals: *Democratization*, *East European Politics*, *Eurasian Geography and Economics*, *Europe-Asia Studies*, *European Politics and Society*, *Geopolitics*, *Global Affairs*, *Problems of Post-Communism* and *The International Spectator: Italian Journal of International Affairs*.

Our sincere thanks also go to the authors of the reprinted articles for their important contribution to the analysis of the Eastern Partnership and EU-Eastern neighbours relations at large. Their findings, many of which found their way into this volume, have enriched the scholarly debate and made it more vibrant.

In a highly populated field of scholarship such as the one that this volume seeks to address, striking a balance is never easy. Thus, our approach towards selecting already published material and reprint has been guided solely by our subjective perspective on the topic of this volume, its evolution over the past years, and our editorial view on how best to structure this book.

Foreword

Academic reflections such as this volume provide an excellent overview and in-depth analysis of the Eastern Partnership (EaP) framework and are a valuable tool for developing EU policy-making in an informed and relevant way. This volume's focus, revolving around both enduring issues and emerging challenges of relations between the EU and Eastern neighbours within and beyond the EaP, cuts across multiple structural and relational aspects that are crucial for the EaP's future.

As both the scholarly and think-tank debate on the matter continue, this volume also engages with some of the emerging five priorities areas that were recently outlined in a Joint Communication to be confirmed by the 2021 EaP Summit:

- Building resilient and integrated economies and improving connectivity;
- Strengthening the rule of law and security;
- Boosting the Green transition;
- Digital transformations;
- Supporting inclusive societies.

As the new EaP framework takes shape, there is clearly strong support by many that it is important to put people first and to deliver tangible benefits in people's lives and address their concerns. Today, over ten years into the EaP, one could reasonably ask what has this framework achieved.

The EU put in place far-reaching Association Agreements and Deep and Comprehensive Free Trade Areas with Georgia, Moldova and Ukraine, and it has also established a visa-free regime. The EU has also concluded a new Comprehensive and Enhanced Partnership Agreement with Armenia. Negotiations on a new agreement with Azerbaijan are ongoing. And the EU has continued to support the people of Belarus. In this context, differentiation and inclusivity are and will remain at the heart of the EaP framework. As this edited volume sees the light of day, it can be confidently said that the EaP has brought about tangible benefits for the citizens across the six EaP countries indeed.

The EU has helped sustain economic development over the past 12 years by supporting more than 70,000 small and medium enterprises in the region, leveraging €2 billion worth of loans and creating more than 30,000 jobs.

Economic development is closely linked to investing in people. Young people need all the relevant skills and qualifications in order to take active part in a rapidly changing labour market. Strengthening investment in young people's skills, entrepreneurship and employability remains a priority for the EU. Erasmus+ has already enabled nearly 25,000 academic exchanges with students from EaP countries. The first European School beyond the EU borders (Tbilisi, Georgia) opened its doors in 2019 to over 30 of the brightest students from across all six partner countries, providing them with an invaluable educational opportunity.

Significant progress has been made as regards improving transport links and infrastructure, and boosting energy resilience and efficiency. The Trans-European Transport Network (TEN-T) Investment Action Plan identifies priority investments, estimating the construction of 4,800 km of roads, but also putting in place, or modernising, railroads, ports and logistical centres in the region by 2030. This will enable further economic growth and jobs creation across EaP countries, and help bring societies closer together.

The EU has a strong track record in supporting energy efficiency transformation in the region, by working hand in hand with local authorities. To date, nearly 400 municipalities have signed up to the EU's Covenant of Mayors climate and energy goals. This is the highest number of signatories in any part of the world. This will help reduce CO_2 emissions in the EaP region.

Challenges remain in two key areas: democracy and security. The EU has a strong ambition to strengthen democratic structures, improve citizens' access to functioning and effective justice systems, tackle corruption and provide free and independent media. To deliver on this in the coming years, political ambition to drive through reforms will be key, in particular the unwavering political will of government stakeholders in all EaP partner countries. Achieving resilience will always be the result of political engagement of our partners in the Eastern neighbourhood – at both state and societal levels – rather than a matter of EU resource allocation alone.

Second, the EU continues to be faced with challenges in the field of security, such as disinformation, hybrid threats or protracted conflicts. More efforts are needed to address these challenges and, therefore, contribute further to strengthening resilience.

Resilience as the overarching policy framework of the EaP proves more relevant than ever, in particular amidst a pandemic that is likely to bring about lasting economic and social consequences. 'Team Europe' is a concrete example of the efforts to tackle SARS-CoV-2, as regards both the health impact and the long-term socio-economic consequences of the crisis. It brings together the full range of expertise, financial assistance and political clout to address an unprecedented global crisis. In support of EaP partners, the EU undertook an unprecedented exercise of thorough re-purposing of financial assistance shortly after the outbreak of the pandemic, mobilising in just ten weeks a considerable amount of EU financing. Not least thanks to such agility and responsiveness, it is hardly surprising that results of a recent opinion poll have demonstrated that the EU is considered the most trusted external actor by 60% of people in the EaP countries.

Engaging with citizens and civil society stakeholders remains key for the EU in advancing the EaP policy. Being in close and regular contact with academic and think-tank networks is part and parcel of this engagement. Insightful studies like this volume, edited by Andriy Tyushka and Tobias Schumacher, as well as debates like the High-Level Think Tank Event of July 2020, are only the latest examples of these efforts. They provide a necessary and much appreciated platform to further develop and deepen cooperation with the scholarly community in EU Member States and across the partner countries, as we generate knowledge-based policies and develop the post-2020 deliverables to take the EaP policy to the next level.

Kathariná Mathernová
Deputy Director General for Neighbourhood Policy
and Enlargement Negotiations, European Commission

Introduction

The European Union, its Eastern Neighbourhood and an evolving structured engagement within and beyond the Eastern Partnership Framework

Tobias Schumacher

On 18 June 2020, EU Heads of State and Government and their counterparts from the six Eastern Partnership (EaP-6) countries – Armenia, Azerbaijan, Belarus, Georgia, Moldova, and Ukraine – met for the first time since they had gathered at the EaP Summit on 24 November 2017 in Brussels. Due to the global SARS-CoV-2 pandemic, the meeting took place in the form of a video conference and, while addressing the multi-layered repercussions of COVID-19 on local healthcare and socio-economic systems, as well as the response by the EU and its EaP interlocutors, revolved exclusively around assessing the current state of the EaP and its future. Following up on an EaP foreign affairs ministers meeting, held less than a week before, the gathering represented the first opportunity to take issue with the Joint Communication, published by the European Commission and the High Representative of the Union for Foreign Affairs and Security Policy (HR/VP) on 18 March 2020, entitled 'Eastern partnership policy beyond 2020: Reinforcing Resilience – an Eastern Partnership that delivers for all' (European Commission and HR/VP 2020). Initially presented by European Commissioner for Enlargement and Neighbourhood Relations Olivér Várhelyi and HR/VP Josep Borrell, the document offered proposals for the long-term objectives of the EaP beyond 2020 and served as a basis for discussion at the December 2021 EaP Summit whose main purpose was to define and adopt the framework's future policy priorities.

The video conference was a first step towards finalization and adoption of a revised EaP framework and a first attempt at preparing for the 2021 Summit. It represented a logical continuation of the high-level conference of 14 May 2019 that had marked the tenth anniversary of the EaP and, at the same time, was the starting point of a public consultation process, destined to motivate stakeholders from EU Member States and the EaP-6 to submit their views on the framework's future strategic direction (Schumacher 2020). This consultation process, put in motion by then Commission President Jean-Claude Juncker and Commissioner for Neighbourhood and Enlargement Negotiations Johannes Hahn, replicated the 2014–2015 public review process of the European Neighbourhood Policy (ENP) (Furness et al. 2019) and was motivated by the ambition to increase inclusiveness and fill with life the notion of co-ownership, propagated for years by the EU (Wolczuk 2017: 7).

The celebratory mood, displayed by EU decision-makers at the May 2019 high-level conference, and the participatory character of the ensuing public consultation process leading to the 2020 Joint Communication and the 2021 EaP Summit, could not, however, conceal at least two important dichotomies: first, ever since the EaP was created, it has been exposed to a plethora of critical voices demanding substantial change and pointing out that the framework, in its original format and structure, was ill-conceived. Scholars and think tankers alike regularly articulated a perceived need 'to move into a higher gear' (de Waal and Youngs 2015) and called for submitting the EaP to 'deep rethinking' (Gromadzki 2015), refreshing (Casier et al. 2014), and even reviving (Carp and Schumacher 2015). At the same time, though, and except for the 2019 consultation process and the corresponding 2021 EaP Summit, as well as the decision, taken in November 2017, to implant into the EaP so-called '20 Deliverables for 2020' – a work plan destined to generate tangible results for citizens in the field of economy, governance, connectivity, and society –, throughout the past 12 years, the EaP has demonstrated remarkable resilience and immunity towards societal and governmental calls for reform.[1]

This is directly linked to the second dichotomy which is marked by the long-standing existence of differing and, to some extent, even diametrically opposed approaches to the EaP. Among the EaP-6, Azerbaijan and Belarus are positioned at one end, as they have been regarding the EaP mainly as a tool for enhancing their external legitimacy and utilizing it for exclusively transactional purposes to extract tangible material economic and financial gains while outrightly rejecting conditionality-related aspects. This is contrasted by the motivations of regimes in Ukraine, Georgia, and, in a certain sense, Moldova (henceforth referred to as 'the associated EaP-3'), all of which are situated at the other end, as they are linked with the EU through Association Agreements (AAs) that aim at political association, economic integration, and legislative approximation. For more than a decade, these regimes have been oscillating between issuing a minimum and a maximum set of demands, ranging from the replacement of a supposedly narrow AA-centred approach by an 'Association *plus*' that revolves around deeper sectoral integration into at least the EU's Energy and Digital Unions and the Schengen Area, as well as the creation of bilateral customs unions, to straightforward demands for a clear-cut EU membership perspective. This is complemented by Armenia, whose Comprehensive and Enhanced Partnership Agreement (CEPA) of 24 November 2017 places it somewhere between these two ends, by providing for deeper cooperation with the EU in a variety of policy fields and issue areas without, however, entailing a viable economic integration perspective into the EU's Internal Market.

The heterogeneous interests of the EaP-6 and their variegated views on both the nature and future of the EaP have been exposed to equally diverse and fragmented attitudes and positions on the part of EU Member States. The majority of them regard cooperation in the context of the EaP as a journey without a predetermined destination and, therefore, more often than not, have placed emphasis on practices of partnering rather than partnership and on cooperation rather than on supporting EaP countries to become future EU members. Put simply: whereas in their view the EaP is what partners make of it, other Member States, such as, for example, Poland and the Baltic countries, support considerably closer ties with all EaP-6 and have, time and again, underlined that the EaP needs to be an instrument preparing particularly the associated EaP-3 for EU membership. Against this backdrop, it did not come as a surprise that most EU Member States regarded the May 2019 high-level conference and the public consultation merely as an opportunity to manifest (a) that the EaP was still alive and operational, (b) their on-going commitment to help EaP regimes transform and modernize their political and economic systems, and that (c) focusing on the generation of tangible transformation dividends was the sole way forward.

Obviously, these divergent interests had to have an impact on the 2020 Joint Communication itself. Notably, it almost inevitably omitted the charting of an undisputable *raison d'être* for the EaP – like other EaP-related documents, issued throughout the years by the European Commission and the European External Action Service (EEAS), or the Council, for that matter. In other words, also this document does not engage with the key question the EaP has been exposed to virtually since its inception, notably whether association, in all its different manifestations, is an end in itself or, instead, a means to an end that can provide all EaP countries with truly tailor-made, performance-based, and unmistakeably defined offers in response to their respective ambitions and expectations. Instead, and while portraying differentiation, greater ownership, enhanced focus, and greater flexibility – the four cornerstones of the 2015 ENP review – as the EaP's 'key achievements' (European Commission and HR/VP 2020: 2), the Joint Communication borrows extensively, and rather uncritically, from the EU Global Strategy's focus on resilience-building (HR/VP 2016). In this way, it perpetuates the much-quoted 'resilience turn' (Joseph and Juncos 2019) in EU foreign policy and contributes to the further cementing of neoliberal 'de-responsibilization' practices (Joseph 2016: 370), increasingly visible in EU-neighbourhood relations in recent years.

Seen from this perspective, the 2020 Joint Communication and the process leading to it are embedded in multiple and multi-layered dichotomies, two of which are touched upon above, and follow established path dependencies, but also embody and exemplify the unabated duality of continuity and change in the EU's proliferating forms of structured engagement with the EaP-6.

This volume acknowledges this feature and embraces, through its design and structure, both a retrospective and prospective outlook and, therefore, a longer and wider view on the EaP and EU relations with the EaP-6.

On the one hand, it concentrates on the identification and analysis of enduring issues that have been affecting the evolution, implementation, and outcomes of the EaP. On the other hand, this volume addresses emergent trends and challenges, while providing a scholarly platform for the articulation of contending views on these. To this end, and instead of following one coherent research design, this volume brings together a curated set of Web-of-Science-sourced and methodologically sampled journal articles published until the end of 2020 across distinct disciplinary outlets.[2] It aims to provide these studies with a space to speak to, and engage with, one another. This is in keeping with the notion that there exists a rich and highly diverse body of scholarly literature on the EaP, EU-EaP countries relations, and EaP countries as such, and that it merits to be looked at and interpreted in an inclusionary fashion. In order to account for more recent developments in the further evolution and implementation of the EaP, this volume combines the chosen reprinted articles with an additional original contribution. Looking backwards and providing, in a synthesized fashion, a critical and thorough assessment of the first 12 years of the EaP in practice, this book also thinks forward: in its third part, it features one newly added, stand-alone chapter that discusses, mainly from a practical policy perspective, achievements and shortcomings in a longitudinal perspective, and sheds some light on perceptions and misperceptions of what the EaP is and can realistically deliver. Moreover, this volume offers a set of synthesizing conclusions that both touch upon the broad contours of the scholarly and policy-oriented *acquis* on the EaP (2009–2020) and critically address multiple modalities of future relationship formats. It does so against the backdrop of altering regional and neighbour-specific scope conditions and an increasingly fragmented, post-Brexit EU that is struggling to carve out a more tangible role in the contested geo-strategic space beyond its Eastern frontiers. Two original and comprehensive annexes, produced with the help of computer-assisted qualitative content analysis (CAQDAS), featuring the five EaP Summit Declarations adopted during 2009–2017 and the existing body of EaP scholarship, produced between 2009 and late 2020, complete this volume. More concretely, with a total of nine figures, tables, and diagrams, the first annex offers visualizations of quantified data and hitherto unpublished findings as to which policy and cooperation issues gained/lost discursive salience over the course of time. The second annex provides for an annotated, topic-related bibliography, covering the period from 2009 until the end of 2020. In order to map both the evolution and the varied contribution of the existing scholarship on the EaP, this annex provides a structured analysis of spatial and temporal characteristics of the evolution of EaP scholarship, its disciplinary and methodological diversity, issues covered, and their salience. It also supports the discussion by offering rich visual material (altogether 30 figures and tables) that draw on the data mined from content and bibliometric analyses. As such, this volume also aims to serve as a 'go-to' reference source for anyone interested in the scholarly analysis of the many and multi-layered dimensions of the EaP since it was created.

With its eclectic approach, this book is intended to complement other collective or single-authored volumes that address, either from an empirical and exclusively descriptive-analytical or theory-informed perspective, select aspects of the EaP as such. For instance, most recently, Rouet and Pascariu (2019) have brought together numerous, hitherto unheard voices with a view to discuss conceptual and policy-focused dimensions of the EaP, the EU's eastern neighbourhood, and individual EaP countries through the lens of resilience. Even though many of the contributions are disconnected from the book's presumptive conceptual lens, these chapters, as well as some of those that are – or at least claim to be – rooted in the volume's conceptual underpinnings, make an interesting contribution on some unexplored dimensions in the broader context of EU–Eastern neighbourhood relations, such as hierarchy, economic resilience, as well as the link between resilience and regime durability. Another collective volume, recently edited by Papadimitriou et al. (2019), addresses only Ukraine from among all EaP-6, next to Central European countries as well as Uzbekistan. Though this volume does not give equal salience to the remaining EaP countries, it uses Ukraine as a valuable case study to discuss the determinants and conditions that affect EU performance in post-communist Europe, as well as potential differences in the projection of EU power between EU enlargement policies and the ENP. Of a more generic nature is the volume, edited by Fawn, published in 2019. As is reflected by its title – *Managing Security Threats along the EU's Eastern Flanks* – its main focus lies on the identification and discussion of security threats in the EU's (wider) Eastern neighbourhood and how the EU – in comparison to other external actors – has been addressing them within and beyond the confines of the ENP. Prior to that, Korosteleva et al. (2018) have offered an important post-structuralist reading of the EU's role in parts of the Eastern neighbourhood by exploring the boundaries, as well as the interplay, of 'the politics' and 'the political' and how these categories operate in relation to defining and locating the 'Self' and the 'Other' in parts of the EU's Eastern neighbourhood. Whereas chapters choose policy fields and issues such as institutional dynamics, security, and cross-border mobility as areas of their interrogation, or Azerbaijan as a single case study, the chapters in Flenley and Mannin (2018) draw on the insights of the Europeanization literature and apply the latter on the four policy dimensions economy, energy, migration, and language, and – as far as EaP countries are concerned – put the (empirical) lens on Belarus, Moldova, and Ukraine. In contrast, the volume by Kerikmäe and Chochia (2016), omitting a guiding framework of analysis, oscillates between, on the one hand, descriptive-analytical and often essayistic chapters that address issues in areas such as association, free trade, migration, environment, and innovation, and, on the other, almost exclusively legalistic accounts of some public and private law-related aspects that underpin bilateral relations between the EU and select EaP countries. Migration- and cross-border-related dynamics in the EU's Eastern neighbourhood feature in the volume by Liikanen et al. (2016) but are largely disconnected from scholarly debates on the EaP as such.

Among the very few monographs that deal, in one way or another, with the EaP, virtually all of them focus, to different degrees, on relational aspects, an EU-centric analysis of norms diffusion or influence and power projection at large – often in indirect or direct juxtaposition to Russia's competing interests and politics in EaP countries (Delcour 2017). More recent monographs concentrate convincingly on the study of the complexities of EU-induced domestic institutional change in Ukraine and Moldova (Nizhnikau 2018) or the analysis of EU democracy promotion efforts in five out of six EaP countries, highlighting the limited effects of EU policies on regime trajectories and how the former are conditioned by a multitude of domestic and transnational factors (Buscaneanu 2016). These studies are preceded by Korosteleva's monograph (2012), aimed at disentangling the notion of 'partnership' in EU-Eastern neighbours relations and drawing on the 'external governance' scholarship, as well as Delcour's early contribution (2011) on the EU's milieu-shaping attempts and temporary ambition to foster regionalization in what is considered as the 'post-Soviet space'.

The EaP: emergence, structure, and evolution of a complex policy framework

The creation of the EaP, formally launched at the first Prague EaP Summit in May 2009, is the outcome of both intense advocacy on the part of individual EU Member States and their subsequent pursuit of favour exchanging, veto playing, and issue linkage. By the same token, the EaP did not – as is discernible so often in past EU foreign policy initiatives – come into being as a result of a thorough and carefully undertaken country- or region-specific needs assessment. As far as advocacy is concerned, it is noteworthy that such efforts were already under way while the EU was still in the process of finalizing the 2004/2007 enlargement round and, with it, the final contours of the ENP. Already in January 2003, Poland, at the time still an accession country, submitted a non-paper with its 'proposals concerning the future shape of the enlarged EU towards the new eastern neighbours',[3] in which it argued for the strengthening of EU relations with future Eastern neighbours; the replacement of the EU's Partnership and Cooperation Agreements with Ukraine, Belarus, and Moldova by wide-ranging AAs; the inclusion of the Russian Federation into the European Economic Area; and a future EU membership promise for Ukraine. This non-paper was swiftly dismissed by other EU Member States' governments. Yet, it marked the beginning of a vibrant attempt – led mainly by Poland – to sensitize other Member States and EU institutions for the felt need to instil greater differentiation into the ENP and offer Eastern European neighbours – as opposed to non-European Southern neighbours – closer and more institutionalized ties. The situation only changed once Germany, in the context of its EU Council Presidency in the first half of 2007, proposed the creation of an 'ENP Plus'[4] – a broad proposal for deeper relations with EU neighbours, entailing the additional conclusion of sectoral agreements – and, more importantly, when French President Nicolas Sarkozy began pushing for the establishment of a Mediterranean Union/Union for the Mediterranean (UfM) in 2007/2008. Wary of potential veto playing by EU Member States' governments that did not regard the Mediterranean as a foreign policy priority, France, like other mainly southern European Member States, suddenly found itself in a position where it could no longer afford to ignore Polish-led policy advocacy efforts and oppose the launch of a more structured framework for EU engagement in Eastern Europe (Schumacher 2011).

Unlike the UfM (Bicchi and Gillespie 2011), the EaP was not endowed with its own secretariat, a secretary general or a rotating presidency, even though Poland, for example, has repeatedly called, in the past 12 years, for the creation of such joint institutions (Czaputowicz 2019). Also, the EaP was not endowed with its own exclusive and long-lasting funding streams but has been subject mainly to the European Neighbourhood and Partnership Instrument (ENPI, 2007–2014) and its successor, the European Neighbourhood Instrument (ENI, 2014–2020), as well as other, though not neighbourhood-specific EU financial instruments (Bossuyt et al. 2018).[5] This exposure has, throughout the years, consolidated a situation in which Eastern and Southern neighbours *de facto* competed with each other over limited financial aid, due to, first and foremost, the much-quoted 'north-south differentiation' (Gillespie 1997: 72), or even north-south split' (Behr and Tiilikainen 2015), in EU foreign policymaking towards Eastern Europe and the Southern Mediterranean.

At the same time, the EaP's scope is much broader and more ambitious than the project-based UfM, which is rooted in the principle of reinforced cooperation and leaves it to the discretion of EU Member States to involve themselves. Revolving around a two-track structure, and as can be seen in Chart I.1, the EaP features a bilateral track, composed of the three sub-tracks (a) political association and economic integration, (b) enhanced mobility, and (c) sectoral cooperation and a multilateral track. The latter is organized along (a) thematic platforms in the fields of democracy and good governance, economic integration/convergence, and energy security; (b) major stakeholders forums; and (c) the so-called flagship initiatives, addressing integrated border management, small- and medium-sized enterprises, electricity markets, environmental governance, and PPRD-East matters (that is, Prevention, Preparedness and Response to Natural and Man-made Disasters in the Eastern Partnership Countries).

Notwithstanding the breadth and sophistication of the EaP framework, the EU never clarified and, therefore, left unanswered the question of how the EaP relates to, and is linked with, the ENP, under whose 'roof' it is situated. On the occasion of the 2009 EaP Prague Summit, the inaugural Joint Declaration stipulated that the EaP constitutes a 'specific Eastern dimension of the European Neighbourhood Policy' (Council of the EU 2009); this was preceded by a similar statement on the part of the European Commission, which stated that the EaP would be 'respecting the character of the ENP as a single and coherent policy' (Commission 2008). In practice, though, it turned out that these lofty statements could not preclude the entire ENP from being negatively affected by the many divisions among EaP participants – emerging at regular intervals prior to, and during, virtually every EaP Summit. Emblematically, disagreements have

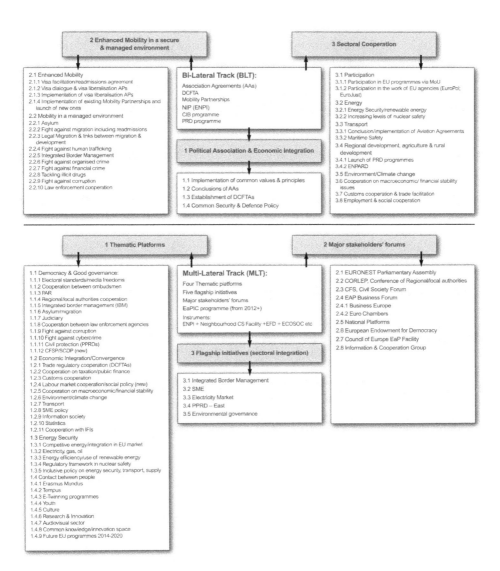

Chart I.1 The structure of the EaP framework.
Source: Casier et al. (2014).

been resurfacing over the same enduring issues, notably: (a) the EU's unwillingness to offer reform-minded EaP frontrunners an EU membership perspective and unequivocally commit to associated partners' 'European aspirations', as stipulated in the preamble of their respective AAs; (b) the unresolved Nagorno Karabakh conflict; (c) Russia's meddling in the domestic affairs of EaP countries and its corresponding violation of international law; as well as (d) the domestic situation in autocratically governed Belarus and the country's role in the EaP and, by extension, the ENP at large. In particular, as far as Belarus is concerned, the conceptual mismatch between the EaP and the ENP and with regard to the country's status in both frameworks is striking. It underlines the persisting lack of agreement among EU Member States' governments and the European Commission. The British-Danish letter to the Council of 28 January 2002 proposed granting Belarus – just like Moldova and Ukraine – a 'special neighbours status' that would provide for 'trade liberalization, closer relationships in Justice and Home Affairs, and/or privileged political dialogue with deeper cooperation in CFSP' in exchange for reforms (quoted after Tulmets 2017: 30). In contrast, on 9 December 2004, i.e. at a time when the ENP had already been launched, the European Commission declared that Belarus was a different partner and that the ENP 'is open to Belarus and all Mediterranean countries including Libya once they have met the necessary conditions for inclusion' (Commission 2004: 5). This wording, in conjunction with the Commission's December 2006 communication on the strengthening of the ENP (Commission 2006a), which omitted any mention of Belarus entirely, and the Commission's subsequent non-paper, entitled 'What the European Union could bring to Belarus' (Commission 2006b), created the impression that Belarus was not formally included in the ENP. Yet, as is argued elsewhere, EU Member States 'made the tactical choice in early 2004 to institutionalise the status quo of EU-Belarus relations in the ENP with the intention to counter pressure by prospective Member States to strengthen relations with Belarus, Ukraine and Moldova' (Bosse 2018: 291). That Belarus' hybrid status, sitting on the fence between the EaP and the ENP, became eventually consolidated is owed to Poland and Sweden – the lead advocates of the EU's 'critical engagement' approach. In 2008/2009, they convinced other (more critical) EU Member States' governments to agree on a compromise that, henceforth, meant letting Belarus become part of the EaP's multilateral track while formally not incorporating it – not even after early 2016 – into the framework's bilateral track, thus consolidating the ambiguity related to the conceptual linkage between the EaP and the ENP. The decision of the illegitimate regime of Alexander Lukashenko in the summer of 2021 to withdraw Belarus from the EaP at a time when the EU – in spite of its latest set of restrictive measures it has imposed on the Belarusian regime – still seemed willing to continue its collaboration with Belarus at least in the context of the EaP, serves as yet another stark reminder of the fact that the EU had never came to terms with Belarus' hybrid status in the ENP.

The EU and its Eastern neighbours: enduring regional issues and a growing menu of choice

The discussion above leads directly to the many and multi-layered issues addressed by the reprinted articles/chapters in this volume, dealing with regional dynamics and bilateral aspects of EU relations with the six EaP countries. As far as the former are concerned, seven overarching themes stand out that have been characterizing the debate on the EaP and that also shine through and inform, albeit to different degrees, the first six articles reprinted in Part I of this volume. The first two themes – *the EU's ideal Self* and *Eastern Europe as one space* – are inextricably linked with one another. The latter revolves around a striking ambiguity in the scholarly engagement with the EaP: 12 years into the study of EU engagement beyond its eastern borders, epistemological consensus over the nature and constituting parameters of the space the EaP targets continues to remain absent. Existing and predominantly used depictions, ranging from 'Eastern neighbourhood/Eastern neighbours' and 'Eastern neighbourhood region' to 'post-Soviet' states or the 'post-Soviet space/region', are not a matter of mere semantics. Instead, and apart from the fact that they point to a felt need to label the object of study, they hint at attached meanings scholars consciously or sub-consciously, implicitly or explicitly subscribe to, and they contribute to the perpetuation of corresponding – often incomplete, flawed, or outdated – connotations and attributes. Whereas the use of 'Eastern neighbours/Eastern neighbourhood' is rooted in an EU-centric perspective, it almost inevitably serves the – intended or unintended – purpose of demarcating the 'Self' from the 'Other'. This applies also to the used notion of 'post-Sovietness', a term that suffers from considerable inbuilt oxymoronic characteristics. On the one hand, it is meant to capture a new socio-political reality as a transition period of sorts between what is seen as 'Sovietness' and 'Europeanness'. On the other, the prefix 'post' implies the 'triumph' of one state of being over a previous, supposedly inferior one while 'Sovietness' points to the continuous existence of supposedly unique legacies – structural, behavioural, attitudinal, discursive – that are presumably distinct and perceived as being out of line with those that are seen to be 'European', or rather 'EUropean'. These variegated meanings become even more problematic when linked to the term 'region' and the inherent belief that the EaP-6, let alone the vast geographic area that is believed to form the so-called 'post-Soviet space', represent *one* region.

Given EaP countries' different socio-political development stages and transition trajectories, their different geographic and geopolitical positionings, and their limited interdependence, but also in light of the need to more systematically break with simplifying and inherently Eurocentric attempts to define the nature of EU behaviour beyond its borders, this volume acknowledges these limitations. Thus, Chapter 1, a reprint of an article published in 2018 by Cristian Nitoiu in *Europe-Asia Studies*, and Chapter 2, a reprint of an article published by Laure Delcour in 2015 in *Problems of Post-Communism*, while still resorting to the 'post-Sovietness' terminology, do offer alternative angles. Whereas Nitoiu demonstrates how the concept of the 'ideal Self' helps to identify EU framing practices of its standard-setting behaviour, policies, and influence in EaP countries and the way they share or even embrace it, Delcour's contribution is a stark reminder of the fact that there is more to region-building than just mere labelling or externally driven dynamics, such as the EaP. In fact, she highlights that local conditions, in particular actors constellations and domestic preference formation, in processes leading to region-building are at least of equal importance as are international stimuli and pressures.

In this sense, Delcour's contribution is not just exemplary of other studies with similar foci, published elsewhere (Delcour 2008, 2011; Simão 2012). It is also directly linked with the third theme of this volume, i.e. *the logic of great power competition: EU vs. Russian region-building attempts* and the fact that EaP partner countries, exposed to both EUropean and Russian influence (Ademmer et al. 2016), find themselves caught in the middle. Though the EU, in devising the EaP, was responsive and managerial rather than strategic and proactive (Smith 2019), it would be misleading to conclude that it lacks geopolitical underpinnings and purpose. Even if it may have been the case that the EU, in the period prior to the inauguration of the policy framework, lacked geopolitical interest in Eastern Europe, geopolitics showed an interest in the EU, most notably when the 2008 August war between Georgia and Russia broke out. Thus, *the geopoliticization of the EaP* appears not just to have become inevitable in the practical development and pursuit of the framework. It also has come to represent another major theme in the scholarly debate and this volume. Chapter 4, a reprint of an article by David Cadier, published in 2019 in *Geopolitics*, discusses this phenomenon at length and in great detail, emphasizing that, while Russia's actions in Ukraine have certainly contributed to the deepening and reinforcement of the EaP's geopoliticization, this dynamic was neither exclusively exogenous nor just reactive. Rather, as Cadier highlights, it also has important foundational roots in intra-EU processes and discourses, destined to push back Russian influence and, by the same token, 'win over' Eastern European countries.

Arguably, the debate on EU influence and performance in Eastern Europe (Baltag and Romanyshyn 2018) relates – though not exclusively – to what could be coined *the EaP: enlargement policies without enlargement*, the fifth major theme. It is represented in this book by Chapter 3, a reprint of an article published by Börzel and Lebanidze in *East European Politics* in 2017. Since its inception, the EaP has been utilizing mechanisms that *de facto* have their roots in EU enlargement policies though, to date, the EU has been adamant about not granting any of the EaP countries the prospect of membership. Undoubtedly, the most salient mechanism has been what Börzel and Lebanidze call 'democratic conditionality', and they argue that unless the latter meets pro-democratic reform coalitions in the respective target country and the oft-cited stability/democratization dilemma is absent, the EU is prone to act as a status-quo power than a transformative force. This, as they demonstrate, has led to a prioritization of (authoritarian) stability over uncertain democratic change.

Obviously, the usage of enlargement policy-related mechanisms and tools has not only been addressed by several studies through the lens of EU democracy promotion in EaP countries but also cultivated a rich academic discourse on *the EaP and its effects on the ground*, the sixth major theme this volume is embedded in and seeks to reflect. Recent scholarship has – long overdue – shifted the focus away from power- and external governance-inspired examinations of EU action to the unintended consequences of its external engagement. Chapter 5, a reprint of Tom Casier's article, published in 2019 in *The International Spectator*, represents this emergent body of literature and, by distinguishing between internal and external unintended consequences, sheds light on a hitherto unexplored aspect within the EU's ENP. He argues that, internally, the ENP's unchanged geographic scope has generated tension between, on the one hand, the EU's goal of maintaining, and even strengthening, privileged relations with EaP countries and, on the other, recognizing the Russian Federation as an equal partner, especially as regards regional affairs. Externally, according to Casier, this has fostered exposure to two different and even opposing strategic environments, namely a cooperative, though asymmetric one (as far as most EaP countries are concerned), and a competitive one (in what regards Russia). While, as Casier points out, the EU has actively sought to reinforce EU 'normative hegemony' (Haukkala 2008) towards EaP countries and mitigate some negative unintended effects, continuous attempts on the part of Russia to challenge this hegemony leave the former with significant 'capacity of choice'.

Lastly, the seventh major theme identifiable in the scholarly study of the EaP until late 2020, and informing this volume, revolves around the idea of reconsidering and reconstituting the EaP – that is: *bringing 'the political' back in,* particularly in the context of ontological security. Drawing mainly on the works of Edkins (1999) and Dillon (1996), and based on the assumption that there is a need to comprehend the formative processes that shape the current European security order and, likewise, to make the EaP supposedly more relevant and effective, Chapter 6 by Licínia Simão – a reprint of an article published in 2017 in *East European Politics* – maps the relevant agents in the symbolic power struggles that underpin European security and identifies the 'forms of capital they mobilise in the process of restructuring of the European order'. This allows for an improved understanding of EU policies towards EaP countries and, according to Simão, shows that the EU promotion of practices of depoliticized forms of politics resonates more with 'the maintenance of hegemonic and hierarchical forms of stability and order'. Obviously, as she finds, this is problematic for several reasons and creates dilemmas relating to (a) limitations of future enlargement in times of uncertainty, (b) the reproduction of imperial patterns in relations between the EU centre and its Eastern peripheries and corresponding identity-building processes, and (c) the intersubjective nature of security.

Part II of this volume shifts the focus of attention to the scholarly discussion of relational aspects in the context of the EaP and offers important insights into key characteristics and challenges that the EaP's bilateral track with the EaP-6 has been exposed to already for more than a decade. While each chapter adopts a different conceptual/empirical lens, all of them have in common that – directly or indirectly – they inevitably touch upon the seven themes outlined above, generating a sense of mutual engagement and debate as well as, unavoidably, tangential overlap. In selecting relevant articles published until late 2020, this volume tried to minimize such overlaps, but, at the same time, acknowledges the near impossibility of avoiding these entirely.

The first three chapters of Part II single out the associated EaP-3 and address matters such as the pursuit of EU structural power projection and support for state-building and modernization among EaP countries (Ukraine), the (detrimental) effects of elite-oriented EU policies in its Eastern neighbourhood (Moldova), and the link between contested statehood and EU actorness (Georgia). Chapter 7, a reprinted article by Kataryna Wolczuk, published in 2019 in *Eurasian Geography and Economics*, argues that Ukraine's Euromaidan had a profound impact on EU-Ukraine relations, particularly in what regards the EU's wide-ranging support for domestic reforms in the country. Taking issue with EU state-building ambitions, she shows not just that the EU-Ukraine AA exceeded the Ukrainian state's implementation capacity and that, therefore, the EU particularly supported public administration reform and capacity-building. What is more, she explores the extent to which implementation of the AA and Ukraine's path towards European integration 'have become tantamount with (re)building the state structures in Ukraine'. Chapter 8, a reprinted article by Ryhor Nizhnikau, published in 2016 in *Global Affairs*, examines EU policies towards Moldova – an EaP country that suffers from state capture, oligarchism, and endemic corruption – in juxtaposition to Russia's. Nizhnikau demonstrates how the EU has been pursuing an almost exclusively elite-centred approach that tied EU policies to the presence of a highly chameleonic and adaptive, though non-committal pro-corruption elite and also how this approach contributed to the consolidation – rather than reform – of dysfunctional state institutions and political instability. He thus argues that 'EU-driven efforts to implement substantial institutional changes were (ab)used to take control over state institutions and to reallocate rents between the entrenched elites'. Examining whether contested statehood represents a hindering condition for EU actorness, Chapter 9, a reprinted article published by Madalina Dobrescu and Tobias Schumacher in *Geopolitics* in 2020, examines EU engagement in the fields of migration and mobility, trade, and conflict management in Georgia – policy arenas where the implications of different understandings of sovereignty, legitimate authority, and territoriality are most salient. Like Nizhnikau in his study of EU-Moldova relations, Dobrescu and Schumacher find significant contradictions in the EU's policies to Georgia, an EaP country where the EU had many opportunities to deal with contested territories, i.e. Abkhazia and South Ossetia. They conclude that, in an attempt to accommodate Georgia's 'problematic sovereignty', the EU, within and beyond the confines of the EaP, has adopted a flexible approach, marked by incoherence as well as ignorance towards the irreconcilable interests of the conflict parties, generating a 'fractured record' of EU actorness.

Chapters 10 and 11, embedded in the geopoliticization argument discussed further above, address EU policies towards Armenia and Belarus – the two EaP countries that are members of the Russia-led Eurasian Economic Union (EAEU) and the Collective Security Treaty Organization (CSTO). Chapter 10, a reprinted article published by Alena Vieira and Syuzanna Vasilyan in *European Politics and Society* in 2018, adopts a comparative cross-country lens in its examination of EU- and Russia-imposed conditionalities. Vieira and Vasilyan show that the latter have been differential, and they also provide evidence that Armenia and Belarus reacted differently to these external pressures mainly as a result of a mix of factors, such as regime type, geopolitical considerations, their predisposition to integration dynamics, and existing stakes in the economic and energy spheres. Their key finding, the fact both Armenia and Belarus have been able to influence the shape and content of the EU's and Russia's conditionalities, is important in its own right. It underscores the agency of EaP countries and their capability to defy their geopolitical 'in-betweenness' and marginality and, therefore, it qualifies more narrowly conceived studies that treat EaP countries as mere subjects of externally imposed policies. To some extent, this contrasts with the argument put forward by Elena Korosteleva in Chapter 11, a reprinted article originally published in 2016 in *Democratization*. Embedded in the debate on EU democracy support, and indirectly drawing on the functional governance model proposed elsewhere (Freyburg et al. 2015), Korosteleva reveals substantive changes in the way the EU has been trying to promote democratic norms, regulations, and practices of international order in Belarus up until 2015. According to her, it shifted from high- to low-level politics, adopted a technocratic and sector-oriented focus, and displayed greater versatility and inclusiveness as far as its used instruments and inclusiveness in its structures are concerned. In spite of the absence of substantive and regular bilateral dialogue prior to the lifting of most EU restrictive measures in February 2016 and the ensuing temporary rapprochement (lasting until August 2020), EU efforts have, as is argued by Korosteleva, 'succeeded in fostering much-needed space for reciprocal learning and critical reasoning'. In her view, this is much noteworthy, as it may have far 'greater transformative potential than manufacturing a single collective will for democracy building'.

Chapter 12 features a reprinted article by Eske Van Gils on the rather overlooked dynamics of strategic interactionism in the context of the EaP more generally and in EU-Azerbaijan relations in particular (Van Gils 2019), published in *Europe-Asia Studies* in 2018. Just like Chapter 10, it takes issue with EaP countries' agency and, more broadly, the EaP's presumptive principle of 'joint ownership'. Applying a model of bargaining power, Van Gils analyses Azerbaijan's resistance to the EU-proposed AA and both Azerbaijan's and the EU's negotiation behaviour in agreeing on a future contractual framework for relations that can replace the outdated Partnership and Cooperation Agreement of 1999. According to her, the quest for dialogue, as displayed by the Azerbaijani regime in bilateral deliberations with the EU, rather than grudgingly succumbing to EU unilateralism, holds considerable potential as a behavioural model also for other EaP countries – provided their respective regimes

(a) are in a position to capitalize on their (supposedly existing) economic resources; (b) use their negotiation skills effectively; (c) can draw on domestic constituencies that advocate clear discourse and issue strong demands; (d) foster 'the perceptions of the Self [that] facilitate[s] an assertive stance in international relations'; and (e) find themselves in a constellation where an agreement with the EU is not the only 'game in town'.

Part III and thus Chapter 13 seek to take stock of EaP deliverables and drawbacks in a longitudinal perspective. By drawing on a goal-oriented framework for foreign policy analysis, Andriy Tyushka and Tobias Schumacher survey key EaP developments during the period 2009–2020, with an eye on the framework's 'joint goals', objectives and salient policy issues as jointly advanced and implemented by the EU and the EaP-6. In addition to assessing the pursuit of the EaP's broad strategic goals, i.e. political association and economic integration, the chapter also evaluates progress in implementing the *'20 Deliverables for 2020' and* offers insight into the discussion on the post-2020 course of the EaP.

Drawing on the many findings in the reprinted articles/chapters and the two Annexes gathered in this volume, as well as the increasingly burgeoning literature on the EaP, the concluding chapter by Andriy Tyushka is seeking to spell out some avenues for the EaP's future design.

Against the backdrop of the emergence of a revised EaP framework in early 2021, there is hope among governmental and non-governmental actors in both EU Member States and EaP countries alike that future relations between the EU and the vast space beyond its eastern borders will be more inclusive and dialogical, generate more tangible and mutually beneficial (material and immaterial) results, and, most of all, diminish existing misperceptions and many of the enduring issues hampering the EaP, as discussed by the contributors in this volume. The recently concluded structured public consultation process on the future of the EaP demonstrates the EU's increasing readiness to engage in self-reflection and consider alternative views. This also implies listening more thoroughly to critical academic voices and learning from the past. It is the hope that this volume can make a modest contribution to this hopefully emerging process.

Notes

1 In September 2018, as well as in Spring 2020, the European Commission and the EEAS reviewed potential progress under the '20 Deliverables for 2020'. These were, however, rounds of internal monitoring and not destined to lead to any reforms or revisions of neither the Deliverables nor the EaP framework as such.
2 358 journal articles on the Eastern Partnership and EU-Eastern neighbours' relations, published between 2009 and 2020, were sampled from over 80 academic journals indexed in WoS SSCI & ESCI. See *Annex 2* for details on the sampling method and bibliometric analysis.
3 See 'Non-paper z polskimi propozycjami w sprawie przyszłego kształtu polityki rozszerzonej EU wobec nowych wschodnich sąsiadów' in: *Polityka rozszerzonej Unii Europejskiej wobec nowych sąsiadów*, Warsaw: Fundacja im. Stefana Batorego, 2003, pp. 93–107, available at: www.batory.org.pl/doc/nowi_s.pdf
4 See Frankfurter Allgemeine Zeitung, 2 July 2006.
5 An exception is the Eastern Partnership Integration and Cooperation (EaPIC) programme, in force between 2012 and 2013, whose main aim was to provide increased support to governmental stakeholders from EaP partner countries engaging in institutional and sector reforms based on the principle of 'more for more'.

References

Ademmer, E., Delcour, L., and Wolczuk, K. (2016). Beyond geopolitics: exploring the impact of the EU and Russia in the contested neighborhood. *Eurasian Geography and Economics, 57* (1), 1–18.

Baltag, D. and Romanyshyn, I. (2018). The Challenge of Analysing the Performance of the European Neighbourhood Policy. In *The Routledge Handbook of the European Neighbourhood Policy*, ed. by T. Schumacher, A. Marchetti, and T. Demmelhuber. London and New York: Routledge, pp. 39–49.

Behr, T. and Tiilikainen, T. (2015). Introduction. In *Northern Europe and the Making of the EU's Mediterranean and Middle East Policies: Normative Leaders or Passive Bystanders?* ed. by T. Behr and T. Tiilikainen. London and New York: Routledge, pp. 1–10.

Bicchi, F. and Gillespie, R. (2011). The Union for the Mediterranean: Continuity or Change in Euro-Mediterranean Relations? *Mediterranean Politics, 16*(1: Special Issue). https://www.tandfonline.com/toc/fmed20/16/1

Bosse, G. (2018). EU-Belarus Relations in the Context of the European Neighbourhood Policy. In *The Routledge Handbook of the European Neighbourhood Policy*, ed. by T. Schumacher, A. Marchetti, and T. Demmelhuber. London and New York: Routledge, pp. 290–301.

Bossuyt, F., Kostanyan, H., Orbie, J., and Vandecasteele, B. (2018). Aid in the European Neighbourhood Policy. In *The Routledge Handbook of the European Neighbourhood Policy*, ed. by T. Schumacher, A. Marchetti, and T. Demmelhuber. London and New York: Routledge, pp. 415–432.

Buscaneanu, S. (2016). *Regime Dynamics in EU's Eastern Neighbourhood: EU Democracy Promotion, International Influences, and Domestic Contexts*. Houndmills, Basingstoke: Palgrave Macmillan.

Carp, S. and Schumacher, T. (July 2015). From Survival to Revival: The Riga Summit 2015 and the revised ENP. *Egmont Security Policy Brief, 65*: 1–6.

Casier, T., Korosteleva, E., and Whitman, R. (2014). Building a Stronger Eastern Partnership. Towards an EaP 2.0. *Global Europe Centre Policy Paper*, University of Kent.

Commission of the European Communities (2004). *Communication from the Commission to the Council on the Commission's Proposals for Action Plans Under the European Neighbourhood Policy (ENP)*, Brussels, 9 December, COM(2004)795 final.

Commission of the European Communities (2006a). *Communication from the Commission to the European Parliament and the Council on Strengthening the European Neighbourhood Policy*, 4 December, COM(2006)726 final.

Commission of the European Communities (2006b). *Non-Paper 'What the European Union Could Bring to Belarus'*, 5 December 2006. Available online at: http://ec.europa.eu/external_relations/belarus/intro/ non_paper_1106.pdf. Last accessed: 30 November 2020.

Commission of the European Communities (2008). *Communication from the Commission to the European Parliament and the Council, Eastern Partnership*. Brussels, 3 December, COM (2008)823/4.

Council of the EU (2009). *Joint Declaration of the Prague Eastern Partnership Summit*. Brussels, 7 May, 8435/09 (Presse 78).

Czaputowicz, J. (2019). Future of the Eastern Partnership: The Polish view. *Euractiv*, 13.05.2019.

Delcour, L. (2008). A Missing Eastern Dimension? The ENP and Region-Building in the Post-Soviet Area. In *Pioneer Europe? Testing EU Foreign Policy in the Neighbourhood*, ed. by L. Delcour and E. Tulmets. Baden-Baden: Nomos, pp. 159–177.

Delcour, L. (2011). *Shaping the Post-Soviet Space? EU Policies and Approaches to Region-Building*. Farnham and Abingdon: Ashgate.

Delcour, L. (2017). *The EU and Russia in Their 'Contested Neighbourhood': Multiple External Influences, Policy Transfer and Domestic Change*. London and New York: Routledge.

De Waal, T. and Youngs, R. (2015). Reform as Resilience: An Agenda for the Eastern Partnership. *Carnegie Europe*, 14.05.2015.

Dillon, M. (1996). *Politics of Security: Towards a Political Philosophy of Continental Thought*. London: Routledge.

Edkins, J. (1999). *Poststructuralism & International Relations: Bringing the Political Back In*. Boulder, CO: Lynne Rienner.

European Commission and HR/VP (2020). *Eastern Partnership Policy Beyond 2020. Reinforcing Resilience - an Eastern Partnership that delivers for all*. JOIN (2020) 7 final, 18 March. Available online at: https://eeas.europa.eu/sites/eeas/files/1_en_act_part1_v6.pdf. Last accessed: 24 November 2020.

Fawn, R. (ed.) (2019). *Managing Security Threats along the EU's Eastern Flanks*. Basingstoke: Palgrave.

Flenley, P., and Mannin, M. (Eds.) (2018). *The European Union and its eastern neighbourhood: Europeanisation and its twenty-first-century contradictions*. Manchester: Manchester University Press.

Freyburg, T., Lavenex, S., Schimmelfennig, F., Skripka, T., and Wetzel, A. (eds.) (2015). *EU Democracy Promotion by Functional Cooperation: The European Union and Its Neighbourhood*. Houndmills, Basingstoke: Palgrave.

Furness, M., Henökl, T., and Schumacher, T. (2019). Crisis, Coordination and Coherence: European Decision-Making and the 2015 European Neighbourhood Policy Review, *European Foreign Affairs Review*, 24(4): 447–468.

Gillespie, R. (1997). Northern European Perceptions of the Barcelona Process. *Revista CIDOB d'Afers Internacionals*, 37: 65–75.

Gromadzki, G. (2015). The Eastern Partnership after Five Years: Time for Deep Rethinking. *EPRS Study*. European Parliament, 21.02.2015. Available online at: http://www.europarl.europa.eu/RegData/etudes/ STUD/2015/536438/EXPO_STU(2015)536438_EN.pdf.

Haukkala, H. (2008). The European Union as a regional normative hegemon: the case of European Neighbourhood Policy. *Europe-Asia Studies*, 60 (9), 1601–1622.

High Representative for Foreign and Security Policy of the EU and Vice-President of the European Commission (HR/VP). (2016). *European Union Global Strategy. Shared Vision, Common Action: A Stronger Europe. A Global Strategy for the European Union's Foreign and Security Policy*. Available at: http://eeas.europa.eu/archives/docs/top_stories/pdf/eugs_review_web.pdf. Last accessed: 25 November 2020.

Joseph, J. (2016). Governing through Failure and Denial: The New Resilience Agenda. *Millennium – Journal of International Studies*, 44(3): 370–390.

Joseph, J. and Juncos, A. (2019). Resilience as an Emergent European Project? The EU's Place in the Resilience Turn. *JCMS: Journal of Common Market Studies*, 57(5): 995–1011.

Kerikmäe, T. and Chochia, A. (eds.) (2016). *Political and Legal Perspectives of the EU Eastern Partnership Policy*. Heidelberg: Springer.

Korosteleva, E. (2012). *The European Union and Its Eastern Neighbours: Towards a More Ambitious Partnership?* London and New York: Routledge.

Korosteleva, E., Merheim-Eyre, I., and van Gils, E. (eds.) (2018). *The Politics and 'The Political' of the Eastern Partnership Initiative: Reshaping the Agenda*. London and New York: Routledge.

Liikanen, I., Scott, J.W., and Sotkasiira, T. (eds.) (2016). *The EU's Eastern Neighbourhood: Migration, Borders and Regional Stability*. London and New York: Routledge.

Nizhnikau, R. (2018). *EU Induced Institutional Change in Post-Soviet Space: Promoting Reforms in Moldova and Ukraine*. London and New York: Routledge.

Papadimitriou, D., Baltag, D., and Surubaru, N.C. (eds.) (2019). *The European Union and Central and Eastern Europe. Assessing Performance*. London and New York: Routledge.

Rouet, G., and G. Pascariu (eds.) (2019), *Resilience and The EU's Eastern Neighbourhood Countries: From Theoretical Concepts to a Normative Agenda*, London: Palgrave Macmillan.

Schumacher, T. (2011). Germany and Central Eastern European Countries: Laggards or Veto-Players? *Mediterranean Politics*, 16(1: Special Issue): 79–98.

Schumacher, T. (2020). The EU and Its Neighbourhood: The Politics of Muddling Through. *JCMS: Journal of Common Market Studies*, *58* S1 (The JCMS Annual Review of the European Union in 2019): 187–201.

Simão, L. (2013). Region-Building in the Eastern Neighbourhood: Assessing EU Regional Policies in the South Caucasus. *East European Politics*, *29*(3): 273–288.

Smith, M. (2019). The Geopolitics of the EU's Partnership Diplomacy: Strategic, Managerial or Reactive? *International Politics*, *56*: 288–303.

Tulmets, E. (2017). Rationalist and Constructivist approaches to the European Neighbourhood Policy: A Growing Prevalence of Interests over Identity? In *Theorizing the European Neighbourhood Policy*, ed. by S. Schunz and S. Gstöhl. London and New York: Routledge, pp. 25–41.

Van Gils, E. (2019). *Azerbaijan and the European Union*. London and New York: Routledge.

Wolzcuk, K. (December 2017). Perceptions of, and Attitudes towards, the Eastern Partnership amongst the Partner Countries' Political Elites. *Eastern Partnership Review*, *11*: 1–12.

Wolczuk, K. (2019). State Building and European Integration in Ukraine. *Eurasian Geography and Economics*, *60*(6): 736–754.

Part I
The EU's Eastern Partnership and regional dynamics

Enduring issues and contending perspectives

The European Union's 'Ideal Self' in the Post-Soviet Space

Cristian Nitoiu

During the last two decades, one of the cornerstones of the foreign policy of the European Union (EU) has been represented by the development of a strong presence in its neighbourhood (Raik & Dinesen 2015). The 2003 Security Strategy[1] and the recent 2016 Global Strategy[2] highlighted the need to show that the EU can play a major role in the international arena by first establishing a strong presence in the neighbourhood and proving the union's effectiveness in the region. This broad aim has been translated in various initiatives towards the neighbourhood such as the European Neighbourhood Policy (ENP),[3] the Eastern Partnership (EaP),[4] and the Union for the Mediterranean (UfM).[5] As part of the European neighbourhood, the post-Soviet space has thus received significant attention from the EU, which aimed to shape both the domestic and foreign policies of the countries in the region. However, the EU's track record of shaping developments in the post-Soviet space has been at best mixed (Ademmer 2015), given the reluctance of some post-Soviet states to go beyond rhetoric in adapting their policies as well as EU member states' unwillingness and lack of commitment to fully support the union's approach to the region (Nilsson & Silander 2016). EU overtures have also been received with scepticism by some post-Soviet states, which tend to see EU policy towards the region as deeply unilateral, asymmetrical, and without regard for the specificities or needs of each country (Delcour 2010). Most of the findings from the open literature refer to the EU's ability to promote its integration project in the post-Soviet states, that is, the range of rules, norms, and regulations that characterise its governance system (Schimmelfennig & Scholtz 2008). Less scrutiny has been directed towards the way the EU's identity in world politics has informed its approach towards the post-Soviet space, and how this identity has been perceived by the states in the region (Gstöhl & Schunz 2017).

The EU's identity in world politics is even more complex than that of nation states. As an economy-driven project, the EU has also sought to achieve a united foreign policy that would underpin a strong presence in the international arena. The literature tends to point to the fact that the EU's identity has been, to a large extent, shaped by its self-perception[6] rather than by interactions with other states or the structure of world politics (Checkel & Katzenstein 2009). The most notable exception here is the United States, as its attempts to portray the EU as a normative, civilian cosmopolitan or ethical power have aimed to place it as both a key transatlantic partner and as a viable and strong alternative in world politics (Rynning & Jensen 2010).

This essay focuses on the role of the perceptions of the self (the ideal self) in world politics in order to analyse the EU's approach towards the post-Soviet eastern neighbours (Armenia, Azerbaijan, Belarus, Georgia, Moldova and Ukraine). Moreover, the essay examines how the states in the post-Soviet space perceive and interpret the EU's identity, and explain why they share or reject various aspects of it. More specifically, it explains similarities and differences between the EU's ideal self and the perceptions of the post-Soviet states regarding EU identity in world politics. In broad terms, the ideal self is the benchmark that states aspire to and against which their actions are judged. Moreover, it is one of the main drivers that informs how states should behave ideally in international relations, in this way constraining the range of national interests, foreign policy strategies, or decisions that policymakers can adopt.[7] Thus, the concept of the 'ideal self' allows us to identify how the EU frames its ideal behaviour, policies, and influence in the post-Soviet space. Identifying the EU's ideal self in the post-Soviet space allows this essay to examine the way in which it is shared or embraced by the post-Soviet states. Consequently, this essay makes a twofold contribution to the literature. On the one hand, it sheds light on the way ideal self-representation (that is, the ideal self) informs the foreign policies of international actors. On the other, it contributes to the growing body of scholarship on the post-Soviet space by examining the way in which the EU's ideal self is perceived by the post-Soviet states and informs their own foreign policies.

The essay presents an overview based on a larger research project that looks in detail at the way the foreign policies of the post-Soviet states interpret the EU. As such, this essay does not provide in-depth analyses of individual states, but rather maps the way the ideal self of the EU is perceived by and reflected in the foreign policies of post-Soviet states. Nevertheless, the essay focuses on individual post-Soviet states in order to substantiate claims about how the EU's ideal self is perceived in the region. More broadly, the validity of this approach is underlined by the fact that these states have faced similar challenges in developing their foreign policies in the post-Soviet era: they have had to balance between the interests of multiple powerful external actors (United States, Russia, EU), while the EU's policies towards them have generally remained consistent (Boedeltje & van Houtum 2011; Beauguitte *et al.* 2015; Gnedina 2015). This approach also provides space for both comparisons between the post-Soviet states and a series of generalisable insights. This research uses official documents and statements, secondary data from media and academic reports, together with participant observations from interviews conducted with experts and policymakers between 2011 and 2016 in Brussels, London, Berlin, Moscow, and across the post-Soviet space. The essay proceeds by presenting the concept of the ideal self in the next section and then applying it to the EU's approach towards the post-Soviet space. The following section evaluates how the EU's ideal self is perceived by the countries in question and how these perceptions inform the different processes of foreign policymaking. The essay's core argument—namely that which postulates that the post-Soviet states have an instrumental view of the EU in their foreign policies—can be explained both by how the EU's ideal self is constructed and the traditional multi-vector foreign policies of the countries in the region. The last section outlines and discusses the findings of the essay.

Perceptions of the self (ideal self) in world politics

The identity of a state in world politics is conceptualised here as encompassing an intersubjective and a self-referential dimension. These two dimensions are inherently interlinked and inform each other. The intersubjective dimension draws on the constructivist approach to international relations, whereby interactions with other actors in the international arena play a key role in shaping states' identities in world politics (Lebow 2008; Schoen 2008). In the same vein, interactions with the structure of international relations—primarily the ideas, rules, norms, and values that originate from this structure—share (as some would argue) equal weight in influencing a state's identity (Zehfuss 2006). In this sense, the literature tends to point to various mechanisms through which the intersubjective character of identities is performed in practice: for example, socialisation, learning, and recognition (Checkel & Katzenstein 2009). Examining the intersubjective aspects of identity is important as it highlights how interactions in the international arena, with other states or various norms, rules, and processes, change state identities and behaviours in world politics (Nabers 2011). This essay is interested in the self-referential aspects of states' identities in world politics. The main reason for the focus on self-referential aspects, as pointed out in the literature, is that the EU has been generally unresponsive to external pressures or realities when constructing its foreign policy in the last 25 years and has developed a narrative that, in many interpretations, seems devoid of political reality (Korosteleva 2016; Youngs 2017). While the intersubjective aspects are more outward-oriented, the self-referential ones are more inward-oriented and imply a greater openness on the part of the actor when it comes to the evolution of identity in world politics. The self-referential aspect (or the ideal self) is the narrative that states create in order to portray to other actors an idealised image of how they behave in and interpret international relations. Conversely, in this essay, the ideal self is also considered to serve, in broad terms, as a benchmark for states themselves. While the ideal self tends to be stable, changes appear due to long-term intersubjective aspects of identity that incrementally spill over and influence perceptions of the ideal self, or in the case of crisis or windows of opportunity where actors within the state have the ability or are forced to alter the narrative of the ideal self (Harnisch 2011).

In their ideal self-representation, states and other international actors perceive themselves as promoting (and embodying) a certain model or set of values. The ideal self sets the broad parameters within which a state's foreign policy is formulated and executed. The ideal self also contains expectations regarding the roles that an actor should play in the international arena. More generally, according to Harnisch 'roles are social positions (as well as a socially recognised category of actors) that are constituted by ego and alter expectations regarding the purpose of an actor in an organised group' (Harnisch 2011, p. 8). Besides roles, the way international actors ascribe meanings, frame, and understand various key concepts in international relations—the international system, status in world politics, the nature of power, legitimacy, responsibility—is intrinsically shaped by their ideal self (Slaughter 2005; Evans 2009; Lake 2011; Bisley 2012; Goddard & Krebs 2015; Heimann 2015; Terhalle 2015; Flockhart 2016; Mattern & Zarakol 2016).

The ideal self can also be seen as an overarching vector in a state's foreign policy, as it provides more or less clearly articulated guidelines for policymakers. It tends to be stable as it develops gradually and incrementally, based on historically situated knowledge and experience of international relations. However, sudden changes lead policymakers to reframe the ideal self. For example, the 9/11 attacks made fighting global terrorism the key priority in US foreign policy and consolidated the legitimacy of interventionism and the responsibility to protect (R2P) principle in this respect as an integral part of the American ideal self (Buzan 2004). Crises in themselves may or may not lead to changes in the state's ideal self but they will accelerate reframing. Russia during Putin's third presidential term (2012–2018) offers another example, as it started to reframe the ideal self that presents an assertive Moscow whose great power status is widely recognised

(Sakwa 2015). This process started in the aftermath of the coloured revolutions in the post-Soviet space (Saari 2014).

States can pursue their ideal self in world politics in an intentional manner by developing strategies and trying to put them into practice. For example, the EU understands an integral part of ideal self to be the spread of its norms and values in world politics, and, first proving that it can act in this manner in its immediate neighbourhood (Prodi 2002; Council of the European Union 2003; Mogherini 2017). Such a broad aspiration, in turn, has informed the development of the EU strategy towards the neighbourhood and a myriad of initiatives such as the ENP, EaP, and the UfM (Schumacher 2015). Conversely, it is on the basis of inertia, rather than intentional effort, that their ideal self can guide states. For example, Russia's actions in the post-Soviet space during the early 1990s, such as support for separatist movements in the newly independent countries or its lacklustre commitment for regional initiatives, did not seem to be informed by an overarching strategy (Bukkvoll 2001).

Although the ideal self of states tends to be stable, there is considerable variation in the way policymakers understand and translate this into foreign policy strategies. Firstly, it can be framed in an explicit manner in which states define a series of steps or strategies for pursuing the ideal self—in this way rallying domestic actors and sending well-defined messages to external ones. During the Cold War, the United States and the Soviet Union constructed clear and rigid dichotomous foreign policy strategies bent on countering each other's influence (Leeds & Mattes 2007). Their ideal self was essentially propagating their ideology and way of life around the world. Framing the 'Other' as an existential threat allowed policymakers to rally their societies as a whole in the ideological Cold War confrontation. Secondly, states can have an ambiguous understanding of the ideal self, which can lead to various interpretations by domestic actors and other states. This may occur due to increasing polarisation among domestic political elites or following significant internal crises or events. For example, after the breakup of the Soviet Union, the new post-Soviet states had the choice of adopting a European liberal path or embracing a conservative (closer to Russia) direction (White & Feklyunina 2014). This intense level of polarisation has led to a very ambiguous understanding of the ideal self, which in practice translated into dysfunctional multi-vector strategies in post-Soviet foreign policymaking. Thirdly, the ideal self can be translated in flexible foreign policy strategies that can be easily reframed in the event of unsuccessful policy outcomes. The 2003 Security Strategy, the ENP, and the EaP had ambitious and flexible goals—promoting democracy and stability in the neighbourhood, managing migration, and respectively tackling global climate change—that were quickly downgraded when it became obvious that the EU could not live up to them (Schumacher 2015).

The ideal self has a temporal dimension linked to the way policymakers understand it and frame foreign policy strategies. States that identify their ideal self in the past will seek to shape the current order so as to replicate the moment of attainment of their ideal self. Those that perceive their ideal self in the present will seek to maintain and advance the current world order. States that wish to break from the past have an abstract view of their ideal self and perceive that it will be realised in the future. However, those that see their ideal self as breaking with the past still identify negatively with an ideal self located in their historical experience. For example, in the initial decades following its creation the EU's ideal self was framed in contrast with the experience of the two world wars and the lack of peace on the European continent. The past thus became a negative signifier for the EU's ideal self, from which the EU sought to break away (Zielonka 2008).

The ideal self shapes the way states' foreign policies balance the need to preserve the national interest and the desire to better the life of people living in other states. The first, inward, approach focuses on furthering domestic needs and devising a foreign policy that maximises the benefits of interaction with other international actors. The second, and arguably less salient, outward tendency emphasises empathy and altruism, prompting states to be sensitive to and reflect on the way in which they can tend to the domestic needs of other international actors (De Zutter 2010). Priorities such as tackling global climate change, alleviating global poverty and social inequality, and international aid and development are some of the key hallmarks of an outward-oriented ideal self.

In terms of the key concepts of international relations, the essay focuses on legitimacy: the way the ideal self of states prescribes the limits of legitimate and responsible behaviour in world politics (Buchanan & Keohane 2006; Mayer & Vogt 2006; Evans 2009). The internal dimension highlights that states' foreign policies need to be legitimate and responsible in front of their citizens in promoting their interest. The external dimension of legitimacy emphasises the way states consider international norms and other states' interests in acting in international relations. The more sensitive a state is to these aspects, the more legitimate its behaviour becomes (Goddard & Krebs 2015). Hence, legitimacy beyond national borders is based on the beliefs or consent of other societies as external normative standards. As the next section will show, focus on the concept of legitimacy is justified by the fact that debates regarding the EU's legitimacy have been increasingly salient in the literature.

The EU's ideal self in the post-Soviet space

The EU's primary role in the post-Soviet space (framed in its ideal self) underscores its ability and duty to act as a normative power that emphasises the promotion of values rather than interests (Füle 2010a; Haukkala 2011). However, the failure to make a clear distinction between values and interests has not only confused other actors—such as Russia or the post-Soviet states—but also led to confusion within EU policymaking circles, with particular reference to the scope and aims of the Union's policy. Firstly, the EU has partly disguised the promotion of its economic and security interests (mainly in the areas of migration, human trafficking and energy) behind the discourse of normative power, that is, the promotion of 'universal' norms such as human rights, democracy, and the rule of law. It has done this in an asymmetrical manner, always assuming that its values are morally superior to those of other states; value promotion, in other words, has gone mostly one way (Delcour 2010). At the other end of spectrum, Russia has furthermore denounced with regularity the promotion of EU values as an unfair intrusion into the internal affairs and political systems of other, sovereign, states (Gretskiy et al. 2014). Post-Soviet states have in turn mixed views regarding the promotion of EU normative power. On the one hand, they seem attracted by the benefits of European integration (Korosteleva et al. 2017) but, on the other, they stress that the EU's model is asymmetrical and unilateral, and that its acceptance does ultimately antagonise Russia (Youngs 2017). Hence, the post-Soviet states have been constrained to choose between the EU and Russia's hegemony. In turn, the leaders of some of these countries (such as Georgia, Moldova and Ukraine) have used a pro-European narrative for electoral purposes and frequently adopted democratic reforms symbolically, without really aiming to implement them (Cantir & Kennedy 2015; Delcour & Wolczuk 2015a; Dragneva & Wolczuk 2015).

Throughout the post-Soviet space, the EU's ideal self has been pursued in a largely intentional manner. Following the 2004 and 2007 enlargements, the union started to build and formalise various initiatives beyond its new borders. This deliberate move meant to highlight that the EU could be an effective actor in the neighbourhood and thus play an enhanced role globally, making the ENP a testing ground for more global policies (Council of the European Union 2003, 2008). Consequently, throughout the last decade, the EU has developed its formal approach towards the post-Soviet space by gradually adding various layers of economic and political integration in a bid to shape both domestic and regional developments, for example, Association Agreements (AAs) and Deep and Comprehensive Free Trade Areas (DCFTAs).[8]

The EU has understood its ideal self in rather flexible terms, which have allowed it to set ambitious goals or foreign policy strategies and downgrade them when reality failed to match them (Schumacher 2015). Some examples include the EU's ambitious goals in tackling climate change, which were downgraded after the failure to set the agenda at the 2009 Copenhagen summit (Bäckstrand & Elgström 2013), the ever-present desire to create a working European defence union, which tends to be put aside in times of adverse conditions (Bickerton 2011), or its approach to migration, which has been reframed several times and arguably made less cosmopolitan during the recent refugee crisis (Heisbourg 2015). In the post-Soviet space in particular, the EU rebranded its approach to promoting 'deep' democracy, justice system reform, or even altered the terms of the DCFTAs and AAs in order to match the operational failure encountered when implementing these treaties (Schumacher 2015). The constant reframing of the EU's understanding of the ideal self is partly influenced by the complex nature of decision-making in foreign policy, where the interests and views of the 28 member states need to be accommodated. At the same time, during the last decade, the post-Soviet space, and the international arena as a whole, have been characterised by increasing disorder, with many events making stable foreign policy strategising rather redundant.

Moreover, the growing assertiveness of Russia in the region and its unpredictability is forcing the EU to reconsider its presence in the eastern neighbourhood. The constant reframing of the EU's strategies in the post-Soviet space, based on the flexible understanding of its ideal self, has damaged its image and reputation in the region. In this sense, the literature indicates that the post-Soviet states tend to see the EU as an incoherent and sometimes weak foreign policy actor that lacks willingness and commitment to put its goals and strategies into practice (Freire & Kanet 2012; Chaban et al. 2013).

The EU ideal self differs from that of nation states as the EU claims to be promoting its values in an altruistic manner. This ideal self resides in the EU's ability to bring peace and prosperity on the continent and reunite Europe, hence presupposing EU moral superiority over other states (Diez 2005). The EU has sought to promote its integration model in the post-Soviet space, an approach justified by the more than half a decade of peace and economic development on the European continent. However, due to the current economic crisis, the increasingly disordered neighbourhood, Russia's assertiveness in foreign policy, and the lack of effectiveness of the ENP or the EaP, the EU's ideal self has become the pre-crisis EU which successfully enlarged to Central and Eastern Europe (CEE)—that is, the recent past. The EU's ideal self is thus located in a period in which it viewed Russia as inherently weak.

On the surface, the EU seems to have an outward understanding of its ideal self, as it discursively emphasises the promotion of universal values and economic development throughout the world. However, in practice, its approach towards the post-Soviet space has been rather inward looking, as most of the EU's policies and initiatives have bent on promoting its own interests (European Commission 2003, 2015; Ferrero-Waldner 2005). Behind the rhetoric of the need to engage with partner countries and be open to their needs, the EU has largely overlooked the desires and specific conditions of the post-Soviet states when tailoring its approach towards the region (Edwards 2008). Conversely, policies such as the ENP and the EaP have been frequently branded as asymmetric, as they draw mostly on the EU's unilateral understanding of what is best for the neighbourhood countries (Haukkala 2011).

In terms of legitimacy of behaviour in world politics, the EU ideal self tends to frame the use of force as a measure of last resort, not a common foreign policy tool. Thus, the EU sees itself as promoting a distinct type of normality in international relations, which, unlike the norms upheld by nation states, focuses on the need to employ non-military and non-coercive tools in foreign policy (European External Action Service 2016). This perception is in stark contrast with the way major international actors, including the United States, Russia and China, view military action or the potential to use military power: as a legitimate aspect of international relations (Bisley 2012). Nevertheless, the EU is a keen supporter of the R2P principle (European Parliament 2013a; Kadelbach 2014) and, in line with this commitment, it has sent peacekeeping missions to various parts of the world (European Parliament 2013a).

Noteworthy here is the fact that the EU's ideal self frames the promotion of its norms in world politics as inherently legitimate, even though they may not be shared by other countries and cultures (Solana 2008; Council of the European Union 2010; Ashton 2012). Significant criticism has been directed towards the EU's promotion of norms, namely, that portraying them as universal insulates the union from criticism that it acts in an asymmetric and illegitimate way (De Zutter 2010; Sjursen 2011; Tonra 2011).

The EU's ideal self and the foreign policies of the post-Soviet states

This section examines the various ways in which post-Soviet states perceive the identity of the EU in world politics and how their foreign policies reflect the EU's ideal self. In doing so, it explains similarities and differences between the EU's ideal self and the perceptions of EU identity in world politics held by post-Soviet states. What unites the foreign policies of post-Soviet states is their tendency to instrumentalise relations with the EU to attain various benefits (economic, recognition of their status in world politics, acknowledgment as part of Europe). In its ideal self, the EU applies a similar instrumental logic regarding the post-Soviet states; that is, while extending the EU integration project to certain countries in the region might not bring significant added value when it comes to trade, enlargement has the potential to prove the EU's weight in international relations. As the section will show, this instrumental approach also underlines the roles that post-Soviet states assign to the EU in the region.

The previous section noted that the EU's ideal self stresses the importance of creating and maintaining a strong presence in the neighbourhood, including the post-Soviet space. Developing such a presence has been considered a prerequisite for proving the EU's ability to shape key issues and events on the international agenda. The ideal self underscores the EU's duty to help the countries in the neighbourhood democratise and develop fully functional economies (European Commission 2003, 2010; Füle 2010b; Council of the European Union 2011). Promoting its norms and values is seen as a key mechanism for effectively exercising this role. By having stable, democratic, and prosperous countries in the eastern neighbourhood, the EU not only manages to prove that it can shape in positive terms the domestic political settings of other countries, but also enhance the security of the region and prevent any threats that might originate from the post-Soviet space spilling over to member states. Particularly, the EU's ideal self does not put significant emphasis on the union's interests in the post-Soviet space. Nevertheless, the post-Soviet states envisage a series of roles, which in some cases overlap, for the EU in the region (see Table 1): normative power, mediator, liberal power, trade power and partner, bargaining chip, or defender against Russia.

One of the most important roles that post-Soviet states attribute to the EU is that of trade partner and economic power. These perceived roles are the key drivers behind the desire of the states in the region to establish strong economic partnerships with the EU. Nevertheless, post-Soviet states have had to balance between pursuing sustainable trade partnerships with the EU and accepting the norms and regulations that the EU seeks to simultaneously and unilaterally export. Most of the post-Soviet states have had to sign some sort of free trade area or partnership and cooperation agreement with the EU that allows them access to the common market. Signing the DCFTA has been indeed one of the key goals of the foreign policies of Ukraine (Maksak *et al.* 2017), Moldova (Ministry of Foreign Affairs and European Integration 2010), and Georgia (Kakachia & Cecire 2013), and has been widely presented in public discourse as a major achievement (Ademmer 2015). Belarus (Ministry of Foreign Affairs of the Republic of Belarus 2017) and Armenia (Ministry of Foreign Affairs of the Republic of Armenia 2017) have advocated for Eurasian integration to be made compatible with the EU's integration project, which would allow them to reap the benefits of an economic partnership with the EU while aligning themselves with Russia in foreign affairs (European Parliament 2013b). Azerbaijan (Pashayeva 2015), on the other hand, has sought a more equal type of trade deal with the EU that would take into account its privileged position as the possessor of significant natural resources. Thus, Baku has been adamant that it should not receive similar treatment or deals as Moldova or Belarus, and that unlike the other post-Soviet states, it should have a say regarding the substance of agreements with the EU. However, the recent decrease in oil prices has limited Baku's bargaining position in relation to the EU (Jafarli 2016). On the whole, the EU's perceived economic role has been its greatest asset in influencing both the domestic and foreign policies of post-Soviet states.

Some post-Soviet states perceive the EU as a mediator in their relationship with other important external actors in the region such as Russia, China and the United States. The EU is seen to have the potential to play an independent role and mediate possible conflicts or agreements. This is to a larger degree the case for post-Soviet states that are positioned more remotely from the EU—both in their geographical location, but also in terms of being subject to weak pressure and low demands from the EU. Azerbaijan is a good example, as it relies on mediation from the EU in solving various tensions with other external actors, such as Turkey or Russia (Mehdiyeva 2011; Kazantsev 2015). Moreover, the slightly lower level of interest from the EU in shaping domestic changes in those countries allows the union to be able to play the role of a mediator. Azerbaijan (Khidayatova 2015) has sought to use the EU to access various multilateral forums, such as the World Trade Organization. The diplomatic mediation of the conflict in Eastern Ukraine with the participation of Germany and France, has allowed Belarus to claim that it has achieved greater status and reputation on the European continent.

Table 1.1 *The Presence Of Role Expectation And Legitimacy In The Eu's Ideal Self And The Post-Soviet States' Perceptions Of The Eu*

	The EU's ideal self	Armenia	Azerbaijan	Belarus	Georgia	Moldova	Ukraine
Normative power	Strong	Medium	Weak	Weak	Medium	Medium	Medium
Mediator	Weak	Weak	Medium	Medium	Medium	Medium	Weak
Liberal power (negative view)	Weak	Strong	Strong	Strong	Medium	Medium	Medium
Trade partner and power	Medium	Medium	Strong	Medium	Strong	Strong	Strong
Bargaining chip	Weak	Strong	Medium	Strong	Weak	Medium	Weak
Defender against Russia	Weak	Weak	Medium	Weak	Medium	Medium	Strong
Legitimacy							
Promoting norms or values	Strong	Weak	Weak	Weak	Medium	Medium	Medium
Use of force	Weak	Strong	Strong	Medium	Medium	Medium	Strong

Note: Author's own evaluation.

At the same time, in their interactions with the EU, these states have put significant emphasis on ensuring that their views and interests have equal weight in any future deals or partnerships.[9] Being in an equal partnership with the EU is seen as a source of empowerment in the international arena. Azerbaijan has sought to develop foreign policies independent of the influence of external actors, sustained by the export of its abundant natural energy resources (Mehdiyeva 2011). The perception of equality has allowed Baku to claim a sense of distinctiveness in interacting with the EU or Russia. However, as the recent fall in global oil prices shows, Azerbaijan's ability to project its individual foreign policy is sensitive to global markets, which forced it to engage with the EU's demands and ask for negotiations on a new partnership (Ledger 2016).

The EU is also perceived as a liberal power that is intent on promoting its own values as part of the relationship package. This role is seen in the region in negative terms, as the EU's unilateral promotion of norms and values often collides with the interests, preferences and political culture of elites who thrive in more or less authoritarian states. To that extent, most post-Soviet states tend to resist and discourage the EU from taking on this role, or link their acceptance of it to various benefits from the EU. Post-Soviet states such as Belarus (Ministry of Foreign Affairs of Ukraine 2015) and Azerbaijan (Ministry of Foreign Affairs of the Republic of Azerbaijan 2015) emphasise the importance of sovereignty and each country's right to independently determine the range of norms and values that influence its political system or foreign policy. Other external actors, including Russia and China, while opposing the promotion of liberal values, tend to be more attractive foreign policy partners for these post-Soviet states (Kazantsev 2015).

The EU is also perceived in the post-Soviet space as a potential bargaining chip. This role is primarily associated with the multi-vector foreign policies of the post-Soviet states, through which they try to balance the interests of more powerful external actors, such as the EU or Russia. These states aim to cooperate with the EU in such a way as not to upset their relationships with other external actors. They try to maximise benefits from external actors and, at times, play them against each other and initiate 'bidding wars' between Russia and the EU (Contessi 2015; Gnedina 2015). For example, among the EaP states, Armenia (Delcour & Wolczuk 2015b) and, to some extent,

Belarus (White & Feklyunina 2014), currently have the most developed multi-vector foreign policies. Although their membership in the Eurasian Economic Union (EEU) might point to the fact that they have chosen to align their foreign policy with Moscow, maintaining a good and workable relationship with the EU is also a key goal for these countries (Lane & Samokhvalov 2015). Moreover, in the case of Belarus, developing closer relations with the EU and accepting some of its conditionality has been a way of ensuring a measure of independence from Moscow (Rankin 2016). In the case of Armenia, the Nagorno-Karabakh conflict with Azerbaijan and subsequent Russian support means that the EU's influence is rather constrained. However, its relations with the EU are much stronger than those of Belarus or Azerbaijan, and the country stated its interest in achieving complementarity between Eurasian and European integration (Cornell 2017).

The 'bargaining chip' role implies that the threat of establishing closer cooperation with the EU or the promise of limiting ties with the union have been used by post-Soviet states in order to secure more favourable deals in their relationship with Russia. The most prominent example is Belarus' increasing willingness to cooperate with the EU and accept aspects of its conditionality. For President Lukashenka, maintaining a sustainable and effective dialogue with the EU has become, since the start of the Ukraine crisis, a key foreign policy goal. This can be seen as part of Belarus' attempts to resist further political integration into the EEU and maintain its relative independence from Russia (Korosteleva 2015a). Armenia has also tried to keep the option of European integration on the horizon despite its entrenchment in Eurasian integration, for similar reasons to Belarus: to resist ceding more sovereignty to the EEU (Delcour & Wolczuk 2015b). Ukraine during the time of Yanukovich is another example of a post-Soviet state that perceived the EU as a bargaining chip in its relations with Russia. To a large extent, Yanukovich pursued the AA and DCFTA with the EU as a way of gaining independence from Russia, and also to strengthen its bargaining position with the Kremlin (Fesenko 2015). Being seen as a bargaining chip has not given the EU any significant influence over the foreign policies of post-Soviet states, in practice rendering it a passive actor.

The EU is perceived as a normative power, which aims to help the countries in the region democratise and develop through the promotion of its governance system or values. Countries that share this perception look to the EU for financial support, expertise, and technical assistance with the implementation of democratic reforms. Some states even aspire to be part of the EU: Georgia, Ukraine and Moldova regard the EU as the 'gold standard' or model for upholding universal norms and values, and for promoting modernisation (Cadier 2014). Moreover, public opinion in these countries usually tends to distrust national politicians and views the recommendations and benchmarks set by the EU as golden standards for their countries' development (Jarábik & Yanchenko 2013; Korosteleva 2013, 2014, 2015b). Just as it did in the CEE post-communist states, the 'return to Europe' narrative is also present in debates within some post-Soviet states (Edwards 2008). Arguments favouring a European path stress the positive influence that the EU can have on economic, social, and political developments, as well as the pride being formally part of 'civilised' Europe elicits.

At the same time, politicians in some of the European-oriented post-Soviet states have adopted pro-EU rhetoric in order to win or secure political power. Currently, Georgia, Moldova and Ukraine see integration in the EU as their ultimate foreign policy goal. Following the departure of Yanukovich in 2014, Ukraine is entrenched in a self-assumed European path. The country has embraced European integration as its main foreign and domestic goal for the foreseeable future, with the perceived end to facilitate democratisations, making Ukraine part of 'civilised' Europe and modernise, while simultaneously keeping Kyiv at bay from future Russian aggression (Dragneva & Wolczuk 2015). In all three states European integration is seen as a way of leaving behind the legacies of the Soviet Union and the post-Soviet mentality (Delcour 2015).

Despite the rhetorical commitment to adopting 'superior' EU values, little progress has been made in actually implementing the EU's rules and values or adapting their political systems. One supposed benefit of EU integration is an end to the corruption and mismanagement of state funds symptomatic of the post-Soviet space as a whole (Popescu 2010). Nevertheless, while the leaderships of most post-Soviet states have subscribed to EU values, norms, and regulations on paper and, in their discourse, they have failed or been unwilling to implement their European commitments (Ademmer 2015). For example, following the departure from power of the communist party in Moldova, the country was presented as a 'model student' by the EU due to the speed and the commitment with which leaders in Chisinau seemed to have adopted EU rules and regulations (Baltag & Smith 2015). However, this was not matched by policy practice, and Moldova slowly developed into one of the most corrupt regimes in the region, with $1 billion of government funds disappearing from Moldovan banks (Tanas 2015). In comparison to Ukraine, Moldova and Georgia have not completely embraced a pro-European path as they still acknowledge the need to have a workable relationship with Moscow (Adzinbaia 2015).[10] At the same time, the post-Soviet states have complained that the promotion of EU norms is unilateral, as also recognised by the 2015 revision of the EaP (European Commission 2015). To a large extent this role matches the one framed in the EU's ideal self. However, even the few post-Soviet states that seem to embrace this role have made only limited steps in implementing the range of values norms and regulations demanded by the EU.

Finally, the EU is perceived as a defender of European values, and a protector against Russian aggression, be it military, economic, or cultural. Most of the post-Soviet states fear in various degrees the potential loss of independence and sovereignty to Moscow (Bechev 2015). In particular, states that have current conflicts with Russia or had conflicts in the past—Azerbaijan, Georgia, Moldova and Ukraine—would like to see more EU involvement in regional security. However, the EU has not been prepared to take up the challenge, partly in order not to further unsettle its relations with Russia, but also due to differences in how to deal with Russia (European Parliament 2014; House of Lords 2015). Although it is hardly characteristic of the EU's ideal self to view its own role as a deterrent of Russian aggression, this role increases the effectiveness for the EU's conditionality in the region, as the post-Soviet states do not have the option of balancing the EU with Russia.

Framed in the ideal self, the EU's understanding of the legitimacy of the use of force in world politics and of the promotion of norms or values are not shared by any of the post-Soviet states. The EU perceives the use of force as a measure of last resort, while the promotion of its (universal) norms to other international actors is seen to be legitimate. Post-Soviet states that are faced with conflicts or with the constant threat of conflict or internal separatism (Ukraine, Azerbaijan, Armenia) frame the use of force as a legitimate and normal tool in world politics. Those states not experiencing immediate threats tend to regard the use of force as a measure of last resort (for example, Belarus). This view is also based on the fact that these countries wish to avoid any type of military confrontation with the various external powers that surround them; in the case of Belarus, Russia. On the other hand, the promotion of EU norms is perceived to be legitimate by countries that support the EU's role as a normative actor in the region (Georgia, Ukraine and Moldova). Importing EU norms is seen as a way to be integrated in the liberal world community and be part of Western civilisation (Barkanov 2015). All post-Soviet states in various degrees argue that the EU promotes its norms asymmetrically and tries to impose them unilaterally. In the more extreme version, this narrative of resisting EU norm promotion is equivalent to maintaining state independence and sovereignty (Sakwa 2014). Moreover, even those that view the promotion of EU norms to be legitimate have had problems in actually implementing the norms and regulations adopted from the EU. Consequently, the EU's view of legitimate behaviour in world politics (be it concerning the use of force or promotion) is shared by the post-Soviet states only when it matches with their interests or their needs. This further strengthens the idea that post-Soviet states tend to instrumentalise the EU in their foreign policies.

Discussion and conclusions

In the context of increasing disorder and conflict across the post-Soviet space, this essay has aimed to shed light on the way the EU's identity is perceived by and reflected in the foreign policies of the countries in the region. The concept of 'ideal self' can be understood as an overall vector in foreign policy that guides the way international actors ought to ideally behave in world politics. Focus on the ideal self allowed the essay to identify the ways the EU frames its ideal behaviour in the post-Soviet space and those in which the EU's ideal self underscored the union's main role as a normative power. In relation to legitimacy, the EU views the use of force in world politics to be legitimate only as a measure of last resort, while the external promotion of universal norms is perceived to represent legitimate behaviour. The essay also explored the way in which the EU's identity is perceived and reflected in the foreign policies of the post-Soviet states. In doing so it aimed to account for the similarities and differences between the perception of the post-Soviet states and the EU's ideal self. The analysis presented an overview from a broader research project that looked in detail at the foreign policies of the post-Soviet states. While the essay presents insights from individual post-Soviet states, the emphasis is rather on identifying and explaining similarities or differences between the ways the foreign policies of these states reflect the EU's ideal self.

The analysis highlights that there are more differences than similarities in the way the post-Soviet states reflect the EU's ideal self. For example, the EU's role as a normative power in the region is shared by only a few states (Georgia, Moldova, Ukraine), for which being part of the EU represents a key foreign policy goal. The post-Soviet states tend to perceive a wider range of roles for the EU in the region: liberal power, security provider, bargaining chip. These roles nevertheless overlap in line with the different interests of the post-Soviet states and their specificities. Moreover, when it comes to legitimate and responsible behaviour no post-Soviet state shares the EU's understanding of the legitimacy of the use of force and the external promotion of norms or values. Most post-Soviet states have instrumentalised their relations with the EU, trying to get as many benefits as possible. Their foreign policy has reflected the EU's ideal self primarily in cases where it suited their interests or presented costs. As the post-Soviet states have been surrounded by multiple powerful external actors, siding in foreign policy with one has the potential of alienating the others and potentially suffering dangerous consequences. In the case of Ukraine, for example, the mismatch between the EU's ideal self in the region and Kyiv's own perception of the EU's role has contributed to the Ukraine crisis in the sense that, since the departure of Yanukovich, the leadership expected more of the union than it received.

The EU's approach towards the post-Soviet region has been informed to a larger extent by own realities rather than by interactions with other states or the structure of world politics. In practice, the intersubjective aspects of the EU's identity have been less pronounced than its ideal perceptions of the self. The construction of the ideal self can thus account for the reasons why the EU is instrumentalised by the post-Soviet states. Firstly, the EU's ideal self tends to be rather flexible, changing its often ambitious goals when they do not match reality and political outcomes. Although the EU perceives itself as upholding and promoting universal norms and values, as well as rules and regulations leading to economic development in the post-Soviet space, in practice it has turned a blind eye to, for example, the corrupt practices of supposedly pro-European policymakers from the region. At the same time, the EU frequently ignored setbacks in democratic reforms in pro-European countries such as Ukraine and Moldova, creating the impression of double standards in its approach towards the eastern neighbourhood. Hence, the flexible interpretation of the ideal self on the part of the EU has made the post-Soviet states question their commitment and adopt an instrumental approach, thus contributing to low ownership from the post-Soviet states of the ENP or the EaP, and to their instrumentalisation of relations with the EU.

Secondly, the EU's ideal self also emphasised the moral supremacy of the EU, regarding EU norms and values as superior to those of the neighbourhood in the post-Soviet space. In practice, the EU's approach mirrored its own institutional make-up and ideal self, ignoring the diversity of views and interests present in the post-Soviet space. EU centrism pushed the post-Soviet states to view the union more as an instrument for achieving various ends rather than a genuine partner (Cadier 2015). Moreover, only until recently with the revision of the 2015 ENP, the EU started to revise its ideal self in the post-Soviet space and be more sensitive to the region, in a move underlined by the realisation that the EU neighbourhood has transformed from a ring of friends to a ring of fire.

Thirdly, on the surface the EU's ideal self has a very well-defined outward dimension, in that unlike nation states it is more altruistic and pays more attention to the wellbeing and interests of other people. As Moga (2017) shows, this characterisation paved the way for EU policymakers and institutions deeply ingrained in the narrative underlying the EU ideal self to be at the helm of the EU's approach towards the post-Soviet space.

Viewing the EU as an instrument for achieving various ends should not be considered to be solely influenced by the EU. On the one hand, the EU is employed by those segments of the post-Soviet elites who want to score electoral points by either declaring their allegiance to the EU (in pro-European countries), opposing the European integration (in more pro-Russian countries), or pointing to the EU as a scapegoat in order to push forward unpopular policies (Delcour 2015). On the other hand, the post-Soviet states have a tradition of balancing their relations with the great powers, employing an opportunistic approach whereby they play these powers against each other in order to get as many benefits as possible. Hence, instrumentalising relations with more salient international actors is also down to the opportunistic tendency of the post-Soviet states. The analysis also provides the basis for understanding the ideal self of external actors and how it is reflected in the foreign policies of the post-Soviet states. The assumption in this case would be that, besides the clash of interests and norms between external actors, regional conflicts are also a result of the contradictory ways in which the ideal self of the external actors framed their roles in the post-Soviet space.

Notes

1. The 2003 Security Strategy highlighted the EU's ambition to play a key role in world politics, and the expectation that it would manage to influence its neighbourhood following the 2004/2007 'big bang' enlargement to Central and Eastern Europe. For more details see: 'European Security Strategy—A Secure Europe in a Better World', 12 December 2013, available at: https://europa.eu/globalstrategy/en/european-security-strategy-secure-europe-better-world, accessed 27 March 2018.
2. The 2016 Global Strategy stresses the fact that world politics has become less stable than a decade ago and requires a different approach from the EU. The emphasis is on the need to develop an approach based on principled pragmatism, where the EU has more limited ambitions in international relations and seeks to pursue its interests in foreign policy. For more details see: 'EU Global Strategy', available at: https://europa.eu/globalstrategy/en/global-strategy-foreign-and-security-policy-european-union, accessed 9 May 2018.
3. The ENP was launched by the EU in 2003 and sought to provide a framework for the union to cooperate with the neighbourhood tastes. The main goal was to promote stability and democracy in the neighbourhood, while also helping the states in the region to develop. The ENP was revised following the Arab Spring in 2011, and then in the context of the Ukraine crisis and the migrant crisis in 2015. For more details see: 'European Neighbourhood Policy', available at: https://ec.europa.eu/neighbourhood-enlargement/neighbourhood/overview_en, accessed 27 March 2018.
4. The EU launched the EaP in 2009 on the initiative of Poland and Sweden. The initiative is part of the ENP, but seeks to further enhance cooperation on trade and political issues with the post-Soviet states of Armenia, Azerbaijan, Belarus, Georgia, Moldova and Ukraine. For more details see: 'Eastern Partnership', available at: https://eeas.europa.eu/topics/eastern-partnership_en, accessed 27 March 2018.
5. Similar to the ENP, the main aim of the UfM is to create stability and integration in the Mediterranean region. It was established in 2008 as an intergovernmental forum consisting of European countries and states from the Mediterranean basin. For more details see, 'Union for the Mediterranean', available at: https://eeas.europa.eu/diplomatic-network/union-mediterranean-ufm_en, accessed 27 March 2018.
6. The essay considers the EU to have achieved actorness in world politics. To that extent references to the EU's foreign policy or to its self-perception in international relations focus on areas where a high level of agreement exist among the member states and the EU's institutions—the neighbourhood is one of these areas.
7. This essay posits that both states and other types of international actors such as the EU are constrained in their foreign policy by the 'ideal self'. However, for practical reasons the term 'state' is used throughout.
8. The AAs are treaties that set out the framework for cooperation between the EU and non-EU states; DCFTAs are enhanced trade agreements that the EU has offered to Ukraine, Georgia and Moldova.
9. *EU Consultation: 'Towards a New European Neighbourhood Policy'*, Heinrich–Böll–Stiftung e.V., 2015, available at: https://eu.boell.org/sites/default/files/towards_a_new_european_neighbourhood_policy_fin.pdf, accessed 20 June 2017.
10. Moldova wants to Improve Relations with Russia—Deputy PM', *TASS*, 31 May 2016, available at: http://tass.ru/en/world/879285, accessed 20 June 2017.

References

Ademmer, E. (2015) 'Interdependence and EU-demanded Policy Change in a Shared Neighbourhood', *Journal of European Public Policy*, 22, 5.

Adzinbaia, Z. (2015) 'Georgia's Normalization of Relations with Russia Murky as Ever', *Georgia Today*, 27 August, available at: http://georgiatoday.ge/news/1089/Georgia%E2%80%99s-Normalization-of-Relations-with-Russia-Murky-as-Ever, accessed 20 June 2017.

Allen, D. & Smith, M. (1990) 'Western Europe's Presence in the Contemporary International Arena', *Review of International Studies*, 16, 1.

Ashton, C. (2012) 'Speech on EU Foreign Policy towards the BRICS and other Emerging Powers', European Parliament, 1 February, available at: http://eeas.europa.eu/images/top_stories/020212_brics.pdf, accessed 20 June 2017.

Bäckstrand, K. & Elgström, O. (2013) 'The EU's Role in Climate Change Negotiations: from Leader to "Leadiator"', *Journal of European Public Policy*, 20, 10.

Baltag, D. & Smith, M. (2015) 'EU and Member State Diplomacies in Moldova and Ukraine: Examining EU Diplomatic Performance Post-Lisbon', *European Integration Online Papers (EIoP)*, 19, 1.

Barkanov, B. (2015) 'Crisis in Ukraine: Clash of Civilizations or Geopolitics?', in Kanet, R. E. & Sussex, M. (eds) *Power, Politics and Confrontation in Eurasia: Foreign Policy in a Contested Region* (Basingstoke, Palgrave Macmillan).

Beauguitte, L., Richard, Y. & Guérin-Pace, F. (2015) 'The EU and its Neighbourhoods: A Textual Analysis on Key Documents of the European Neighbourhood Policy', *Geopolitics*, 20, 4.

Bechev, D. (2015) 'Understanding the Contest Between the EU and Russia in Their Shared Neighborhood', *Problems of Post-Communism*, 62, 6.

Bickerton, C. J. (2011) *European Union Foreign Policy: From Effectiveness to Functionality* (Basingstoke, Palgrave Macmillan).

Bisley, N. (2012) *Great Powers in the Changing International Order* (Boulder, CO, Lynne Rienner Publishers).

Boedeltje, F. & van Houtum, H. (2011) 'Brussels is Speaking: The Adverse Speech Geo-Politics of the European Union Towards its Neighbours', *Geopolitics*, 16, 1.

Browning, C. S. (2006) 'Small, Smart and Salient? Rethinking Identity in the Small States Literature', *Cambridge Review of International Affairs*, 19, 4.

Buchanan, A. & Keohane, R. O. (2006) 'The Legitimacy of Global Governance Institutions', *Ethics & International Affairs*, 20, 4.

Bukkvoll, T. (2001) 'Off the Cuff Politics—Explaining Russia's Lack of a Ukraine Strategy', *Europe-Asia Studies*, 53, 8.

Buzan, B. (2004) *The United States and the Great Powers: World Politics in the Twenty-First Century* (Cambridge, Polity).

Cadier, D. (2014) 'Eastern Partnership vs Eurasian Union? The EU–Russia Competition in the Shared Neighbourhood and the Ukraine Crisis', *Global Policy*, 5, s1.

Cadier, D. (2015) 'Policies Towards the Post-Soviet Space: The Eurasian Economic Union As An Attempt To Develop Russia's Structural Power?', in Cadier, D. & Light, M. (eds) *Russia's Foreign Policy: Ideas, Domestic Politics and External Relations* (New York, NY, Palgrave Macmillan).

Cantir, C. & Kennedy, R. (2015) 'Balancing on the Shoulders of Giants: Moldova's Foreign Policy toward Russia and the European Union', *Foreign Policy Analysis*, 11, 4.

Chaban, N., Elgström, O., Kelly, S. & Yi, L. S. (2013) 'Images of the EU beyond its Borders: Issue-Specific and Regional Perceptions of European Union Power and Leadership', *JCMS: Journal of Common Market Studies*, 51, 3.

Checkel, J. T. & Katzenstein, P. J. (eds) (2009) *European Identity* (Cambridge, Cambridge University Press).

Contessi, N. P. (2015) 'Foreign and Security Policy Diversification in Eurasia: Issue Splitting, Co-alignment, and Relational Power', *Problems of Post-Communism*, 62, 5.

Cornell, S. E. (ed.) (2017) *The International Politics of the Armenian-Azerbaijani Conflict: The Original 'Frozen Conflict' and European Security* (Basingstoke, Palgrave Macmillan).

Council of the European Union (2003) *A Secure Europe in a Better World—European Securityss Strategy*, available at: http://www.consilium.europa.eu/uedocs/cmsUpload/78367.pdf, accessed 20 June 2017.

Council of the European Union (2008) *Report on the Implementation of the European Security Strategy—Providing Security in a Changing World*, available at: http://www.consilium.europa.eu/ueDocs/cms_Data/docs/pressdata/EN/reports/104630.pdf, accessed 20 October 2016.

Council of the European Union (2010) *Conclusions on Eastern Partnership*, available at: http://www.consilium.europa.eu/uedocs/cms_Data/docs/pressdata/EN/foraff/117327.pdf, accessed 20 June 2017.

Council of the European Union (2011) *Joint Declaration of the Eastern Partnership Summit*, available at: http://www.consilium.europa.eu/uedocs/cms_Data/docs/pressdata/en/ec/124843.pdf, accessed 20 June 2017

De Zutter, E. (2010) 'Normative Power Spotting: an Ontological and Methodological Appraisal', *Journal of European Public Policy*, 17, 8.

Delcour, L. (2010) 'The European Union, A Security Provider in the Eastern Neighbourhood?', *European Security*, 19, 4.

Delcour, L. (2015) 'Between the Eastern Partnership and Eurasian Integration: Explaining Post-Soviet Countries' Engagement in (Competing) "Region-Building Projects"', *Problems of Post-Communism*, 62, 6.

Delcour, L. & Wolczuk, K. (2015a) 'Spoiler or Facilitator of Democratization?: Russia's Role in Georgia and Ukraine', *Democratization*, 22, 3.

Delcour, L. & Wolczuk, K. (2015b) 'The EU's Unexpected "Ideal Neighbour"? The Perplexing Case of Armenia's Europeanisation', *Journal of European Integration*, 37, 4.

Diez, T. (2005) 'Constructing the Self and Changing Others: Reconsidering "Normative Power Europe"', *Millennium—Journal of International Studies*, 33, 3.

Dragneva, R. & Wolczuk, K. (2015) *Ukraine Between the EU and Russia: The Integration Challenge* (Basingstoke, Palgrave).

Edwards, G. (2008) 'The Construction of Ambiguity and the Limits of Attraction: Europe and its Neighbourhood Policy', *Journal of European Integration*, 30, 1.

European Commission (2003) *Wider Europe—Neighbourhood: A New Framework for Relations with our Eastern and Southern Neighbours*, available at: http://eeas.europa.eu/enp/pdf/pdf/com03_104_en.pdf, accessed 20 June 2017.

European Commission (2010) 'Implementation of the Eastern Partnership: Report to the Meeting of Foreign Affairs Ministers, December 13, 2010', available at: http://www.eeas.europa.eu/eastern/docs/eap meeting_foreign_affairs_131210_en.pdf, accessed 20 June 2017.

European Commission (2015) *Review of the European Neighbourhood Policy*, available at: http://www.eeas.europa.eu/eastern/docs/eap_meeting_foreign_affairs_131210_en.pdf, accessed 20 June 2017.

European External Action Service (2016) *Shared Vision, Common Action: A Stronger Europe*, available at: https://eeas.europa.eu/top_stories/pdf/eugs_review_web.pdf, accessed 20 June 2017.

European Parliament (2013a) *European Parliament Recommendation to the Council on the UN Principle of the 'Responsibility to Protect' ('R2P')*, available at: http://www.europarl.europa.eu/sides/getDoc.do?pubRef=-//EP//TEXT+REPORT+A7-2013-0130+0+DOC+XML+V0//EN, accessed 20 June 2017.

European Parliament (2013b) *European Parliament Resolution of 12 September 2013 on the Pressure Exerted by Russia on Eastern Partnership Countries (in the Context of the Upcoming Eastern Partnership Summit in Vilnius)*, available at: http://www.europarl.europa.eu/sides/getDoc.do?type=TA&reference=P7-TA-2013-0383&language=EN, accessed 20 June 2017.

European Parliament (2014) *European Parliament Resolution of 6 February 2014 on the EU–Russia Summit*, available at: http://www.europarl.europa.eu/sides/getDoc.do?pubRef=-//EP//TEXT+TA+P7-TA-2014-0101+0+DOC+XML+V0//EN, accessed 20 June 2017.

Evans, G. (2009) 'Russia, Georgia and the Responsibility to Protect', *Amsterdam Law Forum*, 1, 2.

Ferrero-Waldner, B. (2005) *Implementing and promoting the European Neighbourhood Policy*, available at: http://eeas.europa.eu/enp/pdf/pdf/sec_2005_1521_en.pdf, accessed 20 June 2017.

Fesenko, V. (2015) 'Ukraine: Between Europe and Eurasia', in Dutkiewicz, P. & Sakwa, R. (eds) *Eurasian Integration—The View from Within* (Abingdon, Routledge).

Flockhart, T. (2016) 'The Coming Multi-order World', *Contemporary Security Policy*, 37, 1.

Freire, M. R. & Kanet, R. E. (eds) (2012) *Competing for Influence: the EU and Russia in post-Soviet Eurasia* (Dordrecht, Republic of Letters).

Füle, Š. (2010a) *The EU: a Force for Peace, Stability and Prosperity in Wider Europe*, available at: http://europa.eu/rapid/press-release_SPEECH-10-706_en.htm?locale=en, accessed 20 June 2017.

Füle, Š. (2010b) *The European Union and Eastern Europe: Post-Crisis Rapprochement?*, available at: http://europa.eu/rapid/pressReleasesAction.do?reference=SPEECH/10/728&format=HTML&aged=0&language=EN&guiLanguage=en, accessed 1 October 2016.

Fumagalli, M. (2007) 'Ethnicity, State Formation and Foreign Policy: Uzbekistan and "Uzbeks Abroad"', *Central Asian Survey*, 26, 1.

Gnedina, E. (2015) '"Multi-Vector" Foreign Policies in Europe: Balancing, Bandwagoning or Bargaining?', *Europe-Asia Studies*, 67, 7.

Goddard, S. E. & Krebs, R. R. (2015) 'Rhetoric, Legitimation, and Grand Strategy', *Security Studies*, 24, 1.

Gretskiy, I., Treshchenkov, E. & Golubev, K. (2014) 'Russia's Perceptions and Misperceptions of the EU Eastern Partnership', *Communist and Post-Communist Studies*, 47, 3–4.

Gstöhl, S. & Schunz, S. (eds) (2017) *Theorizing the European Neighbourhood Policy* (Abingdon, Routledge).

Harnisch, S. (2011) 'Role Theory: Operationalization of Key Concepts', in Harnisch, S., Frank, C. & Maull, H. (eds) *Role Theory in International Relations: Approaches and Analyses* (Abingdon, Routledge).

Haukkala, H. (2011) 'The European Union as a Regional Normative Hegemon: The Case of European Neighbourhood Policy', in Whitman, R. G. (ed.) *Normative Power Europe: Empirical and Theoretical Perspectives* (Basingstoke, Palgrave Macmillan).

Heimann, G. (2015) 'What does it take to be a Great Power? The Story of France Joining the Big Five', *Review of International Studies*, 41, 1.

Heisbourg, F. (2015) 'The Strategic Implications of the Syrian Refugee Crisis', *Survival*, 57, 6.

House of Lords (2015) *The EU and Russia: Before and Beyond the Crisis in Ukraine*, available at: https://www.publications.parliament.uk/pa/ld201415/ldselect/ldeucom/115/115.pdf, accessed 20 June 2017.

Jafarli, N. (2016) 'Azerbaijan: Approaching Crisis Point', *ECFR Wider Europe Forum*, available at: http://www.ecfr.eu/article/commentary_azerbaijan_approaching_crisis_point5096#, accessed 20 June 2017.

Jarábik, B. & Yanchenko, H. (2013) 'What Eastern Europeans think about the Democratic Transition: Understanding Values and Attitudes', *Globsec Policy Briefs*, available at: http://www.cepolicy.org/publications/what-eastern-europeans-think-about-democratic-transition-understanding-values-and, accessed 20 June 2017.

Kadelbach, S. (2014) 'The European Union's Responsibility to Protect', in Hilpold, P. (ed.) *The Responsibility to Protect (R2P)* (Leiden, Brill).

Kakachia, K. & Cecire M. (eds) (2013) *Georgian Foreign Policy. The Quest for Sustainable Security* (Tbilisi, Konrad-Adenauer-Stiftung), available at: http://www.kas.de/wf/doc/kas_37002-1522-1-30.pdf, accessed 20 June 2017.

Kazantsev, A. (2015) 'Central Asian Perspectives on Eurasian Regionalism', in Dutkiewicz, P. & Sakwa, R. (eds) *Eurasian Integration—The View from Within* (Abingdon, Routledge).

Khidayatova, A. (2015) 'EU to support Azerbaijan's joining WTO', *Trend*, 1 April, available at: http://en.trend.az/azerbaijan/business/2378862.html, accessed 20 June 2017.

Korosteleva, E. A. (2013) *Belarus and the Eastern Partnership: A National Values Survey* (Canterbury, University of Kent).

Korosteleva, E. A. (2014) *Moldova's Values Survey: Widening a European Dialogue in Moldova* (Canterbury, University of Kent).

Korosteleva, E. A. (2015a) 'Belarus between the EU and the Eurasian Economic Union', in Dutkiewicz, P. & Sakwa, R. (eds) *Eurasian Integration—The View from Within* (Abingdon, Routledge).

Korosteleva, E. A. (2015b) *Moldova's Focus Groups: Widening a European Dialogue in Moldova* (Canterbury, University of Kent).

Korosteleva, E. A. (2016) 'The European Union, Russia and the Eastern Region: The Analytics of Government for Sustainable Cohabitation', *Cooperation and Conflict*, 51, 3.

Korosteleva, E. A., Van Gils, E. & Merheim-Eyre, I. (2017) '"The Political" and the ENP: Rethinking EU Relations with the Eastern Region', in Gstöhl, S. & Schunz, S. (eds) *Theorizing the European Neighbourhood Policy* (Abingdon, Routledge).

Lake, D. A. (2011) *Hierarchy in International Relations* (Ithaca, NY, Cornell University Press).

Lane, D. & Samokhvalov, V. (eds) (2015) *The Eurasian Project and Europe: Regional Discontinuities and Geopolitics* (Basingstoke, Palgrave Macmillan).

Lebow, R. N. (2008) 'Identity and International Relations', *International Relations*, 22, 4.

Ledger, R. (2016) 'The EU's Lack of Unity and Strategy is being felt in Azerbaijan', *Euro Crisis in the Press*, 28 July, available at: http://blogs.lse.ac.uk/eurocrisispress/2016/07/28/the-eus-lack-of-unity-and-strategy-is-being-felt-in-azerbaijan/, accessed 20 June 2017.

Leeds, B. A. & Mattes, M. (2007) 'Alliance Politics during the Cold War: Aberration, New World Order, or Continuation of History?', *Conflict Management and Peace Science*, 24, 3.

Maksak, H., Shelest, H., Koval, N. & Koval, M. (eds) (2017) *Ukrainian Prism: Foreign Policy 2016* (Kyiv, Friedrich Ebert Foundation), available at: http://library.fes.de/pdf-files/bueros/ukraine/13244.pdf, accessed 20 June 2017.

Matlary, J. H. (2006) 'When Soft Power Turns Hard: Is an EU Strategic Culture Possible?', *Security Dialogue*, 37, 1.

Mattern, J. B. & Zarakol, A. (2016) 'Hierarchies in World Politics', *International Organization*, 70, 3.

Mayer, H. & Vogt, H. (2006) *A Responsible Europe?: Ethical Foundations of EU External Affairs* (Basingstoke, Palgrave Macmillan).

Mehdiyeva, N. (2011) *Power Games in the Caucasus: Azerbaijan's Foreign and Energy Policy towards the West, Russia and the Middle East* (London, I.B.Tauris).

Menon, A. (2011) 'Power, Institutions and the CSDP: The Promise of Institutionalist Theory', *JCMS: Journal of Common Market Studies*, 49, 1.

Ministry of Foreign Affairs and European Integration (2010) *Moldova Just a Step Away from the EU*, available at: http://www.mfa.gov.md/interviews-en/479415/, accessed 20 June 2017.

Ministry of Foreign Affairs of the Republic of Armenia (2017) *Foreign Policy*, available at: http://www.mfa.am/en/foreign-policy/, accessed 20 June 2017.

Ministry of Foreign Affairs of the Republic of Azerbaijan (2015) *Statement by the MFA of the Republic of Azerbaijan Regarding the So-Called 'Elections'*, available at: http://guam-organization.org/en/node/1695, accessed 20 June 2017.

Ministry of Foreign Affairs of the Republic of Belarus (2017) *Priorities of the Foreign Policy of the Republic of Belarus*, available at: http://mfa.gov.by/en/foreign_policy/priorities/, accessed 20 June 2017.

Ministry of Foreign Affairs of Ukraine (2015) *Belarus Supports Sovereignty and Territorial Integrity of Ukraine*, available at: http://mfa.gov.ua/en/press-center/news/38955-belarus-supports-sovereignty-and-territorial-integrity-of-ukraine, accessed 20 June 2017.

Moga, T. L. (2017) 'The Role of Bounded Rationality in Explaining the European Neighbourhood Policy: The Eastern Dimension', in Gstöhl, S. & Schunz, S. (eds).

Mogherini, F. (2017) *Speech by Federica Mogherini at the Munich Security Conference*, available at: https://eeas.europa.eu/headquarters/headquarters-homepage_en/20832/Speech%20by%20Federica%20Mogherini%20at%20the%20Munich%20Security%20Conference, accessed 20 June 2017.

Nabers, D. (2011) 'Identity and Role Change in International Politics', in Harnisch, S., Frank, C. & Maull, H. (eds) *Role Theory in International Relations: Approaches and Analyses* (Abingdon, Routledge).

Najšlová, L. (2010) 'The EU in the Wider Black Sea Region: Clumsy but Attractive?', in Henderson, K. & Weaver, C. (eds) *The Black Sea Region and EU Policy: The Challenge of Divergent Agendas* (Farnham, Ashgate).

Nilsson, M. & Silander, D. (2016) 'Democracy and Security in the EU's Eastern Neighborhood? Assessing the ENP in Georgia, Moldova, and Ukraine', *Democracy and Security*, 12, 1.

Pashayeva, G. (2015) *The EU–Azerbaijan Relationship: Current Status and Future Outlook*, available at: https://jamestown.org/program/the-eu-azerbaijan-relationship-current-status-and-future-outlook/#!, accessed 20 June 2017.

Popescu, N. (2010) *EU Foreign Policy and Post-Soviet Conflicts: Stealth Intervention* (Abingdon, Routledge).

Prodi, R. (2002) *A Wider Europe—A Proximity Policy as the Key to Stability*, available at: http://europa.eu/rapid/press-release_SPEECH-02-619_en.htm, accessed 20 June 2017.

Raik, K. & Dinesen, R. L. (2015) 'The European Union and Upheavals in its Neighborhood: A Force for Stability?', *International Journal of Public Administration*, 38, 12.

Rankin, J. (2016) 'EU Lifts most Sanctions Against Belarus Despite Human Rights Concerns', *The Guardian*, 15 February, available at: https://www.theguardian.com/world/2016/feb/15/eu-lifts-most-sanctions-against-belarus-despite-human-rights-concerns, accessed 20 June 2017.

Rynning, S. & Jensen, C. P. (2010) 'The ENP and Transatlantic Relations', in Whitman, R. G. & Wolff, S. (eds) *The European Neighbourhood Policy in Perspective: Context, Implementation and Impact* (London, Palgrave Macmillan).

Saari, S. (2014) 'Russia's Post-Orange Revolution Strategies to Increase its Influence in Former Soviet Republics: Public Diplomacy *po russkii*', *Europe-Asia Studies*, 66, 1.

Sakwa, R. (2014) *Frontline Ukraine* (London, I.B. Tauris).

Sakwa, R. (2015) 'Politics and International Affairs in Putin's Third Term', in Sakwa, R., Galeotti, M. & Balzer, H. (eds) *Putin's Third Term: Assessments Amid Crisis* (Washington, DC, Center on Global Interests), available at: http://globalinterests.org/wp-content/uploads/2016/04/Putins-Third-Term_CGI.pdf, accessed 12 April 2018.

Schimmelfennig, F. & Scholtz, H. (2008) 'EU Democracy Promotion in the European Neighbourhood', *European Union Politics*, 9, 2.

Schoen, H. (2008) 'Identity, Instrumental Self-Interest and Institutional Evaluations', *European Union Politics*, 9, 1.

Schumacher, T. (2015) 'Uncertainty at the EU's Borders: Narratives of EU External Relations in the Revised European Neighbourhood Policy Towards the Southern Borderlands', *European Security*, 24, 3.

Sjursen, H. (2011) 'The EU's Common Foreign and Security Policy: The Quest for Democracy', *Journal of European Public Policy*, 18, 8.

Slaughter, A.-M. (2005) *A New World Order* (Princeton, NJ, Princeton University Press).

Solana, J. (2008) 'Address by Javier SOLANA, EU High Representative for the Common Foreign and Security Policy, at the European Union Monitoring Mission (EUMM) Headquarters in Georgia', available at: http://eeas.europa.eu/delegations/georgia/press_corner/all_news/news/2008/20080930_01_en.htm, accessed 20 June 2017.

Tanas, A. (2015) 'Moldova Detains Former PM in Parliament Over $1 Billion Fraud', *Reuters*, 15 October, available at: http://www.reuters.com/article/us-moldova-protests-filat-idUSKCN0S91BY20151015, accessed 20 June 2017.

Terhalle, M. (2015) *The Transition of Global Order: Legitimacy and Contestation* (London, Palgrave Macmillan).

Tonra, B. (2011) 'Democratic Foundations of EU Foreign Policy: Narratives and the Myth of EU Exceptionalism', *Journal of European Public Policy*, 18, 8.

White, S. & Feklyunina, V. (2014) *Identities and Foreign Policies in Russia, Ukraine and Belarus* (London, Palgrave Macmillan).

Youngs, R. (2017) *Europe's Eastern Crisis: The Geopolitics of Asymmetry* (Cambridge, Cambridge University Press).

Zehfuss, M. (2006) 'Constructivism and Identity. A Dangerous Liaison', in Guzzini, S. & Leander, A. (eds) *Constructivism and International Relations: Alexander Wendt and His Critics* (Abingdon, Routledge).

Zielonka, J. (2008) 'Europe as a Global Actor: Empire by Example?', *International Affairs*, 84, 3.

Between the Eastern Partnership and Eurasian Integration

Explaining Post-Soviet Countries' Engagement in (Competing) Region-Building Projects

Laure Delcour

Introduction

This article intends to enrich the understanding of region-building processes in the post-Soviet space by explaining why countries engage in regional projects and highlighting the critical connections between external and internal drivers of integration. Based upon an analysis of the drivers behind Armenia's and Moldova's commitments to Eurasian integration and association with the European Union, respectively, it develops a more nuanced approach to region-building in the post-Soviet space, whereby partner countries are not only objects but also subjects of policies implemented by external actors.

Over the past few years, region-building projects initiated by the European Union (EU) and Russia in the former USSR have increasingly drawn academic attention. While pointing to the profoundly different approaches developed by the EU and Russia in their "common neighborhood," scholars have also brought nuance to analyses of the EU and Russia as being fundamentally different actors (Averre 2009; Casier 2013). More recently, with the development of the EU's and Russia's hard-law economic integration projects in the post-Soviet space (Dragneva and Wolczuk 2013), attention has shifted toward the consequences of their policies for the countries of their common neighborhood (Delcour and Wolczuk 2013). This is because the EU's and Russia's regional projects —more specifically, the EU's Deep and Comprehensive Free Trade Area and the Russia-driven Eurasian Economic Union —are mutually exclusive,[1] thus compelling partner countries to make a choice that commits them to an enhanced relationship with either player while de facto restricting links with the other.

One of the consequences of the EU–Russia rivalry is that the "common neighborhood" now seems deeply divided between those countries that have joined the Eurasian Economic Union (i.e., Belarus and Armenia) and those that have signed the Association Agreements (AAs) and the Deep and Comprehensive Free Trade Agreements (DCFTAs) offered by the EU under the Eastern Partnership (i.e., Georgia, Moldova, and Ukraine). Since 2013, both Russian and EU actors have increasingly referred to their common neighborhood in terms of geopolitical choice.[2] This sharply contrasted geopolitical picture is underpinned by three interconnected ideas. First, the analytical focus on EU–Russia competition suggests that developments in the region are now primarily framed by external actors' interests and policies; according to this view, it is external stimuli and pressures that drive partner countries' engagement in regional integration projects. Second, since the EU's and Russia's policies are identified as key drivers of change, engagement in regional projects is often presented as a path that cannot be reversed by partner countries themselves. Third, the emphasis is often placed on the selection of a regional project by one or another country, thus implicitly suggesting that the selected option is not subject to internal debates and that it is endorsed by the country as a whole.

However, the focus on external drivers neglects complex dynamics at stake in partner countries and leads to an over-simplification. In particular, it fails to explain differential engagement by post-Soviet countries and it overshadows ambiguities and shifts in partner countries' attitudes vis-à-vis regional projects.

What, then, drives partner countries' responses to the EU's and Russia's regional initiatives? What factors explain their European or Eurasian choice? And to what extent do partner countries' seemingly clear-cut choices reflect a consensus among political elites and societies?

This article explores why partner countries engage in regional projects in the EU's and Russia's "common neighborhood." In the process, it unpacks the critical connections that tie together external and internal drivers of engagement into regional projects. As the article argues, engagement in one or the other project is not just the outcome of external actors' stimuli and pressures; it is also tightly connected to partner countries' socio-economic needs, structural constraints influencing their foreign policies, and elites' preferences. After all, the EU's and Russia's regional projects do not take place in a vacuum. First, they are embedded in a longer history of relations that has contributed to shaping partner countries' attitudes to both actors. Second, the reception of these projects crucially hinges on their resonance with existing reforms as well as costs and benefits for the ruling elite and the country as a whole. Therefore, externally driven regional initiatives delve into domestic practices, constellations of actors, and preferences. In essence, since the EU's and Russia's projects are mutually exclusive, the decision to join one or the other project ultimately lies with each of the six countries at stake. While the decision of these countries is certainly shaped by external players' stimuli and pressures, it derives primarily from elites' interpretation of these stimuli and pressures. This calls for rebalancing the examination of factors behind partner countries' involvement in either the Eurasian Economic Union or the deep economic integration scheme foreseen under the Eastern Partnership.

The article scrutinizes the interplay of external policies and domestic contexts in two countries that have made opposite choices in terms of deep economic integration, namely Armenia and Moldova. It is based upon an examination of policy documents, key speeches by decision-makers, existing surveys on attitudes to regional projects, and semi-structured interviews conducted in the countries between 2011 and 2014. The first section examines the factors that have been identified in the literature on regionalism to explain the reasons why states choose to engage in regional integration projects. The article then proceeds to apply these explanations to the cases of Armenia and Moldova. Finally, based upon the findings emerging from the two case studies, the article offers broader conclusions on the mechanisms that shape countries' involvement in regional projects in the post-Soviet space.

Explaining the selection of a regional project in a context of competition

In the vast literature on regionalism that has developed since the end of the Cold War (e.g., Fawcett and Hurrell 1995; Mattli 1999; Hettne, Inotai, and Sunkel 1999; van Langenhove 2011), the post-Soviet space has remained largely unexplored, with only a few exceptions (Libman 2007; Malfliet et al. 2007; Libman and Vinokurov 2012; Wirminghaus 2012). This is perhaps unsurprising given the dynamics that have prevailed there over the past two decades. A number of regional-cooperation or regional-integration projects have emerged since the 1990s,[3] but most of them have either failed or stalled. This is for various reasons, including lack of leadership, absence of effective institutions, competing interests of countries involved in these projects, or divergent political and economic trajectories of post-Soviet countries (Delcour 2011; Wirminghaus 2012). In essence, regionalism has thus been "ephemeral" in the former Soviet Union (Wirminghaus 2012, 25).

However, the projects launched (or re-activated, in the case of the Eurasian project) in 2009–2010 have drastically changed the picture. In contrast to their predecessors, these are hard-law integration projects involving commitments that bind partner countries to the regional core (Dragneva and Wolczuk 2013; Delcour and Wolczuk 2013). While the European Neighborhood Policy launched by the EU in 2003–2004 was initially developed on the basis of political, nonbinding instruments (e.g., Action Plans offering guidance for reforms in each partner country), the Eastern Partnership (operational since 2009) undoubtedly marks a shift in both the scope and the depth of relations with partner countries. The new contractual framework consisting of AAs together with DCFTAs is premised on massive legal approximation with the EU *acquis communautaire* (Van Elsuwege and Petrov 2014). Therefore, if effectively implemented (and despite the lack of a membership perspective), these agreements will bind Moldova, Georgia, and Ukraine to the EU's rules, standards, and values, thus fostering a common legal and political referential between these countries and the EU (Delcour 2011).[4] In contrast to previous initiatives in the post-Soviet space, the Eurasian Customs Union, although premised on a fragmented legal basis, mirrors a shift toward "'hard law' characteristics" (Dragneva 2013, 41). It includes a supranational institution, the Eurasian Economic Commission, with extensive powers in key areas such as trade policy, customs, and technical regulations, and whose decisions have direct effect. The launch of the Eurasian Economic Union[5] is a further step toward deepening integration by removing barriers to the movement of labor and capital and extending approximation to new policy areas (e.g., competition). In sum, while the EU's transformative engagement in the neighborhood bears region-building implications, the Eurasian project involves far-reaching regional integration.

Both projects are in principle aligned with international norms, primarily those of the World Trade Organization (WTO). Therefore, the standards promoted by the Eurasian Economic Union and the EU are expected to be compatible,[6] if not similar. This is also because Russia has not developed any alternative template and actually uses WTO's and EU's norms (even if selectively) as a template for its own reforms. This mirrors Russia's hybrid identity as a subaltern to the West and a postcolonial/postimperial state in the former USSR (Morozov 2014); in other words, as a norm-taker and norm-maker. Nonetheless, while being premised on compatible technical standards, the two region-building projects have actually developed as parallel processes (Vilpišauskas et al.

2012, 12), de facto resulting in competing region-building projects (Makarychev 2012). What, then, drives partner countries' decision to engage in one or the other project?

The literature on regionalism offers useful insights to grasp the motivations behind partner countries' choice. This is because of two factors.

First, despite the fact that the concept of regionalism is highly diverse, scholars have come up with definitions that are well suited to understand regional *processes in the making*, as is especially the case in the post-Soviet space, since both the Eurasian project and the Eastern Partnership are still at an early stage of implementation. Following Tanja Börzel's definition, regionalism is understood here as "the processes and structures of region-building in terms of closer economic, political, security and socio-cultural linkages between states and societies that are geographically proximate" (Börzel 2012, 255).

Second, the literature has tried to both connect and disentangle the various levels affecting and being affected by regionalism. The analysis of internal and external driving forces lies at the core of the narratives that have been put forward to account for the "making" of regions. In his study of approaches to region-building, Neumann (1994, 1999) develops a continuum stretching from inside-out to outside-in explanations. Regions can first emerge in an inside-out dynamic, as an imagined community and a political project borne by regional political actors (Neumann 1999). They can also derive from economic and institutional factors, for example, transaction costs and the demand for institutional change and integration (Mattli 1999). In a reversed, outside-in perspective, regions can be shaped by external influences. While the former approach focuses on the role of internal factors (e.g. cultural similarity) and actors, the latter emphasizes systemic, geopolitical explanations (Neumann 1999, 120–21). It rests on the premise that regionalism can be diffused around the world. This means that external stimuli are powerful enough to prompt region-building, regardless of local specificities. Clearly, in the post-Soviet space the two major region-building projects mirror an outside-in dynamics whereby external actors engage neighbors only to a limited extent, and instead develop their instruments for the neighborhood (Makarychev 2012, 3). However, the analysis of the EU's and Russia's policies alone does not suffice to explain why, for instance, Georgia, Moldova, and Ukraine have engaged with the EU's project, while Belarus and Armenia have made a different choice.

In order to bridge this gap, there is a need to "open the 'black box' of the state" (Börzel 2012, 259) and bring domestic preferences and structures back into the analysis. Therefore, the approaches that have developed toward the middle of the continuum identified by Neumann (i.e., connecting internal and external drivers of region-building) are of specific interest for the purposes of the present article. Three major explanations have been put forward as to why and how states engage into regional projects.[7]

In a first account inspired by functionalist and neo-functionalist theories, states join regional initiatives because they are interdependent. Applied primarily to the European integration process, functionalist and neo-functionalist research has pointed to the role of supranational institutions (e.g., the High Authority in the European Coal and Steel Community) and the spill-over process in encouraging countries to expand existing cooperation to adjacent areas. In the post-Soviet space, growing interdependence with the neighborhood has been identified as a factor prompting the expansion of EU external governance (Lavenex and Schimmelfennig 2009, 793). At the same time, interdependence with other governance-providers (e.g., Russia) may strongly constrain the selection and adoption of EU rules (Lavenex and Schimmelfennig 2009, Dimitrova and Dragneva 2009). Following this account, economic, political, and sociocultural interdependencies (either with the EU or Russia) determine countries' engagement with the Eastern Partnership or the Eurasian integration process.

The second explanation, inspired by liberal inter-governmentalism, offers a two-level grid of analysis. It ascribes a central role to states' preferences, which, in turn, are shaped by domestic constellations of actors. Any decision on regional cooperation or integration thus results from decisions made by states through a bargaining process that reflects their relative power. While also applied primarily to the European integration process, liberal inter-governmentalism offers interesting insights for the purposes of our analysis in that it shifts the attention to both the state level and especially the infra-state level of analysis. It is thus well equipped to account for the role of vested interests and the connections between state and oligarchic groups in the selection of a regional project, or the existence of "hooks" that can be used by external actors in both the design and implementation of their policies (Stewart 2009, 806).

Finally, a third explanation inspired by constructivism places the emphasis on ideational (instead of material) factors. In line with constructivist approaches, regions are constructed through socialization and the building of (regional) identities based upon ideas, norms, and values. Partner countries' engagement in one or the other regional project would thus stem from a sense of common identity, whether it derives from interstate practices or is encouraged by international organizations (Adler 1997, 345).

In sum, theories of regionalism have been developed with other parts of the world in mind than the post-Soviet space. Therefore, while they offer useful insights into how states engage into regional projects, reconciling these theories with post-Soviet realities may prove complex since, in essence, they are not sensitive to the local post-Soviet specificities. With this in mind, the next section applies the three accounts discussed above to the cases of Moldova and Armenia.

Deconstructing moldova's choice in favor of european integration

The signature of an Association Agreement with the EU in June 2014 only seems to confirm Moldova's long-standing choice in favor of EU integration, defined as "an irreversible strategic objective"[8] of the country's foreign and domestic policy. However, while it has remained at the top of the Moldovan agenda over the past decade, the engagement in European integration has significantly evolved and is not as clear-cut as it may seem at first glance. While unveiling the rationale behind Moldova's European choice, this section also points to persisting tensions that may undermine the country's commitment under specific domestic and regional conditions.

Moldova's engagement with the EU is not new. In 2002 (i.e., four years after the Partnership and Cooperation Agreement with the EU entered into force), the government adopted a European Integration Concept Paper and in 2003 it established a National Commission for Legal Approximation (Gutu 2006, 8). Cooperation with the EU significantly expanded under the European Neighborhood Policy (ENP) with the adoption of an Action Plan in 2005. This coincided with the adoption of a European strategy (even if never ratified by the Parliament; Korosteleva 2010, 1273). The signature of the Action Plan with the EU was also followed by corresponding domestic implementation documents (yearly European Integration Agenda Priorities). The Eastern Partnership substantially expanded and deepened the scope of cooperation, especially through the enhancement of the contractual framework (the Association Agreement and DCFTA signed in June 2014) and the offer (which materialized in April 2014) of a visa-free regime. Moldova thus emerged as a frontrunner in terms of integration with the EU. This is especially illustrated by the visa-liberalization process: the country was the first Eastern Partnership country to meet all EU bench-marks and to have Schengen visas lifted for its citizens.

This brief overview of EU–Moldova relations seems to suggest that the commitment to EU integration has been both continuous and consensual. However, a closer examination of the factors behind this choice also reveals cleavages within the country.

From the outset, Moldova's choice in favor of EU integration was sustained by a sense of shared identity. The sense of belonging to Europe is tightly interconnected with the country's Romanian heritage, which played a key role (even if complex; see Parmentier 2004) in Moldova's statebuilding after the USSR's collapse. It was explicit in official speeches upon the launch of the ENP, at a time when the country had a Communist government:

> We have remained faithful to the firm desire ... to fully integrate ourselves in the great European family. The idea of European Integration became the national idea of the Republic of Moldova.[9]

As shown by policy documents on EU integration, Moldova's commitment to integration with the EU was also underpinned by the strong resonance of EU political values and norms:

> The Republic of Moldova is strongly committed to the course of European integration. It remains committed to universal values of democracy, respect for human rights, rule of law and economic freedom.[10]

Beyond the ruling elite, the country's choice of European integration was included in the program of all major political parties in 2003 (Korosteleva 2010). In fact, there was little opposition to the EU vector in Moldova in the early years of the ENP: EU integration was supported by a vast majority of Moldovan citizens (around 70 percent).[11] This apparent consensus even under communist rule was reinforced by increasing tensions with Russia (e.g., over trade).

Economic interdependence also helps explain Moldova's choice. Like Armenia, Moldova still retains a high degree of interdependence with Russia in migration and energy flows.[12] Nonetheless, the geographical structure of Moldovan trade significantly changed in the late 1990s– early 2000s.[13] Whereas until then Russia and other post-Soviet countries figured prominently in Moldova's trade, in 2007 the EU accounted for 50.6 percent of the country's exports and 45.6 percent of its imports—a percentage that has not substantially changed ever since.[14] This is because of two factors. First, a 2006 Russian embargo on Moldovan products further decreased the share of Russia in the country's external trade. Second, trade with the EU increased as a result of several factors, including the extension of trade preferences beyond GSP+ level (thus giving most Moldovan products free access to the EU market, Bosse 2010) and Romania's accession to the EU. Therefore, in line with the literature (Lavenex and Schimmelfennig 2009), Moldova's engagement with the EU is expected to derive from its stronger interdependence with the EU than with any other power.

Nevertheless, this account does not explain persisting gaps in the fulfillment of the country's commitment vis-à-vis the EU until the end of the 2000s. While strong inter-dependence is expected to provide the EU with an effective leverage over the country, throughout the 2000s Moldova's engagement under the ENP was not sustained by effective and consistent implementation. Despite the substantial expansion of relations, the country fell short of translating the commitments into practice (Korosteleva 2010, 1275). The EU itself reported limited progress in transferring its rules and norms to Moldova (Bosse 2010, 1306). While overall the implementation of legislation was much slower in Moldova than in some other ENP countries, the adoption of laws in line with EU demands stumbled against vested interests in sensitive areas such as judicial reform and the fight against corruption (Niemann and de Wekker 2010, 25).

The arrival into power of the Alliance for European Integration after the July 2009 elections, which coincided with the launch of the Eastern Partnership, gave a new impetus to the relationship with the EU. The new Moldovan authorities perceived the EU's enhanced offer under the Eastern Partnership as a pathway to modernization—a perception that is widely shared by the general public, for whom the EU is primarily associated with economic prosperity (Korosteleva 2010, 1281). During the negotiations for an Association Agreement together with a DCFTA, Moldovan authorities proved both receptive to EU demands and, unlike some other Eastern Partnership countries, reluctant to bargain despite the short-term costs to be incurred as a result of compliance with EU demands.[15] Moldovan authorities actually adopted a proactive stance in terms of implementation, combining the adoption of an EU-compliant legal framework and its actual application.[16] This is because, in their view, EU-driven reforms would bring substantial benefits to the country. For instance, as a result of the DCFTA with the European Union, Moldova's GDP was projected to increase by 5.4 percent and its exports to the EU by 16.2 percent.[17] The first economic indicators published after the (still partial) elimination of EU quotas and other barriers seem to confirm that Moldova is already benefiting from the easier access to the EU market.[18]

For the ruling elite, the benefits of EU integration are not only economic, but also political and societal. In Moldova as in Armenia, the EU's offer is perceived as a model for the country's modernization. Compliance with EU standards is expected to enhance the competitiveness of Moldovan products and to substantially increase investment flows to Moldova. In Moldova, integration with the EU has also been seen as a means to strengthen the country's leverage over the breakaway region of Transnistria (Kratochvil and Tulmets 2010, 93). In particular, the authorities' decision to invite Transnistrian officials to the DCFTA negotiations (as observers) was premised on the assumption that the agreement would make Moldova more attractive to Transnistrian citizens; so far, however, these expectations have not materialized.

Thus, EU integration is clearly filtered through the prism of Moldova's interests. As the country moves closer to the EU it also becomes more vocal on EU accession—an objective that had been explicitly stated since the 1990s, yet which has not been matched by actual implementation of EU rules and norms (Phinnemore 2006). In contrast, compliance with EU demands to complete negotiations on association, the free trade area, and visa liberalization has led the country to reiterate its aspirations in a clearer and more assertive way:

> European integration is an offer for all citizens of Moldova, while joining as a full member of the European Union is the end point of our European journey.[19]
>
> I am absolutely confident that offering a membership perspective to the Eastern Partnership countries that are willing, eligible and capable of performing it is a matter of urgent necessity. It will not cost you very much to offer at this stage

membership perspective, but it will have a very important, mobilising effect on those countries in order to continue the course of pro-European reforms, to mobilize all the resources and to have a sense of direction and objective.[20]

At the same time, while Moldova has performed very well in terms of advancing its relationship with the EU, the connection with internal reforms remains unclear.[21] The adoption and implementation of reforms lags behind in those policy areas that are politically sensitive, in particular the fight against corruption and justice sector reform (Parmentier 2014). This is also because of the absence of political costs imposed by the EU on the ruling elite for noncompliance in these areas. In essence, the EU has not exerted any pressure (apart from the soft recommendations contained in the annual progress reports)[22] on the country's pro-European elite and oligarchs. This has negatively affected the EU's image within civil society.[23] This is combined with the EU's perceived proximity with the ruling elite (in a country where trust in public institutions is especially low and has even declined since the 2013 political crisis)[24] and "poor" communication with civil society (Bosse 2010, p.1303). In essence, the EU's support to Moldovan authorities has had counterproductive effects, inter alia by pushing a few political and societal actors (including the Communist Party, PCRM) toward Eurasian integration (Sobják 2013, 5).

Tensions around European integration have been brought to the fore by the emergence of the Eurasian Customs Union (ECU) and the growing rivalry between the EU and Russia. Since 2013, Russia has stepped up pressure over Moldova to deter the country from further integration with the EU. It has done so by adjusting its own policies and by empowering anti-EU actors inside Moldova.

First, the changes recently introduced in Russian migration legislation may severely impact Moldova's post-compliance efforts with the EU's visa-liberalization demands. Since early 2014, tighter limitations for labor migration have been in application in Russia, de facto excluding the possibility of exiting from Russian territory after a 90-day period and re-entering straightaway. Amendments to the Federal Law on the Legal Status of Foreign Citizens in the Russian Federation in November 2014 introduce both administrative liability for foreign citizens who violate Russian migration legislation and mandatory state finger-print registration of foreign citizens who apply for a license to work. These conditions may actually result in the deportation of the bulk of Moldovan migrants.[25] An overwhelming majority of them (around 70 percent) indeed stay and work in Russia illegally.

Second, Russia has not only supported those Moldovan political and societal actors (e.g., the Church, the PCRM) that are less lenient toward EU values. It has also facilitated the emergence of new "hooks" (Stewart 2009) inside the country, including the Party of Socialists (PSRM), that are in favor of canceling the Association Agreement signed with the EU. If anything, divisions regarding foreign-policy orientation surfaced with the November 2014 parliamentary elections. Despite a tight majority in favor of parties supporting EU integration, the PSRM (whose leader, Igor Dodon, met with Vladimir Putin in Moscow during the electoral campaign) has emerged as the single largest party. Another key element in Russia's policy of "managed instability" (Tolstrup 2009) is the increasing use of breakaway and autonomous regions as pressure points over Moldova. Russia's policies vis-à-vis Transnistria and Gagauzia build upon both their specific (non-Romanian) identity within Moldova and their close economic links with the Russian Federation. In these regions, Russia is seen as both a protector against (the perceived threat of) a Moldovan unitary state based upon Romanian heritage and an alternative to integration with the EU. Besides supporting the breakaway region of Transnistria (Devyatkov 2013) and anchoring it further to its own legislation, Russia has sought to empower pro-Russian forces in the autonomous region of Gagauzia. The organization of a referendum on the Eurasian Customs Union in 2014 (with 98 percent of voters in favor of joining the ECU) and the election of a governor supported by Russia in March 2015 are vivid examples of Russia's counteracting power. In essence, Russia's policies are meant to compromise Moldova's capacity to pursue EU integration. They seem to (partly) bear fruit. According to a survey conducted in April 2014, 45 percent of the Moldovan population is in favor of joining the ECU while 44 percent support integration with the EU.[26]

In essence, all three factors identified in the first section of this article contribute to explaining both the choice of EU integration and its limitations, yet they do so to different degrees. First, as suggested by liberal inter-governmentalism, the Moldovan authorities (especially since 2009) have been pursuing EU integration as the result of a cost-benefit analysis; however, this framework does not explain the weak adoption and application of EU-driven reforms in specific sectors despite the pressure of domestic groups (e.g., oligarchs, civil society organizations) in favor of reforms. Second, growing economic interdependence with the EU is an important factor; yet, as Moldova retains other forms of interdependence with Russia (e.g., migration), this factor alone fails to explain the country's choice. Finally, as indicated by constructivism, Moldova's engagement with the EU stems from a sense of common identity; but this sense is not shared by Transnistria and Gagauzia—and Russia has largely built its policy upon this dissonance.

Armenia's half-hearted engagement with eurasian integration

In the post-Soviet space, Armenia is widely perceived as one of Russia's closest allies. Since the collapse of the Soviet Union, the country has been Russia's key partner in the South Caucasus (Delcour 2014). The two countries are linked by close military cooperation as well as substantial trade and migration flows.[27] Over the past two decades, Armenia has taken part in all Russian-led regional initiatives in the post-Soviet area, especially (considering the geopolitical context of the country) security schemes such as the Collective Security Treaty Organization (CSTO). Therefore, in light of the country's multiple ties with Russia, it is perhaps unsurprising that on September 3, 2013, President Serzh Sargsyan announced that Armenia would also join the far-reaching economic integration scheme recently set up by Russia. One year later, in October 2014, the Armenian president signed the accession treaty to the Eurasian Economic Union.

Nonetheless, as in Moldova, there were complex attitudes toward regional integration projects in Armenia. A closer examination of Armenia's policies between 2010 and 2013 indeed reveals two successive, yet contradictory, moves that are both fraught with inherent tensions: a rapid adoption of EU institutional and legal templates under the Eastern Partnership (Delcour and Wolczuk 2015), before the president abruptly, at the end of 2013, decided to join the Eurasian integration project. This section scrutinizes three factors behind the government of Armenia's changing positions: the country's structural constraints (and especially perceptions thereof); the resonance of regional models; and elites' preferences.

Owing to its strategic alliance with Russia, Armenia was broadly perceived as a laggard in the European Neighborhood Policy; however, between 2010 and 2013 the country increasingly sought to expand political and economic cooperation with the EU. Faced with an imperative need to modernize, Armenia considered the EU's enhanced offer under the Eastern Partnership with great interest (Wolczuk 2011), and among domestic actors a consensus emerged regarding the benefits of closer relations with the EU. Armenia's interest in EU templates did not remain purely declarative but translated into an extensive adoption of EU standards (Delcour and Wolczuk 2015). Between 2010 (when negotiations were launched for an Association Agreement with the EU) and 2013, the country carried out substantial reforms in line with EU demands on legal approximation. Armenia actually caught up to some other countries that were considered more advanced under the ENP. In particular, the country quickly completed the negotiations for a DCFTA, which entailed meeting the EU's tough conditionality on trade-related issues. At the same time, Armenia was a case of silent Europeanization (Delcour and Wolczuk 2015). Unlike some other Eastern partners, it was not vocal in highlighting its achievements in the sphere of European integration and it never expressed any membership aspirations. This is because Armenia simultaneously maintained and even expanded its security cooperation with Russia.[28] ("We are not in a position to yell 'EU!' because of our security situation," one civil society expert explained.)[29] Whereas the country viewed the security partnership with Russia and the adoption of EU reform templates as compatible, it kept a low profile, given Russia's increasing irritation at the EU policies in the Eastern neighborhood (Delcour and Wolczuk 2015).

The clear-cut choice announced by President Sargsyan on September 3, 2013, put an end to closer economic integration with the EU, yet it actually overshadows persistent interrogations about the country's regional integration strategy. The decision came as a surprise not only to the EU, but also to the Armenian elites.[30] Whereas the president justified his decision with the need for a consistent foreign policy based upon coherent alliances,[31] the move has received a mixed reaction within Armenian circles involved in EU affairs, even though it did not trigger massive demonstrations.[32] While being also connected to the transformation of the ECU into a Eurasian Economic Union, the difficult negotiation process with the ECU suggests that the country was not eager to join the Eurasian project. Formally, however, major steps were undertaken with the adoption of a road map in December 2013, the approval of the corresponding action plan for implementation in January 2014, and finally the signature of the accession treaty to the Eurasian Economic Union in October 2014. Nonetheless, during negotiations, Armenia actually requested exemptions from customs duties on 900 commodity groups. This huge number reflects the government's concerns about the economic consequences of accession into the Eurasian project (Delcour 2014). As noted by then–Prime Minister Tigran Sargsyan, as a consequence of accession to the Eurasian Economic Union, Armenia will have to reconsider its World Trade Organization commitments, which entails starting negotiations with the WTO. As also openly emphasized by the prime minister, the average import customs duty is 2.4 percent in Armenia, while it is three times as much in the ECU; joining may therefore cause price increases in Armenia.[33] In contrast, according to a study commissioned by the European Union, a DCFTA with the EU would have resulted in a 2.3 percent increase in GDP, or income gains amounting to € 146 million (ECORYS/CASE 2013, 13–14). In addition, in the medium-to-long term, a free trade area with the EU would have strengthened the country's geopolitical situation by offering a leverage vis-à-vis Turkey.[34] Thus, it was clearly in Armenia's interest to sign the Association Agreement, while accession to the Eurasian Union may be detrimental to the country's economy.

What, then, explains Armenia's seemingly paradoxical attitudes? Why has the country given an impetus to compliance with EU templates despite its security alliance with Russia? Why has the Armenian president turned to Eurasian integration in spite of the costs to be incurred by the country?

The normative resonance of the EU's offer as a model for modernization is a key factor explaining both Armenia's rapprochement with the EU from 2010 and its persisting hesitations to join the Eurasian project. The "European model of development" was identified as a path to follow at the highest political level as early as 2007.[35] As illustrated in President Sargsyan's discourse, Armenian elites perceived European templates as highly legitimate:

> We have stated more than once that European direction is our priority. In recent years, we have registered considerable success in that area. European Union has not only become one of our most important partners in the world but also plays a significant role inside Armenia, assisting us in the implementation of the reforms and in strengthening economic and overall stability of the country.[36]

While EU templates have a high normative resonance in Armenia, their adoption has also coincided with elites' strategies. The 2008 presidential elections in Armenia triggered massive protests against alleged electoral fraud. The harsh reaction of incumbent authorities resulted in a sharp political polarization, in a context of severe economic crisis and lack of reforms. A few months later, the country's regional situation sharply deteriorated in the wake of the conflict in Georgia and the failed rapprochement with Turkey. Against this background, modernization *à l'européenne* was viewed by the ruling elite as a strategy to advance its political interests and ensure its survival (Börzel and Risse 2012, 8–9). This is also because the EU's offer under the Eastern Partnership did not (at least initially) entail political costs for the incumbent authorities: the EU mainly focused on sectoral conditionality related to trade *acquis* (Delcour and Wolczuk 2015).

In this context, it is also important to note that Russia was never viewed as a potential partner in Armenia's modernization process. Even though the country has embarked on the Eurasian integration project, the resonance of EU norms and values remains high.[37] In his speech at the Eastern Partnership summit in Vilnius, almost three months after his decision to join the ECU was made public, President Sargysan clearly emphasized the role of EU templates for Armenia:

> Building and strengthening Armenian nationhood upon European model has been the conscious choice of ours, and that process is hence irreversible.[38]

However, Armenia's Europeanization has stumbled against the perceptions of structural constraints (primarily security threats) with which the country is confronted. Armenia's successive engagements can only be understood by taking into account the continuous prioritization of the Nagorno-Karabakh issue and, as a corollary, the country's preparedness to live with the (negative) consequences of the conflict.

This conflict has structured Armenia's foreign policy since the country's independence and continues to pose an essential threat to Yerevan.[39] Due to the conflict, the country's borders with two of its four neighbors have been closed since the beginning of the 1990s. By breaking up trade and energy flows and disrupting transport links, the blockade imposed by Azerbaijan and Turkey has only aggravated Armenia's landlocked situation. This has made Armenia even more vulnerable to external shocks, a weakness that was exposed by the 2008 conflict between Russia and Georgia when the major transit route for Armenia's trade was disrupted. In a context where Armenia has to address major regional threats in order to ensure its survival, Russia has clearly been viewed as the sole guarantor of the country's security (Delcour 2014). The special relationship between Moscow and Yerevan has been built around military cooperation, with Russia offering both bilateral and multilateral security guarantees. These apply only to the territory of Armenia and not to Nagorno-Karabakh. However, both Russia's military presence in Armenia (with the 102nd military base located in Gyumri and an airbase at Yerevan's Erebuni Airport) and Yerevan's CSTO membership are viewed as strong deterrents against Azerbaijan initiating operations against Nagorno-Karabakh (ibid.).

While the country continued implementing reforms in line with EU standards in 2012–2013, it became increasingly aware of the EU's limitations in terms of providing security. The Safarov extradition case,[40] in particular, was a blow to Yerevan's perceptions of the EU and, for that matter, of NATO (ibid.). Armenia then realized that decisions by some EU member states could—even if unintentionally—bring additional insecurity without triggering any condemnation by the bloc.[41] This led to a decline in positive attitudes toward the EU, as illustrated by the increase of distrust vis-à-vis the EU from 17 percent to 28 percent between 2011 and 2013.[42]

It is in this context of growing disillusion with the EU as a normative foreign policy actor that Russia started increasing its pressure for the country to join the ECU—an option initially ruled out by Armenia.[43] Armenia was significantly affected by Russia's simultaneous use of three different yet equally powerful levers: demographic drain through the program "Compatriots Living Abroad," reactivated in 2012[44]; massive arms sales to Azerbaijan in spring 2013, followed by Vladimir Putin's visit to Baku in August; and an increase of gas prices by 50 percent in July 2013 (Delcour 2014). Ultimately, given both the salience of the Nagorno-Karabakh conflict and its regional vulnerability, the country had little choice but to accommodate Russian requirements. Clearly, it is Armenia's prioritization of the conflict that resulted in a multifaceted dependency vis-à-vis Russia and, following pressure from Russia, prompted the country's engagement with the ECU at the end of 2013.

Nonetheless, the depth of this engagement still needs to be ascertained. The Armenian authorities' discourse still reflects the complementarity principle that structured the country's diplomacy over the past decade and prompted the rapprochement with the EU:

> Our major objective is to form such mechanisms with the European Union that on the one hand would reflect the deep nature of our social-political and economic relationship, and on the other—would be compatible with other formats of co-operation.[36]

Complementarity is still supported by the Armenian public, as illustrated by recent surveys.[45] Those parts of the Armenian administration engaged in the EU integration process are also in favor of a continuous engagement with the EU and stress that the Association Agreement/DCFTA would have brought substantial benefits for Armenia.[46]

Civil society is more vocal in condemning the president's decision, considering that it will only result in an increased dependence vis-à-vis Russia. Some NGOs also stress the negative consequences of Armenia's shift because of the Karabakh conflict and point to the escalation of tensions since the end of 2013.[47]

At the same time, Russia is widely seen as the security guarantor by the general Armenian public, whereas there is little knowledge of the EU and its Eastern Partnership. Negotiations with the EU were conducted with small groups of experts, with hardly any explanations of their consequences and benefits to the population. For many, despite the resonance of the EU's model, it still seemed natural to join the economic integration scheme initiated by Moscow,[48] since Armenia is already a member of the Russian-led security organization. Overall, long-term economic benefits of a more balanced foreign policy are clearly outweighed by the country's urgent and vital need for a security umbrella,[49] which explains its engagement (even if hesitant) in the Eurasian project.

In sum, the main explanations identified in the first part of this article interrelate in a complex way in Armenia. Unlike in Moldova, there is no sense of common identity with the EU (nor, for that matter, with Russia). Yet the EU's offer as a model for modernization has been resonating strongly in Armenia, something that scholarly observers seem unable to explain in the absence of strong pressure from domestic groups in favor of EU-driven reforms. Despite this resonance however, the domestic consensus on the overarching foreign-policy priority (the Nagorno-Karabakh conflict), combined with security dependence vis-à-vis Russia and the latter's pressure on Armenia, explain the shift toward Eurasian integration.

Conclusion

In a regional context increasingly shaped by the EU's and Russia's competing region-building projects, this article has shifted attention to the factors explaining the (opposite) choices made by Armenia and Moldova. In particular, it has shown that the reception of, and engagement with, the Eastern Partnership and the Eurasian Union are filtered by three elements: the resonance of the EU's and Russia's offers in terms of norms and identities; structural interdependencies and the resulting expected benefits or constraints in terms of selecting a regional project; and the preferences of domestic actors, whether the ruling elite, business, civil society, or the general public.

The article points to a differential role of these factors in Armenia and Moldova. In Armenia, in the absence of any explicit reference to shared identity with either the EU or Russia, I identify strong security dependence on Russia as a key factor (despite the persisting normative resonance of the EU model); yet this is only because of the country's (consensual) prioritization of the Nagorno-Karabakh conflict. In Moldova, all three sets of factors contribute to explaining the country's choice in favor of EU integration, while at the same time pointing to persisting tensions. Clearly, the country's trade and political interdependence is stronger with the EU than with Russia; however, Russia can rely upon powerful levers to exert pressure on Moldova. Although in Moldova there is a widespread feeling of shared identity with the EU, Transnistria and Gagauzia stand as obvious exceptions that Russia exploits (based upon existing interdependencies with these regions) to undermine the country's commitment to Europe. Finally, while EU norms and values resonate strongly in Moldova, the country's regional engagement is primarily driven by a quest for benefits expected from EU integration—be they economic or political, such as an increased leverage over Transnistria.

In sum, all three explanatory accounts identified in the introduction contribute (even though to different degrees) to explaining Armenia's and Moldova's involvement in regional projects. However, they do so only partially as they fail to fully take into account local conditions. By focusing on the domestic factors behind region-building, the article shows that the range of factors explaining countries' choices is actually much broader (and their interaction more complex) than suggested by existing theories. In fact, the article sheds light on a multifaceted and sometimes dialectical relationship between external and internal drivers leading to engagement into regional projects. It highlights multiple cleavages in partner countries' attitudes, which dovetail with persisting uncertainty in Russia's and EU's projects, especially given the fact that both of them are at an early stage of implementation. These findings open new research avenues. They signal the need for deeper scrutiny of the infra-state level, namely actors' constellation and preference formation shaping countries' engagement in region-building projects. The findings also call for further exploration of the actual implementation of EU and Eurasian Union demands once agreements committing partner countries to regional projects are fully into force and transitional arrangements come to an end.

Acknowledgments

The author would like to thank the participants of a research seminar at the Centre for EU Studies, Ghent University, and two anonymous referees for their comments on an earlier version of this article.

Notes

1. The Deep and Comprehensive Free-Trade Areas proposed by the EU are compatible with any free-trade agreements, including those signed in the framework of the Commonwealth of Independent States (CIS). However, membership of the Eurasian Customs Union implies for member countries a loss of sovereignty over trade policy and sets common tariffs which are incompatible with the elimination of tariffs planned under the DCFTA.
2. See, for example, the discourse by members of the European Parliament Elmar Brok and Jacek Saryusz-Wolski: "It is not at all a trade dispute, but a very serious political conflict with a geopolitical background. It might endanger the whole Eastern Partnership project of the EU, undermine the commitment and determination of our Eastern Neighbours, and it risks to provoke a domino effect, " at www.elmarbrok.de/archives/russia-ukraine-trade-war-eu-must-act-and-defend-ukraine-elmar-brok-mep-and-jacek-saryusz-wolski-mep (accessed October 25, 2014); and by Russian Minister of Foreign Affairs Sergey Lavrov: "The authors of the Eastern Partnership initially assured us that this project has no confrontational component. … However, they soon started to bring this question up with our joint neighbors with the European Union: you should decide who you are with—Europe or Russia." See "Russia—EU: Time to Decide," *Kommersant*, February 13, 2014, available at http://www.mid.ru/brp_4.nsf/0/54255BA2D3C5628C44257C7F00323A39 (accessed November 30, 2014).
3. Niklas Wirminghaus (2012, 25) has counted 39 initiatives of regional integration in the post-Soviet space between 1991 and 2010. Out of these, 36 gave birth to regional organizations.
4. Moldova, Georgia, and Ukraine signed Association Agreements (together with DCFTAs) in June 2014.
5. The treaty creating the Eurasian Economic Union was signed on May 29, 2014. The Union was launched in January 2015.
6. It should be noted that the process of norms' and standards' formulation is still ongoing, especially in light of the recent creation of the Eurasian Economic Union.
7. The explanations inspired by realist views are left outside the scope of this article because of their emphasis on large states' interests and power. In the realist view, regions are seen

either as a means of domination or as an alliance aimed at increasing the power of the region-builder. In either case, realist (or power-based) approaches neglect the motivations of small states for joining regional projects.

8 Official website of the Republic of Moldova, at www.moldova.md/en/europa/ (accessed May 12, 2014).
9 Natalia Gherman (then the Republic of Moldova's ambassador to Austria), "The European Option of the Republic of Moldova" (speech before the Diplomatic Academy, Vienna, March 12, 2003), 2–3.
10 See the Ministry of Foreign Affairs of the Republic of Moldova, European Integration Agenda Priorities for 2008 (in English), p. 1, at http://www.mfa.gov.md/basic-documents/- (accessed October 4, 2014).
11 See the data cited by Valeriu Gheorghiu in "Moldova on the Way to the European Union: Distance Covered and Next Steps To Be Done" (Chisinau, Institute of Public Policy, 2005), 3, available at http://www.ipp.md/download.php?file=cHVibGljL2JpYmxpb3RlY2Ev ODMvZW4vTW9sZG92YVdheUVVLnBkZg%3D%3D (accessed May 18, 2014).
12 According to the World Bank, 284,330 Armenian migrants live in Russia (World Bank Migrants Stock matrix, 2010); yet the actual figure may be higher. Remittances from migrants living in the Russian Federation amounted to USD827M in 2012 (World Bank bilateral remittances matrix, 2012), at siteresources.worldbank.org/INTPROSPECTS/Resources/334934-1110315015165/Bilateral_Remittance_Matrix_2012_Final.xlsx (accessed April 18, 2014).
13 See the data in Ana Popa, Valeriu Prohnitchi, Alex Oprunenco, "Evolution of Exports of the Republic of Moldova to the European Union: The Role of Trade Regimes" (Chisinau: Expert Grup, April–August 2008), 6.
14 In 2013, the EU accounted for 46.4 percent of Moldova's overall trade, 49.8 percent of its exports, and 45.2 percent of its imports, according to data from the European Commission's Directorate General for Trade, "European Union, Trade in Goods from Moldova," available at http://trade.ec.europa.eu/doclib/docs/2006/september/tradoc_113419.pdf (accessed October 23, 2014).
15 Author's interview, EU delegation to Chisinau, May 2012.
16 Author's interviews, Ministry of Foreign Affairs of the Republic of Moldova, May 2012 and 2014. See also the Minister of Foreign Affairs' speech before the Civil Society conference, Eastern Partnership Summit, Vilnius, November 2013: "We hope that 90 percent of the association agreement will be implemented before its ratification."
17 ECORYS/CASE, Trade Sustainability Impact Assessment in support of negotiations of a DCFTA between the EU and Georgia and the Republic of Moldova, Rotterdam, 2012.
18 For instance, wine exports to the EU grew by 26 percent as compared to 2013. See Expert Grup, "Kakovy pervye resultaty soglashenii ob associatsii mezhdu Moldovoj i EC," graphic presentation available at http://www.budgetstories.md/rezultate-aa-ru/ (accessed November 25, 2014).
19 "Premier Leanca: European Integration—An Offer for All Moldovan Citizens," speech by Prime Minister Leanca before the Moldovan Parliament for the ratification of the Association Agreement with the EU, July 2, 2014, available at http://trm.md/en/politic/leanca-integrarea-europeana-este-o-oferta-pentru-toti-cetatenii-republicii-mol dova (accessed July 3, 2014).
20 From the Euractiv interview with Moldovan Deputy Prime Minister Natalia Gherman, "Moldova Deputy PM: EU Membership Perspective Is 'a Matter of Urgent Necessity' for Eastern Countries," at www.euractiv.com/europes-east/moldova-deputy-pm-eu-membership-interview-534188 (accessed May 15, 2014)
21 Author's interview, EU delegation to Chisinau, May 2012.
22 See, for example, "Moldova is invited to: intensify the fight against corruption at all levels," European Commission/High Representative for Foreign Affairs and Common Security Policy; "Implementation of the European Neighbourhood Policy in the Republic of Moldova. Progress in 2013 and Recommendations for Action," March 27, 2014, at http://eeas.europa.eu/enp/pdf/2014/country-reports/moldova_en.pdf (accessed April 7, 2014).
23 Focus group organized in Chisinau, May 2014.
24 The crisis burst out in February 2013 when Prime Minister Vlad Filat announced that his party (the Liberal-Democratic Party of Moldova) would withdraw from the government

and asked for a new coalition agreement to be signed. Yet a few weeks later a motion of no confidence filed by the Communist Party was passed and Filat's cabinet was dismissed. In April, President Timofti appointed Iurie Leanca (until then Minister of Foreign Affairs) as acting Prime Minister.

25 Author's interview, Ministry of Foreign Affairs of the Republic of Moldova, May 2014.
26 See Barometer of Public Opinion, April 2014 (Institute for Public Policy, Chisinau, Moldova), at http://www.ipp.md/libview.php?l=en&idc=156&id=681 (accessed November 10, 2014)
27 Russia accounts for approximately 25 percent of Armenia's trade; data, according to data from the European Commission's Directorate General for Trade, 2014, at http://trade.ec.europa.eu/doclib/docs/2006/september/tradoc_113345.pdf (accessed October 23, 2014). According to the World Bank, 493, 000 Armenian migrants live in Russia (World Bank Migrants Stock matrix, 2010) and 90 percent of remittances to Armenia come from migrants living in the Russian Federation. Remittances totalled USD827M in 2012 (World Bank bilateral remittances matrix, 2012), at siteresources.worldbank.org/INTPROSPECTS/Resources/334934-1110315015165/Bilateral_Remittance_Matrix_2012_Final.xlsx (accessed April 18, 2014).
28 In 2012, Armenia for the first time held a CSTO Collective Rapid Reaction Force (CRRF) exercise on its territory, which tested elite units by simulating a response to an aggression against a member state. In 2010, Armenia had agreed to extend the lease on the Gyumri base, which is home to S-300 anti-aircraft missiles and Mikoyan MiG-29 fighters and where approximately 3,000 Russian soldiers are stationed until 2044 (Delcour 2014).
29 Interview with a civil society expert, Yerevan, November 2011.
30 Interviews with Armenian civil servants, Yerevan, February 2014.
31 "Participating in one military security structure [i.e. CSTO] makes it unfeasible and inefficient to stay away from the relevant geo-economic area." President of the Republic of Armenia, at www.president.am/en/press-release/item/2013/09/03/President-Serzh-Sargsyan-working-visit-to-Russian-Federation (accessed March 25, 2014).
32 Focus group with civil society experts, Yerevan February 2014.
33 "We have to monitor our business competitiveness in CU—Armenia PM," http://news.am/eng/news/201568.html, March 28, 2014 (accessed April 4, 2014).
34 Author's interview, EU official, EU delegation to Armenia, Yerevan, February 2014.
35 The "adoption of a European model of development" was explicitly mentioned in Armenia's 2007 National Security Strategy. See "National Security Strategy of the Republic of Armenia, approved at the session of National Security Council at the RA President office on January 26, 2007," at http://www.mfa.am/u_files/file/doctrine/Doctrineeng.pdf (accessed March 15, 2014).
36 President Sargsyan, speech before the plenary meeting of the 20th Congress of the European People's Party (EPP), Marseille, December 7, 2011, available at www.president.am/en/foreign-visits/item/2011/12/07/news-344/ (accessed December 30, 2011).
37 Author's interviews with Armenian civil servants, Yerevan, February 2014 and March 2015.
38 President of the Republic of Armenia, Speech at the third Eastern Partnership Summit, Vilnius, November 29, 2013, at http://www.president.am/en/press-release/item/2013/11/29/President-Serzh-Sargsyan-speech-at-the-third-Eastern-Partnership-summit/ (accessed January 10, 2014).
39 "The key issue of the National Security of the Republic of Armenia is the settlement of the Nagorno Karabakh conflict" (National Security Strategy of the Republic of Armenia, 2007).
40 An Azerbaijanai officer, Ramil Safarov, brutally murdered an Armenian lieutenant with an axe in Hungary in 2004 and was imprisoned there until 2012, when Hungary decided to extradite him to Azerbaijan. Safarov received a hero's welcome upon returning to Azerbaijan. He was pardoned by Azerbaijani president Ilham Aliyev (despite contrary assurances made to Hungary), promoted to the rank of major, and given an apartment and over eight years of back pay. Armenia reacted by suspending ties with Hungary.
41 The EU expressed its concern, but did not condemn either Hungary's decision or Aliyev's move. See statement by the spokespersons of EU High Representative Catherine Ashton and Commissioner Štefan Füle on the release of Ramil Safarov, September 3, 2012, A389, at

http://europa.eu/rapid/press-release_MEMO-12-642_en.htm?locale=en (accessed January 15, 2013).

42. Data from Caucasus Resource Research Centre, Caucasus Barometer, available at http://crrc-caucasus.blogspot.fr/2014/10/do-armenians-still-view-integration.html (accessed October 14, 2014).

43. See e.g. Garen Arevian, "Armenia Again Rules Out Entry into Russian Customs Union," at http://www.accc.org.uk/armenia-again-rules-out-entry-into-russian-customs-union/ (accessed April 15, 2014).

44. This program is based on a 1999 Federal Law considering everyone who ever held a Soviet passport as a "compatriot." Hayk Hovhannisyan, "As Armenia Moves Closer to the EU, Russia is Taking Advantage of the Country's Economic and Geopolitical Vulnerabilities to Maintain its Influence," LSE, July 30, 2013, at http://blogs.lse.ac.uk/europpblog/2013/07/30/armenia-russia/ (accessed October 25, 2013).

45. According to a poll conducted in June 2014 by the Civitas Foundation, 51 percent of the population believes that "Armenia should deepen relations both with Europe and Russia," compared to 34 percent answering that Armenia should deepen relations with Russia only and only 4 percent responding that Armenia should deepen relations with the EU only. The poll data are available at http://www.civilitasfoundation.org/cf/ (accessed October 10, 2014).

46. Author's interviews in Yerevan with civil society experts and civil servants, February 2014.

47. Eastern Partnership Civil Society Forum, "Armenian National Platform position on the decision of RA authorities to join Eurasian Economic Union" (September 25, 2014, Yerevan), at http://eap-csf.eu/en/news-events/news/anp-position-on-decision-of-ra-authorities-to-join-eurasian-economic-union/ (accessed October 18, 2014).

48. See Alin Ozinian, "Armenia's Security Dilemma Brings It to Eurasian Union," *Today's Zaman*, December 2, 2013, at http:// www.todayszaman.com/op-ed_armenias-security-dilemma-brings-it-to-eurasian-union-by-alin-ozinian-_332920.html (accessed October 24, 2014).

49. "The reactions by the opposition—'We do not want Russia'—will no longer be heard if they come to power because it is all about Armenia's security conundrum rather than being a supporter or an opponent of the West or Russia," ibid.

References

Adler, Emanuel. 1997. "Seizing the Middle Ground: Constructivism in World Politics." *European Journal of International Relations* 3, no. 3: 319–63.

Averre, Derek. 2009. "Competing Rationalities: Russia, the EU and the 'Shared Neighbourhood.'" *Europe-Asia Studies*, 61, no. 10: 1689–1713.

Börzel, Tanja A., Lukas Goltermann, Mathis Lohaus, and Kai Striebinger, eds. 2012. *Roads to Regionalism*. Farnham: Ashgate.

Börzel, Tanja A., Thomas Risse. 2012. "From Europeanisation to Diffusion: Introduction." *West European Politics* 35, no. 1: 1–19.

Bosse, Giselle. 2010. "The EU's Relations with Moldova: Governance, Partnership or Ignorance." *Europe-Asia Studies* 62, no. 8: 1291–1309.

Casier, Tom. 2013. "The EU–Russia Strategic Partnership: Challenging the Normative Argument." *Europe-Asia Studies* 65, no. 7: 1377–95.

Delcour, Laure. 2011. *Shaping the Post-Soviet Space? EU Policies and Approaches to Region-Building*. Farnham: Ashgate.

———. 2014. "Faithful but Constrained? Armenia's Half-Hearted Support for Russia's Regional Integration Policies in the Post-Soviet Space." In *Geopolitics of Eurasian Integration*. London School of Economics: IDEAS Reports, at http://www.lse.ac.uk/IDEAS/publications/reports/pdf/SR019/SR019-Delcour2.pdf (accessed July 3, 2014).

Delcour, Laure, and Kataryna Wolczuk, 2013. "Eurasian Economic Integration and Implications for the EU's Policy in the Eastern Neighbourhood." In *Eurasian Economic Integration: Law,*

Policy, and Politics, eds. Rilka Dragneva and Kataryna Wolczuk. Cheltenham: Edward Elgar, 179–203.

———. 2015. "The EU's Unexpected 'Ideal Neighbour'? The Perplexing Case of Armenia's Europeanisation." *Journal of European Integration* 37, no. 4: 491–507.

Devyatkov, Andrey. 2012. "Russian Policy Toward Transnistria: Between Multilateralism and Marginalization." *Problems of Post-Communism* 59, no. 3: 53–62.

Dimitrova, Antoaneta, and Rilka Dragneva. 2009. "Constraining External Governance: Interdependence with Russia and the CIS as Limits to the EU's Rule Transfer in the Ukraine," *Journal of European Public Policy* 16, no. 6: 853–72.

Dragneva, Rilka. 2013. "The Legal and Institutional Dimensions of the Eurasian Customs Union." In *Eurasian Economic Integration. Law, Policy and Politics*, eds. Rilka Dragneva and Wolczuk, Kataryna. Cheltenham: Edward Elgar, 34–60.

Dragneva, Rilka, and Kataryna Wolczuk, eds. 2013. *Eurasian Economic Integration. Law, Policy and Politics.* Cheltenham: Edward Elgar.

ECORYS/CASE. 2012. *Trade Sustainability Impact Assessment in Support of Negotiations of a DCFTA Between the EU and Georgia and the Republic of Moldova.* Study for the European Commission. Rotterdam, at http://trade.ec.europa.eu/doclib/docs/2012/november/tradoc_150105.pdf.

———. 2013. *Trade Sustainability Impact Assessment in Support of Negotiations of a DCFTA Between the EU and the Republic of Armenia.* Study for the European Commission, Rotterdam, at http://trade.ec.europa.eu/doclib/docs/2013/october/tradoc_151862.pdf.

Fawcett, Louise, and Andrew Hurrell. 1995. *Regionalism in World Politics: Regional Organization and International Order.* Oxford: Oxford University Press.

Gutu, Oxana. 2006. "Moldova's Convergence with the *acquis*: A ProGrowth and Pro-Integration Strategy." *CEPS Working Document* no. 238. Center for European Policy Studies. Brussels.

Hettne, Björn, András Inotai, and Osvaldo Sunkel, eds. 1999. *The New Regionalism*. Volume 1. *Globalism and the New Regionalism.* Basingstoke: Macmillan/ New York: Saint Martin's Press.

Korosteleva, Elena. "Moldova's European Choice: 'Between Two Stools'?" *Europe-Asia Studies* 62, no. 8: 1267–89.

Kratochvíl, Petr, and Elsa Tulmets.2010. *Constructivism and Rationalism in EU External Relations.* Baden-Baden: Nomos.

Lavenex, Sandra, and Frank Schimmelfennig. 2009. "EU Rules Beyond EU Borders: Theorizing External Governance in European Politics." *Journal of European Public Policy* 16, no. 6: 791–812.

Libman, Alexander. 2007. "Regionalisation and Regionalism in the Post-Soviet Space: Current Status and Implications for Institutional Development." *Europe-Asia Studies* 59, no. 3: 401–30.

Libman, Alexander, and Evgeny Vinokurov. 2012. *Holding Together: Twenty Years of Post-Soviet Integration.* Basingstoke: Palgrave Macmillan.

Malfliet, Katlijn, Lien Verpoest, and Evgeny Vinokurov, eds. 2007. *The CIS, the EU and Russia.* Basingstoke: Palgrave Macmillan.

Makarychev, Andrey. 2012. "Russia and the EU: Competing Region-Building Projects." *DGAPanalyse*, no. 1 (March). Berlin: German Council on Foreign Relations.

Mattli, Walter. 1999. *The Logic of Regional Integration: Europe and Beyond.* Cambridge: Cambridge University Press.

Morozov, Viatcheslav. 2014. "Subaltern Empire? Toward a Postcolonial Approach to Russian Foreign Policy," *Problems of Post-Communism* 60, no. 6: 16–28.

Neumann, Iver B. 1994. "A Region-Building Approach to Northern Europe." *Review of International Studies* 20, no. 1: 53–74.

———. 1999. *Uses of the Other: The "East" in European Identity Formation.* Minneapolis: University of Minnesota Press.

Niemann, Arne, and Tessa de Wekker. "Normative Power Europe? EU Relations with Moldova." *European Integration online Papers (EIoP)* 14, article 14, at http://eiop.or.at/eiop/pdf/2010-014.pdf.

Parmentier, Florent. 2004. "État, politique et cultures en Moldavie." *Revue internationale et stratégique* 54, no. 2: 152–60.

———. 2014. "Moldova." *Geopolitics of Eurasian Integration*. London School of Economics: LSE IDEAS Reports at http://www.lse.ac.uk/IDEAS/publications/reports/pdf/SR019/SR019-Parmentier.pdf (accessed July 3, 2014).

Phinnemore, David. 2006. "Moldova: A Step Too Far for EU Enlargement?" Paper presented at the European Consortium for Political Research (ECPR) 3rd Pan-European Conference on EU Politics, September 21–23, at Bilgi University in Istanbul, Turkey.

Sobják, Anita. 2013. "Is Moldova Tired of Being the Success Story of the Eastern Partnership?" *PISM Policy Paper* no. 20 (68). Warsaw: Polish Institute of International Affairs.

Stewart, Susan. 2009. "The Interplay of Domestic Contexts and External Democracy Promotion: Lessons from Eastern Europe and the South Caucasus." *Democratization* 16, no. 4: 804–24.

Tolstrup, Jakob. 2009. "Studying a Negative External Actor: Russia's Management of Stability and Instability in the 'Near Abroad.'" *Democratization* 16, no. 4: 922–44.

Van Elsuwege, Peter, and Roman Petrov, eds. 2014. *Legislative Approximation and Application of EU Law in the Eastern Neighbourhood of the European Union: Towards a Common Regulatory Space*. London: Routledge.

Vilpišauskas, Ramunas, RaimondasALišauskas, Laurynas Kasčiūnas, Živilė Dambrauskaitė, Vytautas Sinica, Ihor Levchenko, and Victor Chirila. 2012. *Eurasian Union: A Challenge for the European Union and Eastern Partnership Countries*. Vilnius, Lithuania: East European Studies Centre.

Van Langenhove, Luk. 2011. *Building Regions. The Regionalization of the World Order*. Farnham: Ashgate.

Wirminghaus, Niklas. 2012. "Ephemeral Regionalism: the Proliferation of (Failed) Regional Integration Initiatives in Post-Soviet Eurasia." In *Roads to Regionalism*, eds. Tanja A. Börzel, Lukas Goltermann, Mathis Lohaus, and Kai Striebinger. Farnham: Ashgate, 25–44

Wolczuk, Kataryna. 2011. "Perceptions of, and Attitudes Towards the Eastern Partnership Amongst Partner Countries' Political Elites." *Eastern Partnership Review* no. 5. Tallinn: Estonian Center of Eastern Partnership.

"The transformative power of Europe" beyond enlargement

The EU's performance in promoting democracy in its neighbourhood

Tanja A. Börzel and Bidzina Lebanidze

1. Introduction

The failure of the European Union (EU) to promote democracy and the rule of law in its neighbourhood regions has been widely acknowledged. Ten years after the inception of the European Neighbourhood Policy (ENP), most of the neighbours both in the East and in the South show the same or the lower quality of democratic development. A few exceptions notwithstanding (Georgia, Moldova, and Ukraine in the East and Tunisia in the South), the EU is surrounded by authoritarian regimes and failed states.

Much of the academic literature argues that an absence of "golden carrot" of membership perspective and a lack of coherence in EU's external governance circumscribe the transformative power of the EU in its neighbourhood. However, whereas the lack of membership perspective may explain the overall ineffectiveness of the ENP, it cannot explain why some of the neighbouring states have democratised more than others. This paper argues that it is not so much the lack of a membership perspective but the inconsistency in applying other forms of conditionality which undermines the EU's performance in promoting democracy in the post-Soviet and the Mediterranean region. In the large majority of cases where the EU applies democratic conditionality as the key instrument of its external democracy promotion, we can observe improvements in democratic quality or a democratic breakthrough in the neighbourhood countries. The main problem for the EU's transformative power, however, is the selective sanctioning of non-compliance with democracy standards caused by conflicting objectives. We identify two conditions for the EU's application of democratic conditionality: *the absence of a democratisation-stability dilemma* and the *presence of pro-democratic reform coalitions*. If neither of these conditions is given, the EU is more likely to act as a status-quo power prioritising (authoritarian) stability over uncertain (democratic) change.

The paper starts by demonstrating that the EU has successfully applied democratic conditionality within the framework of its ENP. The first part maps all the cases, in which violations of democratic standards by ENP countries occurred and how the EU responded. The empirical analysis reveals that there is significant variation with regard to the application of democratic conditionality and its effectiveness.

The second part discusses the extent to which the existing literature has failed to acknowledge the EU's inconsistent use of democratic conditionality and its differential effect on democratic developments in its Eastern and Southern neighbourhood. We then introduce the absence of a democratisation-stability dilemma and the presence of pro-democratic reform coalitions as the main factors that have affected the consistent and effective application of EU democratic conditionality in the European neighbourhood. The fourth part demonstrates how these two factors account for the differential performance of the EU in promoting democracy. Overall, we can see substantial inter-regional differences triggered, first of all, by the democracy-stabilisation dilemma. Its absence explains why the EU has been more consistent in the application of democratic conditionality in the Eastern neighbourhood. Our empirical analysis also finds that the consistent application of democratic conditionality has always resulted in a democratic opening or an improvement in democratic quality if it empowered pro-democratic reform coalitions. The paper concludes with summarising its most important findings and a discussion of some avenues for future research.

2. EU democratic conditionality in the European neighbourhood

In this section, we map the consistency and effectiveness of EU democratic conditionality in Eastern and Southern neighbourhood countries and discuss the main factors that have affected the two phenomena. Since the ENP is about "everything but institutions", the EU has to offer neighbouring countries other incentives in return for domestic reforms, such as advanced access to the Internal Market, visa liberalisation, and increased financial aid (Langbein and Börzel 2013). In the context of this "neighbourhood conditionality" (Borell et al. 2012, 75), consistency presupposes that the promotion of democracy and the rule of law is not compromised by other foreign policy goals of the EU, such as stability, energy security, or trade. As we will see in the remainder of this paper, it is exactly this "substantive inconsistency in seeking to promote both effective and democratic governance" (Börzel and van Hüllen 2014, 1033), which undermines the democracy-promoting potential of conditionality under the ENP. We understand consistency of EU conditionality as to what extent the EU rewards democratic progress (positive conditionality) or sanctions the lack thereof (negative conditionality) in neighbourhood countries. EU conditionality is effective if the application of negative or positive incentives is followed by an increase in quality of democracy or by a democratic breakthrough in the country targeted by EU conditionality.

The case of the ENP supports the main argument of this paper that EU democratic conditionality is effective if it is consistently applied. During the electoral revolutions in Georgia and Ukraine in the early 2000s, the EU and the US played a key role by not acknowledging the results of rigged ballots and limiting the playing field of corrupt and authoritarian incumbent regimes. At the same time, they empowered civil society actors, youth groups and opposition movements through various capacity-building measures and policy advising (Börzel, Pamuk, and Stahn 2009; Wilson 2007). In Georgia's 2003 "Rose Revolution", the EU and the US have even employed financial sanctions against the government of Eduard Shevardnadze. The EU postponed the disbursement of new credits, which caused a budget crisis short before the elections (RFE/RL 2002a, 2002b). The US followed suit and announced the reduction in financial aid just one month before the elections (RFE/RL 2003). Amidst mounting external pressure and large-scale street protests, the government of Shevardnadze collapsed and the political opposition claimed victory. In Ukraine, the EU avoided financial sanctions, but it denounced the results of the 2004 presidential elections and made future relations with Kyiv conditional on the democratic outcome of the crisis and on the quality of democracy in Ukraine (RFE/RL 2004b, 2004c). Both the EU and the US openly called for election reruns (European Parliament 2004) and NATO uninvited the Ukrainian foreign minister saying that it was not willing to "legitimize the existing government" (RFE/RL 2004a). As in the case of Georgia, the Ukrainian government bowed to external pressure and agreed to rerun the second round of elections between governmental candidate Victor Yanukovych and opposition challenger Victor Yushchenko, which ended with the latter's victory (Karatnycky 2005). Hence, the overall, critical position of the West was instrumental for the success of the "Color Revolutions" in Georgia and Ukraine.

A few years later, the EU again stepped up its democratising pressure in both Georgia and Ukraine. In Georgia, together with the US and the NATO, it tried to secure the democratic conduct of the crucial 2012 parliamentary elections by persuading the incumbent regime to participate in the electoral power transition. For instance, the White House used the meeting between Georgian president Mikhail Saakashvili and US president Barack Obama to urge the former in an unprecedented clear language to support "the formal transfer of power" (Sherwood-Randall 2012). On their part, the EU High Representative Catherine Ashton and the Commissioner for Enlargement Štefan Füle in their joint statement explicitly mentioned the linkage between the democratic conduct of elections and "the quality and intensity of the relations with the EU in the future" just a few days before the 2012 elections (Ashton and Füle 2012).

Similarly, in Ukraine the EU reactivated democratic conditionality in 2010 after the newly elected president Victor Yanukovych started to roll back the democratic reforms introduced by his predecessor. Moreover, since the inception of the Eastern Partnership Initiative, Brussels has become more determined and consistent in its insistence on democratic reforms from Kyiv. The EU used the negotiation process on the Association Agreement (AA) to address the lack of democratic change. It made the ratification of the AA with Kyiv conditional on specific demands, including the release of former Ukrainian Prime Minister Julia Timoshenko from prison and "tangible progress" of the government in the areas of justice, elections, and other reforms outlined in the EU-Ukrainian Association Agenda (European Commission 2013b). Ukrainian government refused to accept EU demands and turned towards Russia instead. However, its decision sparked the pro-European large-scale protests called later "Euromaidan", which ended up in a power change with President Yanukovych fleeing the country (Marples and Mills 2015).

In Moldova, the EU encouraged the pro-European political forces in Moldova to build a new governmental coalition after the long period of political crisis in 2013 (Rinnert 2013). In 2015, the EU responded very harshly to the corruption scandal involving the Moldova's politicians. It has frozen financial assistance to Moldova and criticised the government for not implemented the required reforms (EurActiv 2015). Next to the EU, the International Monetary Fund and the World Bank have also stopped their lending (EurActiv 2015).

In Armenia and Azerbaijan, in contrast, the EU has never invoked democratic conditionality consistently. Although the European Parliament and the Organization for Security and Co-operation in Europe have criticised the Azerbaijani government for violating basic principles of democracy and the rule of law, the EU has intensified its energy and trade relations with Azerbaijan. Likewise, the EU has never made financial and technical assistance to Armenia conditional on political reforms. Similar to Azerbaijan, the EU limited itself to criticising elections without resorting to sanctions. The EU together with the US and the Western institutions accepted the disputed results of every election since 2003 without much protest. Some authors consider this Western indifference as the most important reasons for the survival of the Armenian authoritarian regime (Levitsky and Way 2010).

Belarus has been the only European neighbourhood country where EU conditionality has been applied but completely failed. The life-long President Alexander Lukashenko has built the most oppressive regime. The EU has applied democratic conditionality against "Europe's Last Dictator" (Reuters 2012). After multiple falsified elections and the brutal crackdown on political opposition and peaceful protesters, the EU introduced a wide range of sanctions against the Lukashenko government. They included the exclusion of Belarus from the EU GPS system as well as visa bans and asset freezes of governmental officials (Bosse 2012b). The EU also applied strong diplomatic and political pressure by "naming and shaming" the Lukashenko regime as Europe's only remaining dictatorship and criticising the outcome of each election as flawed (Bosse 2012a; Bosse and Korosteleva-Polglase 2009). Yet, the overall strategy of the EU and more broadly of the West towards Belarus has been ineffective. A major issue, of course, is the role of Russia, which has been boosting the autocratic pro-Russian regime of Alexander Lukashenko undermining the leverage of the EU (Ambrosio 2009b; Tolstrup 2009). Moreover, the democratic conditionality applied by the EU has been undermined by other Western institutions providing politically unconditional financial support to stabilise the regime of Lukashenko. Personal sanctions were accompanied by financial credits of the IMF, the World Bank, and other international financial institutions, which, especially during the global financial crisis in 2007–2008, had stabilised the economic situation in the country and strengthened the regime of President Alexander Lukashenko (VOA 2009). Finally, the EU's application of democratic conditionality has also been inconsistent. Unlike the US, for instance, the EU refused to extend the sanctions to include big state-owned enterprises – a backbone of Belarusian economy. The sanctions have not touched the trade area either. EU investments have continued to flow into the Belarusian economy and the trade has increased since the introduction of sanctions (Reuters 2013).

Unlike in the Eastern neighbourhood, the EU has hardly applied democratic conditionality to its Southern neighbours. Even the alleged Arab Spring barely altered the EU's reliance on political dialogue and assistance (van Hüllen 2015). Tunisia has been the only country where the EU decided to apply positive conditionality after the Arab Spring (Balfour 2012). The EU supported the Tunisian regime change by doubling its financial support from an average of 80 million in 2011 to 150–160 million in 2013 and by diverting it rather meaningfully under the changed circumstances (Pierini 2014). It also sent an observation mission to monitor the first post-Arab Spring elections in 2011, increased the financial assistance for reforms of the judiciary and for capacity building of civil society, and proposed to update contractual relationship to "Privileged Partnership" and the Deep and Comprehensive Free Trade Area (DCFTA) (European Commission 2013a). Tunisian civil society has been also supported by extensive transnational exchanges and various programmes launched by the EU member states and the EU civil society organisations (Dandashly 2014, 43). Thus, although the EU refrained from invoking negative conditionality, it succeeded in locking in democratic reforms through positive incentives and close cooperation with political actors.

In Egypt, the EU stepped up financial assistance after the fall of the Mubarak regime and tried to assist new government in democratic transitions. Egyptian authorities, however, declined the EU's offer to monitor the parliamentary and presidential elections (Dandashly 2014, 48). Likewise, they turned a cold shoulder to the EU's attempt to incentivise democratic reforms by proposing to start negotiations on DCFTA and Mobility Partnership. When the military ousted democratically elected president Morsi's and amid continuing violence against MB, the EU stepped up its criticism and even threatened to suspend the financial assistance (Dandashly 2014). But it stopped short of cutting it due to fears of damaging political dialogue with Egypt (Pawlak and O'Donnell 2013).

The other two Arab Spring countries – Libya and Syria – had only been included in the capacity-building component of ENP receiving selective financial assistance. After their authoritarian regimes had collapsed in the Arab Spring revolts, the two states quickly elapsed in total chaos. In Algeria, Jordan, and Morocco, the EU has been supportive of incremental reform process initiated by their regimes to deflect or accommodate protest rather than introduce democratic change (van Hüllen 2012; Youngs et al. 2008). To sum up, empirical evidence from the ENP countries suggests a strong correlation between the consistent application of democratic conditionality and its effectiveness (Table 1). Whenever the EU used democratic conditionality, it has been followed by democratic progress or democratic breakthrough. Georgia, Moldova, Tunisia, and Ukraine are among the few countries that have been consistently subject to EU democratic conditionality; they show the highest level of democratic development and are rated as the only non-authoritarian countries in both neighbourhood regions (Bertelsmann Stiftung 2012; The Economist Intelligence Unit 2013; Freedom House 2015c). Moreover, they are the sole ENP countries that have experienced successful democratic breakthroughs over the last decade. Tunisia has witnessed the main successful Arab Spring transition, Georgia and Ukraine experienced the electoral revolutions in 2003

Table 3.1 Consistency and effectiveness of democratic conditionality.

	Effectiveness	
Consistency	*Democratic opening/democratisation*	*Authoritarian stability/authoritarian backlash*
Democratic conditionality	Georgia *Rose Revolution 2003* Georgia *2012 electoral power transition* Moldova *2009 Twitter Revolution 2013 political crisis* Ukraine *2004 Orange Revolution* Ukraine *2010–2013 Authoritarian backlash/Euromaidan* Tunisia *Arab Spring protests and democratic transition*	Belarus *Multiple fraudulent elections/protests*
Stability/Security over Democracy		Algeria *Arab Spring protests* Armenia *post-electoral protests 2003, 2004, 2008, 2013* Azerbaijan *Multiple fraudulent elections/protests* Egypt *Arab Spring protests and Counterrevolution 2011–2013* Georgia *authoritarian backlash* Jordan *Arab Spring protests* Libya *Arab Spring protests, Civil War* Morocco *Arab Spring protests* Syria *Arab Spring protests, Civil War*

and 2004, and Moldovan post-election protests resulted in a "Twitter Revolution" in 2009. Besides, all four states have experienced electoral power transition. Belarus has been the only neighbourhood country that has resisted the EU's transformative power. Yet, application of democratic conditionality has been inconsistent and undermined not only by Russia but other Western actors stabilising the Lukashenko regime. If the EU's performance as an external democracy promoter relies on consistent democratic conditionality, the question this paper needs to answer is why in the majority of the cases the EU has refrained from applying democratic conditionality in the first place and acted as stabilising rather than a transformative power (Table 1).

3. Explaining (in)effectiveness and (in)consistency of EU democratic conditionality

3.1. The golden carrot and the EU's lack of consistency

The academic literature largely blamed the absence of "the golden carrot" – the EU membership perspective for EU's ineffectiveness in promoting democracy in the ENP countries through democratic conditionality (Börzel and Böttger 2012; Haukkala 2010; Lehne 2014; Schimmelfennig and Scholtz 2008; Whitman and Wolff 2010). Indeed, the absence of a membership perspective or, in Fukuyama's (2005, 86) words, "the most successful exercise of soft power in the world today", has been the main difference between the ENP and the Enlargement policy framework. However, whereas the absence of golden carrot might have an overall negative impact on "neighbourhood Europeanization" (Gawrich, Melnykovska, and Schweickert 2009) and on the effectiveness of democratic conditionality under the ENP, the low attractiveness of incentives cannot explain the intraregional differences since they have been constant for all neighbouring countries.

Next to the low attractiveness of incentives, many authors consider a lack of coherence to circumscribe the transformative power of the EU in its neighbourhood (Baracani 2009; da Conceição-Heldt and Meunier 2014; Noutcheva 2014). Coherence refers to the capability of the EU to overcome institutional complexities and "speak with a single voice" in the foreign policy arena (da Conceição-Heldt and Meunier 2014; Noutcheva 2014; Thomas 2012). Hence, complexities of institutional governance of the ENP could be seen as the main reason behind the EU's failure to transform its neighbourhood as it limits the effectiveness of democratic conditionality through its inconsistent application. "The institutional pluralism of EU foreign policy-making" (Noutcheva 2014, 21) characterised by "a high number of actors with a low level of political power" (Bicchi 2014, 320), weakens the overall actorness of the EU and, hence, the EU's consistency in applying democratic conditionality and its effectiveness. Accordingly, the EU's limited influence on democracy in the ENP is blamed on disagreements among its member states about when and how to invoke democratic conditionality (Noutcheva 2014, 34). Yet, the (high) degree of coherence inside the EU does not always correlate with the effectiveness of the EU's application of democratic conditionality. For instance, the EU has been quite coherent in putting democratising pressure on the authoritarian regime of Alexander Lukashenko in Belarus, yet failed to achieve any results.

In sum, neither the absence of a membership perspective nor the EU's incoherence can explain *when* the EU invokes democratic conditionality consistently and *when* is it effective. To fill this gap in the literature, we developed a two-step argument. First, we argue that EU is more likely to invoke democratic conditionality when there is no democracy-stability dilemma, which makes the EU prioritise stability over pushing for uncertain democratic change. Second, democratic conditionality is only likely to be *effective* if it can empower pro-democratic local actors. In the remainder of the paper, we will show how their presence or absence shapes the consistency and effectiveness of EU democratic conditionality.

3.2. The democratisation-stability dilemma

The major source of the EU's inconsistency in promoting democracy under the ENP is what Annette Jünemann aptly described as the "democratization-stability dilemma" (Jünemann 2004; cf. Youngs 2002). Since the majority of the EU neighbours are authoritarian or semi-authoritarian countries, democratisation is likely to trigger instability at least in the short run, which is exactly the opposite of what the EU wants to achieve in its neighbouring regions. Thus, promoting democratic governance, on the one hand, and, effective governance aiming at securing peace and stability, on the other, may become conflicting objectives of the ENP (Börzel and van Hüllen 2014; Grimm and Leininger 2012). Accordingly, the consistency of the EU democracy promotion under ENP tends to fall victim to the democratisation-stability dilemma (Börzel and van Hüllen 2011, 2014). In its newest revision of the ENP, the EU has tacitly acknowledged that the democratisation-stabilisation dilemma limits its transformative power in the European neighbourhood (European Commission 2015, 2).

At the same time, the EU's preference for stability outweighs its preference for democracy promotion only if destabilisation is associated with acute threats, which might have immediate spillover effects inside the EU. Here lies the important difference in how the EU treats its Eastern and Southern neighbourhood. The recent ENP review identified a number of threats, which the EU considers as the most dangerous to its security: uncontrolled migration, terrorism and radicalisation, energy security, and organised crime (European Commission 2015). They are associated to a greater extent with the Mediterranean than the post-Soviet space. This is particularly the case for the two most pressing among them, uncontrolled migration and transnational terrorism.

The EU prioritising security challenges mirror the concerns of European publics. According to the Eurobarometer 2015, immigration is the number one concern among Europeans (Eurobarometer 2015, 15). Thirty-eight per cent consider it as the most important issue (Eurobarometer 2015, 15). Even prior to the Paris attacks, 17% ranked terrorism fifth place among the EU-wide concerns (Eurobarometer 2015, 15). None of the issues related to the Eastern Neighbourhood Countries (ENC) has made it among the top 10.

The dangers of uncontrolled migration and terrorism dragged the EU into a "Faustian bargain" with the authoritarian regimes of the Mediterranean. For decades, they have worked with the EU on combating terrorism, fighting illegal migration, and maintaining peace and stability on its Southern borders (Dandashly 2014, 38). In return, the EU increased economic incentives and autonomy in domestic matters. After the Arab Spring revolts, the EU continued to stick to its "security and stability driven" agenda prioritising "security concerns" over uncertain democratic openings (Dandashly 2014, 38). The new regimes abolished the migration control deals the EU had struck with the ousted dictators (Noutcheva 2014, 20). Ongoing power struggles between rivalling factions heightened the threats of uncontrolled migration and transnational terrorism.

Accordingly, the EU sought to re-establish border controls and pacify its Southern flank. The stability-driven approach of the EU has undermined its rhetorical support for the democratic forces of the Arab Spring. The EU had promised to abandon its "short-termism" of supporting authoritarian regimes as the only "guarantee of stability in the region" (Füle 2011) and to give way to the EU's promotion of "deep democracy" by providing "three M's" – money, market access, and mobility (Ashton 2011). It launched several new programmes including "A Partnership for Democracy and Shared Prosperity with the Southern Mediterranean" (European Commission 2011a) and Support for Partnership, Reforms and Inclusive Growth (SPRING) based on the "more for more" principle (European Commission 2011b). In practice, however, the EU has "deprioritised" democracy-related issues tolerating authoritarian backlash where it promised more political stability (Dandashly 2014, 40).

EU's reluctance was a sign of its limited leverage in Egypt vis-à-vis other actors and its predominant focus on stability and security issues. Egypt has been geopolitically a very important state for the EU as a "regional bulwark against terrorism" (Kausch 2015, 21) and as the main ally of Israel in the Middle East. Besides, local domestic players did not show much enthusiasm to cooperate with the EU on democracy issues. The violent developments of the Arab Spring revolts have further exacerbated the risks of state collapse in Egypt (Kausch 2015).

In Algeria, the authoritarian regime has been regarded by the EU "as the lesser of two devils" compared to the "likely alternative: a radical Islamist regime" (Çelenk 2010, 183). Besides, the Algeria is the EU's third largest gas supplier after Russia and Norway (Mokhefi 2014). The much-hailed stability of the country is endangered by various risks such as "domestic terrorism, increasing ethnic conflict, and growing regional insecurity" (Mokhefi 2014, 1).

Similar to Algeria, Jordan has been long considered as an "oasis of stability" in the Southern neighbourhood (Echagüe 2008, 37). The EU has emphasised Jordan's role of as "a very valuable partner in the Middle East peace process" as well as in fighting terrorism (ENPI 2007, 6, 17). Moreover, the EU has acknowledged the trade-off between stability and democratisation in Jordan: "… located between two major conflict zones, Jordan's path towards democracy and greater respect for human rights is not an easy one" (ENPI 2007, 18). Thus, destabilised security situation and regional conflicts have provided Jordan "with respite from any pressure for reform" (Echagüe 2008, 37).

In Morocco, finally, the main priorities of the EU have been "migration, anti-terrorism co-operation, regional conflicts [and] trade" (Kausch 2008, 9). In order not to endanger the stability of the incumbent regime, the EU democracy promotion agenda and the ENP Action Plan for Morocco were rather modelled on "careful liberalization" (van Hüllen 2012, 118) and on "selective political reforms in carefully chosen areas" (Kausch 2008, 9). As a manifestation of EU's stability-driven agenda, the EU's ambassador to Morocco conceded that the EU did not negotiate in the area of human rights since it was "a sovereign issue dealt with by the Moroccan government" (EurActiv 2013). In light of Arab Spring unrests Morocco was considered as an "oasis of stability" (Pham 2013) and as a privileged EU partner.

The stability-democratisation dilemma has been less of an issue in the Eastern neighbourhood. Nevertheless, the EU was often reluctant to push incumbent regimes towards democratisation. For instance, the EU continued its very cautious approach towards Armenia – a pragmatic pioneer of the ENP (Börzel and Lebanidze 2015). Armenian ruling elites, which have been in power since 1998, have been cooperative on a number of important issues which was essential for preserving peace and stability in the South Caucasus region – maintaining peace over Nagorno–Karabakh conflict and embracing the restoration of diplomatic relations between Armenia and Turkey. Besides, Armenia managed to build stable economic and political institutions and to achieve double digit annual economic growth for several years. Hence, the EU was careful not to endanger the stability of the Armenian regime by pushing it towards rapid democratisation. In a similar vein, the EU refrained from criticising authoritarian practices of the new government under President Mikhail Saakashvili and closed eyes on the questionable conduct of the 2008 presidential and parliamentary elections. In the midst of deteriorating relations with Russia, the EU was not very keen on regime change in a country which not only had aspirations for EU membership but was in the process of rebuilding its state institutions from the scratch after years of state erosion under Shevardnadze (Lebanidze 2014).

Rather than concerns about political stability, the unwillingness of the EU to invoke democratic conditionality towards Azerbaijan has been based on a sober self-assessment of the EU as lacking the transformative power vis-à-vis energy-rich country. Since the resource-rich regime in Baku does not show any serious interest in closer relations with the EU, there is hardly any sizeable reward Brussels could offer in return for costly democratic reforms (Kobzova and Alieva 2012; Paul 2015).

To conclude, in both the Eastern and the Southern neigbourhood, the inconsistency of the EU in applying democratic conditionality has been the result of a stability-democratisation dilemma, which, however, varies significantly between the two regions. In the Southern neighbourhood, instability has been associated with more severe and imminent threats to the EU such as uncontrolled migration and terrorism. In the eastern neighbourhood, the risks have been more moderate since the region has no tradition of terrorism and massive uncontrolled migration. Accordingly, the EU has refrained completely from using negative conditionality in the case of its Southern neighbours, and only applied positive conditionality to Tunisia. In the Eastern neighbourhood, by contrast, its approach was more mixed depending on domestic conditions, to which we turn next.

3.3. Pro-democratic reform coalitions

The domestic level of political liberalisation and presence of pro-reformist domestic actors are considered by many authors as a precondition for the EU's effective democracy promotion (Börzel and van Hüllen 2014; van Hüllen 2015; Schimmelfennig, Knobel, and Engert 2006). As in the case of the democratisation-stability dilemma, the Eastern and Southern neighbourhood differ quite substantially with regard to these factors.

In Georgia, pro-Western reform-oriented political elites have been in power uninterruptedly since the 2003 "Rose Revolution". They have not always embraced democratic norms, especially when their political power was threatened. For instance, the post-Rose Revolution government under Saakashvili resorted to controversial tactics to win the 2008 presidential and parliamentary elections (Lebanidze 2014). Similarly, the new government of "Georgian Dream" tried to prosecute members of the former government and censor the opposition media (TI Georgia 2015). Nevertheless, both previous and current governments have failed to consolidate the state power in their hands due to broad public opposition (Menabde 2015; TI Georgia 2015).

In Ukraine, the 2004 "Orange Revolution" brought into power a reform-oriented but fragmented elite unable to tackle corruption and necessary political and economic reforms. When Victor Yanukovych got elected president in 2010, he attempted to rollback democratic reforms and reorient the country towards Russia. However, similar to Georgia, the Ukrainian civil society and the broader public mobilised and ultimately forced Yanukovych out of power in the violent protests dubbed later as "Euromaidan" (Marples and Mills 2015). Nonetheless, neither the new government has been able to tackle the main problems of endemic corruption and an unchecked oligarchic influence on Ukrainian politics (Dempsey 2016).

Moldova, finally, has shown more similarities to Ukraine than to Georgia. Its politics has been fragmented and chaotic which ensured the pluralistic political scene but failed to tackle endemic corruption and the lack of reforms. In 2009, the country experienced its own version of "colour revolution" when the protests erupted after the seemingly unclean parliamentary elections (Freedom House 2013). Although the protests failed to overthrow the government, the differences inside ruling communist party regarding the replacement of the term-limited president Vladimir Voronin and subsequent defection of former parliament speaker to the opposition allowed the pro-EU opposition parties to build a governmental coalition after the repeated parliamentary elections in 2010 (Freedom House 2013). Nonetheless, continuing infightings inside the government and recent protests against the corruption scandals underscore the fragility of Moldovan domestic politics (BBC 2015).

Domestic conditions for democratisation in Armenia, Azerbaijan, and Belarus were less favourable. In Azerbaijan and Belarus incumbent regimes managed to build stable authoritarian systems and silence political opposition. The revenues from vast energy resources allowed the Azerbaijani government to build effective clientelistic networks controlling political processes in the country. Similarly, Belarusian president Alexander Lukashenko preserved Soviet-style economic structures which generated relatively higher average income and kept the political expectations of the population in check. In contrast to Azerbaijan and Belarus, Armenia has a rather vibrant civil society and strong tradition of pro-democratic public protest. Yet, Armenian ruling elites have never shown any interest in democratic reforms and have managed to consolidate their power to the extent that Armenian opposition has so far been unable to upset it be means of elections or street protests (Börzel, Pamuk, and Stahn 2009).

To summarise, in the Eastern neighbourhood the domestic conditions for democratisation have been more favourable in Georgia, Moldova, and Ukraine. In the three states, domestic actors within or outside government have supported democratic reforms, and an active civil society and political opposition have been mobilising to push for more change or resists backlash. In Azerbaijan and Belarus, such endogenous drivers of democratic change have been absent. The autocratic governments were not interested in democratic reforms, pro-democratic actors were silenced, and civil society remained passive. Armenia has had a stronger civil society and opposition, which, however, failed to alter the dominant position of the regime that managed to preserve its power by means of political oppression and effective clientelistic networks.

Domestic conditions for democratic development have been even less favourable in the Southern neighbourhood. Before the Arab Spring revolts, Israel has been the only democracy in the region. The Arab Spring protests have shaken the dominant positions of many autocrats and led to regime change in some countries. The revolts have evolved very differently, though, highlighting crucial variation among the Arab countries with regard to the existence of endogenous democratisation processes.

Among the Southern neighbours, Tunisia, with its "well-established political parties, strong unions and highly educated middle class" (Dandashly 2014, 41), has been the only country whose domestic conditions were favourable enough to make EU democratic conditionality effective. It has remained sufficiently stable, has had some "governance capacities" and has possessed pro-democratic domestic agents which the EU could empower (Börzel, Risse, and Dandashly 2014, 151). Besides, the adherence to a moderate strand of Islam (Pierini 2014) and an established culture of political dialogue and compromise among the main political players (Sharqieh 2013) made Tunisia an outlier in terms of reduced risks of political instability in the process of democratisation.

In Egypt, in contrast, the military, the Muslim Brotherhood (MB), and secular-liberal forces failed to establish an endogenously driven consensus-based process of democratic transition, which could be supported by the EU. Unlike Tunisia's moderate Muslim Ennahda party, Egypt's MB, which had come to power after the post-Arab Spring parliamentary and presidential elections, failed to achieve national consensus, ruled instead heavy-handedly, and alienated potential allies among secularists and liberals contributing to the "schism between the Islamists and the rest of society" (Ghanem 2014, 17). Moreover, in contrast to Tunisia's military, which was largely depoliticised, Egyptian military has remained a key political player both before and after the Arab Spring and ensured the return to "the pre-2011 status quo" after the 2013 bloody coup d'etat against the MB and the democratically elected post-Arab Spring president Mohammed Morsi (Mietzner 2014, 436).

The domestic conditions for democratisation in the remaining Southern neighbourhood countries have been even worse. The attempts to remove long-term dictatorships through public revolts have evolved into the civil wars and political fragmentation in Syria and Libya, exacerbating further the stability-democratisation dilemma. In the remaining Arab countries, the opposition to the incumbent autocratic regimes has been weak. The resource-rich authoritarian regime of Algeria managed to pacify the civil unrests during and after the Arab Spring by increasing public spending by 25% and introducing cosmetic changes such as lifting of the country's state of emergency being in force since 1992 (Khan and Mezran 2014). The Jordan and Moroccan royal families, finally, hold extensive political and economic powers, and despite frequent social protests, the opposition in both countries has so far been unable to challenge the dominant position of the incumbent regime (Freedom House 2015a, 2015b).

To conclude, Georgia, Moldova, Ukraine, and Tunisia have been the only four countries in the European neighbourhood where the domestic conditions were conducive for the effectiveness of EU democratic conditionality. The rest were marred by political instability and civil wars with no perspective for applying democratic conditionality in the first place (Syria, Libya), lacked reform-oriented domestic players the EU could empower (Armenia, Egypt), or had well-entrenched authoritarian systems and relatively weak opposition (Belarus, Azerbaijan, Algeria, Jordan, Morocco).

4. Conclusions

This paper argued that the EU's performance in promoting democracy in its neighbourhood is not so much compromised by the lack of a membership perspective but the inconsistent use of alternative incentives. We demonstrated that the EU is likely to consistently apply democratic conditionality if it does not have to choose between democratisation and stability and if it can empower pro-democratic reform coalitions.

Overall, we can identify three groups of states in the European neighbourhood, which differ from each other both in terms of consistency and effectiveness of EU democratic conditionality (Table 2). The biggest group is comprised of all Southern neighbours, with the exception of Tunisia, and of Azerbaijan and Armenia in the East. In these countries, domestic conditions for consistency and effectiveness of EU democratic conditionality have been unfavourable. The EU faces a democratisation-stability dilemma. In the southern neighbourhood, migration control and terrorism have been the main concerns of the EU. In Azerbaijan, energy interests had utmost priority, and in Armenia the freezing of the Nagorny–Karabakh conflict and restoring diplomatic relations with neighbouring Turkey. Thus, it is not surprising that EU has never invoked democratic conditionality in the first place. But even if it had, the absence of pro-democratic reform coalitions would have rendered democratic conditionality ineffective.

The second group identified in the paper consists only of Belarus, where the EU applied democratic conditionality but not consistently. To be fair, the case of Europe's last dictatorship is overdetermined given the role of Russia in boosting Lukashenko's regime (see below).

The third group is formed by Georgia, Moldova, Tunisia, and Ukraine, the four ENP countries where the EU applied democratic conditionality consistently and effectively. They have been sufficiently stable and featured pro-democratic reform coalitions the EU could empower.

While our findings confirm the importance of pro-democratic reform coalitions for the effectiveness of EU conditionality, we disagree with the External Europeanisation literature that the EU's transformative power in the European Neighbourhood has to

Table 3.2 Three groups of ENP states.

Algeria 2011 Arab Spring protests	Stability-democratisation dilemma – **high**
Armenian 2003, 2004, 2008, 2013 post-electoral protests	Pro-democratic reform coalitions – **absent**
Azerbaijan Multiple fraudulent elections/protests	Democratic conditionality – **absent**
Egypt 2011–2013 Arab Spring protests and Counterrevolution	Effectiveness – **absent**
Georgia 2008 authoritarian backlash	
Jordan 2011 Arab Spring protest	
Libya since 2011 Arab Spring protests, Civil War	
Morocco 2011 Arab Spring protests	
Syria since 2011 Arab Spring protests, Civil War	
Belarus Multiple fraudulent elections/protests	Stability-democratisation dilemma – **low**
	Pro-democratic reform coalitions – **absent**
	Democratic conditionality –**inconsistent**
	Effectiveness – **low**
Georgia 2003 Rose Revolution	Stability-democratisation dilemma –**low/medium**
Georgia 2012 electoral power transition	Pro-democratic reform coalitions – **present**
Moldova 2009 Twitter Revolution; 2013 political crisis	
Ukraine 2004 Orange Revolution	Democratic conditionality – **consistent**
Ukraine 2010–2013 Authoritarian backlash/Euromaidan	Effectiveness – **high**
Tunisia 2011 Arab Spring protests and democratic transition	

rely on a membership perspective. If consistently applied, the EU has alternative incentives on offer to promote and protect democratic change. Next to the weakness or absence of endogenous democratic forces, it is, hence, the democratisation-stability dilemma that presents the greatest challenge to the EU's performance in promoting democracy, particularly in its Southern neighbourhood.

Since the EU resorted to democratic conditionality in Belarus where domestic reform coalitions were clearly not in place, we conclude that the democratisation-stability dilemma is the more decisive factor in accounting for *when* the EU invokes democratic conditionality in the first place (figure 1). The presence of pro-democratic reform coalitions then accounts for the effectiveness of EU democratic conditionality and, hence, serves as a necessary condition for the EU performing as a transformative rather than a stabilising power.

The case of Belarus also points to an additional factor that could affect the EU's performance in promoting democracy – the presence of illiberal regional powers. Powerful regional actors, which provide alternative models of reference or alternative sources of assistance, can also undermine the transformative power of the EU in its neighbouring states (Risse and Babayan 2015). In the Eastern neighbourhood, Russia has sponsored authoritarian incumbent elites in Armenia, Belarus, and Ukraine under Presidency of Leonid Kuchma and Victor Yanukovych (Ambrosio 2009a; Tolstrup 2009, 2013; Vanderhill 2013). In a similar vein, Russia tried to destabilise the statehood of Georgia, Moldova, and Ukraine by military, economic, and political means. Yet, this had a double effect on democratisation process of these states probably not intended by the Russian regime. On the one hand, ethno-territorial conflicts fuelled by Russia weakened their overall reform-capacity and made their integration into the Euro-Atlantic structures more difficult and the consistent use of EU democratic conditionality less likely. On the other hand, however, Russia has been pushing the post-Soviet regimes towards the EU, increasing the EU's leverage, and making them more vulnerable to EU democratic conditionality (Ademmer, 2016; Börzel, 2015; Lebanidze 2016). The exception is Armenia, where Russia prevented the regime from establishing closer ties with the EU. It blocked Armenia's attempt to sign the AA with the EU and forced Yerevan to join the Eurasian Customs Union instead. We find a similar ambivalent effect for Saudi Arabia acting as a "counter-revolutionary" force in a number of Arab Spring countries (Hassan 2015). In Egypt, Saudi Arabia has established itself as the main patron of Egyptian military supporting the counterrevolution against the Muslim Brotherhood and the installation of military rule under Abdel Fattah el-Sisi (Hassan 2015). Tunisian political elites, in contrast, view the growing influence of the Golf State with suspicion. Saudi Arabia has been often considered as

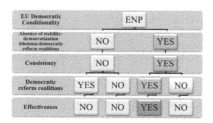

Figure 3.1. Decision tree for EU consistency and effectiveness in the ENP countries.

a supporter of "Salafization" (Sons and Wiese 2015). The Tunisian government has been very cautious in granting Saudi business access to its market turning to the EU for economic and financial assistance.

Illiberal regional powers may undermine the EU's transformative power decreasing the chances of the EU making consistent and effective use of democratic conditionality – but they can also have the opposite effect. What Georgia, Moldova, Tunisia, and Ukraine have in common are pro-democratic reform coalitions which are absent in Armenia, Belarus, and Egypt. Future research needs to explore more systematically how domestic factors, such as pro-EU elites and pro-democratic reform coalitions, influence the interaction between the EU and illiberal regional powers in trying to influence their shared neighbourhood according to their diverging political and economic interests (Lebanidze 2016).

Finally, much of the EU's democratic conditionality in the ENP states has been *ex post* in nature (Ghazaryan 2014). Unlike punitive *ex ante* conditionality, ex-post conditionality draws on the provision or withdrawal of support as a reaction to (non-)compliance with democratic norms (Ghazaryan 2014; Magen 2006). In contrast to its clearly defined enlargement criteria, the EU's neighbourhood conditionality has often been vague and ill-defined. Hence, it is more difficult to isolate its causal effect. Further research is needed to conceptualise, operationalise, and empirically assess the components of neighbourhood conditionality cross-country and cross-time.

Disclosure statement

No potential conflict of interest was reported by the authors.

Funding

Research for this paper has been supported by the FP7 programme of the EU for the project 'Maximizing the integration capacity of the European Union: Lessons and prospects for enlargement and beyond (MAXCAP)' [grant number 320115].

References

Ademmer, Esther. 2016. *Russia's Impact on EU Policy Transfer to the Post-Soviet Space – The Contested Neighbourhood*. London: Routledge.

Ambrosio, Thomas. 2009a. *Authoritarian Backlash: Russian Resistance to Democratization in the Former Soviet Union*. Post-Soviet Politics. Farnham, England: Ashgate.

Ambrosio, Thomas. 2009b. *Authoritarian Backlash: Russian Resistance to Democratization in the Former Soviet Union*. Post-Soviet politics. Farnham, England: Ashgate.

Ashton, Catherine. 2011. "What Next in North Africa?" Accessed October 14, 2015. http://www.nytimes.com/2011/03/19/opinion/19iht-edashton19.html.

Ashton, Catherine, and Štefan Füle. 2012. "Joint Statement by High Representative/Vice-President Catherine Ashton and Commissioner Štefan Füle, on EU-Georgia Relations and the Upcoming Elections." Accessed October 20, 2015. http://europa.eu/rapid/press-release_MEMO-12-640_en.htm?locale=en.

Balfour, Rosa. 2012. "EU Conditionality after the Arab Spring." Accessed October 14, 2015. http://www.epc.eu/documents/uploads/pub_2728_papersbalfour_for_euromesco16.pdf.

Baracani, Elena. 2009. "The European Neighbourhood Policy and Political Conditionality: Double Standards in EU Democracy Promotion?" In *The External Dimension of EU Justice and*

Home Affairs: Governance, Neighbours, Security, edited by Thierry Balzacq, 111–132. Palgrave Studies in European Union politics. Basingstoke: Palgrave Macmillan.

BBC. 2015. "Moldova Anger Grows over Banking Scandal." Accessed February 24, 2016. http://www.bbc.com/news/world-europe-34244341.

Bertelsmann Stiftung. 2012. "Bertelsmann Transformation Index 2012." Verlag Bertelsmann Stiftung. Bicchi, Federica. 2014. "The Politics of Foreign Aid and the European Neighbourhood Policy Post-Arab Spring: 'More for More' or Less of the Same?" *Mediterranean Politics* 19 (3): 318–332. doi:10.1080/13629395.2014.959758.

Borell, Mireia, Ron Boschma, Vassilis Monastiriotis, and Edzard Wesselink. 2012. "Report on ENP Policy Conerning its Objectives and Policy Measures over Time." Accessed October 19, 2015. http://www.ub.edu/searchproject/wp-content/uploads/2012/02/SEARCH-Deliverable-1.2_DEF.pdf.

Börzel, Tanja. 2015. "The Noble West and the Dirty Rest? Western Democracy Promoters and Illiberal Regional Powers." *Democratization* 22 (3): 519–535. doi:10.1080/13510347.2014.1000312.

Börzel, Tanja, and Katrin Böttger. 2012. "Conclusion: The Power to Transform Lies in the Detail." In *Policy Change in the EU's Immediate Neighbourhood, a Sectoral Approach*, edited by Tanja Börzel and Katrin Böttger. 1. Aufl 93, 163–171. Baden-Baden: Nomos.

Börzel, Tanja, and Vera van Hüllen. 2011. "Good Governance and Bad Neighbours? The Limits of the Transformative Power of Europe." KFG Working Paper Series 35. http://userpage.fu-berlin.de/kfgeu/kfgwp/wpseries/WorkingPaperKFG_35.pdf.

Börzel, Tanja, and Vera van Hüllen. 2014. "One Voice, One Message, but Conflicting Goals: Cohesiveness and Consistency in the European Neighbourhood Policy." *Journal of European Public Policy* 21 (7): 1033–1049. doi:10.1080/13501763.2014.912147.

Börzel, Tanja, and Bidzina Lebanidze. 2015. "European Neighbourhood Policy at the Crossroads: Evaluating the Past to Shape the Future." *MAXCAP Input Paper* (13).

Börzel, Tanja, Yasemin Pamuk, and Andreas Stahn. 2009. "Democracy and Stability? EU and US Engagement in the Southern Caucasus." In *Promoting Democracy and the Rule of Law: American and European Strategies*, edited by Amichai A. Magen, Thomas Risse-Kappen, and Michael McFaul, 150–184. Basingstoke: Palgrave Macmillan.

Börzel, Tanja, Thomas Risse, and Assem Dandashly. 2014. "The EU, External Actors, and the Arabellions: Much Ado about (Almost) Nothing." *Journal of European Integration* 37 (1): 135–153. doi:10.1080/07036337.2014.975993.

Bosse, Giselle. 2012a. "A Partnership with Dictatorship: Explaining the Paradigm Shift in European Union Policy Towards Belarus." *JCMS: Journal of Common Market Studies* 50 (3): 367–384.

Bosse, Giselle. 2012b. "The EU and Belarus: Perpetual Tango All over Again?" Accessed July 18, 2016. http://www.epc.eu/documents/uploads/pub_2940_the_eu_and_belarus.pdf.

Bosse, Giselle, and Elena Korosteleva-Polglase. 2009. "Changing Belarus? The Limits of EU Governance in Eastern Europe and the Promise of Partnership." *Cooperation and Conflict* 44 (2): 143–165.

Çelenk, Ayşe A. 2010. "Promoting Democracy in Alegria: The EU Factor and the Preferences of the Political Elite." In *The European Union's Democratization Agenda in the Mediterranean*, edited by Michelle Pace and Peter Seeberg, 176–193. London: Routledge.

da Conceição-Heldt, Eugénia, and Sophie Meunier. 2014. "Speaking with a Single Voice: Internal Cohesiveness and External Effectiveness of the EU in Global Governance." *Journal of European Public Policy* 21 (7): 961–979. doi:10.1080/13501763.2014.913219.

Dandashly, Assem. 2014. "The EU Response to Regime Change in the Wake of the Arab Revolt: Differential Implementation." *Journal of European Integration* 37 (1): 37–56. doi:10.1080/07036337.2014.975988.

Dempsey, Judy. 2016. "Judy Asks: Is Ukraine a Lost Cause?" Accessed February 25, 2016. http://carnegieeurope.eu/strategiceurope/?fa=62866.

Echagüe, Ana. 2008. "Jordan." In *Is the European Union Supporting Democracy in its Neighbourhood?* edited by Richard Youngs, Jos Boonstra, Julia C. Vizoso, Ana Echagüe, Balázs Jarábik, and Kristina Kausch, 33–54. Spain: Priority Producción, Diseño y Comunicación S.L.

ENPI. 2007. "Jordan Strategy Paper 2007–2013. National Indicative Programme 2007–2010." Accessed March 2, 2016. http://trade.ec.europa.eu/doclib/docs/2007/october/tradoc_136445.pdf. EurActiv. 2013. "'EU's Support for Morocco Not Conditional on Human Rights', Ambassador Says." Accessed December 23, 2015. http://www.euractiv.com/east-mediterranean/eu-support-civil-society-morocco-news-531376.

EurActiv. 2015. "EU Freezes Funding for Moldova." Accessed December 23, 2015. http://www.euractiv.com/sections/europes-east/eu-freezes-funding-moldova-316202.

Eurobarometer. 2015. "Public Opinion in the European Union: Standard Eurobarometer." Accessed December 3, 2015. http://ec.europa.eu/public_opinion/archives/eb/eb83/eb83_first_en.pdf.

European Commission. 2011a. "A Partnership for Democracy and Shared Prosperity with the Southern Mediterranean." COM(2011) 200 final.

European Commission. 2011b. "EU Response to the Arab Spring: The SPRING Programme." Accessed December 22, 2015. http://europa.eu/rapid/press-release_MEMO-11-636_en.htm.

European Commission. 2013a. "EU's Response to the "Arab Spring": The State-of-Play after Two Years." Accessed February 26, 2016. http://europa.eu/rapid/press-release_MEMO-13-81_de.htm.

European Commission. 2013b. "Signature of Association Agreement with the EU Will Depend on Ukraine's Performance." Accessed October 28, 2015. http://europa.eu/rapid/press-release_IP-13-436_en.htm.

European Commission. 2015. "Review of the European Neighbourhood Policy." Accessed December 3, 2015. http://eeas.europa.eu/enp/documents/2015/151118_joint-communication_review-of-the-enp_en.pdf.

European Parliament. 2004. "European Parliament Resolution on the Result of the Elections in Ukraine." Accessed July 3, 2015. http://www.europarl.europa.eu/sides/getDoc.do?type = MOTIO N&reference = B6-2004-0196&language = ET.

Freedom House. 2013. "Freedom in the World 2013. Moldova." Accessed February 24, 2016. https://freedomhouse.org/report/freedom-world/2013/moldova.

Freedom House. 2015a. "Freedom in the World 2015. Algeria." Accessed March 2, 2016. https://freedomhouse.org/report/freedom-world/2015/algeria.

Freedom House. 2015b. "Freedom in the World 2015. Morocco." Accessed March 2, 2016. https://freedomhouse.org/report/freedom-world/2015/morocco.

Freedom House. 2015c. "Nations in Transit 2015: Democracy on the Defensive in Europe and Eurasia." Accessed July 9, 2015. https://freedomhouse.org/sites/default/files/FH_NIT2015_06.06.15_FINAL.pdf.

Fukuyama, Francis. 2005. "'Stateness' First." *Journal of Democracy* 16 (1): 84–88.

Füle, Štefan. 2011. "Speech on the Recent Events in North Africa." Accessed July 18, 2016. http://europa.eu/rapid/press-release_SPEECH-11-130_de.htm.

Gawrich, Andrea, Inna Melnykovska, and Rainer Schweickert. 2009. "Neighbourhood Europeanization Trough ENP: The Case of Ukraine." Accessed March 2, 2016. http://www.polsoz.fu-berlin.de/en/v/transformeurope/publications/working_paper/WP_03_August_Melnykovska_Gawrich_Schweick ert.pdf.

Ghanem, Hafez. 2014. "Egypt's Difficult Transition: Why the International Community Must Stay Economically Engaged." Global Economy and Development Working Paper 66. Accessed December 19, 2015. http://www.brookings.edu/~/media/research/files/papers/2014/01/egypt-transition-economy-ghanem/arab-econpaper1hafez-v3_mr.pdf.

Ghazaryan, Nariné. 2014. *The European Neighbourhood Policy and the Democratic Values of the EU: A Legal Analysis/Nariné Ghazaryan*. Modern Studies in European Law, Vol. 41. Oxford: Hart.

Grimm, Sonja, and Julia Leininger. 2012. "Not All Good Things Go Together: Conflicting Objectives in Democracy Promotion." *Democratization* 19 (3): 391–414. doi:10.1080/13510347.2012.674355.

Hassan, Oz. 2015. "Undermining the Transatlantic Democracy Agenda? The Arab Spring and Saudi Arabia's Counteracting Democracy Strategy." *Democratization* 22 (3): 479–495. doi:10.1080/13510347.2014.981161.

Haukkala, Hiski. 2010. "Explaining Russian Reactions to the European Neighbourhood Policy." In *The European Neighbourhood Policy in Perspective: Context, Implementation and Impact*, edited by Richard G. Whitman and Stefan Wolff, 161–177. Basingstoke, England: Palgrave Macmillan.

van Hüllen, Vera. 2012. "Europeanisation Through Cooperation? EU Democracy Promotion in Morocco and Tunisia." *West European Politics* 35 (1): 117–134. doi:10.1080/01402382.2012.631317.

van Hüllen, Vera. 2015. *EU Democracy Promotion and the Arab Spring: International Cooperation and Authoritarianism*. Governance and Limited Statehood. Basingstoke: Palgrave Macmillan.

Jünemann, Annette, ed. 2004. *Euro-Mediterranean Relations after September 11: International, Regional, and Domestic Dynamics*. London: Frank Cass. http://site.ebrary.com/lib/alltitles/docDetail.action?docID = 10093984.

Karatnycky, Adrian. 2005. "Ukraine's Orange Revolution." *Foreign Affairs* 84: 35–52.

Kausch, Kristina. 2008. "Morocco." In *Is the European Union Supporting Democracy in its Neighbourhood?* edited by Richard Youngs, Jos Boonstra, Julia C. Vizoso, Ana Echagüe, Balázs Jarábik, and Kristina Kausch, 9–31. Spain: Priority Producción, Diseño y Comunicación S.L.

Kausch, Kristina. 2015. "Egypt: Inside-out." In *Geopolitics and Democracy in the Middle East*, edited by Kristina Kausch, 21–35. Spain: Artes Gráficas Villena.

Khan, Mohsin, and Karim Mezran. 2014. "No Arab Spring for Algeria." Accessed December 21, 2015. http://www.atlanticcouncil.org/images/publications/No_Arab_Spring_for_Algeria.pdf.

Kobzova, Jana, and Leila Alieva. 2012. "The EU And Azerbaijan: Beyond Oil." Accessed June 3, 2015. http://www.ecfr.eu/page/-/ECFR57_EU_AZERBAIJAN_MEMO_AW.pdf.

Langbein, Julia, and Tanja A. Börzel, eds. 2013. "Introduction: Explaining Policy Change in the European Union's Eastern Neighbourhood." Special issue. *Europe-Asia Studies* 65 (4). doi:10. 1080/09668136.2013.766042.

Lebanidze, Bidzina. 2014. "What Makes Authoritarian Regimes Sweat? Linkage, Leverage and Democratization in Post-Soviet South Caucasus." *Southeast European and Black Sea Studies* 14 (2): 199–218. doi:10.1080/14683857.2014.905040.

Lebanidze, Bidzina. 2016. "Bringing the Puzzle Together: Russia, EU and the Post-Soviet Democratic Failure." Dissertation, Free University Berlin.

Lehne, Stefan. 2014. "Time to Reset the European Neighbourhood Policy." Accessed July 18, 2016. http://carnegieendowment.org/files/time_reset_enp.pdf.

Levitsky, Steven, and Lucan Way. 2010. *Competitive Authoritarianism: Hybrid Regimes after the Cold War*. Problems of International Politics. New York: Cambridge University Press.

Magen, Amichai. 2006. "The Shadow of Enlargement: Can the European Neighbourhood Policy Achieve Compliance?" Accessed July 10, 2016. https://cddrl.fsi.stanford.edu/sites/default/files/No_68_Magen.pdf.

Marples, David R., and Frederick V. Mills, eds. 2015. *Ukraine's Euromaidan: Analyses of a Civil Revolution*. Soviet and Post-Soviet Politics and Society 138. Stuttgart, Germany: Ibidem. http://search.ebscohost.com/login.aspx?direct = true&scope = site&db = nlebk&AN = 982187.

Menabde, Giorgi. 2015. "Georgian Government Accused of Attempts to Shut Down Opposition TV Channel." *Eurasia Daily Monitor* 12 (193). Accessed February 24, 2016. http://www.jamestown.org/single/?tx_ttnews%5Btt_news%5D = 44524&tx_ttnews%5BbackPid%5D = 7&cHash = 8268a3 123493c5c1a7724fee3e427034#.Vs4BFVXhChc.

Mietzner, Marcus. 2014. "Successful and Failed Democratic Transitions from Military Rule in Majority Muslim Societies: The Cases of Indonesia and Egypt." *Contemporary Politics* 20 (4): 435–452. doi:10. 1080/13569775.2014.968473.
Mokhefi, Mansouria. 2014. "Algeria – an Unsteady Partner for Europe." Accessed March 2, 2016. http://www.ecfr.eu/page/-/ECFR110_ALGERIA_MEMO.pdf.
Noutcheva, Gergana. 2014. "Institutional Governance of European Neighbourhood Policy in the Wake of the Arab Spring." *Journal of European Integration* 37 (1): 19–36. doi:10.1080/07036337.2014.975987.
Paul, Amanda. 2015. "The Eastern Partnership, the Russia-Ukraine War, and the Impact on the South Caucasus." IAI Working Paper 15/06.
Pawlak, Justyna, and John O'Donnell. 2013. "Europe Shies Away from Cutting Aid for Egypt." Accessed December 22, 2015. http://www.reuters.com/article/us-egypt-protests-eu-idUSBRE97K0WE20130821.
Pham, Peter. 2013. "Moroccan 'Exceptionalism' Deserves Support." Accessed December 23, 2015. http://www.the-american-interest.com/2015/08/05/moroccan-exceptionalism-deserves-support/. Pierini, Marc. 2014. "EU Foreign Policy in the Arab World: Three (Bad) Examples." Accessed December 5, 2015. http://carnegieeurope.eu/publications/?fa = 56071.
Reuters. 2012. "Belarus's Lukashenko: "Better a Dictator than Gay"." Accessed December 18, 2015. http://www.reuters.com/article/us-belarus-dicator-idUSTRE8230T320120304.
Reuters. 2013. "Belarusians in Exile Calls for EU Ban on Belaruskali and Belarusian Potash Company." Accessed August 4, 2014. http://www.reuters.com/article/2013/09/05/belarusians-in-exile-idUSnBw055161a + 100 + BSW20130905.
RFE/RL. 2002a. "Newsline – July 1, 2002." Accessed August 4, 2013. http://www.rferl.org/content/article/1142707.html.
RFE/RL. 2002b. "Newsline – October 10, 2002." Accessed August 4, 2012. http://www.rferl.org/content/article/1142777.html.
RFE/RL. 2003. "Newsline – September 26, 2003." Accessed August 4, 2012. http://www.rferl.org/content/article/1143010.html.
RFE/RL. 2004a. "Newsline – December 9, 2004." Accessed March 24, 2013. http://www.rferl.org/content/article/1143297.html.
RFE/RL. 2004b. "Newsline – November 24, 2004." Accessed March 24, 2013. http://www.rferl.org/content/article/1143288.html.
RFE/RL. 2004c. "Newsline – November 29, 2004." Accessed March 24, 2013. http://www.rferl.org/content/article/1143289.html.
Rinnert, David. 2013. "The Republic of Moldova in the Eastern Partnership From 'Poster Child to 'Problem Child'" Accessed July 18, 2016. http://library.fes.de/pdf-files/id-moe/10184.pdf.
Risse, Thomas, and Nelli Babayan. 2015. "Democracy Promotion and the Challenges of Illiberal Regional Powers: Introduction to the Special Issue." *Democratization* 22 (3): 381–399. doi:10. 1080/13510347.2014.997716.
Schimmelfennig, Frank, Heiko Knobel, and Stefan Engert. 2006. *International Socialization in Europe: European Organizations, Political Conditionality, and Democratic Change*. Palgrave Studies in European Union Politics. Basingstoke, England: Palgrave Macmillan. http://site.ebrary.com/lib/alltitles/docDetail.action?docID = 10263437.
Schimmelfennig, Frank, and Hanno Scholtz. 2008. "EU Democracy Promotion in the European Neighbourhood: Political Conditionality, Economic Development and Transnational Exchange." *European Union Politics* 9 (2): 187–215.
Sharqieh, Ibrahim. 2013. "Tunisia's Lessons for the Middle East: Why the First Arab Spring Transition Worked Best." Accessed December 5, 2015. https://www.foreignaffairs.com/articles/tunisia/2013-09-17/tunisia-s-lessons-middle-east.
Sherwood-Randall, Liz. 2012. "President Obama Meets with Georgian President Mikheil Saakashvili." Accessed July 18, 2016. http://www.whitehouse.gov/blog/2012/02/03/president-obama-meets-georgian-president-mikheil-saakashvili.

Sons, Sebastian, and Inken Wiese. 2015. "The Engagement of Arab Gulf States in Egypt and Tunisia since 2011 Rationale and Impact." DGAP Analyse 9.

The Economist Intelligence Unit. 2013. "Democracy Index 2013: Democracy in Limbo." Accessed July 9, 2015. http://www.eiu.com/public/thankyou_download.aspx?activity = download&campaignid = Democracy0814.

Thomas, Daniel C. 2012. "Still Punching Below Its Weight? Coherence and Effectiveness in European Union Foreign Policy*." JCMS: Journal of Common Market Studies 50 (3): 457–474. doi:10.1111/j.1468-5965.2011.02244.x.

TI Georgia. 2015. "Rustavi 2's Timeline in the Aftermath of the 2012 Parliamentary Elections." Accessed February 24, 2016. http://www.transparency.ge/en/node/5656.

Tolstrup, Jakob. 2009. "Studying a Negative External Actor: Russia's Management of Stability and Instability in the 'Near Abroad'." Democratization 16 (5): 922–944. doi:10.1080/13510340903162101.

Tolstrup, Jakob. 2013. Russia vs. the EU: The Competition for Influence in Post-Soviet States. Boulder, CO: FirstForumPress.

Vanderhill, Rachel. 2013. Promoting Authoritarianism Abroad. Boulder, CO: Lynne Rienner.

VOA. 2009. "Belarus Gets $2.5 Billion Credit Line from IMF." Accessed July 18, 2016. http://www.voanews.com/content/a-13-2008-12-31-voa58/401507.html.

Whitman, Richard G., and Stefan Wolff, eds. 2010. The European Neighbourhood Policy in Perspective: Context, Implementation and Impact. Basingstoke, England: Palgrave Macmillan. http://www.worldcat.org/oclc/294885550.

Wilson, Andrew. 2007. "Ukraine's Orange Revolution, NGOs and the Role of the West*." Cambridge Review of International Affairs 19 (1): 21–32. doi:10.1080/09557570500501747.

Youngs, Richard. 2002. "The European Union and Democracy Promotion in the Mediterranean: A New or Disingenuous Strategy?" Democratization 9 (1): 40–62. doi:10.1080/714000237.

Youngs, Richard, Jos Boonstra, Julia C. Vizoso, Ana Echagüe, Balázs Jarábik, and Kristina Kausch, eds. 2008. Is the European Union Supporting Democracy in its Neighbourhood? Spain: Priority Producción, Diseño y Comunicación S.L.

The Geopoliticisation of the EU's Eastern Partnership

David Cadier

Since the outbreak of the Ukraine crisis in 2014, the notion that the EU and Russia are engaged in a geopolitical contest over their common neighbourhood and that the Eastern Partnership (EaP) is Brussels' instrument in this context appears 'common sense'. Moscow's zero-sum approach and hard power projection in its 'near abroad' have certainly been apparent; they are well documented and abundantly commented upon. Several analysts have also recently denoted, however, a growing—albeit non-comparable—tendency on the part of the EU to adopt a geopolitical posture towards its Eastern neighbourhood (Kazharski and Makarychev 2015; Nitoiu 2016; Youngs 2017). In a recent study investigating both the EU's reaction to the Ukraine crisis and the impact of the crisis on EU foreign policy, Richard Youngs (Youngs 2017, 6–7) finds that EU support for certain political values and reforms is increasingly "pursued as a geopolitical comparative advantage over Russia" and "superimposed with a layer of geostrategic diplomacy". In documenting the same pattern, other scholars have notably pointed to Brussels' relaxing, in an apparent bid to compete with Moscow's influence, of its conditionality towards Ukraine to incentivise Viktor Yanukovych to sign the Association Agreement (AA) (Kazharski and Makarychev 2015, 334–35) and of its benchmarks of engagement with Belarus by lifting its sanctions in February 2016 in spite of a lack of progress on the human rights front (Charap and Colton 2017, 119–21; 175). What is more, the EaP itself is now, in fact, routinely represented as a containment policy in the Western press: the AA with Ukraine is described as a "bulwark against Russian aggression" (Robinson 2016) while the visa-free regimes with Ukraine and Georgia are presented as ways "to help [countries of the post-soviet space] as they try to move away from Moscow's orbit" (Baczynska 2016).

This evolution in the self-understandings and media narratives around the EaP begs question as neither in its original purpose, actual content or effects on the ground does the reality of the policy correspond to such representation. Two established experts on EU external relations concur in stressing that the European Neighborhood Policy (ENP), of which the EaP is the Eastern branch, was "stripped of any geo-political considerations" in its design and that it "has not been a geopolitical power projection project in the crude sense of the term" (Haukkala 2016, 6; Howorth 2017, 6; see also: Youngs 2017, 50–64). The ENP hardly amounts, indeed, to a policy consciously seeking—or able—to project hard power and was not created based on a logic of competition for territories. Quite simply, if the EU really did want to 'take over' countries of the post-Soviet space, it would offer them membership. Yet the ENP and EaP have precisely been engineered above all as *alternatives* to enlargement (Dannreuther 2006). In addition, paradoxically, what analysts generally reproach to the EU in the context of the Ukraine crisis is, actually, to have failed to appreciate the geopolitical dynamics at play in the Eastern neighbourhood and the potential repercussions of the EaP in this context (Auer 2015, 760; Howorth 2017, 8; Haukkala 2016, 7; MacFarlane and Menon 2014; House of Lords 2015). They point, in other words, to the EU's *lack* of geopolitical thinking in this context. How to account, then, for the aforementioned evolution in the representation of the EaP? How to explain, in particular, the discrepancy between, on the one hand, the geopolitical framing of the EaP in public discourses and, on the other hand, the non-geopolitical content of the policy and absence of geopolitical contingency planning in its implementation? What are the implications and consequences of this 'geopoliticisation' of the EaP?

The traditional explanation advanced in both academic and policy debates is that EU policies in the Eastern neighbourhood have become geopolitical because Russia has perceived, denounced and responded to them as such (see for instance: European Commission 2014). While certainly accurate in its characterisation of Moscow's reception of—and reaction to—the EaP (Gretskiy, Treshchenkov and Golubev 2014), this explanation is insufficient to fully account for why the policy has been framed as geopolitical by European actors themselves. First, there is a difference between acknowledging that your interlocutor sees your mutual interaction as a gunfight and starting seeing your own hand as a gun. There is a difference between recognising that Russia's reactions to the EaP (and to the EU–Ukraine AA in particular) has turned EU–Russia interactions in the Eastern Neighbourhood as a geopolitical contest and representing the EaP as a geopolitical instrument in this contest. Second, one would need to explain why this pattern of exogenous speech act (or externally transposed meaning) happened in that instance and not others: why would European actors adopt Moscow's characterisation of their own policies in the case of the EaP but not, let's say, of the war in Kosovo, the situation of Russian speakers in the Baltic states or the Maidan revolt? Such transposition is particularly difficult to explain in the case of the EaP when one agrees that Russia's protestations against this policy were often "disingenuous" and hardly "withstanding serious scrutiny" (Haukkala 2016, 660). Third and most crucially, the traditional explanation overlooks the fact that, as this article shows, enunciations of the geopolitical storyline on the EaP can be traced in European discourses *before* the outbreak of the Ukraine crisis (late 2013) and, even, before the launch of the EaP (May 2009).

With a view to advance a more complete and more accurate explanation, this article purports to unpack the geopolitical storyline and analyse its elevation as a prevalent narrative in European public discourse when referring to the EaP—what is conceptualised here as the *geopoliticisation* of the EaP. Directly drawing on that of securitisation (Waever 1995), this notion is set forth to designate the discursive construction of an issue or policy as a geopolitical matter. Relying on discourse analysis theories from the International Relations literature, but also engaging with critical geopolitics to some extent, this article aims to denaturalise the geopolitical narrative around the EaP by contextualising the discursive practices that have underpinned it and by shedding light on the conditions that have favoured its emergence and prevalence. I argue that the geopoliticisation of the EaP was not simply exogenous, but also carried forward from within the European policy community by discourse entrepreneurs who, based on their own political subjectivities and policy agenda, came to frame the EaP as an endeavour aimed at 'winning over' countries of the Eastern neighbourhood and at 'rolling back' Russia's influence. The concept of discourse coalition (Hajer 1993; Howorth et al. 2000; Howarth and Torfing 2005) is called upon to designate, and integrate in the analysis, both these entrepreneurs and the main storylines they promoted.

It is important to stress that the geopolitical storyline on the EaP was never taken up as such in EU official communications. This, however, should be read more as a manifestation of the EU's traditional ambiguity than as a mark of the narrative's total irrelevance in Brussels. As emphasised by Merje Kuus (2015), who shows that EU foreign policy is characterised by a "variegated practical use of [geopolitical] concepts", the neutrality of the official narrative often serves the function of patching up variations in the dispositions and agendas of European policy professionals. I argue in fact that, because it was enounced by actors with significant social capital within the European political community (notably foreign ministers from EU member states) and as EU foreign policy discourse cannot be summed up to that of its institutions, it contributed to shape the structure of signification in which EU policies towards the Eastern Neighbourhood were articulated and implemented. This article thus sheds light, through the case of the EaP, on the broader pattern of geopoliticisation of EU–Russia relations that has started to receive attention in relation to other issue areas, such as energy (Casier 2016). It also provides some elements of understanding on Europe's internal debates over the on-going "discursive competition between the various actors within the post-Soviet geopolitical field over the reworking of longstanding Cold War categories" (Toal 2017, 41).

The argument is developed in four successive steps. The first section presents the analytical framework employed and its two central concepts of discourse coalition and geopoliticisation. In a second step, the rationale, content and effects of the EaP are briefly analysed, with a view to emphasise their essentially non-geopolitical nature (provided that one adopts a minimalist definition of geopolitics, as this article does). The third section constitutes the bulk of the empirical contribution of the article. It unpacks the geopoliticisation of the EaP in European policy discourses by focusing on two specific contexts: national discussions in EU member states before the launch of the EaP in May 2009 and pan-European debates before the outbreak of the Ukraine crisis in late 2013. For the first context or arena, I focus on the cases of Poland and the Czech Republic, two countries that have played an important role in pushing for the EaP initiative and in promoting it at the EU level. Although the activism of the former is the one that has been the most decisive in that regard, I actually focus on the latter above all as the facts that the Czech Republic is less geopolitically exposed than Poland and that its Eastern policies underwent salient changes in the period studied both render geopoliticising moves more visible there. The years around the launch of the EaP constituted a period important and rich in terms of discursive articulation as Czech and Polish policy-makers had to 'sell' the EaP both to their domestic constituencies and to other member states.[1] In studying their articulatory practices, I rely on the qualitative content analysis of public speeches and of private, semi-directed interviews with diplomats and policymakers.[2] The goal here—and in discourse analysis more generally—is not to pretend to reveal what policy-makers 'really believe' but to trace which codes and organisational metaphors are used when speaking about the EaP and identify which chains of connotations and storylines are shared and reproduced throughout. The second context studied is that of European and transatlantic policy debates on the EU's AA with Ukraine and on EU-Russia relations in the common neighbourhood more generally. There, I focus more precisely on two metaphors redundant in policy-makers' declarations and think tanks productions from *before* the outbreak of the Ukraine crisis. The conclusion discusses the consequences and implications of this geopoliticisation of the EaP for EU external relations.

Discourse Coalition and Geopoliticisation: An Analytical Framework

Discourse theory understands discourse as being constitutive of social reality rather than a mere reflection of it.[3] As emphasised by Lene Hansen, "policy discourses are inherently social because policymakers address political opposition as well as the wider public sphere in the attempt to institutionalize their understanding of the identities and policy options at stake" (Hansen 2006, 1). Discourse provides the context in which these policy articulations are set (Diez 2014, 320). The notion of articulation refers here both to the act of formulating a policy and of endowing it with meaning, for instance by relating to certain markers of political culture or national identity (Weldes 1999, 98–103; Laclau and Mouffe 2001). By ascribing meaning, discourse makes the world intelligible and creates interpretative dispositions for actors, but it also "operationalizes certain regime of truths while excluding other possible mode of identities and actions" (Milliken 1999, 229). In that sense, discourse contributes to set the limit of legitimate, meaningful and practicable policy: it enables certain choices while disabling others (Diez 2014).

Meaning is neither immanent nor fixed, but constantly established, negotiated and contested through political struggle (Diez 2014; Hansen 2006; Larsen 1997). This leads discourse theories and poststructuralism in particular to underline the contingency and precariousness of politics and, as such, to seek to denaturalise and problematise the present. In this context, the discourse analyst's task is to "plot the course of these struggles to fix meaning at all levels of the social" (Jørgensen and Phillips 2002, 24) and, in particular, to study the "rhetorical strategies inherent in discourses [that] contribute to the way social facts are perceived" (Carta and Morin 2014, 296; See also: Howarth et al. 2000, 3; Foucault 2014). This article relies on discourse theory in as much as it seeks to unpack the struggles around the 'fixing of the meaning' of the EaP and to unveil, in particular, the 'rhetorical strategies' of discourse entrepreneurs in that context.

In studying the production, reproduction and contestation of meaning, discourse analysis stresses its relational dynamic. As emphasised by Jutta Weldes,

> Meaning is created and temporarily fixed by establishing chains of connotations among different linguistic elements. In this way, different terms and ideas come to connote or to summon one another, to be welded into associative chains that make up an identifiable whole. [...] The chains of association established between such linguistic elements [...] are socially constructed and historically contingent rather than logically or structurally necessary. (Weldes 1999, 98)

Such chains of connotations can be identified in European policy debates on Russia and the post-Soviet space. For instance, characterising a policy through 'linguistic elements' belonging to the 'associative chain' (or structure of meaning) of the Cold War discourse amount to 'connote' Russia as an adversary and the common neighborhood as theatre for the rivalry between two blocs.[4] Similarly, speaking of the Baltic states as "frontline states"—as the discourse entrepreneurs studied below have tended to do since the 2000s—amount to indirectly frame Russia as an enemy and EU-Russia relations as a conflict, since if there is a front then there must be a conflict and an enemy. Thus, discourse theories invite to pay attention not just to term uttered but also to the non-uttered terms and ideas associated to it (Neumann 1996; Walker 1993).

This conception of meaning production, which is embraced by many IR discourse analysts but also by several scholars of critical geopolitics, thus invites placing the analytical focus on actors, their discursive practices and their rhetorical strategies. To designate social actors and their positions, the Essex School set forth the concept of discourse coalition, which refers to "the ensemble of a set of storylines, the actors that utters these storylines, and the practices that conform to these storylines, all organized around a discourse" (Hajer 1993, 47; For an overview of the Essex School's approach, see: Howarth et al. 2000). Linguistic elements such as representations, storylines or organising metaphors (in Essex School's parlance: 'nodal points') glue political subjectivities and it is around them that discourses are articulated.[5] The discourse coalition framework reveals itself particularly useful to map the various political subjectivities in the EU context: James Rogers (2009), for instance, linked the advent of the notion of Europe as a 'global power'— which came to replace that of 'civilian power' in the definition of EU Grand Strategy—to the action of a discourse coalition of "euro-strategists". Similarly, Kuus (2015, 47; see also: Kuus 2014) places the emphasis on the agency of policy professionals, which lies in the "gradual collective crafting of phrases, agenda and lines of reasoning", and posits that the "terminology that circulates in EU settings reflects in part the power among them". The EU constitutes, indeed, an "open and heterogeneous discursive environment" which can be studied either by analysing "the main features of the EU discursive field" or the "contiguous discursive practices" of actors (Carta and Morin 2014, 303, 307). This article focuses on the latter, though not so much at the level of EU institutions but at that of the "wider semantic field [that] includes the member states' polities" (Carta and Morin 2014, 307). More specifically, it places the spotlight on member states' representatives, politicians, media and think tanks. Both IR discourse analysts (Hansen 2006; 7; Diez 2014, 330) and scholars of critical geopolitics (Ó Tuathail and Agnew 1992, 194; Toal 2017, 39–41) tend to favour a large analytical angle when it comes to studying actors' discursive practices.

This article studies how the discursive practice of a specific group led to a 'geopoliticisation' of the EaP. That notion directly draws on that of securitisation, developed by the Copenhagen School and based, to a large extent, on the theoretical foundations presented above. Understanding security as a *speech act*, Ole Waever defines a securitising move as one by which an issue is discursively framed as a security problem and, thereby, removed from the sphere of normal politics (Waever 1995, 67). Its success is mediated by factors that are internal ("following the grammar of security") as well as external ("features of the alleged threat" and "social capital of the enunciator") (Buzan, Wæver and De Wilde 1998, 33). The notion of geopoliticisation is thus used here to designate the discursive construction of an issue or policy as a geopolitical matter. It can refer both to the discursive practices framing a policy in geopolitical terms and to the resulting outcome in terms of crystallisation of meaning. As for securitisation, the success of a geopoliticising move is seen as being mediated by the speech's internal adherence to the 'grammar' and 'dialects' of geopolitics and by the position of authority of the geopoliticising actor. Its concrete operationalisation requires, however, to specify what is meant by geopolitics.

Tracing the 'Geopolitical' in the EaP's Rationale, Content and Impact

The notion of geopolitics has been used and abused—but rarely specified—in reference to EU-Russia relations in the post-Soviet space. It has come to mean anything, and everything, related to power politics, realpolitik, influence, hard power, imperialism or conflict. Though not confined to this context or issue-area (see: Deudney 1997, 93;

Sloan and Gray 1999, 1), this indeterminacy is particularly problematic in that case. First, while its use in the context of the Ukraine crisis itself, to refer to the annexation of Crimea or the conflict in the Donbas, appears rather straightforward, its applicability to the ENP and the EaP is less evident and should be qualified. Second, the term geopolitics has been heavily connoted in these debates and often invoked to criticise Russia's—but also the EU's (See for instance: Boedeltje and van Houtum 2011)—policies in the neighborhood. Just as the term 'normative' lost some of its conceptual value in the analysis of EU foreign policy after becoming somehow associated with "doing good" (Sjursen 2013), the term 'geopolitics' has been increasingly associated with 'doing bad'.

Geopolitics can refer to a body of theories, to the academic discipline of political geography or to a set of state practices (including discursive ones) in international affairs. The latter aspect, of concern here, is also the most difficult to operationalise: the term is abundantly used outside of the scholarly community and, even there, its contours can be broad. The most encompassing conceptualisation includes the practice by which states and their representatives spatialise international politics, order the space at their border and define relations with their neighbours. This definition is favoured in particular by the critical geopolitics scholarship, whose ontological and epistemological positions are, as briefly evoked, close to the ones adopted by the present article, except that the latter's theoretical framework borrows from the international relations literature rather than from political geography. For instance, if one refers to Gearóid Ó Tuathail and Agnew (1992) seminal article and to the key notions it introduced, geopoliticisation can be understood as a form of 'practical geopolitical reasoning' and discourse coalitions as being composed of 'intellectual of statecrafts'.[6] The present article is not just concerned with geopolitics as mode of reasoning or writing however, but also with geopolitics as a *policy character* attributed to the EaP. Thus, when unpacking the latter, a minimalist definition of geopolitics is favoured, one that allows to better grasp possible differences between the content of EaP policies and their framing, and thereby emphasise possible geopoliticising patterns more clearly.

In this understanding, a geopolitical endeavour is one that displays the following features: projecting or seeking to deter *hard power*; reflecting objectives or concerns related to *territoriality*; and consisting in actions taken against, or at least decided in consideration of, *other powers*.[7] A first criteria pertains to the *type of power* deployed and draws in particular on Luttwak's classic differentiation between geopolitics as a competition for territories and geoeconomics as a competition for markets (Luttwak 1990). Extrapolating on this, Wigell and Vihma conceptualise geopolitics and geoeconomics as two different geostrategies that mobilise different means (military vs economic), proceed according to different logics (confrontation vs selective accommodation), and provoke different reactions (counterbalancing or bandwagoning vs under-balancing) (Wigell and Vihma 2016; Vihma 2018; For a critique, see: Sparke 2018). A second criteria relates to the *territorialised* setting of the competition or power projection endeavour. A policy that seeks or amounts to control or integrate an external territory can, by essence, be regarded as geopolitical. In that sense, the EU enlargement *is* a geopolitical process under this criteria.[8] A third criteria concerns *external actors*: a policy can be considered geopolitical when it is decided or designed not just in relation to the territory where it is deployed, but also to external powers that may be present or influential on this territory or bordering it.

Neither in their rationale, content or effects, the EaP and the ENP display evident geopolitical features as defined above. Launched in 2004, the ENP aims to foster the "economic integration and political association" of states of the neighbourhood (East and South) with the EU (European Commission 2004; see also: Whitman and Wolff 2010; Schumacher, Marchetti and Demmelhuber 2017). Security considerations were in part driving this new policy: the underlying rationale was to attempt to stabilise the periphery rather than risk seeing it destabilise the EU (Rupnik 2007). However, the kind of threats against which the EU wanted to guard itself by investing in the ENP was above all non-military and de-territorialised (Christou 2010). As these threats were often striving on governance failures, encouraging and supporting state reforms in the neighborhood was seen as a way to enhance the EU's security and, in this endeavour, Brussels sought to reproduce the transformative power it successfully yielded in the enlargement process—yet *without* offering membership. Membership was not explicitly excluded, as ambiguity allowed to maximise incentives for neighbours and accommodate those EU member states rooting for further Eastern enlargement, but in reality it was largely excluded by the time the EaP was launched in 2009.[9] The EaP's does partly proceed from a geo-strategic rationale, namely stabilising the periphery (Browning and Joenniemi 2008), but it can be regarded as geopolitical only in the maximalist understanding of the term, not in the minimalist definition adopted here.

To foster domestic reforms, the EaP offers a set of incentives that can be summed up by the so-called 'three Ms': Markets (sectorial access to the EU internal market), Money (financial aid and loans), and Mobility (visa facilitation). Thus, it is best described, in our view, as a structural power endeavor[10]—the concept of 'soft', 'normative' or 'civilian' power are also sometimes used in the literature, yet never that of 'hard power'. The will to shape domestic markets towards the approximation of EU norms and standards partly reflects a desire to make them more amenable for EU businesses; thus the EaP does entail an offensive component in that sense, but a geo-economic one. It is above all internal drivers and dynamics have been key in bringing about the EaP: path-dependency on the part of EU institutions (Kelley 2006) and the will to increase their agenda-setting capacity in Brussels for the member states who promoted it (notably Poland, see below).[11] As such, at least in the form in which it was designed by EU Commission and adopted by all EU member states, in its content the EaP is not geared *against* other powers—if anything, analysts tends precisely to reproach this policy with neglecting the role of other regional powers, such as Russia or Turkey (Auer 2015; Beauguitte, Richard and Guérin-Pace 2015).

Similarly, the impact of the EaP has been largely undirected and unspecific, which makes it difficult to use it instrumentally. Concrete empirical studies find that the EU did manage to foster some degree of compliance and convergence in the Eastern neighbourhood, but that this change is above all policy-specific and largely uncorrelated with membership prospects or the level of interdependence with the EU (Langbein and Börzel 2015). More than geopolitical association with either the EU or Russia, domestic actors' preferences, calculations and decisions remain the key mediating factor accounting for sectorial reforms and policy change (Ademmer, Delcour and Wolczuk 2016). Furthermore, the sources of EU transformative power are multiple and not all Brussels-controlled (e.g. donor organisations, multinational corporations, national governments) and Russia, while having most often prevented the kind of domestic policy change advocated by the EU in the Eastern neighbourhood, has actually also facilitated it in some specific instances by pushing, out of considerations for its own agenda and benefits, local actors to adopt EU norms and standards (See: Ademmer 2016; Tolstrup 2014). All this speaks against the prevailing images of EU–Russia relations in the

Eastern neighbourhood as a 'geopolitical clash between two blocks' or of the EaP as 'geopolitical instrument' in this battle (Cadier 2014).

The Geopoliticisation of the EaP in National and Pan-European Contexts

Yet, both have become increasingly represented as such in European policy debates. The section below represents a first, and necessarily incomplete, attempt at undertaking a genealogy of this geopoliticising discourse. In order to be as representative as possible, it focuses on two different contexts (understood here both as setting and time period): national discussions in two EU member states around the launch of the EaP in May 2009 and pan-European debates before the outbreak of the Ukraine crisis in late 2013.

Geopolitical Argumentations on the EaP in EU Member States: The Cases of Poland and the Czech Republic

I first look at domestic discourses in Poland and the Czech Republic, notably in the years before and around the launch of the EaP. Although the involvement and influence of the former has been most substantial in shaping the EaP, the empirical focus is actually placed on the latter, for three reasons. First, albeit not comparable to that of Warsaw, Prague's contribution has nonetheless been meaningful, and yet received little attention. The Czech Republic has, for instance, produced a non-paper on the Eastern dimension of the ENP in 2007 and it was in Prague, during its holding of the rotating Presidency of the EU Council, that the EaP was launched in May 2009 (Tulmets 2014, 205–8). Second, a clear variation in Czech Republic's policies towards the Eastern Neighbourhood can be identified: while the region was largely absent from its foreign policy radar until the mid-2000s, a new focus and activism is notable from that period onwards (Weiss 2011; Tulmets 2014; 167). This marked policy change allows to reflect on the factors that prompted it as well as on the discursive practices of the actors who promoted this new preference. Third, contrary to Poland, the Czech Republic does not share any borders with the post-Soviet space (at least since Czech Republic's separation from Slovakia in 1993) and its historical relationship with Russia has been less recurrently and profoundly conflictual than in the case of Poland. In principle, the geostrategic imperatives being less pressing, one could hence expect Czech diplomats' default discourse on the EaP to be less geopolitically tainted than that of their Polish counterparts, and thus for geopoliticising moves to be more visible.

Poland

Poland has undeniably been the main shaper behind the EaP initiative: its first proposal to develop EU policies towards the post-Soviet space dates back from 2003 (that is, even before its own accession to the EU or the creation of the ENP) and what came to be known as the 'Polish-Swedish proposal' of 2008 eventually constituted the backbone of the EaP ('Polish-Swedish Proposal on the Eastern Partnership' 2008). As such, Poland's self-understanding of this initiative, and its successful efforts in promoting it at the EU level, have been abundantly studied (see for instance: Copsey and Pomorska 2014; Kaminska 2014; Natorski 2007). Hence, they will only be briefly reflected upon here.

Geopolitical thinking has been central to Poland's investment in EU Eastern policies and common to both its political and foreign policy elites. The Eastern neighbourhood is, indeed, regarded in Warsaw as zone of vital importance for national security: a Ukraine free from Moscow's influence has long been considered a cardinal and necessary protection against the potential revival of Russia's imperialism (Natorski 2007, 80; Kuzniar 1993). The investment in the Eastern dimension of the ENP also proceeded, more generally, from a desire to have stable, peaceful and reformed states at its immediate border.[12] Combined, these two objectives have translated into Poland's support for the European integration of its two Eastern neighbours, Belarus and especially Ukraine, "sometimes more determinedly than the neighbors themselves"(Szczepanik 2011, 63). In this context, a Polish diplomat, who was heading the EU department at the Polish MFA at the time of the launch of the EaP, described the initiative's goal as being to "prepare these countries for [approximating] the *acquis communautaire*" and thus "help them to get ready" for accession.[13] Beyond policy objectives, the EaP was also articulated at times with markers of Poland's national identity: in a speech to the Polish Parliament in 2008, the then Foreign Minister Radosław Sikorski presented it as a way to "fulfill the legacy" of the Jagiellonian era (cited in: Szczepanik 2011, 55; see also: Sikorski 2013), during which the Polish-Lithuanian Commonwealth administrated parts of contemporary Ukraine and Belarus.

In summary, the Polish discourse on the EaP was at least partially articulated around geopolitical metaphors: the initiative was occasionally framed by policy-makers and diplomats as a buffer against a feared resurgence of Russia's neo-imperialism, as a way to domesticate the space at Poland's borders and a mean to prepare countries of Eastern neighborhood for EU membership. Casting the light on these geopolitical storylines does not amount to claim that Poland's investment in the EaP was strictly and only engineered *against* Russia: it was also certainly conceived *for* the Eastern neighbourhood countries at its borders and *for* Poland itself. Warsaw was, indeed, pursuing to a great extent intra-European objectives, namely carving out for itself a niche of specialisation in EU structures and increasing thereby its agenda-setting capacity in Brussels. Nevertheless, the geopolitical framing by Polish officials of the proposed EaP initiative contributed to shape its meaning—to the extent that the proposal had to be adjusted so as to be 'sold' at the EU level and accepted by all member states. Nathaniel Copsey and Pomorska (2014, 439–40) show indeed how, in an endeavour to de-politicise the initiative and infuse it with a dose constructive ambiguity, Poland deliberately toned down the rhetoric at the EU level and set, for the EaP, modest bureaucratic and administrative goals.

The Czech Republic

Czech Republic's involvement and influence in shaping the EaP has been less substantial than Poland's. Nevertheless, it represents an even more instructive case for the approach specifically developed in this article.

As in Poland, intra-EU objectives explain, to a significant extent, Prague's investment in the EaP in the mid-2000s: it was regarded by Czech diplomacy as a pathway towards future Eastwards enlargement (one of its priorities at the time, see: Government of the Czech Republic 2006), as a way to cultivate a "market niche" at the EU level and as an ideal flagship policy for its Council Presidency (Kratochvíl and Horký 2010, 77). This change was, however, also more specifically impulsed from within the Czech foreign policy elite by a distinct group, based on the agendas and worldviews of its members. This group reunited two main sociological profiles: the former dissidents, who were advocating a stronger Czech involvement in the Eastern neighbourhood based on their democratisation agenda (Cadier and Mikulova 2015, 84–87), and the 'Atlantists' (or 'hawks'),[14] who saw it as a way to contain Russia's regional influence. The latter group was especially dominant in Czech foreign policy structures in the second half of the 2000s as testified by its holding of key positions in the MFA and by a number of atlantist decisions taken in that period, but also by the fact the atlantist discourse had acquired quasihegemonic status.[15] This group can be characterised as a *discourse coalition* in the sense that its member's political subjectivity are articulated around a set of distinctive storylines, metaphors, and narratives -the concept is thus used below to refer both to the group and to these discursive positions. Several of these storylines and metaphors are of a geopolitical texture and, as such, stood out in the Czech political discourse. As noted by Petr Drulák (2013, 98), who studied the discursive practices of this group with reference to another policy area, namely missile defense, but whose insights are equally valid for the case of the EaP, "the Atlantist foreign policy elite which came to power in 2006 had in general been more sensitive to the Russian threat than its predecessors and more open to geopolitical argumentation".

The Atlantist discourse coalition played a decisive role in putting the Eastern Neighbourhood on the agenda of Czech foreign policy and in framing it in geopolitical terms. Its leading figure, Alexandr Vondra, who around that time held the positions of Minister of Foreign Affairs (2006–2007) and of Deputy Prime Minister for European Affairs (2007–2009), called on in 2006 to "reinforce the country's diplomatic presence" in the Eastern neighbourhood, depicting the region as a "natural geographic priority" (Vondra 2006) even though, as mentioned, it had been absent from Prague's radar until then. Mr Vondra and his collaborators were active in promoting this preference inside and outside the foreign policy system (Kratochvíl and Tulmets 2009, 81). As such, they articulated this policy around specific symbols and self-understandings that are central to the Czech political culture, thereby endowing the EaP with certain meanings and providing a script to refer to it. These articulations and script were apparent in the discursive practice of diplomats and policy-makers.[16] In the content analysis of speeches and interviews, three storylines were identified in particular.

First, the investment in the EaP was often presented as made necessary by Russia's return to the canons of power politics in the post-Soviet space since the mid-2000s. In making this point, a diplomat invoked Czech Republic's historical "sensitivity to signals that Russia is trying to re-create its geopolitical ambitions, if not imperial position".[17] The image of the return evokes a continuity between the USSR and Russia as well as in the essantial nature of their policies: the correlated securitisation and essantialisation of Russia is, indeed, one of the landmark of the Czech atlanticisit discourse (Cadier 2012). For instance, a former foreign minister argued in private that Russia's long-term policy was to "re-establish the Soviet empire" while the Chief of Staff of another foreign minister asserted that "there is only one Russia".[18] In this containment narrative, the theme of energy security was also often invoked: it is, at the same time, a domain where Russia policies have been heavily securitised in European debates (Ciută 2010, 130–31) and an argument set forth by Czech advocates of the EaP (Vondra 2008).

Second, the EaP was sometimes framed as a *rollback* policy of Russia's influence in the post-Soviet space. In the words of a diplomat, who directly contributed to the drafting of the aforementioned 2007 Non-paper and who explicitly presented himself as belonging to the atlantist group, the objective of this initiative was to "disconnect" EU policies towards the Eastern neighbourhood from those pertaining to Russia, since colliding the two was amounting to "pushing [EaP countries] in the arms of Russia". In this context, he described the EaP as an attempt to "change the situation of these countries" and explained Moscow's negative reaction by the fact that this policy might lead the EU to "take EaP countries away from Russia, while they [Russia] still think that it's theirs".[19] More crucially, this representation of the EaP as a tool in a regional battle for influence also somehow transpired in some of the declarations of Karel Schwarzenberg, the Foreign Minister at the time. In February 2009, he warned Belarus that the recognition of (Russia-occupied) Abkhazia and South Ossetia would jeopardise its chances to be included in the EaP initiative to be launched three months later (Lobjakas 2009). Similarly, pointing to one of the Minister's declaration on (non-aligned but undemocratic) Azerbaijan (Schwarzenberg 2008), Petr Kratochvíl and Ondřej Horký note some "highly ambiguous statements" on the Eastern neighbourhood on the part of Czech diplomacy, which they explain by the conflicting aim of erecting a "protective belt of countries between the Czech Republic and Russia" and of promoting democracy in the region (Kratochvíl and Horký 2010, 77).

Third, the investment in the EaP was represented as a pathway towards the European integration of post-Soviet states. The need to work towards this integration was not only articulated with the containment narrative presented above but also, more profoundly, with Czech Republic's own geostrategic position and national identity. A mental map whereby the country is depicted as being on the "edge" of Europe and constantly risking to "fall" into an abyss was often mobilised in advocating further enlargement as well as the EaP.[20] This abyss was traditionally characterised as the 'East', which in the Czech political discourse refers less to a geographical space than to ontological categories defining the alienated past of the Czech Republic (i.e. communist, non-democratic and satellised to Russia)[21]—in other words to the meaning the notion had acquired in the 'Return to Europe' narrative. In this context, supporting the political and economic transformation as well as geopolitical emancipation of post-Soviet countries through the EaP was represented as a way to further 'push back' the East and thus consolidating Czech Republic's 'Return to Europe' (Cadier 2012).

In summary, in the discourse of the Czech Atlantist coalition, the EaP was at least partially articulated as policy of *containment* of Russia's geopolitical ambitions in Central Europe, of *rollback* of its influence in the Eastern neighbourhood, and of *preparation* of post-Soviet countries accession to the EU. As for Poland, pointing to these geopolitical storylines should not lead to oversimplify Prague's position: the Czech Republic, too, was pursuing intra-EU objectives and its discourse on the EaP was also articulated with non-geopolitical markers, such as the country's national role conception (democracy promotion), historical identity (successful post-communist transition) or national identity (Western). In addition, it is important to take into account the specific context in which this geopoliticising discourse was uttered. On the one hand, it should be recalled that some of these EaP debates happened in the wake of the Russo-Georgian war of August 2008, an event that boosted politicians' and media attention towards the Eastern neighbourhood and often led them to apprehend the region first and foremost through the prism of Russia's foreign policy behaviour. On the other hand, the promoters of the EaP were pursing an internal agenda of generating support for a new preference—namely a greater Czech involvement in the Eastern neighbourhood—and as such there is always a possibility that they might have been tempted to instrumentalise the Russia question to advocate this preference. The mere eventuality of advocacy motives does not invalidate the argument developed here, however, since the point is not to pretend to unveil Czech policy-makers' thinking on the EaP—let alone to dispute their interpretations of regional politics—but to stress that, regardless of intent, these articulatory practices contributed to shape the structure of meaning in which this policy was formulated and implemented.

Several intermediary conclusions can be drawn from the analysis—and comparison—of the Czech and Polish cases. First, instances of geopolitical framing of the EaP were unveiled in both national contexts, including in the period preceding the official launch of the EaP (i.e. before May 2009). Further comparative research on the situations in other EU member states would be welcome, but this finding is already significant in itself as the two countries played an important role in conceiving and promoting the EaP. In considering additional cases, it would notably be useful to investigate whether and to what extent there is a correlation between the geopolitical framing of the EaP and national positions on Russia. It would be interesting, for instance, to determine whether there has been a similar tendency to geopoliticise the EaP on the part of policy-makers from Western member states such as the UK or Sweden, who do not share Central European countries' geopolitical situation or Cold War history, but that have nevertheless adopted similar (i.e. critical) positions on Russia at the EU level.

Second, although enunciations of the geopolitical storyline on the EaP was denoted in both national contexts, the comparison between the Polish and Czech cases also revealed differences in how it emerged and was promoted, which calls for contextualised analysis of each Central European state's positions on the EaP and Russia, rather than lumping them together in a single, homogenous category.[22] In Poland, geopolitical reasoning around the EaP has been pervasive and featured at both the practical and formal levels— to the extent that it was difficult to link geopoliticising practices to a specific and distinct discourse coalition. In the Czech Republic by contrast, whose territory is less exposed from a geo-strategic point of view and where geopolitics had in fact generally *not* featured prominently in political thinking (Drulák 2013, 2006), geopolitical argumentation featured mainly at the practical level and could be attributed to a distinctive discourse coalition. In this context, the concept of geopoliticisation revealed particularly useful to capture and integrate in the analysis the articulatory practices of this coalition as well as their implications in terms of meaning production.

Pan-European and Transatlantic Debates on the EaP and on the Signing of an EU Association Agreement with Ukraine

Instances of geopoliticisation of the EaP have not been confined to the Polish and Czech contexts—nor to the time period around the launch of the initiative—but appeared in broader and latter contexts. This second sub-section traces enunciations of the geopolitical story line in transatlantic and pan-European debates in the year preceding the outbreak of the Ukraine crisis. It does not pretend to be able provide a comprehensive, systematic and definitive analysis of such a wide and diverse array of debates. Rather it focuses on two illustrative signposts, the '*Europe Whole and Free*' metaphor and the '*Battle for Ukraine*' narrative, which are denaturalised and contextualised. These two signposts have often been mobilised by the members of a broader, pan-European and transatlantic discourse coalition that encompasses, among others, the groups studied in the Czech and Polish contexts. This coalition is mainly composed of state representatives, policymakers, think tank analysts and journalists who coalesce around certain political subjectivities and policy objectives, such as the normative attachment to strong security and political links with the US, the support to democracy promotion policies and a critical attitude towards Russia (On this group, see for instance: Mikulova and Simecka 2013; Schaller 2005). They share a number of discursive practices that have been articulated, maintained and reproduced on the occasion of public speeches, participation to policy conferences, op-eds or declaration to the press. As witnessed in the case of the Czech Republic, their discourse on the Eastern neighbourhood tends to be marked in particular by a correlated securitisation of Russia and geopoliticisation of the EaP.

The first signpost is the chain of association regularly established between the EaP and the 'Europe Whole and Free' metaphor. Coined by the US President George H. Bush in May 1989, this programmatic slogan was largely meant to counter Gorbachev's 'Common Home' motto and embody Washington's political vision for the European order (Hoagland 1989). More specifically, the phrase "rearticulated in positive terms a longstanding Cold War aspiration to roll back the Soviet Empire on the European continent" (Toal 2017, 5). Later on, under the Clinton Presidency, this leitmotiv was elevated as a parable for NATO's enlargement, which was presented as creating the institutional architecture to realise this vision. John O'Loughlin (1999) points, for instance, to a 1997 report from the US State Department where, in advocating NATO enlargement to the US Congress, the Department describes this enlargement as serving the "broader goal of a peaceful, undivided and democratic Europe".

In 2013, American members from the aforementioned discourse coalition have been invoking the same motto in voicing their support to the EaP, which they presented as a natural continuation and incarnation of this historical dynamic, and Russia as a spoiler attempting to prevent its advent. For instance, in a hearing to the US Senate, the Executive Vice President of a Washington think tank influential on European affairs declared:

> The EU's Eastern Partnership initiative and future NATO enlargement do not necessarily overlap, but they can be mutually reinforcing just as NATO and EU enlargements have been in the post-Cold War period. Indeed, the Eastern Partnership is the latest instrument of a common transatlantic grand strategy [...] After 45 years of Cold War, we forged a bipartisan US policy to fulfill our original national aims of 1945. We nearly achieved our goal, with NATO and EU enlargement, the twin instruments of this strategy to secure a Europe whole, free, and at peace. [...] At the same time, the United States and the EU should anticipate and counter possible Russian efforts to derail these nations' move toward Europe.[23]

This association between the EaP and the 'Europe Whole and Free' metaphor was stable enough to be invoked in similar terms by the US Assistant Secretary of State for European and Eurasian affairs as well as by a Senior Democrat member of the Committee on Foreign Relations.[24] The invocation of slogans and symbols in an endeavor to generate support for policies is obviously quite common. It remains that the articulation of the EaP around a metaphor associated with US-URSS rivalry in Europe and NATO enlargement amount to connoting the policy geopolitically.

The second signpost relates to the framing, in the months preceding the Ukraine crisis, of the EU-Russia geo-economic competition in the shared neighbourhood as a geopolitical one. From Spring to Fall of 2013, tensions were mounting between Brussels and Moscow around the signing by Ukraine of an AA with the EU: after several years of negotiations, the Ukrainian President seemed suddenly ready to pull the plug on the process, out of domestic calculations and because of Russia's pressure.[25] In this context, various commentators and notably members of the studied discourse coalition, characterised the situation as a geopolitical 'battle' for Ukraine in which the EaP was the EU's 'weapon'. For instance, in June of that year (i.e. before the imposition of trade restrictions by Moscow), the Lithuanian foreign minister, whose country was to hold the EU Council Presidency and host the EaP Summit in November, described it in the following terms:

> This is a geopolitical battle for Europe, if I may, and we should win Ukraine. We can continue intellectual debates about human rights and things like that but we will find ourselves on the side of losers (cited in: Peach 2013).

Similarly, in a press article from early August, a journalist and columnist with substantial experience and visibility on matters related to Central and Eastern Europe characterised Ukraine's decision to sign an AA with the EU as being about "countering Russia's influence" and insisted that, as such, it "mattered to Europe" (The New York Times 2013). In that article, the Lithuanian foreign minister is also cited on its depiction of the EU Agreement with Ukraine: it is "not just technical negotiations with just another partner; it is a geopolitical process". In the following months, as Russia rhetorical and coercive pressure on Ukraine intensified and as EU– Russia tensions grew contingently, the mainstream European press often resorted to geopolitical metaphors borrowed from the lexicon of the Cold War to characterise the situation[26]: "bloc"; "win over Ukraine"; "geopolitics unfolding in real time"; "Yalta"; "drawing Ukraine away from Russia's sphere of influence"; "going west" (Chaffin 2013; The Economist 2013b, 2013c). Relying on comparable framing and making similar recommendations, some think tank analysts called on the EaP to take a "bolder strategic direction" in the "geopolitical contest with Russia" so as to avoid seeing countries of Eastern Europe becoming "puppets of the Kremlin" (Techau 2013). These three illustrative utterances of the 'battle for Ukraine' narrative are both representative of the variety in profiles of its enunciators (policy-makers, journalists and think tankers) and symptomatic as regard the period of their utterance (i.e. *before* the outbreak of the Maidan movement and Russia's military intervention).

Without amounting to a full fledge radiography of the pan-European and transatlantic debates on the EaP, the focused analysis of these two specific signposts shed light on the occurrence of geopoliticising practices in this arena as well. It also revealed a proximity, in terms of storylines mobilised and meaning conveyed, with what was observed in the primary empirical case study devoted to the Czech Republic and Poland. This could somehow be interpreted as the mark of an increased influence of Central European member states on EU policy debates on Russia, which has been documented elsewhere.[27] More profoundly though, what this rhetorical proximity actually reveals is that the geopoliticisation of the EaP cannot be summed up to an uploading, at the EU level, of Central European foreign policy elites' practical geopolitical reasoning: this geopoliticisation has been promoted and sustained by the discursive practices of a broader, transatlantic discourse coalition that relied on much more extensive resources in terms of knowledge production.

Conclusion

The practical geopolitical reasoning around the EaP has been articulated, promoted and reproduced within the European polity by an identifiable discourse coalition, as early as in the year of the launch of the initiative and the months preceding the outbreak of the Ukraine crisis. The strength of this geopoliticising move—a notion set forth in this article to characterise the discursive construction of an issue as a geopolitical problem—has stemmed from its adherence to the 'grammar' of geopolitics (reproducing the dialect of the Cold War in particular), from the 'social capital' of its enunciators (state representatives up to the level of foreign ministers and commentators with significant policy and media visibility), and from the 'feature of the threat' (geopolitical texture of Russia's own objectives and foreign policy behaviour). In addition to the impact of the Ukraine crisis and of Russia's actions in that context, this geopoliticising discourse and its effects constitute a complementary explanation of the growing EU tendency to approach its Eastern neighbourhood through a geopolitical prism. At the very least, this pre-existing discourse enabled this tendency, endowing it with meaning as well as with a script and a certain degree of legitimacy.

Through the case of the EaP, this article complements previous studies on the broader political framing of EU-Russia relations. As noted by Tom Casier, this framing is increasingly characterised by "one-sided negative geopolitical reading obfuscating underlying complexity" and tends to produce, as such, "abstract enemy-like structures" (Casier 2016, 773). From a theoretical point of view, thanks to its emphasis on actors' discursive practices and to its understanding of meaning as being relational, a discourse analysis lens, built around the notions of articulation, geopoliticisation and discourse coalition, allowed to shed light on how these structures emerge and are maintained and reproduced. The notion of geopoliticisation provided a conceptual link between discursive practices and policy implications while that of discourse coalition permitted to integrate actors in the analysis and explanation, without falling in the pitfalls of, either, generalising indiscriminately about a national or regional policy community (as is sometimes done about Central Europe) or of denouncing a 'cabal' of individuals (as conspiracy theories tend to do). More specifically, the concept of discourse coalition allowed both to distinguish discourse entrepreneurs within a national context —namely that of the Czech Republic—and to study their links or integration with actors beyond that context. From an empirical point of view, the case of the EaP showed a tendency on the part of European actors to geopoliticise not just Russia's behaviour but also, to some extent, the EU's own policies. As such, it permits to account, at least partially, for the notable discrepancy between the "defensive nature" of the ENP and the "wildly ambitious rhetoric" that accompanied its Eastern branch in particular (Haukkala 2016, 5).

The geopoliticisation of the EaP has implications for how this policy has been implemented and for regional politics more broadly. It is important, however, not to misrepresent these consequences or to overinflate them to the extent of denying the impact of other factors or the agency of other actors, as is sometimes done in the debates on the Ukraine crisis. In emphasising that patterns of discursive geopoliticisation of the EaP pre-date the outbreak of this conflict, this article has argued that this discourse cannot be interpreted simply as a reaction to Russia's coercive actions in Ukraine. What it has *not* argued, though, is that this discourse has, alone and in itself, *caused* the outbreak of the Ukraine crisis. Indeed, this crisis cannot be summed up to a mere and mechanical externality of the EU-Russia geo-economic competition in the post-Soviet space or to its geopolitcisation in some European quarters, although this competition and this discourse certainly played a role of incubator. Counter-factual reasoning is useful to illustrate this point: if Yanukovych had signed the AA but remained in power Russia would probably not have annexed Crimea; if he had not signed the AA but the Maidan had not happen, the EU would have probably looked the other way. It was above all dynamics internal to Ukraine and Russia that led the crisis to escalate and take the dramatic proportions we know. The dysfunctional and corrupt nature of Ukraine's state structure led internal divisions and disagreement over the AA to escalate into a revolt and to the fall of the government. Prompted in great deal by this fall, Russia's military intervention was also itself driven by strategic objectives and domestic drivers unrelated to the EaP (Allison 2014; Cadier and Light 2015). Similarly, while it might have been partly influenced by it, it's hard to see why Russian policy-makers' perceptions and interpretations of the EaP would have been solely determined by the geopoliticising discourse presented in this article: they have also been exposed, indeed, to EU official communication as well as to other (i.e. non-geopolitical) discourses on the EaP while, in addition, idiosyncrasies specific to the Russian domestic context—such as the shift in Russia's ideational representation of the EU and the growing tendency to characterise the latter as an 'ontological other'(Makarychev and Yatsyk 2015; Neumann 2016)— might have played a role in shaping these perceptions.

It remains that the actual and specific consequences of the geopoliticisation of the EaP are nonetheless significant, yet often overlooked. First, it provided ample rhetorical ammunitions to Moscow's denunciation of the EU's alleged 'expansionism' and to its framing of the EaP as a 'sphere of influence' policy: some of the geopolitical utterances transcribed above have, in fact, been explicitly showcased by Russian officials (see for instance: Deutsche Welle 2009; Pop 2009). Second and most crucially, the geopoliticising discourse sent the wrong signal to local elites in the Eastern neighbourhood, about an EU determination to 'prevail' over Russia in 'winning over' these states (which was not confirmed when the conflict escalated militarily), but also more problematically about Brussels' willingness to lower or even set aside the EaP's conditionality criteria and benchmarks for reform in order to do so. During the pivotal weeks of Fall 2013, this went beyond simply conveying an impression at the level of public discourse in fact, as proponents of the geopolitical storyline invoked it in EU decision-making deliberations: during a series of crucial meetings, "Poland and Lithuania persuaded other member states—most crucially Germany—to drop the conditions attached to the [Association] agreement [with Ukraine] as Russia's success in enticing Yanukovich away from the EU became clear" (Youngs 2017, 118). In that context, the "main motivation for Lithuania [and, arguably, for Poland] was geopolitical: it saw 2013 as a crucial moment for preventing Ukraine's fall into Russia's sphere of influence" (Raik 2016, 247). Yet, abandoning the EaP's conditionality criteria out of geopolitical thinking undermines EU policies in the region and deserves their long-term objective of promoting reforms, not least as it feed the partial reform equilibrium in these countries and allow local elites to use the EU-Russia contest to divert attention away from reforms (Cadier and Charap 2017). Tellingly, as early as April 2013, a prominent Ukrainian expert, asked about how the EU could help her country, called on Brussels to "agree a pause in the enlargement debate", "deliver a clear message to Ukraine" and "stop with the unnecessary rhetoric about competition over Ukraine with Russia" (Shumylo-Tapiola 2013; see also: Kudelia 2013). Third, one can only wonder to what extent the essentialist script articulated by the geopolitcising discourse coalition fed into the EU's relative blindness regarding both the evolution of Russia's foreign policy and the strategic implications of the EaP. It is rather paradoxical indeed that while securitising Russia as a dangerous and immutable geopolitically-driven foe, this coalition did not anticipate or warned against Moscow's potential geopolitical reaction to the EaP. Whether the EU has a strategic interest or moral imperative in confronting Russia geopolitically over the orientations of the countries of the Eastern neighbourhood is a political question to be settled by member states and their representatives. In any case, regardless of the ends actually agreed upon, framing as a geopolitical mean in that competition a policy (the EaP) that is not equipped for such use appears un-strategic. In sum, this article has thus provided a theoretical and empirical account of a pattern of geopolitical thinking that has the potential to somehow weaken, rather than strengthen, the EU's strategic posture in its Eastern neighbourhood.

Notes

1. As emphasised by Kuus (2015, 47, 36), "geopolitical argumentation [is a] politicised form of analysis crafted for specific reasons in specific places". Hence, claims about the world are to be "studied in terms of where they are produced and where they circulate", which calls for "empirically detailed case studies".
2. Most of the interviews cited have been conducted in Prague and Warsaw during two main periods: early 2009 and Spring 2013. More profoundly, the article draws on a more extensive, year-long empirical fieldwork conducted in Prague by the author in the year 2008–2009.
3. What is presented here is only a very brief account of a rich, dense and diverse literature. It places the emphasis in particular on what is often designated as the post-structuralist branch of discourse analysis. For a detailed overview of discourse analysis theories and methods, see for instance Carta and Morin (2014), Dunn and Neumann (2016), Jørgensen and Phillips (2002), and Milliken (1999).
4. The Cold War can, indeed, be understood as a configuration defined by a "particular discursive structure [where] the East–West relationship is constructed as one of hostility and clash of political, economic and social orders" (Risse 2011, 599).
5. As defined by Frank Fisher (2003, 87), storylines "function to condense large amounts of factual information inter- mixed with the normative assumptions and value orientations that assign meaning to them".
6. Ó Tuathail and Agnew (1992, 194) distinguish practical geopolitical reasoning (that of practitioners, statespersons, politicians) from formal geopolitical reasoning (that of strategic thinkers and public intellectuals). While the latter tend to have "highly formalized rules of statement", the former relies on "narratives and binary distinctions found in societal mythologies".
7. This minimalist definition is close to Deudney's (1997) 'realist' definition ("power competition between major states in peripheral areas") and to what Ó Tuathail and Agnew (1992, 191) designate as the 'classic' definition ("actions taken against other powers, such as invasions, battles and the deployment of military force").
8. Kazharski and Makarychev (2015, 334) note for instance that, by integrating Romania and Bulgaria in 2007, the EU became a geopolitical actor in the Black Sea.
9. As noted by Hiski Haukkala (2016), rather than an aspirational power projection endeavor, the ENP amounts to an "essentially defensive policy meant to stave off demands, expectations and obligations both from new members and prospective neighbours".
10. In Susan Strange's (1994, 24–25) classic definition, structural power refers to the "power to shape and determine the structures of the political economy within which other states, their political institutions and their economic enterprises" have to operate. (Strange 1994, 24–25)
11. To be sure, the coming into being of the EaP was not totally disjointed from geopolitical events, as it is in the official resolution adopted in reaction to the Russo-Georgian conflict of August 2008 that the European Council asked the Commission to accelerate the set up of this policy (European Council 2008). Yet, this should be less read as a

retaliatory move or strategic response to the conflict than as the outcome of intra-European bargaining: the member states advocating the imposition of sanctions against Russia after the conflict accepted to lift their demand in exchange for the acceleration of the EaP initiative.

12 Comparing to Germany's rational in supporting the 2004 EU enlargement, a Polish diplomat, who is said to have been one of the co-author of the 2006 internal MFA document that latter constituted the basis of the Polish-Swedish proposal, emphasised that it was in "Poland's interest to have civilized states at its borders". Interview at the Polish Ministry of Foreign Affairs, Warsaw, May 2013.
13 Interview with a Polish diplomat, London, April 2013.
14 The label Atlantists is used here as it is the one favoured by Czech analysts (see for instance Drulák 2013) as well as by practitioners claiming their belonging to this group (interviews conducted by the author).
15 On this group and its members, their discourse and their influence, see: (Cadier 2012).
16 As noted by Drulák (2013, 96–97), the Atlantists' geopolitical rhetoric was indeed mainly observable in private conversations and off-record discussions with policy makers, but rarely present in public discourse. It featured, in other words, at the level of practical rather than formal geopolitical reasoning.
17 Interview at the Security Department, Ministry of Foreign Affairs of the Czech Republic, June 2009.
18 Interview with a former Foreign Minister of the Czech Republic, Prague, February 2011; Interview at the Minister's Office, Ministry of Foreign Affairs of the Czech Republic, May 2013.
19 Interview with a diplomat, Embassy of the Czech Republic to the United States, May 2010.
20 Interview at the South-Eastern Europe Department, Ministry of Foreign Affairs of the Czech Republic, July 2009.
21 Thus, by projecting Czech Republic's own image onto post-Soviet countries, advocates of the EaP invoked a historical responsibility and moral imperative for Prague to support their transition as well as European integration. (Tulmets 2014)
22 For detailed and comparative case studies on other Central and Eastern European EU member states, see Kuus (2007), Raik (2016), and Tulmets (2014). Kirsti Raik (2016, 247) explains for instance that "the Baltic support to European-oriented reforms in the Eastern neighbourhood merged value-oriented and geopolitical motivations" and that this "geopolitical motive to support Eastern neighbors represents continuity in the old existential security problem".
23 "A US Strategy for Europe's East: Testimony by Damon M. Wilson", Hearing on *A Pivotal Moment for the Eastern Partnership: Outlook for Ukraine, Moldova, Georgia, Belarus, Armenia, and Azerbaijan*, US Senate Committee on Foreign Relations (Subcommittee on European Affairs), 14th November 2013. Available at: https://www.foreign.senate.gov/imo/media/doc/Wilson_Testimony.pdf
24 Testimony by Assistant Secretary of State for European and Eurasian Affairs Victoria Nuland, Hearing on *A Pivotal Moment for the Eastern Partnership: Outlook for Ukraine, Moldova, Georgia, Belarus, Armenia, and Azerbaijan*, US Senate Committee on Foreign Relations (Subcommittee on European Affairs), 14th November 2013. Available at: https://www.foreign.senate.gov/imo/media/doc/Nuland_Testimony_REVISED.pdf; Eliot Engel, "United States Must Stand Firm Against Russian Bullying in Europe", Oped on the Eastern Partnership, available at: https://democrats-foreignaffairs.house.gov/news/press-releases/engel-op-ed-eastern-partnership
25 To pressure the government in Kyiv, Moscow notably instigated a custom blockade at the Russo-Ukrainian border in August (The Economist 2013a)
26 The invocation of Cold War imagery obviously served the purpose of attracting the attention of Western audiences in spite of their lack of acquaintance with the region and of the technical complexity of the EU's Association Agreements.
27 Merje Kuus (2015) cites, for instance, two European policy professionals—one from a (formerly) 'new' and one from an 'old' member state—who concur in noting that the member states from Central and Eastern Europe have "strongly influenced" the EU's position and discourse on Russia, notably towards greater "geopolitical argumentation".

Funding

This work was made possible financially by the funding received in the framework of the The Transatlantic Post-Doc Fellowship for International Relations and Security (TAPIR).

References

Ademmer, E. 2016. *Russia's impact on EU policy transfer to the post-soviet space: The contested neighborhood.* New York: Routledge.

Ademmer, E., L. Delcour, and K. Wolczuk. 2016. Beyond geopolitics: Exploring the impact of the EU and Russia in the "contested neighborhood". *Eurasian Geography and Economics* 57(1):1–18. doi:10.1080/15387216.2016.1183221.

Allison, R. 2014. Russian "deniable" intervention in Ukraine: How and why Russia broke the rules. *International Affairs* 90(6):1255–97. doi:10.1111/1468–2346.12170.

Auer, S. 2015. Carl Schmitt in the Kremlin: The Ukraine crisis and the return of geopolitics. *International Affairs* 91(5):953–68. doi:10.1111/1468–2346.12392.

Baczynska, G. 2016. EU unblocks visa-free travel for Ukraine, Georgia. *Reuters.* December 8, 2016. http://www.reuters.com/article/us-ukraine-crisis-eu-idUSKBN13X0QI.

Beauguitte, L., Y. Richard, and F. Guérin-Pace. 2015. The EU and its neighbourhoods: A textual analysis on key documents of the European neighbourhood policy. *Geopolitics* 20 (4):853–79. doi:10.1080/14650045.2015.1075512.

Boedeltje, F., and H. van Houtum. 2011. Brussels is speaking: The adverse speech geo-politics of the European Union towards its neighbours. *Geopolitics* 16(1):130–45. doi:10.1080/14650045.2010.493791.

Browning, C. S., and P. Joenniemi. 2008. Geostrategies of the European neighbourhood policy. *European Journal of International Relations* 14(3):519–51. doi:10.1177/1354066108092311.

Buzan, B., O. Wæver, and J. De Wilde. 1998. *Security: A new framework for analysis.* Boulder CO: Lynne Rienner Publishers.

Cadier, D. 2012. 'L'invention d'une tradition de politique étrangère: Choix et préférences de politique étrangère de la République Tchèque (2004–2009)'. unpublished PhD Thesis, Institut d'Etudes Politiques de Paris (Sciences Po), Paris.

Cadier, D. 2014. Eastern partnership vs. Eurasian Union? The EU–Russia competition in the shared neighbourhood and the Ukraine crisis. *Global Policy* 5(October):76–85. doi:10.1111/1758–5899.12152.

Cadier, D., and S. Charap. 2017. The polarisation of regional politics: The impact of the EU–Russia confrontation on countries in the common neighbourhood. In *Damage assessment: EU–Russia relations in crisis*, eds. Lukasz Kulesa, Ivan Timofeev, and Joseph Dobbs, 9–16. London: European Leadership Network.

Cadier, D., and M. Light. 2015. Conclusion: Foreign policy as the continuation of domestic politics by other means. In *Russia's foreign policy: Ideas, domestic politics and external relations*, eds. D. Cadier and M. Light, 2015th ed., 204–16. Palgrave Macmillan.

Cadier, D., and K. Mikulova. 2015. European endowment for democracy: Institutionalizing central and eastern European democracy promotion model at the EU level?. In
Democratization in EU foreign policy: New member states as drivers of democracy promotion, eds. B. Berti, K. Mikulova, and N. Popescu. Oxon; New York: Routledge.

Carta, C., and J.-F. Morin. 2014. Struggling over meanings: Discourses on the EU's international presence. *Cooperation and Conflict* 49(3):295–314. doi:10.1177/0010836713494995.

Casier, T. 2016. Great game or great confusion: The geopolitical understanding of EU–Russia energy relations. *Geopolitics* 21(4):763–78. doi:10.1080/14650045.2016.1185607.

Chaffin, J. 2013. EU steps up courtship of Ukraine to wield more influence in East. *Financial Times.* September 25, 2013. https://www.ft.com/content/826d3322-25f1-11e3-8ef6-00144feab7de.

Charap, S., and T. J. Colton. 2017. *Everyone loses: The Ukraine crisis and the ruinous contest for post-soviet Eurasia*, 1st ed. New York: Routledge.

Christou, G. 2010. European Union security logics to the East: The European neighbourhood policy and the eastern partnership. *European Security* 19(3):413–30. doi:10.1080/09662839.2010.526110.

Ciută, F. 2010. Conceptual notes on energy security: Total or banal security? *Security Dialogue* 41(2):123–44. doi:10.1177/0967010610361596.

Copsey, N., and K. Pomorska. 2014. The influence of newer member states in the European Union: The case of Poland and the eastern partnership. *Europe-Asia Studies* 66(3):421–43. doi:10.1080/09668136.2013.855391.

Dannreuther, R. 2006. Developing the alternative to enlargement: The European neighbourhood policy. *European Foreign Affairs Review* 11(2):183–201.

Deudney, D. 1997. Geopolitics and change. In *New thinking in international relations theory*, ed. M. W. Doyle and G. J. Ikenberry, 91–123. Boulder: Westview Press.

Deutsche Welle. 2009. EU's new Eastern partnership draws Ire from Russia. March 21, 2009. http://www.dw.com/en/eus-new-eastern-partnership-draws-ire-from-russia/a-4116554.

Diez, T. 2014. Setting the limits: Discourse and EU foreign policy. *Cooperation and Conflict* 49(3):319–33. doi:10.1177/0010836713494997.

Drulák, P. 2006. Between geopolitics and anti-geopolitics: Czech political thought. *Geopolitics* 11(3):420–38. doi:10.1080/14650040600767883.

Drulák, P. 2013. Czech geopolitics: Struggling for survival. In *The return of geopolitics in Europe?: Social mechanisms and foreign policy identity crises*, ed. S. Guzzini, 1st ed., 77–100. Cambridge: Cambridge University Press.

Dunn, K. C., and I. B. Neumann. 2016. *Undertaking discourse analysis for social research*. Ann Arbor: University of Michigan Press.

European Commission. 2004. European Neighborhood Policy Strategy Paper, Communication from the European Commission. COM. (2004), 373.

European Commission. 2014. Speech by President Barroso at the conference paving the way for a European energy security strategy. http://europa.eu/rapid/press-release_SPEECH-14-400_fr.htm?locale=en.

European Council. 2008. Extraordinary European council: Presidency conclusions'. 12594/2/08 REV 2. http://www.consilium.europa.eu.

Fischer, F. 2003. *Reframing public policy: Discursive politics and deliberative practices*. Oxford: OUP Oxford.

Foucault, M. 2014. *L'archéologie du savoir*. Paris: Editions Gallimard.

Government of the Czech Republic. 2006. Programové Prohlášení Vlády. https://www.novinky.cz/specialy/dokumenty/96921-dokument-programove-prohlaseni-vlady.html.

Gretskiy, I., E. Treshchenkov, and K. Golubev. 2014. Russia's perceptions and misperceptions of the EU Eastern partnership. *Communist and Post-Communist Studies* 47(3–4):375–83. doi:10.1016/j.postcomstud.2014.10.006.

Hajer, M. A. 1993. Discourse coalitions and the institutionalization of practice: The case of acid rain in Britain. In *The argumentative turn*, eds. Frank Fischer, and John Forester, 43–76. Durham: Duke University Press.

Hansen, L. 2006. *Security as practice: Discourse analysis and the Bosnian war*. London: Routledge.

Haukkala, H. 2016. A perfect storm; or what went wrong and what went right for the EU in Ukraine. *Europe-Asia Studies* online (March):1–12. doi:10.1080/09668136.2016.1156055.

Hoagland, J. 1989. Europe's destiny. *Foreign Affairs* 69(1):33–50. doi:10.2307/20044286.

House of Lords. 2015. The EU and Russia: Before and beyond the crisis in Ukraine. European Union Commttee 6th Report of Session 2014–15, UK House of Lords. http://www.publications.parliament.uk/pa/ld201415/ldselect/ldeucom/115/115.pdf.

Howarth, D., A. J. Norval, Y. Stavrakakis, E. Laclau, and A. Ehrlich. 2000. *Discourse theory and political analysis: Identities, hegemonies, and social change*. Manchester: Manchester University Press.

Howarth, D., and J. Torfing. 2005. *Discourse theory in European politics: Identity, policy and governance*. New York: Springer.

Howorth, J. 2017. "Stability on the Borders": The Ukraine crisis and the EU's constrained policy towards the eastern neighbourhood. *JCMS: Journal of Common Market Studies* 55 (1):121–36. doi:10.1111/jcms.12448.

Jørgensen, M. W., and L. Phillips. 2002. *Discourse analysis as theory and method*. 1st ed. London; Thousand Oaks: SAGE Publications Ltd.

Kaminska, J. 2014. *Poland and EU enlargement: Foreign policy in transformation*. New York: Palgrave Macmillan.

Kazharski, A., and A. Makarychev. 2015. Suturing the neighborhood? Russia and the EU in conflictual intersubjectivity. *Problems of Post-Communism* 62(6):328–39. doi:10.1080/10758216.2015.1057077.

Kelley, J. 2006. New wine in old wineskins: Promoting political reforms through the New European neighbourhood policy. *JCMS: Journal of Common Market Studies* 44(1):29–55. doi:10.1111/j.1468-5965.2006.00613.x.

Kratochvíl, P., and O. Horký. 2010. Eastern promises? Czech ambiguity in the European neighbourhood. In *The quest for the national interest: A methodological reflection on Czech foreign policy*, eds. Petr Drulák and Mats Braun, 71–86. Frankfurt am Main: Peter Lang.

Kratochvíl, P., and E. Tulmets. 2009. La politique orientale de la République Tchèque et la Politique Européenne de Voisinage. *Revue D'études Comparatives Est-Ouest* 40(01):71–98. doi:10.4074/S0338059909001041.

Kudelia, S. 2013. EU-Ukraine association agreement: Yanukovych's two-level games | PONARS Eurasia. PONARS Eurasia. September 20, 2013. http://www.ponarseurasia.org/article/eu-ukraine-association-agreement-yanukovych%E2%80%99s-two-level-games.

Kuus, M. 2007. *Geopolitics reframed: Security and identity in Europe's eastern enlargement*. 2007. New York: Palgrave Macmillan.

Kuus, M. 2014. *Geopolitics and expertise: Knowledge and authority in European diplomacy*. Chichester, West Sussex; Malden: Wiley-Blackwell.

Kuus, M. 2015. Crafting Europe for its neighbourhood: Practical geopolitics in European institutions. In *Perceptions of the EU in Eastern Europe and sub-Saharan Africa – Looking in from the outside*, eds. V. Bachmann and M. Müller, 34–50. Basingstoke: Palgrave Macmillan.

Kuzniar, R. 1993. The geostrategic factors conditioning Poland's security. *The Polish Quarterly of International Affairs* 2(1):9–28.

Laclau, E., and C. Mouffe. 2001. *Hegemony and socialist strategy: Towards a radical democratic politics*. 2nd ed. London; New York: Verso.

Langbein, J., and T. A. Börzel, eds. 2015. *Explaining policy change in the European Union's Eastern neighbourhood*. London: Routledge.

Larsen, H. 1997. *Foreign policy and discourse analysis: France, Britain and Europe*. New York: Routledge.

Lobjakas, A. 2009. EU foreign ministers discuss eastern partnership. *Radio Free Europe/Radio Liberty (RFERL)*. February 23, 2009. http://www.rferl.org/a/EU_Foreign_Ministers_Discuss_Eastern_Partnership/1497826.html.

Luttwak, E. N. 1990. From geopolitics to geo-economics: Logic of conflict, grammar of commerce. *The National Interest* 20:17–23.

MacFarlane, N., and A. Menon. 2014. The EU and Ukraine. *Survival* 56(3):95–101. doi:10.1080/00396338.2014.920139.

Makarychev, A., and A. Yatsyk. 2015. Refracting Europe: Biopolitical conservatism and art protest in Putin's Russia. In *Russia's foreign policy: Ideas, domestic politics and external relations*, eds. D. Cadier and M. Light, 2015th ed., 138–55. Basingstoke: Palgrave Macmillan.

Mikulova, K., and M. Simecka. 2013. Norm entrepreneurs and Atlanticist foreign policy in central and Eastern Europe: The missionary zeal of recent converts. *Europe–Asia Studies* 65 (6):1192–216. doi:10.1080/09668136.2013.813681.

Milliken, J. 1999. The study of discourse in international relations: A critique of research and methods. *European Journal of International Relations* 5(2):225–54. doi:10.1177/1354066199005002003.

Natorski, M. 2007. Explaining Spanish and Polish approaches to the European neighbourhood policy. *European Political Economy Review* 7(Summer):63–101.

Neumann, I. B. 1996. Self and other in international relations. *European Journal of International Relations* 2(2):139–74. doi:10.1177/1354066196002002001.

Neumann, I. B. 2016. Russia's Europe, 1991–2016: Inferiority to superiority. *International Affairs* 92(6):1381–99. doi:10.1111/1468-2346.12752.

The New York Times. 2013. The Kremlin tries charm to counter E.U. August 5, 2013. http://www.nytimes.com/2013/08/06/world/europe/06iht-letter06.html.

Nitoiu, C. 2016. Increasingly geopolitical? The EU's approach towards the post-soviet space. *Journal of Regional Security* 11(1):9–32.

Ó Tuathail, G., and J. Agnew. 1992. Geopolitics and discourse. *Political Geography* 11 (2):190–204. doi:10.1016/0962-6298(92)90048-X.

O'Loughlin, J. 1999. Ordering the "Crush Zone": Geopolitical games in post-cold war Eastern Europe. *Geopolitics* 4(1):34–56. doi:10.1080/14650049908407636.

Peach, G. 2013. Linas linkevicius – diplomatic stalwart. *POLITICO*. June 26, 2013. http://www.politico.eu/article/diplomatic-stalwart/.

Pop, V. 2009. EU expanding its "sphere of influence," Russia says. *Euobserver*. March 21, 2009. https://euobserver.com/foreign/27827.

Polish-Swedish Proposal on the Eastern Partnership. 2008. June 2008. http://www.euneighbours.eu/library/content/polish-swedish-proposal-eastern-partnership.

Raik, K. 2016. Liberalism and geopolitics in EU–Russia relations: Rereading the "Baltic factor". *European Security* 25(2):237–55. doi:10.1080/09662839.2016.1179628.

Risse, T. 2011. Ideas, discourse, power and the end of the cold war: 20 years on. *International Politics* 48(4–5):591–606. doi:10.1057/ip.2011.20.

Robinson, D. 2016. Dutch threaten to sink EU-Ukraine trade and security deal. *Financial Times*. December 9, 2016. https://www.ft.com/content/713641f0-bd4e-11e6-8b45-b8b81dd5d080.

Rogers, J. 2009. From "civilian power" to "global power": Explicating the European Union's "grand strategy" through the articulation of discourse theory. *JCMS: Journal of Common Market Studies* 47(4):831–62. doi:10.1111/j.1468-5965.2009.02007.x.

Rupnik, J., ed. 2007. *Les banlieues de l'Europe*. Nouveaux Débats. Paris: Presses de Sciences Po.

Schaller, J. 2005. Neoconservatives among us? A study of former dissidents' discourse'. *Perspectives* 25(December):43–62.

Schumacher, T., A. Marchetti, and T. Demmelhuber, eds. 2017. *The Routledge handbook on the European neighbourhood policy*. Milton Park, Abingdon, Oxon; New York: Routledge.

Schwarzenberg, K. 2008. Osvícený Panovník Není Nejhorší Řešení. Ministry of Foreign Affairs of the Czech Republic. http://www.mzv.cz/jnp/cz/o_ministerstvu/archivy/clanky_a_projevy_ministru/clanky_a_projevy_ministra_schwarzenberga_1/osviceny_panovnik_neni_nejhorsi_reseni.html.

Shumylo-Tapiola, O. 2013. Why does Ukraine matter to the EU? *Carnegie Europe* (blog). April 16, 2013. http://carnegieeurope.eu/2013/04/16/why-does-ukraine-matter-to-eu-pub-51522.

Sikorski, R. 2013. Address by the minister of foreign affairs on the goals of Polish foreign policy in 2013. http://www.mfa.gov.pl/en/news/address_by_the_minister_of_foreign_affairs_on_the_goals_of_polish_foreign_policy_in2013_.

Sjursen, H. 2013. A foreign policy without a state? accounting for the CFSP. In *Rethinking Foreign Policy*, eds. Fredrik Bynander and Stefano Guzzini, 123–36. London: Routledge.

Sloan, G., and C. S. Gray. 1999. Why geopolitics? *Journal of Strategic Studies* 22(2–3):1–11. doi:10.1080/01402399908437751.

Sparke, M. 2018. Geoeconomics, globalisation and the limits of economic strategy in statecraft: A response to Vihma. *Geopolitics* 23(1):30–37. doi:10.1080/14650045.2017.1326482.

Strange, S. 1994. *States and markets*. London: Continuum.
Szczepanik, M. 2011. Between a romantic "Mission in the East" and Minimalism: Polish policy towards the Eastern neighbourhood. *Perspectives* 19(2):45–66.
Techau, J. 2013. Why the Eastern partnership is crucial for the EU and the West. *Carnegie Europe* (blog). October 9, 2013. http://carnegieeurope.eu/strategiceurope/?fa=52913.
The Economist. 2013a. Ukraine and Russia: Trading insults'. August 24, 2013. https://www.economist.com/news/europe/21583998-trade-war-sputters-tussle-over-ukraines-future-intensifies-trading-insults.
The Economist. 2013b. Looking to the West. October 3, 2013. https://www.economist.com/news/europe/21587260-russian-intransigence-has-helped-ukraines-integration-europe-looking-west.
The Economist. 2013c. West or East? October 3, 2013. https://www.economist.com/news/leaders/21587228-european-union-should-sign-deal-ukrainebut-only-if-yulia-tymoshenko-freed-west-or.
Toal, G. 2017. *Near abroad: Putin, the West and the contest over Ukraine and the Caucasus*. Oxford: Oxford University Press.
Tolstrup, J. 2014. *Russia vs. the EU: The competition for influence in post-soviet states*. Boulder: Lynne Rienner Publishers.
Tulmets, E. 2014. *East central European foreign policy identity in perspective: Back to Europe and the EU's neighbourhood*. Basingstoke: Palgrave Macmillan.
Vihma, A. 2018. Geoeconomic analysis and the limits of critical geopolitics: A new engagement with Edward Luttwak. *Geopolitics* 23(1):1–21. doi:10.1080/14650045.2017.1302928.
Vondra, A. 2006. Projev Ministra Vondry Na Poradě Velvyslanců ČR. http://www.mzv.cz/jnp/cz/o_ministerstvu/archivy/clanky_a_projevy_ministru/clanky_a_projevy_ministra_vondry_2006/porada_velvyslancu_cr.html.
Vondra, A. 2008. Foreign policy priorities of the Czech presidency. Vláda ČR. https://www.vlada.cz/scripts/detail.php?id=45498.
Waever, O. 1995. Securitization and desecuritization. In *On security*, eds. Ronnie Lipschutz, 46–86. New York: Columbia University Press.
Walker, R. B. J. 1993. *Inside/outside: International relations as political theory*. Cambridge: Cambridge University Press.
Weiss, T. 2011. Projecting the Re-discovered: Czech policy towards Eastern Europe. *Perspectives* 19(2):27–44.
Weldes, J. 1999. *Constructing national interests: The United States and the Cuban missile crisis*. Minneapolis: University of Minnesota Press.
Whitman, R. G., and S. Wolff, eds. 2010. *The European neighbourhood policy in perspective: Context, implementation and impact*. Basingstoke: Palgrave Macmillan.
Wigell, M., and A. Vihma. 2016. Geopolitics versus geoeconomics: The case of Russia's geostrategy and its effects on the EU. *International Affairs* 92(3):605–27. doi:10.1111/1468-2346.12600.
Youngs, R. 2017. *Europe's Eastern crisis: The geopolitics of asymmetry*. Cambridge; New York: Cambridge University Press.

The Unintended Consequences of a European Neighbourhood Policy without Russia

Tom Casier

A substantial part of foreign policy deals with the unintended consequences of an actor's domestic and foreign policies. It is reactive rather than the outcome of well-designed proactive strategies. Yet it is an under-researched topic. Drawing on Olga Burlyuk's conceptualisation of unintended consequences (2017), this article explores how the decoupling of Russia from the European Union's policies versus former Soviet states contributed to the emergence of significant unplanned internal and external outcomes.

In terms of theory, this article seeks to add two elements to Burlyuk's concept of unintended consequences. First, the article reflects on the way actors deal with the unintended consequences of their policies in order to reach certain objectives. Different modes of managing these unintended consequences are distinguished. Second, they are seen as part of a process: a chain of external action, unintended consequences and the management of the latter. As a result, while dealing with the threefold question, what, why and how, of this Special Issue (see Introduction), the emphasis of this contribution is on the latter: how unintended consequences are managed by the EU. In doing so, the article sheds new light on the EU's role as an international actor, arguing that it is characterised by an unusual balance between the intended and unintended impact of its policies. Furthermore, it opens a new perspective on the Union's policies *vis-à-vis* it eastern neighbours.

The case presented is the decoupling of the EU's foreign policy towards Russia from that towards other former Soviet states[1] in 2003–04. Throughout the 1990s, the European Union's policy towards the countries in the area was fairly monolithic, characterised by similar policy objectives, instruments, funds, etc. It also tended to respect a certain hierarchy whereby Russia would come first, Ukraine second, followed by other former Soviet states. The decoupling[2] of Russia from the EU's policy towards East European states (in the framework of the European Neighbourhood Policy and Russia's decision not to join) had profound unintended consequences for both the EU's policy and its relations with Russia. The article concludes with some reflections on the agency of the Eastern Partnership countries experiencing these consequences.

Conceptualising unintended consequences

Building on Olga Burlyuk's framework for studying unintended consequences of EU external action (2017), this article uses the following conceptual distinctions.[3] First, intended versus unintended consequences, whereby the latter are defined as "outcomes of purposive action(s) which are not directly intended by an actor" (Burlyuk 2017, 1012). Second, internal consequences are distinguished from external ones, with internal unintended consequences referring to consequences of foreign policy or external action for the actor itself, in this case the EU. External unintended consequences are those that affect the target of the action, third actors or the broader system or environment (1015). The third concept is the management of unintended consequences. This refers to the intentional action an actor takes in response to the unintended consequences it has generated. Two assumptions underpin this idea: one, an actor may or may not take action to steer the unintended consequences in a certain direction; two, an actor may take a variety of actions, from mitigating the unintended consequences to reinforcing them.

On the basis of this set of concepts, this article engages in the exploration of a broader process which could be presented ideal-typically as a chain: *external action – unintended consequences – management of unintended consequences*. Self-evidently, this representation is an analytical simplification of a complex process of multi-level transnational interactions. As Olga Burlyuk has noted, unintended consequences may be both "single" or "cumulative" (Burlyuk 2017, 1014). In the latter case, they may have a more systematic and durable effect. For example, asymmetrical economic relations may generate a more stable form of economic dependence. Most of the analysis in this article focuses on this type of cumulative consequences.

The very idea of (cumulative) unintended consequences is certainly not absent from the discipline of International Relations. In structural realism, for example, it is present in Waltz's concept of security dilemma (Waltz 1979), where the increase in capabilities of one state with the purpose of increasing its own security and chances of survival, has unintended consequences for the security of other states, who see their relative security diminished. In liberalism, it appears, for example, in Keohane and Nye's theory of complex interdependence (1989), where asymmetrical interdependence between two countries generates higher costs for the dependent country and gives the other country effective control over outcomes. Also, the concept of unintended consequences has long been present in research on EU external action, without being theorised as such. In his theory of normative power Europe, for example, Ian Manners refers to "contagion" as an unintentional form of norm diffusion by the EU (Manners 2002, 244–245). Sandra Lavenex distinguishes between intentional and non-intentional mechanisms of EU functional rule extension (Lavenex 2014, 889), with the latter resulting from indirect socio-economic forces.

Unintended consequences cannot be understood by looking only at the actor 'causing' them, but are also a function of the processes in the external environment (the context, the willingness of the 'receiving' countries to undergo or resist the impact, learning, etc.). Equally, the effect of unintended consequences will be determined by the way they interact with the objectives, activities and perceptions of third actors. As a result, unintended consequences are by definition complex and diffuse, in terms of both their origin and their impact on receivers.

The EU and unintended consequences

It may be hypothesised that the balance between the intended and unintended *external* consequences of its foreign policy is quite peculiar in the case of the EU. As an economic giant, it generates strong economic dependence for most of its neighbours, in comparison to the fairly limited intended impact that is created because of a weakly developed foreign policy. This may explain the particular importance of structural foreign policy for the EU, that is, "a foreign policy which, conducted over the longterm, seeks to influence or shape sustainable political, legal, socio-economic, security and mental structures" (Keukeleire and MacNaughtan 2008, 25). The ultimate aim is not one of control, as in conventional foreign policy, but to promote "a more favourable international environment by pursuing and supporting long-term structural changes" (Keukeleire 2003, 47). As stated by Arnold Wolfers, the EU's foreign policy is tilting towards "milieu goals" rather than "possession goals" (Wolfers 1962, 73).

Three (interrelated) forms of external, cumulative unintended consequences are of key importance for the EU in its relations with neighbouring countries: effects of (economic) dependence, externalisation, and attraction.

The first form of unintended consequences refers to the *costs generated by asymmetrical interdependence*. This holds in particular in the economic field. The EU is an economic giant, on which most of its neighbours are dependent for trade and investments. This generates tremendous unintended consequences for neighbouring economies. Drawing on Keohane and Nye, this can be seen in a transnational perspective, disconnected from interstate relations. According to them, interdependence produces "reciprocal (although not necessarily symmetrical) costly effects of transactions" (Keohane and Nye 1989, 9) When this interdependence is asymmetrical, that is when potential costs are higher for one party than for the other, this creates a potential source of influence (10–11).

Second, there are the *externalisation effects* of the EU's policies. Lavenex and Uçarer define externalities as "the positive or negative external effects of an activity on other actors or activities than the one originally intended" (Lavenex and Uçarer 2004, 438). Domestic policies will produce certain effects across the border.[4] The income support granted under the Common Agricultural Policy, for example, may lead to the dumping of EU agricultural products in third countries and eventually disrupt local markets. Obviously these externalisation effects are interwoven with interdependence. Generalising, we can assume the impact of externalities to grow with stronger dependence. This is particularly clear in the field of trade (Dodini and Fantini 2006). The alignment of new EU member states with the Common External Tariff had consequences for trade with its neighbours, thus changing opportunity structures. Strong export dependence on the EU will push companies and states to accept the standards and rules of the EU, eventually affecting preferences, legislation and opportunity structures.

A third form of unintended consequences results from *attraction*. "The EU exercises influence and shapes it environment through what it is, rather than through what it does" (Maull 2005, 778). The EU may be attractive for certain states as a model of integration, for the wealth it generates or for its soft security guarantees. Through the possible prospect of membership, the EU exerts a magnetic force or "gravitational pull" (782) on some eastern neighbours. Even just the subjective perception of a prospect within the neighbouring state to accede to the EU over the mid- or longer term will strongly determine its willingness to adopt the rules and norms of the latter.

Managing unintended consequences

To understand the process of unintended consequences and the EU's reaction to it, reflection is required about different modes of post factum management of unintended consequences.[5] EU external policies, such as enlargement and the ENP/EaP (European Neighbourhood Policy/Eastern Partnership), may be regarded as structural policies which seek to 'manage' the unintended externalisation effects of EU policies and make their impact more purposive, intentional, in particular with the objective of producing domestic reform in order to prepare countries for membership (in the case of enlargement policy) or for privileged relations (in the case of the ENP).

One can distinguish between different modes of managing unintended consequences, depending on whether and how an actor reinforces or mitigates them.[6] The EU does this in a particular way. It is predominantly a regulatory actor (Majone 1994) and its policy towards its neighbours is heavily oriented towards the transfer of rules. Because of this, it has a strong institutionalist reflex. In the case of the ENP/EaP, it seeks to extend part of the *acquis communautaire* beyond its borders. As mentioned above, this is typically a long-term structural policy, aimed at transforming legal, administrative and political systems in neighbouring countries in its own image. The strategy is one of weak or partial integration, where countries get partially included in the EU's regulatory and economic sphere, but without receiving the prospect of full membership. In other words, the EU aims at exporting its model rather than extending it to new countries, which would open the doors for membership.

The management of unintended consequences is itself a function of the capacity of an actor, in relation to other relevant actors and within a certain context. This means that the capacity to manage unintended consequences is ultimately also a form of power.[7]

Case: the decoupling of the EU's Russia and Eastern Europe policies

Against this conceptual background, this article explores the unintended consequences of the decoupling, in 2003–04, of the EU's policy vis-à-vis Russia from its policies towards the other East European former Soviet states. The latter remained part of the EU's European Neighbourhood Policy (ENP), while a separate Strategic Partnership was established with Russia. For simplicity sake, I will refer to both the ENP and the Eastern Partnership (EaP) states, even though the EaP dimension was only added in 2009.[8] The case will be presented as part of the ideal-typical process chain mentioned: external action – unintended consequences – management of unintended consequences. The EU's policy towards Russia and Eastern European countries was split as the result of Moscow's withdrawal from the ENP project. Despite this split, the EU did not alter its policy, something that will be explained below as a non-decision.

A simplified summary of the case and the main argument is presented in Figure 1 below.

Figure 5.1 Summary of the 'unintended consequences' model and its applications to the case of the EU's decoupling of its East European policies

In terms of Olga Burlyuk's classification, the unintended consequences were unanticipated and diachronic. Plausibly, they resulted in the first place from path dependence (and thus ignorance) and the "imperious immediacy of interests" (Burlyuk 2017). No doubt the institutional complexity of the EU, which makes a radical strategic overhaul difficult, played a crucial role.

The unintended consequences of decoupling EU policies vis-à-vis Eastern Europe and Russia

A non-decision

In 2003, the EU was preparing a new policy of privileged relations with the neighbours of the soon-to-be-enlarged Union, aiming at stability and avoiding new dividing lines in Europe. The Russian Federation was originally included in the ENP blueprint and was generally expected to join. However, despite the fact that negotiations with Russia had progressed substantially, at the last moment Moscow decided not to join the ENP. The country was increasingly lukewarm to an EU-centric policy, in which it was considered just one of the EU's many neighbours and put in the same basket with small countries such as Moldova and Tunisia. As a result, the EU's Russia policy was *de facto* decoupled from its policy towards its eastern former Soviet neighbours (Wolczuk 2009). Nevertheless, the EU continued with the ENP without Russia, developing a separate policy for Russia, in which Brussels and Moscow recognised each other as Strategic Partners.

The EU's decision not to alter its neighbourhood policy can be regarded as a non-decision. It has been defined as "the exclusion of some alternatives from the agenda of collective choice because dominant values make them politically impossible for the moment" (Rose and Davies quoted in McCalla-Chen 2000, 34).

In the original concept of Bachrach and Baratz (1963), non-decision was linked to the idea of "mobilisation of bias". It suggests that certain issues are systematically kept out of decision-making through certain dominant values or procedures to benefit a small elite of decision-makers. Yet several authors have argued that it may also occur for unconscious reasons, such as incompetence or attachment to something highly valued (for example maintaining good relations with both Russia and other eastern neighbours). In our case, non-decision was probably mainly a form of 'accommodation', where actors fail to pursue issues of interest or concern and instead accept or adjust to the existing situation (McCalla-Chen 2000, 35). Little or no trace was found of a profound discussion or new initiatives within the EU to revise policies towards the eastern neighbours because of Russia's decision to withdraw from the ENP. The EU simply seems to have acquiesced in the new situation and, confronted with the implications of Russia's decision, opted for inaction rather than redesigning its policies vis-à-vis post-Soviet states.

It is beyond the scope of this article, but it could be argued that the complexity of EU decision-making and the risk of disrupting balances among multiple decision-makers by changing delicate long-negotiated compromises made the EU more prone to accommodation. Radically changing a policy that is the result of years of difficult negotiations between all member states and EU institutions was not an evident option. It required a sense of urgency. In the case of Moscow's decision not to join the ENP, this sense of urgency was lacking. Relations with Russia were good at this point. Enthusiasm over the idea of a Strategic Partnership abounded. There was a lack of anticipation of the possible consequences in the longer term.

Internal and external unintended consequences

The unintended consequences of the decoupling and the decision to pursue the Strategic Partnership with Russia as well as an unchanged European Neighbourhood Policy with the other eastern neighbours were twofold. *Internally*, a tension developed between the two policies. With the eastern ENP countries, the EU developed a structural foreign policy (Keukeleire and MacNaughtan 2008) aimed at long-term structural reforms. The neighbours were to converge their laws, norms and institutional practices to those of the EU. Policies were predominantly EU-driven. With Russia, on the other hand, the EU engaged in a Strategic Partnership covering four Common Spaces of cooperation. This partnership was based on equality and frank recognition of each other's interests. It was a form of strategic diplomacy (Smith *et al.* 2016), driven by interests rather than norms, and based on 'constructive engagement'.

The tension between the two policies resided in their incompatibility. The ENP, as a form of structural diplomacy, sought to reshape its eastern neighbours in the EU's image, extending the EU's legal and economic system. However, these neighbours were equally a part of the neighbourhood of Russia, with which the EU had a Strategic Partnership. Establishing a form of far-reaching association with exactly those countries where Russia claimed to have legitimate "privileged interests" – in the words of President Medvedev (2008) – inevitably undermined the EU's credibility as Russia's strategic partner and the other way around. Before the Ukraine crisis of 2014, this inherent tension in the EU's eastern policy fuelled divisions among member states. Some, like Germany and the Netherlands, prioritised relations with Russia; others, such as Poland and Lithuania, put EaP countries like Ukraine first.

The major *external* unintended consequence was that the decoupling of policies fundamentally reshaped relations with Russia. Because of the combination of the Strategic Partnership and the ENP, the EU operated in two different strategic contexts in its relations with East European neighbours. The tension between the EaP and the Strategic Partnership fed negative opinions in Moscow about the EU's intentions (Casier 2016a). Arguably it fuelled the geopolitical suspicion that was clearly gaining ground in Russia and gave it a degree of legitimacy. When the Eastern Partnership was launched, Foreign Minister Lavrov accused the EU of 'building a sphere of influence'. Later on he claimed that the EU was forcing Kyiv to sign agreements (Haukkala 2015, 34). In this context, it became easier for the Russian government to exploit "the situation if not of conflict then of controversy between Russia and the West" and "the idea of Russia as some sort of besieged castle" (Volkov quoted in House of Lords 2015, 21).

As a result, a dynamic developed whereby both countries increasingly regarded each other's policies in the neighbourhood with mistrust. Any form of enhanced regional cooperation (whether the EaP or the Eurasian Economic Union) came to be regarded in a zero-sum context, as a potentially inimical act weakening the interests of the other (Casier 2016a). This resulted in "a culmination of tensions" (Haukkala 2015, 25) and "recurrent rounds of escalation – a costly spiral of action and reaction" (Charap and Troitskiy 2013, 51).

It goes without saying that this evolution cannot be attributed solely to the EU's decoupling of policies and its non-decision to adapt the ENP to the changed situation. This alone cannot explain the confrontation with Russia a decade later. As argued above, unintended consequences cannot be ascribed to only one actor; they are the result of complex, diffuse processes in the external environment and the choices and policies of various actors. The causes of the conflict over Ukraine are multiple and changing Russian policies have played a substantial role in creating a competitive strategic environment. As argued elsewhere (Casier 2016a), we cannot understand the confrontation in EU–Russia relations without understanding the complex dynamic which developed over the years giving rise to a "logic of competition". Thus, the point here is that the decoupling of the EU's policies towards its eastern neighbours did not cause the competition, but that it has been a facilitating factor for the development of competitive dynamics.[9]

In this respect, Joan DeBardeleben (2018) refers to a fundamental paradigm shift in relations between the EU and Russia. Initially, the EU–Russia Strategic Partnership developed within a paradigm of a "common/greater Europe": "the relationship revolved around contested visions of a common integrated [greater European] space, but with agreement on some fundamental principles" (115). Because of a lack of a "shared vision of how the relationship should unfold within the larger European space", this paradigm gave way to a new paradigm of "competing regionalisms" (115). The latter was characterised by mutually exclusive integration projects, competing regulatory norms and a securitisation of the relationship (129).

DeBardeleben situates the beginning of the shift in the years before the Ukraine crisis, but describes it as crystallising with the confrontation over Ukraine (115). She argues that Putin's proposal (Putin 2011) to establish a Eurasian Union was an attempt to restore the balance between the EU and Russia within the (dysfunctional) common Europe paradigm. Formally, the Strategic Partnership was based on equality, but in terms of economic strength the imbalance was considerable: size-wise the Russian economy was roughly equal to the Italian economy. Moreover, the EU was a highly integrated organisation of 28 member states, while Russia was basically on its own. By establishing a Eurasian Union, Russia's capabilities would be increased and the EU–Russia Strategic Partnership more balanced. This, in turn, would allow Russia to restore some of its lost influence in the postSoviet space. Yet, when the ECU was established in 2010, this was not received very well by the EU. The Union refused to negotiate trade matters with the ECU and many in the West perceived the Russian integration initiative as a crypto geopolitical project. Rivalry over the neighbourhood thus became a determining factor in EU–Russia relations.

Managing unintended consequences

As mentioned in the conceptual section, the EU's management of its unintended consequences can ideal-typically be analysed along two different continuums. First, the degree to which the EU actively seeks to steer the unintended consequences of its action or presence. Here the options vary from inaction to active steering. Second, the proactive steering of unintended consequences may take two different forms: the EU seeks either to reinforce the outcomes which are seen as positive or beneficial (for example, reinforcing democratisation tendencies in neighbouring countries or promoting investment opportunities for EU-based companies) or to mitigate the consequences seen as negative (for example, compensating for the negative economic effects of EU enlargement by giving neighbours facilitated access to the Single European Market).

How did the EU seek to manage the unintended consequences of the decoupling of its East European policy? A distinction should be made between management of the internal unintended consequences of the decoupling and management of the external effects on its neighbours. As to the former, and as argued above, the EU basically chose inaction. It did not fundamentally alter its policies, but just accepted the new unintended situation. Little was done inside the EU to coordinate or reconcile its contradictory ENP/EaP policies with its Russia policy. This was not helped by the "diffusion of competencies" (David et al. 2013, 3) within the EU vis-à-vis Russia, but equally vis-à-vis the EaP states.

There is a classic "legal and procedural duality" between Common Foreign and Security Policy (CFSP) and other external policies (Wouters and Ramopoulos 2013, 2). In the case of Russia policies, this duality is particularly strong with an imbalance in favour of certain Directorate-Generals (DGs) like Energy and Trade, at the expense of the European External Action Service (EEAS), expected to set out the broader, strategic line. Furthermore, coordination mechanisms between EaP and Russia policies are weak. As a result, no mechanisms were set up to consult Russia on the development of ENP/EaP policies, despite Russia's regular demands for consultation. For example, no triangular negotiations were held during the negotiation stage of the Association Agreements with Ukraine, Georgia and Moldova.[10]

As for the external effects, an interesting discrepancy emerged in the management of the unintended consequences of the EU's policies towards its EaP neighbours and Russia. With the ENP/EaP countries (at least the willing partners Georgia, Moldova and Ukraine), the EU generally has a high degree of unintended impact through externalities and attraction (see above). *Ab initio*, there were many unintended domestic, in particular economic, effects of the EU's economic size and eastern enlargement. With high shares of their exports going to the EU, the neighbouring states have little choice but to adapt to the economic policies of Brussels. For example, the products they export have to adapt to the regulatory environmental, hygienic or technical standards. As a result of this sort of processes, domestic opportunities and choices in EaP countries are determined by economic dependence on the EU.

With the asymmetrical ENP/EaP policy, the EU is simultaneously steering, mitigating *and* reinforcing the unintended consequences generated. It steers because it actively seeks to transform the political and economic systems of its neighbours through conditionality, rule transfer and a normative agenda (promoting democracy, the rule of law, etc.). It mitigates by creating opportunities for (selective) free trade and better market access, allowing neighbours to join certain EU programmes or offering visa liberalisation. Finally, it also reinforces the unintended consequences when they are beneficial for the EU, thus promoting its own interests.

This is done, first of all, by exporting a considerable part of its *acquis communautaire*, aiming at the approximation of laws in the target country. Thus, the EU anchors associated neighbours in its own economic and regulatory sphere and extends that sphere without enlarging the Union. Secondly, EU interests are fostered by negotiating a Deep and Comprehensive Free Trade Area (DCFTA) that arguably reflects predominantly EU economic interests. It is clear that both elements have a strong asymmetry in favour of the EU. Also certain EaP flagship initiatives (energy, border management) are predominantly policies reflecting EU interests. The simultaneous mitigation and reinforcement of the unintended consequences of EU policies creates a certain ambiguity in the EU's policy, as it tries to reconcile diverging goals.

With Russia, the management of unintended consequences is rather different, but then, the consequences are substantially different and much more complicated. The situation is one of a strong economic asymmetry between the EU and Russia, favouring the EU, combined with energy dependence favouring Russia. With the Strategic Partnership, the EU dropped the normative agenda in its relations with Russia. Equally, instruments of rule transfer and conditionality became marginalised. This can be seen as the result both of Russia's opposition and of less asymmetrical relations. It implies that there has been only a limited (attempt at) steering the domestic consequences in Russia. Nor has there been much mitigation of the negative unintended consequences of the EU's dominant economic presence. Rather those seen as beneficial for the EU (and the other way around for Russia) have been reinforced and this has further strengthened an agenda framed in terms of interests.

The agency of the EaP countries

Both unintended consequences and the way they are managed are a function of the actor's capacity in relation to other relevant actors. This holds not only for the actor producing the unintended effects (in this case, the EU), but also for the target of its action and third parties (the EaP countries and Russia). All three categories have the capacity for action. While this article has focused mainly on the capacity of the EU to steer, reinforce or mitigate its unintended consequences, the EaP states and Russia also have a degree of agency. In the case of Russia, it has already been described how the clashing objectives in the EU's policies versus its eastern neighbours created fertile ground for Russia to exploit an image of the West pursuing an anti-Russian policy and seeking to create a sphere of influence in the former Soviet space.

But the EaP countries also have a degree of agency that allows them to use unintended consequences to their advantage. This holds for both the external and internal unintended consequences of the EU's decoupling of policies. Externally, the development of two different strategic contexts – competitive zero-sum with Russia and cooperative with EaP countries – allowed some of the latter to exploit threat images of Russia to seek closer integration with the EU or obtain certain advantages.

Ukraine, for example, actively tried to obtain a prospect for EU accession during the Association negotiations. While it did not achieve this (the Association Agreement only "welcomes" Ukraine's European choice), it did manage to use the new strategic context to get clear and more explicit recognition of its European identity from the EU. The two-pronged strategic context formed a conducive environment for Ukraine to stress its distinct identity vis-à-vis Russia.

As for the unintended consequences inside the EU, EaP countries were put in a position where they could make use of the internal divisions that the decoupling of policies had generated within the EU. This split allowed them to pursue their interests or influence agendas by collaborating with those member states that promoted an 'EaP first' policy, such as Lithuania and Poland.

But the agency of the EaP countries also lies in their capacity to adopt EU policies selectively. Undeniably, several EaP states have been subject to strong "adaptational pressure" (Börzel and Risse 2012) resulting from the economic asymmetrical interdependence and "normative hegemony" (Haukkala 2008) of the EU. But, while this could be expected to lead to considerable guaranteed leverage on the part of the EU, in practice this has often been eroded by a selective or superficial adoption of EU-imposed conditions. The lip service paid by some elites has led, for example, to limited success in combating corruption in some countries or to the creation of "procedural" ballot box democracies rather than sustainable "substantive" democracies (Pridham 2000).

Finally, the EaP countries have a considerable degree of agency precisely because of the competition that arose between the EU and Russia over their common neighbourhood. The EU's impact could only be effective if it was not undermined by Russia's influence or deliberate policies. Its conditionality could only be effective if it was not neutralised by Moscow's promises for similar or greater benefits – so-called "crossconditionality" (Schimmelfennig and Sedelmeier 2004). Russia deliberately tried to undermine the effectiveness of the EU's normative hegemony in the region, challenging it on different fronts: through control (destabilising Ukraine), alternative institutional arrangements (the Eurasian Economic Union), and claims of genuine Europeanness, pursued by means of a "paleoconservative" ideology (Morozov 2018), which in many ways represents an alternative to the EU's normative agenda.

As many constraints as this may have implied, it also provided EaP countries with the possibility of balancing and a degree of choice (Makarychev 2018) – and different choices they have made. Three willing partners (Georgia, Moldova and Ukraine) signed Association Agreements with the EU in 2014. Armenia has opted for membership of the Eurasian Economic Union, but has chosen to combine this with continued collaboration with the EU, signing a Comprehensive and Enhanced Partnership Agreement (CEPA) with Brussels. Belarus, in turn, has opened up to the EU, in particular since the Ukraine crisis, seeking some kind of counterbalance to its close links to Russia. Azerbaijan, finally, has shown only selective interest in collaboration with either the EU or Russia. The extremely varying 'success' of the EU vis-à-vis the different EaP countries can only be understood in the light of the countries' capacity of agency.

Conclusion

This article has built on Olga Burlyuk's conceptualisation of unintended consequences, extending her model to a larger process linking external action, unintended consequences and the (intended) management thereof.

The case presented has dealt with the unintended consequences of the EU's nondecision to change the ENP after Russia was decoupled from it with the creation of a separate Strategic Partnership in 2003–04. It has been argued that *internally* this created an inherent tension in the EU's East European policy: the ENP's objective of creating privileged relations and association with the eastern neighbours was incompatible with the Strategic Partnership's promise of equal partnership and respect for Russian interests, as Moscow saw privileged interests in the former Soviet space as a key priority. *Externally* this contributed to the development of two different dynamics: cooperative but asymmetrical relations with certain EaP countries versus a competitive context for the development of relations with Russia. The development of a logic of competition between Brussels and Moscow had multiple and complex causes and cannot therefore be attributed exclusively to the decoupling of the two policies, but it was one of the facilitating factors.

The article argues that there are different modes of management of unintended consequences. First, an actor can decide to steer its unintended effects actively or not to act. Second, the modes of management of unintended consequences may vary on a spectrum that ranges from mitigating to reinforcing.

The EU has actively sought to reinforce its normative hegemony towards EaP countries, while at the same time mitigating certain negative unintended effects of its dominant economic position. Yet, those countries have the capacity to erode or reinforce the EU's policies. Moreover, in the competitive strategic context that has come into existence, Russian foreign policy actively seeks to challenge the EU's hegemony and to undermine its effectiveness. Apart from imposing considerable constraints, it also leaves the EaP countries with a considerable capacity of choice, which is reflected in highly differentiated degrees of cooperation with the EU.

Notes

1. Excluding the three Baltic states.
2. The term is taken from Wolczuk 2009.
3. Part of this article draws on earlier work, in particular Casier 2015 and Casier 2016b.
4. See also Reslow's contribution to this Special Issue.
5. Post-factum management is referred to in the Introduction of the Special Issue as "reaction" rather than "anticipation".
6. As this article focuses on post-factum management of unintended consequences, the term "avoidance", suggested in the Introduction of this Special Issue, will not be used. Reinforcing and mitigating are considered the end points of a spectrum of options and not a dichotomous choice.
7. Barnett and Duvall (2005, 42) define power as "the production in and through social relations, of effects that shape the capacities of actors to determine their circumstances and fate".
8. The EU formulated two core objectives for its neighbourhood policy (ENP): avoiding new dividing lines in wider Europe and creating stability in the neighbourhood (European Commission 2004). It sought to do so by establishing "privileged relations" with its Eastern and Southern neighbours. The Eastern Partnership (EaP) did not change these objectives in a fundamental way. It was launched in 2009 as one of the two ENP dimensions "to create the necessary conditions to accelerate political association and further economic integration between the European Union and interested partner countries" (Council of the European Union 2009).
9. Moreover, understanding the crisis in relations between Russia and the Euro-Atlantic community also requires that other actors be taken into account, such as the US, NATO and Ukraine. This is however beyond the scope of this article.
10. The EU's reason for not consulting with Russia during the negotiations on the Association Agreements, notwithstanding their potential impact on its trade, was mainly framed in terms of not giving Russia a veto right in the negotiations. Yet, it can be doubted whether consultation by definition implies granting a veto right. Interestingly, triangular negotiations were held between the EU, Ukraine and Russia about the implementation of the EU-Ukraine Association Agreement, after it was signed.

References

Bachrach, P., and Baratz, M. 1963. Decisions and Nondecisions: An Analytical Framework. *American Political Science Review* 57 (3): 641–51.

Barnett, M., and Duvall, R. 2005. Power in International Politics. *International Organization* 59 (Winter): 39–75.

Börzel, T., and Risse T. 2012. From Europeanisation to Diffusion: Introduction. *West-European Politics* 35 (1): 1–19.

Burlyuk, O. 2017. The 'Oops!' of EU Engagement Abroad: Analyzing Unintended Consequences of EU External Action. *Journal of Common Market Studies* 55 (5): 1009–1025.

Casier, T. 2015. National Level: How the EU and Russia Manage their Unintended Impact on their Common Neighbours. In A. Obydenkova and A. Libman, eds. *Autocratic and Democratic External Influences in Post-Soviet Eurasia*. Farnham: Ashgate: 89–108

Casier, T. 2016a. From Logic of Competition to Conflict: Understanding the Dynamics of EU-Russia Relations. *Contemporary Politics* 22 (3): 376–394.

Casier, T. 2016b. The EU and Russia. From a Marriage of Convenience to Confrontation. In M. Smith, S. Keukeleire and S. Vanhoonacker, eds. *The Diplomatic System of the European Union: Evolution, Change and Challenge*. Abingdon: Routledge: 129–145.

Charap, S., and Troitskiy, M. 2013. Russia, the West and the Integration Dilemma. *Survival* 55 (6): 49–62.

Council of the European Union. 2009. *Joint declaration of the Eastern Partnership Summit. Prague, 7 May 2009*. 8435/09 (Presse 78), 7 May. http://www.consilium.europa.eu/uedocs/cms_data/docs/pressdata/en/er/107589.pdf

David, M., Gower, J., and Haukkala, H. 2013. Introduction. In M. David, J. Gower and H. Haukkala, eds. *National Perspectives on Russia*: 1–12. Oxon: Routledge.

DeBardeleben, J. 2018. Alternative Paradigms for EU-Russian Neighbourhood Relations. In T. Casier and J. DeBardeleben, eds. *EU-Russia Relations in Crisis. Understanding Diverging Perceptions*: 115–136. London: Routledge:

Dodini, M., and Fantini, M. 2006. The EU Neighbourhood Policy: Implications for Economic Growth and Stability. *Journal of Common Market Studies* 44 (3): 507–532.

European Commission. 2004. *Communication from the Commission. European Neighbourhood Policy. Strategy paper*. COM(2004) 373final, 12 May.

Haukkala, H. 2008. The European Union as a Regional Normative Hegemon: The Case of European Neighbourhood Policy. *Europe-Asia Studies* 60 (9): 1601–1622.

Haukkala, H. 2015. From cooperative to contested Europe? The conflict in Ukraine as a culmination of a long-term crisis in EU-Russia relations. *Journal of Contemporary European Studies* 23 (1): 25–40.

House of Lords. 2015. European Union Committee, 6th Report of Session 2014–15, *The EU and Russia: before and beyond the crisis in Ukraine*, HL Paper 115, 2015. https://publications.parliament.uk/pa/ld201415/ldselect/ldeucom/115/115.pdf

Keohane, R., and Nye, J. 1989. *Power and Interdependence*. New York: Harper Collins.

Keukeleire, S. 2003. The European Union as a Diplomatic Actor: Internal, Traditional, and Structural Diplomacy. *Diplomacy and Statecraft* 14 (3): 31–56.

Keukeleire, S., and MacNaughtan, J. 2008. *The Foreign Policy of the European Union*. Basingstoke: Palgrave Macmillan.

Lavenex, S., and Uçarer, E. 2004. The External Dimension of Europeanization: The Case of Immigration Policies. *Cooperation and Conflict* 39 (4): 417–34.

Lavenex, S. 2014. The power of functionalist extension: how EU rules travel. *Journal of European Public Policy* 21 (6): 885–903.

Majone, G. 1994. The Rise of the Regulatory State in Europe. *West European Politics* 17 (3): 77–101.

Makarychev, A. 2018. *Incomplete Hegemonies, Hybrid Neighbours: Identity games and policy tools in Eastern Partnership countries*, CEPS Working Document no. 2018/02. Brussels: CEPS. https://www.ceps.eu/publications/incomplete-hegemonies-hybrid-neighbours-identity-games-and-policy-tools-eastern

Manners, I. 2002. Normative Power Europe: A Contradiction in Terms? *Journal of Common Market Studies* 40 (2): 235–258.

Maull, H. 2005. Europe and the New Balance of Global Order. *International Affairs* 81 (4): 775–799.

McCalla-Chen, D. 2000. Towards an Understanding of the Concept of Non-Decision Making and its Manifestation in the School Sector. *Educational Management & Administration* 28 (1): 33–46.

Medvedev, D. 2008. Interview given by Dmitry Medvedev to Television Channels Channel One, *Rossia*, NTV [Transcript], 31 August 2008. http://en.kremlin.ru/events/president/transcripts/48301

Morozov, V. 2018. Identity and Hegemony in EU-Russia Relations: Making Sense of the Asymmetrical Entanglement. In T. Casier and J. DeBardeleben, eds. *EU-Russia Relations in Crisis. Understanding Diverging Perceptions*: 30–49. Abingdon: Routledge.

Pridham, G. 2000. *The Dynamics of Democratization. A Comparative Approach*. London: Continuum.
Putin, V. 2011. Novyi integratsionnyi proekt dlia Evrazii – budushchee, kotoroe rozhdaetsia. *Izvestiia*, [A new integration project for Eurasia. The future that is born today] 3 October. http://www.izvestia.ru/news/502761.
Schimmelfennig, F., and Sedelmeier, U. 2004. Governance by Conditionality: EU rule transfer to the candidate countries of Central and Eastern Europe. *Journal of European Public Policy* 11 (4): 661–679.
Smith, M., Keukeleire, S., and Vanhoonacker, S. eds. 2016. *The Diplomatic System of the European Union: Evolution, Change and Challenges*. Abingdon: Routledge.
Waltz, K. 1979. *Theory of International Politics*. New York: Addison Wesley.
Wolczuk, K. 2009. Implementation without Coordination: The Impact of EU Conditionality on Ukraine under the European Neighbourhood Policy. *Europe-Asia Studies* 61 (2): 187–211.
Wolfers, A. 1962. *Discord and Collaboration. Essays on International Politics*. Baltimore: Johns Hopkins Press.
Wouters, J., and Ramopoulos, T. 2013. *Revisiting the Lisbon Treaty's Constitutional Design of EU External Relations*. Working Paper no. 119. Leuven: Centre for Global Governance Studies.

Bringing "the political" back into European security

Challenges to the EU's ordering of the Eastern Partnership

Licínia Simão

Introduction

Mainstream studies of European Union (EU) security actorness have developed along two central strands. The first has focused on the normative and rule-based approach to European integration, which translated into the establishment of an enlarged security community among European countries (Deutsch et al. 1957; Wæver 1998). The second has focused on the technologies of security which the EU has gradually set in place, namely through the development of its military tools (Bono 2004; Hyde-Price 2004; Kaldor, Martin, and Selchow 2007; Menon 2009), but also its governance and soft security approaches (Kirchner 2006; Lavenex and Schimmelfennig 2009). These approaches raise important issues regarding the EU's security actorness – its nature and capabilities – and yet, they only narrowly address the processes through which such understandings of security come about in the EU, as well as their constitutive nature of the social order which sustains such understandings.

This article uses a post-structuralist approach to map the "symbolic power struggles" (Villumsen Berling 2012, 453) which explain the nature of the social order underlying European security, particularly in the case of the Eastern Partnership (EaP) initiative. This approach is influenced by Bourdieu's concepts of *field*,[1] *capital*,[2] and *symbolic power*[3] (Bourdieu 1990), and how the latter two are activated in order to remake hierarchies of power within the former. In this article, the *field* we are seeking to map out is the field of European security, which has been fast changing since the end of the Cold War (Williams 2007; Villumsen Berling 2012). We argue that the *field* is still being reshaped by constant struggles among different actors in their ambitions to be perceived as legitimate and relevant agents in the process of shaping a new social order. Dominant narratives can be identified at specific times and on specific dimensions of security, but ultimately, a fastchanging reality has made this field a highly contested one. By analysing the EaP from a security perspective, we place this EU policy within a broader logic of regional security provision, clearly acknowledged in EU official discourse since its inception in 2003 as the European Neighbourhood Policy (ENP), which has become empirically visible with the unfolding Georgian and Ukrainian crises.

Another central conceptual distinction we resort to in our analysis is the one between *the political* and *politics*, as elaborated in works by Michael Dillon and Jenny Edkins. The authors define "the political" as "a period where a new social and political order is founded" (Edkins 1999, 7),[4] it is the allowing of human possibilities, the *struggle*

(Bourdieu 1990), "the plural ' how' dedicated to keeping the taking place of that possibility open" (Dillon 1996, 6). This meaning of "the political" as possibility, as reordering and contestation, contrasts with an understanding of "politics" as an institutionalised technological exercise of governmentality (Foucault 1997a, 1997b), to close contestation in order to maintain the established authority. By uncovering the possibilities inherent in bringing "the political" back into the design of European security, particularly in the context of the EU's increasing engagement with its eastern neighbours, we seek to understand the prospects of redesigning the existing security field, the agents who actively seek to shape it, and the forms of power (or *capital*) they exercise in the process.

Given that the EU emerged as a central security actor in the post-Cold War European security order, it should be perceived as an agent committed to the preservation of the existing hierarchy of power within this established social field – namely by exerting symbolic power. The EU's approach to security, combining normative, soft approaches with the increasing use of the military instrument for humanitarian goals and crisis response, has established several forms of capital which can be legitimately exercised in the field of European security. This process is also fundamental for the EU's social identity as a relevant security agent. By being recognised as a legitimate agent by other players in the field, such as the United Nations, the US, and NATO, but also Russia and other former-Soviet and the former-Warsaw Pact states, the EU has entered the European security field and, we would argue, has come to dominate it. The escalating crisis in relations with Russia can be seen as a result of a struggle between agents in this field, vying for dominant discourses and resources. Russia's understanding of the EU's security role in Europe has gradually changed, seeing the Union as an exclusionary force against perceived Russian interests. The EU's Global Strategy, presented in 2016 (European Union 2016), articulates clearly the importance of the EU in the European security order and Russia's role as a challenger. Moreover, it also underlines greater EU autonomy as an important step towards assuring security, as well as promoting greater resilience in neighbouring countries.

The article proceeds with the presentation of the conceptual framework linking the notions of "the political" and security. It then moves on to see how these two notions have been articulated in the social field of European security in the post-Cold War context and maps the competing agents and approaches, which are especially relevant to understanding the EaP. The third section focuses on the EaP as an illustration of a *depoliticised* dimension of the EU's security promotion and how Russia has become a central actor advocating for the re-*politicisation* of the EU regional security policy, exposing its hegemonic and hierarchical nature. The article concludes by positing dilemmas of politicisation for the EaP from a security perspective.

The political moment and the search for security: irreconcilable processes?

Edkins (1999) starts her book on "Poststructuralism & International Relations: Bringing the Political Back in" by making a distinction between the concepts of "the political" and "politics". The author reads both concepts in light of Max Weber's notion of "politics and bureaucracy" and links them to Slavoj Žižek's work on "the political and subjectivity". From these perspectives, she sees politics as the daily management of decision-making by bureaucrats, the design and implementation of technologies of power and governance. This is a normalising process (highlighting the primacy of established norms), designed to administer and order human communities (Edkins 1999, 19). Politics also legitimises the prevailing order, but it does not question its origins, or the power struggles inherent to its development and maintenance. In order to understand the latter's main aspects and the origin and process of establishing subjectivities, one must look at the moment of "the political" (Edkins 1999, 7). This is the moment when order breaks down and politics ceases to exist as previously established. In these crucial moments, bureaucrats are no longer at the centre of the political process, but leadership is instead fundamental in order to redesign the frames of reference for the new social order that is about to take place. This is a relational process, and authority/leadership is recognised as legitimate as a result of its ability to provide meaning and structure to social relations, namely through discourse. This results in the establishment of new structures of politics, normalising life and constraining human possibilities according to the new understandings of identity, belonging, power, and justice, which are valued by the political community (Edkins 1999).

In order to illustrate this point, we can refer to the political moment in European security, opened by the fall of the Soviet Union and the end of the Cold War. The established bureaucracies and norms had to be revised and adjusted to a new reality. NATO's central security role was contested, as was the understanding that security was largely a military, state-based affair. European integration, challenging the central role of the state in international affairs and the movement towards broader understandings of security, facilitated by policy makers and academics, meant that new forms of social order and capital were promoted anew and recognised as valid. In that process, new actors emerged and were allowed into the field of security, aiming to establish new rules and hierarchies of power. Political leadership was articulated by politicians like Mikhail Gorbachev (underlining cooperative security through the idea of a "common European house"), Gro Harlem Brundtland (advocating for sustainable development as part of global security governance efforts), or academics like Bary Buzan who argued for broader concepts of security (such as Human Security). All of these actors used the opportunities provided by the new context to challenge the existing views on security to develop a new direction for action, and to embed new structures in the field of global and European security.

In Bourdieu's terms, "the political" is a process through which new social fields are created and reshaped – being the latter of particular interest to our argument. Agency is a fundamental element in that it is through the activation of different forms of capital and their recognition by other agents in the field that power constellations and meanings are transformed (Bourdieu 2004, 34). Villumsen Berling (2012) argues that the 1990s were a moment of active political contestation of the security field in Europe, which led to the emergence of new agents, but also to the valorisation of other forms of capital, besides the military, which had been at the centre of the Cold War's understanding of security in the European continent (Buzan and Hansen 2009, 156–183). Villumsen Berling also argues that think tank and academic constructivist perspectives made their way into the social field (Villumsen Berling and Bueger 2013) and eventually even challenged NATO's military dominance. This notion of struggle within a given social field resonates with a creative moment (the moment of human possibility) inherent in the political, and contrasts with order, predictability, and knowledge, which are the founding stones of security, actively sought through politics. By opening the social field to new agents, these processes engage directly with the issues of *othering* and *differentiation* – that is, with the external perspectives – to be gradually internalised by the new field and to establish a new agreed normal.

Michael Dillon's work also sheds light onto the difficult relationship between "the political" and security. According to Dillon (1996, 6), "the political" should be the "how" that allows human possibilities to develop; allowing human freedom to turn into possibilities. The reason why "the political" can be seen as contrary to security is because struggle and contestation, uncertainty and fear, inherent in the lack of a fixed structure of social order, are fundamentally at odds with security's desire for familiarity, predictability, stability, and knowledge. Dillon (1996, 17) goes as far as stating that today's "hypertrophic register of security" is a "monumental enterprise of power-knowledge" consuming all thought and all human life. He argues that security is the ordering principle of modern civilisation and the response to the human desire of order, truth, certainty, stability, and permanence. Security is thus fundamentally linked to the desire of all-encompassing knowledge and control over the unknown, over change, and the security endeavour seems to have been sequestered by politics, and its desire for preservation, order, and stability.

Security relations also take place in the context of power asymmetries and hierarchies, inherent to the fields of action and meaning. This is relevant for several reasons. First, power asymmetries allow established agents to reproduce and reinvent their capital for the sake of self-preservation (Villumsen Berling 2012, 463). New agents seeking to enter the field are thus constrained to comply with the existing views of order and security, especially if the forms of capital they can mobilise are either rejected or contested by more powerful agents. Thus, the establishment of shared norms and rules is always the result of a bargaining process among different actors. For instance, concerns of sovereignty and ethnic nationalist conflicts, which are still fundamental to many of the countries on the EU's borders, have reluctantly been addressed by the EU foreign policy. This is partly because of how the EU and its members conceptualise security as deriving from a liberal democratic and capitalist order, which provides limited tools to address these forms of insecurity. Bargaining between the EU and EaP countries is addressed by van Gils (2017) in more detail.

Second, power asymmetries are also important due to the subjective dimension of security and identity building. The production of authoritative/valid knowledge (security) rests upon a hierarchy of relations, placing certain agents and their discourses and perspectives at the centre and others at the margins of the system of belief, norms, and power (the fields, in Bourdieu's terms). We can thus conceive international security as a process of identity building, where the centre is perceived as having legitimate concerns for action, while the periphery is seen as having a legitimate obligation to contribute to the stability of the centre. This dimension reinforces power asymmetries, by defining security and insecurity as separate conditions and by prescribing a path out of insecurity that requires others to become like "Us". The secure "Us" is the liberal democratic and capitalist West, whereas the insecure other is the violent and disordered periphery (Buzan and Hansen 2009, 167) – a view proposed among others by the democratic peace theory (Russett 1993; Brown, Lynn-Jones, and Miller 1999; Mansfield and Snyder 2005).

As we have mentioned, the production of secure subjects implies the production of insecure ones too. But it is in this shared essence of human condition, whereby we only know ourselves because we understand the insecurity of the *other*, that we can have the ambition to think security and insecurity together (Dillon 1996, 19) – and we can aim to achieve a shared notion of "normal".[5] This is a narrow window to overcome the apparently irreconcilable nature of the political and security, since the *other* cannot be totally unknown to us, as it is part of who we are and our identity can only make sense in relation with the *other*. As William Connolly observed, "to redefine its relation to others, a constituency must also modify the shape of its own identity" (in Dillon 1996, 3). This is painfully visible in the way the EU has dealt with the flows of migrants and refugees reaching its shores and how its decisions affect normative Europe's image. Issues about the EU's identity have recurrently been related to its international security actorness, reflecting exactly this understanding.

Ultimately, the fundamental question posed to European security, and which the concept of the political elaborates, is what type of political community is the EU advancing? Is the EU focusing on a restrictive political and security community, with hard borders on the outside and exclusionary principles – what Richmond (2000, 54) has called a "communitarian model"? Or is the EU capable of conceptualising (in)security as an interdependent process, rooted in hybrid identities, reflecting what Booth (2005, 109) has called "ethical universalism or cosmopolitanism"? In order to pursue the latter, the return of "the political" and the dismantling of the technologies of politics and governmentality, which constrain it, become necessary. Nowhere is this need more visible than in the present-day relations between the EU and Russia. The ambition of establishing an ethical and cosmopolitan basis for European security, reflecting a diverse array of understandings and perspectives, requires the dismantling of the mechanisms entrapping alternatives under hegemonic western practices. The EU's commitment to democratic principles also in international relations and multilateralism could work as important references to the debates on European security, beyond views of great power balance.

The field of European security: redesigning the boundaries of "the political"

The previous section linked the political moment and the processes of politicisation to the definition of the boundaries and components of different social fields in the broader context of security. We now turn to the analysis of the social field of European security, in order to understand the major moments of politicisation and depoliticisation that have taken place since the end of the Cold War. This competition for authority in shaping and structuring the social field is the process through which we come to assess the development of the EaP and its contribution to European security.

The focus of this analysis is thus on the struggle for a central stake in defining the "legitimate security logic in Europe" (Villumsen Berling 2012, 462) – the establishment of a political moment, as proposed by Dillon and Edkins. This perspective helps to understand how the new security order takes shape, how agency is exercised, how new norms come into existence, and how material resources are used. What forms of capital are valued at a given moment and how does their use shape a given field?

Since power distribution in the European field of security is uneven and the valorisation of a given capital (power) is relational, it is fundamental for an agent to be recognised by other authoritative agents as a legitimate player in the field. Legitimacy is derived from the valorisation of the capital the agent commands and to its access to the field. The EU's security model of peace through trade, of democracy and human rights, and of cooperative approaches has been perceived as a powerful example and a source of legitimacy for the Union's actorness as a regional security actor (Lucarelli 2002; Hill and Smith 2011, 435– 457). But there is an instrumental dimension to the valorisation of specific forms of capital, since agents who command certain forms of established capital in the field may perceive change as a form of survival. Villumsen Berling (2012, 469) underlines the strategic practice of conversion and redefinition of capital in fast-changing fields, as was the field of European security in the 1990s. Thus, she argues that, for instances, military power, which had been valued during the Cold War as the most important source of capital (and legitimacy in the hierarchical structure of the field), was reinvented for humanitarian purposes, linking it to other forms of capital which began to be valorised.

With this process, agents who relied on military capital for authority within the field, such as NATO, US, and Russia, needed to reposition themselves. The 1990s saw important changes in terms of the discursive valorisation of different forms of capital. Economic capital and soft power, linked to democratic norms and human rights, became more relevant (Thomas 2000; Chouliaraki 2007). The peace dividend created the expectation that social progress, empowerment of the citizens, and cooperative relations would become the structuring features of the international system, and more specifically, of the European context (Hettne and Söderbaum 2005). Nationalism, sovereignty, and balance among great powers were largely marginalised as no longer relevant sources of (in)security. As these forms of capital became valorised, new agents entered the field, and others remained outside of it. The EU was now perceived as a relevant actor for the provision of security, rooted in social stability, economic prosperity, and the promotion of norms and values (Stefanova 2005; Diez, Stetter, and Albert 2006). Other agents such as the Council of Europe and the Organization for Security and Co-operation in Europe became more prominent.

Enlargement has been regarded by EU policy-makers as the most successful foreign policy tool of the EU (Prodi 2002; European Commission 2003; The Economist 2007), exactly because it provided irrefutable evidence of the EU's effectiveness in providing security in the continent. The European Commission became a fundamental agent, by promoting a technocratic approach to geopolitical transformation. The roots of this depoliticised approach are recognisable in Mitrany's functionalist view of international relations, as a means to limit national states' power and shifting the subjectivity of international politics to international institutions. However, there remained a geopolitical motivation behind the processes of governmentality promoted by the EU, through which member states can be seen to advance their own interests (Moravcsik and Vachudova 2003; Skålnes 2005). This also signalled the return to politics, as bureaucrats assumed larger roles shaping the field of European security. Security in Europe was reconceived through the lenses of governmentality, including regulation, oversight, and prescriptive reform (Schimmelfennig and Sedelmeier 2004). This also echoed the global liberal agenda, which promoted good governance as a central element of conditionality for financial assistance (Kapur 2001; Soederberg 2003) and through the growing mechanisms of post-conflict state-building (Barnett 2006). Although the role of bureaucracies in advancing policy goals is not new in itself, the qualitative difference in the post-1990s EU approach to regional peace and stability is the gradual removal of political authority and leadership as the main vectors shaping the EU policy. Thus, although decisions such as the "big bang" enlargement of 2004 were the result of political deliberations of EU Member States, the shape and pace of the process was ultimately defined by Commission bureaucrats (Hooghe 2001).

Throughout most of the 1990s, Russia's role in the social field of European security was rather marginal, both because military power was undervalued and because Russia was not capable of mobilising economic and normative resources of its own. Its most important contribution to European security was to the cease-fire agreements and management of the conflicts in the former-Soviet space (Duffield 2003, 261–266) as well as the management of nuclear arsenals in the former-Soviet Union. However, the former were hardly acknowledged as part of the European security agenda at the time and were mainly perceived as being part of a separate Eurasian security context, where Russia was granted tacit leadership and responsibility. Arguably, it has been the gradual inclusion of post-Soviet countries into the European security field which not only imported the protracted conflicts into EU and other western-dominated institutions' agendas, but also created an added layer of conflict with Russia itself.

The 2000s saw the emergence of contradictory dynamics in the security field. Although military power had become less relevant during the previous decade, NATO nevertheless remained a central actor, especially in Europe, both through its interventions in the Balkan wars and through its enlargement processes (Kay 1998). Following 9/11, a fast remilitarisation of international relations pushed to the centre of the field the industrial military complexes and private security companies, creating pressure for domestic policing and militarisation, under the threat of terror (Dalby 2003). Russia began a process of political and economic consolidation, which reverberated regionally and internationally. These contradictions and the powerful discourse on global terror opened the possibility for a new process of rapid hyper-securitisation of many aspects of social and political life in Europe (and elsewhere) (Dillon 2007).

The world became a geography of insecurities, in which the EU was an inspiring exception. This provided it with self-appointed additional responsibilities and legitimacy for normative and institutional expansion, but also potential challenges regarding the centrality of its approach to security. Building on the success of enlargement, the EU developed a Neighbourhood Policy, premised on the idea that the Union had a responsibility to share the benefits of enlargement beyond the new member states. Prodi (2002), the then President of the European Commission was actively voicing this idea, present in many of the EU's official ENP documents. The European Security Strategy of 2003 extended this idea of a responsibility to participate actively in the promotion of security at a global level (Council of the European Union 2003). No doubt this vision of the need for a proactive EU, stabilising the countries in the neighbourhood, was shaped by the fears and insecurities associated with the global war on terror (Holm 2004; Christou 2010; Eder 2011). Thus, the EU responded to the new demands emerging from the field with mechanisms and instruments rooted in depoliticised approaches and the expansion of its governance systems. Because of this bias, however, the EU often perceived the security threats experienced by its neighbours through bureaucratic and normative lenses, and responses to the hard security threats were largely absent from the EU's neighbourhood policy (Simão 2014).

This new configuration of narratives, approaches, and instruments pushed forward a delicate balance between military, economic, financial, and normative forms of capital, which were deeply intertwined. The political economy of security, using the tools of transnational liberalism and the opportunities of globalisation (Agnew and Corbridge 1995), legitimised the bureaucratic expansion of democracy and ordered societies, based on the rule of law, and in the European case, by adopting EU regulations and norms from the EU *acquis* – that is, the externalisation of EU norms and governance (Lavenex 2008; Lavenex and Schimmelfennig 2009). In this process, agency has been amplified, including the European Commission, but also agencies linked to the management of the EU's external border and member states, including those from Central and Eastern Europe. The latter were particularly active in instigating the Commission and fellow Member States in developing the EaP, making available financial and bureaucratic resources and building on the normative capital accumulated from their successful transitions (Tulmets 2014).

Russia's role in the 2000s, however, changed considerably with the arrival of President Putin to the Kremlin. Russia was now endowed with the capital of political leadership at a time when the international political economy also valued Russia's natural resources, increasing energy interdependence between the EU and Russia and rapidly increasing its financial resources. Based on a new-found pride, Russia sought to also gradually command normative power, promoting a multipolar world order and challenging the self-perceived benevolent nature of Western hegemony. The ultimate goal was to reposition Russia on the global scene as a great power, and in order to achieve that, control over the near abroad became a fundamental stepping stone (Freire 2011). This contrasted directly with the ENP, whereas anti-Russian sentiment, promoted by some of the new EU Member States, created resentment in Moscow. The most visible moments when purposeful western action sought to unsettle Moscow's influence and promote the democracy-security nexus were the colour revolutions in Georgia and Ukraine, in 2003 and 2004, respectively. Russia sought to expose western support as a form of subversive action against the basic principles of sovereignty and non-interference in domestic affairs. The events in Ukraine, as well as the EU's reaction and involvement in these, are discussed elsewhere in this issue.

It is in this increasingly contested social field that the EaP comes about, as part of the EU's reaction to the war in Georgia, in 2008. This marks a turning point in European security, which is now being continued in the current conflict in Ukraine. If on the one hand the EU's approach and vision of regional security continues to be deeply rooted in the promotion of governmentality, reform, and conditionality (the "more for more" principle, benchmarking, reporting and monitoring), on the other hand, Russia has exposed the deeply hegemonic nature of this process and has successfully politicised what the EU sought to keep as a technocratic process. The next section looks in more detail at these dynamics, assessing the EaP's contribution to the reshaping of the European security order ("the political"), and the challenges faced by the EU as it seeks to redefine security identities in this context.

The death of "the political" and the triumph of "politics": the EaP and European security

The EaP was the EU's response to the critiques to the ENP, namely its attempt at "one-size-fits-all" policy and the limited political and financial resources available to support reforms. Moreover, the conceptual ambiguity of the ENP and the EaP, hinged between enlargement and the EU's external relations, affected policy-making and identity-building processes throughout the European continent. Analysing these incoherencies, Edwards (2008) talks about how different EU agents sponsored competing understandings of what the ENP might entail for regional security, and how it would reach such goals. Simão (2013) has looked at how regional approaches can be reconciled with differentiation. Other issues include: what legitimacy is there for conditionality in the absence of membership perspectives? And how to redesign EU foreign and security policies in the pan-European context short of enlargement? EU institutions were thus aware of the need to move beyond technocratic approaches, based on the scripts of enlargement, but were very much entrapped by old perceptions of the post-Soviet space and of its own transformative power.

In order to strengthen differentiation, the EaP was set up as a separate policy framework for the eastern neighbours: their European identity and some partners' European aspirations were acknowledged by the Council of the European Union (2009) following the 2008 war in Georgia and reaffirmed at the Vilnius summit, in November 2013 (Council of the European Union 2013). The EU also improved positive incentives for reforms, namely allocating significantly more funds, and establishing a new host of programmes, tools, and initiatives that have made the EaP more dynamic, engaging non-state actors as stakeholders in the process in a less hierarchical and state-centred approach (Korosteleva, Natorski, and Simão 2013).

Despite these improvements, Korosteleva's analysis of the concept of partnership at the heart of the EaP provides important clues to explain why the EaP remains a problematic tool for the promotion of an emancipatory and ethical universalist view of security, as conceptualised by Booth (2005). Korosteleva (2011, 244, 258, footnote 7) argues that the conceptual deficiencies of the original ENP still linger in the EaP. In her view, these include "a critically disincentivised form of partnership, which continues to be ill defined and EU-owned, thus causing further EU-isation of the region and so precipitating security dilemmas for the contested neighbourhood". Although the author does not explain how the security dilemmas develop from the EU-isation of the region, this formulation seems to suggest that the fundamental problem is the EU's focus on security through governmentality and bureaucratic management, which implies a perpetuation of hegemonic, ahistorical, and apolitical dynamics. Such views reinforce the EU's dominant position in the field of European security, by reproducing the models dominated by its institutions. It further perpetuates hierarchies of insecurity and a restrictive definition of normal, lacking alternatives for more inclusive dialogue.

However, the EaP operates in a very different political context than enlargement. Thus, the way this project relates to competing visions of the pan-European security order is distinct (Christou 2010). While the end of the Cold War allowed the EU to become a predominant agent in the social field of European security and to shape global understandings of peace and security, the current context is one of competing multipolarity of rising powers, set on denouncing what they perceive as hegemonic and imperialist features of this western-centric global order (Börzel 2015).[6] Particularly in the European context, Russia is no longer a weak actor and has increasingly mobilised new forms of social capital to shape understandings of security. By mobilising military means to address regional issues (Reuters 2016; Stratfor 2016), Russia has sought to re-politicise the EU's approach to regional security, namely regarding the issue of frozen conflicts. Also, Russia has acted as a model for authoritarian regimes, creating its own version of "sovereign democracy" and "managed capitalism". These normative differences with the EU's model are visible, for instance, in Belarus (Korosteleva 2015) or Armenia (Freire and Simão 2013).

On the other hand, by undertaking a self-perceived depoliticised and technocratic view to regional security, the EU is increasingly perceived as being out of touch with the security concerns of its neighbours. Their context poses important challenges to their sovereignty and territorial integrity, including issues of ethnic nationalist mobilisation and institutional weakness. The EU's handling of the territorial conflicts in Georgia, Moldova, and Azerbaijan is illustrative of this mismatch, prioritising economic and political reforms over conflict resolution and by not engaging directly (for instances in Nagorno-Karabakh) or engaging reactively (as is the case in Abkhazia and South Ossetia) (see, for example, Sasse 2010; Simão 2014). Under the EaP, the EU has engaged with highly politicised issues, including visa regimes, border management, and energy, to name the most salient. In doing so, the EU has also sought to differentiate and to learn lessons during the process and transfer that knowledge to its relations with other partners (see Delcour 2012). These dynamics could translate into a more palpable partnership with neighbouring countries, where the politicisation of European security could be managed, but no substantive proof exists that such a partnership is developing. The list of projects funded under the EaP multilateral platforms further enhances this understanding that a depoliticised approach is preferred (European Commission 2013).

We argue that European integration has addressed security issues not in a political, but rather in a de-politicised manner – via technical approaches devoid of mechanisms of contestation (Edkins 1999). Despite the EaP's clear geopolitical design, it remained premised on a non-critical narrative of democratisation and economic integration with the EU as a means to promote stability. By presenting the EU's neighbourhood policies as an uncontested means of achieving security in Europe, reproducing the achievements of enlargement, EU institutions sought legitimation. But, as Haukkala (2016, 657, 658) has argued, the 2004 enlargement to Central and Eastern Europe differs from the EaP in three major aspects: the willingness and ability of local elites to engage in reforms; the influence of historical legacies facilitating the process of Europeanisation; and the favourable geopolitical environment.

A Foucauldian critique of technocratic governmentality is a claim for the return of "the political"– and thus a form of public contestation of the contents and forms of security, in order to secure legitimisation currently amiss in the EU approach. This is a major challenge to the EU's way of doing politics in many areas, not just security, as discussed elsewhere in this volume. Edkins insists that depoliticisation should be understood as the closure of contestation and promotion of an established order and authority. In the eastern neighbourhood, for example, when authority of both the EU and Russia is essentially contested, it is imperative to bring "the political" back into the realm of public policy, government management, and resource allocation, rather than remove it from debate.

Equated with uncertainty, disorder, underdevelopment, weak institutionalism, violent nationalism, the periphery of Europe has been seen as a threat, requiring protection and normative alignment with EU standards (see Simão and Dias 2016). However, the means to achieve it caused much confusion. Moreover, this conception of the Other's subjectivity has been largely managed by the Commission's bureaucracy, creating a narrative about the threats and fantasising about what it should become, and how to achieve it. This vision has clearly lacked a participatory dimension and was asymmetrically established, in a "politics-ised" rather than a "political" way.

The political struggle for influence in the definition of European security has become antagonistic and incompatible in many ways. This has been a fight, led by Russia and reproduced by other actors, forcing the shaping of the European security field by other forms of capital, which the EU does not command. Russia has resorted to a form of subversive strategy – the "Tricks of the Weak" – recognising the dominant rules of the game but seeking to subvert them, challenge their meaning, and expose their contradictions (see de Certeau 1984; see also Dunn and Bobick 2014, 409). Thus, we have Russia's "humanitarian" wars in South Ossetia and Crimea as a way to challenge the West's own narrative about the principle of Responsibility to Protect and humanitarian intervention.

Further undermining the credibility of the EU's (and western) security model is the drive by many EU states for self-preservation, in the context of the financial crisis of 2008 and the migration crisis affecting the Union since 2012. These events have sown the seeds for future challenges to the EU's relevance for European security. External challenges will continue to antagonise EU views of security through governmentality and bio-politics, including challenges to the implementation of the EaP Association

Agreements, weakening its real and symbolic meaning, in the absence of membership perspectives. Internal divisions and the emergence of transnational nationalist and xenophobic movements further contribute to weakening the EU's normative image and its potentially positive impact in the development of new, more solidary, and emancipating forms of cosmopolitan security.

These challenges, however, may eventually lead to re-politicisation of the European public space, reflected in the demands for stronger intra-EU democratic accountability and the need to reform EU security and ENP approaches. This is an opportunity for the EU to re-think its security project along more inclusive lines, in which its neighbouring countries will be crucial elements – addressing the processes of othering, differentiation, and normalisation. How the EU manages to institutionally include them in this new political moment is open for discussion (see, for example, Schmidt 2006; Nicolaïdis 2013). Another issue is how EU security policies will balance pushes for remilitarisation, both from Russia, and some EU member states, with its historical focus on civilian and normative instruments. What seems certain is that the current way of projecting security through ordering and bureaucratic politics, if anything, will erode the EU's legitimacy as a relevant regional security actor and will fail to provide objective security in the European context. The drafting of the EU's Global Strategy took these political struggles into consideration (as argued by Anthony, Grand, and Lewis 2015, 11), and engaged with all relevant stake-holders, within and outside the EU.

Conclusion

This article puts forward new approaches to the study of European security, informed by post-structuralist perspectives on international politics and international security. The argument for using these approaches rests on the need to understand the formative processes that shape the current European security order and to make the EaP more relevant and effective. The constitution of a field of security practices in Europe, where the EU has had a leading role since the end of the Cold War, was analysed looking at the processes of *de-politicisation* underpinning the EU's technocratic approaches. It is our contention that such an analysis would better prepare us to identifying the fundamental contradictions in the EU's policies, namely the EaP, and to seeking ways to resolve them. Considering the major ongoing crisis in Ukraine and serious implications for the EU if it continues "business as usual" in its neighbourhood, the *re-politicisation* (the need to bring "the political" back in) of European security comes across as much needed in order to renegotiate regional identities and understandings of normality.

Building on the eclectic combination of scholars from social theory and political sociology, this article intended to understand how security is being defined in Europe. By mapping the relevant agents in the "symbolic power struggles" underlying European security, and by identifying the forms of capital they mobilise in the process of restructuring of the European order, we were able to place the EU's policies towards its eastern neighbours in the broader context of security restructuring in Europe. It became clear that the EU's promotion of a depoliticised form of politics resonates more with the maintenance of hegemonic and hierarchical forms of stability and order, than with partnership and emancipating forms of security. This is problematic in many ways, not least due to the subjectivities it creates, but also because of the lack of objective results in providing security.

By conceptualising security in Europe as being dependent on the successful hegemonic domination of its vision of security, through democratic and liberal capitalist expansion, the EU falls into several complex dilemmas. The first is related to the institutional and political limitations of further enlarging in a context of uncertainty about the meaning of European integration and economic and financial crisis. The second is the undemocratic and hegemonic nature of its external project, reproducing imperial patterns of relations between the centre and periphery, and the consequences it entails for the development of political identities in Europe. This relates to the third dilemma, which is premised on the intersubjective nature of security, meaning that how each agent perceives its (in)security varies, as does what is worth securing. By promoting a model of security that values an ideal type of democracy and economic progress, the EU fails to acknowledge that *there is no* ideal type of democracy and economic development, that plurality of experiences of peaceful political management and political and social progress can be achieved and that any human (social and political) project needs to be historically contextualised (Fierke, [2007] 2012, 157, 158). Such a dialogue of differences requires *re-politicisation* of European security, in order to reach a new set of norms guiding political relations in Europe, acceptable to all.

Notes

1 Bourdieu perceived the social world as being composed of a variety of distinct "fields" of practice, each with its own set of rules, knowledge, and forms of capital. Fields can overlap but they remain relatively autonomous and have specific positions of power and practices, which are constantly contested by new players looking for dominance.
2 Bourdieu defined three major forms of capital, which could be mobilised: economic capital, cultural capital, and social capital.

> Depending on the field in which it functions, and at the cost of the more or less expensive transformations which are the precondition for its efficacy in the field in question, capital can present itself in three fundamental guises: as economic capital, which is immediately and directly convertible into money and may be institutionalized in the form of property rights; as cultural capital, which is convertible, on certain conditions, into economic capital and may be institutionalized in the form of educational qualifications; and as social capital, made up of social obligations ("connections"), which is convertible, in certain conditions, into economic capital and may be institutionalized in the form of a title of nobility. (Bourdieu 1986)

3 Symbolic power is defined as being composed of "ideological systems that specialists produce in and for the struggle over the monopoly of legitimate ideological production" (Bourdieu 1991, 168).
4 For further discussion, see the introduction to this volume.
5 See discussion of "normalisation" in the introduction to the volume.
6 Flockhart (2016) has argued in favour of the concept of "multi-order system", suggesting significant differences among clusters of states forming distinct orders. Her research builds on the English School concepts of primary and secondary institutions and, although highly relevant for the debate on the way European powers relate to others and the norms they support, we maintain here the concept of multipolarity. In our view, multipolarity refers to the emergence of distinct forms of contestation to the norms and institutions supported by liberal western powers, as well as the establishment of alternative models of ordering international relations. Whether these can be clustered as specific orders in itself or not is not directly relevant for our argument.

Disclosure statement

No potential conflict of interest was reported by the authors.

Funding

The author acknowledges funding for research from the Marie Skłodowska-Curie Innovative Training Networks (ITN-ETN) of the European Union's Horizon 2020 research and innovation programme, under grant agreement "CASPIAN – Around the Caspian: a Doctoral Training for Future Experts in Development and Co-operation with Focus on the Caspian Region" and Research Executive Agency [642709 – CASPIAN – H2020-MSCA-ITN-2014].

References

Agnew, John, and Stuart Corbridge. 1995. *Mastering Space: Hegemony, Territory and International Political Economy*. London: Routledge.
Anthony, Ian, Camille Grand, and Patricia Lewis. 2015. *Towards a New European Security Strategy? Assessing the Impact of Changes in the Global Security Environment*. Report prepared for the European Parliament's Subcommittee on security and defence. EP/EXPO/B/SEDE/FWC/2013-08/Lot6/05, June 2015 – PE 534.989.
Barnett, Michael. 2006. "Building a Republican Peace: Stabilizing States after War." *International Security* 30 (4): 87–112.
Bono, Giovanna. 2004. "Introduction: The Role of the EU in External Crisis Management." *International Peacekeeping* 11 (3): 395–403.
Booth, Ken. 2005. "Introduction to Part 2." In *Critical Security Studies and World Politics*, edited by Ken Booth, 109–112. London: Lynne Rienner.
Börzel, Tanja A. 2015. "The Noble West and the Dirty Rest? Western Democracy Promoters and Illiberal Regional Powers." *Democratization* 22 (3): 519–535.
Bourdieu, Pierre. 1986. "The Forms of Capital." In *Handbook of Theory and Research for the Sociology of Education*, edited by J. Richardson, 241–258. New York: Greenwood.
Bourdieu, Pierre. 1990. *The Logic of Practice*. Cambridge: Cambridge University Press.
Bourdieu, Pierre. 1991. *Language and Symbolic Power*. Edited and Introduced by John B. Thompson, Translated by Gino Raymond and Matthew Adamson. Cambridge: Polity Press.
Bourdieu, Pierre. 2004. *Science of Science and Reflexivity*. Cambridge: Cambridge University Press.
Brown, Michael E., Sean M. Lynn-Jones, and Steven E. Miller, eds. 1999. *Debating the Democratic Peace*. Cambridge, MA: MIT Press.
Buzan, Barry, and Lene Hansen. 2009. *The Evolution of International Security Studies*. Cambridge: Cambridge University Press.
Chouliaraki, Lilie, ed. 2007. *The Soft Power of War*. Amsterdam: John Benjamins.
Christou, George. 2010. "European Union Security Logics to the East: The European Neighbourhood Policy and the Eastern Partnership." *European Security* 19 (3): 413–430.
Council of the European Union. 2003. *A Secure Europe in a Better World. European Security Strategy*. Brussels, December 12.
Council of the European Union. 2009. *Joint Declaration of the Prague Eastern Partnership Summit*. Prague, May 7, 8435/09 (Presse 78).
Council of the European Union. 2013. *Eastern Partnership: The Way Ahead, Joint Declaration of the Eastern Partnership Summit*. Vilnius, November 28–29, 17130/13 (OR. en), PRESSE 516.
Dalby, Simon. 2003. "Calling 911: Geopolitics, Security and America's New War." *Geopolitics* 8 (3): 61–86.
de Certeau, Michel. 1984. *The Practice of Everyday Life*. Berkeley: University of California Press.
Delcour, Laure. 2012. "What Influence Does the European Union have in its Eastern Neighbourhood? Assessment and Prospects for the Eastern Partnership." *Études Européennes*, February 16 (online).

Deutsch, Karl, Sidney A. Burrell, Robert A. Kann, Maurice Lee Jr, Martin Lichterman, E. Lindgren Raymond, Francis L. Loewenheim, and Richard W. Van Wagenen. 1957. *Political Community and the North Atlantic Area. International Organization in the Light of Historical Experience.* New York: Greenwood Press.

Diez, Thomas, Stephan Stetter, and Mathias Albert. 2006. "The European Union and Border Conflicts: The Transformative Power of Integration." *International Organization* 60 (3): 563–593.

Dillon, Michael. 1996. *Politics of Security: Towards a Political Philosophy of Continental Thought.* London: Routledge.

Dillon, Michael. 2007. "Governing Terror: The State of Emergency of Biopolitical Emergence." *International Political Sociology* 1 (1): 7–28.

Duffield, John S. 2003. "Regional Conflict Management in Europe." In *Regional Conflict Management,* edited by Paul F. Diehl and Joseph Lepgold, 239–268. Lanham, MD: Rowman & Littlefield.

Dunn, Elizabeth C., and Michael S Bobick. 2014. "The Empire Strikes Back: War Without War and Occupation Without Occupation in the Russian Sphere of Influence." *American Ethnologist -Journal of the American Ethnological Society* 41 (3): 405–413.

Eder, Franz. 2011. "The European Union's Counter-terrorism Policy Towards the Maghreb: Trapped Between Democratisation, Economic Interests and the Fear of Destabilisation." *European Security* 20 (3): 431–451.

Edkins, Jenny. 1999. *Poststructuralism & International Relations: Bringing the Political Back in.* Boulder, CO: Lynne Rienner.

Edwards, Geoffrey. 2008. "The Construction of Ambiguity and the Limits of Attraction: Europe and its Neighbourhood Policy." *Journal of European Integration* 30 (1): 45–62.

European Commission. 2003. *Wider Europe – Neighbourhood: A New Framework for Relations with our Eastern and Southern Neighbours.* Communication from the Commission to the Council and the European Parliament. Brussels, March 11. COM (2003) 104 final.

European Commission. 2013. *Panorama of EU Regional Programmes and Projects Eastern Partnership and Russia.* Luxemburg: Publications Office of the European Union.

European Union. 2016. *Shared Vision, Common Action: A Stronger Europe. A Global Strategy for the European Union's Foreign and Security Policy.* Brussels, June.

Fierke, Karen M. [2007] 2012. *Critical Approaches to International Security.* Cambridge: Polity.

Flockhart, Trine. 2016. "The Coming Multi-order World." *Contemporary Security Policy* 37 (1): 3–30.

Foucault, Michel. 1997a. *'Il faut défendre la société'. Cours au Collège de France 1976.* Paris: Gallimard/Seuil.

Foucault, Michel. 1997b. "Security, Territory, and Population." In *Ethics: Subjectivity and Truth,* edited by Paul Rabinow, 67–71. New York: The New Press.

Freire, Maria R. 2011. *A Rússia de Putin: Vectores Estruturantes de Política Externa.* Coimbra: Almedina.

Freire, Maria R., and Licínia Simão. 2013. "' From Words to Deeds': EU Democracy Promotion in Armenia." *East European Politics* 29 (2): 175–189.

van Gils, Eske. 2017. "Differentiation Through Bargaining Power in EU–Azerbaijan Relations: Baku as a Tough Negotiator". *East European Politics.* doi:10.1080/21599165.2017.1322957.

Haukkala, Hiski. 2016. "A Perfect Storm; Or What Went Wrong and What Went Right for the EU in Ukraine." *Europe-Asia Studies* 68 (4): 653–664.

Hettne, Björn, and Fredrik Söderbaum. 2005. "Civilian Power or Soft Imperialism? EU as a Global Actor and the Role of Interregionalism." *European Foreign Affairs Review* 10 (4): 535–552.

Hill, Christopher, and Michael Smith. 2011. *International Relations and the European Union.* 2nd ed. Oxford: Oxford University Press.

Holm, Ulla. 2004. *The EU's Security Policy Towards the Mediterranean: An (Im)possible Combination of Export of European Political Values and Anti-terrors Measures?* DIIS Working Paper, n° 13.

Hooghe, Liesbet. 2001. *The European Commission and the Integration of Europe: Images of Governance.* Cambridge: Cambridge University Press.

Hyde-Price, Adrian. 2004. "European Security, Strategic Culture, and the Use of Force." *European Security* 13 (4): 323–343.

Kaldor, Mary, Mary Martin, and Sabine Selchow. 2007. "Human Security: A New Strategic Narrative for Europe." *International Affairs* 83 (2): 273–288.

Kapur, Devesh. 2001. "Expansive Agendas and Weak Instruments: Governance Related Conditionalities of International Financial Institutions." *The Journal of Policy Reform* 4 (3): 207–241.

Kay, Sean. 1998. *NATO and the Future of European Security.* Lanham, MD: Rowman & Littlefield.

Kirchner, Emil J. 2006. "The Challenge of European Union Security Governance." *Journal of Common Market Studies* 44 (5): 947–968.

Korosteleva, Elena A. 2011. "Change and Continuity: Is the Eastern Partnership an Adequate Tool for the European Neighbourhood?" *International Relations* 25 (2): 243–262.

Korosteleva, Elena. 2015. "The EU and Belarus: Democracy Promotion by Technocratic Means?" *Democratization* 23 (4): 1–23.

Korosteleva, Elena, Michal Natorski, and Licínia Simão, eds. 2013. *The European Neighbourhood Policy in the Eastern Region: The Practices Perspective.* London: Routledge (Special Issues as Books Series).

Lavenex, Sandra. 2008. "A Governance Perspective on the European Neighbourhood Policy: Integration Beyond Conditionality?" *Journal of European Public Policy* 15 (6): 938–955.

Lavenex, Sandra, and Frank Schimmelfennig. 2009. "EU Rules Beyond EU Borders: Theorizing External Governance in European Politics." *Journal of European Public Policy* 16 (6): 791–812.

Lucarelli, Sonia. 2002. *Peace and Democracy: The Rediscovered Link. The EU, NATO and the European System of Liberal-democratic Security Communities.* Final Report Research project funded by the NATO Euro-Atlantic Partnership Council Individual Research Fellowships – 2000-2002 Programme. Florence: Forum on the Problems of Peace and War. http://www.nato.int/acad/fellow/00-02/Lucarelli%27s.pdf.

Mansfield, Edward, and Jack Snyder. 2005. *Electing to Fight: Why Emerging Democracies go to War.* Cambridge, MA: MIT Press.

Menon, Anand. 2009. "Empowering Paradise? The ESDP at Ten." *International Affairs* 85 (2): 227–246.

Moravcsik, Andrew, and Milada A Vachudova. 2003. "National Interests, State Power, and EU Enlargement." *East European Politics and Societies* 17 (1): 42–57.

Nicolaïdis, Kalypso. 2013. "European Democracy and Its Crisis." *Journal of Common Market Studies* 51 (2): 351–369.

Prodi, R. 2002. "A Wider Europe – A Proximity Policy as the Key to Stability." 6th ECSA World Conference, Jean Monnet Project. Brussels, December 5–6. http://europa.eu/rapid/press-release_SPEECH-02-619_en.htm.

Reuters. 2016. "Russia Will Cut Defense Budget by 5% in 2016, RIA Reports." March 6. http://www.reuters.com/article/us-russia-defense-budget-idUSKCN0W80TL.

Richmond, Oliver. 2000. "Emerging Concepts of Security in the European Order: Implications for the Zone of Conflict at the Fringes of the EU." *European Security* 9 (1): 41–67.

Russett, Bruce. 1993. *Grasping the Democratic Peace.* Princeton, NJ: Princeton University Press.

Sasse, Gwendolyn. 2010. "The European Neighbourhood Policy and Conflict Management: A Comparison of Moldova and the Caucasus." In *EU Conflict Management*, edited by James Hughes, 92–109. Oxon: Routledge.

Schimmelfennig, Frank, and Ulrich Sedelmeier. 2004. "Governance by Conditionality: EU Rule Transfer to the Candidate Countries of Central and Eastern Europe." *Journal of European Public Policy* 11 (4): 661–679.

Schmidt, Vivien A. 2006. *Democracy in Europe: The EU and National Polities.* Oxford: Oxford University Press.

Simão, Licínia. 2013. "Region-building in the Eastern Neighbourhood: Assessing EU Regional Policies in the South Caucasus." *East European Politics* 29 (3): 273–288.

Simão, Licínia. 2014. "The EU's Conflict Resolution Policies in the Black Sea Area." *Journal of Balkan and Near Eastern Studies* 16 (3): 300–313.

Simão, Licínia, and Vanda Dias. 2016. "The Securitization of the EU's Eastern Neighbourhood: What Role for Russia?" In *Security in Shared Neighbourhoods. Foreign Policy of Russia Turkey, and the EU*, edited by Remi Piet and Licínia Simão, 97–118. London: Palgrave Macmillan.

Skålnes, Lars S. 2005. "Geopolitics and the Eastern Enlargement of the European Union." In *The Politics of European Union Enlargement: Theoretical Approaches*, edited by Frank Schimmelfennig and Ulrich Sedelmeier, 213–234. Oxford: Routledge.

Soederberg, Susanne. 2003. "The Promotion of 'Anglo-American' Corporate Governance in the South: Who Benefits from the New International Standard?" *Third World Quarterly* 24 (1): 7–27.

Stefanova, Boyka. 2005. "The European Union as a Security Actor: Security Provision through Enlargement." *World Affairs* 168 (2): 51–66.

Stratfor. 2016. "Russia Prepares to Tighten Spending in 2016." November 3. https://www.stratfor.com/analysis/russia-prepares-tighten-spending-2016.

The Economist. 2007. "The Ins and Outs. The EU's Most Effective Foreign-policy Instrument has been Enlargement. But how Far can it go?" March 15. http://www.economist.com/node/8808134.

Thomas, Caroline. 2000. *Global Governance, Development and Human Security: The Challenge of Poverty and Inequality.* London: Pluto.

Tulmets, Elsa. 2014. *East Central European Foreign Policy Identity in Perspective: Back to Europe and the EU's Neighbourhood.* Basingstoke: Palgrave Macmillan.

Villumsen Berling, Trine. 2012. "Bourdieu, International Relations, and European Security." *Theory and Society* 41 (5): 451–478.

Villumsen Berling, Trine, and Christian Bueger. 2013. "Practical Reflexivity and Political Science: Strategies for Relating Scholarship and Political Practice." *Political Science & Politics* 46 (1): 115–119.

Wæver, Ole. 1998. "Insecurity, Security, and Asecurity in the West European Non-War Community." In *Security Communities*, edited by Emanuel Adler and Michael Barnett, 69–118. Cambridge: Cambridge University Press.

Williams, Michael C. 2007. *Culture and Security. Symbolic Power and the Politics of International Security.* London: Routledge.

Part II
The EU's bilateral engagement with Eastern Neighbours

A growing menu of choice

State building and European integration in Ukraine

Kataryna Wolczuk

Introduction

The Euromaidan protests of 2013/14 had a range of consequences for Ukraine and international politics. Societal protests, the fall of the Yanukovych regime and Russia's aggression against Ukraine have all prompted some actors within the EU institutions to "act differently" by supporting Ukraine in innovative ways. Indeed, it is one of those paradoxes of history that the latter resulted in a degree of proximity and engagement between the EU and Ukraine, which was exactly what the Kremlin sought to prevent (Delcour and Wolczuk 2015).

Although membership for Ukraine was out of the question, the EU has concluded an Association Agreement (AA), including a Deep and Comprehensive Free Trade Area (DCFTA) with Ukraine.[1] The AA represented a breakthrough in EU-Ukraine relations: it promotes political association and economic integration while facilitating the modernization of the country, leading to, it is hoped, a more stable, well-governed and prosperous country.

It is well recognized that integration into a more advanced organization, such as the EU, enhances the credibility of domestic reforms in the aspiring countries. Aside from the economic gains from trade, benefits include a multiplicity of other goals, including securing the irreversibility of domestic reforms (Kolesnichenko 2009). This is especially so with regard to the EU. As the most densely legalized organization in the world, with a vast array of rules the participating countries need to adhere to, European integration is not only a foreign policy choice but becomes a causal variable in domestic policy making. While European integration represents a formidable challenge for Ukraine, Kyiv entered into this asymmetrical and complex agreement precisely to stimulate domestic reforms of the state and economy.

This article examines the relationship between these two processes: European integration and statebuilding within Ukraine. It will be noted that the EU, cognizant of the challenges facing Ukraine as it sought to integrate with the EU while facing Russia's aggression, has offered an unprecedented "reform stimulus" to Ukraine by supporting public administration reforms and assisting with capacity building in the government in order to overcome state weakness. This support goes well beyond what has typically been offered to the so-called "third countries", namely, countries which are not members nor candidate states.

Relatively little has been written about the EU's impact on domestic change in non-member states, outside the context of accession. Therefore, first section takes stock of the research on the impact of EU "beyond enlargement" and argues that the predominantly EU-focused explanations of the impact do not pay sufficient attention to how domestic and EU-level factors interact to shape domestic dynamics and outcomes. Thereafter, it provides an empirically-grounded account of the raft of measures through which the EU has engaged in statebuilding in Ukraine. The empirics points to a move away from the use of external incentives toward a more complex process of external actors engaging with domestic actors in reform coalitions. In Ukraine, it is argued, the EU has become a key transnational actor, working closely with domestic reformers to create "reform enclaves" inside state institutions to spearhead reforms.

As a result, Ukraine's European integration has become intertwined with statebuilding, as conceptualized by Orenstein, Bloom, and Lindstrom (2008) who proposed the quadruple transition framework – consisting of the nation-state building, democratization, marketization as well as integration. However, crucially they did not advocate simply inserting integration a neglected fourth component into the study of post-communist transition. Instead they suggested that "the project of nation-state building, democratization and marketization has been embedded within transnational agenda and pressures, most importantly but not limited to those of the EU" (Orenstein, Bloom, and Lindstrom 2008, 6). This is particularly relevant to Ukraine, where domestic developments have been deeply shaped by a process of European integration in legal, geopolitical and cultural dimensions (see Wolczuk 2016).

Conceptual framework

Despite their ubiquity, dominant enlargement theories are of limited use for analyzing post-communist transformations and integration with the EU in the post-Soviet countries, owing to their excessive emphasis on conditionality and the membership perspective.

The external incentive model has been widely used to explain EU's impact on domestic change in post-communist countries, in which the key instrument of Europeanization is conditionality (Schimmelfennig and Sedelmeier 2019). The EU offers its norms and rules as conditions that the target states have to fulfill in order to receive a reward. The model views the governments as unitary actors – responding to EU conditionality in a rationalist, instrumentalist way to the external conditions and reward. The simplicity of this model is hindered by a noteworthy limitation: it is premised on a specific configuration of conditions found in East-Central European countries, as retrospectively acknowledged by Schimmelfennig and Sedelmeier themselves (2019). This limits the applicability of the model to other post-communist countries. Indeed, the model fails to explain the EU's role in Ukraine since the Euromaidan.

A more insightful theoretical framework with which to understand the EU's diverse impact in accession countries was provide by Vachudova (2001). She starts by highlighting the EU's passive leverage, defined as the traction that the EU has on the domestic politics of credible candidate states by the sheer virtue of its existence. This certainly resonates in Ukraine. Building on this, she posits that the active leverage of the EU includes the promotion of the political and economic benefits of EU membership, the costs of exclusion, and, by extension the relationship between the EU and non-member states. In her view, it is precisely the force of the EU's passive leverage which explains why potential future EU member states declare EU membership as their foremost foreign policy goal. However, for some states, such as Slovakia and Romania, the membership perspective was not enough to trigger domestic reform, as a result of which the EU had to step in with detailed and explicit pre-accession conditionality (see Vachudova 2001).

However, in these rationalist, institutionalist accounts, the membership perspective remains central and their limitations are exposed when they are applied to the western Balkans and the eastern neighborhood. As regards the former, the offer of membership has been an ineffective stimulus to reform; while when it comes to the latter, in some countries, major reforms have been undertaken even in the absence of a membership perspective. Scholars therefore sought to tweak the models by identifying the specific conditions for the external incentive model work. However, by continuing to focus EU-related factors, to the detriment of domestic politics, despite the mounting evidence that in the case of Turkey and western Balkans, the theories struggle for a more universal applicability (see Giandomenico 2015). Furthermore, the theories fail to account for the role of other regional powers, such as Russia, which has been at the heart of the new impetus behind the EU's relations with Ukraine (see Delcour and Wolczuk 2015; Wolczuk 2016).

Conversely, the EU has been become a powerful transnational actor, even where membership is not on offer, such as through the European Neighborhood Policy (ENP) in 2003–4 and then the Eastern Partnership (EaP) in 2009 – both ambitious and sophisticated policies, using a wide range of instruments and platforms for engagement with EU's eastern neighbors.[2] Both policies were designed to export EU's normative order to the countries outside its borders which are not prospective members. As was the case during the accession process, under the ENP, the neighbors would benefit from developing and modernizing their public policies and economies by anchoring them in the EU model of governance (ENEPO 2007, 9). This process of adopting the EU rulebook (the acquis) in domestic legislation is known as legal harmonization. This process comprises both the "download" of EU rules into the domestic legal order and the creation and restructure of domestic institutions to make them capable of implementing the acquis.

So far, the neighborhood policy has not generated much optimism amongst the scholars. Various analyses regarded it as flawed in that, in particular the EaP failed to endow the EU with sufficient leverage over the countries it seeks to influence. The EaP contained inadequate incentives for states to justify the painful process of adopting the EU's rule-setting agenda – in contrast to the ECE states prior to their accession. Vachudova argued that "the incentives that the EU is offering in exchange for reforms are too modest and too vague to be credible" (2008, 37). Yet even this fails to explain why, despite the lack of the membership perspective, integration with the EU – including the conclusion of the AA – has played such a salient role in domestic politics, up to the mass revolt and overthrow of the authoritarian regime in Ukraine. Neither can it explain the enhanced role of the EU in domestic reforms since the Euromaidan. This article seeks to answer this puzzle by an empirically-grounded investigation, which indicates the mechanism, namely EU's formation of reform coalitions and "reform enclaves" within public administration.

European integration and state weakness

The AA with the DCFTA represents an important shift in Ukraine's relations with the EU: it is an *integration-oriented* agreement (Van der Loo 2016) – but it does not entail nor imply an offer a membership. The AA-DCFTA goes beyond a "standard" FTA agreement by carrying a promise to eliminate non-tariff trade barriers to trade through a legalized, detailed and binding framework for economic and sectoral integration. It also contains provisions about various sectors, such as transport, environment and energy, whereby Ukraine under-takes to align itself with EU rules and standards (e.g. on anti-monopoly policy and food safety standards). In many chapters of the AA, the regulations to be transposed are listed in extensive annexes, which far exceed the main text of the agreement. The conclusion of the AA-DCFTA entails a profound impact on the regulatory framework of the country associated with the EU.

The AA has two roles: firstly, to enable political cooperation and economic integration with the EU and secondly, to drive the modernization of the economy and state institutions of signatory countries (see Dragneva and Wolczuk 2012; Wolczuk et al. 2017). From the EU's perspective, these role are intertwined and mutually reinforcing (European Commission 2008, 4). At the heart of this process is institutional and regulatory convergence with the EU, something which is achieved through the "import of the *acquis*". The density and precision of these undertakings departs from the previously vague and unspecific frameworks for cooperation between the EU and Ukraine (Dragneva and Wolczuk 2014 ; Van der Loo 2016; Van der Loo et al. 2014). Therein lies the actual salience of the AA: it seeks not only to integrate but also to transform the associated countries at the same time (Adarov and Havlik 2016; Emerson and Movchan 2016).

The EU is more effective than any other international organization in inducing domestic change in the process of integration. This is because European integration is a complex and lengthy process involving virtually all parts of the state and which penetrates deep into the state apparatus, ranging from food safety agencies to anti-monopoly policies. Certainly, the 2004–7 enlargement showed that European integration is positively associated with enhancing state capacity in post-communist countries. This is because, in the accession countries, the demands of integration were of such magnitude that sufficient administrative capacity were the *sine qua non* for dealing with the sheer volume of inter-sectoral matters to be dealt within tight time constraints (Fink-Hafner 2005; Lippert et al 2001). The application of EU law has some bearing on almost every aspect of public policy-making and implementation (Grabbe 2001, 1051). In particular, institutional adaptation was a response to the extensive functional pressures arising from the need to organize relations with the EU, formulate negotiating positions, and implement EU policies (Sedelmeier 2006). This process encompassed both general public administration reforms as well as the building of sectoral and horizontal capacity. The EU explicitly demanded from accession countries that they introduce independent professional bodies and protect civil servants from dismissal and extensive political interference. In particular, with regard to public administration reforms, the EU insisted on, first, the adoption of legislation governing the functioning the civil service, second, the creation of a public administration reform strategy and, third, civil servant training (Dimitrova 2005, 82). Thus, the process of accession has spawned both comprehensive public administration reform as well as targeted capacity building to coordinate legal harmonization and accession to the EU. The resulting upgrade to state capacity in East-Central Europe has had a lasting positive effects on administrative capacity and policy making in general, and the implementation of the EU *acquis* in particular (Dimitrova et al. 2019; Sedelmeier 2006).

However, the post-Soviet states – apart from the three Baltic states – were left aside, despite their deep-seated problems. Ukraine shares its state weakness with most other post-Soviet states, including Russia. This commonality points to a deeper systemic legacy of misdevelopment in the Soviet period (see Solnick 1998). The USSR was an all-encompassing but ultimately shallow state, the structures of which were formally preserved and yet atrophied soon after its demise. While all post-communist countries suffered from state weakness and faced similar challenges (see Goetz and Wollmann 2001), East-Central European states conducted public administration reforms in the 1990s, in part to eradicate communist legacies and in part to prepare for EU membership. Ukraine, however, continued to suffer from an "overbloated and yet ineffective apparatus of the state" (Kravchuk 1999).

For all other post-Soviet states, the delay in addressing public administration reforms had profound long-term consequences in terms of state capture – in which various element of the administrative and policy machinery became subordinated to powerful interests – state capacity has been further degraded. More specifically, state capture occurs when economic agents manipulate policy formation and even shape the emerging *rules of the game* to their own advantage (Hellman, Jones, and Kaufmann 2000). Administrative roles in individual ministries or other executive bodies provide ample opportunities for rent extraction in the course of regulatory functions, such as tax collection, licencing, registration, inspections etc. State weakness allows state capture as institutions are infiltrated by predatory networks. These networks corrode the capacity to devise and apply rules in a neutral way and indeed, conversely, seek to devise rules to facilitate rent extraction. As such, state capture further erodes the state capacity to devise, implement and enforce the rules in a competent and neutral way, which is necessary to deliver public goods for the public as a whole (Van Zon 2000). In Ukraine, in the opaque networks of bureaucrats-cum-business, people become powerful veto players "whose agreement is necessary for a change in the status quo" (Tsebelis 2002, 19).

Against this backdrop, European integration became a way to provide a reform stimulus to Ukraine. The Ukrainian officials seeking closer relations with the EU sought to link domestic reform to European integration (Wolczuk 2008, 2009). In particular the Ukrainian officials, who conducted negotiations on the AA (2007–11) sought to ensure that Ukraine's extensive commitments could be used as a leverage to promote domestic reform and thereby change the dysfunctional status quo (Langbein and Wolczuk 2012). Ironically, however, while Ukraine concluded the negotiations during Yanukovych's presidency (2010–14), he systematically and relentlessly hollowed out the state through unprecedented state capture (Dragneva and Wolczuk 2015). The resulting state weakness was vividly exposed during 2014, as analyzed by D'Anieri (2017).

As a result, as Ukraine was concluding a complex and ambitious agreement with the EU, the gap between formal, legal commitment and its capacity to implement that commitment was growing exponentially. By 2014, the scale of domestic change required in Ukraine to strengthen state capabilities in order to pursue integration with the EU was considerably larger than was the case in the East-Central European countries in the 1990s. This dual role of the AA – both as a transformation and integration device – has meant that the agenda for AA implementation is huge in terms of sheer scope, depth of required change, and associated costs for the associated country. Crucially, the challenge of eradicating state weakness per se was explicitly recognized by some in the EU institutions. As a high-level official in the EU Delegation put it:

> The government apparatus is probably too big for the purposes the country needs it to serve. And it is certainly not up to delivering the kind of public service quality that Ukraine requires. We could compare the government's central administration

to a company with 220,000–230,000 employees. It is all but bankrupt, but we need this company regardless because it has, so to say, a monopoly on the product it delivers. So we have to reorganize it (De Groot 2016).

The EU supports Ukraine in "ensuring a stable, prosperous and democratic future for all its citizens" (EEAS 2016), this means, that by implication, it also supports the notion of helping create a state which can deliver the above. As was widely realized in international development, "for donors to simply attend to social and economic needs without sufficient attention to the basic functioning of core political institutions makes no sense" (Carothers and De Gramont 2013, 97).

The Euromaidan, the conclusion of the AA, Russia's aggression against Ukraine, and the influx of new pro-EU actors (i.e. willing domestic actors to engage with), provided a unique situation, within which the EU could have an impact.

Eu's support for statebuilding

European integration – including association – is premised on strong state capacity to enact new rules. State capacity refers to the state's institutional capability to design and carry out a range of public policies that deliver benefits and services to the public and economic actors. Building state capacity entails having a long-term vision that may need to override the short-term political calculus of the political class, which tends to prevail in the post-Soviet states in general. It is particularly important to develop state capacity to implement reforms which is as immune as possible from shifting political configurations within government and parliament (Wolczuk and Zeruolis 2018).

The European Commission has offered assistance to help build state capacity. Four key features of this work are noteworthy. First, the EU engaged in state-building in Ukraine, a task it usually leaves to other transnational actors. Second, through a dedicated taskforce, it has developed a dynamic approach, which is designed around the specific needs of the country. Third, the EU officials have worked with domestic actors to form reform coalitions. However, the EU has not only sought to empower reformers within the government but actually funded an increase in their numbers. All of this is evidence that the EU has a deep understanding not only of the state weakness of Ukraine, but also the dangers it represents to Ukraine's European integration and resilience.

The above mentioned taskforce, the Support Group for Ukraine (SGUA), was an innovation conceived in 2014 under the Barosso presidency of the European Commission, which became operational under Junkers' presidency. It was created as a dedicated unite, consisting both European and national officials from EU member states. Ukraine is the only state, which as a "third country" to the EU, has been allocated such a dedicated taskforce. By 2019, staffed with about 35–37 officials (some of whom are located in Kyiv), the SGUA had launched various innovations, under the stern leadership of Peter Wagner since 2016.

Statebuilding, rather than simply implementation of the AA, became an explicit and ambitious priority of the EU's actions in Ukraine:

> Actions will enable reform in all sectors of public administration and in public finance management, including law enforcement, border, customs and migration management, judiciary and local government. This will result in delivery of

high-quality, secure and user friendly public services to citizens and enterprises, good policy development and strategy, accountability and transparency of state authorities and a motivated, professional, skilled and gender-balanced workforce. New actions will contribute to the rationalisation of state bodies, promotion of cross-sectorial collaboration, and implementation of e-governance (European Commission 2018 2008).

The SGUA has control over design and disbursment of financial assistance since July 2015.[3] This, in conjunction with its responsiveness meant it was well placed to help identify and address reform blockages.

While the EU and its member states are the biggest international donor in Ukraine, the SGUA has coordinated its assistance with other international donors (see Wolczuk and Žeruolis 2018). Thanks to the pooling of various sources, extensive funding has become available to Ukraine, well beyond the narrowly defined country allocation within the context of the European Neighborhood Instrument. While onerous to achieve, close coordination also allows different sources of funding to be "blended", including those of European Bank for Reconstruction and Development (EBRD) and the European Investment Bank. The EU created a multi-donor account, which receives financial contributions from 17 countries and supports various reform activities (De Groot et al. 2019). As the biggest-by-far financial contributor to this financing instrument, the EU has taken a lead in creating the multi-stranded Ukraine Reform Architecture. This architecture involves both Public Administration Reforms (PAR) and a range of other flanking measures to boost capacity within the public administration, which will be analyzed below.

Public administration reform[4]

The need for Public Administration Reforms (PAR) in Ukraine had long been known. However, the ongoing political instability made it difficult to launch and sustain the reform process during 2005–9 (see SIGMA 2006) . Under President Yanukovych (2010–14), political resistance to reforms became stronger. For example, the EU's offer of €100 million budgetary support to PAR, was turned down by Prime Minister Mykola Azarov who was discouraged by the associated conditionality and benchmarking.[5] EU institutions and various EU member states also provided assistance which mainly consisted of technical assistance projects, which were numerous and fragmented, and therefore largely ineffective in terms of reforming state institutions (Wolczuk and Žeruolis 2018). The Euromaidan provided a new impetus for PAR on the understanding that "a thorough reform of public administration is indispensable for the successful implementation of Ukraine's ambitious reform process" (SGUA 2016). A professional, well-motivated and, most importantly, independent civil service can impose limits on state capture and abuse of power by power holders.

Indeed, within weeks of Euromaidan, the European Commission had redistributing financial resources within the EU assistance programmes, such as the European Neighborhood Instrument to create the so-called State Building Contract. The Commission sought to provide support for the creation of an independent, civil service, including, amongst others, separating political positions from administrative positions, and those in the public sphere from those in the private; meritocratic, non-political recruitment; as well aspromoting senior and middle level civil servants, offering employment security and adequate remuneration (European Commission 2014, 5).

While Prime Minister of Ukraine Arseniy Yatsenyuk and European Commission President José Manuel Barroso signed the Financing Agreement for the State Building Contract in 2014, with an allocation of €80 mln to supplement salaries of newly-selected public servants to competitive level.

Working in the background, the EU officials helped ensure that the draft law on the civil service met international benchmarks (see below). The Group provided support to various stakeholders in their quest to have the law, which would subsequently be one of the pillars of Public Administration Reform, adopted by the Verkhovna Rada in December 2015, entering into force on 1 May 2016 (De Groot et al. 2019).

In parallel to the legal basis, the Support Group pushed for PAR asking for an overall strategy and implementation plan, which the EU could provide financial support for. Thus, the EU made assistance conditional upon political buy-in as well as a feasible and clear reform strategy. It is indicative that attempts to draw up such a strategy under Prime Minister Arseniy Yatseniuk (2014–16) were inconclusive. Hence, the offer of financial support was therefore suspended and additional high-level advisers were recruited to steer the process.

The appointment of a new government in April 2016 provided another "window of opportunity" for a renewed impetus. The new Cabinet of Ministers adopted a comprehensive Public Administration Reform Strategy (PARS), together with a corresponding implementation plan, in June 2016. The preparation of the law, strategy and implementation plans involved an inclusive consultation process in which civil society had been encouraged to participate. The new law established competitive selection procedures and a dedicated commission was set up to implement them in July 2016. In order to support the reforms, in late 2017, as part of the "State Building Contract,,, the EU offered €71mln for PAR and €104mln to put in place "a new generation of Ukrainian public servants, organize the government according to European standards, implement best practices in policy-making and advance key sector reforms" (EEAS 2016, 2).

In promoting administrative reforms, the EU has relied on the approach defined by the Support for Improvement in Governance and Management (SIGMA), a joint initiative by the Organization for Economic Cooperation and Development (OECD) and the EU since the 1990s. SIGMA is mainly funded by the European Commission in order to develop a framework for defining and evaluating administrative baseline criteria. The framework was pioneered for the Eastern enlargement candidates and then further expanded, culminating in a comprehensive and elaborate set of principles of public administration grouped into six categories, each with a detailed set of benchmarks and assessments (SIGMA 2017). From mid-2000s, SIGMA had started assessing the capacities to Ukraine from mid-2000 onwards (SIGMA 2017), but Ukrainian and EU officials turned SIGMA standards into explicit and formal benchmarks for PAR in the aftermath of the Euromaidan.

Once the comprehensive Public Administration Reform Strategy (PARS) for 2016–2020 was adopted by the Ukrainian government in June 2016, in December, the European Commission and Ukraine signed a memorandum in support of comprehensive PAR in Ukraine. In return, the EU provided substantial budgetary support to initiate a wholesale reform of its entire public administration. (This PARS was developed in conjunction with OECD's SIGMA in line with the Principles of Public Administration.) Ukraine is also subject to monitoring of the PARS implementation. By request of the Ukrainian government, the SIMGA assessment in 2018 was based on the methodology and indicators developed for the EU candidate countries, which are more rigorous than those designed for ENP countries. The assessment concluded that reform is progressing slowly and is over-ambitious in the short to medium term (SIGMA 2018).

This assessment underscores the fact that comprehensive reforms take time to take root. This is a classic conundrum that the reform process engenders: opting for comprehensive reforms leads to a more fundamental transformation but only in the long terms, while the pursuit of rapid gains is less likely to result in a fundamental transformation. EU officials were only too aware that fundamental reforms are needed but they would take years, if not decades, to accomplish (Dimitrova et al. 2019, 11). So, rather ingeniously EU officials have created "reform enclaves", which can drive specific reforms while the administration as a whole lags behind, something which temporarily results in a two-tier administration.

Multiplying "reform enclaves,, within public administration

In addition to supporting PARS, there have been several important innovations to spearhead reforms within the government both at the political and administrative levels. Working with other international donors, the EU has supported the creation of dedicated reform units within the government. Starting reforms with relatively targeted and carefully selected reform units that manage tasks linked to policy making – including designing and implementing fundamental reforms and pursuing European integration – promise quicker results. Four particular innovations stand out.

First, the EU has funded the Strategic Group of Advisers (SAGSUR), created by the IBRD This high-level advisory group led by Ivan Miklos, the architect of Slovak economic reforms, advises the Prime Minister of Ukraine on strategic key reforms, including pensions, health services etc. The strategy involves the creation of a close-knit group who develop a deep knowledge of the country and work closely with the key officials, providing advice on reform of health-care, education and pensions (Miklos and Kukhta 2019).

Second, the Reform Delivery Office (RDO), which is working with the Prime Minister's office, acts as a permanent advisory body to the Cabinet of Ministers, coordinated by the Prime Minister and headed by the Minister of the Cabinet of Ministers. The RDO is primarily responsible for the development and implementation of the annual government reform plan, overall coordination and ensuring consistency of reform delivery across the Government. The team is particularly focused on the implementation of Ukraine's public administration reform (Miklos and Kukhta 2019; De Groot et al. 2019). In 2017, the RDO prepared the strategic governmental plan such as the Midterm Plan of Reform Priorities for 2017–2020. This is the most comprehensive and realistic plan outlining the reforms of the state and economy, that Ukraine has ever developed (*Kabinet of Ministers*, 2017).

Third, Reform Support Teams (RST) have been created in several ministries. Crucially they consisted of reform-minded Ukrainians, rather than international experts. The RST have a dual role, first, to implement the PARS in their respective ministries and, second, to design, develop and implement relevant sectoral reforms. One of the lessons learnt is that a need for systematic reforms needs to avoid limited, random interventions and instead utilize a strategic, sectoral approach. A sectoral approach is pivotal, because the appropriate use of sectoral reform strategies means that tasks are prioritized and done in the right order to enable reforms to build on each other in a systemic way.

The fourth – and arguably the most important – innovation has been the creation of reform posts within the public administration bodies. Thanks to the scale of its funding, the EU was able to provide what international donors can rarely afford to fund in beneficiary countries, namely, support for reform positions across a number of ministries. Coordinated by the SGUA, ten ministries as well as the Secretariat of the Cabinet of Ministers agreed to participate in a pilot where reform positions were established starting with secretary generals down to technical specialists. Most importantly, the SGUA made support available upon adopting a special recruitment process. This procedure allowed the government to hire people experienced in civil service and external specialists with respective competency and experience in business and non-government sector. Ukraine was offered €104 million in funding; the plan is to recruit around 2000 civil servants in an independent selection process by 2020. Apart from ministries, the Secretariat of the Cabinet, which oversees administrative reforms, is also a beneficiary of the scheme. These initiatives have resulted in the recruitment of new, highly talented public servants positioned in strategic positions across government where they can act as a "reform enclaves'" and act as "agents of change" inside the government in field such as public finance, agriculture, energy efficiency, environment, economic development and infrastructure. By bringing highly competent Ukrainians from outside public administration, lured by with more job satisfaction and better salaries than state positions usually attracted, the EU not only bolstered reformers, but increased their numbers. This is a vast improvement on the old system of "importing" experts.

In engaging in these initiatives, the EU goes well beyond the narrowly defined implementation of the AA. By focusing on the fundamental preconditions for the AA implementation in terms of building state capacity, the EU is playing a more pivotal role than originally expected. Indeed, it has directly contributed to the emergence of stronger domestic institutions, and the strengthening of the capacity of the state to deliver public goods, while increasing its resilience to the transgressions of political elites seeking to secure their own interests.

Indeed, the EU has hoped to curb state capture. Crucially, PARS have been bolstered by anti-corruption reforms as a second plank of its support for statebuilding (see Lough and Dubrovskiy 2018). In this regard, the AA has provided a powerful stimulus for EU officials to focus on tackling long-standing weaknesses and challenges, thereby ensuring that Ukraine's integration with the EU results in tangible results in terms of eradicating long-standing problems Ukraine has faced (Mathernova 2019). Like PAR, the anti-corruption reforms are ongoing and will take years if not decades to succeed, if at all.

Common to all of these initiatives is the focus on generic institutional reform rather than capacity simply to implement the AA -the EU has supported the meaningful rebuilding of the state. This is in contrast to 2004 enlargement, which emphasized "compliance with the acquis", as the East-Central European were further along the path of comprehensive reform than was Ukraine (Dimitrova et al. 2019). Only where candidate states lacked capacity, such as Lithuania, did the EU apply conditionality and provide assistance (see Nakrosis 2003). In the Western Balkans, the EU also prioritized the fundamentals of the rule of law and anti-corruption institutions. Quite interestingly, there is little evidence that the instruments developed for the Western Balkans were transferred directly to Ukraine. Rather, the initiative undertaken in Ukraine was developed by a group of EU officials and experts working in tandem with other international donors, especially the EBRD, and domestic reformers. This support was developed in an indigenous way to deliver a "better-targeted and better-timed support" (Miklos and Kukhta 2019, 4). In comparison to the pre-Maidan period, a seasoned expert assessed the changed approach as follows: "To sum up, the European Commission is implementing a comprehensive, long and apparently well planned pursuit of PAR in Ukraine. It is displaying much-needed leadership and conditionality, which is positively puzzling" (Žeruolis 2018).

Analytical challenges: mechanism and outcomes

As was highlighted above, the limits of the rationalist institutionalist soon became apparent in the aftermath of the 2004–7 enlargements:

> [S]tudying the impact of transnational actors on states with an EU membership perspective turns out to be easy [...]. Beyond the line in the sand that separates these states from the rest of the post-Soviet space, the arrows no longer all point in the same direction, and the impact of transnational actors becomes much more murky. In this it resembles more closely other world regions, such as Latin America, the Middle East, and Africa (Vachudova 2008: 37).

In a similar vain, Sedelmeier (2006) noted the analytical challenge of devising a framework in order to explain just how the EU impacts domestic change in neighborhood states, which lack a membership perspective. The approaches stressing the external incentive have limited utility because they underplay the domestic dynamics and demand for reforms inside the countries. Yet, it is precisely these under-appreciated factors which the EU has been able to capitalize on. In fact, this more nuanced picture was already noted. For Grabbe (2001; 2004) and Epstein (2008) have observed that domestic reformers, in the face of hurdles tend to turn to international organizations and the influence that they bring. This is certainly resonates in Ukraine: working with the EU was seen as the key to addressing the weak indigenous capacity for reform (Wolczuk 2009). While the EU is regarded as more effective than any other international organization in promoting domestic change in non-member states, this is only the case when it has domestic actors with which it can work as argued by Jacoby (2006, 626–35). Despite its relatively weak incentives (in comparison to enlargement), the "modernization through integration" agenda can be effective when there are motivated and committed domestic actors who use the EU for guidance and support. The fact that the EU was responsive to the agenda of these actors is also a key element to the success of the process. Indeed, it is striking how closely the EU officials and experts worked with domestic actors and engaged in reform coalitions across a variety of fields and sectors. As noted by Samokhvalov (2019), these coalitions "transgress formal institutional positions and levels with information and action flows cutting across various dimensions". The utility of the coalitional approach to external influence stems from its linking EU agenda to specific actors at the domestic level because "external influences matter precisely where they best connect with domestic processes, not where they act independently" (Jacoby, 2008: 69) This is certainly how international donors seek to promote reforms in developing countries (see Carothers and De Gramont, 2013).

However, in analytical terms, this precise mechanism by which the process works is hard to discern. As Samokhvalov argues, "even though it is analytically convenient to distinguish various forms of influence, in real life no dimension of EU-Ukraine interaction has been air-tightly isolated from others. They should not be treated separately" (2019). The study of EU's support for statebuilding since the Euromaidan blurs the dichotomy between domestic and international explanations. While external influence – through coalition building – does not always work, when it does it is "particularly hard to see, precisely because it is so bound up with domestic politics", as noted by Jacoby (2008: 71). This complexity and blurring perhaps accounts for the scarcity of analysis of EU's support for Ukraine, something which clearly warrants further investigation.

The second analytical challenge is to gauge the outcomes of the statebuilding agenda pursued. It has become abundantly clear that rebuilding the post-Soviet states is an arduous and drawn-out process (see SIGMA 2018). In Ukraine for sure, within line ministries, rent-extraction provides powerful incentives to resist reforms, which curb the corrupt practices (Van Zon 2000). However, equally important is the sheer scale and complexity of devising and implementing root- and-branch reform across government. Therefore, conceptualizing the domestic impact of European integration in Ukraine five years since the Euromaidan presents a considerable challenge. Rather than rapid, comprehensive and harmonized change, we can observe gradual forms of change such as those delineated in historical institutionalism (Thelen 1999), which argues that while various legal and institutional changes are made, yet they are often fragmented, and are impacted on by elements of the existing system which linger on. So, the new elements are introduced – like reform teams or new directorates – work in conjunction with existing bodies, which are subject to slower reforms. The result is overlapping functions, conflict of interests and so forth. While this dynamic is unavoidable, it results in a particularly complex process which is hard to examine and conceptualize (see Kupriy 2019).

Conclusions

Since the events of 2014, much attention has been paid to the EU's role in deterring Russia's aggression against Ukraine, especially the role of sanctions. Yet arguably, the most important event has been the change in EU-Ukraine relations. For sure, the Euromaidan was instrumental in enabling Ukraine's closer integration with the EU, above all through the conclusion of the AA. However, the significance of integration with the EU goes beyond the narrowly defined implementation of the AA. While the AA embodies long-term aspirations, the EU's innovative and tailored support is proving to be transformational. Aside from any trade benefits resulting from economic integration, some of which are already materializing, for Ukraine the salience of European integration lies not so much in the AA – and trade liberalization in a narrow sense – but above all in the in the stimulus it offers for deeper reforms of the governmental structures. While the process of state building is inevitably slower and more arduous than expected, the underlying rationale for seeking integration with the EU, despite the absence of the membership perspective, has been validated.

By making statebuilding a pre-condition for European integration, the EU innovated and devised a developmental approach, more in tune with the specific needs of the target country. In doing so, the EU's innovations in Ukraine are likely to offer lessons far beyond Ukraine and have wider ramifications for the EU's external action in Eastern Europe and more broadly.

Notes

1. However, the conclusion of the AA was delayed four times (for details see Wolczuk at al. 2017).
2. The ENP is a composite policy, framing relations with Union's neighbors in the east and south. The ENP subsumes a number of initiatives, most notably the Mediterranean Union and the Eastern Partnership, and country-specific bilateral instruments, which are either legally binding (such as new Association Agreements) or are more political in their nature (such as the Association Agendas), as well as various assistance programmes such as the European Neighborhood Instrument.
3. From 2014 to 2017 bilateral assistance to Ukraine – in the context of the European Neighborhood Instrument – was provided in the form of annual Special Measures. For 2017–20, the Single Strategic Framework for 2017–20 was adopted, which includes "good governance" as one of the key priorities for funding.
4. The empirical section is based on first, an analysis of documentary sources as well as on extensive contacts and seminar presentations with EU and Ukrainian officials and experts held by the Ukraine Forum, Russia and Eurasian Programme at Chatham House in London (of which the author is an Associate Fellow) during 2014–19. Most of those meetings were held under the Chatham House rule so information cannot be attributed to specific participants. The participants included, amongst others, Peter Wagner (head of the SGUA), Katarina Mathernova (deputy director general in the European Commission), Oleksandr Saienko (Minister of the Cabinet of Ministers in charge of PAR (2016–19), Ivanna Klimpush-Tsintsadze, deputy Prime Minister for European and Euro-Atlantic Integration (2016–19). The empirical section also draws on extensive information gathered during fieldwork in Kyiv (in May 2018) to prepare a study on the institutional mechanism for the implementation of the AA in Georgia, Moldova and Ukraine for the European Parliament (see Wolczuk 2018). This fieldwork was greatly facilittated by the EU Delegation in Kyiv. The author is deeply grateful to all EU and Ukrainian officials and experts for sharing their insights.
5. Author's interview with EU official, Kyiv, September 2013.

Acknowledgments

The author acknowledges the support this research paper received from the Horizon 2020 research and innovation programme of the EU (project EU-STRAT 'The European Union and Eastern Partnership Countries – An Inside-Out Analysis and Strategic Assessment') under grant agreement number 693382.

Disclosure statement

No potential conflict of interest was reported by the author.

Funding

This work was supported by the Horizon 2020 Framework Programme [693382].

References

Adarov, A., and P. Havlik. 2016. *Benefits and Costs of DCFTA: Evaluation of the Impact on Georgia, Moldova and Ukraine*. Vienna: Vienna Institute for International Economic Studies.

Carothers, T., and D. De Gramont. 2013. *Development Aid Confronts Politics: The Almost Revolution*. Washington D.C.: Carnegie Endowment for International Peace.

D'Anieri, P. 2017. "Anarchy, the State, and Ukraine." In *Paradox of Power the Logics of State Weakness in Eurasia*, edited by J. Heathershaw and E. Schatz, 200–214. Pittsburgh, Pa.: University of Pittsburgh Press.

De Groot, B. 2016. *EU Diplomat: Ukraine's Public Administration Needs New Talent*. Interview for the Ukrainian press. https://euukrainecoop.com/2016/11/01/public-administration/

De Groot, B., M. Maslowska, S. Schleuning, and W. Peter. 2019. "Overcoming Challenges with Innovation. Capacity Building in Transaction Countries – Examples from the Eastern Partnership and Ukraine." *New Eastern Europe*.

Delcour, L., and W. Kataryna. 2015. "Spoiler or Facilitator of Democratization? Russia's Role in Georgia and Ukraine." *Democratization* 22 (3): 459–478. doi:10.1080/13510347.2014.996135.

Dimitrova, A. 2002. "Enlargement, Institution-Building and the EU's Administrative Capacity Requirement." *West European Politics* 25 (4): 171–190. doi:10.1080/713601647.

Dimitrova, A. 2005. "Europeanization and Civil Service Reform in Central and Eastern Europe." In *The Europeanization of Central and Eastern Europe*, edited by F. Schimmelfennig and U. Sedelmeier, 71–91. Ithaca and London: Cornell University Press.

Dimitrova, A., J. Lanbeing, K. Mankokas, and K. Wolczuk 2019. "Learning from Enlargement@ Compring EU Capacity Building and Monitoring under Enlargement with the Implementation of the Association Agreement." EU-STRAT Paper.

Dragneva, R., and K. Wolczuk. 2012. "EU Law Export to the Eastern Neighbourhood." In *EU External Relations Law and Policy in the Post-Lisbon Era*, edited by P. Cardwell, 217–240. The Hague: TMC Asser Press.

Dragneva, R., and K. Wolczuk. 2014. "The EU-Ukraine Association Agreement and the Challenges of Inter-Regionalism." *Review of Central and East European Law* 39: 213–244. doi:10.1163/15730352-00000019.

Dragneva, R., and K. Wolczuk. 2015. *Ukraine between the EU and Russia: the Integration Challenge*. Houndmills and New York, NY: Palgrave Macmillan.

EEAS. 2016. "EU-Ukraine Relations, European External Action Service". accessed 20 July 2019. https://eeas.europa.eu/headquarters/headquarters-Homepage/1937/ukraine-and-eu_en

Emerson, M., and V. Movchan, eds. 2016. *Deepening EU-Ukrainian Relations. What Why and How?* London: Rowman & Littlefield International.

ENEPO. 2007. "Working Paper on Concepts and Definitions of Institutional Development (harmonisation) and Methodology of Measuring Them." *EU Eastern Neighbourhood: Economic Potential and Future Development*, June. doi:10.1094/PDIS-91-4-0467B.

Epstein, R. 2008. *In Pursuit of Liberalism: International Institutions in Postcommunist Europe*. Baltimore: Johns Hopkins University Press.

European Commission. 2008. "*Eastern Partnership*. Communication to the Council and to the European Parliament." *COM (2008) 823 final*, December 3.

European Commission. 2014. "Commission Implementing Decision of 29. 4.2014 Modifying the Commission Decision C(2013) 8059 of 20 November 2013 on the ENPI Annual Action Programme 2013 in Favour of Ukraine to Be Financed from the General Budget of the European Union", Brussels. European Commission. 2018. Summary of the Single Support Framework for EU Support to Ukraine (2018–2020), Brussels.

Fink-Hafner, D. 2005. "Europeanization of the Core Executive in the Transition from EU Accession to Full EU Membership", Paper presented at the EUSA Ninth Biennial International Conference, Austin, Texas, March 31-April 2, 2005.

Giandomenico, J. 2015. *Transformative Power Challenged. EU Membership Conditionality in the Western Balkans Revisited. InSkrifter Utgivna Av Statsvetenskapliga Föreningen I Uppsala194*. Uppsala: Acta Universitatis Upsaliensis.

Grabbe, H. 2001. "How Does Europeanization Affect CEE Governance? Conditionality, Diffusion and Diversity." *Journal of European Public Policy* 8 (6): 1013–1031. doi:10.1080/13501760110098323.

Grabbe, H. 2003. "Europeanisation Goes East: Power and Uncertainty in the EU Accession Process." In *The Politics of Europeanisation*, edited by K. Featherstone and R. Claudio, 303–323. Oxford: Oxford University Press.

Hellman, J., G. Jones, and D. Kaufmann. 2000. "How Profitable Is Buying State Officials in Transition Economies." *Transition* 11: 8–11.

Jacoby, W. 2006. "Inspiration, Coalition, and Substitution. External Influences on Postcommunist Transformations." *World Politics* 58. doi:10.1353/wp.2007.0010.

Jacoby, W. 2008. "Minority Traditions and Post-communist Politics: How do IGOs Matter?." In *Transnational Actors in Central and East European Transitions*, edited by M, Orenstein, S, Bloom, and N. Lindstrom, 111–153. Pittsburgh: University of Pittsburgh Press.

Kabinet of Ministers of Ukraine. 2017. "Seredniostrokovyi Plan Priorytetnykh Diy Uryadu Do 2020 [The Mid-Term Plan of Priority Actions of the Government till 2020." Accessed 18 July 2019. https://www.kmu.gov.ua/ua/npas/249935442

Klaus, G. H., and H. Wollmann. 2001. "Governmentalizing Central Executives in Postcomunist Europe: A Four-country Comparison." *Journal of European Public Policy* 8 (6): 864–887. doi:10.1080/13501760110098260.

Kolesnichenko, A. 2009. "Institutional Harmonization and Its Costs and Benefits in the Context of EU Cooperation with Its Neighbours". *CASE Network Studies and Analyses*, Warsaw.

Kravchuk, R. 1999. "The Law on the Civil Service: A Case Study of Administrative Reform in Ukraine." In *State and Institution Building in Ukraine*, edited by T. Kuzio, R. S. Kravchuk, and P. D'Anieri, 135–154. New York: NY: Martin's Press.

Kupriy, N. 2019. *Public Administration Reform in Ukraine: A Review of Accomplishments*. Ukrainian Prism: Foreign Policy Council. Accessed 20 July 2019. *http://prismua.org/en/pdf/2019-02-8/*

Langbein, J., and K. Wolczuk. 2012. "Convergence without Membership? the Impact of the European Union in the Nieghbourhood: Evidence from Ukraine." *Journal of European Public Policy* 19 (6): 863–881. doi:10.1080/13501763.2011.614133.

Lippert, B., G. Umbach, and W. Wessels. 2001. "Europeanization of CEE Executives: Eu Membership Negotiations as a Shaping Power." *Journal of European Public Policy* 8: 980–1012. doi:10.1080/13501760110098314.

Lough, J., and V. Dubrovskiy 2018. "Are Ukraine's Anti-corruption Reforms Working?" *Research Paper*, London: Chatham House.

Mathernova, K. 2019. "Ukraine and the European Union." In *Reforms in Ukriane after Revolution Fo Dignity: What Was Done, Why Not More and What to Do Next*, edited by M. Ivan. and P. Kukhta, 144–165. Kyiv: Strategic Advisory Group for Support of Ukrainian Reforms.

Miklos, I., and P. Kukhta. 2019. *Reforms in Ukraine after Revolution Fo Dignity: What Was Done, Why Not More and What to Do Next*. Kyiv: Strategic Advisory Group for Support of Ukrainian Reforms.

Nekrosis, V. 2003. "Assessing Governmental Capabilities to Manage European Affairs. The Case of Lithuania." In *The Road to the European Union*, edited by V. Pettai and J. Zielonka, 104–139. Vol. 2. Estonia, Latvia and Lithuania. Manchester: Manchester University Press.

Orenstein, M., S. Bloom, and N. Lindstrom. 2008. "A Fourth Dimension of Transiton." In *Transtional Actors in Central and East European Transitions*, edited by M. Orenstein, S. Bloom, and N. Lindstrom, 1–18. Pittsburgh: University of Pittsburgh Press.

Samokhvalov, V. 2019. "Linking Linkages, Leverage and Others: the Role of Cross-Dimensional Networks in EU Democracy Promotion." *Manuscript in preparation*.

Schimmelfennig, F., and U. Sedelmeier. 2019. "The Europeanization of Eastern Europe: The External Incentives Model Revisited." *Journal of European Public Policy* 1–20. doi:10.1080/13501763.2019.1617333.

Sedelmeier, U. 2006. "Europeanisation in New Member and Candidate States." *Living Reviews in European Governance* 1: 3. Accessed 25 April 2007. doi:10.12942/lreg-2006-3.

SGUA. 2016. *Support Group for Ukraine: Activity Report, the First 18 Months*. Brussels: European Commission.

SIGMA. 2006. "Ukraine Governance Assessment." *OECD, SIGMA Programme*.

SIGMA. 2017. *The Principles of Public Administration*. Paris: OECD. http://sigmaweb.org/publications/Principles-of-Public-Administration_Edition-2017_ENG.pdf

SIGMA. 2018 June. *Baseline Measurement Report: the Principles of Public Administration*. Ukraine: OECD Paris.

Solnick, S. 1998. *Stealing the State. Control and Collapse in Soviet Institutions.* Cambridge Mass.: Harvard University Press.
Thelen, K. 1999. "Historical Institutionalism in Comparative Politics." *Annual Review of Political Science* 2: 369–404. doi:10.1146/annurev.polisci.2.1.369.
Tsebelis, G. 2002. *Veto Players: How Political Institutions Work.* Princeton: Princeton University Press.
Vachudova, M. 2001. *Europe Undivided: Democracy, Leverage, and Integration after Communism.* Oxford: Oxford University Press.
Vachudova, M. 2008. "The European Union: The Causal Behemoth of Transnational Influence on Postcommunist Politics,,. In *Transnational Actors in Central and East European Transitions*, edited by Orenstein, M., S.Bloom and N. Lindstrom, 19–38. Pittsburgh: University of Pittsburgh Press.
Van der Loo, G. 2016. *The EU-Ukraine Association Agreement and Deep Comprehensive Free Trade Area.* The Hague: Brill/Nijhoff.
van der Loo, G., P. Van Elsuwege, and R. Petrov 2014. "The EU-Ukraine Association Agreement: Assessment of an Innovative Legal Instrument", *EUI Department of Law Research Paper No. 2014/09*, July, Florence: European University Institute.
Van Zon, H. 2000. *The Political Economy of Independent Ukraine: Captured by the Past.* London: Macmillan.
Wolczuk, K. 2008. "Ukraine and Its Relations with the EU." In *Ukraine: Quo Vadis*, edited by S. Fisher, 87–118. Vol. 108. Paris: Chaillot Papers (EU Institute for Strategic Studies.
Wolczuk, K. 2009. "Implementation without Coordination: the Impact of the EU Conditionality on Ukraine under the European Neighbourhood Policy." *Europe-Asia Studies* 61 (1): 187–211. doi:10.1080/09668130802630839.
Wolczuk, K. 2016. "Ukraine and Europe: Re-Shuffling the Boundaries of Order." *Thesis Eleven* 136 (1): 54–73. doi:10.1177/0725513616667666.
Wolczuk, K. 2018. "The Development of an Institutional Framework for the Implementation of the Association Agreements in Georgia, Moldova and Ukraine: a Comparative Perspective." *Study*, Brussels: European Parliament.
Wolczuk, K., and D. Žeruolis 2018. "Rebuilding Ukraine: an Assessment of EU Assistance."*Research Paper*, London: Chatham House.
Wolczuk, K., L. Delcour, R. Dragneva, K. Maniokas, and D.Žeruolis. 2017. "The Association Agreements as a Dynamic Framework: between Modernization and Integration." *EU-STRAT Working Paper* Series, Berlin.
Žeruolis, D. 2018. "Association Agreement between the European Union and Ukraine: Improving the Imperfect Framework to Deliver Reforms." *Unpublished Report.*

When Goliath meets Goliath
How Russia and the EU created a vicious circle of instability in Moldova

Ryhor Nizhnikau

The various domestic crises in Moldova raise questions about the role of the European Union (EU) and the Russian Federation (Russia). Are they helping to tackle the deeply rooted problems and promoting the country's development, or are they fostering domestic turmoil in this and other post-soviet countries? Following the launch of the EU's Eastern Partnership (EaP) policy, the post-soviet countries located between Russia and the EU – especially Moldova, Ukraine and Georgia – have once again turned into an arena of geopolitical competition. This development has coincided with an economic downturn and growing political instability in these countries. This is quite the opposite of what the EU's closer cooperation with these countries was intended to achieve. Equally, Russia's support to and promotion of the elites in these countries did little to improve the wellbeing of the societies in its neighbourhood, nor did it increase political stability in Moldova, Ukraine or Georgia.

Yet, it is not merely the geopolitical competition, which explains the growing instability, decreasing prosperity and increasing turmoil, but also the substance of the policies of the two external actors, which arguably pursue similar ends by similar means. Both Russia's and the EU's policies are similar in their goals, strategies and applied mechanisms and are primarily aimed at supporting the loyal (pro-EU or pro-Russia) entrenched elites to help them take and/or stay in power. In both cases, the EU's and Russia's policies help the regime to maintain an uneven playing field to prevent their political opponents from taking power. This article focuses on the case of Moldova and argues that while the external support to the (entrenched) elites brings some political stability (to the regime), in fact the EU and Russia bear some responsibility for reinforcing the negative systemic features of domestic malpractices, with an unaccountable government, state capture, rent seeking and persisting high levels of corruption.

One of the vivid illustrations of the domestic problems and a consequence of the ruling coalition's governance was the theft of $1 billion from the three leading banks in Moldova, which the state had been forced to bail out in 2015 (Higgins, 2015b). The missing money caused a rapid depreciation of the national currency and consequently a decline in living standards for the population. The final straw was a leaked report which made clear that a 28-year-old businessman, Ilan Shor, linked to the ruling coalition, was the main coordinator and beneficiary of what has been later described as a series of transactions which had "no sound economic rationale", having emptied the banks of funds until "they were no longer viable" (Whewell, 2015). Against this background, it is hardly surprising that on 6 September 2015 a new wave of protests started in Chisinau – the "Revolution of Dignity and Truth". Moldovans went out to protest, once again, against widespread corruption in the government. Further protests were organized by the main opposition forces – the Socialist Party and the Our Party – which demanded the dissolution of the Parliament and new elections. The protests continued through the winter and spring 2016 in Chisinau, Belti and Comrat.

The evidence suggests that the government's policies reinforced domestic malaise and increased social injustice. They contributed to growing impoverishment and consequently social unrest, triggering widespread anti-government protests that demanded the elimination of corruption and punishment of the "looters". While these cases point to the domestic sources of trouble, this article argues that the role of external actors is equally important in explaining the current situation in Moldova. To understand recent developments in Moldova and in the post-Soviet space, we need to understand the role played by both the EU and Russia in supporting the leading domestic actors and the political and economic structures and institutions. Like in other post-soviet countries, Moldova's political elites and the political and economic development of the country depend to a large extent on the policies of external actors, in particular the EU and Russia, and the support that they provide to the pro-Russian and pro-European elites. While the success of the current pro-EU coalition depends on technical and material assistance from the EU and other international donors, the Russian government wields also significant political, socio-economic and military leverage. The Moldovan and the Russian political and business elites maintain close links.

The above-described events unfolded after a series of reforms had been actively promoted as part of the EU–Moldova Association Agreement (AA) and the Deep and Comprehensive Free Trade Agreement (DCFTA). Moldova also received a Visa Liberalization Action Plan (VLAP). Despite these reform efforts, Moldova remains a captured state in much the same way as it was before 2009 under the Communist rule: key state institutions remain under the control of oligarchs, which use their access to the government to promote their interests and informally control state institutions (Gamurari & Ghinea, 2014). Dysfunctional political and legal institutions, unaccountable government, weak judiciary and law enforcement continue to persist in Moldova (Gamurari & Ghinea, 2014). Despite the EU's capacity building measures, numerous incentives and socialization efforts by the EU, the Moldovan government failed to build fully functioning democratic institutions – quite similar to the case of Ukraine, while the captured state institutions which capacity was efficiently built were used for more efficient extraction of rents and instruments in political in-infighting for power. Despite the evident malpractices of the Moldovan government (Kyvyrzhyk & Solov'ev, 2016; Transparency International [TI], 2014), the EU, though dissatisfied with the state of affairs (European Council, 2016; Tapiola, 2016) continued to support the regime (European Commission, 2015; European Council, 2016; United Nations Development Programme [UNDP], 2016; UN in Moldova, 2016). The EU's policies thus reinforced the vicious circle.

Russia's policies are similarly designed to support pro-Russian elites and consequently aimed at maintaining the existing system of governance. There is no doubt that Russia is taking the protection of its geopolitical interests in the post-soviet space very seriously. Russia has not only demonstrated determination to apply any force including military in its "near abroad" – the EU's Eastern neighbourhood – but also strongly criticized the further integration with the EU and NATO which it regards as a red line not to be crossed in its zone of "special interest". Moreover, Russian actors learned how to use more subtle instruments to promote their interests and in particular, the incentivizing of local political and economic elites and the promotion of linkages with societal groups, in particular minorities. As the EU supported politically and financially the Alliance for European Integration (AEI) coalition during their rule, Russia became directly involved in Moldovan politics on the eve of and after the Parliamentary elections of 2014 by reorganizing its political support base and helping to build the two large opposition parties (Our Party and Socialist Party), enabling them to efficiently function in the pluralist political system. It also invested in creating a network of grassroots organizations and NGOs.

While it is Russia which is rightly criticized for pursuing destabilizing and assertive policies towards its neighbours, the EU's EaP policies have, as this article argues, generated a similar outcome. The EU sees its current key mission in the stabilization of the region (ENP Review, 2015) and the prevention of the pro-Russian forces from getting in power. To do that, the EU relies on the pro-European ruling elites as the key transmitters of its policies and interests providing them with political and economic incentives. The pro-European elites, in their turn, need the EU and its support to stay in power and maintain control over rents, as the pro-Russian part of the elites need Russia to get into power and get control over rents (Roubanis, 2015). In the following, the policies of the EU and Russia will be scrutinized in terms of their effects on Moldovan state institutions and the development of the country.

Cry havoc: the Eastern Partnership and the EU's policies towards Moldova

Moldova had been regarded as the "key reformer" state in the post-soviet space, and had been deemed to be one of the EU's great success stories (Benedyczak, Litra, & Mrocek, 2015; European Commission, 2011b, 2013a, 2013b; Index, 2013). The pro-European Moldovan government was considered a "star pupil" among the Eastern Partnership countries (New Eastern Europe, 2014; EaP Index, 2014). It was the first to complete the implementation of the Visa Liberalization Action Plan (VLAP) and the first to obtain visa free travel from the EU. It also was among the first to sign the Association Agreement with the EU at the Vilnius Summit. In her Government address to Bundestag on the eve of the Eastern Partnership Summit in Vilnius, Angela Merkel declared that "in spite of some domestic turmoil, the Republic of Moldova has perhaps demonstrated the greatest political will of all the Eastern partners to adopt and implement reforms" (Merkel, 2013). Stefan Füle had commented even earlier on Moldova saying "amazing how much has been achieved" (Litra, 2011, p. 6).

The EU's policies were built on the ambition of Moldova and the EU to enter into intensified political, security, economic and cultural relations. The EU offered clear goals, benchmarks and incentives for compliance. To stimulate reforms, the EU presented a "clear conditions – clear rewards" model (Ghinea, Paul, & Chirila, 2013) also known as the "more for more" principle. The pro-European coalition – the Alliance for European Integration (AEI) – immediately upon coming into power signed a declaration committing Moldova to the path of European integration. The EU offered the coalition more financial support and facilitated global donors' support of $2.6 billion for 2010–2013 already during the first months of the AEI coalition's rule (European Commission, 2011a, p. 44). As a result, the EU politicized its support, becoming directly associated with the AEI coalition and assisting the coalition to win the Parliamentary election in 2014. Moreover, at the high point of the protests in 2015–2016, and the collapse of the pro-European coalition government, it was the US, Romania and the EU, which opposed the snap Parliamentary election (Sholar'; 2016; Tomiuc & Benea, 2016), and supported (though reluctantly) the unlawful Constitutional reform to instate the direct Presidential election to provide more political stability (European Council, 2016). This continuous support led to the politicization of the European integration and the EU in the Moldovan politics.

The negotiations on the Association Agreement were combined with the adoption of a set of special reform priorities identified by the EU for Moldova in May 2010 (the Association Agenda) aimed to strengthen close sectoral cooperation and capacity building measures of the EU (European Commission, 2011b). Besides the official framework, unofficial and official political consultations between EU and Moldovan officials were often held within the EU institutions and various transnational groups (Korosteleva, 2012, p. 109). This framework was similar to the EU's policies towards Ukraine or Georgia (European Commission, 2010, 2012). To help the implementation and to assist the pro-EU elites, the EU primarily focused on building capacities of state institutions by providing direct state building assistance (European Commission, 2011a, 2011b, 2012; Litra, 2011; Siscan, 2012). Moldova became one of the biggest per capita beneficiaries of EU funds with EU assistance amounting to some 5% of GDP, most of which went into institution-building (Ghinea et al., 2013). The key assistance was targeting state institutions through the Comprehensive Institution Building (CIB) programmes, direct budget support, and thematic projects. Out of a 75% increase in funding for 2011–2013, 50% of the additional funds were devoted to CIB and 20% to regional development (Siscan, 2012, p. 44; World Bank, 2010). In line with the VLAP objectives, the government was expected to reform a broad range of institutions – from the civil service and the judiciary to education and health and of course to combat corruption (Index, 2013, p. 86). A total of EUR 1.9 billion (of which EUR 550 million from the EU) was pledged by international donors in support of Moldova only for the period 2010–2013 and added to the EU's targeted support (Siscan, 2012, p. 45–46; World Bank, 2010).

However, the adoption of formal rules by Moldova – as required by the EU – did not translate into real change on the ground. The implementation has been lagging behind in key areas such as the anti-corruption reforms, the judiciary reform, the border management control and the banking sector reform. Moldovan authorities tend to comply with EU recommendations in a minimal manner by establishing the new institutions, but endowing them with insufficient resources. Credible activists were often selected to run the institutions, but granted with unclear responsibilities and new legislation is, as critics argued, made purposefully vague (Gamurari & Ghinea, 2014). Instead of living up to its reputation of "star pupil", Moldova has turned into a problematic EU neighbour, whose systemic failures frequently overshadow the publicized achievements of the government.

The response of the EU to the domestic structural problems has been to reiterate full support to the governing elites in their efforts to implement the European agenda, to strengthen democratic institutions and ensure their integrity and transparency. The so-called "success" reform of the Anti-corruption National Centre (ANC) was hijacked by political interests and the reforms of the functioning of key established institutions have become mismanaged, delayed and politicized (Ghinea et al., 2013). Some important reforms were undermined from the beginning by inadequate funding of newly established institutions and an incompatibility with other domestic legislation. The Penal Code, for example, did not correspond with the tasks of the newly created anti-corruption mechanisms, which were, on top of this, underfunded (Gamurari & Ghinea, 2014). Political interferences have further undermined the anti-corruption reform as implementation deadlines have been frequently considerably delayed (Gurin, 2012, p. 2). As a result, the key institutions, law enforcement and judiciary mostly fell under the control of the power groups and in particular the "shadow cardinal" of Moldovan politics, Vladimir Plahotniuc (Soloviev, 2015).

The EU recognized the multitude of problems. In its communiqués, it showed its concern about the politicization of state institutions, the systemic corruption and lack of independence of the judiciary and law enforcement agencies (European Council, 2016). However, besides temporary freezing of funding, the EU's response to Moldova's numerous political crises and reform problems has not been to fundamentally change its approach. Instead, the EU continued to draw up a new roadmap to the government, helped with the mediation amongst local politicians, provision of conditional assistance to the government and continuous "education" through high-level advisors missions (European Council, 2016). In the EU's view, engaging with the political elites is the best way to reform the country as the opening of its markets and faster growth should promote development, universal values and stability in the neighbourhood (ENP review, 2015).

However, the reaction by Moldova's government to the EU "harshest ever reaction" and to the new roadmap indicates that the need for change was not really felt by the local elites. The statement by the prime minister of Moldova that the EU's recommendations showed that "the direction of the reforms, chosen by Moldova, is right" (Sholar', 2016) makes clear that local elites felt comfortable with the status quo. Indeed, the Moldovan government continued to imitate reforms and ignored at the same time the EU's concrete requirements (European Commission, 2015). The Filip government rejected the de-monopolization of the media law and appointed the crony of Vladimir Plahotniuc as the head of the Supreme Court Chamber without the required open competition (Shupak, 2016a, 2016b). The reform of the public procurement and the prosecution system uncovered the existence of improper influence on the prosecution office (UN in Moldova, 2016). In this regard, the problems of Moldova are not the product of a poor legislation as such, but also the outcome of a culture of tolerance towards corrupt practices (UNDP, 2016). Independent assessments concluded that the problem of corruption should be addressed by more assistance, such as additional "training of representatives of central and local public authorities with a view to a better management of the risks of corruption in public procurement" (UN in Moldova, 2016).

In its review of the EaP (as part of the European Neighbourhood Policy) the EU highlighted the continuing problems with "poverty, inequality, a perceived sense of injustice, corruption, weak economic and social development and lack of opportunity, particularly for young people […as…] roots of instability, increasing vulnerability to radicalization" (ENP review, 2015, p. 3–4). Yet, while recognizing the ineffectiveness of the EU's policies to date, the EU pledged its support to the same solutions that had failure to deliver success. It emphasized the further and deeper involvement of domestic elites in the target countries to "increase opportunities for political dialogue at ministerial level with these partners" and "to jointly set new partnership priorities, which would focus each relationship more clearly on commonly identified shared interests to maximize the benefits for both parties" (ENP review, 2015, p. 4).

In light of the scandals involving the pro-EU political forces, this politicization and direct involvement of the EU in domestic politics backfired. Given the open competition between the EU and Russian integration projects in Moldova, the popularity of the EU significantly dropped. Some 50% of Moldovans were in favour of joining the Eurasian Economic Union in April 2015 (the last official poll in 2015). Only 32% were still in favour of joining the EU, according to the Institute for Public Policy, a local think-tank (Higgins, 2015a). A significant change took place between January 2014 as the scores were 44–40% in the EU's favour (Central European Policy Institute [CEPI], 2014) and November 2014 as the tables were turned, with 43–39% in favour of Moldova joining the Customs Union (Nezavisimyi Informacionnyi Portal [NOI], 2014). In 2009, more than 70% of Moldovans supported the EU integration of Moldova. The poll in February 2016 showed that Our Party and the Socialist Party would receive 32 and 21%, respectively (Moldovanews, 2016).

Unleashing the dogs of war: Russia's policies in Moldova since 2014

In contrast to the EU, Russia had shown little interest and invested little time and effort in Moldova until autumn 2014. Russia had however already been a dominant player in local politics, and exerted its influence through other soft and hard means: for example, the majority of Moldovans watch Russian television channels and Moscow retains a military base in Transdnistria. Russia has built active ties and a support base in Gagauzia, which is the pro-Russian autonomous region in Moldova, populated by Gagauz people and it uses economic incentives and pressures on the Moldovan government. Importantly Russia also created a set of pro-Russian social groups and has actively supported the development of a network of grassroots and proxy organizations including the Orthodox Church (for example, see Lutsevych, 2016). In 2014, as the parliamentary elections in Moldova coincided with the stalemate in the Donbas, the Russian government rediscovered its interest in Moldova. The evidence suggests that the primary aim was to use the momentum to improve its positions in Moldova.

To bring pro-Russian forces back into power and to prevent Moldova's further integration with the EU, the Russian government has employed a diverse set of economic, social and political instruments to promote its political goals in Moldova. Russia became directly involved in Moldovan politics politicizing its support on the eve of the 2014 Parliamentary elections where it promoted the development of new and loyal pro-Russian political forces: Igor Dodon's Socialist Party (PSM) and Renato Usatii's Our Party. The Socialist Party campaigned under the slogan "Together with Russia" and was openly endorsed by Russian President Putin in early November 2014. It was the Socialist Party who negotiated the trade agreements with the Russian government. With Russia's support, PSM received 20.51% of votes in the parliamentary election (Central Electoral Committee [CEC], 2014). This was a striking achievement in comparison to the 4–6% it had obtained in the first half of the year and especially compared to 2011, when PSM won only 0.09% of votes in local councils (E-democracy.md, 2011).

In addition, Russia promoted "Renato Usatii", a charismatic politician at the head of the pro-Russian Our Party. Parallels can be drawn between this "project" and the "green men", given Usatii's Russian connections and Russia's involvement in the creation of the combat wings of pro-Russian forces such as Antifa-Rezist or Russkij Legion, connected to a senior member of Usatii's Party, and Dmitry Rogozin. Renato Usatii has numerous connections to Russia's ruling elites – in particular Russian Deputy Prime Minister Dmitri Rogozin, security services and the previous Russian Railways (RW) chairman Vladimir Yakunin. As soon as Usatii had gained control over the Russian company VPT-NN, it was granted a lucrative $30 million-a-year contact and was made the sole supplier to RW of specialist cutting equipment. Before the 2014 election, with the backing of Moscow's power circles, businessman Usatii stormed into Moldovan politics to become a crucial player.

In terms of economic measures, Russia has used trade carrots and sticks to put extra pressure on the government and to help increase the popular support for pro-Russian forces in Moldova. To do so, Moscow has intensified its economic pressure on Moldova, using both positive and negative conditionality such as opening/banning access to its own market for Moldovan goods or offering to extend or refusing to renew gas contracts and imposing or lifting embargoes for certain groups (Calus, 2014). The import ban caused major protests in Moldova by local farmers during 2014 and 2015 as a result of which many demanded to scrap the free-trade deal with the EU, while others argued that Moldova and the EU must reach a mutually acceptable agreement on export prices with Russia. These import bans were accompanied by new restrictions prohibiting Moldovan workers in Russia from sending home remittances. From 2014, Russia tightened the residency rules for Moldovans arriving in Russia without a work permit. The new rules allow Moldovan migrant workers to stay and work in Russian no more than 90 days during a six-month period (Chawrylo, 2014). In 2015 a mandatory work permit system for all foreign workers from Moldova was introduced, which creates considerable costs for applicants. It obliges all Moldovans wishing to receive a work permit to register upon arrival within 30 days with the Russian Migration Service and to pass a test examining their knowledge of Russian history, legislation and language for a fee (Moldova.ms, 2015).

Russia also got the Moldovan banking sector under its control. Russia is Moldova's largest foreign investor, in 2012 accounting for 23% of all foreign investment in that country (786 million US dollars). The second largest investor is also Russia through Cyprus registered companies (553 million US dollars in 2012) (Calus, 2014). Russian companies control key parts of the Moldovan banking sector that they use for money laundering. (Anti-corruptie.md, 2015a, 2015b). According to Moldovan law enforcement bodies and the investigative journalist organization, the Organized Crime and Corruption Reporting Project (OCCRP), the largest bank, Moldindconbank was involved in activities which enabled at least 18 billion US dollars to be laundered between 2010 and 2014 (OCCRP, 2014; Radu, Munteanu, & Ostanin, 2015).

Equally, Russia remains the exclusive supplier of gas and electricity in Moldova and it controls Moldovagaz, responsible for gas purchases and distribution. Chisinău has, at present, no viable alternatives of gas supplies. Its imports from Romania amount to only 5% of Moldova's demand and any diversification efforts are blocked by Moldovagaz. Since 2011, no new contract with Gazprom on gas supplies has been concluded as the signing of a new agreement was made conditional on Moldova's abstention from the implementation of the EU's Third Energy Package and the withdrawal from the Energy Community (Calus, 2013). "We believe that Moldova must first denounce the protocol on its entry in the EU Energy Charter Treaty", Russian Minister of Energy Novak said in 2012 (EUBusiness, 2012). Upon compliance with its demands, Russia would negotiate and sign a new long-term gas contract with Moldova, which would include a price discount (of allegedly up to 30%) and resolve the issue of the Transnistrian gas bill worth over $4 billion (Popescu & Litra, 2012). Most importantly, without the contract Russia can cut its supplies to Moldova at any moment and force the government to pay back the gas debts owed.

Russia's political and economic influence is reinforced by the Russian media which is used as a tool to increase Russia's influence abroad. Many in Moldova and external observers see propaganda as a weapon in Russia's hands (Allmoldova, 2016; Media-azi, 2015). With a growing discontent over their own government's ability to manage the reform process, many Moldovans are open to the Kremlin's messages that are disseminated in the country by Russian media. Russia's First Channel (Perviy Kanal) and Rossiia 24 are available to all with its open access broadcasting. In addition, rebroadcasts from other Russian TV channels account for about half of the programming on Moldovan cable networks – twice as much as on neighbouring Romania's cable channels. This is important to consider, because in Russian media, European integration is often presented as one of the factors behind the economic hardship that Moldovans experience (Rossiia 24, 2014, 2015a, 2015b) and it is portrayed as a plot aimed at reuniting Moldova with Romania (Tkach, 2014; Vzgliad, 2016). The typical message is that conditions will improve for Moldovans only after they "come to their senses" and return to Russia's "embrace". It often re-translates messages from Russian representatives such as Konstantin Kosachev, chair of the Russian Federation Council's Foreign Affairs Committee, telling Moldovans "to put their interests first, which do *not* contradict Russia's interests, despite what some people want to make Moldova's citizens believe" (Eurasianet, 2015). What is more, Russian TV channels are rebroadcasted in Moldova by the companies under the control of Vlad Plahotniuc, the key force behind the governing coalition (Gogu, 2016).

Finally, Russia has invested in building a grassroots support base including the Church, but also movements such as youth organizations and NGOs (Lutsevich, 2016). Even a few pro-Russian organizations are active, such as the "Russkii Legion" or the "Budjak republic" project in Gagauzia (Calcea, 2015). The leader of the League of Russian Youth, Igor Tuleancev is a close associate of the vice Prime Minister of Russia Dmitrii Rogozin (Solov'ev & Surnacheva, 2014) and has close ties with the Russia's "Motherland" Party, which Rogozin created, and its current head, Russia's State Duma deputy Alexey Zhuravlev. Other organizations linked to Russia and Tuleancev include "Assembly of Peoples of Moldova", "Russian Community of Moldova", the foundation "Commonwealth" and the "Motherland – the Eurasian Union" (Ligarus, 2013, 2015).

In addition, there are training programs for Moldovan young volunteers under the aegis of the Russia-based organization the Soyuz – Nasledniki Pobedi and in a number of youth movements in Moldova, such as "Moldova without Nazism", "Russian history and patriotic club", "Patriots of Moldova", which are encouraged to coordinate their efforts. The latter is a gathering of young Russian patriots willing to take part in military exercises to learn how to defend their territory from external threats including "Romanian fascists", which are supposedly financed through the local branch of the Russian state agency Rossotrudnichestvo, the Russian Centre of Science and Culture and the Russian Embassy in Moldova (Bucataru, 2015, p. 128; Lutsevich, 2016). They also support organizations such as the "People's Front for Moldova", the "Eurasian People's Front" and the "Union of Veterans of Moldova". Many of these organizations are connected to pro-Russian (ex-) Communist Party members or above-mentioned Dmitri Rogozin's allies such as Fedor Gagauz and his United Gagauzia movement.

The role of the Orthodox Church is important given that some 80% of Moldovans trust it as their religious institution (Pravoslavie.ru, 2015). The Moldovan Orthodox Church has very close ties with Russia through the Russian Orthodox Church, to which it is canonically subordinate, and is also dependent on Russia's financial support.

The Russian Embassy in Moldova actively supports the Church's eparchies, such as in Balti. What is more, Gazprombank has even made large donations to help finance local parishes (Azi.md, 2011).

Finally, Russia intensified its support to the Gagauz region after creating a powerful support base for its policies in the autonomous region. The trade embargo on Moldova facilitated the development of parallel ties with Gagauzia, which announced that the region wants to establish "individual ties" with Russia. Gagauzia first received an exemption from the Russian embargo on Moldovan wines and later some exemption from the Russian fruit embargo. Russia provides political and material supports to Gagauzia and controls effectively the key political players in the region. In February 2014, local authorities initiated a referendum in which the Gagauz people voted for the integration of their region into the Eurasian Economic Union. Neither the EU, nor Chisinau were able to convince the local government not to hold the referendum. The speaker of the Popular Assembly (local legislature) of Gagauzia confirmed: "the population wants to be with Russia and to enter the Customs Union". After the referendum, in March 2014, the embargo on alcoholic beverages and agriculture that had been imposed against Moldova was lifted by Russia to benefit just the producers from this autonomous region.

Shortly before the parliamentary elections held on 30 November 2014, Vladimir Putin received the leader of the Socialist Party in Moldova, Igor Dodon, and made sure that he would represent in Chisinau the interests of the Gagauz people. Later, on 30 March 2015, Irina Vlah, singled out by Moscow and strongly favoured from the outset of the selection process (Socor, 2015), was elected the head of Gagauzia. All candidates ran with a pro-Russian program but Vlah's advantage was her direct support by Moscow, being close to Russia's long-time ally Mark Tkachuk and being supported by Igor Dodon (Socor, 2015).

Russia's post-election strategy

Although Russia achieved a lot on the eve of the election, the pro-Russian political forces lost in Moldova due to the unlawful disqualification of the Renato Usatii's party at the last moment, which had been one of the frontrunners in the election. On 29 November 2014, Moldova's supreme court confirmed a ruling that Patria, a party then led by Renato Usatii, should be barred from the election due to alleged financing from abroad, presumably from Russia (Economist, 2014). However, Russia did not stop its attempts to achieve a regime change in Moldova and continued to use its leverage and connections to bring Dodon and Usatii into power. In this regard, after the protests erupted, a three-stage plan was pursued.

First step: to facilitate the breakdown of the pro-European coalition

The arrest of ex-Prime Minister Vlad Filat (Liberal Democratic Party) was the initiative Truth and Dignity, "DA" of the coalition partner Vlad Plahotniuc (Democratic Party), supported by Vladimir Voronin (Communist Party) and Igor Dodon (PSM), who – in turn – seized the opportunity to destabilize the coalition. The same informal alliance of Democrats, Communists and Socialists also brought down the government of Filat's successor, Vladimir Strelets, in late October 2015. Outside the Parliament, Renato Usatii was accused of having launched an attack on Filat and his allies. At the same time, the popular protests originally led by the civic platform "DA" were also reinforced by the Socialists and the Our Party, which later replaced "DA" as the leading protest force in Chisinau. Their key demand was the resignation of the government and the President to hold new Parliamentary election and, in the longer term, to denounce the EU-Moldova Association Agreement.

Second step: to propose a peaceful change through constitutional reforms

The pro-Russian forces tried to dissolve the Parliament and change the Constitution to elect the President of Moldova directly by popular vote. The governing coalition was primarily aiming to prevent the dissolution of the Parliament, as that would lead to the loss of power. The Socialist Party demanded to change the political system by establishing the direct Presidential elections (78th article of the Constitution). This was later supported by Vladimir Filat's party, which had been expelled from the ruling coalition by its pro-European rival, Vlad Plahotniuc, (Filat was sub-sequently arrested having been charged with the theft of one billion from the banks) and the Dignity and Truth movement. PSM initiated the hearing in the Constitutional Court on the article of the Constitution that specifies the procedure to dissolve the Parliament. While it was not in Plahotniuc's interest, he pushed for an alternative referendum proposal to prevent or delay the review of the PSM proposal and prevent the dissolution of the Parliament.

Third step: to build and present a credible alternative leader

The Russian government tried not only to support pro-Russian parties, but also to create a charismatic political leader in Moldova, who could unite the majority of voters on a pragmatic basis. Renato Usatii and Igor Dodon have tried to boost their visibility and popularity in Moldova: they have, for instance, used populist mottos ("expropriate and re-distribute"), they have blocked public roads and participated in official meetings (on behalf of the Moldovan government) with Russian authorities, in which they have negotiated concessions regarding the bilateral Russian–Moldovan trade issues and the removal of Russian sanctions (Rospotrebnadzor [RSVPS], 2015).

In the chaotic political situation and due to a profound lack of trust in its political partners in Moldova, the Russian power circles have been interested in installing a strong and popular pro-Russian president in Moldova that could promote Russia's interests in the country and make anti-Russian policies of future governments impossible. The creation and promotion of such a leader would allow Russia to have a power player with whom to make deals on a wide range of issues. It would also avoid symbolic anti-Russian actions. Usatii was considered to be sufficiently connected and dependent on Russia. Dodon meanwhile provided guarantees of his loyalty by following Moscow's orders and including a number of pro-Russian politicians in his party list (Socor, 2014). As a result, on 29 November 2015, the delegation of both United Russia and Just Russia participated in the PSM Party Congress and thereby institutionalized further the cooperation with the PSM.

A vicious circle

It is clear that the domestic turmoil in Moldova (or Ukraine, or Georgia) is the consequence of the dysfunctional political and legal institutions in the country, state capture by "politically engaged" oligarchs, which use their access to the government to promote their economic interests and seek to increase and consolidate their political power and consequently the pervasive corruption. But it is equally clear that the EU's and Russia's influence has done little to overcome the legacy of the past.

In this regard, returning to the case that triggered the protests in Moldova – the theft of $1 bn from the three largest banks, according to the General Prosecutor Corneliu Gurin it extends back as far as 2007, putting into question almost the whole political elite of Moldova, including five former prime ministers (Whewell, 2015). This illustrates how the entrenched interests and state capture prevail despite the external efforts and even a regime change in 2009. For Corneliu Gurin the main question is "why Banca de Economii was defrauded when it was owned by the state, and why that continued after it came under private control" (Whewell, 2015). Vasile Sarco of Moldova's Office for the Prevention of Money Laundering points not only at the disappearance of the $1bn from the three banks, but also at an earlier $20bn operation which used Moldova to launder dirty money from Russia through Moldova into the EU (OCCRP, 2014; Whewell, 2015).

The prevalence of the entrenched interests predetermines the persistence of the inefficient state system. The established incentive structures and constraints of existing institutions reinforce the prevalence of the entrenched interests, corruption, and competition between the groups in power, which leads to government instability, low state capacity and more corruption. Entrenched interests, supported by the bureaucracy, control the economy and state agencies and are interested in maintaining their dominant positions. As Acemoglu, Ticchi, and Vindigni (2011) show, to maintain this system, elites distribute rents to the bureaucracy and engage in lobbying: they buy votes, use force or co-opt social groups of the population. In the captured state, the coalition between bureaucracy and political elites is natural, as the bureaucrats will support the entrenched elites, because the latter need the former to maintain its political power, while the bureaucracy equally prefers the status quo to keep its power and rents, which it receives from political elites in exchange for support (Acemoglu et al., 2011).

Both Russia and the EU focus in their policies on the support of the elites. The key difference between the political elites in Moldova is the source of external support. While Russia was associated directly with Dodon and Usatii, the EU was associated with the members of the AEI coalition. The key players in both the pro-EU (such as Plahotniuc and Lupu) and pro-Russian political forces (Dodon, Vlah and Usatii) came out of the Voronin entourage and do not differ on the main issues that dominate domestic politics in Moldova. In this regard, Russia's policies and the EU's policies assist the entrenched elites to keep the existing system in place and thus defend the status quo. The outcome of these policies is less stability, both in the medium and longer term. The reason is in particular that external support of inefficient state structures enables the entrenched elites to use state capture and existing patronage networks to create and maintain their constituency by distributing rents. At the same time, the fear of instability, mistrust and geo-political games between the EU and Russia guarantee the survival of the malfunctioning system, which continues to impoverish people and creates a favourable environment for corruption. This eventually creates incentives for the people to take to the streets and protest against the ruling elites. However, even if protests succeed, the new regime, which is supported by similar policies and strategies from the (other) external actor, will resist reform efforts and defend the existing system. The main losers here are the people of Moldova who get poorer, and who stand and freeze in the streets fighting in yet another Colour Revolution for a better future, just to realize that nothing changes, despite all their efforts.

The EU, which seeks prosperity and stability on its borders, has good reasons to try to address the dismal outcomes of its policies and to reassess its experience of inducing change in captured post-soviet democracies such as Moldova, Ukraine and Georgia. Yet, the EU incentive-based approach ("more-for-more") aimed at incentivizing elites and building their capacities is still considered to be a successful mechanism in supporting reforms – as long as the incentives and the conditions are right. The EU policies were designed to promote the implementation of the EU reform agenda by giving the necessary resources to the pro-European government. While this strategy has a huge deficiency in promoting institutional monocropping instead of identifying the real needs of the target state (see for example Evans, 2004; Rodrik, 1999), the second problem was the reliance on domestic elites, which benefit from the extraction of the state resources for personal benefits. In this regard, the problems identified by the EU have persisted partly because of the EU's own strategies for how to reform Moldova, which are beneficial to the entrenched gatekeepers, rather than empowering pro-change societal forces that can help promote the implementation of necessary structural reforms. Instead, the EU-driven efforts to implement substantial institutional changes were (ab)used to take control over state institutions and to reallocate rents between the entrenched elites. The EU's approach will not be able to comprehensively address the sources of instability and instead reinforce the domestic problems unless its strategy changes. The key obstacle, which is the state capture and inability to dismantle the old system of governance in Moldova, will continue to persist partially due to the policies of the support of the entrenched rent seeking elites by both the EU and Russia, and thereby prevent long-term stability.

References

Acemoglu, D., Ticchi, D., & Vindigni, A. (2011). Emergence and persistence of inefficient states. *Journal of European Economic Association*, *9*(2), 177–208. DOI:10.1111/j.1542-4774.2010.01008.x

Allmoldova. (2016). Posol USA. Rossijskaia Propaganda opasna dlia Moldovy. Retrieved from http://www.allmoldova.com/ru/news/posol-ssha-rossijskaya-propaganda-opasna-dlya-moldovy

Anti-corruptie.md. (2015a). 18 bln USD laundered through the judiciary in Moldova since 2010 (I). Retrieved from http://anticoruptie.md/en/investigations/justice/18-bln-usd-laundered-through-the-judiciary-in-moldova-since-2010-i

Anti-corruptie.md. (2015b). 18 bln USD laundered through the judiciary in Moldova since 2010 (II). Retrieved from http://anticoruptie.md/en/investigations/justice/18-bln-usd-laundered-through-the-judiciary-in-moldova-since-2010-ii

Azi.md. (2011). Russian Gazprombank sacrifices over us$5 million for Moldovan Orthodox Church. *Infotag*. Retrieved from http://www.azi.md/en/print-story/19403

Benedyczak, J., Litra, L., & Mrocek, K. (2015). Moldova's success story. Stefan Batory Foundation. Retrieved from http://www.batory.org.pl/upload/files/Programy%20operacyjne/Otwarta%20Europa/Moldova%20success%20story%20-%20policy%20paper%20-%20SBF%20IWP.pdf

Bucataru, V. (2015). Moldova still at the crossroads: Is the European part irreversible? In T. Rostoks and A. Spruds (Eds.), *The different faces of "soft power": The Baltic States and Eastern Neighborhood between Russia and the EU*. LIIA. Retrieved from http://liia.lv/site/docs/LIIA_soft_power_book_web_layout.pdf, pp. 141–161.

Calcea, N. (2015). Russia behind the "Budjak Republic" Separatist Projects in Moldova and Ukraine. *Moldova.org*. Retrieved from http://www.moldova.org/en/russia-behind-budjak-republic-separatist-project-moldova-ukraine/

Calus, K. (2013). The Iasi-Ungheni pipeline: a means of achieving energy independence from Russia? Moldova's attempts at gas supply diversification. *OSW Commentary*. Retrieved from http://www.osw.waw.pl/en/publikacje/osw-commentary/2013-10-11/iasi-ungheni-pipeline-a-means-achieving-energy-independence

Calus, K. (2014). Russian sanctions against Moldova. Minor effects, major potential. *OSW Commentary*. Retrieved from http://www.osw.waw.pl/en/publikacje/osw-commentary/2014-11-06/russian-sanctions-against-moldova-minor-effects-major-potential

Central Electoral Committee [CEC]. (2014). Alegerile parlamentare 30 noiembrie 2014. Retrieved from http://www.cec.md/r/r/

Central European Policy Institute [CEPI]. (2014). CEPI presents a public opinion poll in Chisinau. Retrieved from http://www.cepolicy.org/news/cepi-presents-public-opinion-poll-chisinau

Chawrylo, K. (2014). Russia tightens up residence regulations for CIS citizens. *OSW*. Retrieved from http://www.osw.waw.pl/en/publikacje/analyses/2014-01-15/russia-tightens-residence-regulations-cis-citizens

EaP Index. (2014). European Integration Index 2014 for Eastern Partnership Countries. Retrieved from http://www.eap-index.eu/sites/default/files/EaP%20Index%202014.pdf

Economist. (2014). Moldovans choose Europe, barely. *Economist*. Retrieved from http://www.economist.com/news/europe/21635339-moldovans-choose-europe-barely

E-democracy.md. (2011). Local elections of June 5 and 19, 2011. Retrieved from http://www.e-democracy.md/en/elections/local/2011/

ENP review. (2015). Joint communication review of the European Neighbourhood Policy. *European Commission*. Retrieved from http://eeas.europa.eu/enp/documents/2015/151118_joint-communication_review-of-the-enp_en.pdf

EUBusiness. (2012). Russia sets Moldova gas ultimatum amid EU price row. *EU Business*. Retrieved from http://www.eubusiness.com/news-eu/russia-moldova-gas.ic0

Eurasianet. (2015). Moldova: Examining the Russian media factor in protests. Retrieved from http://www.eurasianet.org/node/75046

European Commission. (2010). EU-Ukraine Association Agenda. *EEAS*. Retrieved from http://eeas.europa.eu/ukraine/docs/2010_eu_ukraine_association_agenda_en.pdf

European Commission. (2011a). *Implementation of the European Neighbourhood Policy in 2010: Sector Progress Report* (Joint Staff Working Paper, SEC 645). Retrieved from http://www.mfa.gov.md/img/docs/progress-report-ENP-sectoral-cooperation-2010.pdf

European Commission. (2011b). *Visa Liberalization Action Plan*. Retrieved from http://www.enpi-info.eu/library/content/action-plan-visa-liberalisation-moldova

European Commission. (2012). Annual action programme for Georgia. *European Commission*. Retrieved from https://ec.europa.eu/europeaid/sites/devco/files/aap-financing-georgia-af-20120827_en.pdf

European Commission. (2013a). *Fifth Report on the implementation by the Republic of Moldova of the Action Plan on Visa Liberalisation*. European Commission. http://ec.europa.eu/dgs/home-affairs/what-is-new/news/news/docs/20131115_5th_progress_report_on_the_implementation_by_moldova_of_the_apvl_en.pdf

European Commission. (2013b). Implementation of the European Neighbourhood Policy in Republic of Moldova Progress in 2012 and recommendations for action. Retrieved from http://eeas.europa.eu/enp/pdf/docs/2013_enp_pack/2013_progress_report_moldova_en.pdf

European Commission. (2015). Implementation of the European Neighbourhood Policy in Moldova: Progress in 2014 and recommendations for actions. Retrieved from http://eeas.europa.eu/enp/pdf/2015/repulic-of-moldova-enp-report-2015_en.pdf

European Council. (2016). Council conclusions on the Republic of Moldova. Retrieved from http://www.consilium.europa.eu/en/press/press-releases/2016/02/15-fac-moldova-conclusions/

Evans, P. (2004). Development as institutional change: The pitfalls of monocropping and the potentials of deliberation. *Studies in Comparative International Development, 38*(4), 30–52.

Gamurari, L., & Ghinea, C. (2014). It has only just begun: EU and anticorruption institutions in Moldova. Retrieved from http://www.epc.eu/documents/uploads/pub_4683_eu_and_anticorruption_institutions_in_moldova.pdf

Ghinea, C., Paul, A., & Chirila, V. (2013). Helping Moldova stay on the EU course: Proposals for a real 'more for more' approach. Retrieved from http://www.epc.eu/documents/uploads/pub_4006_helping_moldova_stay_on_the_eu_course.pdf

Gogu, N. (2016). Who really rules the airwaves in Moldova? https://www.opendemocracy.net/od-russia/nadine-gogu/who-really-rules-airwaves-in-moldova

Gurin, C. (2012). Anti-corruption reforms in the context of the visa liberalization dialogue with the EU. *DGAP*. Retrieved from https://dgap.org/sites/default/files/event_downloads/Corneliu%20Gurin_Anti-corruption%20reforms-1_0.pdf

Higgins, A. (2015a). Moldova eyes Russia's embrace as flirtation with Europe fades. *New York Times*. Retrieved from http://www.nytimes.com/2015/05/22/world/europe/moldova-eyes-russias-embrace-as-flirtation-with-europe-fades.html?_r=0

Higgins, A. (2015b). Moldova, hunting for missing millions, finds only ash. *New York Times*. Retrieved from http://www.nytimes.com/2015/06/05/world/europe/moldova-bank-theft.html?_r=0

Index. (2013). *European Integration Index 2013 for Eastern Partnership Countries*. International Renaissance Foundation. Retrieved from eap-index.eu/sites/default/files/EaP_Index_2013_0.pdf

Korosteleva, E. (2012). *The European Union and its eastern neighbours: Towards a more ambitious partnership?* London: BASEES/Routledge Series.

Kyvyrzhyk, I., & Solov'ev, V. (2016). Leonid Talmach – NM. *Newsmaker*. Retrieved from http://newsmaker.md/rus/novosti/leonid-talmach-nm-nas-vse-vremya-sravnivayut-s-etimi-tremya-bankami-i-vot-eto-samo-22603

Ligarus. (2013). Dmitrij Rogozin prinial Igora Tuleanceva v Dome Pravitel'stva. *Liga Russkoj Molodezhi*. Retrieved from http://ligarus.org/index.php/acti/3266-rogozin-tuleantsev.html

Ligarus. (2015). O nas. *Liga Russkoj Molodezhi*. Retrieved from http://www.ligarus.org/abus.html

Litra, L. (2011). Visa facilitation baseline study. Policy Association for an Open Society. Retrieved from http://eapmigrationpanel.org/files/research/en/Moldovabaseline_Moldova%202011.pdf

Lutsevych, O. (2016). *Agents of the Russian world: Proxy groups in the contested neighbourhood*. Chatham House. Retrieved from https://www.chathamhouse.org/sites/files/chathamhouse/publications/research/2016-04-14-agents-russian-world-lutsevych.pdf

Media-azi. (2015). Media experts are concerned by Russia's use of information as a hybrid war weapon. Retrieved from http://media-azi.md/en/stiri/media-experts-are-concerned-russias-use-information-hybrid-war-weapon

Merkel, A. (2013). Government statement delivered by Chancellor Angela Merkel on the EU's Eastern Partnership Summit to be held on 28/29 November 2013 in Vilnius. *Deutscher Bundestag*. Retrieved from http://www.bundesregierung.de/ContentArchiv/EN/Archiv17/Regierungsrerkl%C3%A4rung/2013-11-18-merkel-oestl-partnerschaften.html

Moldova.ms. (2015). Pamiatka Grazhdaninu Pribyvshemu v Rossiju. *Congress of Moldovan Diaspors*. Retrieved from http://www.moldova.ms/?l=ru&a=80&i=49

Moldovanews. (2016). Socopros: reiting bol'shinstva partii snizils'a. Retrieved from http://moldovanews.md/24022016/obshhestvo/121270.htm

New Eastern Europe. (2014). Moldova: The star pupil of Europe's East? *New Eastern Europe*, 4 (XIII). Retrieved from http://www.neweasterneurope.eu/component/content/article/1014-issue/1309-4-xiii-2014-moldova-the-star-pupil-of-europe-s-east

Nezavisimyi Informacionnyi Portal [NOI]. (2014). Opros: Moldovane kolebljutsja mezhdu Evropeiskim I Tamozhennym Sojuzom. *NOI*. Retrieved from http://www.noi.md/ru/news_id/51002

Organized Crime and Corruption Reporting Project [OCCRP]. (2014). *The Russian Laundromat*. Retrieved from https://www.reportingproject.net/therussianlaundromat/russian-laundromat.php

Popescu, N., & Litra, L. (2012). Transnistria – a bottom-up solution? *ECFR*. Retrieved from http://www.ecfr.eu/page/-/ECFR63_TRANSNISTRIA_BRIEF_AW.pdf

Pravoslavie.ru. (2015). Zhiteli Moldovy bol'she vsego doveriajut Cerkvi – opros. Retrieved from http://www.pravoslavie.ru/82575.html

Radu, P., Munteanu, D. and I. Ostanin. (2015). Grand theft Moldova. *OCCRP*. Retrieved from https://www.occrp.org/en/investigations/4203-grand-theft-moldova

Rodrik, D. (1999, November 8–9). *Institutions for high-quality growth: what are they and how to acquire them*. Paper presented at IMF conference on Second-Generation Reforms, Washington DC.

Rossiia 24. (2014). Eto zhdet i Ukrainu. Kak zhivet Evropeiskaia Moldova. *Rossiia 24*. Retrieved from https://www.youtube.com/watch?v=VARHVwHRDxc&nohtml5=False

Rossiia 24. (2015a). Dodon: Evropeiskaia integraciia v Moldove provalilas. *Rossiia 24*. Retrieved from https://www.youtube.com/watch?v=bLHA1abOF5o

Rossiia 24. (2015b). Telekanal Rossiia 24 o situacii v Moldove. *Rossiia 24*. Retrieved from https://www.youtube.com/watch?v=A-FtPeOIGeY&nohtml5=False

Roubanis, I. (2015). Brussels sees no evil, hears no evil in Moldova? *New Europe*. Retrieved from https://neurope.eu/article/brussels-sees-no-evil-hears-no-evil-in-moldova/

RSVPS. (2015). Talks between Rosselkhoznadzor and Igor Dodon, Chairman of Socialist Party of Republic of Moldova. Retrieved from https://www.fsvps.ru/fsvps/news/14793.html?_language=en

Sholar', E. (2016). Fevral'skaja Rezoljucija. *Newsmaker*. Retrieved from http://newsmaker.md/rus/novosti/fevralskaya-rezolyutsiya-22539

Shupak, I. (2016a). Bystryj Sovet Magistratury. *Newsmaker*. Retrieved from http://newsmaker.md/rus/novosti/bystryy-sovet-magistratury-kak-proshlo-utverzhdenie-mihaya-poalelunzh-kandidatom-n-22339

Shupak, I. (2016b). Ne prikidyvajtes', chto vy takoj etalon. *Newsmaker*. Retrieved from http://newsmaker.md/rus/novosti/ne-prikidyvaytes-chto-vy-takoy-uzh-bolshoy-etalon-22326

Siscan, Z. (2012). Analysis of the EU – Republic of Moldova relations in the context of the EU 2014–2020 financial perspective. *Project Bridge*. Retrieved from http://www.project-bridge.eu/datoteke/Actions2012/BRIDGE-ANALYSIS%20OF%20THE%20EU-MOLDOVA%20RELATIONS.pdf

Socor, V. (2014). Russia's new Moldovan favorite: Igor Dodon's Socialist Party. *Eurasia Daily Monitor*. Retrieved from http://www.jamestown.org/single/?tx_ttnews%5Bswords%5D=8fd5893941d69d0be3f378576261ae3e&tx_ttnews%5Bany_of_the_words%5D=Dodon&tx_ttnews%5Bpointer%5D=1&tx_ttnews%5Btt_news%5D=43150&tx_ttnews%5BbackPid%5D=7&cHash=785e0fc192a31d011abb6fdd64aecafe#.VxAuYLx5j-Y

Socor, V. (2015). Russia Orchestrates Gagauz election in Moldova, ponders the next steps. *Eurasia Daily Monitor*. Retrieved from http://www.jamestown.org/programs/edm/single/?tx_ttnews%5Btt_news%5D=43724&cHash=b9e211386ad234cc650d69902cae47d5#.VxAO1Lx5j-Y

Soloviev, V. (2015). Igra tenej. *Newsmaker*. Retrieved from http://newsmaker.md/rus/novosti/igra-teney-kuda-i-zachem-ushel-iz-parlamenta-vladimir-plahotnyuk-15985

Soloviev, V., & Surnacheva, E. (2014). Moldovaskie golosa. *Kommersant*. Retrieved from http://www.kommersant.ru/doc/2613728

Tapiola, P. (2016). Moldovan citizens deserve independent judiciary. *IPN*. Retrieved from http://ipn.md/ru/politica/75878

Tkach, S. (2014). Moldova protiv fabriki lzhi: shvatka v noiabre. Retrieved from http://www.newscom.md/rus/moldova-protiv-fabriki-lzhi-shvatka-v-noyabre.html.

Tomiuc, E., & Benea, R. (2016). Moldovan opposition vows to keep up protests. *Radio Free Europe*. Retrieved from http://www.rferl.org/content/moldovan-protesters-keep-up-pressure-for-early-elections/27504121.html

Transparency International [TI]. (2014). The National Integrity System Assessment Moldova 2014. *Transparency Moldova*. Retrieved from http://files.transparency.org/content/download/1331/10309/file/2014_NationalIntegritySystem_Moldova_EN.pdf

UN in Moldova. (2016). UNDP and the Council of Europe have assessed the risks of corruption in public procurement and Prosecutor's Office. United Nations Development Programme. Retrieved from http://md.one.un.org/content/unct/moldova/en/home/presscenter/pressreleases/pnud-_i-consiliul-europei-au-evaluat-riscurile-de-corupie-in-ach.html

United Nations Development Programme [UNDP]. (2016). *Assessment Report of corruption risks in public procurement in the Republic of Moldova*. Retrieved from http://www.raport-de-evaluare-a-riscurilor-de-corupie-in-sistemul-achiziiil.html

Vzgliad. (2016). V Moldove razrabotali plan po ob'edineniiu v Rumyniej k 2018 godu. Retrieved from http://vz.ru/news/2016/3/21/800719.html

World Bank. (2010). Rethink Moldova. Retrieved from http://siteresources.worldbank.org/INTMOLDOVA/Resources/Rethink-Moldova-2010-2013-Final-edit-110310.pdf

Whewell, T. (2015). The great Moldovan bank robbery. *BBC*. Retrieved from http://www.bbc.com/news/magazine-33166383

The Politics of Flexibility
Exploring the Contested Statehood–EU Actorness Nexus in Georgia

Madalina Dobrescu and Tobias Schumacher

Introduction

The EU's ability to display actorness towards states affected by limited sovereignty has been put to the test by the large number of EU candidate and neighbouring countries – such as Serbia, Moldova, Ukraine, Azerbaijan, Libya, Palestine, Syria and others – experiencing some form of contestation to independent statehood. The issue of EU actorness is, in turn, inextricably linked to the EU's potential to project influence externally, thus rendering the contested statehood–EU actorness nexus critically important for any discussion of the EU as an international actor. Despite a core body of scholarly works addressing the link between Europeanisation and conflict resolution in divided territories such as Cyprus, Moldova and Georgia (Bouris and Kyris 2017; Coppieters et al. 2004; Kyris 2016; Tocci 2007), the impact of contested statehood on the EU's potential for effective international action remains sparsely explored. The few contributions that engage with the topic have generally identified contested statehood as a condition which limits EU actorness, either because of the poor governance structures of contested states and the increased political costs incurred by domestic elites as a result of sensitive ethno-national identities (Börzel 2015), or because contested statehood often sharpens intra-EU divisions, constraining EU consistency (Papadimitriou and Petrov 2012), and potentially exposing the tension between the EU's normative and strategic goals (Noutcheva 2009).

This article is embedded in the literature addressing the conditions under which the EU performs effectively as an international actor (Hill 1993; Thomas 2012; Zielonka 1998). Specifically, it aims to enquire into whether contested statehood represents a condition that hinders EU actorness, by zooming in on a country where the EU has had ample opportunities to engage with contested territories. Georgia's sovereignty has been challenged by two de facto states – Abkhazia and South Ossetia – for almost three decades, presenting a complex configuration of challenges to statehood. Tbilisi's official aim of reintegrating the two regions is at odds with the entities' self-determination aspirations and long-term goals of independence (Abkhazia) and integration into Russia (South Ossetia). These mutually exclusive objectives complicate not only the conflict resolution process, but also EU involvement in Georgia more generally.

Prior to 2003 the EU's engagement in Georgia was mainly technical and economic, but the favourable context created by the Rose Revolution led to the EU broadening its range of policy instruments: an EU Special Representative for the South Caucasus was appointed in 2003; Georgia, together with Armenia and Azerbaijan, was included in the European Neighbourhood Policy in 2004; and the EU deployed its first ever rule of law mission in the Common Security Defence Policy framework, EUJUST Themis, to Georgia in July 2004. The 2014 Association Agreement pursues a high level of political association and economic integration between the EU and Georgia, thus going beyond the narrow confines of the Partnership and Cooperation Agreement, which had represented the main framework and legal basis for bilateral co-operation since its entry into force in 1999. As the EU–Georgia relationship grew progressively closer, important questions emerged regarding the extent to which Georgia's complex state-hood challenges have complicated co-operation in a number of areas. How has Tbilisi's lack of full control over its territory affected the EU's ability to offer Georgia visa-and trade-free regimes and pursue the rule transfer embedded in these? What are the implications of Abkhazia and South Ossetia's claims for recognition and Russia's pervasive influence in the two entities for EU conflict management policies? These are the central questions that this article grapples with. In tackling them, it acknowledges that 'contested statehood' is not an objective condition, but only produces effects through the perceptions of actors confronted with it. This analysis of the contested statehood–EU actorness nexus therefore implicitly refers to the EU's conception of contested statehood in Georgia.

In order to explore the impact of contested statehood on EU actorness in Georgia – including Abkhazia and South Ossetia – in a comprehensive and systematic manner, the article focuses on three policy sectors: conflict management, migration and mobility, and trade. The case study selection is justified, first, by their salience when it comes to divergent conceptions of sovereignty, legitimate authority and territoriality. In addition, the three policy sectors operate under distinct EU policy and legal frameworks and, interestingly, adopt in practice different interpretations of the EU's conception of Georgia's contested statehood. This in itself represents a significant finding and raises the secondary question of how these distinct interpretations of the territorial applicability of EU rules shape EU actorness in Georgia.

The EU's approach to contested statehood in Georgia was outlined in the December 2009 Non-Recognition and Engagement Policy, which encapsulates the twin objectives of principled adherence to Georgia's territorial integrity and pragmatic engagement with the two unrecognised entities. The Non-Recognition and Engagement Policy explicitly provides for the practical inclusion of Abkhazia and South Ossetia in EU–Georgia co-operation initiatives in the absence of formal recognition but, in reality, the EU has found it difficult to abide both by the letter and spirit of the Policy. As a qualitatively distinct policy area eschewing many of the regulatory pitfalls that complicate the enforcement of trade or migration-related provisions in unrecognised territories, conflict management comes closest to the inclusionary logic of the Policy. The application of migration- and mobility-related provisions to the two de facto states, on the other hand, is enveloped in ambiguity. Migration and mobility policies are only vaguely addressed by the Association Agreement and are actually regulated by distinct legal instruments such as the Mobility Partnership, the Readmission Agreement and the Visa Liberalisation Action Plan, none of which refers to Georgia's contested statehood. The territorial enforcement of this policy area in Abkhazia and South Ossetia is thus merely implied by default. By contrast, Association Agreement stipulations pertaining to the establishment of a Deep and Comprehensive Free Trade Area represent 'the hard core of the economic content [...] with many legally binding obligations undertaken by both parties' (Emerson and Kovziridze 2016, 4), making trade the most highly regulated policy area in EU–Georgia relations. The issue of Georgia's problematic sovereignty (Krasner 2001) is given due consideration particularly with reference to the application of the Deep and Comprehensive Free Trade Area, which is explicitly excluded from enforcement in Abkhazia and South Ossetia. The EU thus appears to display the entire gamut of practical approaches to contested statehood in Georgia – from explicitly including the unrecognised territories in the application of its policy instruments for the purposes of pragmatic co-operation, to inclusion by default and explicit exclusion. This article argues that the EU has gone to great lengths in adjusting its policy and legal frameworks and their practical implementation to accommodate Georgia's contested statehood. This flexible and to some extent inconsistent approach was meant to enhance its actorness in Georgia, but the irreconcilable interests of the conflict parties, together with the EU's inability to concomitantly pursue the two pillars of its Non-Recognition and Engagement Policy, resulted in a fractured record of actorness.

The article draws on primary and secondary sources in English, including EU and Georgian official documents and media reports, as well as 11 semi-structured interviews with EU and Georgian policy-makers, think tank representatives and journalists. Interviews were conducted in English over the phone, via email and in person in Brussels and Tbilisi between April 2013 and July 2018, and served not only to uncover information that was not accessible through other research techniques, but also to triangulate data from other sources. The article is structured as follows: the next section provides a conceptual elaboration of the notions of contested statehood and EU actorness, followed by three empirical sections exploring the ways in which contested statehood in Georgia, and the EU's distinct approaches to it, has affected EU actorness across the conflict management, migration and mobility, and trade policy sectors, respectively. The article concludes with a comparison of the EU's flexible approach to contested statehood in Georgia across the three policy sectors examined.

Setting the Scene

Contested Statehood

Definitions of contested statehood generally take as a starting point a notion of sovereignty according to which states display a combination of strong central authority and consolidated political territoriality. The weakening of either the authority or control dimensions, or both, results in cases of problematic sovereignty and contested, as opposed to confirmed, statehood (Geldenhuys 2009). The approach taken here is rooted in a conceptual understanding of contested state-hood drawing on Krasner's acknowledgement that 'sovereignty is not an organic whole' (Krasner 2001, 2), but rather a combination of different components, all of which are present to different degrees in entities experiencing statehood-related challenges. According to Krasner, there are four attributes of sovereignty that capture the key conditions characterising situations of contested statehood. First, domestic or internal sovereignty requires the existence of a legitimate and effective authority able to govern the polity and exercise effective control over the territory (Krasner 2001, 7). Limited domestic sovereignty can lead to instances of contested statehood typically involving an internationally recognised state authority unable to maintain effective control over the entirety, or parts, of the territory it claims (Papadimitriou and Petrov 2012, 749). As a country that does not control one fifth of its territory, Georgia's domestic sovereignty can be considered severely constrained. If, up until 2008, Tbilisi still controlled parts of Abkhazia and South Ossetia, as a result of the Russian-Georgian war of August 2008, Georgian forces were pushed out of areas such as Upper Kodori in Abkhazia and several villages along the Georgian-South Ossetian border (Blakkisrud and Kolstø 2012, 283). Conversely, the 'deepening institutionalisation' (Broers 2013, 64) and 'potential for an autonomous politics of contestation' (Broers, Iskandaryan, and Minasyan 2015, 10) in the two entities suggest a consolidation of Sukhumi and Tskhinvali's domestic sovereignty, although the two have not been able to establish autonomous political systems and governance structures (Kolstø and Blakkisrud 2008, 493–494 and 497–498).[1]

Second, external sovereignty implies international legal recognition in the absence of which political entities are merely acknowledged as 'unrecognised', 'partially recognised' (Caspersen and Stansfield 2011, 3) or 'de facto' states (Bachelli, Bartmann, and Srebrnik 2004). Such contested territories are usually de facto governed by authorities that have declared independence without benefitting from formal international recognition by a significant part of the international community (as expressed by full membership of the UN) (Papadimitriou and Petrov 2012, 749). Both South Ossetia and Abkhazia initially declared independence from Tbilisi following the conflicts of 1991–1992 and 1992–1993, respectively, and as of August 2008 the independence of the two breakaway regions has been formally recognised by Russia. Nonetheless, the entities are largely considered to be part of Georgia, with only four other UN members except for Russia – Syria, Venezuela, Nicaragua and Nauru – providing recognition.

A third crucial characteristic in determining cases of problematic sovereignty is the autonomy of domestic governing structures from any authoritative external influence. Referred to as Westphalian sovereignty, it requires states to be not only 'de jure independent, but also de facto autonomous' by freely setting up governing structures, determining their own institutions, and appointing officials (Krasner 2001, 11). This is especially relevant when considering Abkhazia and South Ossetia's extensive economic, military and political dependence on Russia, particularly in the framework of the recently concluded Treaties – of Alliance and Strategic Partnership in Abkhazia's case, and Alliance and Integration in South Ossetia's. While the distinction underlines Abkhazia's long-standing quest for independence, as opposed to South Ossetia's aspiration to be incorporated into the Russian Federation, both Treaties largely invalidate the entities' claim to statehood.

Finally, interdependence sovereignty problematises the ability of states to regulate the movement of goods, people and capital across their borders. While a loss in interdependence sovereignty does not necessarily undermine external recognition, it can in practice lead to a compromise of Westphalian sovereignty, which is why Krasner emphasises the importance of any agreements diluting states' control over transborder movements to be concluded freely between international legal sovereigns (Krasner 2001, 9). Georgia's inability to control South Ossetia and Abkhazia's land borders with Russia, as well as Sukhumi's maritime borders with Russia and Turkey, point to a major deficit in its interdependence sovereignty, compounded by Moscow's intensifying borderisation of the internal Administrative Boundary Lines.

EU Actorness

One of the theoretically most valuable contentions of the literature addressing the EU's role as an international actor is that the EU's potential to act effectively in the international arena is shaped both by the functions fulfilled and the capabilities possessed by the Union itself, on the one hand, and the perceptions held of its role by third parties, on the other. Reflecting this approach, Bretherton and Vogler's social constructivist framework envisages EU actorness as the locus of interaction between three elements: opportunity (the structural environment within which the EU acts), presence (the EU's ability to project external influence and shape understandings, expectations and behaviours of others) and capability (the structural prerequisites of an international actor and the actual performance of actor behaviour; Bretherton and Vogler 2006).

The dialectical relationship between agency and structure means that the EU is both source and recipient of various perceptions of the meaning of *opportunity*: it contributes to such understandings through its participation in social interactions while it must respond simultaneously to third parties' perceptions of its role. Conceived of as the ability to project external influence and shape the understandings, expectations and behaviour of others, *presence* situates itself at the frontier between the inside and the outside by depicting how the EU, by virtue of its existence, exerts influence beyond its borders. Drawing on Sjöstedt's work (Sjöstedt 1977, 16), Bretherton and Vogler propose four *capability*-related requirements for actorness: a shared commitment to a set of common values; domestic legitimation of external policies, actions and priorities; the ability to identify priorities and formulate policies, reflected by the concepts of consistency and coherence; and the availability of, and capacity to utilise, policy instruments such as diplomacy, and economic and military tools (Bretherton and Vogler 2006, 30). This article focuses in particular on the last two elements when discussing EU *capabilities*.

Having unpacked its working concepts, the article proceeds with an analysis of the impact of contested statehood, as conceptualised by the EU, on the Union's actorness in the context of its conflict management, migration and mobility, and trade policies.

Conflict Management

The brief war between Georgia and Russia in 2008 provided the EU with the context to acquire a conflict manager role in the region. Apart from its involvement in achieving a ceasefire, the EU took steps to strengthen its *capabilities* on the ground: it appointed a Special Representative for the crisis in Georgia and deployed an EU Monitoring Mission, whose objectives include monitoring the security situation and implementing the Six Point Agreement, establishing contacts between parties and informing EU policy (Sasse 2009, 103). The 2008 war also saw a more politically salient involvement of the EU as an official co-chair of the Geneva International Discussions, together with the UN and the OSCE.

The profound effect of the August 2008 war on the *opportunity structure* within which the EU has acted in Georgia ever since cannot be overemphasised. Of particular relevance for the constantly evolving relation between contested statehood and EU actorness is the shift in focus from the local dimension of the conflicts, which prioritised the self-determination claims of Abkhazia and South Ossetia vis-à-vis Georgia, to the geo-strategic dimension of the 2008 war, which highlights Russia's territorial aggression (Finchova Grono 2010, 11). This shift was accompanied by an increasing relevance of status-related issues, as Abkhazia and South Ossetia's recognition by Russia modified the incentive structure for all the actors involved, as well as making it impossible to return to the pre-war status quo (Merlingen and Ostrauskaite 2009, 25). As the following analysis shows, these two related developments have shaped the distinctive ways in which contested statehood challenges have affected the EU's ability to project influence in Georgia. At the same time, the EU's conception of legitimate statehood and sovereignty, favouring external sovereignty and non-recognition of entities which do not possess this attribute, has imposed significant limits on its actorness.

As a key aspect of contested statehood, the absence of formal international recognition of the two de facto states has had a wide-ranging impact on the EU's *presence* and *capabilities* in the context of its conflict management activities in Georgia. The EU's approach to Abkhazia and South Ossetia has been characterised by efforts to reconcile its support for Georgia's territorial integrity with a degree of engagement with the two entities, as encapsulated by the Non-Recognition and Engagement Policy's objective 'to create the political and legal space within which the EU could relate to the separatist regions […] without compromising the EU's adherence to Georgia's territorial integrity' (Semneby 2014). But while the EU has been a significant source of financial assistance for Abkhazia, and less so for South Ossetia (Vasilyan 2014, 406), this balancing act has become increasingly difficult to maintain since 2008. Some opportunities that could have provided the EU with an increased footprint in the two entities have never materialised because of status-related obstacles, underscoring the Union's structural inability to effectively make use of available policy instruments when confronted with entities lacking external sovereignty. For instance, an EU office in Sukhumi never opened because of political impediments raised by Georgia and Abkhazia, and the possibility of including civil society representatives from Abkhazia and South Ossetia within the Eastern Partnership Civil Society Forum proved impractical, given that the latter is designed to engage with Eastern Partnership members and not unrecognised entities (Freizer 2017, 169).

Perceptions of the EU – and thus its *presence* – in the two entities have suffered as a result of its firm support for Georgian territorial integrity and the resulting failure to give equal consideration to Georgia, Abkhazia and South Ossetia's interests.[2] By privileging a particular notion of legitimate political authority and territoriality, which implicitly subsumes some attributes of domestic sovereignty to the recognition of international legal sovereignty, the EU has generated negative attitudes in Sukhumi and Tskhinvali, undermining its role as conflict mediator. Brussels is perceived as overwhelmingly biased in Georgia's favour (Fischer 2010, 4) and therefore irrelevant to the entities' goals of achieving formally recognised independence (Abkhazia) and integration with Russia (South Ossetia). The de facto authorities have been sceptical of the EU's policy of engagement without recognition, arguing that 'its declarative and political [nature] to some extent provides covering for the Georgian strategy of so-called occupied territories' (Civil Georgia 2011).

The EU Monitoring Mission's mandate – defined as covering Georgian territory within the country's internationally recognised borders, therefore explicitly including Abkhazia and South Ossetia – confirms the EU's resolute support for Georgia's territorial integrity (Finchova Grono 2010, 17), and the 'broadly successful' (de Waal 2017) pursuit of non-recognition of the two entities. This has antagonised Sukhumi and Tskhinvali, who perceive the Mission's mandate as formulated entirely on Tbilisi's terms and in complete disregard of political realities, given that Georgia has not been able to significantly control these regions for more than a decade (Finchova Grono 2010, 18).

Consequently, both Abkhazia and South Ossetia rejected the possibility of EU monitors accessing the two territories and an early EU Monitoring Mission attempt at entering Abkhazia triggered a vehement reaction by the de facto authorities who complained that the 'unauthorised' entry was 'unacceptable' (Civil Georgia 2008). The politically sensitive issue of 'status' of the two breakaway regions has also spilled over into the functioning of policy instruments which should be essentially technical. Although the Incident Prevention and Response Mechanism created at the EU Monitoring Mission's proposal was meant to be a non-political forum that addresses practical challenges to the security of local populations, the de facto authorities and Russian representatives routinely raise politicised issues such as border demarcation.[3] A poignant example of how the functioning of the Incident Prevention and Response Mechanism has been undermined by the instrumentalisation of (non-)recognition was the declaration of the EU Monitoring Mission Head of Mission as persona non grata in Abkhazia, resulting in the suspension of the Mechanism in Gali between April 2012 and May 2016 (Civil Georgia 2012).

The Geneva International Discussions established in the aftermath of the 2008 war have been undermined from inception by the intractability of the conflict parties' positions on status issues. By bringing to the fore the geostrategic dimension of Georgia's conflicts, the 'unipolar recognition' (Broers 2014, 153) by Moscow of Abkhazia and South Ossetia removed the scope for political negotiations between the two entities and Tbilisi, depriving the EU, US, OSCE and UN – all of which unequivocally support Georgia's territorial integrity – of any leverage. Consequently, the Discussions have not been used as a framework for reaching a negotiated agreement between conflict parties but have rather been instrumentalised by participants in order to achieve their respective, irreconcilable, interests.

Another aspect of contested statehood which invariably affects EU actorness is what Krasner would call the absence of Westphalian sovereignty of the two entities. Both are entirely dependent on Russia for their continued existence as de facto states: Moscow provides Tskhinvali and Sukhumi with recognition, security guarantees and financial support. The two breakaway regions are heavily reliant on Russian aid, with contributions from Moscow constituting approximately two thirds of Sukhumi's state budget (O'Loughlin, Kolossov, and Toal 2014, 449), while South Ossetia is almost entirely financed by its northern neighbour, due to its small size and lack of resources (Blakkisrud and Kolstø 2012, 291). Dependence has been further consolidated through the signing of alliance treaties reinforcing Russia's control over the de facto states' military forces and economies (though to different degrees) (Dolidze 2015), as well as through various measures such as issuing Russian passports, investments in healthcare and culture, Russian real estate purchases, intensification of Russian language-teaching, provision of legal assistance, and restoration of air, rail and road traffic (Nixey 2012, 3). On a broader geopolitical level, Russia represents a considerable limitation to EU actorness, to the extent that any attempt by Brussels to change the status quo would amount to altering the regional balance of power. The largely negative perceptions of the EU in the two de facto states (Kvarchelia 2012, 5–6; Stewart 2011, 77) can also be said to reflect an implicit comparison with Russia's role – whose leadership enjoys higher levels of trust in Abkhazia and South Ossetia than their de facto leaders; and whose military presence is supported by an overwhelming majority of Abkhazian and South Ossetian citizens (O'Loughlin, Kolossov, and Toal 2014, 435–437).

Migration and Mobility

Unlike the EU's conflict management policies vis-à-vis Georgia, the EU's migration and mobility policy avoids taking issue with contested statehood altogether. Neither the relevant political and legal frameworks, nor the corresponding instruments used by the EU refer to Georgia's limited sovereignty and territoriality, thus leaving ample room for interpretation as regards the scope of application of the EU's migration and mobility *acquis*.

The latter has progressively expanded over the last two decades, reflecting the EU's efforts at bringing this policy area under Community competencies. The Amsterdam, Nice and Lisbon Treaties brought about the enhancement of EU *capabilities* with respect to external migration and mobility policy and resulted in strengthened actorness in this field (Boswell and Geddes 2011, 9–10). The acquisition of more competencies and the 2008 war altered the *opportunity structure* considerably. Despite its initial reluctance to sign a readmission agreement with Brussels, the new circumstances in which it found itself persuaded Georgia to cooperate with the EU in the field of migration and mobility. The EU's 2006 visa facilitation agreement with Russia – regarded by the Georgian authorities as a move that would entice Georgian citizens living in the separatist entities to apply for Russian passports – but, more importantly, the conflict with Russia, added a sense of urgency to Tbilisi's attempts at gaining the EU's support (Ademmer and Delcour 2015). Subsequently, Georgia rushed to negotiate Readmission and Visa Facilitation Agreements with the EU in November 2008, concluded a Mobility Partnership in 2009, and embarked on a Visa Liberalisation Dialogue with the EU in June 2012. Together with the Visa Liberalisation Action Plan of February 2013, which served as a basis to grant Georgia visafree travel as of March 2017, these regulate EU–Georgia co-operation in the field of migration, mobility and visa, whereas the Association Agreement in its Article 16 refers back only to the implementation of the Readmission and Visa Facilitation Agreements and the parties' commitment to work towards visa liberalisation.

Unlike all other policy fields that are regulated by the Association Agreement, the EU–Georgia migration, mobility and visa *acquis* does not formally rule out application to the two breakaway regions. How can this distinction be explained? According to EU officials in the European Commission and the European External Action Service, a distinction between visa liberalisation and mobility issues on the one hand and all other policy fields regulated by the Association Agreement on the other had to be made, as the former was considered a tool that could contribute to conflict resolution. Both the Commission and the European External Action Service hoped that a liberalised visa and mobility regime would incentivise citizens in the separatist entities to apply for Georgian passports, thus undermining territorial separation and occupation.[4] This notion, however, is detached from the political realities in the regions, as is demonstrated by the fact that visa liberalisation has not had any impact on conflict resolution and the de facto authorities in the two breakaway regions have never shown any interest in exploring the benefits of visa-free travel.[5]

The de facto inclusion into any EU mobility scheme, let alone visa liberalisation, is perceived by the authorities of the two entities as an attempt to undermine the territorial status quo.[6] This was illustrated by recent statements of the respective de facto foreign ministries, which regard the openended offer of EU visa-free travel as a 'crude attempt of Tbilisi authorities to "entice" citizens of the Republic of Abkhazia in the political and legal sphere of Georgia', [employing] 'all sorts of promises and propaganda tricks' (Civil Georgia 2017). This sentiment is underpinned by the lack of support for reintegration with Georgia in both Abkhazia and South Ossetia (O'Loughlin, Kolossov, and Toal 2014, 448), as well as by highly negative public attitudes.[7] Furthermore, Abkhazians and South Ossetians who hold a Russian passport can already benefit from the 2006 EU–Russia agreement on visa facilitation (Achba 2016), though not without encountering difficulties. According to a statement by the de facto foreign ministry of South Ossetia, 'South Ossetians hold Russian citizenship as well, which enables them to travel the world [but] it is the very Georgian authorities and their western sponsors, who create obstacles on entry to the EU countries' (Civil Georgia 2017). Thus, overall, this state of affairs amounts to very little, if any, scope for the EU to realistically employ its capabilities and 'seek ways to share the benefits and opportunities stemming from the EU-Georgia Visa Liberalisation Dialogue [...] with the populations across the administrative boundary lines', as is declared in the EU–Georgia Association Agenda (European Union 2014, 10).

EU actorness suffered already from negative perceptions, and thus weak presence, in Abkhazia and South Ossetia long before the EU began to expand its migration and mobility repertoire. The EU's Non-Recognition and Engagement Policy was initially welcomed by the de facto authorities in Sukhumi (Kirova 2012, 49), then increasingly eyed with suspicion, and eventually rejected. This happened once it had become obvious that the Policy had tacitly abided by the Law of Georgia on the Occupied Territories[8] and failed to dissociate its practical engagement in the migration, mobility and visa field from status questions. As a result, statements such as the one by Georgia's Minister for Reconciliation and Civic Equality that 'we need visa liberalisation mostly for Abkhazia and South Ossetia, so that these people get more interested in Georgia's welfare',[9] shared by European decision-makers in Brussels, do not correspond to attitudinal realities in either Sukhumi or Tskhinvali. Despite this mismatch of perceptions, Georgia's contested statehood and the incomplete control of its internationally recognised borders did not negatively impact on intra-EU debates regarding the decision to grant Georgia visa liberalisation: the Commission and the Council overlooked Georgia's limited domestic sovereignty and the gradual weakening of interdependence sovereignty in particular, and turned a blind eye to the fact that EU demands with respect to concrete provisions stipulated in the Visa Liberalisation Action Plan are, actually, impossible for Georgian authorities to abide by.[10] This means that Brussels left the issue of enforcement across the whole territory of Georgia entirely in the hands of the two de facto states. For example, as a result of the fact that Tbilisi lacks control over the territories of the separatist entities and 20% of Georgia's external borders, Tbilisi (a) is incapable of implementing fully its Integrated Border Management Strategy and Action Plan (Block 2, Visa Liberalisation Action Plan); (b) cannot prevent and fight organised crime, terrorism and corruption that originate in the two breakaway regions and possibly spill over into Georgia and/or beyond Georgia's internationally recognised borders (Block 3, Visa Liberalisation Action Plan); and (c) is unable to ensure unrestricted freedom of movement within Georgia (Block 4, Visa Liberalisation Action Plan).

In sum, despite severe compliance problems with the Visa Liberalisation Action Plan, the Commission recommended to the Council to move Georgia from Annex I of Regulation 539/2001 to Annex II of the same regulation, thus providing for visa-free travel (European Commission 2015). That these recommendations – after some bickering by Germany, France, Italy and Belgium in June 2016 – were approved of by the Justice and

Home Affairs Council on 5 October 2016 underscores that 'it was a political decision' based on the understanding that consistent and strict monitoring and enforcement of Georgian compliance with all benchmarks of the Visa Liberalisation Action Plan on the part of the EU would, after all, 'have implied demarcating Georgia's borders – something both parties wanted to avoid'.[11]

Trade

In contrast to the migration and mobility domain, the EU's trade policy visà-vis Georgia addresses the issue of contested statehood explicitly through the Association Agreement and its corresponding Deep and Comprehensive Free Trade Area stipulations. The Association Agreement, as its predecessor – the Partnership and Cooperation Agreement – singles out trade as the most salient policy field for bilateral co-operation. This is reflected by the large number of titles, articles and protocols relating to trade, business, and economic co-operation. In spite of this general commonality, however, the Partnership and Cooperation Agreement and the Association Agreement differ with respect to how contested statehood has affected the EU's ability to display *presence* and utilise its fully communitarised trade-related *capabilities* vis-à-vis Georgia and the two breakaway regions.

Under the Partnership and Cooperation Agreement, Georgia first benefited from the Generalised System of Preferences and as of 2005 from the Generalised System of Preferences+ (Kakulia 2014, 148). The Deep and Comprehensive Free Trade Area stipulations (provisionally applied since September 2014 and fully in force since January 2017) regulate bilateral trade and, apart from the gradual creation of a deep and comprehensive free trade area, foresee mainly regulatory approximation with EU laws and standards in fields such as, *inter alia*, competition policy, services, public procurement, energy, sanitary and phytosanitary standards. In other words, unlike the Partnership and Cooperation Agreement, the Association Agreement/Deep and Comprehensive Free Trade Trade Area envisages economic integration of Georgia with the EU based on reforms in trade-related areas originating in the principles of the World Trade Organisation. As far as the link between contested statehood and EU actorness is concerned, the Partnership and Cooperation Agreement does not mention Abkhazia and South Ossetia and neither does it contain any references to Georgia's territorial integrity and, therefore, its limited sovereignty. This stands in sharp contrast to the Association Agreement. Article 429 (2) of the Association Agreement adopts straightforward language by specifying that the

> *application of this agreement, or of Title IV (Trade and Trade-related Matters) thereof, in relation to Georgia's regions of Abkhazia and Tskhinvali region/South Ossetia over which the Government of Georgia does not exercise effective control, shall commence once Georgia ensures the full implementation and enforcement of this Agreement, or of Title IV (Trade and Trade-related Matters), thereof, respectively, on its entire territory.* (Official Journal of the EU 2014)

Whereas the omission of such a clause in the Partnership and Cooperation Agreement is not surprising, given that, according to one Georgian interviewee 'territorial issues then were not as acute as they are today',[12] the inclusion of a territoriality clause that singles out trade explicitly, as embodied by Article 429 (2) of the Association Agreement, reflects the extent to which the 2008 war impacted on Georgia's interdependence sovereignty, the territorial scope of EU–Georgia trade and EU actorness.

In practical terms, the omission of a territoriality clause in the Partnership and Cooperation Agreement and the fact that both Abkhazia and South Ossetia's Administrative Boundary Lines' were still permeable until 2008 meant that there were no physical or legal barriers to limit the territorial scope of trade stipulations. In other words, the Generalised System of Preferences/Generalised System of Preferences+ regimes formally applied also to the two breakaway regions, though EU trade with the latter was conducted through Georgian authorities in Tbilisi. In this regard, trade with Abkhazian hazelnuts – Abkhazia's most important agricultural commodity – serves as a relevant example: they crossed the Administrative Boundary Line freely and were also exported by Georgia to European markets for years, despite Sukhumi's efforts in 2007 to ban this cross-Administrative Boundary Line trade (International Crisis Group 2018, 5). Even though the de facto authorities permitted Abkhaz hazelnut exports in 2015, the entry into force of the implementation of Deep and Comprehensive Free Trade Area rules, however, means that the product can no longer be exported to European markets or used as an ingredient for EU-bound, export-oriented products, as local producers are reluctant to obtain a Georgian certificate of origin, given that this 'would be considered an act of national betrayal' (The Economist 2017).

With the outbreak of the 2008 war, the adoption of the Law of Georgia on Occupied Territories and the ongoing borderisation by Russia of the Administrative Boundary Lines ever since, the *opportunity structure* for EU actorness in the field of trade changed significantly. The Law of Georgia on the Occupied Territories makes it compulsory by law for any foreign company or investor to apply for a special permit from the Georgian authorities and penalises foreign businesses or states that open offices in the two breakaway regions without such a permit. Consequently, European businesses that conducted operations in Abkhazia prior to 2008 rushed to terminate existing contracts once the Law of Georgia on Occupied Territories entered into force. Though the authorities in Sukhumi increasingly attempt to diversify Abkhazia's trade links beyond Russia and increase EU imports, these efforts have been unsuccessful, as demonstrated by the fact that during 2008–2016 not a single permit was requested by (EU-certified) foreign trading companies (Public Defender of Georgia 2017, 29).

The EU tacitly allowing Georgian authorities to determine the extent to which the Generalised System of Preferences+ regime was in practice applied to the two breakaway regions, and in particular the EU's compliance with the Law of Georgia on Occupied Territories, negatively influenced perceptions of the EU as a credible trade partner and thus damaged its *presence*. In conjunction with the fact that the inclusion into the Deep and Comprehensive Free Trade Area would have, from the perspective of the separatist entities, implied surrendering to Georgian terms, these factors explain why, to date, neither Abkhazia nor South Ossetia has indicated any interest in the Deep and Comprehensive Free Trade Area.[13] In the words of a former South Ossetian senior official:

> To be honest, few people are interested in these issues for now; South Ossetian society and the state are now trying to resolve other problems, we have other priorities. Georgia's European and Euro-Atlantic integration has brought us only war, death and pain. (Accent 2016)

With a view to swaying both public sentiment and elite perceptions in the separatist entities, the EU has been supporting Deep and Comprehensive Free Trade Area-related talks with the de facto authorities of the two break-away regions on the margins of the Geneva International Discussions, as well as attempts by the Georgian authorities to provide 'information about the benefits of the Association Agreement/Deep and Comprehensive Free Trade Area to the population living in the occupied territories' (Accent 2016). Also, since 2017 EU officials have quietly held talks with the Abkhaz authorities to explore whether and how Abkhazia could, in part or fully, partake in the Deep and Comprehensive Free Trade Area regime (International Crisis Group 2018, 25). Yet, these efforts demonstrate the extent to which the *opportunity structure* continues to constrain EU actorness in the trade domain: first, the recent exploratory talks were embedded in the Georgian government-led initiative 'A Step to a Better Future: Peace Initiative, Facilitation of Trade Across Dividing Line', announced in early April 2018 (Georgia Today 2018). The resignation of Georgian Prime Minister Kvirikashvili in mid-June 2018 (RFE/RL 2018) – a key supporter of both the initiative and the EU's informal talks with Sukhumi – entails the risk that the Initiative will be discontinued by the new Georgian government, thus limiting the EU's room for manoeuvre for further engagement with Abkhazia.[14] Second, a possible extension of the Deep and Comprehensive Free Trade Area to Abkhazia (or South Ossetia, which, to date, has rejected similar talks), is, from the perspective of Sukhumi, inextricably linked to the issue of trust, as the Abkhaz leadership and entrepreneurs alike fear that it would touch upon status questions and undermine Abkhazia's quest for independence (International Crisis Group 2018, 18). Third, the prospect of letting Sukhumi benefit from the Deep and Comprehensive Free Trade Area is also eyed with suspicion by Tbilisi itself, as such a decision may be interpreted by the former as a sign of indirect recognition. Fourth, unlike Moldova's breakaway region of Transnistria, whose economy is dependent on trade with Moldova and the EU, and therefore had a strong motivation to participate in the Deep and Comprehensive Free Trade Area regime (International Crisis Group 2018, 19), Abkhazia, let alone South Ossetia, does not have similar economic incentives that could outweigh status-related concerns.[15]

Conclusion

This article has enquired into the impact of Georgia's contested statehood, as conceptualised by the EU, on the Union's *presence* and *capabilities*, as well as addressing the extent to which distinct interpretations of the territorial applicability of EU rules shape its actorness in Georgia.

The EU embraces a conception of legitimate statehood and territoriality which favours external sovereignty, and thus international legal recognition, above all other types of sovereignty discussed in this article. In practice though, the EU has approached Georgia's contested statehood through the twin pillars of non-recognition and engagement. The concomitant pursuit of these two objectives has proved challenging, compelling the EU to become creative with respect to the territorial applicability of its different policy fields in Georgia. The examination of the contested statehood–EU actorness nexus across the conflict management, migration and mobility, and trade policy areas, has revealed that the EU adopts a flexible, and to some extent inconsistent, approach to Georgia's contested statehood: conflict management policies explicitly include the unrecognised territories of Abkhazia and South Ossetia; migration and mobility instruments omit any reference to Georgia's contested statehood, implying the default inclusion of the de facto states in visa liberalisation; and trade explicitly excludes them from the implementation of the Deep and Comprehensive Free Trade Area as long as the Georgian government cannot ensure full enforcement in these territories. Although this flexible approach was meant to accommodate Georgia's contested statehood, the irreconcilable interests of the conflict parties, together with the EU's privileging of international legal recognition, resulted in a fractured record of actorness: strong EU actorness towards the 80% of territory controlled by the Georgian government, and low – if any – actorness towards the two unrecognised entities.

In the field of conflict management, despite the EU's principled adherence to engaging Abkhazia and South Ossetia in confidence-building initiatives aimed at addressing the dividing lines of the conflicts, in practice its actorness towards the two de facto states has been severely hampered by its strict pursuit of non-recognition, as well as by Russia's pervasive role in the two entities. Not only have Abkhazia and South Ossetia's lack of external sovereignty prevented the EU from using a wide range of available *capabilities* in the de facto states, but the EU's uncompromising support for Georgia's territorial integrity and, by extension, its dismissal of Sukhumi and Tskhinvali's recognition claims have undermined the EU's *presence* in these regions, where it has come to be perceived as biased in Tbilisi's favour. Moreover, cooperating with the secessionist authorities in conflict management has been aggravated by Abkhazia and South Ossetia's limited Westphalian sovereignty, amounting to an overwhelming economic, military and political dependence on Russia.

As regards migration and mobility, the limitations to Georgia's domestic and interdependence sovereignty, and thus the Georgian authorities' inability to control the country's external borders, did not preclude the EU from formulating and implementing policy action, culminating even in concrete and explicit rule transfer in the framework of visa liberalisation. This suggests that the EU was willing to overlook Tbilisi's inability to fully implement the Visa Liberalisation Action Plan, in order to be able to deploy any actorness at all vis-à-vis Georgia in this policy field.

By contrast, the conditions under which Brussels granted visa liberalisation to Georgia prevented the EU from achieving even the slightest degree of EU actorness towards Abkhazia and South Ossetia. The ambiguity surrounding the territorial application of visa liberalisation, underlined by the absence of any mention of Georgia's contested statehood by any of the relevant policy instruments, suggests that the EU fell back on its default position of implicitly treating the two unrecognised entities as part of Georgia. The result of this default inclusion has been a rejection by Abkhazia and South Ossetia of EU *capabilities*, which effectively require residents of these territories to acquire Georgian passports. While the EU regards this as a potential conflict resolution mechanism, the de facto authorities consider it an attempt to undermine their claim for recognition. The negative perceptions thus generated have severely undermined the EU's *presence* in the two de facto states.

Unlike conflict management and migration and mobility, two policy areas with – explicit or implicit – territorial applicability to Abkhazia and South Ossetia, rule transfer in the field of trade is limited to the territory controlled by the Georgian government. The insertion within the Association Agreement of a territoriality clause that covers the entire agreement, but refers specifically to trade-related matters, serves the purpose of explicitly excluding the two unrecognised entities from the application of any Deep and Comprehensive Free Trade Area-related provisions as long as they remain outside Tbilisi's control. Although embracing a different practical interpretation of the EU's approach to Georgia's contested statehood than that applied to conflict management and migration and mobility, the trade sector has presented similar opportunities and challenges for EU actorness. On the one hand, the territoriality clause responded to Georgian concerns that exports originating in the two de facto states will be conducted through authorities in Tbilisi, creating the regulatory framework for the EU to deploy its trade *capabilities* in Georgia. On the other hand, similarly to the visa-free regime, the prospective inclusion of Abkhazia and South Ossetia into the Deep and Comprehensive Free Trade Area effectively amounts to them operating under Tbilisi's authority. Against this background, the two entities have firmly rejected the EU's trade-related *capabilities* and their negative perceptions of its role as a trade partner have been reinforced, resulting in insignificant EU *presence*.

By exploring the contested statehood–actorness nexus with respect to the EU's conflict management, migration and mobility, and trade policies in Georgia, this article has sought to shed light on the complex articulations of EU international actorness under conditions of problematic sovereignty. The flexible interpretation of the territorial applicability of the three policy fields aimed to enable the EU to exercise actorness in Georgia, even though this was effectively restricted to 80% of the territory, while at the same time allowing for the possibility to further engage Abkhazia and South Ossetia. Given the EU's own rigid conceptions of sovereignty and territoriality and the intractability of the conflict parties' positions, contested statehood emerged as a constraining condition for EU actorness only as far as the two de facto states were concerned, while it appears not to have had any discernable negative impact on EU actorness in Tbilisi-controlled territory.

Notes

1. We use the terms 'Sukhumi' and 'Tskhinvali' as these are the most common in English and correspond to the relevant scholarly terminology. While acknowledging that these forms are disputed by the conflict parties, our choice is pragmatic and should not be interpreted as a political statement.
2. The EU itself admits it is not a neutral actor, phone interview European External Action Service officials (12 January 2017).
3. Interview Georgian Ministry of Defence official, Tbilisi (29 July 2016).
4. Interview European Commission official, Brussels (22 February 2018); Phone interview European External Action Service official (26 June 2018).
5. Phone interview Tbilisi-based journalist and civil society activist (16 December 2016); Phone interview European External Action Service official (20 December 2016).
6. Interview Delegation of the European Union to Georgia official, Tbilisi (26 April 2013).
7. According to an Abkhaz citizen, 'Georgia lost any moral and legal right to rule Abkhazia [and it] will never again be a part of the Georgian state', quoted in (Garb 2009, 238).
8. The Law of Georgia on the Occupied Territories, initiated by Georgia's President Mikhail Saakahashvili, was adopted on 23 October 2008 and criminalises the separatist entities' relations with the outside world.
9. Quoted in Agenda.Ge. 2015. Georgia ready for Visa-Free Travel to Europe. *JAMnews*. 18 December. See also AgendaGe. 2015. Will Abkhazians and Ossetians benefit from EU visa liberalization? 19 December.
10. E-mail interview former European External Action Service official (27 December 2016).
11. Phone interview Georgian think tank representative (5 July 2018).
12. Phone interview Georgian think tank representative (2 July 2018).
13. Phone interview official in the Office of the State Minister of Georgia for European and Euro-Atlantic Integration (9 December 2016).
14. Phone interview European External Action Service official (26 June 2018).
15. Here, the comparison with Transnistria is revealing, as it further underlines the EU's privileging of external sovereignty and the potential practical implications of this approach to contested statehood. Transnistria's willingness to trade through the Moldovan authorities

largely explains why, and despite the existence of an identical territoriality clause in the EU-Moldova AA, the EU was in a position to extend the DCFTA to Transnistria. Despite the absence of an effective mechanism for the full verification of compliance by Transnistrian companies with DCFTA rules (Secrieriu 2016), Tiraspol's principled acceptance of Moldova's authority appears to have satisfied the EU's concern for the respect of sovereignty and territorial integrity. Contrastingly, Abkhazia and South Ossetia's refusal to be treated as integral parts of Georgia makes it improbable to find a compromise solution for the application of the DCFTA to these territories.

References

Accent. 2016. *When Sukhumi and Tskhinvali are able to trade freely with EU*. March 9.
Achba, A. 2016. *Abkhazia: Russia's tight embrace*. Brussels: European Council on Foreign Relations. September.
Ademmer, E., and L. Delcour. 2015. With a little help from Russia? The European union and visa liberalisation with post-Soviet states. *Eurasian Geography and Economics* 57 (1):89–112. doi:10.1080/15387216.2016.1178157.
Bachelli, T., B. Bartmann, and H. Srebrnik. 2004. *De facto states: The quest for sovereignty*. London: Routledge.
Blakkisrud, H., and P. Kolstø. 2012. Dynamics of de facto statehood: The South Caucasian de facto states between secession and sovereignty. *Southeast European and Black Sea Studies* 12 (2):281–98. doi:10.1080/14683857.2012.686013.
Börzel, T. 2015. Building sand castles? how the EU seeks to support the political integration of its new members, accession candidates and Eastern neighbours. Maximizing the integration capacity of the European Union: Lessons of and prospects for enlargementand beyond (MAXCAP) Working Paper Series 9.
Boswell, C., and A. Geddes. 2011. *Migration and mobility in the European Union*. Basingstoke: Palgrave Macmillan.
Bouris, D., and G. Kyris. 2017. Europeanisation, sovereignty and contested states: The EU in northern Cyprus and Palestine. *The British Journal of Politics and International Relations* 19 (4):755–71. doi:10.1177/1369148117727534.
Bretherton, C., and J. Vogler. 2006. *The European Union as a global actor*. London: Routledge.
Broers, L. 2013. Recognising politics in unrecognised states: 20 years of enquiry into the de facto states of the South Caucasus. *Caucasus Survey* 1 (1):59–74. doi:10.1080/23761199.2013.11417283.
Broers, L. 2014. Mirrors to the world: The claims to legitimacy and international recognition of De Facto States in the South Caucasus. *Brown Journal of World Affairs* XX (II):145–59.
Broers, L., A. Iskandaryan, and S. Minasyan. 2015. Introduction: The unrecognised politics of de facto states in the post-Soviet space. In *The unrecognised politics of de facto states in the post-Soviet space*, ed. L. Broers, A. Iskandaryan, and S. Minasyan, 5–16. Yerevan: Caucasus Institute and International Association for the Study of the Caucasus.
Caspersen, N., and G. Stansfield. 2011. *Unrecognized states in the international system*. London: Routledge.
Civil Georgia. 2008. *EU monitors want access to Abkhazia, S.Ossetia*. November 5.
Civil Georgia. 2011. *Sokhumi criticizes EU's Abkhaz policy*. January 18.
Civil Georgia. 2012. *Sokhumi slams EUMM head*. April 25.
Civil Georgia. 2017. *Sokhumi, Tskhinvali reject Tbilisi's EU Visa liberalization offer*. February 3.
Coppieters, B., M. Emerson, M. Huysseune, T. Kovziridze, G. Noutcheva, N. Tocci, and M. Vahl. 2004. *Europeanization and conflict resolution: Case studies from the European periphery*. Gent: Academia Press.
de Waal, T. 2017. Enhancing the EU's engagement with separatist territories. *Carnegie Europe*, January 17.

Dolidze, T. 2015. *Deliberately integrated: South Ossetia headed for and into Russia*. Brussels: CEPS.
Emerson, M., and T. Kovziridze. 2016. *Deepening EU-Georgian relations. What, why and how?* London: Rowman & Littlefield.
European Commission. 2015. Fourth progress report on Georgia's implementation of the action plan on visa liberalization. 684 final. Brussels.
European Union. 2014. *Association agenda between the European Union and Georgia*. Brussels.
Finchova Grono, M. 2010. Georgia's conflicts: What role for the EU as mediator? The initiative for peacebuilding (IfP). International Alert.
Fischer, S. 2010. The EU's non-recognition and engagement policy towards Abkhazia and South Ossetia. Seminar Report. European Union Institute for Security Studies. Brussels. December 1–2.
Freizer, S. 2017. The revised European neighbourhood policy and conflicts in the south caucasus: The EU's growing transformation role. In *The revised European neighbourhood policy. Continuity and change in EU foreign policy*, ed. D. Bouris and T. Schumacher, 157–76. Basingstoke: Palgrave Macmillan.
Garb, P. 2009. The view from Abkhazia of South Ossetia ablaze. *Central Asian Survey* 28 (2):235–46. doi:10.1080/02634930903034856.
Geldenhuys, D. 2009. *Contested states in world politics*. Basingstoke, New York: Palgrave Macmillan.
Georgia Today. 2018. *PM announces new peace initiative "step toward a better future"*. April 4.
Hill, C. 1993. The capability-expectations gap, or conceptualizing Europe's international role. *Journal of Common Market Studies* 31 (3):305–28. doi:10.1111/j.1468–5965.1993.tb00466.x.
International Crisis Group. 2018. Abkhazia and South Ossetia: Time to talk trade'. Crisis Group Europe Report, 249. May 24. Brussels: The International Crisis Group.
Kakulia, M. 2014. Georgia's experience on developing trade and trade policy measures with the European Union. *East European Studies* 5:137–60.
Kirova, I. 2012. *Public diplomacy and conflict resolution. Russia, Georgia and the EU in Abkhazia and South Ossetia*. Los Angeles: Figueroa Press.
Kolstø, P., and H. Blakkisrud. 2008. Living with non-recognition: State- and nation-building in south Caucasian Quasi-states. *Europe-Asia Studies* 60 (3):483–509. doi:10.1080/09668130801948158.
Krasner, S. 2001. *Problematic sovereignty: Contested rules and political possibilities*. New York: Columbia University Press.
Kvarchelia, L. 2012. Perceptions of the EU in Abkhazia and prospects for the EU–Abkhazia engagement. Analytical Report, Centre for Humanitarian Programmes (Sukhumi) and Conciliation Resources (London).
Kyris, G. 2016. *The Europeanisation of contested statehood: The EU in northern Cyprus*. Oxon, New York: Routledge.
Merlingen, M., and R. Ostrauskaite. 2009. EU peacebuilding in Georgia: Limits and achievements. Leuven Centre for Global Governance Studies: Centre for the Law of EU External Relations. Working Paper 35. The Hague: T.M.C. Asser Institute.
Nixey, J. 2012. *The long goodbye: Waning Russian influence in the south Caucasus and central Asia, briefing paper*. London: Chatham House.
Noutcheva, G. 2009. Fake, partial and imposed compliance: The limits of the EU's normative power in the western Balkans. *Journal of European Public Policy* 16 (7):1065–84. doi:10.1080/13501760903226872.
O'Loughlin, J., V. Kolossov, and G. Toal. 2014. Inside the post-Soviet de facto states: A comparison of attitudes in Abkhazia, Nagrony Karabakh, South Ossetia, and Transnistria. *Eurasian Geography and Economics* 55 (5):423–56. doi:10.1080/15387216.2015.1012644.
Official Journal of the European Union. 2014. AssociationAgreement between the European Union and the European Atomic Energy Community and their Member States, of the one part, and Georgia, of the other part. *Official Journal of the European Union* L/261.

Papadimitriou, D., and P. Petrov. 2012. Whose rule, whose law? contested statehood, external leverage and the European union's rule of law mission in Kosovo. *Journal of Common Market Studies* 50 (5):746–63. doi:10.1111/j.1468-5965.2012.02257.x.

Public Defender of Georgia. 2017. *Analyses of the law of Georgia 'on occupied territories' and recommendations.* Tbilisi. February 9.

RFE/RL. 2018. *Georgian Prime Minister resigns after antigovernment protests.* June 13.

Sasse, G. 2009. The European neighbourhood policy and conflict management: A comparison of Moldova and the Caucasus. *Ethnopolitics* 8 (3–4):369–86. doi:10.1080/17449050903086971.

Secrieriu, S. 2016. Transnistria Zig-zagging towards a DCFTA. PISM Policy Paper 4/145.

Semneby, P. 2014. The EU, Russia and the South Caucasus – building confidence. *Russia in Global Affairs* 1.

Sjöstedt, G. 1977. *The external role of the European community.* Famborough: Saxon House.

Stewart, E. J. 2011. Mind the normative gap? The EU in the south Caucasus. In *Normative power europe. Empirical and theoretical perspectives*, ed. R. G. Whitman, 65–82. London: Routledge.

The Economist. 2017. *Of nationalists and nuts. Georgia and Abkhazia are making Nutella's job harder.* October 19.

Thomas, D. C. 2012. Still punching below its weight? coherence and effectiveness in European union foreign policy. *Journal of Common Market Studies* 50 (3):457–74. doi:10.1111/j.1468-5965.2011.02244.x.

Tocci, N. 2007. *The EU and conflict resolution: Promoting peace in the backyard.* Oxon, New York: Routledge.

Vasilyan, S. 2014. "Moral power" as objectification of the "civilian"/"normative" "EUlogy": The European union as a conflict-dealer in the south Caucasus. *Journal of International Relations and Development* 17 (3):397–424. doi:10.1057/jird.2013.10.

Zielonka, J. 1998. *Explaining Euro-paralysis: Why Europe is unable to act in international politics.* Houndmills, Basingstoke: Macmillan Press.

Armenia and Belarus

Caught between the EU's and Russia's conditionalities?

Alena Vieira and Syuzanna Vasilyan

Introduction

Within the EU's Eastern neighbourhood comprising six countries in the post-Soviet area, namely, the geographically defined Eastern European Ukraine, Moldova, Belarus, and the South Caucasian Armenia, Azerbaijan and Georgia, Armenia and Belarus stand out due to their close relations with Russia.[1] These are the only two European Union's (EU) Eastern Partnership (EaP) states that are also part of the Russia-led Eurasian Economic Union (EAEU). While Armenia and Belarus differ in terms of reasons, nature and objectives of their relationship with Moscow, they share a similarity of close security ties, as well as economic and energy dependency on Russia.[2] This common feature sets the tone for Armenia's and Belarus' engagement with the EU, while also raising the question of how much of EU conditionality, and of what kind, could be absorbed by countries in such a position. The issue is intriguing since Armenia's and Belarus' close relationship with Moscow has not precluded their cooperation with the EU, as reflected in their participation in the European Neighbourhood Policy (ENP) and the EaP, albeit to a different extent.[3]

In the dynamically evolving field of the EU external governance and the ENP/EaP studies, single-case studies of Armenia (Delcour, 2017; Vasilyan, 2017) and Belarus (Bosse, 2012; Korosteleva, 2013) have been already carried out. While there is also a smaller number of contributions exploring EU's and Russia's influence on each of the two individual countries (Delcour, 2017; Vasilyan, 2017; Vasilyan & Petrossian, 2014), these studies have not specifically focused on the reception of Russia's *versus* EU's conditional approaches in Belarus and Armenia. In addition, a comparative analysis of Armenia and Belarus has been rare (cf Dragneva, Delcour, & Jonavicius, 2017).

By firstly assessing the policies of Russia and the EU towards their shared neighbourhood and, secondly evaluating their respective reception in Armenia and Belarus the article carries out a double comparison. It allows to demonstrate that, on the one hand, the conditionalities imposed by the EU and Russia towards the two countries have differed. On the other hand, it shows that Armenia and Belarus have reacted to Russia's and the EU's conditional approaches in a different way, something reflected in the fact that only Armenia and not Belarus signed an advanced agreement with the EU, the Comprehensive and Enhanced Partnership Agreement (CEPA), in November 2017. This divergent pattern of conditionality reception in two EaP countries urges for exploration of factors responsible for it on the part of the individual EaP states, which is especially crucial in light of the 2015 revision of the ENP and the ensuing EU aspirations to develop a more differentiated and flexible set of policy tools towards its neighbours.

This article starts with a short account of the EU's and Russia's conditional approaches towards the two countries that serves to establish turning points in their changing positions towards the common neighbourhood. While tracing the evolution of EU engagement with its neighbours towards its most recent expression in the Association Agreements (AA) and Deep and Comprehensive Free Trade Areas (DCFTA), it also investigates the Russian foreign policy shift away from the affinity-based and towards a pragmatism-oriented position. It finally looks into the role played by the EAEU, developed initially as the Eurasian Customs Union (EACU), but nevertheless displaying ambition to become a full-fledged Eurasian Union. The reaction of two EaP states is then analysed by applying analytical framework proposed in the introduction to this special section, in addition to identifying further factors relevant to the reception of the EU and Russian policies in Armenia and Belarus in specific policy areas.

EU's and Russia's policies towards shared neighbourhood: the legacy of two decades

Both the EU and Russia have been faced with the dilemma of how to define a new approach towards their common neighbourhood following the dissolution of the Soviet Union. The EU's initial stance in the beginning of the 1990s has been mostly oriented towards finding a mode of cooperation with Russia, with the EU's Eastward enlargement occupying most of the place on the political agenda. Russia's own position set the premium on the cooperation within the Commonwealth of Independent States (CIS), extending advanced cooperation in military (industrial) field, as well as in the areas of education and culture, and the movement of people (labour) to Russia in addition to trade and financial assistance, to its most eager members. Russia's emerging policy towards its 'near abroad' was based upon socio-cultural affinity rather than conditionality, aiming at cultivating a 'collective we' with these states without, however, stipulating a clearly defined set of cooperation conditions and rewards. Such affinity-based engagement allowed for flexibility in dealing with pressing bilateral problems, as reflected in the intricate Russia-Belarus barter schemes to resolve pressing energy debt issues (Balmaceda, 2014). Along with social, economic and political ties, Russia's privileged position in terms of influencing its neighbours had a strong cultural and linguistic dimension, with the Russian language as a *lingua franca* facilitating the relations. A factor especially relevant to fostering bilateral relations was the presence of the Russian media, as most of Russian TV and radio channels had been widely broadcasting both in Belarus and Armenia. Multiple ways were therefore available to convey Russian narratives as an integral part of its 'soft power' influence in its 'near abroad'. The EU hardly enjoyed a similar tool of projection of its image or influence in the region at that time. However, while being aware of its advantage over the EU in terms of influence over its 'near abroad', Moscow was not interested to capitalise upon it: the EU's incipient policy towards CIS states was not viewed as a threat to what Russia has considered its traditional zone of influence (*cf* Schmidt-Felzmann, 2016).

In the initial phase of the evolution of EU's and Russia's policies towards the post-Soviet states, as the EU was channelling its Technical Assistance to the Commonwealth of Independent States (TACIS) programme, starting from 1991 onwards,[4] there was no overlap between the EU's and Russia's approaches towards their neighbours. Originally, TACIS comprised humanitarian and technical assistance provided unconditionally to CIS countries (Vasilyan, 2006), and it was only in the TACIS regulation adopted in 1996 that the EU referred to negative conditionality, by stipulating 'the possibility of suspending an assistance… in cases of violation of democratic principles and human rights' (European Commission, n.d.). The associated 'Western template' for reforms in different spheres, was not contested by Moscow. More generally, TACIS aimed to help CIS countries, including Russia, revive infrastructurally, economically and politically after the demise of the Soviet Union. In this spirit, EU initiatives like the additional Transport Corridor Europe-Caucasus-Asia (TRACECA) and Inter-State Oil and Gas Transportation to Europe (INOGATE) also targeted the whole former Soviet space with the objective of creating a transportation and energy hub stretching from the EU to the Newly Independent States (NIS) (Vasilyan, 2006).

Meanwhile, since the 1990s, the EU and its member states have stood out as zealous democracy promoters in the eastern part of its neighbourhood channelling funding both through state and non-state actors (Vasilyan, 2010c). For the latter the European (Initiative later to be renamed into) Instrument for Democracy and Human Rights (EIDHR), Non-State Actors and Local Authorities (NSA&LA), Decentralised Cooperation have served as relevant budget lines. Recently these have been augmented by the funding provided directly to non-state actors by the European Endowment for Democracy (EED).[5] Armenia has been one of the beneficiaries of such funding with the adoption of 'soft norms' taking place at the bottom (Vasilyan, 2010c).

However, even in this initial stage of interaction, in stark contrast to converging views in Moscow and the West on the course of Russia's and CIS states' internal political and economic reforms, tensions emerged between the parties in the area of conflict resolution, especially in the post-Soviet space. For instance, in the case of the resolution of the Nagorno-Karabakh conflict within the frames of the Organization for Security and Cooperation in Europe (OSCE) Minsk Group,[6] frictions surfaced between Russia and Sweden as co-chairs over choice of venue or differing initiatives in the mid-1990s (De Waal, 2003).[7]

The adoption, conclusion and ratification of the first PCAs between 1994 and 1996 marked an important turning point in the evolution of the EU conditionality towards the post-Soviet countries. The PCAs established the so-called 'suspension clauses' as well as 'evolutionary clauses' paving the way to a FTA in the future (Russia, Ukraine, Belarus and Moldova),[8] thereby reinforcing the role of the (positive and negative) EU conditionality in promoting reforms. Its subsequent application has not always been consistent, however, as manifest in negative political conditionality (i.e. sanctions) applied to Belarus,[9] which stood in contrast to exclusively positive conditionality extended to Armenia. As for Russia, its approach towards CIS countries, continued to be affinity-based, informal, and was developed on an *ad hoc* basis, with specific benefits for the cooperation-oriented partners defined individually for every bilateral relationship, and often subject to (re)negotiation. The reinforcement of a 'collective we' towards the post-Soviet states continued to be the main rationale of Russia's engagement, as manifest in Gazprom's pricing policy for Russian natural gas export to individual neighbouring countries (Balmaceda, 2014).[10]

The years 2000 introduced a turn in EU-Russian relations and a rethinking, on the part of Russia, of the EU/Western recommendations as a blueprint for Russia's reforms (Schmidt-Felzmann, 2016). NATO intervention in Kosovo in 1999, and the subsequent recognition of independence by the US and a majority of EU member-states created a new political context for conflict-resolution efforts in Chechnya, as well as Abkhazia, South Ossetia and Nagorno-Karabakh. NATO enlargement to Central Eastern European countries between 1996 and 2004 was making pro-Western oriented Georgia after its Rose Revolution (2003) and Ukraine after its Orange Revolution (2004) hopeful of their accession bid, while simultaneously raising the wariness of Moscow (Vasilyan, 2010b). Negotiations over consequences of the EU enlargement for Russia, which included the issue of Kaliningrad transit and trade aversion, demonstrated a clash of interests between Russia and the EU. All of the aforementioned changes reinforced the belief in Moscow that it could no longer rely on the West as an agenda-setter for Russia's reforms, so that the EU conditionality and EU ensuing position of policy-maker (*vis-à-vis* Russia as a policy-taker) were now reconsidered in Moscow.

This new phase in EU-Russia relations went hand in hand with a rethinking of Russia's relations towards the CIS countries. A 'pragmatisation' of Russian foreign policy was announced by Russian Security Council Secretary Sergey Ivanov in 2001 (Vieira, 2016), with Russia now putting its foreign policy to the service of its own (economic) development, thereby abstaining from the previous practice of subsidising its (south-)eastern neighbours. In the mid-2000s, Gazprom's pricing policy towards the 'near abroad' changed radically, and Gazprom came to gradually acquire gas and oil transmission networks in Moldova, Belarus and Armenia (Babayan, 2015). Russia's affinity-based approach originally aimed at fostering a 'collective we' was now giving place to a new style of interaction, with Russia's own interests coming fist. However, it continued to lack any clear set of conditions for Russia's CIS partners' compliance.

Faced with the need to find new, more effective cooperation modes with its politically defined neighbours following its eastward enlargement, the EU launched the ENP in 2003– 2004. This new EU policy was founded upon positive political conditionality, with the prospect of the 'EU internal market and further integration and liberalisation to promote the free movement of persons, goods, services and capital (four freedoms)' (European Commission, 2003). Following the ENP review in response to the Arab Spring, the EU introduced the so-called 'more for more' principle in 2011, stipulating a closer relationship with neighbours displaying a more advanced reform progress. This resulted in additional funding for Armenia (together with Georgia and Moldova) owing to the country's good performance as assessed by the EU in 2012 and 2013 (Vasilyan, 2018).[11] While Belarus remained outside the ENP, EU's relations with Armenia had been codified in the EU-Armenia Action Plan (AP), a political document building upon the legal PCA foundation and listing the 'priorities for action' in all the domains of public life (Ibid.).

The ENP aimed at the introduction of 'partial' positive conditionality (Vasilyan, 2010a), implying incremental provision of additional funding, extension of projects and budget lines, access to programmes and agencies short of the membership 'carrot'. However, it has been often criticised for inconsistency, including at the point of the acceptance into this policy of Armenia and Azerbaijan in following Georgia's Rose Revolution, in spite of the lack of democratic progress in the two countries (Babayan, 2015). The positive conditionality approach underpinning the ENP, which was additionally reinforced in the 'more for more' principle, has been actively debated in the expert community. Hale (2012) recommended to pursue the 'more-for-less' principle for rendering influence over authoritarian states, such as Azerbaijan. For the sake of proportionality it has been suggested to offer least for most, e.g. Georgia, less for more, e.g. Armenia, and most for least, e.g. Azerbaijan (Vasilyan, 2010c). In addition, while the main aspiration of the AP was to reinforce the EU conditionality, uncertainty regarding specific conditions and rewards for neighbour states' compliance was recognised as a weak point (Delcour, 2017).

As the ENP introduced the logic of 'competition for reforms', with 'frontrunners' and laggards among six EaP states identified in every monitoring phase, all six of them politically, economically and culturally close to Russia, EU's policy and the reform efforts of the former Soviet states started to be closely followed in Moscow. In response and building upon pragmatism as a new principle of Russia's foreign policy, Moscow started to employ its own-styled negative functional conditionality, by calling upon the established linkage(s) with its neighbours, which eventually led to (re)appearance of a number of sectoral 'trade wars' (over milk, meat, wine, energy, etc) (Korosteleva, 2013; *cf* Samokhvalov, 2016). Russia's approach stood in stark contrast with the ENP offer underpinned by positive conditionality, a contrast further reinforced by the Russia-Georgia war over Abkhazia and South Ossetia in 2008, which attested to Russia's capacity to resort to military measures *vis-à-vis* the states in its 'near abroad'. In 2009, responding to the new Russian assertiveness as well as to the growing concerns of the Russia's neighbours, the EU launched the EaP establishing the prospect of further political association, economic integration and legal convergence between the EU and the six participating states. The original Polish-Swedish idea of a special relationship between the EU and the countries to its East eventually assumed the contours of AA and a DCFTA, in addition to the focus on multilateral cooperation (Vasilyan, 2010a).

Russia's subsequent position can be characterised as further consolidation of Russia's *ad-hoc* negative functional conditionality. One of its manifestations was recurrent trade conflicts with both EU-oriented countries such as Ukraine and pro-Russian states (Koroste-leva, 2013). Heads of Russia's food safety agency (Rosselkhoznadzor) as well as consumer protection agencies (Rospotrebnadzor) became faces and voices of Russia's unpredictable trade conflicts with Russia's neighbours. Internal administrative adjustments reflected the new importance of the agencies: in 2012, Rosselhosnadzor was made directly responsible to the federal government, in contrast to its previous subordinated position at the ministry of health (Black, 2015, p. 110).

The revamp of the Eurasian project, in the form of the EACU and afterwards the EAEU (and potentially the Eurasian Union) offered another response to the evolving EaP, which demonstrated the double-track nature of Russian engagement. On the one hand, Moscow indicated that it had developed its own negative functional conditionality, with an associated package of 'sticks' and 'carrots' now extended to the prospective members/outsiders of the Eurasian project. The case in point were the sensitive Russia-Belarus gas transmission network negotiations eventually leading to what has become known as an 'integration discount', of the price of natural gas in return for Belarus' participation in the Eurasian project (Vieira, 2017).[12]

On the other hand, Moscow demonstrated willingness to supplement its previous *ad hoc* approach towards its 'near abroad' with an institutionalised basis for the relations. In stark contrast with the previous integration initiatives on the post-Soviet space, where the cooperation was primarily grounded in Russia's aspiration to cultivate the 'collective we' on the basis of informal trade-offs, EACU/EAEU cooperation included an actual implementation of the institutionalised and legalised norms. For instance, the EACU became *de facto* operational very fast, introducing new legislation in a number of fields (Delcour & Wolczuk, 2014). This created new terms of engagement with Russia for its Eurasian partners such as Belarus and Armenia.

By the moment of EAEU's entrance into force in 2015, in light of the rapidly evolving events in Ukraine, the Eurasian integration had been experiencing a setback (Vieira, 2016). Russia's actions in Ukraine demonstrated that Russia was determined to resist unilateral application of the EU conditionality in the EaP countries. At the same time, Russia's Eurasian partners were now more cautious in taking steps towards deepening integration, while also raising questions on Russia's overall integration commitment and objectives. A linear evolution of the Eurasian initiative was no longer a viable plan, as the parties have in fact regressed in terms of their integration efforts in a number of fields. This has not only led to sporadic setbacks in trade and economic matters (such as the occasional milk and meat 'wars' between Russia and Belarus); in 2016 and 2017, checkpoints have been introduced between the two EAEU member states, undermining the common custom space while also indicating Belarus' resistance to the Russian functional conditionality (Vieira, 2016). All these events eventually raised new questions on the mechanisms and dynamics of the Eurasian integration process, once again bringing to the forefront the issue of the Russian (and the EU) conditional approaches.

The EU in its turn recognised the need to develop a more differentiated approach towards its neighbours, including by rethinking its engagement with the EaP countries also participating in the EAEU, thus paving the way towards EU-Armenia CEPA as a new precedent formalising the EU-EaP states relationship. However, Russia continued to insist on the right to interpret the extent of compatibility between two integration blocs (Dragneva et al., 2017, p. 16).

The EU, Russia and Armenia: policies with loose strings

The case of Armenia illustrates a vivid difference of perception of the EU and Russia as influential external actors. The Armenian elite, political parties and the public have perceived the EU as a political and economic bloc, with Russia and the Collective Security Treaty Organization (CSTO) considered as vital security partners (Vasilyan, 2011). The Armenian National Security Strategy has appreciated cooperation with all the possible global and regional actors, yet, naming only Russia as a 'strategic' ally (Ministry of Foreign Affairs of the Republic of Armenia, 2007, in Vasilyan & Petrossian, 2014). This can be attributed to the fact that, as a result of the Armenian Genocide under the Ottoman Empire, Russia per se has been viewed as a saviour and the subsequently established Armenian Soviet Socialist Republic (ASSR) as a safe haven, which entitled Armenians to statehood.[13] The EU and its member states, including France, Germany, the UK and Italy, along with the US have thus been new-comers to a region previously subject to imperial incursions by the regional powers, especially Russia, Turkey and Iran as successors of the Russian, Ottoman and Persian Empires. In the face of the lingering Nagorno-Karabakh conflict as a domestic and foreign policy priority, and in its condition of a small state, Armenia has been keen to navigate in the 'known terrain' configured by conventional relations with states rather than recent international actors with cumbersome bureaucratic machinery such as the EU. However, the country has also welcomed EU's programmes, projects and initiatives (contrary to other states, such as Belarus).

While the official discourse recognises the country as 'European', Armenia's nation- and state-building is to be attributed to the Soviet period. At the same time, the size of its diaspora has made the Armenian identity multi-layered, branched among the American, European, Eurasian, North-American, and Middle Eastern ones. With the largest

Armenian communities residing in Russia, the US and France in the mentioned order, and thereby representing important constituencies and interest groups in the respective countries, the Armenian government sought cooperation with all (Vasilyan, 2011).[14] This led to facing the differential conditionalities of the EU and Russia tied to their political identities, as assumed in the approach adopted in the present special section. Therefore, even with consideration of the historical ties and contemporary political context, no exclusive reception of Russia's versus the EU conditionality has been taking place.

In comparison to the enlargement policy currently exercised towards the (potential) candidate countries, especially in the Western Balkans with embedded negative conditionality, and in contrast to EU sanctions against Belarus, the EU has only applied positive conditionality towards the South Caucasian countries, including Armenia (Vasilyan, 2018). Despite being classified as 'partial democracy' (Freedom House, 2016) due to its electoral malpractices, Armenia was able to benefit from the good disposition of the EU, who had been inclined to reward the apprenticeship of better democratic practices.[15] Meanwhile, Russia had not imposed any negative conditionality on Armenia either. An episode of an application of functional EU conditionality can be considered the Mobility Partnership Agreement with Armenia (2011), when the EU has attached the repatriation of illegal migrants as a condition for offering visa facilitation and especially potential visa liberalisation for temporary migration. Eventually, the Visa Facilitation Agreement signed in 2012 and the Readmission Agreement signed in 2013, entered into force at the same time in January 2014. In contrast, the Russian Compatriots Programme as of 2009 had provided an unconditional offer for permanent labour immigration, something that had been facilitated by demographic shifts in the Russian aging population (Vasilyan, 2017; Vasilyan & Petrossian, 2014).[16]

Meanwhile, domestic acceptance/resistance to the policies of the EU and Russia can be illustrated by internal political dynamics. The country has witnessed a number of public rallies over the past few years.[17] The case in point are protests in Yerevan in September 2013, that even though of a less magnitude than the Euromaidan in Ukraine, nevertheless united hundreds in front of the presidential residence following the presidential announcement regarding the country's change of foreign policy course (Grigoryan, 2013). Different from the colour revolutions in Ukraine, Georgia and Kyrgyzstan, Armenia's civic activism at the bottom has been frequent, and aimed at revealing the malpractices in domestic economic, social and political governance. With Russia involved in the country via the assets it holds in Armenia's energy (electricity and gas) and transportation networks, in addition to banking, insurance and telecommunications, and considering Russia's share of foreign direct investment (FDI) and its role as the second trade partner (after the EU), as well as security ally with a military base in Armenia's second largest town Gyumri, Moscow had been a target of some civic protests, either directly or indirectly (Vasilyan, 2017; Vasilyan & Petrossian, 2014).

In the energy sphere, in spite of the public protests, Gazprom gained complete control over Armenia's gas distribution network in December 2013. As a result of the subsequent protests against mismanagement and corruption following the electricity price hike in June 2015, the gas price offered to Armenia was lowered to 165 USD per thousand cubic metres in September the same year (Radio Free Liberty, Radio Europe, 2015, in Vasil-yan, 2017) making Armenia the top beneficiary ahead of Belarus (Vasilyan, 2017). Further, in April 2016 it was dropped to 150 USD (Arka News Agency, 2016). The Electric Networks of Armenia (ENA) acquired by RAO UES in 2006 was sold to the Tashir Group owned by a Russian-Armenian billionaire in mid-2015, something that allowed the Armenian government to make a pledge to subsidise the expenditures up to 31 July 2016, switching to compensation of families living below the poverty line as of August 2016. Unlike Georgia, who is a member to the Energy Charter Treaty promoted by the EU, Armenia is an observer (Vasilyan, 2018). In short, in the energy domain, the relevant interests have determined the reception of EU and Russian conditionality.

In the security sphere, Russia has been Armenia's primary ally. This 'bandwagoning' exercise has been juxtaposed to the Azerbaijan-Turkey and US-Georgia alliances. In the meantime, Armenia (although not a formal party) and Azerbaijan, which/who has recurrently threatened with the use of force, have pursued an arms-race resulting in escalation in the context of the Nagorno-Karabakh conflict (Vasilyan, 2010b). The EU has not provided conflict-resolution focused assistance to Armenia or Azerbaijan through the National Indicative Programs (NIPs), the programming instruments under the ENP, distributing its funding proportionally among different domains instead. The August 2008 war over Abkhazia and South Ossetia reaffirmed Russia's leading position as a mediator via the Maindorf Declaration in the presence of Russian, Armenian and Azeri Presidents (Vasilyan, 2013). However, Armenian public's hopes that Russia's recognition of the independence of Abkhazia and South Ossetia would be followed by Moscow's identical posture *vis-à-vis* Nagorno-Karabakh, remained unfulfilled. Russia's role as a major mediator was nevertheless reinstated in the aftermath of the April 2016 war launched by Azerbaijan over Nagorno-Karabakh, with Russia convening a meeting in Moscow with the presence of the Iranian Foreign Minister.[18] Having tried to maintain 'parity' between Armenia and Azerbaijan, Russia has provided weaponry (for free or at discounted rates) to the former and sold to the latter (Kucera, 2015). In the meantime, up to 2013, Armenia aligned with more CFSP declarations issued by the EU than the neighbouring Azerbaijan or even Georgia (Vasilyan, 2018). Yet, Armenia's economic condition and the security environment have *a priori* made it susceptible to accepting Russia's potential conditionality.

The constitutional amendments following the 2015 referendum were approved by the CIS observers, with the EU delegation 'calling for investigations' amidst allegations of fraud (ArmeniaNow 2015 and Delegation of the European Union to the Republic of Armenia 2015 in Vasilyan, 2017). The envisaged transition from the presidential to a parliamentary type of regime in circumstances when the incumbent president was heading the majority Republican Party has raised suspicions regarding the intention of the latter to find a covert tactic for keeping on to power (Ibid.). The envisaged signing of the AA had raised public expectations over potential amelioration of the political climate via improvement of electoral practices, human rights and governance, so that the retreat from these principles has led to public disenchantment. At the same time, while Armenia has been lagging behind other EaP countries such as Georgia and Moldova in terms of the overall democracy score, in the EAEU it still fares best, both politically, despite the stagnation since 2013 (Freedom House, 2016) and as a relatively more liberal economy (Vasilyan, 2017). Without any reform incentive from the top, and democracy not being a criterion for accession into the EAEU, '(b)lockage' of transition to democracy has been taking place in the past few years (Vasilyan, 2016). As a result of retreat from the path of closer 'integration with' the EU (Vasilyan, 2017), Armenia has experienced stagnation of the reform-prone stamina.

The turning point marked by the shift of Armenia's foreign policy choice towards entering the EACU in 2013 and eventually becoming a member of the EAEU in 2015 was not accompanied by formal negative conditionality on the part of the EU or positive conditionality by Russia. While the visit by President Sargsyan to Moscow at the brink of his declaration regarding the change of Armenia's foreign policy course led to public reflections on a possible push by President Putin, the Armenian leadership has denied any pressure exerted by Moscow. Rather, the preference for the EACU/EAEU was justified on security grounds, in the sense that Armenia's membership in the CSTO presupposed conformity with its participation in a regional economic grouping that had a similar member-state composition (Vasilyan, 2017).

Meanwhile, the accession to the EACU did not go smoothly. Due to Azerbaijan's lobbying, Kazakhstan and Belarus objected to Armenia's membership, expressing reluctance to see the potential extension of the EACU to Nagorno-Karabakh, which does not have a customs checkpoint with Armenia. This was resolved with the Russian statement articulated by the Head of the Eurasian Economic Commission Viktor Khristenko that an external country could not determine matters pertaining to a regional bloc, implying that Armenia's membership would take place against all odds (Asbarez, 2013). This implied that Russia preferred to keep the Nagorno-Karabakh conflict de-securitised in the EAEU framework. Moreover, the Armenian bureaucrats had to de-learn what they had apprehended from the European counterparts in the process of approximation to the rules, standards and practices with the EU and learn what was put forth by the EAEU colleagues (Vasilyan, 2017). This has led to complications in functional adaptation through 'hard norms', despite the political determination to proceed. Additionally, while Belarus as a founding member could have a say over the nature of the EACU and the EAEU being a norm-setter together with Russia and Kazakhstan, Armenia, together with Kyrgyzstan were late-comers, thereby becoming norm-takers.

Paradoxically, Armenia had become a front-runner in terms of adoption of the required EU legislation in line with the necessary positive functional conditionality, with a best record of approximation to the EU *acquis* by adoption of hard norms in addition to soft norms. Given the fact that the Armenian government's position indicated that the relationship with the EU constituted a priority, the pre-Vilnius summit declaration by President Sargsyan was met with disappointment in Brussels. However, the EU expressed respect for the partner's choice (Panarmenian.Net, 2013). The already negotiated AA and the DCFTA had to be abandoned and a new unprecedented type of a document was to be developed, eventually taking the shape of the CEPA. The EU therefore did not hesitate to continue with sectoral cooperation with Armenia in those spheres of interest whereby no clash between Armenia's relations with the EU and membership obligations in the EAEU would be detected. These ranged from reform of the justice sector, public administration, private sector to engagement with civil society. The sectoral cooperation was accompanied by a funding scheme, the Single Support Framework, which replaced the NIP, yet again devoid of any negative conditionality (Vasilyan, 2018).

The tacit levers which Russia may have utilised *vis-à-vis* Armenia in September 2013 draw on the above-mentioned stakes. Moreover, the entwinement between the Armenian and Russian elites allows inferring that any informal reference by the Russian leadership to these issues would have made the Armenian authorities comply with a Russia-favoured policy choice. While previously Armenia had managed to oscillate between Russia and the EU, the decision on accession to the EAEU had reshaped Armenia's former 'complementary' foreign policy into a 'supplementary' one, i.e. with unequal weight in foreign policy now distributed in favour of Russia and the EACU/EAEU with the relevant domestic repercussions (Vasilyan, 2014). In the meantime,

Armenian political actors and the public watched the Maidan from a distance, wary of any radical change potentially leading to a crisis. Albeit having retained stability, public distrust in the political processes grew in Armenia, irrespective as to whether these have been tilted towards the EU, which is associated with scepticism *qua* the values, especially, minority rights it intends to transpose, or Russia *qua* loss of sovereignty-related concerns (Vasilyan, 2011).

The EU, Russia and Belarus: conditional approaches in a zero-sum game?

At first approximation, Belarus represents a clear case of acceptance of Russia's and the rejection of the EU's conditional approaches. Since the mid-1990s, Russia's policies have been viewed as appropriate and even legitimate in Belarus, while the EU conditionality rejected along with other Western approaches, proposals and offers. The EU and the West were determined to apply negative normative conditionality on the increasingly authoritarian Belarusian regime since the mid-1990s. Brussels came to adopt 'one of the most complete CFSP sanctions regimes in force', in addition to reducing the political dialogue and the interaction with the Belarusian authorities (but not the opposition or civil society) to its minimum, which included the suspension of the PCA (Bosse, 2012, p. 374; Portela, 2011, p. 487).[19] Both internally and in relationship with Moscow, Belarus' confrontation with the West had featured as an important factor in improving the position of Belarusian leadership. Under these circumstances, the EU political conditionality had become 'unacceptable in principle' (Rontoyanni & Korosteleva, 2005, p. 217). Policies and offers coming from Moscow, on the contrary, were met positively, independent of whether they were associated with hard or soft norms. In this sense, the Belarusian leadership came to support all Russia-led regional initiatives, such as CIS, CSTO and the Eurasian project. Belarus' reaction to EU's and Russia's conditional approaches resembled the logic of a zero-sum game, in which the choice for embracing Russia's conditional approaches was embedded into an affinity-based relationship with Moscow, while rejecting the conditionality of the EU served to reaffirm Belarus' explicit denial of any EU potential to exert its influence. It is in this sense that the nature of Russia and the EU as actors with two different political identities can be argued to determine Belarus' reception of Russia's and the rejection of EU conditionality.

This account of a decade of Belarus' limited contact with the West, however, needs to be reconsidered in light of the evolving Russian and EU approaches. Starting from the mid-2000s, the acceptance of Russian conditional offers and initiatives had become much less 'commonsensical' in Belarus, as manifest in growing bilateral disagreements between the two closest allies, including recurrent trade wars, Belarus' de-alignment from Russia in the matters of recognition of Abkhazia and South Ossetia as well as cooperation within the CSTO (Busygina, 2018). Meanwhile, EU recognised that the effects of its negative normative conditionality in Belarus had been limited, which eventually paved the way to the EU' engagement with the country in the late 2000s, the opening of the European Commission's Delegation in Minsk, Belarus acceptance to the EaP (multilateral dimension), and the launch of functional cooperation. The latter has included 'structured discussions' on energy (Portela, 2011, p. 494), and some years later, visa facilitation talks and the European Dialogue on Modernisation (2012). The EU has also increased its financial support in Belarus. Targeted sanctions have been suspended in 2008, although expanded once again following the worsening of the political climate in Belarus in 2010 (Bosse, 2012, p. 376; 2018). In February 2017, Belarus unilaterally introduced a visa-free regime for citizens of all EU countries (for short-term visitors) (while Armenia introduced the same measure in January 2013). In spite of the constant episodes of political downturn, the new position assumed by the Belarusian leadership indicated that the reception of Russia's and EU's conditional approaches was hardly taking place in accordance with the logic of a zero-sum game, as one could have suggested before.

As for Russia's conditional offers, starting from the mid-2000s, their reception, while continuously viewed in largely positive terms in Belarus, was not any more related to the issue of appropriateness, to the extent that the rejection of Russia's conditionality was not any more considered an illegitimate option. As argued elsewhere (Vieira, 2014, 2016), even Belarus' initial wholehearted embracement of Russia's affinity-based conditional approaches has been founded upon a specific trade-off, in which Belarus' alliance commitments have been exchanged against economic and politico-diplomatic support of Moscow to the Belarusian regime.[20] Accordingly, Russia's shift away from an affinity-based position towards pragmatism led the Belarusian leadership to revise its posture towards Moscow (Danilovich, 2006, p. 147), even though this did not lead to a foreign policy change commensurate with a committed reorientation towards the West.

This new Belarus perspective on Russia's conditional approaches explains the mixed record of Belarus' implementation of Eurasian agreements, where the progress in terms of adoption and implementation of the agreed arrangements has coincided with a growing number of trade conflicts between Russia and Belarus, including over industrial machinery, milk products and meat, not to mention oil and gas issues (Korosteleva, 2013, p. 240). The unpredictable timing and the unclear reasons behind the 'trade wars' reinforced the belief of the Belarusian leadership that the Eurasian integration process would remain a subject of negotiations, independent of whether it was underpinned by soft or hard norms. Uncertainty over the course of Eurasian integration was reinforced by Russia's own controversial decisions, such as Russia's proposal in 2013 to adopt sanctions against Ukraine in Moldova, as a common 'Eurasian' measure, which eventually was not supported by other EACU members, including Belarus (Vieira, 2016). Similarly, Russia's decisions on anti-sanctions against the EU and the US, taken in 2014 amid the economic hardship and a new series of Russia-Belarus 'trade wars', were also not joined by Belarusian leadership, who instead decided to revise its own commitment to the Eurasian integration project, eventually causing another round of bilateral trade conflicts and introduction of border checks with Russia that were undermining the integrity of a common customs space (Vieira, 2016, 2017).

A less straightforward position on the reception of the Russian conditionality has however not meant acceptance of the conditionality of the EU. While the Belarusian leadership had acknowledged the quality of EU norms, never questioning their credibility or associated incentives and indeed often referring to the EU as a model in the talks within the CSTO and CIS frameworks (Vieira, 2014), the transposition of the EU regulatory framework was hardly a priority. Rather, the Belarusian leadership was eager to use the prospect of compliance with the EU conditionality as a bargaining chip against Russia. Given the sensitivity in Moscow to any EaP state rapprochement with the EU, which was reinforced by the events in Ukraine, the Belarusian leadership did not need to actually implement the EU *acquis*. To achieve its goals of raising stakes in the negotiation game with Moscow, some measures indicating openness to dialogue with Brussels in the spirit of 'functional cooperation' would be sufficient. In this sense, one could argue that the Belarusian elites have been able to reaffirm their agency by identifying a certain space of manoeuvre stemming from the conditional approaches of Russia and the EU. An additional factor facilitating the *rapprochement* between Minsk and Brussels has been the position assumed by the Belarusian leadership on the Ukraine crisis (Busygina, 2018), which included divergence from the official Moscow narrative, demonstrating a pro-Ukrainian orientation (Vieira, 2015), as well as Belarus' investment and engagement in the peace negotiation process. All of this has made the traditional EU focus on sanctioning the Belarusian authoritarian regime a less urgent matter.

As far as the adoption of soft rather than hard norms is concerned, the tendency has been towards the adoption of the former rather than the latter. While the legal basis (PCA), as a foundation for the potential transfer of hard norms, continues to be missing in EU-Belarus relationship, soft norms represent a sufficiently suitable fit for the Belarusian leadership's objective to use the EU conditionality as an instrument in its relationship with Moscow. In addition, opting for soft rather than hard norms in relations with the EU can be seen as a safer option: the events in Ukraine demonstrated how fast and how easy the adoption of hard norms, such as AA/DCFTA, could be politicised and even securitised in Moscow. Growing preference for the soft norms can be identified in the case of the Eurasian integration project as well, corresponding to the resistance to the institutionalisation of regulatory Eurasian norms, as in the case of the roadmap towards the common currency in the EAEU framework (Vieira, 2016). This tendency can be attributed to the aspiration of the participating countries to leave as much room for negotiation as possible, given the uncertainty related to Russia's interpretation of its Eurasian commitment (Dragneva et al., 2017, p. 10). An exception which reinforces the importance of distinguishing between cooperation in different policy areas has been the energy issue and the prospect of the Eurasian energy market, an especially sensitive matter to Belarus given the high dependence of the latter on Russia's gas and oil. In the framework of 2014–2015 EAEU negotiations, contrary to the Russian position indicating preference to leave undefined the establishing of short-term targets and roadmaps in the EAEU founding documents (Vieira, 2016), Belarus insisted on the adoption of more specific provisions. The failure of the Russian leadership to move towards harder regulation of the energy matters led the Belarusian leadership once again to revisit its Eurasian commitment.

Finally, considering the possible role of security conditionality, Belarus as Russia's ally, could be expected to act upon alliance conformity. The latter could be either a result of Russia's exercising alliance coercion as a specific form of security conditionality (Schweller, 1994) or Belarus' voluntary compliance in accordance with its interpretation of the alliance obligations. Thus far however, Belarus' alliance with Russia has not led to an unrestricted reception of Russian conditional approaches, as already indicated above. In military-strategic terms, Belarus importance to Moscow results from its geostrategic position and the direct border to NATO countries as well as connection to Russia's Kaliningrad exclave. Even though Belarus is dependent on Moscow in terms of the modernisation of its armed forces and military equipment, this cooperation structure does not always allow for the asymmetry necessary for Russia's exercising alliance coercion, something that finds confirmation in Belarus' resistance to Russia's plans to construct an airbase on Belarusian territory in 2016. In addition, as indicated above, the understanding of an alliance obligation in Belarus has been intertwined with political, economic, trade and energy aspects and a possibility to (re)negotiate the terms of Russia's conditionality. This specific context of the reception of Russian conditional approaches in Belarus has also influenced Belarus' expectations within the Eurasian project, and its setbacks combined with the instability created by the events in the neighbouring Ukraine eventually urged the Belarusian leadership to revise its alliance obligations towards Russia.

Conclusions

The present contribution, which aimed to provide an assessment of the reception of the EU's and Russia's conditional approaches in Armenia and Belarus, allows us to draw a number of conclusions. First of all, the EU and Russia, have both evolved in terms of their policies towards the shared neighbourhood since the 1990s, and have become increasingly aware of the implications and tensions provoked by their respective conditional approaches. In this respect, the launch of the EaP and an offer of AA and DCFTA, followed by the revamping of the Eurasian project, in spite of all the differences between the two approaches, represent important turning points in the evolution of the EU's and Russia's shared neighbourhood'.

In accordance with the analytical approach adopted in the special section, the present contribution has explored the importance of individual conditionality dimensions in the reception of the EU and Russian conditional approaches. Regarding the role EU and Russia as actors of different political nature and the corresponding identity dynamics in the region, the present analysis confirms that both external actors indeed prove to be critically important to the countries in EU's and Russia's shared neighbourhood: both serve as anchors for a variety of processes ranging from identity-building to economic modernisation. A reflection of this is the reception in both Armenia and Belarus of at least some (functional) conditionality from Russia and the EU. This conclusion is in tune with a further finding concerning another conditionality dimension, namely that of security. Here, the centrality of security cooperation in the bilateral relationship with Russia, i.e. the formal military alliance underpinning both Russia-Armenian and Russia-Belarus relations does not determine the reception of conditionality from just one of the two actors (Russia) to the detriment of another (EU). A case in point is Armenia and its advanced state of reception of the EU functional conditionality as manifest in the CEPA.

Confirmation of the importance of identity dynamics as a foundation for the reception of EU and Russian conditional approaches comes with some qualifiers. Firstly, neither Armenia nor Belarus have been passive receivers of the existing conditional approaches. Secondly, while both Belarus and Armenia, just as many other EaP states, can be said to display an internal identity split, manifest in the Europhile and Russophile orientations, which are present in both countries, the reception of EU conditionality in the two cases has been different. While Armenia has been able, for a long time, to absorb the EU conditionality and could thus enjoy the 'carrots' offered by both Russia and the EU, Belarus has been moving away from its exclusive reception of the Russian conditionality only starting from the mid-2000s.

The present study also allows us to confirm receptivity towards soft norms in the reception of Russian conditional approaches. As shown in the case of Armenia, soft norms correspond to Russia's aspiration to maintain its hegemonic position resulting from its role as a security guarantor, primary economic investor, trade partner and labour destination, as well as a cultural trendsetter. On the other hand, the EaP states participating in the Eurasian project seem to rely on soft norms or at least to resist the hard norms, as a means to avoid getting entrapped into a disadvantageous agreement with Russia (a concern that seems to be absent from the EaP states interactions with the EU). Belarus' position towards the common Eurasian energy market, however, shows that hard norms can also be seen as a guarantee of Russia's Eurasian commitment. This proves that the structure of interests may be more important than the general tendency towards the receptiveness of soft rather than hard norms. More generally, the present tendency towards soft rather than hard norms is demonstrative of the uncertainty regarding (the scope of) the Eurasian commitment of the participating countries.

The case of Armenia provides important evidence of the EaP states' unproblematic acceptance of hard norms embodied in the EU conditionality. Once certain of the compatibility between the offers of the two external actors, Armenia was keen on deepening relations with the EU by pursuing the closest possible integration, most vividly represented in the approximation to the EU *acquis*, without questioning any EU offer irrespective of its nature as a hard or soft norm and eventually embarking upon the course of substantial reforms. The EU, in its turn, followed the progress made by the country on its way to closer integration by offering additional funding and providing access to EU agencies and programmes.

In addition to the analysis of individual conditionality dimensions in the reception of Armenia and Belarus, the comparative analysis undertaken in this contribution allows shedding light over the reasons behind both Russia and the EU recurring to practicing negative (political) conditionality towards Belarus, while only extending positive conditionality to Armenia. A more authoritarian nature of the Belarusian regime as compared to Armenian, and its initial course of confrontation with the West provides part of the answer, but it is as important to consider that the geopolitical proximity has made Belarus, immediate geographical neighbours of both the EU and Russia, more relevant to Brussels and Moscow, thereby raising the stakes and urging both external actors to look for ways to influence the behaviour of the Belarusian leadership, with the reverse being applicable to Armenia, which is geographically detached from both. Moreover, in Armenia, both the EU and Russia have favoured stability through preservation of the status quo. Negative conditionality towards Armenia might have implied shattering the frozen Karabakh conflict, whereas Belarus does not have any security hotbed. Finally, with Belarus acting as the energy corridor between the two foreign actors, both have tried to exercise influence by asserting 'power', be it 'normative' of the EU or 'traditional' of Russia *vis-à-vis* each other. Armenia being landlocked and resource-poor, which was additionally reinforced by the fact that it had largely surrendered its energy infrastructure to Russia, and has not received such attention by either the EU or Russia.

These interests on the part of EU and Russia contribute to the explanation of the use of negative conditionality towards Belarus and non-use of the latter *vis-à-vis* Armenia. While both Belarus and Armenia have been reliant on both the EU and Russia as primary trade partners, the inter-dependence with Russia has led to recurrent trade wars in the case of Belarus, contrary to Armenia, who has evaded such tensions. Most importantly, even if both Armenia and Belarus are members of the EAEU, the former has entertained 'integration with' the EU as a foreign policy priority until the presidential declaration made in 2013. Subsequently, this has been manifested in Armenia's continued inclination to pursue closest possible cooperation with the EU through CEPA in the areas, which do not collide with the obligations it has undertaken as a member of the EAEU.

To conclude, the present contribution has once again demonstrated the need to depart from a thinking of EU or Russian conditionalities in their common neighbourhood in terms of 'competition', or in terms of the conditionality's (in)effectiveness on (one of the) supply side (s). More attention should be paid to the way the conditionality is translated into actual policy outcomes in the individual participating countries instead. Both the cases of Belarus and Armenia demonstrate that while being caught in between the EU and Russia, and likely to remain so due to their geographic, security and energy characteristics, the two EaP countries participating in the EAEU have been able to change the eventual shape and content of both the EU's and Russia's conditionalities extended to them.

Notes

1 This contribution is partly supported by the Research Center in Political Science (CICP) (UID/CPO/00758/2013) and the Portuguese Foundation for Science and Technology and the Portuguese Ministry of Education and Science through national funds. The authors would like to thank the editor and two anonymous reviewers for their time and effort leading to the present publication.
2 Russia-Belarus military alliance established by the Union Treaty (1997) has with time evolved into a common defence system, including air defence and joint military planning (Vieira, 2014). Russia-Armenia security relations initially based on a Friendship Treaty (1997) for mutual assistance in case of a potential military attack, allowing Russian guards to protect Armenia's borders with Iran and Turkey (Vasilyan, 2010b), have more recently developed towards a joint air defence system agreement (2015) and a Joint Task Force agreement (2016) (Vasilyan, 2018). Both Armenia and Belarus are highly dependent on the Russian energy. In addition to the natural gas, Russia's oil, refined and exported to the EU, generates critical export revenue for Belarus (Balmaceda, 2014).
3 While Armenia has demonstrated aspiration to integrate more closely with the EU, coming close to pre-signing the AA, including the DCFTA, but retreating from this foreign policy course in 2013 (Vasilyan, 2017) and eventually signing the Comprehensive and Enhanced Partnership Agreement (CEPA), Belarus has only participated in the multilateral track of the EaP, and its relations with the EU evolved without a PCA (Vieira, 2014).
4 Besides the EaP states, TACIS also covered Russia and the Central Asian countries.
5 The EED was established in 2013 replicating the US National Endowment for Democracy (Vasilyan, 2018).
6 The Minsk Group was a body set-up at the 1994 Budapest summit to deal with the mediation process of this conflict.
7 Both parties displayed willingness to exert influence via agenda-setting. Eventually, although Sweden remained a participating state of the Minsk Group, it was replaced by France as a co-chair in 1996 (Vasilyan, 2013). Besides the co-chairing Russia, France and the United States (US), the Minsk Group comprises Sweden, Germany, Italy, Finland, as well as Belarus and Turkey as participating states.
8 These clauses linked upholding human rights and democracy to an increase in trade access and deepening of relations in general, while also stipulating a unilateral suspension of the agreement in the event of its 'material breach' (Bosse, 2012, p. 369; Hillion, 2000, p. 1220).
9 EU sanctions imposed on Belarus since 1996 included visa bans, freezing of assets of certain individuals, economic sanctions on Belarusian companies, withdrawal of privileges under the Generalised System of Preferences, in addition to limiting the political dialogue. Sanctions never included a stoppage of the oil and/or gas flow into the EU, even 'given the fact that income from such sales was so critical for the Lukashenka regime' (Balmaceda, 2014, p. 63).
10 In 2006, the difference in pricing policy for the natural gas of Ukraine versus Belarus constituted 55 versus USD 95 per thousand cubic metres (Balmaceda, 2014).
11 These revisions covered the time period of Armenia's participation in the EaP (see below).
12 The price was lowered from USD 286 for thousand cubic metres in 2011 to 166 per thousand cubic metres in 2012.

13 Being among the oldest ethnic civilisations, Armenia thrived as a kingdom in the 1st century BC during the reign of Tigran the Great, then briefly in 1918–1920 as a part of the Transcaucasian Democratic Federative Republic, afterwards of the Transcaucasian Federated Soviet Socialist Republic and subsequently, as the ASSR.
14 The number of Armenians residing abroad surpasses the number of those in the country by about twice.
15 The EU approach has differed from the approach of the US, which imposed negative conditionality on Armenia (Vasilyan, 2010c).
16 This Programme covering travel, housing, job placement, among other factors was however ceased in 2012 due to the concerns raised by the Armenian government reflecting the public discontent over emigration (Hakobyan, 2012).
17 The civic rallies carried out since November 2007 have been against potentially negative environmental consequences of mining. The illegal construction in the Mashtotz Park in Yerevan led to protests in February 2012. Further, rallies were held against the pension reform in January 2014, demolition of buildings having historical significance in Yerevan in June 2014, extradition of a Russian servicemen who murdered an Armenian family in Gyumri in January 2015, the rise of public transport fares in June 2015, and the electricity price hike in July 2015. A distinct kind of protest in the form of an armed occupation of a police station took place in July 2016 (Vasilyan, 2016).
18 While Iran had been neutral *vis-à-vis* the Nagorno-Karabakh conflict due to its large Azeri population, as well as its marginalisation owing to the Western sanctions, after the nuclear deal reached through the Geneva process, Iran has become a more active regional player.
19 Subsequently, Brussels has reached out to the Belarusian civil society and the opposition, by supporting media programmes, backing the opening of the Office for Democratic Belarus in Brussels, sustaining the European Parliament's Delegation for relations with Belarus (Vasilyan, 2018) and the support to the European Humanitarian University, which moved to Vilnius after it was closed down in 2004 in Minsk.
20 This has allowed to classify Belarus' relationship with Russia as 'bandwagoning for profit' (Schweller, 1994, p. 74; *cf* Vieira, 2016).

References

Arka News Agency. (2016, August 11). Daily says Russian Gazprom suggests cutting price of natural gas for Armenia. Retrieved from http://arka.am/en/news/economy/daily_says_russian_gazprom_suggests_cutting_price_of_natural_gas_for_armenia/

Asbarez. (2013, November 8). Karabakh has place in customs union, says Russian official. Retrieved from http://asbarez.com/116005/karabakh-has-place-in-customs-union-says-russian-official/

Babayan, N. (2015). *Democratic transformation and abstraction: EU, US and Russia in the South Caucasus*. Abington: Routledge.

Balmaceda, M. (2014). *Living the high life in Minsk Russian energy rents, domestic populism and Belarus' impending crisis*. Budapest: Central European University Press.

Black, J. (2015). *The Russian presidency of Dmitry Medvedev, 2008–2012: The next step forward or merely a time out?* Abingdon: Routledge.

Bosse, G. (2012). A partnership with dictatorship: Explaining the paradigm shift in European Union policy towards Belarus. *JCMS, 50*(3), 367–384.

Bosse, G. (2018). EU -Belarus relations in the context of the European neighbourhood policy. In T. Schumacher, A. Marchetti, & T. Demmelhuber (Eds.), *Handbook of the European neighbourhood policy* (pp. 290–301). Abdington: Routledge.

Busygina, I. (2018). *Russia-EU relations and the common neighbourhood: Coercion vs. authority*. London: Routledge.

Danilovich, A. (2006). *Russian-Belarusian integration: Playing games behind the kremlin walls*. Aldershot: Ashgate.

Delcour, L. (2017). *The EU and Russia in their 'contested neighbourhood': Multiple external influences, policy transfer and domestic change*. Abington: Routledge.

Delcour, L. & Wolczuk, K. (2014). Eurasian economic integration: Implications for the EU Eastern policy. In R. Dragneva & K. Wolczuk (Eds.), *Eurasian economic integration: Law, policy, politics* (pp. 180–203). Cheltenham: Edward Elgar.

De Waal, T. (2003). *Black garden: Armenia and Azerbaijan through peace and war.* New York and London: New York University Press.

Dragneva, R., Delcour, L., & Jonavicius, L. (2017, November). Assessing legal and political compatibility between the European Union engagement strategies and membership of the Eurasian Economic Union. EU-STAT Working Paper Series No. 7. Retrieved from http://eu-strat.eu/wp-content/uploads/2016/05/EU-STRAT-Working-Paper-No.7.pd

European Commission. (2003, March 11). Wider Europe-neighbourhood: A new framework for relations with our Eastern and Southern neighbours. Communication to the council and the parliament, Brussels.

European Commission. (n.d.). Council adopted new regulation to launch TACIS 1996. Retrieved from http://europa.eu/rapid/press-release_IP-96-559_en.htm

Freedom House. (2016). Nations in transit: Armenia 2016. Retrieved from https://freedomhouse.org/report/nations-transit/2016/armenia

Grigoryan, M. (2013, September). Armenia: Customs union commitment risks EU cooperation chances. *Eurasianet.* Retrieved from http://www.eurasianet.org/node/67482

Hakobyan, J. (2012). End of "compatriots"?: Government says Russian immigration program unacceptable for Armenia. Retrieved from https://www.armenianow.com/society/40234/russian_program_compatriots_concerns_armenia_labor_migration

Hale, J. (2012, May). Brussels, open society Institute Discussion Paper. Retrieved from https://www.opensocietyfoundations.org/sites/default/files/eu-relations-azerbaijan-20120606.pdf

Hillion, C. (2000). Institutional aspects of the partnership between the EU and the newly independent states of the former Soviet Union—Case studies of Russia and Ukraine. *Common Market Law Review, 37*(5), 1211–1235.

Korosteleva, E. (2013). Belarusian foreign policy in a time of crisis. In V. Feklynina & S. White (Eds.), *The international economic crisis and the post-Soviet states* (pp. 232–252). Oxon: Routledge.

Kucera, J. (2015, June 19). Russia trying to maintain 'parity' in arms sales to Armenia, Azerbaijan. Retrieved from www.eurasianet.org/node/73936

Ministry of Foreign Affairs of the RoA. (2007). Foreign policy. Retrieved from www.mfa.am/en/foreign-policy/

Panarmenian.Net. (2013, September 4). EU wants Armenia's explanation over customs union. Retrieved from http://www.panarmenian.net/eng/news/169553/

Portela, C. (2011). The European Union and belarus: Sanctions and partnership? *Comparative European Politics, 9*(4–5), 486–505.

Radio Free Europe, Radio Liberty. (2015, September 8). Armenian leaders gets $200 million loan, gas price cut from Russia. Retrieved from www.rferl.org/content/armenian-leader-gets200-millionloan-gas-price-cut-from-russia/27232478.html

Rontoyanni, C., & Korosteleva, E. (2005). Belarus: An authoritarian exception from the model of post-communist democratic transition? In T. Flockhart (Ed.), *Socializing democratic norms: The role of international organizations for the construction of Europe* (pp. 209–213). Basingstoke: Palgrave Macmillan.

Samokhvalov, V. (2016). Ukraine and Eurasian regionalism: A case of holding together integration. In D. Lane & V. Samokhvalov (Eds.), *The Eurasian project and Europe: Regional discontinuities and geo-politics* (pp. 169–184). Basingstoke: Palgrave Macmillan.

Schmidt-Felzmann, A. (2016). The breakdown of the EU's strategic partnership with Russia: From strategic patience towards a strategic failure. *Cambridge Review of International Affairs, 29*(1), 99–127.

Schweller, R. (1994). Bandwagoning for profit: Bringing the revisionist state back in. *International Security, 19*(1), 72–107.

Vasilyan, S. (2006). The policy of regional cooperation in the south Caucasus. Working Paper 24, Buenos Aires, Argentinean Center of International Studies.

Vasilyan, S. (2010a). The 'European' 'Neighbourhood' 'Policy' (ENP): A holistic account. In D. Bailey & U. Wunderlich (Eds.), *Handbook on the European Union and global governance* (pp. 177–187). London and New York: Routledge.

Vasilyan, S. (2010b). A cacophony: The EU's security policy towards the south Caucasus. In K. Henderson & C. Weaver (Eds.), *The black sea and EU policy: The challenge of divergent agendas* (pp. 87–107). Farnham: Ashgate.

Vasilyan, S. (2010c). 'The European Union as an impotent democracy-promoter in the south Caucasus?' European Consortium for Political Research (ECPR) 5th Pan-European Conference on EU Politics, Porto, Portugal (June 23–26).

Vasilyan, S. (2011). The external legitimacy of the European Union (EU) in the south Caucasus. *European Foreign Affairs Review, 16*(3), 341–357.

Vasilyan, S. (2013). 'Moral power' as objectification of 'civilian'/'normative' EUlogy: EU as a conflict-dealer in the south Caucasus. *Journal of International Relations and Development, 17*(13), 397–424.

Vasilyan, S. (2014). 'Armenia from a foreign policy of complementarity to supplementarity? A sandwich story!' International Affairs Forum, Washington, DC: Centre for International Relations. Retrieved from http://www.ia-forum.org/Content/ViewInternalDocument.cfm?ContentID=8084

Vasilyan, S. (2016). "Armenia (B)Locked in Transition?!" Paper presented at a workshop organized by Maastricht University, Brussels, Belgium, October 6–7, 2016.

Vasilyan, S. (2017). "Swinging on the pendulum": Armenia in the Eurasian Economic Union and with the European Union. *Problems of Post-Communism, 64*(1), 32–46.

Vasilyan, S. (2018). *The European Union as a 'moral power' in the south Caucasus*. London: Palgrave Macmillan.

Vasilyan, S., & Petrossian, S. (2014). Russia's policy towards the south Caucasus: Triangulation of domestic, border and foreign logics. In L. Asta (Ed.), *Challenges and perspectives of contemporary Russia* (pp. 37–66). Padova: Digital Academic Press.

Vieira, A. (2014). The politico-military alliance of Russia and Belarus: Re-examining the role of NATO and the EU in light of the intra-alliance security dilemma. *Europe-Asia Studies, 66*(4), 557–577.

Vieira, A. (2016). Eurasian integration: Elite perspectives before and after the Ukraine crisis. *Post-Soviet Affairs, 32*(6), 566–580.

Vieira, A. (2017). A tale of two unions: Russia–Belarus integration experience and its lessons for the Eurasian Economic Union. *Journal of Borderlands Studies, 32*(1), 41–53.

The European Union and Belarus
Democracy promotion by technocratic means?

Elena A. Korosteleva

Introduction: "still waters" or incremental change?

Is Belarus an unwavering constant in international relations: an authoritarian maverick, continuously isolated from the West, and increasingly entangled with the Russian – now Eurasian – sphere of influence? Indeed, on the surface, there seems to be business as usual: for two decades Freedom House has referred to the country as "the least free, or fair" in Europe,[1] while scholarly accounts customarily depict it as "the last dictatorship in Europe",[2] with Alexander Lukashenko remaining as de facto president since 1994.

Belarus' relations with the international community and, especially, with its larger western neighbour – the European Union (EU) – have shown little sign of change since the mid-1990s, and at best could be described as spasmodic: for every intention to co-operate, there always seems to be a counter-action to thwart it. For example, an initially enthusiastic ratification of Belarus' Partnership and Cooperation Agreement (PCA) with the EU in 1995 ended in suspension only two years later, owing to its declining human rights record.[3] A subsequent rapprochement in 1999 – as part of the "Responsible Neighbourhood" strategy – instead concluded in the signing of a Union Treaty with Russia.[4] Efforts for more dialogue under the European Neighbourhood Policy (ENP) in 2004 and a subsequent Eastern Partnership Initiative (EaP) in 2009,[5] yielded only partial involvement of Belarus, in a non-binding multilateral track of regional cooperation. A Joint Interim Plan carrying substantial financial incentives, but straightjacketed by political conditionality,[6] disintegrated after the 2010 presidential election. The 2012 Dialogue on Modernization, targeting civil society, to date, as claimed, has had only a limited effect.[7] A sense of impasse around EU-Belarus relations has now grown into a *sense of fatigue* amongst policymakers, donors, and even practitioners, resulting in half-measures normally short of action and commitment.[8] Donors are particularly wary of Belarus-focused discussions, and presently there seems to be a tacit acceptance of the established status quo.

Meanwhile, Belarus' relations with its eastern neighbours have predictably expanded, albeit more often through compulsion, rather than by free will. By 2007 Belarus was co-opted into negotiation over the Eurasian Customs Union (ECU) with Russia and Kazakhstan, which took force in 2010.[9] By May 2014 the ECU member-states signalled a joint agreement on the prospective launch of the Eurasian Economic Union (EEU), to come into effect in January 2015.[10]

So, as it seems, Belarus' domestic and international relations remain emphatically stagnant, reflecting a predictable status quo, or do *they?*

Two critical disjunctures challenge a seemingly enduring order. The first disjuncture refers to the government's quiet but persistent discourse of resistance to Russia's overbearing influence, manifested in three long years of sabotaging the launch of the ECU and petty wars over trade and economic issues;[11] in re-shaping the Eurasian course into a *cumulative integration* narrative to stay connected with both the East and the West;[12] in a recently increasing dialogue with the EU;[13] and more tellingly, in publicly endorsing Petro Poroshenko's leadership in Ukraine and objecting to Russia's demands for extending an economic and political embargo to the country.[14]

The second disjuncture is by far more emblematic of existing undercurrents at work, exposing profound longitudinal changes[15] in public opinion and behaviour associated with growing levels of affinity and interest in the EU, as well as the public's gradual legitimation of European standards and fostering of a new European identity – "We are part of Europe", a narrative hitherto absent from a public "story-telling". This indicates an ongoing process of socialization into a European discourse and a wider European space, manifested at different levels and by different actors. In turn, this may also suggest that the EU, despite a limited official dialogue, might have been doing something "right", to be able to succeed in expanding the boundaries of public space and even engendering a new sense of identity. This triggers a range of questions, with three perhaps being of particular relevance: (1) what has been the EU's strategy to date, especially in the circumstances of no political dialogue; (2) how does this translate into public/government narratives; and (3) essentially, if there are changes, why now and what of democracy?

Hence, this article sets out to examine recent changes in EU policy towards the region, and Belarus in particular, to uncover causalities at work, which may be, at least partially, responsible for the social transformation that is occurring in the country. In particular, the article contends that the "opening" of government and public narratives – the "story-telling" of their daily lives – is a consequence of the continuing and persistent practice of engagement by the EU, but not through high-level politics and value-taxing conditionality. This proves some vocal critics wrong who believe that they are "betraying" EU values "when partnering dictatorships".[16] Instead it is rather the enablement via codified, regulatory, and interest-driven exposure of individuals at different levels, through sector cooperation, to the workings of European democracy, which makes a difference. These changes, reflected in altering patterns of public behaviour and a growing sense of identity, necessitate further discussion of democracy promotion as a non-linear process of social empowerment which works with local issues on an individual level, and of international assistance, which inculcates international norms into people's daily practices and narratives, thus approximating their space to that of "the international". Whatever the assumptions or their justifying rationalities, they invariably challenge the established political (value-driven) underpinnings for democracy promotion, and necessitate a discussion of social empowerment *anew*, and by *other means*, which are uncovered below.

The EU approach: towards social empowerment and norm codification

Since the launch of the ENP in 2004, the EU had struggled to secure allegiance from the partner countries in the east.[17] The policy went through several iterations with the same limited effect: its further differentiation, including the initiation of the EaP, raised more concerns than provided solutions to the dwindling support by the eastern neighbours.[18]

In 2011, however, the European Commission substantively revisited its approach to the eastern region,[19] which marked a turning point in EU engagement.[20] Three particular aspects are worth noting here: First, the new measures have become *more complex and versatile*, expanding the panoply of instruments, programmes, and actors, to lock partners into an enduring reciprocal relationship. Second, the new approach became more *inclusive* in targeting all levels of society, especially regionally and locally, ensuing EU visibility and internalization of European standards. Third, and perhaps most instructively here, the EU approach has become more *technical*, sector-driven, and low-key, gradually depoliticizing conditionality, but enabling the codification of norms and their inculcation into the daily practices of Belarusian people. Let us observe the context of the occurring change.

The 2011 and onwards iteration of the EaP approach turned a *two-track approach* into a complex matrix of *enablement*, supported by a new "more for more" format of cooperation.[21] Primarily, the bilateral track offered legally binding Association Agreements (AA) to the willing parties, which, after a series of recent setbacks and postponements, have now been signed with Ukraine, Georgia, and Moldova.[22] The AAs, structured along the three principal dimensions of fostering political association/free trade area (DCFTA), mobility partnerships, and sector cooperation, lay the groundwork for an ambitious integrationist agenda, especially in terms of expanding the single European market and making EU institutional structures more accessible.[23] These binding initiatives were supported by a wide range of financial instruments and structural programmes, including the European Neighbourhood Instrument (ENI),[24] the Neighbourhood Investment Facility, the EAP Integration and Cooperation Facility, Civil Society Facility (CSF), European Endowment for Democracy (EED), European Investment Bank's (EIB) external mandate and the EU-financed Council of Europe Eastern Partnership Facility, which jointly approximated €1 billion in loans and grants for 2011–2013 alone![25]

Admittedly, the EU *bilateral track* does not officially apply to Belarus. At the same time, the EU succeeded in making important contractual inroads into the country, via technical assistance and sector cooperation, amounting to almost €60 million under the ENPI for 2012–2013 alone;[26] this thus related to a sixfold increase in funding available for 2007–2011. The range of structural programmes has also expanded. In particular, the bilateral 2012–2013 roadmap for Belarus aimed at enhancing mobility and sector cooperation. The ensuing talks on visa facilitation (including bilateral actions of individual member states) and readmission agreements gradually yielded a positive response from the government.[27] Under sector cooperation the EU has initiated talks on the Baltic Energy Market Interconnection Plan to establish a regulatory and institutional framework promoting energy efficiency and increasing renewable energy use (C.2.a.) and has introduced a strategic framework for EU-Belarus customs cooperation which was agreed and endorsed in 2011 (C.7).[28] Belarus was also included as an observer in the Northern Dimension Partnership; and is now an active participant of the Partnerships on Environment and on Transport and Logistics. The Market Economy Status assessment, launched in Belarus in 2010, prepares the ground for structural reforms and economic stabilization. To address regional economic and social disparities, new pilot regional development programmes were recently added[29] offering over €10 million in support and investment. This is in addition to the Comprehensive Institution Building (CIB) programmes addressing public administration reforms, which totalled €5 million for 2012–2013. The Delegation of the European Commission to Belarus was upgraded to a fully-fledged EU Delegation in the course of 2011, and is now an active interlocutor between the government and non-state actors in Belarus. The EIB has also extended its lending mandate to Belarus; this assistance has at a minimum increased twofold since 2010.[30]

These concrete roadmap targets – although still officially limited in scope and coverage – do not simply aim to lock partners into a "more for more" modality of cooperation and self-censorship; they also promote decentring and local initiative which embrace all levels of society – civil society, businesses, local authorities, central government, and national parliaments. This has clearly facilitated some local activism in Belarus, especially amongst business interests and non-state actors.[31]

At the same time, Belarus' full engagement with the EU has been chiefly facilitated by *the EaP multilateral track*.[32] Since 2011 the track has come to operate its own instruments and infrastructure.[33] It is precisely its *inclusive* nature that allows further individuation of EU policies in support of local activism and democracy. Notably, in all six EaP countries, CSF, national platforms, Business Forum,[34] CORLEAP,[35] and EURONEST[36] have provided civil society organizations and other stakeholders with a chance to articulate their needs, and facilitate reforms at the level of the individual countries. Many local actors are now regular and active participants in various EaP informal and formal consultations and meetings.[37]

This panoply of instruments and actors (especially CSF, EED, and special measures) have continuously covered Belarus, including at the time of diplomatic crises which followed the 2010 and 2012 elections. Through thematic platforms alone, Belarus received in aid over €300 million worth of funding (some *ongoing* since 2001), having become fully integrated with good governance, people-to-people, and socio-economic projects.[38] A *European Dialogue on Modernization* with Belarusian society was launched at the European Commission's initiative on 29 March 2012,[39] and now involves, via specific projects, over 747 non-governmental organizations alone who engage with EU-level activities.[40] The dialogue offers the exchange of views and inculcation of EU practices into stakeholders at various levels. The agenda of meetings is set by the Belarusian stakeholders, identifying priorities for support and investment in the forthcoming years; and the language of decision-making is output-driven, and codified to European standards. The first meeting of the dialogue took place in Poland on 16–17 April 2012 and focused on the issues of privatization and entrepreneurship.[41] In 2013 the dialogue, for example, initiated two new programmes for Belarus: BELMED – supporting reforms in the health care system (€8 million) and RELOAD-2 offering support for regional and local development in two regions – Grodno and Minsk (€3.5 million). Although limited in terms of direct contact with higher-level officials, the dialogue is effective at lower levels (including respective ministries), and helps regional authorities, in particular, to identify and promote development strategies, and support local communities through training and grant-identifying strategies.[42] As the Belarusian Ministry of Foreign Affairs confirms, there are currently 59 ongoing projects (with over 150 successfully completed in the past ten years, and many ongoing on the European Commission assessment!) being implemented in Belarus under EaP initiatives, especially in the areas of border modernization and customs infrastructure, energy, transport, environment, education, and culture, the overall budget of which has quadrupled since 2010.[43]

Finally, and most importantly, many of these initiatives simply focus on sector cooperation, avoiding high-level politics and instead connecting multiple stakeholders, within and outside the country, to encourage their socialization into international practices, and to facilitate an independent mode of thinking. As Petrova and Raube observe,[44] a single added value of EURONEST is perhaps less about the output, but much more about the process of their communication, which enables a new language of norms, new narratives of deliberation, and prospectively, a new modus operandi, conducive to fostering reciprocal learning space and future dialogue. This mode of engagement – low-key, depoliticized, and technocratic – is relatively new, but has already proven effective by enabling a greater number of local actors, and increasing their levels of awareness, appreciation, and affinity with EU standards, as the next section conveys. It is perhaps unsurprising that the EU *bilateral initiatives* for Belarus for 2014–2017 propose to include projects focusing on social inclusion, environment, and local and regional economic development, with the indicative support of €90 million,[45] which, if anything, should further enable reasoned and responsive citizenship and raise awareness about people's social rights and economic benefits of cooperation. In this framing, the technocratic means of democracy promotion becomes social empowerment, rather than a defeat of the EU's normative agenda, as some commentators of this approach would contend.[46]

The above examination of the advantages of continued EU technocratic engagement is not at all to claim that this non-linear approach has been impervious to fallacy: the events in Ukraine explicitly challenge this position. It is clear that the complex and inclusive matrix of engagement, although innovative and versatile in the opportunities it offers, still lacks the mechanisms of ensuring implementation and commitment to the course. It also struggles to outpace Russia in offering, and committing partners to accept, alternative choices. At the same time, and no matter how imperfect the overall model of EU external engagement still is, it is a decisive step forward in trying to engage more inclusively, predicating on the needs of partner countries and their people. Belarus' case is very instructive here: despite the overall lack of strategy, and political dialogue, the aforementioned activities have triggered some substantial undercurrents, which may, with time, erode the existing architecture of the deadlocked relations between the EU and Belarus, nudging the latter towards more dialogue and cooperation. As Commissioner Fü̈le has commented, the EaP, despite its setbacks and shortcomings, offers a much-needed "inclusive process" of enablement and allows countries like Belarus, deterred by other commitments, still to be part of the wider European project.[47] These of course may well be far-reaching objectives, especially in the light of the immense damage caused by the war in Ukraine, Russia's annexation of Crimea, and a continued regional dispute between the EU and Russia. Nevertheless, the changing modus operandi does help to reignite hopes and combat decision-making fatigue vis-à-vis Belarus at the international level. No matter how small-scale or confined the above activities may seem, they reveal what "still waters" hide well – the practices at work which are inspired by new instruments and actors, and which eventually may lead to the emergence of new social structures to challenge the seemingly inviolable surface of the existing status quo. How do the above activities translate into a public modus operandi?

Population: EU legitimacy writ large?

As discussed elsewhere,[48] public legitimation is one of the most essential requirements for fostering sustainable democracy. It works as a measure of acceptance and support for the established political order, a kind of subscription to a professed normative course. It also serves as a means to keep governments accountable, when it comes to evaluating their performance and deliberating on a new course. Hence, exploring the nature of public discourse as a composite of citizens' daily narratives is an important exercise, which may expose some causality at work and render a clearer view on public recognition of the impact of EU policy as well as the validity of the government's course, and the perception of the self. All these aspects, in correlation with EU policy practices examined earlier, should shed a new light on the current debate about the nature and strategies of democracy promotion.

Based on extensive and subject-focused research, conducted in the country between 2009 and 2013,[49] the findings of which were also corroborated by a number of other sources,[50] the following trends become identifiable via crosstemporal analysis of public behaviour and attitudes, and are explored below:

1   there has been a significant rise in public awareness and cognizance of the EU as a polity, its institutions and policies;
2   there is a growing sense of clarity and recognition of EU competencies in specific areas, and their mapping against the needs and interests of the population;
3   most essentially, a new sense of identity is being forged premised on a more critical evaluation of the self, acceptance of European standards, and interrogation of government rationale for one-dimensional policy eastwards. To this end, relations with Russia (and the ECU) are no longer seen as a default option for Belarus.

First, a cross-temporal analysis of public opinion explicitly reveals a positive and substantive shift of preferences towards the EU, in cross-temporal comparison. This is primarily reflected in higher levels of awareness, more discernible knowledge of EU structures and policies, more interest in EU affairs, more appreciation of EU support, and most importantly, a more identity-based narrative vis-à-vis the EU. In particular, the levels of public awareness about the EU as a polity have reached 97%, an absolute majority (+4%), allowing the facilitation of a more discernible understanding of the EU structures, institutions, and activities. Respondents display higher cognizance in detailing EU functions, policies, and multilevel actors, in comparison with any other international organizations cited in the survey. They could name without difficulty all member states of the EU, its key institutions and geographical outposts of power. This is further reinforced by growing interest in EU affairs (49%; +5%), against a similar drop in that of Belarus-Russia and the Commonwealth of Independent States. An astonishing two-fold increase is observable in the positive image of the EU within the country (55%). Twice as many respondents are now familiar with the EaP initiative (39%), and correctly name countries and their progress under the ENP framework. Moldova and Georgia are listed as the frontrunners, while Ukraine is observed as "problematic" and Belarus as "a laggard", "to be ashamed of" (+4%). The EU is increasingly associated with "hope" (+5%) and "enthusiasm" (+10%); replacing the "indifference" (−6%) and "mistrust" (−3%) of the past.

Second, changing attitudinal positions of respondents also render greater clarity to EU objectives, policies, and intentions towards the country, which translate directly into public appreciation and recognition of EU competencies in some specific areas, while mapping them against those of the ECU. Notably, EU support is now seen as corresponding more closely to the interests of both the government and people (a two-fold rise since 2009), and there is an increasing overlap between what Belarusians perceive to be "most pressing issues" of the day and where the EU could adequately help. More specifically, while living costs, working conditions, meagre pensions, and a crumbling health system are regarded as imminently failing and in need of urgent support, it is believed that Belarus could learn more from the EU in the areas of economic reform (81%), social protection (66%), effective governance (63%), and independence of the judiciary (61%). This is particularly striking when compared to a set of areas where the ECU's competencies and aid are believed to be complementary: trade (70%), economic reforms (51%), tourism (38%), and energy security (29%). This comparison indicates the EU's growing credibility with the general public, and deeper public understanding of EU and ECU competencies. A clear mapping out of the competencies of the EU and the ECU seems to have taken place in public narratives, and more often than not, they are viewed in their distinctiveness and complementarity, allowing for the development of synergies and their legitimation.

Greater clarity about the EU's intentions towards the country in turn generates closer affinity with the former as a polity and a major power. In particular, a third of the respondents have now come to assert that the EU is an *important strategic partner*, which is comparable with those pledging support for the ECU and Russia (39%), with the latter historically enjoying strong public support. In public assessment of the EaP's relevance and effectiveness, twice as many respondents have found that partnership now fully corresponds to *the interests* of Belarus' government and its people. On average, a 10% rise is observed amongst those who affirm that the EaP is premised on *common* values (43%), common economic and political interests (39%), common security interests (45%), and mutual trust (56%). Further legitimation of the EU is manifested in a sharp two-fold decline in those respondents who initially contended that Belarus-EU cooperation was in the EU's interests only. A tenth of the population have heard about the programme on modernization initiated by the EU in March 2012. Many respondents noted particular progress in the areas of trade, cross-border cooperation, student exchange, and economic opportunities; a fifth pledged that this cooperation fully corresponds to the interests of the people (+7%). These rather affirmative reflections are radically different to those in 2009, which displayed more indifference and fear. In a relatively short period of time, the transformation in attitudinal and behavioural patterns is truly astounding, especially given the non-existent bilateral dialogue between the EU and Belarus under the EaP, and the growing presence of the ECU and Russia in Belarus' domestic politics.

Third and most instructive, is the rise of a new critical identity amongst Belarusians. A new narrative, which expresses growing public affinity with the EU, can be summed up as "We are Europeans", and "We are part of Europe", which hitherto had no precedent. In parallel, changes in public self-perception also become apparent, associated with a more critical (and even negative) view of Belarus' external policies, and its single-vector move eastward. In particular, an increasing number of respondents disapprove of the course of Belarus' foreign policy (+6%), and critically assess Belarus' image abroad (31%, a two-fold rise since 2009). Many believe that Belarus may no longer be seen as a suitable and important partner to their neighbours, and especially to the EU (52%; +5%). Some begin to view their country as a security threat to the neighbourhood (+4%), expressing increasing vulnerability and a sense of insecurity about their future. It is important to note that this progressively negative self-assessment coincided with the *increasing mobility* of the population as a whole. A growing number of respondents now travel abroad (+5%), and have been to the EU more than once (+4%). This is against a considerable decline of those (−20%) who had never travelled outside the country.

Russia and the ECU continue to be viewed favourably as Belarus' foreign policy priority, but this is no longer exclusive, and is manifested in many different ways. For example, when faced with the choice between the EU and Russia/ECU, the respondents no longer unequivocally support the latter, as was the case in 2009. Only one-third express their full preference for the continued union with Russia/EEU (a drop of 24%), while another third expresses a closer affinity with the EU (a rise of 15%). Only 23% see benefits of working exclusively with the ECU (a drop of 27%), and the majority (37%) believe that partnership with both polities would be of greater benefit for the country.

In summary, five years on (2009; 2013) public legitimation of the EU is clearly on the rise, reflecting positive changes in attitudinal preferences and behavioural patterns. Particularly noticeable is the rising ideational affinity of the respondents with the EU, and their now comparable treatment of the EU with that of the ECU and Russia. In 2009, as the survey shows, the population was largely uninterested and uninformed about the EU: every fifth respondent had difficulty in naming EU member states, every second failed to locate the EU's headquarters. This radically altered by 2013, attesting to the efforts and benefits of the EU's continued low-key engagement with the people, at different levels of the social hierarchy. The inclusive and versatile nature of EU projects, instruments, and sector cooperation, directly or otherwise, succeeded in awakening a long overdue interest and urge for cooperation, as well as in producing an astounding array of various actors who begin to question the established status quo, and those who actively advocate for reciprocal learning space with the EU, and other neighbours.

These new narratives, to a degree, are mirrored by government discourse, openly recognizing the need to pursue a multi-vector foreign policy. As Lukashenko formally declared in 2008, "the 'Golden Rule' of our foreign policy is *multi-vectoredness* and interest in reciprocal contracts... We are equally keen on cooperating with both the East and the West, and especially the EU".[51]

This discourse – of tacit resistance and clandestine diversification – continues, even at the sight of a closer approximation with the ECU and the future EEU, which Belarus feels compelled to ratify given pressure from Russia.[52] Government discontent with its increasing co-optation by Russia into a binding space of the ECU/EEU has been detected on several occasions, including criticism of Yanukovich's actions towards Maidan, endorsing Poroshenko's presidency, and refusing to support Russia's economic embargo of Ukraine, as mentioned earlier. By now it seems to have become a regular feature of Belarus' policy-making eastward.

This is not to say that these disjunctures – in public and government discourses – recently emergent in Belarus' external relations are fully institutionalized to challenge the established order. Much more work is still needed, especially in terms of developing synergies, through shared practices and reciprocal learning, to assure gradual convergence between normative foundations of the EU and Belarus. As the survey indicates, the uncompromising differences, which go back to prehistory, cultural traditions, and ways of living remain acute, explicitly differentiating between the models of liberal democracy and those of non-liberal type.[53] At the same time, signs of convergence, especially in the socio-economic terrain, and the potential complementarity of the two regional projects – the EaP and the ECU – are gradually translating into the daily narratives of citizens and their governments, indicating their potential.

New normative visions, even when simply associating with more stability, prosperity, and security rather than highly politicized values of European democracy, cannot be imposed externally, even by means of the most sophisticated social/ideational engineering. It is important on this occasion to recognize and accept the very existence of the non-liberal Other, who can only be *socialized* rather than compelled into a "shared mode" of thinking, if sustainable relations are to endure. On the part of the EU, this understanding is slowly be forged, whereby political conditionality, although still mooted, is now complemented by a technocratic campaign of codification and inculcation of norms and practices into the daily lives of individuals. The EU is expanding its presence in Belarus, and the benefits of incremental socialization are beginning to show. At the same time, the EU is still a considerable distance away from understanding that the pursuit of cooperation is not simply about propping up the same political initiatives with new or more instruments or implementing them in a unilateral manner. It is a lengthy and painstaking process of change through continued assistance, but with no immediate or significant outcomes to justify commitment. However if commitment is there, social empowerment and norm inculcation may do wonders, which is further explored below.

Further discussion: social empowerment by technocratic means?

What does the above discussion tell us about the causality of change and of a changing (and contested) nature of democracy promotion? So far we have registered a transforming nature of EU democracy promotion strategy towards Belarus. The analysis of EU engagement with the country did not only uncover its continued and even increasing levels of engagement undertaken in the circumstances of limited political dialogue under a much-criticized ENP/EaP. Most crucially, the analysis reveals substantive change in the EU's modus operandi – from high to a low-level politics – which became more technocratic (and sector-focused), more versatile in its instruments, and more inclusive in its structures. The crucial question here is whether this shift in EU governance has had any positive effect on regime performance in Belarus?

Further, in our analysis, we also observed a gradual change in public attitudes and behavioural patterns, which more recently began to manifest as closer affinity with the EU, expressed through rising levels of public awareness, cognizance, interest, and emotive approval. There has also been a better understanding of the EU as a neighbour and a polity, and important mapping of interests and capacity, by the respondents, has taken place. Most instructively however, there have been significant shifts in identity formation, inclusive of a more critical view of the self, and a more quizzical view of the other – the EU and the ECU/Russia in this particular case. A newly emergent public narrative conveys more "European-ness" amongst the Belarusians, and the urge to become more open-minded and inclusive of both the West and the East, to avoid a hitherto privileged treatment of Russia as a default option.

The above processes of course may or may not be connected; after all, establishing transparent causality in the ontology of beings has always been tricky (some would even argue impossible).[54] At the same time, given the coincidence of the time periods – of the shift in EU governance and a subsequent shift in public opinion – as well as the respondents' concrete references to EU-specific measures and projects, the bourgeoning number of actors who associated with their activities positively, one might confidently rationalize the occurring changes in their causal connectivity. Does it imply that democracy promotion by technocratic means has a precedent today and may even be more effective in some cases? Then what about the "values-driven" approach: is a more functionalist engagement towards less-democratic states, tantamount to propping up "the last dictatorship in Europe", which has so far shown no official remorse or backtracking of its policies?

These questions are worth unpacking here to clarify a number of important tenets for understanding democracy promotion and practice.

Recently, several scholars[55] have begun to observe critical shifts towards more "functional" and "institutionalized" engagement of the EU with autocratic regimes in the Middle East and North Africa, and in the eastern region, and with Belarus and Azerbaijan in particular. This development, as Bosse argues in particular,

> is potentially serious, as it appears to mark the beginning of the end of the EU's ambition to act as a successful democratizer in its immediate neighbourhood, and perhaps even the end of the democratizing paradigm in the EU's foreign policies more generally.[56]

Furthermore, she contends, the EU strategy of functional cooperation "remains fuzzy" and ad hoc, and simply submits to what is possible to achieve under the "circumstances" – controversial goals of ensuring economic and geopolitical benefits for some parties.[57] The wider picture, however, reiterates a scholarly concern about the EU's credibility as a "force for good", and may even underscore "*de facto* acceptance ... of the limits of Union's role as a 'successful democratizer' when the prospect of membership is not within reach".[58] These potentially serious concerns over the EU's undermining of its own creed, when "partnering with dictatorships", raise equally serious questions. First, if the current EU policies towards modern autocracies are not working or effective, as many recent cases come to attest, should the EU then withdraw from further engagement with a country-in-question in order to avoid unpleasant compromises and save its integrity? Surely, a formal recognition of its defeat over securing some legitimation in a country would be an even greater de facto blow to the EU's credibility as a global democracy promoter? Conversely, if the EU's policies are not delivering in a particular case, would it not be more expedient to diversify and offer a more tailored, non-linear, and even inclusive, if necessary, approach in order to facilitate more interest and understanding of intentions? Perhaps, when analysing these complex and contested issues of democracy promotion, it may be advisable to consider a wider picture, and when tracing cross-temporal longitudinal developments, also to try and connect multiple societal layers of evidence, within and outside the country, to realize what is truly at stake, or hidden below the surface. As the analysis in this article demonstrates, the EU's changing modus operandi to that of a low-key and more technocratic engagement, which has extended to all levels of society, and been interest/sector-based, has yielded a sea-change transformation in public acceptance of the EU as an equally important player in the eastern region (in conjunction with Russia), and in behavioural patterns by displaying more self-awareness and critical reasoning. So, is it, on the part of the EU, recognition of defeat or rather a differentiated tactic to make democracy promotion work? How does it matter, and, more essentially, what needs to be done after these initial steps are undertaken to promote more enduring practices of democracy? Using the above evidence, we will consider two particular conceptual dimensions here: one of continued practice of international assistance, and one of social empowerment.

Belarus' case is particularly instructive for discussing the relevance of *continued* practice of international engagement. Owing to its declining human rights record, the country had practically lived in isolation from the West for almost a decade until the introduction of the ENP with its two-track engagement. This policy yielded no positive results and, as some would argue,[59] on the contrary caused regime endurance ("rallying around the flag"), pushing the country deeper into Russia's embrace. The ENP and especially the EaP have opened up new opportunities for engagement. As the above evidence attests, the new nonlinear approach perhaps counter-intuitively, especially in the absence of political dialogue, induced public socialization and recognition of the EU as an alternative partner to Russia. These policy objectives are clearly long-term, and may be unjustifiably costly for the incremental and often less-visible outcomes they render. At the same time, the policy of international assistance – low-key and technocratic – speaks volumes, first, about the committing party (the EU in this case), and the result when it comes to bearing fruit when finally connected with "the hearts and minds" of the target countries. But not just *any* international assistance is conducive to the enduring democratic process, and hence its theorization is of great importance, especially in the light of recent events in Ukraine. As Jahn argues in her seminal work on rethinking democracy promotion:

> One of the weaknesses of democracy promotion has been its tendency to focus on "impulses, strategies, impacts", to frame the issue either as a matter of foreign policy on the part of liberal states or as a matter of domestic political development in target states. What this framing leaves undertheorised, however, are the relations *between* sponsors and targets, that is its international dimension.[60]

It is precisely the framing of international assistance that the article seeks to test on the case of EU–Belarus relations, in order to better understand the undercurrents at work, and also to explicate the nexus between the international policies of democracy promotion and the changing practices of its reception and implementation in Belarus. Often, a focus on producing a single collective will to overthrow a regime may not necessarily engender practices which would add up to making changes feasible or enduring. As Jahn contends, "while [actions] are often successful in establishing democratic institutions, these institutions are subsequently and frequently used to pursue decidedly illiberal policies".[61] Indeed, as the evolution of the EU's policy towards Belarus testifies, the lack of structured and inclusive engagement during the early days of the ENP, and especially during the time of Belarus' isolation, had been unproductive, and almost detrimental to the interests of all parties concerned. The role of "the international", as Jahn insists, is decisive and, simultaneously, sensitive, and has not been sufficiently theorized in conjunction with "the other" – the target country:

> the international order provides the framework demarcating the possibilities and limits of political and economic development for individual states suggesting that policies of democracy promotion must address these systemic constraints in addition to, and in combinations with, their propaganda of particular strategies on the part of targets and sponsors.[62]

When applied to the case of Belarus, what appears to be decisively positive is the EU's continued functional engagement – especially through sector cooperation under CIB and cross-border cooperation, as well as regional development programmes and small-scale projects – which now provides a new language of norms and regulations, and engenders new practices, and in some cases, structures. But the instances of joint practice are still new in Belarus, and their frequency should be positively encouraged. For example, it remains unclear why EURONEST has rejected Belarus' participation in its forums, the value of which, as Petrova and Raube have argued, is essentially about emulating EU practices and inculcating good governance.[63] Being dressed up in a language of higher politics, this presents itself as a clearly missed opportunity to develop joint practices between the EU and Belarus' stakeholders. There also seems to be little incentivization occurring to integrate Belarus more closely in the World Trade Organization (WTO) economic community, now that is part of the ECU. Otherwise, nudging the country towards further economic reforms to meet the WTO criteria for membership could have offered another (and yet) missed opportunity to inculcate international norms into Belarus' daily practices. As Jahn argues, practitioners of democracy promotion "should care at least as much about the WTO" as they do about the impact of assistance for elections or support for civil society".[64]

If "the international" matters for codifying people-to-people contacts, and socializing them into the practices of "good governance", and not as spasmodic occasions but rather as a continuing effort, social empowerment – another dimension explored in this article – works differently but relatedly, to ensure translation of "interpretive practices" into respective "performing acts" of the individuals.[65] As Chandler argues, the analytical framing of "social empowerment" has been lately revisited to recognize and explore non-linear approaches to democracy promotion. In these frameworks, he contends, the logic works inside-out, driven by public resilience when "the personal becomes political".[66] This is however not in the sense of politicizing the issues concerned with the working of democracy, but rather in a reverse order, breaking down democracy to the level of "the individual" to make it relevant to their daily lives:

> Individuals and communities are to be empowered to reflexively work on their personal choices and practices in order to effect political change. "Political problems" are thereby "depoliticized" and represented as "personal problems" which can be dealt with by empowered individuals and communities.[67]

Democracy, as the new debates affirm, is much more than voting in elections and constitutionalizing norms. It is about "the public and individuals and their behaviour and understanding on an 'everyday' level". It is less about building institutions – although they matter to help affix pertinent practices – but more so about "the social production of reflexive autonomous subjects".[68] It is also less about dragging the problems of democracy (or the lack of it) into the realm of high politics, through "naming and shaming", or bullying target countries into submission to improve their "democratic performance" by external means. The binary/dichotomous narratives of political conditionality to date have been problematic in their effectiveness and sustainability, normally leading to shallow executive decision-making (Ukraine in early 2000s), or shutting down boundaries for reciprocation altogether (Belarus until now).

Perhaps what matters instead is fostering *daily practices* of normality for and by individuals, who when engaged, for example in a problem-solving process of their households, develop new knowledge of "good governance" or simply share "good practices" to become more able to solve and less tolerant of the existing inadequacies in their daily lives, including mismanagement, inequality, corruption, or abuse. This is where de-politicization of democracy – "the rule of people, by the people and for the people" – is truly vital. As Chandler contends further:

> Democratic politics in a non-linear age is less concerned with representation than with the development of social reasoning. The "power" which "the people" are seen to require today is social empowerment: the power to take reasoned and responsive decisions in their everyday lives... In this framing, there is no limit to the extension of democracy through social capacity-building, the "powering" of communities or the empowerment of decision-making individuals.[69]

Gradual change that we begin to observe in public attitudes and behavioural patterns in Belarus attests to the merits of this approach and also renders some useful insights into how low-level pragmatic engagement with various local stakeholders may alter public understanding of politics, and bring clarity to workings of democracy. To give an example, electoral politics in Belarus hitherto revolved around a single issue of building an opposition to the regime: that is, in separating those who desire change from those who would like to keep the status quo of Lukashenko's regime. This dichotomous politics of garnering a single collective will hitherto has yielded limited interest and commitment from the wider public. In partnership with a neighbouring branch of the National Democratic Institute, local activists began to alter their tactics of electoral campaigning during 2013–2014. This included issue-based politics, raising problems not of democracy promotion but rather those that were relevant to specific constituencies, and even broken down to the level of individual people. Levels of interest in mobilization and activism began to grow exponentially, even engulfing authorities in seeking solutions to specific "local problems".[70]

The same could be said about engaging local interest in various projects of sector cooperation – CIB, CSB, BELMED, RELOAD, just to name a few successful initiatives. Not only do they socialize people into the new practices of "good governance" and help to improve social welfare, they also expand public knowledge and develop critical reasoning about the self and the order of things, which soon enough will be challenged through the rise of a new collective identity of the "future Significant We"[71]; perhaps even along the lines of "We are part of pan-European space". What we see now are only the seeds of technocracy, the results of which, to be sure, we will not be awaiting for long: new narratives today may become new practice tomorrow, synergizing public resilience and government vision into a new sustainable democratic future.

Conclusion

As the old English proverb goes, "still waters run deep", and exploring this simple wisdom has been instructive in the case of Belarus. On the surface, we seem to observe a long-standing political impasse associated with a seeming lack of progress in EU-Belarus relations, which for 20 years have seen no major change, and are presently further constrained by the new developments eastwards, and the forging of the Eurasian space.

As the above analysis has shown, the surface appears deceptive, revealing deep undercurrents at work. Two particular disjunctures – in government and public narratives – have been instructive to help establish real undercurrents at work. They first associate with a profound shift in the EU's engagement with less-democratic regimes, which, in the case of Belarus, has been enduring, more complex, and versatile in the use of new instruments; more inclusive in targeting multiple actors; and more substantive in depoliticizing democracy promotion to the level of low-key technocratic engagement and sector cooperation.

This counter-intuitive non-linear approach, paradoxically, and in opposition to much scholarly criticism, succeeded in bringing about some crucial changes in public and government narratives. This is mostly associated with positively transforming public affinity with Europe, more clarity with mapping out joint needs and interests, and more motivation for forging a wider European identity, hitherto missing from public narratives.

These changes may seem insignificant at a glance. At the same time, for those who believe in inculcation of values through continued reciprocation and joint practices, and those with stakes in public resilience and social empowerment, these changes would undoubtedly become most important signifiers of synergies that are finally being sown. The outcomes posit a new turn in democracy promotion politics – long-term, and technocratic – that is, building democracy by *other* means and via continuing exposure to the international norms and regulations, and their inculcation not necessarily into grand stately structures, but rather, into the small but meaningful lives of individuals.

Disclosure statement

No potential conflict of interest was reported by the author.

Notes

1. http://www.freedomhouse.org/report/freedom-world/1998/belarus#.VA2SZMJdV8E
2. Wilson, *Belarus*; Bennett, *The Last Dictatorship in Europe*.
3. Council of the European Union, *Regulations* (EC) No. 552/97.
4. Ulakhovich, "Belarus-Evropeiskiy Soyuz," 3; Danilovich, *Russian– Belarusian Integration*.
5. De facto Belarus was excluded from the framework of bilateral cooperation; while its multilateral regional engagement had been aided by curtailed funds from the European Neighbourhood and Partnership Instrument (ENPI) 2007–2013 and from 2014, the European Neighbourhood Instrument (ENI). For more information visit http://www.enpi-info.eu/ENI
6. European Commission, *ENP Package – Belarus*.
7. See Yahorau's analysis 2013; and also a CFS position paper http://www.eap-csf.eu/assets/files/News/National_Platform_Position_Paper_2013_EN.pdf
8. Author's interviews with European Commission officials and members of the European Parliament.
9. Dragneva and Wolczuk, *Russia, the Eurasian Customs Union and the EU*, 5.
10. http://rt.com/business/162200-russia-bealrus-kazakhstan-union/
11. Korosteleva, "Belarusian Foreign Policy in a Time of Crisis."
12. Minister of Foreign Affairs, Vladimir Makey's interview, 23 July 2013, http://www.belta.by/ru/all_news/politics/Makej-v-Brjussele-podtverdil-printsipialnye-podxody-Belarusi-k-razvitiju-otnoshenij-s-ES_i_641904.html. and Deputy Minister of Foreign Affairs, Alena Kupchyna's speech at the Baku EaP summit: http://mfa.gov.by/en/press/news_mfa/fcdf6f3a68f1fd19.html
13. For recent developments see http://www.belinstitute.eu/en/node/2280
14. Lyutova and Tovkailo, *Vedomosti*, 30 June 2014: www.vedomosti.ru/newsline/news/28324261/ukraina-radelila-tamozhennyj-soyuz
15. The causation of change is a complex phenomenon which may be triggered by a number of factors. In Belarus' case, a growing public predisposition to the EU should not be solely attributed to the latter's policies alone but rather considered in a wider geostrategic and economic context to account, for example, for Russia's politics. The focus of this article however is on the EU factor, which takes discussion of causation beyond its scope.
16. Bosse, "A Partnership with Dictatorship."

17 Korosteleva, *The European Union and its Eastern Neighbours*; Delcour, "The Institutional Functioning of the Eastern Partnership."
18 This, of course, has been further challenged by the events in Ukraine, and the EU's slow reaction to Russia's aggression.
19 European Commission, *A New Response to a Changing Neighbourhood.*
20 As transpired from the author's interviews with senior EU officials, the 2011 revisions indeed signified a "new turn" in EU policies to the neighbourhood, partially for the reasons presented in the text; but more so for the new momentum of partnership they had inspired.
21 European Commission, *The Bilateral Dimension*; European Commission, *The Multilateral Dimension.*
22 http://eeas.europa.eu/top_stories/2014/270614_association_agreement_en.htm
23 This track has been compromised by the EU's politicization of the AA with Ukraine on the eve of the Vilnius summit.
24 A new instrument which in 2014 succeeded the European Neighbourhood and Partnership Instrument: http://www.enpi-info.eu/main.php?id=27348&id_type=1
25 European Commission, *ENP: Working towards a Stronger Partnership.*
26 Not only has this sum in some cases quadrupled in the past two years, it also equals about 15% of Belarus' nominal gross domestic product for 2010, excluding loans and other investments.
27 http://mfa.gov.by/en/press/news_mfa/d9b701481c909233.html
28 European Commission, *The Multilateral Dimension.*
29 ENPI, *Belarus: National Indicative Programme 2012–13*, Annex 3.
30 ENPI, *Belarus: National Indicative Programme 2012–13*; ENPI, *National Indicative Programme 2012–13 for Belarus.*
31 In July 2013 the business forum staged a series of unsanctioned meetings protesting some of the government's decisions regarding the ECU, see http://www.rferl.org/content/Belarusian_Market_Vendors_Strike_Against_New_Regulations/1358394.html. The National Platform recently met up to identify new targets for the modernization plan for Belarus: http://www.eap-csf.eu/en/national-platforms/belarus/
32 See Casier, Korosteleva, and Whitman, *Building a Stronger Eastern Partnership*, 6 and 8.
33 European Commission, *The Multilateral Dimension*; European Commission, *A Road to the Autumn 2013 Summit.*
34 This incidentally was set up at the Belarusian initiative in 2011. See MFA statement at http://mfa.gov.by/en/organizations/membership/list/f1d2b5ac3e69e36f.html
35 Conference of the Regional and Local Authorities for the Eastern Partnership, see http://cor.europa.eu/en/activities/Pages/corleap.aspx
36 The EURONEST Parliamentary Assembly is a forum to promote political association and further economic integration between the EU and the East European partners, see http://www.euronest.europarl.europa.eu/euronest/
37 Petrova and Raube, "The EaP, EuroNest and the Inter-Parliamentary Cooperation in the EU Neighbourhood."
38 http://eeas.europa.eu/delegations/belarus/documents/eu_activities_in_belarus.pdf
39 European Commission, *EU Cooperation for a Successful Eastern Partnership.*
40 http://ec.europa.eu/europeaid/sites/devco/files/eap-flyer-results.pdf, 4.
41 European Commission, *ENP Package – Belarus.*
42 European Commission, *New EU Support on Health and Development for Belarusian People.*
43 European Commission, *A Road to the Autumn 2013 Summit*; European Commission, *EU Cooperation for a Successful Eastern Partnership.*
44 Petrova and Raube, "The EaP, EuroNest and the Inter-Parliamentary Cooperation in the EU Neighbourhood."
45 European Commission, Press Release, 8 September 2014, 3.
46 Bosse, "A Partnership with Dictatorship"; Youngs, "European Approaches to Democracy Assistance"; Kubicek, *The European Union and Democratization.*
47 Füle, "ENP – Priorities and Directions for Change."
48 Duncan, *Democratic Theory and Practice*, Introduction.
49 The 2008 survey was funded by the ESRC (RES-061-25-0001) as part of a large project "Europeanising or Securitising the Outsiders: Assessing the EU's Partnership-Building Approach with Eastern Europe": http://www.aber.ac.uk/en/interpol/research/

research-projects/europeanising-securitising-outsiders/researchfindings/. A similar survey was executed in June 2013, with the support of the Office for a Democratic Belarus (ODB). The survey included 1000 respondents, and was stratified, random, and representative of the Belarusian population aged 18+ (urban and rural) by nationality, sex, religion, age, and education. For more information see http://www.kent.ac.uk/politics/gec/research/documents/gec-belarus-survey-brief-2013.pdf
50. EU Neighbourhood Barometer East: euneighbourhood.eu/wp-content/uploads/2013/03/ENPIreport_wave2_East.pdf and NISEPI http://www.iiseps.org/analitica
51. Lukashenko, Speech Delivered at the Meeting with BSU Students.
52. http://www.kyivpost.com/content/russia-and-former-soviet-union/russia-belarus-kazakhstan-and-armenia-are-about-to-ratify-the-eurasian-economic-union-364921.html (accessed 17 September 2014).
53. The new debate on democracy promotion underscores the need to pluralize and contextualize the concept for its promotion to be enduring. See Kurki for a more recent discussion on the contestation and pluralization of different types of democracy, "Democracy and Conceptual Contestability," 365.
54. Kurki, *Causation in International Relations*.
55. Joffe, "The European Union, Democracy and Counter-Terrorism in Maghreb"; Youngs, "European Approaches to Democracy Assistance"; Pace, "Paradoxes and Contradictions in EU Democracy Promotion in the Mediterranean"; Bosse, "A Partnership with Dictatorship."
56. Bosse, "A Partnership with Dictatorship," 367.
57. Ibid., 379.
58. Ibid., 380.
59. Korosteleva, *The Impact of Targeted Sanctions on Belarus*.
60. Jahn, "Rethinking Democracy Promotion," 686–687.
61. Ibid., 692.
62. Ibid., 702–703.
63. Petrova, and Raube, "The EaP, EuroNest and the Inter-Parliamentary Cooperation in the EU Neighbourhood."
64. Jahn, "Rethinking Democracy Promotion," 703.
65. Adler and Pouliot, *International Practices*.
66. Chandler, "Democracy Unbound?," 43.
67. Ibid., 44.
68. Ibid., 46.
69. Ibid., 56.
70. Michael Murphy (NDI), Presentation at "Belarus Reality Check", Latvian Ministry of Foreign Affairs, Riga, 11 September 2014.
71. Flockhart, "Complex Socialization."

Bibliography

Adler, Emanuel, and Vincent Pouliot, eds. *International Practices*. Cambridge: Cambridge University Press, 2011.

Bennett, Brian. *The Last Dictatorship in Europe: Belarus under Lukashenko*. London: Hurst, 2011.

Bosse, Giselle. "A Partnership with Dictatorship: Explaining the Paradigm Shift in EU Policy towards Belarus." *Journal of Common Market Studies* 50 (2013): 367–384.

Casier, Tom, Elena Korosteleva, and Richard Whitman. *Building a Stronger Eastern Partnership: Towards an EaP 2.0*. University of Kent: Global Europe Centre Policy Paper, 2012.

Chandler, David. "Democracy Unbound? Non-linear Politics and the Politicization of Everyday Life." *European Journal of Social Theory* 17 (2014): 42–59.

Council of the European Union. *2027th Council meeting, 10368/97 (C/97/269)*. Brussels, 1997. http://europa.eu/rapid/press-release_PRES-97-269_en.htm?locale=en.

Danilovich, Alexander. *Russian– Belarusian Integration: Playing Games behind the Kremlin Walls*. Aldershot: Ashgate, 2006.

Delcour, Laure. "The Institutional Functioning of the Eastern Partnership: an Early Assessment." *Eastern Partnership Review*, No.1. Tallinn: Estonian Centre of Eastern Partnership, 2011.

Dragneva, Rilka, and Katarzyna Wolczuk. *Russia, the Eurasian Customs Union and the EU: Cooperation, Stagnation or Rivalry?* Briefing Paper, 2012/01. London: Chatham House, 2012.

Duncan, Graham. ed. *Democratic Theory and Practice*. Cambridge: Cambridge University Press, 1983.

European Commission. *A New Response to a Changing Neighbourhood*, Joint Communication to the European Parliament, the Council, the European Economic and Social Committee and the Committee of the Regions, JOIN (2011) 303. Brussels, 25 May 2011.

European Commission. *Eastern Partnership Roadmap 2012–13: The Bilateral Dimension*, Joint Communication to the European Parliament, the Council, the European Economic and Social Committee and the Committee of the Regions, JOIN (2012) 109 final, Brussels, 15 May 2012a.

European Commission. *Eastern Partnership Roadmap 2012–13: The Multilateral Dimension*, Joint Communication to the European Parliament, the Council, the European Economic and Social Committee and the Committee of the Regions, JOIN (2012) 108 final, Brussels, 15 May 2012b.

European Commission. *Eastern Partnership: A Road to the Autumn 2013 Summit*, Joint Communication to the European Parliament, the Council, the European Economic and Social Committee and the Committee of the Regions, JOIN (2012) 13 final, Brussels, 15 May 2012c.

European Commission. *ENP Package – Belarus*, MEMO/13/244, Brussels, 20 March 2013a.

European Commission. *ENP: Working towards a Stronger Partnership*, Joint Communication to the European Parliament, the Council, the European Economic and Social Committee and the Committee of the Regions, JOIN (2013) 4 final. Brussels, 20 March 2013b.

European Commission. *EU Cooperation for a Successful Eastern Partnership*. Brussels: DEVCO, 2012d.

European Commission. *New EU Support on Health and Development for Belarusian People*, 25 July, IP/13/743. Brussels, 2013.

European Commission. "The Commission Sets out Cooperation Priorities for the Eastern and the Southern Neighbourhood." Press Release. Brussels, 8 September 2014.

European Neighbourhood and Partnership Instrument (ENPI). *Belarus: National Indicative Programme 2012–13*. Brussels: European Union, 2012.

European Neighbourhood and Partnership Instrument (ENPI). *National Indicative Programme 2012–13 for Belarus: Concept Note*. Brussels: European Commission, 2011.

Flockhart, Trinity. "'Complex Socialization': A Framework for the Study of State Socialization." *European Journal of International Relations* 12 (2006): 89–118.

Füle, Stefan. "ENP – Priorities and Directions for Change," Speech/13/661, Warsaw: Annual Conference of Polish Ambassadors, 25 July 2013.

Jahn, Beate. "Rethinking Democracy Promotion." *Review of International Studies* 38 (2012): 685–705.

Joffe, George. "The European Union, Democracy and Counter-Terrorism in Maghreb." *Journal of Common Market Studies* 46 (2008): 147–171.

Korosteleva, Elena. "Belarusian Foreign Policy in a Time of Crisis." *Journal of Communist Politics and Transition Studies* 27 (2011): 566–587.

Korosteleva, Elena. *The European Union and its Eastern Neighbours: Towards a More Ambitious Partnership?* London: Routledge, 2012.

Korosteleva, Julia. *The Impact of Targeted Sanctions on Belarus*. Brussels: DG for External Affairs, 2012. http://www.iris-france.org/docs/kfm_docs/docs/observatoire-voisinage-europeen/2012-05-impact-of-targeted-sanctions-on-belarus.pdf

Kubicek, Paul. *The European Union and Democratization*. London: Routledge, 2002.

Kurki, Milja. *Causation in International Relations: Reclaiming Causal Analysis*. Cambridge: Cambridge University Press, 2008.

Kurki, Milja. "Democracy and Conceptual Contestability: Reconsidering Conceptions of Democracy in Democracy Promotion." *International Studies Review* 12 (2010): 362– 387.

Lukashenko, A. Speech Delivered at the Meeting with BSU Students, Press Release No. 49929, 12 February 2008, http://www.president.gov.by/press49929.print.html

Pace, Michelle. "Paradoxes and Contradictions in EU Democracy Promotion in the Mediterranean: The Limits of EU Normative Power." *Democratization* 16 (2009): 39–58.

Petrova, Irina, and Raube. "The EaP, EuroNest and the Inter-Parliamentary Cooperation in the EU Neighbourhood." Paper Presented at the UACES Conference, September 1–3, 2014.

Ulakhovich, Vladimir. "Belarus-Evropeiskiy Soyuz: Sotrudnichestvo v Novykh Usloviyakh." Paper Presented at Joint German-Belarusian Conference "New Policy towards Belarus." Minsk: Belarusian State University, 2003.

Wilson, Andrew. *Belarus: the Last European Dictatorship*. New Haven and London: Yale University Press, 2011.

Yahorau, Andrei. "Dialogue Limited to Technical and Diplomatic Level: Belarus." PASOS assessment, 2013. http://www.eap-csf.eu/assets/files/Articles/Web/Roadmapreports/Belarus%20roadmap%20monitoring%20csf%20nov%202013%20(3).pdf

Youngs, Richard. "European Approaches to Democracy Assistance: Learning the Right Lessons?" *Third World Quarterly* 24 (2003): 127–138.

From 'Unilateral' to 'Dialogical'
Determinants of EU–Azerbaijan Negotiations

Eske Van Gils

RELATIONS BETWEEN AZERBAIJAN AND THE EUROPEAN UNION (EU)[1] have become more and more intense over the past decades. Cooperation is particularly smooth in the area of energy supply as well as trade. However, in recent years there has been discussion over the future of relations, in particular the limits to cooperation as well as the legal foundation for these relations.

Relations between the EU and Azerbaijan are presently conducted within the Eastern Partnership framework (EaP) (European Commission 2010b), which involves political and economic cooperation between the EU on the one hand, and Belarus, Ukraine, Moldova, Armenia, Georgia and Azerbaijan on the other (European Commission 2010b, p. 6). Bilateral relations are still based on the legally binding Partnership and Cooperation Agreement (PCA) from 1996, which entered into force in 1999 and has been renewed since. In this sense, relations can only develop and expand within the boundaries set by this PCA.[2] With the inclusion of Azerbaijan in the European Neighbourhood Policy (ENP) and the EaP in 2004 and 2009 respectively, the two sides have discussed possible follow-up agreements that could serve as a legal basis for relations. While the PCA is mostly technical in nature, with an emphasis on material objectives such as cooperation in the field of trade and energy supply, the objectives of the ENP and EaP have an additional, transformative aspect and aim at support for economic (market) reforms and values promotion.[3]

In 2009 the EU started searching for a replacement for the PCAs. In 2010, a new type of legal framework for the EaP countries was proposed: the Association Agreement (AA). Georgia, Ukraine and Moldova signed an AA in 2014;[4] Armenia intended to sign the agreement but then opted for integration into the Eurasian Customs Union instead (Gardner 2013; Eurasian Economic Commission 2015). The Azerbaijani government initially started the negotiations with the EU for an AA but decided against it in 2013, wanting instead a tailor-made policy adjusted to its own interests and objectives. It therefore proposed two alternative frameworks: first, the Strategic Modernisation Partnership (SMP) in 2013, which the EU soon dismissed; and second, in 2015, the Strategic Partnership Agreement (SPA). The latter was taken into consideration by the EU, and negotiations commenced in 2016. Initially this seemed a bargaining victory for Azerbaijan, considering the unprecedented nature of the situation, with a partner state proposing such an initiative, and Baku's assertive tone. However, since 2016 the EU and the Azerbaijani government have been involved in a negotiation process that required concessions and at times pragmatism, as will be set out in the analysis later on in this essay.

The essay intends to make two main contributions. First, it will add to the literature on EU external relations and the limits to the EU's transformative power by analysing the actions and interests of a third country, namely Azerbaijan, rather than only seeking explanations for the EU's reduced influence in the EU's own behaviour and motives. The second contribution to the literature will be an insight into how Azerbaijan has been a forerunner in resisting the EU's agenda. In the past few years, several other smaller states in the region have followed its example, albeit in a more moderate way (for example, Armenia and Belarus). Relations between Brussels and Baku are therefore particularly interesting because they appear to be illustrative of a broader change in power dynamics between the EU and neighbouring countries. While the EU still adheres to a largely EU-centred agenda for relations with its Eastern neighbours, Azerbaijan only wants close cooperation with the EU on its own terms (van Gils 2018). Azerbaijan is not the only country to desire a more equal relationship with the EU; its position, however, stands out due to Baku's open challenge to the *status quo*.[5] The Azerbaijani government has tried to alter negotiation practices, to move from a unilateral to a more dialogical decision-making process. Yet since 2013, when the AA was rejected, there have been several remarkable shifts in the negotiation dynamics. At times, Baku seems to have successfully reached its aim; yet in other stages of the negotiations the EU has re-established itself as the main actor. The question arises: how can these dynamics be explained? A possible answer might be found in the concept of 'bargaining power', which captures both the EU's and Azerbaijan's material and immaterial sources of power. As such, the case of Azerbaijan is simultaneously both an outlier and an illustration of a larger, upcoming change in the region, and can thus help us to understand the mechanisms of resistance to the EU's policies by smaller states in the EU's neighbourhood.

The aims of this essay are to therefore analyse, first, what changes in dynamics have occurred in negotiations over the AA, SMP and SPA; second, if, and to what extent, these dynamics can be explained by the framework of 'bargaining power'; and third, what these findings on EU–Azerbaijan relations tell us about the broader context of changing power relations between the EU and post-Soviet states. The essay will argue that Azerbaijan's growing leverage has allowed it to resist the EU's unilateral mode of policy-making to a certain extent, and that it has partially succeeded in enforcing more dialogical forms of policy-making. However, this power seems conditional on a number of factors, which are outlined in the bargaining power model. A change in conditions in recent years—notably Azerbaijan's weakened economic position since 2015—may affect significantly the outcome of the ongoing negotiations over the SPA.

The essay also covers the three 'tectonic shifts' that are discussed in this Special Collection. Firstly, while Azerbaijan is a relatively young and small state, its more assertive stance in international politics can be seen as part of a larger emergence of new powers. Second, the country is seen as an important player in several transnational issues: the EU and United States particularly value Azerbaijan as a strategic ally in a volatile and unstable region, and Azerbaijan is also an ally of Russia, Turkey, Iran and Israel. With growing religious tensions in the wider region, President Ilham Aliyev's secular regime is appreciated by Western states.[6] Another main transnational issue that links Azerbaijan to, among others, Europe and the US is the supply and trade of energy. One would expect this to lead to an increase in the level of partnership and reciprocity in relations, yet what can be observed is that the policy remains mostly unilaterally set by the EU, without equal regard for the interests and perceptions of Azerbaijan. This essay finds that, in response, the Azerbaijani government tries to influence the policy-making process and even to hinder the implementation of EU policies that are not in its interests. Third, the essay will argue that the institutional architecture of relations should be reconsidered, and perhaps gradually move from an EU-dominated agenda to a more inclusive one. The research presented here is therefore situated in the broader framework of the EU's changing external relations, and possible obstacles to the EU's desired transformative effect.[7]

The following section will discuss each of the three agreements that have been negotiated since 2010: from the discussion and rejection of the AA to the proposal of the SMP and the negotiations over the SPA since 2015. Subsequently, the essay will present a model of bargaining power as a conceptual framework to answer the main question about changing negotiation dynamics. Next, the essay will analyse these negotiations in light of the different elements of this model. In its conclusion, the essay will reflect on the significance of these findings for relations between the EU and the broader emerging Eurasian space.

Negotiations over three agreements

Between 2010 and 2017, three different agreements were negotiated as possible follow-ups to the PCA. What follows is a brief discussion of the context of these subsequent negotiations and the proposed agreements. The aim of this section is to shed light on the unique situation posed by these developments.

Association Agreement (2010–2013)

As discussed in the introduction, after 2010 the EU aimed to sign an AA with Azerbaijan. Association Agreements have the aim of bringing partner states' legislation in a number of policy areas in line with the EU's standards (Della Sala 2015, p. 167). Signing an AA would effectively update the legal basis for bilateral relations between the EU and Azerbaijan, which would facilitate deeper political and economic cooperation (European Commission 2010c).

Negotiations between the EU and Azerbaijan on the AA started in July 2010 (European Commission 2010c). The EU identified a specific range of chapters that did not require any negotiations, since both parties were already aligned in a number of areas, including energy and technical cooperation.[8] Negotiations on the other chapters proved more difficult. First of all, the EU had a mostly regional policy framework in mind, whereas Azerbaijan wanted a more differentiated framework that represented its own interests better. Furthermore, AAs have a strong transformative dimension, in that they aim at significant political and economic reform in the partner states (EU Council 2014). This normative dimension can also be seen in the EU's policies towards the post-Soviet region more broadly, as demonstrated by Siddi in his contribution to this collection of essays. As a consequence, the Baku government perceived that the agenda was set mostly unilaterally by the EU and did not sufficiently include Azerbaijani interests. Specifically, the two key issues at stake in the negotiations over all three suggested agreements have been the inclusion of a political and values dimension (desired by the EU, in line with its transformative objectives) and that of a stronger reference to the Nagorno-Karabakh conflict (Azerbaijan's wish, based on the belief that more active EU engagement would benefit the conflict resolution process).[9]

The Azerbaijani government has indicated numerous times that while it seeks in-depth cooperation with the EU, it has no interest in extensive integration through further institutionalisation of relations. This lack of interest is predominantly based on the country's (economic) independence, its relations with Russia and Baku's reluctance to include the transmission of values as part of the relationship (Babayev 2014, pp. 61–2). The government only wants to cooperate on three specific conditions: any integration must be on equal terms; there must be economic benefits; and Azerbaijan must exert some direct influence over bilateral decision-making processes.[10] These conditions were not met in the AA negotiations, leading Baku to reconsider the partnership in the shape as foreseen by the AA,[11] and to aim for a 'lighter' alternative agreement instead. Government representatives announced at the Vilnius Summit in November 2013 that the planned signing would not proceed (Della Sala 2015, p. 167). Instead, the government proposed a SMP: an agreement tailor-made for bilateral relations between Brussels and Baku.

Strategic Modernisation Partnership (2013–2015)

On 4 April 2013 a draft of the SMP was proposed by Azerbaijan as an alternative to the EU's AA. This proposed agreement addressed all of Azerbaijan's three key objections against the AA. The SMP would not be legally binding (as opposed to the AA), and the PCA would remain the legal basis for relations (Rettman 2013). Furthermore, the SMP would largely follow the lines of the EaP but exclude the parts on 'democratization, human rights and freedoms'.[12] A SMP would thus allow Azerbaijan to be selective in the areas of cooperation,[13] and lead to less cooperation rather than more, as opposed to the AA.[14] Apart from largely omitting the value-based dimension of an AA, the SMP would further differ from such agreement in that Azerbaijan's territorial integrity, relating to the Nagorno-Karabakh conflict, would be mentioned (Rettman 2013).[15]

The EU received the SMP proposal with scepticism. One interviewee expressed doubts, about whether Azerbaijan really wanted a Strategic Partnership comparable to that of other states, as existing Partnerships with countries such as China or the United States mean more cooperation with the EU rather than less.[16] Furthermore, if the SMP largely followed the lines of the AA, this should then include the issues of human rights and transparency. Thus, it was clear from the EU side that Azerbaijan wanted to exclude these issues from the realm of cooperation.[17] However, according to one of our interviewees, Baku was willing to include the human rights dimension in the SMP.[18] The proposed text contained a reference to political reform and the promotion of democracy (Rettman 2013). Yet, without having sighted the text, it can be assumed that, unlike the AA, the proposed SMP did not require the same level of commitment to these two processes.

The EU rejected the SMP in 2015.[19] In response to the halt to SMP negotiations, the EU prepared another document to bridge the period until Azerbaijan 'provided clarity' about what it wanted from either an AA or Strategic Partnership.[20] This Strategic Modernisation Agreement was a working document with no legally binding power, and was to be agreed between the Commission and the Azerbaijani government. Therefore, it would be restricted to those areas in which the Commission has competence. The document contained a matrix with all goals for the future, and seemed to meet demands from both parties by including references to human rights and democracy and to the territorial integrity of Azerbaijan.[21] Azerbaijan did not sign the document because it disagreed with the language used concerning the Nagorno-Karabakh conflict.[22]

Strategic Partnership Agreement (post-2015)

In May 2015, the process received fresh impetus when the Azerbaijani government proposed a new agreement at the Riga Summit.[23] This Strategic Partnership Agreement

(SPA) would be the second proposed alternative to the AA that aimed to update the legal basis of relations.[24] In contrast to the SMP, this time the EU was willing to seriously consider Azerbaijan's proposal. However, it took until November 2016 for the European External Action Service (EEAS) to obtain a mandate for negotiations from member states in the EU Council (2016). Negotiations began in February 2017 (EU Council 2018).[25]

Again, the objectives from both sides were to increase cooperation and, again, the contested issue was whether or not to include chapters referring to values and to Nagorno-Karabakh.[26] Initially, the fact that the EU was prepared to consider the proposal seemed a bargaining victory for Azerbaijan. However, in the course of negotiations, the EU managed to convince Azerbaijan to include a chapter on democracy and human rights,[27] an important goal for Brussels. With the negotiations still ongoing at the time of writing (Gotev 2018), it is unclear as of yet whether Azerbaijan can successfully put the Nagorno-Karabakh conflict on the agenda. The Azerbaijani side has stated that the inclusion of references to the conflict is crucial.[28]

In July 2018 the EU and the Azerbaijani government signed a document called the Partnership Priorities, which, as it replaces the current ENP Action Plan (European Commission 2018a), can be seen as a step towards setting the agenda for cooperation until the legal basis for relations is updated. The priorities listed for cooperation in the next few years represent the EU's as well as Azerbaijan's interests but show that the EU has been the most successful of the two in advocating its own interests: the first priorities listed relate to 'good governance, the rule of law and human rights', and the functioning of civil society is mentioned multiple times (European Commission 2018b). Priorities of more interest to the Azerbaijani government concern economic diversification and energy trade, as well as the implementation of the Mobility Partnership (European Commission 2018b). The Nagorno-Karabakh conflict is not mentioned in the document at all (European Commission 2018b), even though the conflict was raised by government officials in most, if not all, official meetings with the EU in the year preceding the signing of the document.[29] While Partnership Priorities are not legally binding and could therefore be seen as less important to the Azerbaijani government, it is nonetheless telling that the authorities in Baku have agreed to sign these priorities without the document containing any references to the Nagorno-Karabakh conflict.[30]

It is thus clear that the SPA, at least initially, established a clear tendency towards a dialogical form of negotiations, yet the negotiations reverted to a more unilateral tendency from 2016, as reflected in the 2018 Partnership Priorities document. The next section will introduce a conceptual framework to help us unpack the dynamics of these negotiations, to understand whether, why and how the two parties managed to successfully defend their interests.

A new model of bargaining power to assess negotiation dynamics

This brief overview suggested that negotiations over all three agreements have revolved around similar issues: the EU seeks to secure a political and values dimension in each agreement, while Azerbaijan wants more dialogical, rather than unilateral, negotiations, to ensure representation of its own interests, namely less attention on the values dimension and a more prominent position for the Nagorno-Karabakh conflict.

The desire for more dialogical relations seems unnecessary when looking at the official narrative. Bilateral relations between the EU and Azerbaijan are officially founded on partnership, a core concept in the EaP (Korosteleva 2011). It is argued that genuine partnership should consist of reciprocity in relations: attention to the interests and policy priorities of both actors (Weber *et al.* 2007), and joint ownership of the policy (Korosteleva 2011, p. 5; Khasson 2013, p. 334). In theory there should be equal input from the EU and Azerbaijan in their bilateral relations. Yet in practice, while the relationship has certainly developed in that direction, we observe that the proposed policies, and therefore the negotiation practices, remain very one-sided. Azerbaijan views itself as an equal if not stronger partner than the EU (Franke *et al.* 2010) and therefore disagrees with the EU-centred policies and the perceived lack of dialogue.

What makes this situation so unique is that the case of the SMP and SPA represents the first instance in which a non-EU actor has proposed an agreement anticipating the EU's initiative.[31] Moreover, EU readiness to negotiate the SPA is in stark contrast to its unwillingness to discuss the SMP, while the two agreements themselves do not substantially differ. After Azerbaijan's initial successes, Brussels now appears to have regained a stronger position in the negotiations. Azerbaijan is assertive and does not accept the *status quo*, while the EU is not used to being confronted in this way by its smaller partners. Regarding a follow-up agreement for the PCA, both actors are thus actively seeking to promote their own interests.

How can we explain the changing dynamics in negotiations between the EU and the Azerbaijani government over a follow-up to the PCA in this rather rare case of EU external relations? The concept of bargaining power may prove useful to address this question. As a concept borrowed from negotiation and conflict mediation literature (Jervis 1976; Zartman & Rubin 2002), bargaining power is here understood as the ability to influence the outcome of relations to one's own benefit, either through the ability to affect the policy-making process or through the capacity to curb the competitive influence of other actors.[32] The notion of bargaining power has been applied in the context of the EU's external relations in a limited number of studies (Zartman 1978; Elgström & Jöohnsson 2005). The concept is often used to study EU decision-making processes or fixed-stage negotiation processes in international politics.[33] By viewing the policy-making process as a form of negotiation, it becomes possible to take into account all actors involved, and to capture both their input and the other parties' response to that input, allowing us to assess both what enables and what prevents actors from exerting influence in political relations. The innovation here is that the concept is used to analyse an ongoing process of 'interdependent decision-making' (Sjöstedt 1979, p. 279) between two parties on an international level, in a non-linear process with no clearly defined stages, start or end point, as opposed to, for example, negotiations on conflict resolution or clearly defined scenarios for international bargaining.

Using the concept in this way has the advantage of granting the EU and Azerbaijan equal analytical relevance. Usually EU external relations are only studied from the EU perspective. For instance, the external governance approach is very helpful in categorising relations between the EU and partner countries in terms of forms of cooperation and levels of EU influence (Lavenex 2004; Börzel 2010),[34] but it has several limitations compared to bargaining power in the context of this study. While this approach allocates space for the partner states in the outcome of the process, the centre of the analysis is still the EU's position and behaviour, and it is still assumed that the EU can choose for, or decide upon, a specific form of governance in relations with an external actor. Governance can thus only explain the EU's policies, not Azerbaijan's resistance to them. Also, the existing literature on external governance mostly looks at policy outcomes rather than policy-making, while this essay aims to unpack the very process of negotiation and bargaining in EU–Azerbaijan relations. Similar limitations apply to the notion of 'decentring'. Bechev and Nicolaïdis assess how relations between the EU and neighbouring countries can be improved by allocating a greater role to the partner states in designing and implementing the policies (Bechev & Nicolaïdis 2010, pp. 490–91). The desire for decentring certainly captures the Azerbaijani government's motivation for its aims and actions in relations with the EU, but is not useful in understanding the actual process of bringing about a more decentred *modus operandi*.

Therefore, the bargaining power concept will be applied to shed light on the interaction between the EU and Azerbaijan and to understand why and how power dynamics changed during the course of this interaction. The notion can give us insight into the strategies and instruments used by Baku and Brussels to influence the policy-making process. It may illuminate the ways in which the Azerbaijani government tries to make negotiations more dialogical and the measures taken by the EU to secure its dominant position. To analyse bargaining power in EU–Azerbaijan relations, five core aspects have been identified as particularly relevant. Some of these have a material basis (the power base); others are non-tangible in nature (negotiation skills and capacity as well as perceptions of the Self and Other) or refer to non-material considerations affecting an actor's room for manoeuvre (domestic context and available alternatives). The analysis uses an interpretivist approach and the five elements are not to be seen as independent variables but rather as dimensions that all contribute to a broader picture of the interaction during negotiations.

The first element is the actors' power base, the most material form of power in the bargaining power model. The EU traditionally enjoys an asymmetry in relations with smaller neighbouring and candidate countries; in the case of Azerbaijan, there seems to be a more symmetrical relationship or at least a less asymmetrical mode than in relations with other states in the EaP. This power base has played out differently over time, as will be shown in the empirical segments of this essay. Notably, between 2010 and 2015, oil prices were high and Azerbaijan's economy boomed; the 2016 economic downturn naturally affected the country's power base in a negative manner. The second important element of bargaining power is negotiation skill and capacity. Diplomacy, lobbying and winning political support can all be put under this category (Goldmann 1979, p. 29; Melissen 2005). Both the EU and Azerbaijan have used this element extensively with regards to the AA, SMP and SPA negotiations. Azerbaijan is an unusual partner for the EU in that it has a comparatively strong diplomatic body for the country's size and its relatively young statehood. This relative strength seems to play out favourably for Baku in relations with Brussels. A third element of an actor's bargaining power is the domestic context, which sets the boundaries and expectations for the negotiation process (Turner 1992, p. 233).[35] Relevant variables can be opportunities, internal legitimacy, consensus among EU member states and tensions between institutions on a (supra)national level. Fourth, perceptions of the Self and Other are crucial to an actor's bargaining power. Perceptions of the Self are important because of the domestic dimension: negotiators have to behave in accordance with the role and expectations that they consider to apply to themselves as an actor. Perceptions of the Other, in turn, legitimise certain actions or policies towards other actors (Diez 2005, p. 629). The fifth and last element of the bargaining power model is the attractiveness of alternative options. The availability of alternatives also potentially affects the receptiveness of partner countries to EU influence and *vice versa*; having alternatives affects the offers an actor makes in negotiations since there is less need to compromise (Tutzauer 1992, p. 73). Alternative options may also affect the perception of the Self.

Importantly, some facets of these five elements may overlap or may be interlinked. For instance, domestic factors will also inform an actor's perception of the Self and may influence its negotiation skills. An actor's power base directly influences its negotiation capacity too, whereas the availability of alternatives can be dependent on the perception of the Self and the Other.

What we expect to find on the basis of this bargaining power model is that increased bargaining power for Azerbaijan would allow its government to enforce more dialogical forms of decision-making, to be measured by representation of its main priorities, namely, more attention on the Nagorno-Karabakh conflict and less emphasis on values promotion. More bargaining power for the EU would facilitate in turn the continuation of more unilateral modes of negotiation, resulting in a strong values-promotion dimension to a negotiated agreement, and less commitment to engage directly in conflict resolution regarding Nagorno-Karabakh.

Bargaining power and the negotiations over time

When applying the bargaining power model to negotiations over the AA, SMP and SPA, we find that the five elements have a clear role in explaining the negotiation dynamics.

Power base

The power base—the actors' material sources of power—is less asymmetrical than could be expected on the basis of Azerbaijan's population, territory and GDP in comparison to those of the EU. Two key factors are energy and the subsequent economic interdependence between the two sides (Nuriyev 2008; Gahramanova 2009).

While both actors are economically independent, there is at the same time a great interdependency between Brussels and Baku. Azerbaijan's energy is sought by the EU, in particular as a means of diversifying supply and reducing its reliance on Russia, while Azerbaijan needs the EU as a customer for this energy (European Commission 2015a).[36] In absolute numbers, the trade balance remains in favour of the EU, but energy is a valuable asset for Azerbaijan, as demonstrated by the repeated references to the country's importance in EU official documents and statements (European Commission 2015a).[37] Therefore, we can still speak of a certain power balance in terms of economic interdependence. Simultaneously, energy plays an indirect role in the bargaining power model in that it facilitates self-reliance for Azerbaijan; in other words, the EU's model of financial conditionality as a means for political reform will not be effective with regard to Azerbaijan (Simão 2012, p. 198). This higher degree of mutual dependence has placed Baku in a much more solid bargaining position compared to other states in negotiations over a follow-up agreement to the PCA. Between 2010 and 2015, Azerbaijan enjoyed economic growth amidst worldwide economic contraction, including in the EU, where the economy performance alternated times of crisis to slow recovery (World Bank 2017a, 2017b). This relative symmetry might explain why Azerbaijan felt able to reject the AA, advancing an alternative agreement. The EU's weakened position also reduced its attraction for cooperation and legal approximation, as it had less to offer in economic terms, than previously (Kavalski 2012, p. 84).

This balance has altered, however, since the economic downturn that hit Azerbaijan in 2015, following a drop in oil prices worldwide.[38] The country's economy relies on energy revenues for over 65% (Jafarli 2016) and in December 2015 the government was forced to unpeg the Azerbaijani manat from the US dollar (Agayev 2015) and to devaluate the currency by 32% (Farchy 2015). The resulting inflation led to small-scale protests[39] and forced the government to intervene over bread prices in an attempt to maintain domestic stability (Salimova 2016). The Azerbaijani government realised that a diversification of its economy was necessary, in an endeavour that received some modicum of EU support.[40] Azerbaijan's reduced economic independence diminished the country's power base, affecting in turn the negotiation dynamics. Moreover, the EU's need for energy diversification lessened as oil prices fell. Import of Azerbaijani goods into the EU declined by more than 28% in 2016, and EU exports to Azerbaijan dropped even further, by over 45% (EC DG Trade 2017). This likely places the EU in a more favourable bargaining position, as possibly evidenced by the fact that Baku agreed in 2017 to include a chapter on democracy and human rights into the latest agreement under negotiation.[41]

In short, until 2015, economic interdependence meant that the EU and Azerbaijan were negotiating from similar power bases. The post-2015 economic downturn diminished Azerbaijan's power base relative to the EU, altering in turn the negotiation dynamics in favour of Brussels.

Negotiation skill and capacity

As a large and experienced negotiator, the EU naturally outweighs Azerbaijan in terms of negotiation skill and capacity. Yet, one of the features that makes Azerbaijan stand out in the post-Soviet region is its disproportionate negotiation strength as a relatively small power. The government has invested heavily in diplomatic capacity in recent years, and uses lobby and public relations activities in Brussels and other European capitals to advance its own interests (ESI 2012; Knaus 2015).

A strategy of first resort used by the Azerbaijani government is to postpone or call off negotiations. Negotiations over the legal framework for relations have so far taken place during official visits and at EaP Summits.[42] In 2013 a number of official meetings were held in Baku and Brussels to discuss the SMP.[43] Then Commissioner for the ENP Štefan Füle stressed the EU's willingness to develop relations with Azerbaijan further. In reality, this seemed conditional on relations developing in accordance with the EU's design. While Füle stated that Azerbaijan agreed that 'negotiations on the AA and the document on a SMP run in parallel and are complementary',[44] the EU's plan remained to sign only the AA at the Vilnius Summit in November 2013 (Rettman 2013). Moreover, according to interviews with Azerbaijani representatives, it transpires that Azerbaijan saw the SMP as an alternative to the AA, rather than a parallel development. Despite diplomatic attempts at streamlining,[45] the Vilnius Summit instead showed the differences between the EU and Azerbaijan regarding their vision of the future.

In the period 2014–2015, the Azerbaijani government backed down on two occasions from signing the SMP, as the document's references to the Nagorno-Karabakh conflict were unsatisfactory for the government. At the same time, the EU did not wish to continue negotiating the SMP either, because of the demand for references to the conflict.[46]

The Riga EAP Summit in May 2015 showed the difficult nature of negotiations. Azerbaijan did not expect any new agreements to be signed at the summit.[47] One day before the start, President Aliyev decided not to participate, and the Minister of Foreign Affairs and the head of the presidential administration attended instead.[48] European newspapers reported this as a protest against the EU's criticism of human rights in Azerbaijan (Walker 2015) while other commentators believed the reasons given by the president to be genuine, namely that he was busy with the final preparations for the European Games and a fire that occurred in an apartment block in Baku on 18 May.[49] Indeed, any protest by Azerbaijan would most likely be made explicitly, as a negotiation tactic.

A second tactic used by the authorities in Baku was to use a critical situation to its own advantage and change the power dynamics. The SPA negotiations had a very difficult start. The EEAS decided to send a mission to Baku in September 2015, to explore options for the SPA.[50] However, several days before the mission, a critical resolution on Azerbaijan was approved by the European Parliament, condemning the state of democracy and human rights in the country (European Parliament 2015). In response, the Azerbaijani government asked the EEAS to postpone the mission (European Parliament 2015). Thus, by approving a resolution criticising the Azerbaijani authorities, the European Parliament inadvertently passed the initiative to Baku: the EEAS had to wait for approval to come to the Azerbaijani capital to talk about the former's proposal.[51] This decision, however, added pressure to the relations.[52]

Baku's proactive promotion of Azerbaijan's interests is another example of its diplomatic capacity. Not only was the issue of Nagorno-Karabakh raised in nearly every meeting with the EU, the Ministry of Foreign Affairs furthermore engaged in what its spokesperson called a 'digital diplomacy policy': 'issues related to the foreign policy of our country were delivered to the wider public and relevant inquiries were responded to in an operative manner', while at the same time 'disinformation' was responded to, 'by using the right of reply were [sic] provided'.[53] Azerbaijan's interest group abroad, the European Azerbaijan Society (TEAS), organises many activities in European capitals to raise awareness of the Nagorno-Karabakh conflict.[54] The effectiveness of this proactive stance is open to question, given the reduced financial means available following the economic downturn. Up until 2017 the Azerbaijani government maintained that a satisfactory reference to the conflict was a precondition for signing any new agreement; however, the 2018 Partnership Priorities (albeit not comparable to a new legal basis for relations) do not mention the conflict even once (European Commission 2018c).

While the AA and SMP were being negotiated simultaneously, both sides appeared to have similar bargaining power: the negotiations, as a consequence, ended in a deadlock. Goldmann's distinction between offensive and defensive power (Goldmann 1979) suggests that neither side had the offensive power to successfully change the agenda;[55] all they could do was to apply their defensive power by postponing negotiations and rejecting proposed agreements. Yet at first sight, the fact that the EU was willing to negotiate the SPA, and that the EEAS seemed to be taking this proposal much more seriously than it did the SMP, points to Azerbaijan's increased bargaining power. The 2015 downturn may have changed these dynamics, however, leaving Azerbaijan in a more vulnerable position; for instance, having to make concessions on the values dimension, as described earlier. It is too early to tell how this new dynamic has affected the use of specific negotiation strategies. Overall, the government's tactics have not changed. However, following the 2017 Laundromat scandal, the government's lobbying attempts have been brought into disrepute, which may have led to the reduced effectiveness of such a strategy; furthermore, lobbying in the policy world is costly and the economic downturn may have affected the government's ability to finance such activities (van Gils 2018).

Domestic context

The domestic context plays an important role in determining the two actors' priorities—values promotion (EU) and the agenda-setting of the Nagorno-Karabakh conflict (Azerbaijan). These priorities can be related to the EU's and Azerbaijani government's support bases.

The issues of legitimacy and constituency are interpreted differently by the Azerbaijani government and EU institutions, mostly as the former has a more direct relation to its citizens than the latter do towards the 28 EU member states. Supranational actors (EEAS, the EU Delegation in Baku, the European Parliament and the European Commission) need to take into consideration the viewpoints and interests of the member states, which in turn have their own respective constituencies in the form of citizens and the electorate.

One of the main concerns of the Azerbaijani government is maintaining legitimacy on a domestic level, to ensure regime survival and resilience (Dimitrov 2013): its behaviour in negotiations over the agreements is immediately affected by this necessity. For the EU, legitimacy is a more indirect and longer-term asset, yet its credibility both at domestic and international levels is equally crucial. As will be shown in the following section on perceptions, credibility and roles significantly affect the EU's behaviour in relations with Azerbaijan. Both sides are as such similarly restrained in their room for manoeuvre by domestic pressures and their anticipation of potential threats to their legitimacy or credibility. Closely connected to these domestic priorities is the fact that signing the AA was not a viable option for Azerbaijan. As mentioned above, one of the points of disagreement over the AA as well as the SMP was the manner in which they referred to the Nagorno-Karabakh conflict. Since resolving the conflict is a national priority, having the matter included in any future agreement signed with the EU is crucial to the Azerbaijani government's internal legitimacy.

Securing this legitimacy could also be a factor in the government's preference to hold SPA negotiations in Baku rather than in Brussels. Whereas the AA and SMP were discussed in various locations, the first SPA negotiations were held in Baku, with the government letting the EEAS delegation wait for an invitation to come to Baku, after the issue of the European Parliament's resolution on human rights in Azerbaijan. This move reflected Azerbaijan's strong bargaining power position at the time. In February 2017 President Aliyev did go to Brussels, although he cancelled a meeting with the European Parliament because it was hosting an event on human rights in Azerbaijan.[56] Such national assertion in the matter of negotiating the SPA may have served to enhance the government's domestic legitimacy, too.

The EU's options to negotiate the SMP with Azerbaijan were limited because the member states had only given the EU a mandate to negotiate an AA.[57] At the same time, the EEAS also realised that if negotiations over the AA were to remain deadlocked, there would be a point at which the member states would request a change of mandate.[58] While the EEAS did not have a mandate to negotiate the SMP alongside the AA, it did obtain a mandate for the SPA in 2016 (EU Council 2016). The domestic context may also shape the EU's preference for a regional approach over individual country agreements, with the EU aspiring to further regional integration in the South Caucasus (Babayev 2014, p. 108). This preference for a regional approach could also be a result of the fact that the EU member states simply could not reach consensus on a country-specific policy towards Azerbaijan, considering that they have different interests at stake and cooperate with Baku to varying degrees, and therefore continued to advocate the AA, which did have such regional rather than country-specific focus. The Council's decision to provide a mandate for the SPA negotiations in 2016 will be explained in the next section on perceptions.

For both the EU and the Azerbaijani government, domestic factors thus played a significant role in determining whether or not the proposed agreements were acceptable. It appears that the disagreement over the reference to the Nagorno-Karabakh conflict and to values led to the discontinuation of negotiations over both the AA and the SMP. It remains to be seen how the two actors will include these issues in negotiations over the SPA, as the negotiations are still ongoing at the time of writing.

Perceptions of the Self and Other

Perceptions and misperceptions appear to be a powerful influence in negotiations over the AA, SMP and SPA. Interestingly, both actors perceived themselves to be more powerful than the other. That the EU thinks of itself as the strongest actor is probably not surprising. Azerbaijan's perception of itself as insufficiently acknowledged is more striking, especially in comparison to other, less assertive states in the EaP. This notion seems to have played a key role in the AA negotiations in particular. Azerbaijan has a strong desire for acknowledgement and respect as a serious player in international politics,[59] in line with its self-perception as a growing economic and political power,[60] which is (partially) based on its oil revenues since the 2000s (Babayev 2009, p. 83).

The Azerbaijani government has strengthened its narrative about the country's meaningful place in the international community. Government officials often refer to the country's perceived importance, particularly Azerbaijan's 'strategic importance' for the EU.[61] A public statement by President Aliyev in early 2018 asserting Azerbaijan's identity as a 'dignified and reliable partner in the world' is indicative of this narrative.[62] Government-supported media regularly report on when and how Azerbaijan is positively referred to in international media or by international actors. This narrative is further supported by Azerbaijan showcasing itself as a resource-rich and proactive country, for instance, through organising large international events (Ismayilov 2012; van Gils 2018). The government invests heavily in public relations to promote Azerbaijan abroad; at home, large infrastructural investments have been made, particularly in Baku's city centre.[63]

According to Azerbaijani government sources, by failing to give Azerbaijan 'any ownership of the project' and by not including any of Azerbaijan's key priorities, the AA was in effect not meeting the condition of acknowledging Azerbaijan as an equal international partner.[64] In the EU account, Azerbaijan had decided not to sign the AA; in the Baku version, the EU put Azerbaijan in the position of having to reject it.[65] In a slightly different narrative, the government considered non-exclusive programmes with the EU, such as the AA, to be 'too low profile'[66] and believed that modernisation would be possible without EU support (Babayev 2014, p. 62). This attitude was typical of the period 2010–2015, when Azerbaijan's economic growth facilitated such an assertive and confident stance.

228 THE EUROPEAN UNION AND ITS EASTERN NEIGHBOURHOOD

The EU also sees itself as the stronger actor in bilateral relations with Azerbaijan as well as other states in its neighbourhood. Conceptualisations of the EU's international role, such as Normative Power Europe (Manners 2002), provide valuable insight into the way the EU perceives itself as an actor in international relations. This self-representation may be one possible explanation for the EU's behaviour in relations with other actors, including Azerbaijan (Orbie 2008, p. 2). It also translates into objectives that are often transformative and political in nature, among others: support for market economic reform and free trade; encouragement for WTO accession; and promotion of democracy and human rights. As these are the underlying principles of the EU's own institutional project, Brussels is adamant to have them included to a certain extent in the agreements under negotiation with Azerbaijan, as they are seen as 'universal' values.[67]

The EU knows that Azerbaijan perceives itself as a stronger actor but believes this to be misguided, mostly due to the lack of awareness of what the relationship has on offer.[68] Regarding the SMP specifically, the EU argued that Strategic Partnerships would be exclusively reserved for great powers—including Russia.[69] The EU's willingness to negotiate the SPA in 2015, then, seems to be a U-turn. For the EU, the SMP was not acceptable but since negotiations over the SPA started in 2017, it seems that Brussels has acknowledged that it has no alternative but to negotiate with Azerbaijan. When asked about the reason for this changed attitude towards Azerbaijan's first and second proposed alternative agreement, one interviewee referred to the urge to update the PCA as well as the changed emphasis of the renewed European Neighbourhood Policy.[70] The ENP's new strategy, presented in November 2015, officially allows for more differentiation between country policies (EC & HR/VP 2015), which would allow the EU to consider alternative frameworks, such as the SPA.[71] Indeed, the Azerbaijani negotiators have perceived the current European Commission as more 'pragmatic'.[72] Despite this pragmatic approach, the EU would still prefer to have signed an AA with all political dimensions included but realised that this was not realistic in relations with Azerbaijan.[73]

Availability of alternative options

For both the EU and Azerbaijan, a follow-up to the PCA is important.[74] This means that no agreement is not an option, but at the same time there does not seem to be a rush to find a follow-up agreement. This provides both sides with space for negotiation. Yet simultaneously, both sides have made clear that they have had strong reasons for not signing the proposed agreements so far. As stated previously, for the EU, incorporating a values dimension is crucial; for Azerbaijan, so is the absence of a strong political approach and, in addition, the inclusion of stronger references to the Nagorno-Karabakh conflict.

In addition, Azerbaijan was reluctant to sign the AA because of its foreign policy strategy of 'balancing', which requires a multi-vectored policy aimed at maintaining positive relations with many different powers in the region.[75] The late President Heydar Aliyev established this strategy in order to maintain good relations with all surrounding neighbours. The EU is therefore an important partner but not the only one. The Azerbaijani government feared that signing formal mechanisms offered by the EU, such as an AA or DCFTA, would send the wrong signal to other crucial partners, especially Russia (Della Sala 2015, p. 167).[76] Moscow would perceive an AA as 'one step away from EU membership'.[77] Nearly all Azerbaijani interviewees referred to the previous experiences of Georgia, Armenia and, most recently, Ukraine, in trying to forge closer relations with the EU, to show why Azerbaijan as a post-Soviet state should not sign any other formal agreement with the EU. There is great doubt as to whether the EU would ever come to Azerbaijan's aid (Cornell 2011, p. 392), a feeling that was strengthened after the EU's inaction when Ukraine and Georgia requested Brussels' help following Moscow's military interventions.[78] The alternative agreements are seen as a way of enabling further cooperation with the EU while avoiding upsetting Russia, by giving the Partnership essentially the same content as an AA but with a different name, making it seem less formal.[79]

Unlike Armenia, Azerbaijan has rejected membership of the Eurasian Economic Union (EEU). At the same time, however, Azerbaijan seeks to maintain good trade relations with the Eurasian bloc (Glazyev & Tkachuk 2015, p. 74). The EEU is therefore not seen as a real competitor by the EU with regard to Azerbaijan. Some have argued however, that if Turkey were to enter a special relationship with the EEU, this might also open the door for Baku (Trudos International 2016). Meanwhile, there has been increased economic cooperation between Azerbaijan and Turkey, and between Azerbaijan, Iran and Russia.[80] This reduces Azerbaijan's need to cooperate with the EU and is gradually strengthened its bargaining position in this respect.

Conclusion

Since 2010, three different proposed agreements have been negotiated between the EU and Azerbaijan to form the new legal basis for relations, replacing the PCA currently in place: the AA, SMP and SPA. Negotiations over all three agreements faced the same problematic points: the EU insists that there should be a chapter referring to values, particularly democracy and human rights, while the Azerbaijani government does not want too much emphasis on values in any future agreement, and instead wants more focus on the Nagorno-Karabakh conflict, which in turn is undesirable for Brussels.

The Azerbaijani side has argued that EU proposals are too unilateral and not dialogical in that they do not sufficiently take into account Azerbaijan's interests. Seen from another angle, one could argue that since neither side is willing to compromise on the key issues mentioned above, both parties appear 'unilateral' in their own way. To an extent it could be stated that Azerbaijan has succeeded in representing its interests; however, a values chapter will most likely still be included in the SPA, showing that the EU remains the strongest actor. Still, the fact that the AA was challenged by Azerbaijan in the first place has created a unique situation in relations with the EU.

We can observe different tendencies in the negotiations over time, and the question asked in this essay was, therefore, how can we explain these changing dynamics? To answer this question, the essay introduced a new model of 'bargaining power' to analyse the interactions and negotiation dynamics between Brussels and Baku. It was found that bargaining power can be gained and lost quickly, and that five aspects are vital to explain Azerbaijan's and the EU's behaviour in negotiations, and to assess their success in having their key interests represented.

The first vital aspect is the power base of both actors, with both sides' bargaining power significantly affected by their economic performance. This seems to have led to a stronger position for the Azerbaijani government prior to 2015; but to a weakened stance after. In terms of negotiation skill and capacity, the second aspect, it was argued that while the EU is traditionally a strong and experienced negotiator, Azerbaijan has used its non-material resources in the smartest way possible to maximise its leverage.

Regarding the domestic context of actors, the third aspect, for both the EU and the Azerbaijani government domestic constituents played a significant role in determining whether or not the proposed agreements were acceptable, especially in terms of values and the Nagorno-Karabakh conflict, as these issues also impact on legitimacy. The fourth aspect of the bargaining power model is actors' perceptions of the Self and Other. Generally, both Brussels and Baku appear to feel that they hold the stronger position in negotiations—or at least they keep up that appearance. These (mis)perceptions seem to stay firm across the different agreements that were negotiated. While other aspects of bargaining power have changed, and the perception of the Other has transformed over time as well, the perceptions of the Self (at least, those admitted to the outside world) appear remarkably constant. The last bargaining power dimension is the availability of alternative options. Here, both actors remained rather weak, since both agreed on the necessity of a follow-up agreement to the PCA. Neither Brussels nor Baku appear to have any significant alternatives, since Azerbaijan has declared it does not wish to join the EEU, and the EU had no other means to induce Azerbaijan to sign the AA.

Some would question that there have been any remarkable dynamics, and indeed, over the years there has been no significant change from the EU side: Brussels has consistently applied a policy based on a combination of strategic interests and values promotion (Youngs 2009, 2010; Kotzian *et al.* 2011) and has explicitly named this 'principled pragmatism' in the EU Global Strategy (EEAS 2016, p. 16). What this analysis has shown however, is that the situation is more nuanced and that there are more aspects to be considered than strategic interests alone: the non-material dimensions, such as domestic context and perceptions, matter more than often thought. Moreover, apart from factors influencing the EU's behaviour, including stability and continuity in its own policies, there has been considerable change on the other side, namely, in the approach and behaviour of the Azerbaijani government. Its increased bargaining power prior to 2015 led the government first, to reject the AA in 2013, and second, to propose an alternative agreement in 2013, which was unique in the history of EU external relations. Since 2015, as the foundation of Azerbaijan's bargaining power has been reduced somewhat, the government has had to make a number of concessions and has become more accommodating regarding the political dimension of the new agreement, which is what the EU desired. What we see, therefore, is that only viewing the EU perspective is insufficient: taking into consideration the Azerbaijani side of the story is crucial for understanding the dynamics in negotiations over the new legal agreement.

Naturally, over this period the EU remained the actor with most bargaining power. Given the sheer size of the EU and its market, Azerbaijan could not resist the EU's agenda altogether. However, in relative terms we have witnessed that, especially in the period 2013–2015, Azerbaijan has had significant bargaining power and that it has been able to challenge and resist the EU's proposed policies to an extent. Putting the negotiations in a broader perspective, one can see how remarkable and important Azerbaijan's contestations in this negotiation process have been, even if they have not (yet) led in full to the outcome desired by the government in Baku.

Overall, what the analysis of bargaining power made most clear, is that the negotiations over the AA, SMP and SPA are a relevant example of the changing power dynamics between the two sides. While back in the 1990s, the PCA was signed without any difficulties, Azerbaijan has since become a stronger actor with a clear agenda of its own. Baku's reluctance to sign the AA and the fact that it even proposed an alternative, show how the government perceived its own strength. Neither the EU nor Azerbaijan has, so far, had the offensive power to alter the agreements under negotiation to its own benefit; both had the defensive power to reject agreements that did not sufficiently meet their own interests. Nonetheless, that a relatively small country such as Azerbaijan can halt negotiations over such a major agreement and can subsequently induce the EU to negotiate an alternative, is meaningful, even more so because Baku pointed out that it considers the lack of dialogical policy-making, that it perceived as part of the AA, not acceptable.

What can we learn from the case of negotiations between the EU and Azerbaijan that is applicable to the broader region? On the one hand, Azerbaijan is perhaps not representative for the entire Eurasian region, given that the EU has clear transformative objectives in its relations with Azerbaijan.[81] The negotiation strategies used by the government in Baku are thus far also rare for the smaller states in the region. On the other hand, Azerbaijan is not unique in its resistance against a unilaterally set agenda, and there are indications that several countries in the region are becoming more assertive in applying their different (material and non-material) forms of power to enable themselves to co-shape relations with the EU and other actors. Following in Baku's footsteps, the Armenian government negotiated an individual, differentiated agreement in 2017 (EEAS 2017), and Moldovan President Igor Dodon has stated that he wants to reconsider the AA signed in 2014 (Hille & Buckley 2017). Belarus might request a similar pathway at a future date. The Azerbaijani case suggested that the quest for dialogue instead of unilateralism may be successful if countries can capitalise on their economic resources; if they can use their negotiation skill in the most effective way possible; if their domestic constituents push for a clear discourse and strong demands; if the perceptions of the Self facilitate an assertive stance in international relations; and if there are alternative options available. The 'starting point' still seems to be a unilateral policy based on the EU's wish for cooperation, unless the partner state manages to influence the policy through its bargaining power. The question is whether all states in the Eurasian region can meet these conditions.

From the EU's side, this shift in power dynamics seems to be facilitated by the rethinking of its policies towards the neighbourhood, following its economic decline after 2008 and the awareness that previous governance strategies in relations with neighbouring countries were not successful. The 2015 review of the ENP envisaged more differentiation (European Commission 2015b), and the European Commission installed in 2015 appears to be more pragmatic in determining the foundations for relations with the Eurasian region. The more pragmatic approach does bring along an important moral issue, in that key values of the EU may be (partially) sacrificed for the sake of cooperation. Change can be expected, but all sides will have to engage in lengthy negotiations over the final outcomes.

ESKE VAN GILS, *School of Politics and International Relations, University of Kent, Rutherford College, Canterbury, CT2 7NX, UK. Email: e.van-gils@kent.ac.uk*

Notes

The fieldwork for this research was made possible through the generous financial support of the School of Politics and International Relations at the University of Kent, BASEES and UACES. I would like to thank the two anonymous reviewers for their time and effort in reading the first draft of the essay and for making very helpful suggestions. My gratitude is also due to the organisers and participants of the conference 'Beyond Vilnius: The European Union and the Emerging Eurasian Space' at the University of Trento, 29–30 January 2016, for providing such in-depth feedback on the initial version of this essay, to peers at the BASEES Annual Conference 2017, to colleagues at the Global Europe Centre and especially to the guest-editors for their very helpful comments on later drafts.

1. For this case study, the 'EU' refers to the EU actors involved in the negotiations with Azerbaijan, namely the European External Action Service and its delegation in Baku, and the EU Council. Member states, their embassies in Baku, the European Commission and the European Parliament are included in the analysis to the extent that their bilateral contacts with Azerbaijan are relevant to the overall EU-led negotiations on this subject. 'Azerbaijan', in turn, refers to the elements of the Azerbaijani government conducting negotiations with the EU. These are often the highest-level officials, including the president, representatives of the Ministry of Foreign Affairs and members of the presidential administration. There are naturally more actors involved; however, for the sake of clarity this essay only examines bilateral relations at the executive level.
2. Interview with European affiliate 3, July 2014. For reasons of confidentiality, all names and positions of interviewees have been omitted. Interviewees will only be referred to by their broad affiliation ('European', referring to EU institutions as well as national member states; Azerbaijani establishment; or independent expert) in addition to the date of the interview.
3. Interview with European affiliate 3, July 2014.
4. Georgia Ratifies EU Association Agreement', *RFE/RL*, 18 July 2014, available at: http://www. rferl.org/content/georgia-eu-association-agreement-ratification-parliament/25461441.html, accessed 2 October 2014. The AAs would at a later stage be complemented by a Deep and Comprehensive Free Trade Agreement (DCFTA) (European Commission 2008, p. 4). In the case of relations between the EU and Azerbaijan, only the negotiations over the AA are relevant, since the country is not eligible to start DCFTA negotiations until it becomes a WTO member (ECFR 2013; Gstöhl 2015, p. 863).
5. This is a crucial difference between Belarus and Azerbaijan: both Minsk and Baku disagree with the EU's one-sided view on relations, and both countries resist EU pressure to comply with its policy framework and conditions. However, in the case of Belarus the result is that the EU has excluded the country from the bilateral track of the EaP, while Azerbaijan is included as a full partner. The Union has even expressed its wish for further economic and political cooperation with Baku in official documents and on the occasion of numerous official visits (European Commission 2007, 2010a). This scenario leaves space for Azerbaijan to actively resist the *status quo* and to try to influence the policy-making process.
6. Interview with expert 1, July 2014.
7. The analysis is based on the investigation of a range of sources, including policy documents, newspaper archives and other secondary literature. Secondary sources were integrated by a total of 25 interviews, conducted in 2014, 2015 and 2017 in both Baku and Brussels. Twelve respondents were representatives of or affiliated with the different EU institutions and national member states; six were representatives of or affiliated with the government of Azerbaijan; and seven interviewees were independent experts. While the number of interviews is rather limited, they provided comprehensive information, as demonstrated by the fact that a point of data saturation was reached whereby the interviews turned up the same or similar information.
8. Interview with European affiliate 3, July 2014.
9. The EU refers to the OSCE Minsk Group as having the official mandate for the conflict resolution process, and therefore does not wish to become engaged in the process itself, other than through an indirect role as a supporter of the Minsk Group's efforts. The Azerbaijani government, however, wants the EU to take on a more active role, as it has no confidence that the OSCE Minsk Group has the will or capacity to solve the conflict in a manner beneficial to Azerbaijan's interests. The EU's position in this regard conflicts somewhat with its stated desire to become a regional security actor and its commitment to regional security cooperation recorded in the ENP and EaP (Simão & Freire 2013, p. 465). While resolving the conflict would benefit the EU, as regional stability is in its immediate interest (Nuriyev 2008), involvement would also be a delicate matter considering that both Azerbaijan and Armenia are partners of the EU, and Russia would likely not approve of the EU's involvement.
10. Interview with Azerbaijani affiliate 5, May 2014.

11 Interview with Azerbaijani affiliate 5, May 2014.
12 'EU–Azerbaijan: The Game in Modernization', Turan Information Agency, 17 June 2014, available at: http://www.contact.az/docs/2014/Analytics/061700081652en.htm#.VClu3mOx3YU, accessed 29 September 2014.
13 Interview with European affiliate 7, May 2014.
14 Interview with European affiliate 5, May 2014.
15 Interview with Azerbaijani affiliate 3, July 2014.
16 Interview with European affiliate 5, May 2014.
17 Interview with European affiliate 3, July 2014.
18 Interview with Azerbaijani affiliate 3, July 2014.
19 Interview with European affiliate 3, July 2014.
20 Interview with European affiliate 3, July 2014.
21 Interview with European affiliate 3, July 2014.
22 Interview with European affiliate 3, July 2014.
23 Interview with European affiliate 1, October 2015.
24 Interview with European affiliate 1, October 2015.
25 'Azerbaijan, EU to Hold Another Meeting on Strategic Partnership Agreement', *AzerTac*, 25 August 2017, available at: https://azertag.az/en/xeber/1088555, accessed 6 September 2018; 'Baku Hosts Azerbaijan–EU Negotiations', *News.az*, 25 April 2017, available at: http://news.az/articles/politics/121064, accessed 16 June 2017.
26 Interview with European affiliate 1, October 2015.
27 Interview with Azerbaijani affiliate 1, May 2017.
28 Interview with Azerbaijani affiliate 1, May 2017.
29 'Baku Hosts 15th Meeting of EU–Azerbaijan Parliamentary Cooperation Committee', *AzerTac*, 8 May 2018, available at: https://azertag.az/en/xeber/1160813; 'Azerbaijan, EU Discuss Bilateral Cooperation', *AzerTac*, 20 February 2018, available at: https://azertag.az/en/xeber/1138634, accessed 6 September 2018.
30 The importance attached to the conflict is reflected in the fact that the overall majority of official statements, comments and speeches released by the Ministry of Foreign Affairs between January and November 2018 focused in one way or the other on Nagorno-Karabakh (MFA 2018).
31 Interview with European affiliate 1, October 2015.
32 This definition is the author's, constructed on the basis of a range of literature on bargaining power (Zartman 1978; Doron & Sened 2001).
33 Many studies apply bargaining power in light of rational choice theory or game theory, with fixed stages and 'purposeful action' of agents (Doron & Sened 2001, p. 19). This essay does not adhere to this interpretation of the negotiation process.
34 The concept defines a form of relationship between the EU and third countries in which the EU can exert a certain influence in a non-accession framework (Lavenex 2004, p. 680). Different modes of external governance have been conceptualised, including 'hierarchical governance', when relations are top-down and mostly determined by the EU rather than based on equal input from both sides (Boörzel 2010, pp. 191, 198); and 'network governance', whereby views of all actors involved are taken into account (Pierre & Peters 2000, p. 19). Korosteleva argues that genuine partnership should go even a step further, and not be based on governance but on genuinely equal cooperation (Korosteleva 2011).
35 See also Iklé (1985, p. 122).
36 Interview with Azerbaijani affiliate 3, July 2014.
37 Interview with European affiliate 1, October 2015.
38 'How Azerbaijan is Coping with Crisis', *Stratfor*, 20 February 2015, available at: https://www.stratfor.com/analysis/how-azerbaijan-coping-crisis, accessed 6 December 2015.
39 'Arrests as Azerbaijani Police Use Water Cannons, Tear Gas against Protesters', *RFE/RL*, 15 January 2016, available at: http://www.rferl.org/content/azerbaijan-protests-increased-security-popular-discontent/27489831.html, accessed 7 September 2018.
40 Interview with European affiliate 5, May 2014; interview with European affiliate 1, October 2015.
41 Interview with Azerbaijani affiliate 1, May 2017.
42 The AA and SMP had not been discussed in the Cooperation Council of Parliamentary Cooperation Committee, since those meetings had been called off between 2013 and 2016,

following EU criticism over Azerbaijan's human rights record (interview with European affiliate 3, July 2014; European Parliament 2017).
43 Interview with European affiliate 2, July 2014; interview with Azerbaijani affiliate 3, July 2014.
44 EU Refused to Enter into the Strategic Modernization Partnership with Azerbaijan until the Association Agreement is Concluded', *Abc.az*, 31 August 2013, available at: http://abc.az/eng/news/75788.html, accessed 8 September 2014.
45 EU Refused to Enter into the Strategic Modernization Partnership with Azerbaijan until the Association Agreement is Concluded', *Abc.az*, 31 August 2013, available at: http://abc.az/eng/news/75788.html, accessed 8 September 2014.
46 Interview with Azerbaijani affiliate 3, July 2014; interview with European affiliate 1, October 2015.
47 Interview with Azerbaijani affiliate 4, May 2015; 'Azerbaijan, EU Unlikely to Sign Any Document at Riga Summit', *News.az*, 19 May 2015, available at: http://www.news.az/articles/politics/98094, accessed 7 September 2018.
48 Ali Hasanov: Azerbaijani President Will Not Participate in Riga Summit', Azeri Press Agency, 20 May 2015, available at: http://en.apa.az/xeber_ali_hasanov accessed 1 November 2015. azerbaijani_president_will 227319.html,
49 Interview with Azerbaijani affiliate 2, May 2015. The fire in the apartment block was a major incident which left 15 people dead, and led to protests in the country against cheap but unsafe infrastructural adjustments to make the city look more presentable.
50 Interview with European affiliate 1, October 2015.
51 Interview with European affiliate 1, October 2015.
52 Interview with European affiliate 1, October 2015.
53 Azerbaijan Continues Independent, Multidimensional, Balanced and Active Foreign Policy in 2017', *AzerTac*, 28 December 2017, available at: https://azertag.az/en/xeber/1125089, accessed 7 September 2018.
54 See for instance the group's event calendar: https://www.eventbrite.co.uk/o/the-european-azerbaijan-society-teas-1348104131, accessed 7 November 2018.
55 Offensive power is power in which A can chose to make B do something; defensive power is possessed by B and refers to the situation in which A cannot succeed in making B do something (Goldmann 1979, pp. 13–4).
56 Azerbaijan's Aliyev Cancels Brussels Meeting with EU Parliament President', *RFE/RL*, 6 February 2017, available at: https://www.rferl.org/a/azerbaijan-eu-aliyev-partnership-talks-human-rights-pressure/28281494.html, accessed 16 June 2017.
57 Interview with European affiliate 3, July 2014.
58 Interview with European affiliate 3, July 2014.
59 Interview with independent expert 1, July 2014; interview with European affiliate 6, May 2014; and interview with Azerbaijani affiliate 3, July 2014.
60 Interview with expert 1, July 2014.
61 Democratic Processes Taking Place in Azerbaijan are Highly Appreciated by the World Community, President', *AzerTac*, 10 July 2018, available at: https://azertag.az/en/xeber/1178670, accessed 17 September 2018; 'President Ilham Aliyev Received Delegation of European Commission', *AzerTac*, 29 January 2018, available at: https://azertag.az/en/xeber/1132224, accessed 17 September 2018.
62 President Ilham Aliyev: Azerbaijan has Asserted Itself as a Dignified and Reliable Partner in the World', *AzerTac*, 1 January 2018, available at: https://azertag.az/en/xeber/1125637, accessed 17 September 2018.
63 Interview with expert 1, July 2014.
64 Interview with Azerbaijani affiliate 3, July 2014.
65 Interview with Azerbaijani affiliate 3, July 2014.
66 Interview with European affiliate 5, May 2014. It this sense Azerbaijan's reasoning is very similar to that of Russia at the time, when Moscow demanded individual treatment rather than being included in the ENP, because it felt more important to the EU than the other states that are currently included in the Eastern Partnership and European Neighbourhood Policy.
67 Interview with European affiliate 2, July 2014.

68 Interview with European affiliate 4, April 2014.
69 Interview with European affiliate 5, May 2014.
70 Interview with European affiliate 1, October 2015; see also Korosteleva et al. (2015).
71 Interview with European affiliate 1, October 2015.
72 Interview with Azerbaijani representative 1, May 2017.
73 Interview with European affiliate 1, October 2015.
74 Interview with European affiliate 1, October 2015.
75 Interview with Azerbaijani affiliate 5, May 2014.
76 Two interviews with European affiliates 6 and 7, May 2014.
77 Interview with expert 3, May 2014.
78 Interview with expert 2, May 2014; interview with Azerbaijani affiliate 5, May 2014.
79 Interview with expert 3, May 2014.
80 Azerbaijan, Turkey Define Scope of Preferential Trade Deal', *AzerNews*, 6 May 2017, available at: https://www.azernews.az/business/112577.html, accessed 17 June 2017; 'Iran and Azerbaijan to Join Railways as Part of Freight Route', *Reuters*, 5 March 2017, available at: http://www.reuters.com/article/us-iran-azerbaijan-railways-idUSKBN16C0MW?il¼0, accessed 17 June 2017.
81 Similarly clear objectives do not receive the same weight in relations with, for example, the Central Asian states. While they do play a key role in the EU's agenda *vis-'a-vis* Russia, we cannot compare Russia and Azerbaijan in this regard, because of their differing economic and political power.

References

Agayev, Z. (2015) 'Azerbaijan's Shift to Free Float Sends Manat to 20-year Low', *Bloomberg,* 21 December, available at: http://www.bloomberg.com/news/articles/2015-12-21/azerbaijan-moves-to-floating-exchange-rate-letting-manat-tumble, accessed 7 September 2018.

Babayev, A. (2009) 'Der Bergkarabach-Konflikt aus aserbaidschanischer Sicht', in Reiter, E. (ed.) *Der Krieg um Bergkarabach: Krisen-und Konfliktmanagement in der Kaukasus-Region* (Vienna, B€ohlau Verlag).

Babayev, A. (2014) *Weder Krieg noch Frieden im S€udkaukasus: Hintergr€unde, Akteure, Entwickelungen zum Bergkarabach-Konflikt* (Baden-Baden, Nomos).

Bechev, D. & Nicolaïdis, C. (2010) 'From Policy to Polity: Can the EU's Special Relations with its "Neighbourhood" be Decentred?', *Journal of Common Market Studies*, 48, 3.

Börzel, T. (2010) 'European Governance: Negotiation and Competition in the Shadow of Hierarchy', *Journal of Common Market Studies*, 48, 2.

Cornell, S. (2011) *Azerbaijan since Independence* (New York, NY, M.E. Sharp).

Della Sala, V. (2015) 'The EU and the Eurasian Economic Union: Between Partnership and Threat?', in Dutkiewicz, P. & Sakwa, R. (eds) *Eurasian Integration: The View from Within* (Abingdon, Routledge).

Diez, T. (2005) 'Constructing the Self and Changing Others: Reconsidering Normative Power Europe', *Millennium: Journal of International Studies*, 33, 3.

Dimitrov, M. (2013) *Why Communism did not Collapse: Understanding Authoritarian Regime Resilience in Asia and Europe* (New York, NY, Cambridge University Press).

Doron, G. & Sened, I. (2001) *Political Bargaining: Theory, Practice & Process* (London, Sage).

EC DG Trade (2017) 'European Union, Trade in Goods with Azerbaijan', available at: http://trade.ec.europa.eu/doclib/docs/2006/september/tradoc_113347.pdf, accessed 15 June 2017.

EC and HR/VP (2015) *Review of the European Neighbourhood Policy, JOIN (2015) 50 final* (Brussels, European Commission).

ECFR (2013) *Wider Europe: Relations with the Eastern Neighbourhood on Trade and Energy*, available at: http://www.ecfr.eu/scorecard/2012/wider/48, accessed 6 August 2013.

EEAS (2016) *Shared Vision, Common Action: A Stronger Europe: A Global Strategy for the European Union's Foreign and Security Policy* (Brussels, EEAS).

EEAS (2017) *Important Step Forward in EU–Armenia Relations as Bilateral Agreement is Initialled*, 21 March, available at: https://eeas.europa.eu/headquarters/headquarters-homepage_en/23150/Important%20step%20forward%20in%20EU-Armenia%20relations%20as%20bilateral%20agreement %20is%20initialled, accessed 15 June 2017.

Elgström, O. & Jöhnsson, C. (2005) *European Union Negotiations: Processes, Networks and Institutions* (Abingdon, Routledge).

ESI (2012) *Caviar Diplomacy: How Azerbaijan Silenced the Council of Europe—Part 1* (Berlin, European Stability Initiative).

Eurasian Economic Commission (2015) *Armenia is Now in the Eurasian Economic Union*, 2 January, available at: http://www.eurasiancommission.org/en/nae/news/Pages/02-01-2015-1.aspx, accessed 17 September 2018.

European Commission (2007) *European Neighbourhood and Partnership Instrument: Azerbaijan Country Strategy Paper 2007–2013* (Brussels, European Commission).

European Commission (2008) *Communication from the Commission to the European Parliament and the Council: Eastern Partnership {SEC(2008) 2974}* (Brussels, European Commission).

European Commission (2010a) *Implementation of the European Neighbourhood Policy in 2009: Progress Report Azerbaijan* (Brussels, European Commission).

European Commission (2010b) *Implementation of the Eastern Partnership: Report to the Meeting of Foreign Affairs Ministers, December 13, 2010* (Brussels, European Commission).

European Commission (2010c) 'EU Launches Negotiations on Association Agreement with Armenia, Azerbaijan and Georgia', Press Statement IP/10/955, available at: http://europa.eu/rapid/press-release_IP-10-955_en.htm, accessed 16 July 2014.

European Commission (2015a) *Implementation of the European Neighbourhood Policy in Azerbaijan: Progress in 2014 and Recommendations for Actions. SWD (2015) 64 final* (Brussels, European Commission).

European Commission (2015b) *Joint Communication to the European Parliament, the Council, the European Economic and Social Committee and the Committee of the Regions: Review of the European Neighbourhood Policy, SWD (2015) 500 final* (Brussels, European Commission).

European Commission (2018a) *Partnership Priorities between the EU and Azerbaijan Reinforce the Bilateral Agenda*, 11 July, available at: https://ec.europa.eu/neighbourhood-enlargement/news_corner/news/partnership-priorities-between-eu-and-azerbaijan-reinforce-bilateral-agenda_en, accessed 17 September 2018.

European Commission (2018b) *Annex to the Joint Proposal for a Council Decision on the Position to be Taken on Behalf of the European Union within the Cooperation Council (...) with Regard to the Adoption of the EU–Azerbaijan Partnership Priorities, JOIN(2018)24 final* (Brussels, European Commission).

European Commission (2018c) *Joint Proposal for a Council Decision on the Position to be Taken on Behalf of the European Union within the Cooperation Council Established by the Partnership and Cooperation Agreement between the European Communities and their Member States, of the one part, and the Republic of Azerbaijan, of the other part, with Regard to the Adoption of the EU–Azerbaijan Partnership Priorities* (Brussels, European Commission).

EU Council (2014) *Association Agreement between the European Union and its Member States, of the One Hand, and Ukraine, of the Other Part*, 29 May (Brussels, Official Journal of the European Union).

EU Council (2016) 'EU to Launch Negotiations on a New Agreement with Azerbaijan', Press Release, 14 November (EU Council, Brussels).

EU Council (2018) *EU Relations with Azerbaijan*, available at: http://www.consilium.europa.eu/en/policies/eastern-partnership/azerbaijan/, accessed 2 August 2018.

European Parliament (2015) *Joint Motion for a Resolution*: RC-B8–0856/2015, 9 September, available at: http://www.europarl.europa.eu/sides/getDoc.do?pubRef=-%2F%2FEP%2F%2FTEXT%2BMOTION%2BP8-RC-2015-0856%2B0%2BDOC%2BXML%2BV0%2F%2FEN& language EN, accessed 27 September 2015.

European Parliament (2017) 'Final Statement and Recommendations', The EU–Azerbaijan Parliamentary Cooperation Committee Fourteenth Meeting, 2–3 May (Brussels, European Parliament).

Farchy, J. (2015) 'Azerbaijani Manat Collapses after Government Abandons Dollar Peg', *Financial Times*, 21 December, available at: http://www.ft.com/cms/s/0/b5f46eac-a7c4-11e5-9700-2b669a5aeb83.html#axzz3v3djcMem, accessed 22 December 2015.

Franke, A., Gawrich, A., Melnykovska, I. & Schweickert, R. (2010) 'The European Union's Relations with Ukraine and Azerbaijan', *Post-Soviet Affairs*, 26, 2.

Gahramanova, A. (2009) 'Internal and External Factors in the Democratization of Azerbaijan', *Democratization*, 16, 4.

Gardner, A. (2013) 'Armenia Chooses Russia over EU', *Politico*, 3 September, available at: https://www.politico.eu/article/armenia-chooses-russia-over-eu/, accessed 17 September 2018.

Glazyev, S. & Tkachuk, S. (2015) 'Eurasian Economic Union: Achievements and Prospects', in Dutkiewicz, P. & Sakwa, R. (eds) *Eurasian Integration: The View from Within* (Abingdon, Routledge).

Goldmann, K. (1979) 'The International Power Structure: Traditional Theory and New Reality', in Goldmann, K. & Sjöstedt, G. (eds) *Power, Capabilities, Interdependence: Problems in the Study of International Influence* (London, Sage).

Gotev, G. (2018) 'EU and Azerbaijan Agree "Partnership Priorities"', *Euractiv*, 11 July, available at: https://www.euractiv.com/section/azerbaijan/news/eu-and-azerbaijan-agree-partnership-priorities/, accessed 17 September 2018.

Gstöhl, S. (2015) 'Models of External Differentiation in the EU's Neighbourhood: An Expanding Economic Community?', *Journal of European Public Policy*, 22, 6.

Hille, K. & Buckley, N. (2017) 'Moldova Leader Vows to Scrap EU Trade Deal for Moscow-led Bloc', *Financial Times*, 17 January, available at: https://www.ft.com/content/52651bb6-dcd4-11e6-86ac-f253db7791c6, accessed 25 July 2018.

Iklé, F. (1985) *How Nations Negotiate* (London, Harper & Row).

Ismayilov, M. (2012) 'State, Identity, and the Politics of Music: Eurovision and Nation-building in Azerbaijan', *Nationalities Papers*, 40, 6.

Jafarli, N. (2016) 'Azerbaijan: Approaching Crisis Point', *ECFR Wider Europe Forum Commentary*, 10 February, available at: http://www.ecfr.eu/article/commentary_azerbaijan_approaching_crisis_ point5096, accessed 16 June 2017.

Jervis, R. (1976) *Perception and Misperception in International Relations* (Princeton, NJ, Princeton University Press).

Kavalski, E. (2012) *Central Asia and the Rise of Normative Powers: Contextualizing the Security Governance of the European Union, China, and India* (London, Bloomsbury).

Khasson, V. (2013) 'Cross-border Cooperation over the Eastern EU Border: Between Assistance and Partnership under the European Neighbourhood and Partnership Instrument', *East European Politics*, 29, 3.

Knaus, G. (2015) 'Europe and Azerbaijan: The End of Shame', *Journal of Democracy*, 26, 3.

Korosteleva, E. (2011) 'Change or Continuity: Is the Eastern Partnership an Adequate Tool for the European Neighbourhood?', *International Relations*, 25, 2.

Korosteleva, E., van Gils, E., Merheim-Eyre, I. & Mnatsakanyan, I. (2015) 'Towards a European Global Security Strategy: Challenges and Opportunities', House of Lords' call for evidence 'The strategic Review of the EU's Foreign and Security Policy', available at: http://data.parliament.uk/writtenevidence/committeeevidence.svc/evidencedocument/eu-external-affairs-subcommittee/strategic-review-of-the-eus-foreign-and-security-policy/written/22127.html, accessed 6 November 2018.

Kotzian, P., Knodt, M. & Urdze, S. (2011) 'Instruments of the EU's External Democracy Promotion', *Journal of Common Market Studies*, 49, 5.

Lavenex, S. (2004) 'EU External Governance in "Wider Europe"', *Journal of European Public Policy*, 11, 4.

Manners, I. (2002) 'Normative Power Europe: A Contradiction in Terms?', *JCMS*, 40, 2.
Melissen, J. (ed.) (2005) *The New Public Diplomacy: Soft Power in International Relations* (Basingstoke, Palgrave Macmillan).
MFA (2018) 'Press Service: Press Releases, Statements, Comments, Speeches, Articles and Interviews', Ministry of Foreign Affairs of the Republic of Azerbaijan, available at: http://www.mfa.gov.az/, accessed 30 July 2018.
Nuriyev, E. (2008) 'Azerbaijan and the European Union: New Landmarks of Strategic Partnership in the South Caucasus—Caspian Basin', *Southeast and Black Sea Studies*, 8, 2.
Orbie, J. (2008) *Europe's Global Role: The External Policies of the European Union* (Aldershot, Ashgate).
Pierre, J. & Peters, B. (2000) *Governance, Politics and the State* (Basingstoke, Palgrave Macmillan).
Putnam, L. & Roloff, M. (eds) (1992) *Communication and Negotiation. Sage Annual Reviews of Communication Research, vol. 20* (London, Sage).
Reiter, E. (ed.) (2009) *Der Krieg um Bergkarabach: Krisen-und Konfliksmanagement in der Kaukasus-Region* (Vienna, Böhlau Verlag).
Rettman, A. (2013) 'Azerbaijan and EU Race to Agree "Modernisation" Pact', *EU Observer*, 27 September, available at: http://euobserver.com/foreign/121592, accessed 8 September 2014.
Salimova, G. (2016) 'Azerbaijan Government Cuts Break Price in Effort to Dampen Protests', *Kyiv Post*, 15 January, available at: http://www.kyivpost.com/article/content/world/azerbaijan-government-cuts-bread-price-in-effort-to-dampen-protests-405995.html, accessed 7 September 2018.
Simão, L. (2012) 'The Problematic Role of EU Democracy Promotion in Armenia, Azerbaijan and Nagorno-Karabakh', *Communist and Post-Communist Studies*, 45, 1–2.
Simão, L. & Freire, M. (2013) 'The EU in Georgia: Building Security?', *Oficina do CES*, 396, 11. Sjöstedt, G. (1979) 'Concluding Remarks', in Goldmann, K. & Sjöstedt, G. (eds) *Power, Capabilities, Interdependence: Problems in the Study of International Influence* (London, Sage).
Trudos International (2016) *Eurasian Economic Union: Why it Matters* (London, Trudos International).
Turner, D. (1992) 'Negotiator–Constituent Telationships', in Putnam, L. & Roloff, M. (eds) *Communication and Negotiation. Sage Annual Reviews of Communication Research, volume 20* (London, Sage).
Tutzauer, F. (1992) 'The Communication of Offers in Dyadic Bargaining', in Putnam, L. & Roloff, M. (eds) *Communication and Negotiation. Sage Annual Reviews of Communication Research, volume 20* (London, Sage).
van Gils, E. (2018) 'Differentiation Through Bargaining Power in EU–Azerbaijan Relations: Baku as a Tough Negotiator', *East European Politics*, 33, 3.
Walker, S. (2015) 'EU Eastern Partnership Summit will Highlight Failure of Plan to Check Russia', *The Guardian*, 20 May, available at: http://www.theguardian.com/world/2015/may/20/eu-eastern-partnership-highlight-failure-plan-check-russia, accessed 7 September 2018.
Weber, K., Smith, M. & Baun, M. (eds) (2007) *Governing Europe's Neighbourhood: Partners or Periphery?* (Manchester, Manchester University Press).
World Bank (2017a) 'Data: European Union GDP Growth', available at: https://data.worldbank.org/indicator/NY.GDP.MKTP.KD.ZG?locations=EU, accessed 15 June 2017.
World Bank (2017b) 'Data: Annual GDP Growth Azerbaijan', available at: https://data.worldbank.org/indicator/NY.GDP.MKTP.KD.ZG?locations=AZ, accessed 15 June 2017.
Youngs, R. (2009) 'Democracy Promotion as External Governance?', *Journal of European Public Policy*, 16, 6.
Youngs, R. (2010) *The European Union and Democracy Promotion: A Critical Global Assessment* (Baltimore, MD, Johns Hopkins University Press).
Zartman, W. (ed.) (1978) *The Negotiation Process: Theories and Applications* (London, Sage).
Zartman, W. & Rubin J. (eds) (2002) *Power and Negotiation* (Ann Arbor, MI, University of Michigan Press).

Part III

Looking backward

The EU, the Eastern Neighbours and the 'Eastern Partnership' a decade past

Looking backward

Deliverables and drawbacks of the Eastern Partnership during 2009–2020

Andriy Tyushka and Tobias Schumacher

Since 2019, the EU's Eastern European policy in general and the Eastern Partnership (EaP) in particular have been at the crossroads of programmatic and practical rethinking, that is at the stage of revision. In May 2019, the tenth anniversary of the EaP was marked, and while there were many reasons for celebration, there was at least as much ground for critical reflection. Progress achieved in some policy fields and countries alike seemed to be oddly satisfying, whereas in others, including the EaP framework as a whole, numerous problems not only persisted, but were actually reinforced and became intertwined with other emergent challenges. In sum, ten years after its launch, the EaP still meanders in the eyes of most critical observers between success and failure.

Obviously, such a binary assessment is over-simplistic. It appears to be close to infeasible as 'any evaluation of (non-)achievements of such a multi-stakeholder, multi-platform and multi-purpose joint political undertaking cannot be made to fit the simplistic "success or failure" binary', for it is 'an area where details and nuances matter' (Tyushka 2019: 13). It is, furthermore, an area where not only the declared objectives but also the (geo)strategic context in which the EaP was founded and implemented play a significant role. Such parameters have evidently fed into the initiative's founding dilemmas and design faults, including its much-criticized strategic ambiguity, situation-dependency and limited responsiveness. The EU's seemingly inherent problem in its external action, namely whether it should prioritize its interests or values and thus whether it should focus on transforming (democratizing) rather than stabilizing its neighbourhood, in conjunction with the manifold challenges that the pursuit of general and sector-specific 'Europeanization beyond borders' entails have exposed the EaP to two major dilemmas of strategic uncertainty. These keep determining the framework's genuinely reactive and structurally constrained policy design. The first dilemma revolves around the EU's ambition to bring closer its Eastern neighbourhood and transform it while, at the same time, the EU refuses to define a strategic end goal. The second dilemma relates to the (un)intended consequences of the pursuit of a policy framework that is confronted with a growingly assertive Russia which regards the space beyond the EU's eastern borders as its exclusive sphere of influence (van der Togt 2018; Tyushka 2019). Such dilemmas might well be reflective of the 'mutually incompatible basic assumptions about the political organization of the transnational world', as some posit (Beichelt 2014: 357). Moreover, they arguably co-produce what is called 'narrational insecurity' (ibid.: 361–363) in what regards the EaP and the EU's Eastern neighbourhood as such, generating a broad mix of negative consequences for political action. Practically, and as is pointed out in the Introduction to this volume, the EU's Eastern neighbourhood policy has been perplexed by the inexistence, in political terms, of an Eastern European region as such and the highly contested (re)ordering of a geostrategic space that has been moving past 'post-Soviet' towards an uncertain destination (cf. also: Saari and Secrieru 2019). That the EU's approach towards its Eastern neighbours was 'mesmerized by enlargement' (Lightfoot et al. 2016), while lacking the necessary strategic determination and direction, has aggravated the expectations gap among EaP countries and, *ipso facto*, limited the EU's transformative power potential.

Any assessment of the EaP's successes and failures, therefore, has to be reflective of the initiative's founding dilemmas and design constraints. Viewing drawbacks in terms of the EaP's value-added, or impact, shall help overcome the simplistic 'success or failure' binary. In this regard, it is instructive to distinguish between broader achievements and more specific policy deliverables.[1] The same applies to major shortcomings as far as under-performance and un-delivered promises are concerned. This chapter is guided, in its assessment of the EaP's successes and failures, by a *goal-oriented* framework (GOF) for policy analysis, as presented below.

A GOF for (foreign) policy analysis

Categories such as 'success' and 'failure' are under-researched categories in the scholarly literature in International Relations (IR), Foreign Policy Analysis (FPA) and, to a lesser extent, Public Policy Analysis. This comes as a surprise, given that every (public/foreign) policy entails purposive behaviour and, thus, by definition, is goal-oriented, as the 'rational actor model' and the 'logic of appropriateness' accounts suggest (March and Olsen 1989: 23–24; Carlsnaes 2004: 502). Evaluation and assessment of goal attainment is, consequently, at the heart of studying success and failure of any (foreign) policy. Nonetheless, the 'field of foreign policy studies is preoccupied with the processes of foreign policy making and has tended to neglect the outputs of such processes', whereby '[m]ost discussions of foreign policy success and failure are left to journalistic pundits or to scholars writing for journals as *National Interest, Foreign Affairs, Foreign Policy*' and other outlets (Baldwin 2000: 167). The lack of scholarly conceptualizations of 'success' and 'failure', and the related methodological challenges in operationalizing them are evidently responsible for such an analytical gap. As Baldwin (2000: 180) posits in his study on *Success and Failure in Foreign Policy,* '[b]efore criticizing foreign policy failures, one should ponder the meaning of success and failure in foreign policy'. Also, he admits that:

> Estimating the success or failure of policy instruments is difficult because the concept of success is slippery, recipes for success can be misleading, the dimensions of success are multiple, and clear-cut victories or defeats are few.
>
> (Baldwin 2000: 171)

'Success' can be defined in terms of favourable or desired outcomes, (the lack of excessive) costs and positive cost-benefit balances. Furthermore, it is a multi-dimensional and relative notion, which is assessed against the backdrop of other international actors' successes and failures, just as it is a matter of degree (Baldwin 2000: 171–176). A necessary, though not sufficient, component of estimating success is the evaluation of effectiveness in accomplishing goals (Clark 1995: 562; Baldwin 2000: 174). Such a perspective regards foreign policy as an 'output' rather than as 'action'. In what follows, foreign policy goals (FPGs) feature as a central object of analysis and a measure in itself.

In its simplest and ordinary meaning, a FPG is a politically established and officially declared end-state of an (inter)action pursued. In other words, it is what actors want to achieve as part of their formulated foreign policies. Carlsnaes (2002: 335) defines the scope of foreign policy as a goal-driven and goal-oriented complex international activity or interaction:

> [F]oreign policies consist of those actions which, expressed in the form of explicitly stated goals, commitments and/or directives, and pursued by governmental representatives acting on behalf of their sovereign communities, are directed toward objectives, conditions and actors – both governmental and non-governmental – which they want to affect and which lie beyond their territorial legitimacy.
> (Carlsnaes 2002: 335)

Whereas the realist school of thought presupposes the existence of universally shared (and, thus, mutually competing) FPGs, such as survival, security and prestige, other theoretical perspectives, including liberalism and neorealism, point to the existence of salient FPGs beyond survival (Wolfers 1962: 71–72). As regards international cooperation, actors are said to usually pursue goals that stem from dual strategic interests – a security and an economic interest (Slobodchikoff 2013: 64–69). Importantly, FPGs should not be equated with (national) foreign policy interests, even if the latter inform the former. Hill (2003: 119) argues that these are precisely FPGs that can objectify what is an implicit interest in terms of power, security, prosperity and independence, 'all of which can be taken for granted as high-level goals of all states' foreign policy, but which lead to disagreement as soon as discussion becomes more specific'. FPGs convert a general sense of national/foreign policy interests into an operational and prioritized agenda for action. Prioritization and goal setting is, furthermore, done in the context of ascertaining significant/salient foreign policy issues (Alden and Aran 2017: 52).

Just as in IR/FPA, theory-informed analysis of FPGs in European Studies in particular – in contrast to research on (national) interests – represents a niche. Developing an institutionalist approach to EU foreign policy cooperation, Smith (2004: 18) defines it as an action 'oriented toward a specific goal'. Rieker (2013: 160) adds that studying the EU's ability to formulate and pursue goals can contribute to a better understanding of EU actor properties, enriching the popular set of research programs on EU decision-making, administrative and institutional capabilities and foreign policy behaviour. In the case of a unique and complex international actor such as the EU, FPGs are not only expressed in programmatic documents and discourses of EU institutions, they are also anchored in EU constitutional law (Larik 2016). In view of the intergovernmental character of EU foreign, security and defence policies, analysis of the corresponding foreign policy interests, preferences and objectives of the 27 EU Member States renders this field of enquiry highly politicized and fluid. Studies of goal attainment, also as part of the 'success' and 'failure' paradigms, are even rarer. The analytical lens is essentially revolving around the notions of influence, performance or effectiveness. Aiming to build an analytical framework for assessing the EU's influence on global politics in specific issue areas, Schunz (2010: 22), for instance, draws on public policy analysis approaches and develops an avenue for studying the 'EU's concrete foreign policy activities and their effects'. Seeing influence as an ability of influence-wielders to attain their goals, he posits that 'the goal-oriented behaviour of the influence-wielder must be successful: its goal must be attained' (Schunz 2010: 26) for the assessment about influence to become possible. The concept of effectiveness, in turn, is relatively unpopular, not least as it 'is notoriously difficult to analyse and assess' (Hoffmann and

Niemann 2018: 31). The challenge increases when the subject matter does not only revolve around EU FPGs and their attainment, but also around those of its six Eastern neighbours (the EaP-6).

In light of the above, it appears clear that a complete discussion of successes and failures of the EaP during 2009–2019, as far as goal attainment is concerned, and seen from all relevant angles, is impossible within the scope of this chapter. The first legitimate question to ask in this regard is 'whose goals?'. The next question is 'what kind of goals?', i.e. explicitly stated or actually pursued goals? If one were to assume that the EU's actual (implicit) goals behind launching the EaP were 'to tie the Eastern neighbors to the European Union, keep Russia out and EU membership perspective off the table' (Jarábik 2019: 44), one might *prima facie* even have to register success in achieving such goals. When, however, the EU's explicitly stated goals are to be considered, with the neighbourhood's transformation (democratization) topping the agenda, it becomes more complicated to assess whether the policy has been successful at all: not only is the goal itself too broadly formulated and difficult to operationalize. There is also no clarity as to how to evaluate policy change in that '[i]nstead of transformation, [the EU now] speaks of stabilization and differentiation' (Nixey 2019: 33). Is this shift to be positively assessed as an actor's ability to adapt the pursuit of its goals, or is this to be regarded as a complete failure to reach initially set goals? Or does this possibly have to be evaluated as something 'in between', bearing in mind the multiple degrees of success? Multiplied by 6 EaP countries (EaP-6) and 27 EU Member States, respectively, this puzzle risks turning into an endless 'yes… but' exercise in policy output evaluation.

In this chapter, only *explicitly declared joint goals*, as stated by the EU and the EaP-6, are at the centre of analysis. After all, international cooperation is rational – in a goal-oriented, instrumental way. Though the EaP is an EU foreign policy framework, cooperation within it is an integral part of both the EU's and the EaP-6's foreign-political undertakings, guided by explicitly defined joint goals. This chapter, therefore, develops a GOF for foreign policy and cooperation analysis within the EaP. This approach is rooted in the public policy literature and in particular in policy evaluation, as discussed above. This chapter aims at identifying relevant goals of EU-EaP-6 cooperation in the initiative's two tracks and assesses goal attainment in terms of goal-relevant accomplishments, bearing in mind that the spectrum of degrees of goal attainment and the notion of success are themselves multidimensional. Yet, two reservations apply. First, given that policy goals range from being truly broad to being highly specific, it is difficult to bridge policy evaluation perspectives, tools and measures of goal attainment. Second, while intellectually stimulating, the second-order effects, i.e. the effectiveness, of the goals attained in various domestic or international contexts are not addressed. Instead, in what follows, this chapter is primarily concerned with the question of *how effective* the EU and the EaP-6 have been *in pursuing* their joint goals of cooperation in the framework of the EaP's two tracks.

Eastern Partnership goals, objectives and policy issues

Since 2009, the main goal of the EaP has been to 'accelerate political association and further economic integration' between the EU and its Eastern neighbours (EaP Summit Joint Declaration 2009: 6, para.2). Based on this twofold goal, the EaP has sought to: (1) support political and socio-economic reforms of the partner countries (facilitating prosperity and approximation with the EU); (2) promote democracy and good governance; (3) promote stability and multilateral confidence building; (4) strengthen security (including energy security); (5) support economic and social development; (6) encourage people-to-people contacts and to (7) offer additional funding to reduce socio-economic disbalances and increase stability.[2]

Pursuant to this chapter's framework of analysis, EaP goals need to be seen in the broader context of jointly pursued salient issues of EU-EaP-6 cooperation. A thorough content analysis of the Joint Declarations adopted at the five biannual EaP Summits held during 2009–2017 showed that, out of nearly 30 identified policy issues, reference to 'reforms' (with occurrence frequency of 8.92%) tops the cooperation agenda. This is followed by references to 'security' (6.76%), 'political dialogue' (6.62%), 'social dialogue and civil society engagement' (6.62%), 'business and SME development' (6.47%), 'association' (6.04%), 'sustainable development' (5.32%), 'economic integration' (4.89%) and 'legislative and regulatory approximation' (4.75%) as issue areas that are to be pursued multilaterally and bilaterally (Tyushka 2019: 11–13; cf. also *Annex 1, Figure A1.3*). The broadly formulated aims, as well as the variegated focus of the EaP's Joint Declarations (cf. *Annex 1, Figures A1.4 and A1.5*), blurred the understanding of the true nature of the EaP and, accordingly, its targets. In addition, the proliferating 'myths' and misperceptions revolving around the EaP as a policy initiative (Gretskiy et al. 2014; EEAS 2019a) – regardless of whether these were guided by EaP partners' varying expectations or the proliferating, Russia-originating fake discourses about the EaP – undermined the framework's communicative rationality.

First attempts to strategically frame EaP aims and activities ensued in 2015, when, following the EaP Riga Summit, four priority areas were added: (1) stronger economy (economic development and better market opportunities); (2) stronger governance (strengthening of institutions and good governance); (3) stronger connectivity (enhancing connectivity, notably in the areas of transport and energy, and environment and climate change); (4) stronger society (increasing mobility and contacts between people) (EaP Summit Joint Declaration 2015). It was not until the 2017 EaP Brussels Summit, however, that the EaP was given a catalogue of specific objectives and tangible deliverables – the so-called '20 Deliverables for 2020' (European Commission 2017; cf. also *Table 13.2*). Along with the deliverables within the four priority areas, these '20 Deliverables for 2020' also included cross-cutting deliverables, targeting increased engagement with civil society, gender equality and non-discrimination as well as the strengthening of strategic communication and supporting plurality and independence of media. Importantly, each of the 20 deliverables identified focused on improving people's lives in the EaP-6.

Eastern Partnership's broader achievements and major shortcomings

Broadly speaking, evaluations of EaP operations range from optimistic to pessimistic (*NEE* 2019). While the former point to the fact that, against all odds, the EaP showed remarkable resilience, the latter tend to mainly emphasize the project's presumptive irrelevance. Many also considered the EaP a 'paper tiger', read: a policy project with numerous declarations but few outcomes and little impact on the ground.

The EaP as such is not a single EU policy, but a policy framework that conjoins elements of foreign, trade, regional and cultural policies, as well as bilateral cooperation and development aid policies. The confounding effects of these areas of engagement complicate the distilling of a 'genuine EaP effect'. In what follows, the discussion will be guided by the two main goals supposedly defining and guiding the EaP, notably political association and economic integration.

Indeed, *political association* with Eastern neighbours accelerated and endured, mainly in the form of concluded Association Agreements (AAs) or other contractual relations that aim to forge closer ties. However, only some Eastern neighbours – Ukraine, Georgia and Moldova (the associated EaP-3) – became politically associated with the EU through the new-generation AAs and Deep and Comprehensive Free Trade Areas (DCFTAs). For the past two years, Ukraine has been advocating for an update and revision of its AA, not least against the backdrop of the fact that, as of early 2020, overall progress in the implementation of the AA for the period 2014–2024 was 43% (GOCEEAI Ukraine 2020: 11). In contrast, Armenia, drawing on its less ambitious Comprehensive and Enhanced Partnership Agreement (CEPA), seeks to create more jobs and more business opportunities; enhance safety and security; and contribute to a cleaner environment, fairer rules for market operators, as well as to the strengthening of democracy and human rights. By the same token, Azerbaijan is still negotiating a new legal framework for its cooperation with the EU, and the conclusion of at least Partnership Priorities with Belarus was taken off the table as a result of the Belarusian regime's disproportionate and unlawful behaviour in the wake of the presidential elections of 9 August 2020. In fact, Belarus was also the last among all EaP countries to sign a visa facilitation and readmission agreement with the EU in May 2020. Visa liberalization regimes, on the other hand, are in force solely with Ukraine, Georgia and Moldova (cf. *Table 13.1*).

Within this diverse group of EaP countries, several subgroups can be identified, depending on their domestic political dynamics and foreign policy priorities/ambitions, in relation with the EU. Typically, and rather simplistically, a twofold division is made, i.e. into countries associated with the EU – the associated EaP-3, and non-associated eastern partners – Azerbaijan, Armenia and Belarus. However, it is justified to speak of at least four categories of EaP countries as the non-associated ones defy the criteria that characterize the associated EaP-3, notably a 'European choice' (Armenia, Belarus), 'democratization' (Azerbaijan, Belarus), 'orientation towards European integration' (Azerbaijan, Armenia, Belarus) and 'good neighbourly relations' (Armenia, Azerbaijan). At the same time, the associated EaP-3, in spite of their declared commitment to European and Euro-Atlantic integration, differ in what regards the extent to which they comply with AA stipulations and oscillate between a straightforward EU orientation and leanings towards Russia.

Still, EaP countries' involvement in the EaP's *multilateral* track helped maintain broad and collective political and social dialogue. For example, in May 2011, the Euronest Parliamentary Assembly was inaugurated. As a regional inter-parliamentary cooperation assembly, Euronest chiefly serves as a parliamentary diplomacy forum, offering also tracks for informal exchange. As an institutionalized form of cooperation among parliamentarians from EU Member States and EaP countries, it also generates (limited) socialization effects (Petrova and Raube 2016). The EaP Civil Society Forum presents another multilateral platform that promotes socialization and learning and that contributes to the strengthening of civil societies across Eastern partners and civil society links between the EU and EaP countries (Kostanyan and Vandecasteele 2013; Kourtikakis and Turkina 2015).

Notably, the shared drive for furthering their European integration agendas has stimulated *mini-lateral cooperation* – notably among the associated EaP-3. In October 2018, Georgia, Moldova and Ukraine established the Inter-Parliamentary Assembly (IPA) that

Table 13.1 Interlocking Dimensions of EU–Eastern Neighbours Relations (2009–2020)

EU–Eastern neighbours: interlocking dimensions	Ukraine	Moldova	Georgia	Armenia	Azerbaijan	Belarus
EaP policyframework						
Multilateral track	✓	✓	✓	✓	✓	(✓)[a]
Bilateral track	✓	✓	✓	✓	(✓)	✗
Legal and political framework						
Multilateral	EaP Joint Declarations (2009, 2011, 2013, 2015, 2017)					✗
Bilateral	AA/DCFTA (2017)[b]	AA/DCFTA (2017)[c]	AA/DCFTA (2016)[c]	AA/DCFTA (2016)[d]	CEPA (2021)[e]	EU-AZ CP[f]
Joint-institutional framework						
Multilateral	EaP Biannual Summits; *Euronest Parliamentary Assembly*;[g] EaP Civil Society Forum; EaP Multilateral Platforms					
Mini-lateral	Inter-Parliamentary Assembly (2018); Association Trio (2021)			✗	✗	✗
Bilateral	Association bodies	Association bodies	Association bodies	✗	✗	✗
Free trade						
Free movement of goods (industrial & agricultural)	(✓) gradual	✓	✓	✗	✗	✗
EU competition policy extension	✓	✓	✓	(✓)[h]	(?)	✗
Visa and mobility regimes						
Visa facilitation & Readmission	✓ (2014)	✓ (2011)	✓ (2011)	✓ (2014)	✓ (2014)	✓ (2020)
Visa liberalization	✓ (2017)	✓ (2014)	✓ (2017)	✗	✗	✗
Free circulation of capital	(✓) gradual	✓	✓	✓	(?)	✗
Free circulation of services		✓	✓	✓	(?)	✗
Stake in EU system						
EU Programs	✓	✓	✓	✓	✓	✓
EU Agencies[j]	Moderate (6)	Moderate (6)	Moderate (4)	Low (3)	Low (2)	Low (1)
EU Institutions (as ad-hoc invitee or observer)	✓	✓	✓	✗	✗	✗
EaP Countries' Alignment with CFSP Declarations[k]	High (nearly all in 2009; 88% in 2017)	High (nearly all in 2009; 69% in 2017)	Moderate (71% in 2009; 50% in 2017)	Low to none (78% in 2009, non-alignment since 2015)	Low to none (40.5% in 2009, non-alignment since 2014)	n/a
EaP Countries' Contribution to CSDP Missions[l]						
Military CSDP missions	EUNAVFOR Atalanta	EUMAM RCA	EUFOR RCA; EUMAM RCA			
Civilian CSDP missions	EUPM BiH; EUOPOL PROXIMA FYROM	EUTM Mali; EUTM RCA	EUTM Mali; EUAM Ukraine			

(Continued)

EU-Eastern neighbours: interlocking dimensions	Ukraine	Moldova	Georgia	Armenia	Azerbaijan	Belarus
EU Battlegroups	EU BG HELBROC 2011, 2014, 2016; 2018; 2020; EU BG 2010; Visegrad Four EU BG 2016; UK-led EU BG 2016					
Energy Cooperation / EnCT	✓	✓	✓	✓	✗	✗
EU Financial Commitments[m]						
EU Eastern Neighbourhood budget allocations in general	**ENPI** (2007–2014): EUR11.2 bln.; for EU Eastern neighbourhood: ca.6.58 bln.; **ENI** (2014–2020): EUR15.43 bln.; for EU Eastern neighbourhood (est.): EUR 3.02–3.68 bln.; (draft) **NDICI** (2021–2027) EUR79.462 bln. (incl. for neighbourhood in general: ca. EUR 22 bln.)					
ENPI allocations (2007–2010; 2011–2013)[n]	EUR964.1 mln. *(EUR 470.1 mln.)*	EUR482.8 mln. *(EUR494 mln.; EUR 470.1 mln.)*	EUR300.7 mln. *(EUR120.4 mln.; EUR180.3 mln.)*	EUR 255.7 mln. *(EUR 98.4 mln.; EUR157.3 mln.)*	EUR214.5 mln. *(EUR 92 mln.; EUR 122.5 mln.)*	EUR20 mln. *(EUR 20 mln.; n/a)*
ENI allocations (2014–2020)[o]	EUR 1.28–1.55 bln.	EUR 610–746 mln.	EUR 610–746 mln.	EUR 252–308 mln.	EUR139–169 mln.	EUR129–158 mln.
Covid-19 response package (January 2021)[p]	EUR 202 mln.	EUR 128 mln.	EUR 183 mln.	EUR 96 mln.	EUR 31 mln.	EUR 74 mln.

LEGEND: ✓ – given/foreseen; (✓) – conditionally given/foreseen; ✗ – not given/not foreseen.

a In response to the EU's new restrictive measures against the country's business and political elites, Belarus suspended, on 28 June 2021, its participation in the EU's Eastern Partnership initiative.
b The EU-Ukraine AA was initialed on 30.03.2012; concluded – in two separate acts – on 21.03.2014 and 27.06.2014, respectively; provisionally applied since 01.11.2014 and 01.01.2016, respectively; and fully entered into force on 01.09.2017.
c The EU-Moldova AA was initialled on 29.11.2013; concluded on 27.06.2014; provisionally applied since 01.09.2014; and fully entered into force on 01.07.2016.
d The EU-Georgia AA was initialled on 29.11.2013; concluded on 27.06.2014; provisionally applied since 01.09.2014; and fully entered into force on 01.07.2016.
e After Armenia's rejection of a negotiated AA in September 2013, negotiations on a new contractual framework resumed in January 2015. A new agreement, i.e. the EU-Armenia Comprehensive and Enhanced Partnership Agreement (CEPA), was initialed in 2017 and concluded shortly thereafter on 24.11.2017; it became provisionally applied since 01.06.2018 and fully entered into force on 01.03.2021.
f In 2017, the EU and Azerbaijan started negotiations on a Comprehensive Cooperation and Partnership Agreement.
g Due to political reasons, Belarus is not taking part in Euronest PA activities.
h Even though EU competition policy does not extend to Armenia, a member of the EAEU, the EU-Armenia CEPA provides for 'fairer rules', which implies i.a. upholding of competition principles, operation of an independent competition authority, more transparent public procurement, a strong IPR protection system and fairer conditions of employment.
i *Ukraine* (Frontex; EMCDDA; Eurojust; Europol; EASA; EDA); *Moldova* (Frontex; EMCDDA; CEPOL; Eurojust; Europol; EASA); *Georgia* (Frontex; Europol; CEPOL; EASA); *Armenia* (Frontex; CEPOL; EASA); *Azerbaijan* (Frontex; EASA); *Belarus* (Frontex).Source: Own elaboration based on data from: Rimkute and Shyrokykh (2017: 11).
j For instance, EU-EaP Ministerials, ad-hoc observer status with EU Committees.
k Source: Dobrescu 2018: EU official reports.
l Source: Dobrescu 2018: EU CSDP missions' official websites.
m Source: Financing the ENP, https://eeas.europa.eu/headquarters/headquarters-homepage/8410/financing-enp_en. *Note:* No conclusive data available yet on ENI and draft NDICI individual-country allocations.
n Source: Eurostat, https://ec.europa.eu/eurostat/web/european-neighbourhood-policy/background
o Source: Programming of the ENI (2014–2020), https://eeas.europa.eu/archives/docs/enp/pdf/financing-the-enp/regional_south_strategy_paper_2014_2020_and_multiannual_indicative_programme_2014_2017_en.pdf
p Source: EU COVID-19 Solidarity Programme for the Eastern Partnership (Factsheet, January 2021), https://ec.europa.eu/neighbourhood-enlargement/sites/near/files/coronavirus_support_eap.pdf

also contributed to the EU's structured public consultation process in 2019 on the future of the EaP (MFA Ukraine 2019). On 17 May 2021, the three associated EaP countries formalized their mini-lateral cooperation within the EaP with the establishment of the so-called Association Trio — a tripartite format for the enhanced cooperation and co-ordination on the three countries' European integration policies (MFA Ukraine 2021). The interactionism of the associated EaP-3 is additionally driven by *the joint bilateral institutions* established under the AAs, the 'association bodies' with decision-making powers. These include the Association Council, the Association Committee, numerous Sub-Committees, the Parliamentary Association Committee and the Civil Society Platform. In Ukraine's case, annually held EU-Ukraine summits complement the joint-institutional framework (cf. *Table 13.1*).

Participation in EU programs and agencies, too, fosters closer political association. To a varying extent, all EaP countries take part in EU programs, ranging from cultural to scientific and cross-border cooperation. In addition to Erasmus+ and TEN-T/EaP TP programs, in which all EaP-6 are involved, the associated EaP-3 also take part in other programs. For example, Ukraine is part of the EU's Horizon Europe, Creative Europe, Culture Bridges, Copernicus Earth, COSME, European Houses of Culture/Houses of Europe and Cross-Border Cooperation programs. Following a Council decision in 2007, EU Agencies opened up for cooperation with third countries, predominantly from the EU's neighbourhood. Already by 2017, the associated EaP-3 forged moderately broad trans-governmental links with the EU by joining up to six EU Agencies (incl. Frontex, EMCDDA, Eurojust, Europol, EASA and CEPOL). Since 2016 Ukraine is the only non-EU Member State that has also been cooperating with the European Defence Agency (EDA). In contrast, the three non-associated EaP countries kept this cooperation to a near minimum. Whereas all joined Frontex, Azerbaijan and Armenia also adhered to EASA, and Armenia is the only one that is also cooperating with CEPOL (Shyrokykh and Rimkutė 2019: 749; cf. also: *Table 13.1*).

In a certain sense, the associated EaP-3 are increasingly becoming embedded in *EU policy-shaping milieus* – a development that is in the spirit of the AAs, offering 'stakes' in the EU internal market and 'system' (Tyushka 2017: 92–105). Though core EU institutions are closed for third-country participation, throughout the past years, however, novel cooperation formats, such as the EU-EaP Ministerials, bringing together foreign affairs ministers and the EU's High Representative for Foreign and Security Policy and Vice-President of the European Commission (HR/VP), emerged. Moreover, ministers of the associated EaP-3 are occasionally invited as observers to Council meetings and more recently, in May 2020, following the breakout of the SARS-CoV-2 pandemic, Ukraine was even invited to join the EU's Health Security Committee as an observer in pursuit of closer cooperation in the context of the fight against the pandemic (Tyushka 2020: 172).

EU and EaP countries cooperate also with regard to *international and security matters*, including by aligning with Common Foreign and Security Policy (CFSP) decisions and declarations and by contributing to CSDP missions. In so doing, the associated EaP-3 demonstrate relatively high levels of congruence, not least as they adhere to the vast majority of the EU's CFSP declarations, whereas other Eastern partners display low or no interest at all (Mayer 2014). The 2020 Association Implementation Report on Ukraine by the European External Action Service (EEAS) estimates that Ukraine aligned itself with the EU in what regards 81% of its CFSP declarations (EEAS AIR Ukraine 2020b: 9). As far as Georgia is concerned, alignment occurred in 37 out 55 instances. Put differently, in 2019 Georgia aligned itself in 61% of all possible cases, compared to 56% in 2018 (EEAS AIR Georgia 2020a: 5). Moldova's alignment with the EU was recorded in 46 out of 68 EU declarations and Council decisions in 2018, corresponding to a total of 68% (compared to 69% in 2017) (EEAS AIR Moldova 2019b: 6). The

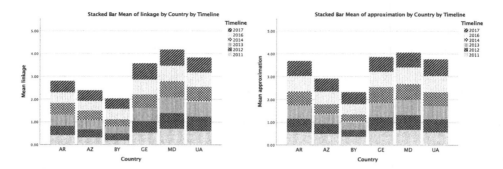

Figure 13.1 a&b. The State of EU–EaP Countries' Linkage and Approximation in 2011–2017. Source: Tyushka (2019: 17).

three countries continue contributing also to EU civilian and military missions. The EaP-6's varied participation in these, as well as the associated EaP-3's generally high alignment with EU CFSP declarations for more than a decade (cf. *Table 13.1*), are irrefutable signs of increasing cooperation and a 'technocratic form of integration into the EU, a sort of *de facto* technocratic membership' (Shyrokykh and Rimkutė 2019: 750). Cross-dimensional data on the EU-EaP countries' *linkage and approximation* confirm this assessment. The annual EaP Indexes for the period 2011–2017,[3] for instance, reveal the following picture (cf. *Figures 13.1 a & b*).

The underlying idea behind these graphs, derived from the democratization literature, is that greater linkage leads to greater progress in democratic development. In turn, greater convergence with both EU norms and international standards is closely associated with progress in EaP countries' European integration, as captured by the approximation measure. The above value-mean representations of general patterns and trends in linkage and approximation should be regarded as relative as the 'leader' and 'laggard' positions tend to fluctuate corresponding to the respective year. In general, however, the dividing line runs between the associated EaP-3 and the non-associated EaP countries such as Azerbaijan and Belarus, with Armenia being situated between the two ends (Tyushka 2019: 16–21).

It is noteworthy that the identified convergence between the EU and EaP countries is essentially EU-centric and asymmetric, and, second, closer political association and the resulting realignment inevitably trigger sovereignty and international security dilemmas. The idea of EU-centric Europeanization comes to connote both the hope for, and haplessness of, the region's transition processes from authoritarian regimes and hybrid democracies to consolidated, EU-style, constitutional democracies. In her study *Russia, the Former Soviet Republics, and Europe since 1989: Transformation and Tragedy*, Graney (2019: 10–11) places the strength of Europeanization processes in Georgia, Moldova and Ukraine very close to those witnessed by Estonia, Latvia and Lithuania. At the same time, Europeanization in Armenia and Azerbaijan is assessed as rather moderately strong, leaving Belarus further behind (ibid.). Domestic official discourses in the associated EaP-3 richly feature the 'frames' of the countries' European identities: 'Georgia is Europe!' and 'Ukraine is Europe!' have not only become frequently occurring ornaments of political speeches. They have also shaped peoples' understandings of belonging and future. For example, Ukraine's 2013/2014 Revolution of Dignity and the following defensive war against Russian hybrid aggression are inextricably linked with Ukraine's European choice. The political symbolism of a 'European choice' and 'Europeanness' proliferates across the associated EaP-3 as well as, to a lesser extent, other reform-oriented 'post-Soviet' countries. Their transformative and state-building agendas, just as popular discourses, have been driven, time and again, by the idea of *'Evroremont'* (literally: 'Eurorepair'), i.e. a transition towards European-style democracy (Seliverstova 2017).

The undisputed achievement of the EaP is the preservation of a generally positive *perception* of the EU as a regional actor and partner (Chaban et al. 2018). 52% of societies in the EaP-6 maintain a positive attitude towards the EU, with 34% remaining neutral and just 10% carrying negative views (EU Neighbours East Survey 2019). Support for the EU varies across EaP countries and has increased in recent years. In 2019, it ranges from 36% in Belarus to 62% in Armenia. In Azerbaijan, the EU enjoys a positive image among 46% of respondents, whereas in the remaining three countries numbers range from 50% (Georgia), 55% (Moldova) to 56% (Ukraine) (ibid.). Moreover, compared to other international organizations involved in the six countries, the EU is the most trusted partner: 58% of respondents in the EaP-6 show confidence in the EU, 44% trust the United Nations, 38% NATO and only 28% the Eurasian Economic Union (EAEU). Thus, one aspect seems obvious: with 12 years into the EaP, there is much more of Europe in all EaP-6 – even if this has not come at the expense of a less present and interventionist Russia.

Perceptions of the Eastern neighbourhood among EU Member States' publics, too, show some noteworthy features, though they are overshadowed by a seemingly lasting enlargement fatigue in general. In 2006, however, a striking majority of EU Member States' citizens (72%) expressed their consent to further, though measured, rounds of EU enlargement (Special EB, 259 2006: 20). Nearly the same number of respondents (70%) agreed that, in parallel to the ongoing enlargement process with Western Balkans countries, the EU should offer other neighbouring countries a different type of relationship that falls short of full membership (Special EB, 259 2006: 21). Currently, EU Member States' citizens remain predominantly opposed to further EU enlargement, as the idea is supported just by some 37% (Standard EB 81, 2014: 143–144). Such attitudes, however, have little, if anything, to do with the perception of the belonging – or (non-) 'Europeanness' – of EaP countries. Instead, they are related to the multi-layered challenges the EU is exposed to from within, of which the recent rounds of enlargement and Brexit are just two among many examples. The EU's 2004/2007 enlargement has not only shifted the EU's gravity centre more eastwards, but also altered the perception of 'Europe' and the 'East' (Schilde 2014) as such, amalgamating the space beyond the new borders into a 'new Eastern Europe'. On the EU's webpage that presents the EU's relations with the countries of the region, titled 'Eastern Europe', the EEAS posits: 'Armenia, Azerbaijan, Belarus, Georgia, The Republic of Moldova and Ukraine are European countries not part of the EU'.[4]

At the same time, there is a significant gap in the EU's role expectation and performance in the security realm – one of the most salient policy fields for EaP countries. Here, the perception of the EU as a security actor (and provider) is much less favourable than that of its role as a transformative force and donor (Axyonova et al. 2018). In terms of hard security, the EU was never framed as a strong security actor in its Eastern neighbourhood (Delcour 2010; Wolczuk and Delcour 2018), in spite of its considerable efforts to contribute to the humanitarian dimension of security conflict-affected areas such as in Ukraine or the recent war between Armenia and Azerbaijan. Partially, this outcome results from the Union's limited power and capabilities in this policy field and a preferred engagement in areas such as (civilian) crisis management, security sector reform promotion, confidence-building measures and other soft security mechanisms (Kuzio 2017; Zarembo 2017). But even soft security as a presumptive policy field has been faced with mounting challenges in recent years, as rising disinformation and populism do not only pose significant problems *per se* but undermine EaP countries' strategic communication and thus mutual understanding (Pawlak 2017).

The EU's motivation to politically associate the EaP-6, and – in one way or another – reorder the geostrategic space they represent, has triggered an unintended consequence and problem the EU has hitherto been unable to confront openly and resolutely: Russia's increased assertiveness and aggressiveness towards its own neighbourhood and, by extension, the EU itself. The 2014 'Ukraine crisis' and the unfolding of a Russia-Ukraine hybrid war, just as Moscow's broad challenge of Brussels' normative hegemony (Haukkala 2008) in what some consider to be a 'shared neighbourhood' (Averre 2009), moved security concerns up on EaP countries' agendas. The relevance of this is hard to overestimate, not least as the future of Europe's security, political and economic order (Raik 2019) hinges upon the future of the EU's Russia and Eastern policy at large.

As regards the EaP's second main goal, i.e. *furthering economic integration*, results are equally mixed and vary both along the associated/non-associated countries dividing line and within each subgroup. Though overall trade dynamics between the EU and EaP countries are positive (EU exports to the EaP-6 increased by 84% during 2005–2016), the volume and structure of trade in individual bilateral relations differ, as do the market orientations of EaP countries (especially as far as Armenia and Belarus are concerned). Whereas Armenia's and Belarus' trade relations with Russia expanded since 2015, mainly at the expense of trade with the EU, the EU remains the most important trade partner for Georgia, though the DCFTA has failed to boost the overall turnover. In fact, over the past five years trade between the EU and Georgia has stagnated, as the EU's share in Georgia's total imports declined from 27.8% in 2014 to 25.6% in 2019. At the same time, Georgian exports to the EU increased by 32% throughout the past five years (as did Georgian exports elsewhere), while the EU's overall share in total Georgian exports remained the same (21.8%). Yet, for the EU as a whole, trade with Georgia is of little significance as it accounts for just 0.07% of total EU external trade (Zygierewicz 2020c: 48). For Moldova, Ukraine and Azerbaijan, though, the EU not only became the most important trade partner, but it also succeeded to steadily expand its share in the three countries' trade balance throughout the past ten years (Saari and Secrieru 2019: 15). Ukraine, drawing on the DCFTA, is perhaps the most telling example of a radical reorientation of external trade structures in so far as it shifted its trade from Russia primarily towards the EU within a very short period of time (Zygierewicz 2020a: 57–59). According to European Commission data,[5] the EU, as Ukraine's largest trading partner, accounts for 40% of the country's trade flows. In turn, in 2019, Ukraine became the EU's second-most important trade partner in what regards organic products, as it nowadays accounts for 10% of all EU organic imports.[6] Positive effects of the DCFTA implementation can also be observed in EU-Moldova economic relations. Already in 2014 Moldova's exports to the EU accounted for 53% of the country's total exports. Until 2019, the figure rose to 66%. An increase, though less tangible, occurred also with respect to Moldova's imports from the EU, notably from 48.3% in 2014 to 49.5% in 2019 (Zygierewicz 2020b: 59–60).

In addition to trade, the variegated economic and sectoral cooperation between the EU and the EaP-6 – ranging from macro-economic cooperation to public finances management, banking, business and tourism to statistics – is seen as being responsible for driving economic integration and convergence at large (Siljak and Nagy 2018; Damen 2019: 19–23). The earlier estimates of potential effects of the EU-EaP-6 trade intensification also suggested a positive impact on regional integration that a greater within-EaP trade could bring (Gylfason et al. 2015). Nonetheless, intra-EaP economic relations have so far remained negligible, with all EaP countries gravitating, in their trade orientations, either towards the EU or Russia. The gradual dismantling of economic barriers between the EU and the EaP-6 (both within and beyond DCFTA formats) has primarily enabled the expansion of trade links but also allowed for increased sectorial cooperation and thus linked trade with necessary domestic reforms as regards business operation, market (de)regulation, decentralization, public administration or public finances management. The 2020 SME Policy Index for Eastern Partnership countries points to observable efforts across the EaP-6 to develop better strategies for small- and medium-sized enterprises' development as well as relevant institution-building (OECD 2020). The assessments of both the regulatory and institutional frameworks confirm the countries' commitment to relevant reform and progress. They also showcase distinct achievements: while Georgia stands out as a leader across the index' many dimensions, the performance of the remaining five EaP countries varies – and does so beyond the 'associated/non-associated' countries' dividing line (OECD 2020: 49–61). The outcomes of economic and sectorial cooperation within the associated EaP-3 also show a variegated record. As the biggest recipient of EU funds and support for SME development under the EU4Business projects, Ukraine has so far demonstrated moderate success in decentralization and deregulation reforms. In contrast, Georgia has retained its leadership in terms of ongoing cooperation projects and the state of its regulatory and institutional frameworks which are most approximated with those of the EU (Zygierewicz 2020c: 16–18, 46–53). With all associated EaP-3 countries having largely managed to stabilize their financial and banking sectors in spite of the financial crises and geopolitical turbulences of the past decade, problematic issues in the financial sector and as regards banking transparency have not been completely eradicated, as Moldova's or Ukraine's track record shows (Zygierewicz 2020a: 62–63, 2020b: 63–64). It should also be pointed out that the moderate progress in macro-economic and sectorial cooperation, including subsequent domestic reforms, shall be regarded against the broader picture of persistent market-incompatible structures and arrangements among business and political elites in the EaP-6 that effectively impede domestic economic growth and EU-EaP-6 convergence.

Lastly, EU *financial aid*, provided in support of bi- and multilateral projects, presents an important value-added of the EaP. Countless statistics on foreign and development aid unequivocally demonstrate that no other international actor has invested in the EaP-6 as much as the EU did. Being the largest donor since the early 1990s, the EU has more than doubled its assistance to the EaP-6 throughout the past decade. For example, since 2014, the EU and both the European Investment Bank (EIB) and the European Bank for Reconstruction and Development (EBRD) have jointly mobilized, in grants and loans, over EUR 15 bn for Ukraine. Effectively, though, EU financial commitments to EaP countries have been tied, to varying degrees, to the principle of conditionality, and therefore, positive and negative incentives related to (non-)compliance with EU values (including the respect for human rights and democracy) and, in the case of the associated EaP-3, the rules and principles of EU internal market accession and association acquis implementation (Bolkvadze 2016; Burlyuk and Shapovalova 2017; Vieira and Vasilyan 2018). As is demonstrated elsewhere, however, this financial assistance has not always generated positive effects. In hybrid regimes, where state capacity is low, EU aid is often associated with adverse effects as it might induce a deterioration of human rights standards, whereas in countries benefiting from high state capacity, positive effects of EU assistance are likelier (Shyrokykh 2017). As four out of six EaP countries – i.e. Ukraine, Moldova, Georgia and Armenia – represent hybrid regimes, it is unsurprising that the EU's record in promoting human rights and democracy, as well as good governance at large, has remained the most contested area of performance – and the least successfully implemented 'deliverable'.

20 deliverables for 2020: state of play

As regards the assessment of EaP goal attainment along the list of stipulated policy deliverables, the binary success/failure lens is, yet again, of little help, not least as mere achievement of a given deliverable does hardly shed any light on the inherent quality or possible nuances. Due to the blatant absence of benchmarks, it remains challenging to identify 'clear-cut victories or defeats', as Baldwin (2000: 171) put it. A certain level of arbitrary assessment is, therefore, to be presumed to form part of the evaluations by the European Commission. In fact, following the 2017 Brussels EaP Summit, achievements and shortcomings of the EaP are chiefly assessed in the context of the *'20 Deliverables for 2020'* – a list of specific objectives and tasks that aim to generate tangible benefits for citizens in the four key priority areas mentioned further above (European Commission 2017).

As became apparent, these 'deliverables' also envisage stronger links between EaP countries' civil societies, the enhancement of mobility, a widening of socio-cultural links, socialization of elites, improved transport connectivity, energy, health and environment, etc. According to the EU, the EaP generated ten achievements with regard to the '20 Deliverables': (a) new bilateral agreements were concluded with most EaP countries; (b) trade and EU investment increased; (c) EaP countries underwent economic development; (d) energy resilience and energy efficiency were enhanced; (e) support for young people was stepped up; (f) transport links and infrastructure improved, including under the EU's TEN-T transport network extension; and (g) visa-free regimes for Georgia, Moldova and Ukraine were adopted (European Commission 2019). Nonetheless, challenges still remain and cut across all priority areas: from maintaining the rule of law, implementing judicial reforms and fighting corruption, to strengthening the environment for civil society and a free and independent media, as well as from increasing societal resilience by countering hybrid threats and disinformation to stepping up the EU's humanitarian engagement in conflict-affected areas, fighting climate change and supporting the protection of the environment (European Commission 2019). The European Commission and HR/VP's joint monitoring report of February 2020 on the implementation of the '20 Deliverables for 2020' pointed to the limited achievements in these five areas while it emphasized progress achieved in the remaining deliverables (European Commission 2020a; cf. also *Table 13.2*).

Notably, among all cross-cutting deliverables and being a deliverable in its own right, the EU's *engagement with civil society organizations* in the EaP-6 is an area of noted progress, not least due to societies' emancipation. In line with EaP objectives, civil societies in the EaP-6 have considerably developed throughout the past decade, repeatedly harnessed the power of the streets and became empowered vis-à-vis state institutions (Bouchet

Table 13.2 '20 Deliverables for 2020': Monitoring implementation progress (February 2020)

'20 Deliverables for 2020'	Implementation status (02/2020)
Cross-cutting deliverables	
1 More engagement with civil society organizations	++
2 Increase gender equality and non-discrimination	+
3 Strengthen strategic communications and supporting plurality and independence of media	++
Stronger economy: *Economic development and market opportunities*	
4 Improve the investment and business environment and unlock Small- and Medium-sized Enterprises' (SMEs) growth potential	++
5 Address gaps in access to finance and financial infrastructure	++
6 Create new job opportunities at the local and regional level	++
7 Harmonize digital markets	++
8 Support intra-regional trade among partner countries and the EU	++
Stronger governance: *Strengthening institutions and good governance*	
9 Strengthen the rule of law and anti-corruption mechanisms	+
10 Support the implementation of key judicial reforms	+
11 Support the implementation of public administration reform	++
12 Stronger security cooperation	++
Stronger connectivity: *Connectivity, energy efficiency, environment and climate change*	
13 Extend the TEN-T core networks, transport	++
14 Increase energy supply security	++
15 Enhance energy efficiency and the use of renewable energy; reduce Greenhouse Gas emissions	+
16 Support the environment and adaptation to climate change	+
Stronger society: *Mobility and people-to-people contacts*	
17 Progress on Visa Liberalization Dialogues and Mobility Partnerships	++
18 Strengthen investment in young people's skills, entrepreneurship and employability	++
19 Establish an Eastern Partnership European school	+++
20 Integrate Eastern Partnership and EU research and innovation systems and programmes	++

Legend: Implementation status (since 2016): +++ (completed); ++ (on track); + (limited progress).
Source: Adapted from: European Commission (2020a).

and Pishchikova 2020). In many areas, they became consolidated drivers for domestic reforms and further EU-EaP rapprochement – even in countries whose regimes have opted for Eurasian integration vectors, such as in Armenia or Belarus.

In terms of facilitating people-to-people contacts, strengthening ties between citizens of third countries and the EU, promoting visa liberalization has been one of the EU's most powerful tools and an important pillar of cooperation among EU and EaP countries (Delcour and Fernandez 2016; Merheim-Eyre 2017). Since 2014 (Moldova) and 2017 (Georgia and Ukraine), citizens from the associated EaP-3 have been enjoying visa-free regimes with the EU. For example, from the start of Ukraine's visa-free regime, i.e. 11 June 2017, until April 2020, Ukrainian citizens had travelled to EU countries nearly 49 mln. times (SBGS Ukraine 2020). With Belarus having successfully finalized its negotiations in 2020, also visa facilitation and readmission agreements have now been concluded with all six Eastern partners (cf. *Table 13.1*).

In contrast, *stronger governance* remains the most problematic deliverables category. The EU's selective approach towards supporting reforms of state institutions and reorganization of state-society relations in EaP-6 has its limits. EU-induced transformation processes in the EaP-6 are being contested both from within and outside, most notably by Russia's promotion of de-democratization trends (Roberts and Ziemer 2018). This led many to argue about the notorious 'regime persistence' in select EaP-6 (Ademmer et al. 2020) or the 'post-Soviet democratic failure' at large (Lebanidze 2020). Multiple external influences, intertwined with numerous linkages and interdependences, thus, seem to be bound to bring about variegated (as regards country-specific and temporal scope) outcomes in regime change and/or resilience. Paradoxically, in EaP countries like Georgia and Ukraine, for example, democratic transformation of political systems ensued not as much due to EU democracy promotion efforts as it did in response to Russia's coercive actions to counter such tendencies in the post-Soviet space (Delcour and Wolczuk 2015). As Georgia and Ukraine, as well as Moldova, are classified in the Democracy Index 2019 as 'hybrid regimes' (*EIU* 2020), the EU's approach to democracy promotion, both within and outside the EU, is undoubtedly in need of reconceptualization.

By far, democratic reforms and the presumptive good governance 'turn' have produced more debate than action across the EaP-6. In her overview of EU democracy promotion efforts in EaP countries, Bosse (2019) highlights Ukraine's and Moldova's zigzags of democratization; Georgia's slowdown of democratic reforms; Armenia's promising democratic experiment, following the 2018 Velvet Revolution; and the absence of democratic change in both Azerbaijan and Belarus. Thus, roughly, three groups can be identified again: the associated EaP-3 representing the group of Eastern neighbours that advanced the most on democratic reforms; Azerbaijan and Belarus that resisted any regime change; and Armenia, showcasing features of both moderate autocratization (2008–2018) and democratization (since 2018–2021) (Bosse 2019: 222). As far as the associated EaP-3 are concerned, relevant progress can indeed be attributed to their political association with the EU even though the AAs do not contain specific chapters on good governance or democratic transition. Instead, references to both the rule of law and good governance-related aspects feature mainly as part of the basic principles or policy approximation areas. The EEAS' most recent annual Association Implementation Report on Ukraine (EEAS AIR Ukraine 2020b) acknowledges that the country continued to advance democratic reforms in spite of Russia's destabilization efforts and the outbreak of the SARS-CoV-2 pandemic.

As confirmed by other reports on the implementation of AAs with Georgia, Moldova and Ukraine, public administration and decentralization belong to those areas that have been positively assessed by the EU, whereas respect for human rights (especially as regards non-discrimination or, in Ukraine's case, protection of rights of civilians affected by the Russia-Ukraine war) shows a mixed record in what regards legal development and implementation. The most problematic areas in the associated EaP-3 remain the rule of law, judicial and law enforcement reforms and the fight against corruption, with Georgia, despite the decreasing pace of anti-corruption reforms since 2019, maintaining its lead among the EaP-6 (Zygierewicz 2020a: 45–56, 2020b: 36–55, 2020c: 37–45).

Whereas the EaP has been instrumental in promoting debates about good governance in the EaP-6 and also contributed to an improved understanding of the nature of 'bad governance', true reforms have, nonetheless, been too sporadic and unconsolidated, justifying why it seems more appropriate to speak of 'good-looking governance' in select areas of engagement. In conjunction with the fact that the rather mixed democratization record of the EU's Eastern neighbourhood does also have to be seen against the backdrop of rising security challenges and the corresponding democracy-security nexus (Nilsson and Silander 2016), it is all the more lamentable that the EaP, as a framework, has never attempted, and therefore never managed, to address these challenges and their effects on neighbours' domestic political development and statehood.

The EaP beyond 2020: a revamped and resilience-oriented agenda

Following the EU's structured public consultation process on the future of the EaP, launched in May 2019, the Joint Communication of the European Commission and the HR/VP of 18 March 2020 defined the broad parameters of the EaP beyond 2020 (European Commission 2020b). Endorsed by the European Council on 20 June 2019 and validated by the EU Foreign Affairs Council on 11 May 2020, they serve as basis for discussions at the upcoming EaP Summit in December 2021, as discussed in the Introduction to this volume. With a view to strengthening the resilience of EaP countries, their state institutions, economies and societies, it is claimed that efforts will be made to achieve five strategic objectives of cooperation post-2020: (1) sustainable, stable and integrated economies; (2) responsible institutions, the rule of law and security; (3) resistance to changing climatic conditions and environmental conditions; (4) sustainable transformation through digitalization; (5) sustainable, equitable and inclusive societies (European Commission 2020b: 4). Translated into concrete policy measures, this will entail, *inter alia*, developing further mutual trade and economic integration; improving the investment climate and mutual access to finance; strengthening connectivity (including transport and infrastructure – but also energy and political dialogue); investing in the social capital of Eastern neighbours; stronger support for reforms (including anti-corruption or justice reform); stepping up of the cross-border fight against organized crime; furthering security sector reform (including public, environmental, cyber/digital or health security) and creating opportunities for greater involvement of organized society in domestic political processes and dialogue with EU partners.

During the meeting of EaP leaders, held on 18 June 2020 in the form of a videoconference, the agenda, as initially jointly proposed by the Commission and the HR/VP, was validated through a voiced commitment on the part of Eastern neighbours to endorse the EaP's post-2020 long-term objectives in the five suggested priority areas. Also, it was agreed to update the framework with a view to adjusting it to emerging realities and catering to neighbours' distinct expectations.[7] In the view of the EU and the EaP-6, these measures are supposed to contribute to the implementation of the EaP's five policy priorities post-2020 and help transform the EaP into a partnership that – in the jargon of the EEAS – creates, protects, greens, connects, empowers and thereby delivers for all.[8]

Conclusions

As this chapter has demonstrated, the success/failure binary, often at the core of public and political discourses when evaluating the EaP, is both fallacious and feckless as an epistemological tool in the context of attempts to assess achievements and shortcomings of an international, multi-stakeholder, multi-level policy project such as the EaP. In the absence of clear-cut definitions and benchmarks, there is no clarity as to what success (and, by extension, failure) means, let alone how it can be measured. This is not surprising, as the operationalization of categories such as success and failure more generally remains an underdeveloped area of IR/FPA analysis in general. Thus, a GOF for policy analysis, as devised in this chapter, appears to be a more suitable tool for a critical discussion of EaP operations in relation to EaP goals and objectives.

In this light, this chapter showed a mixed record of goal attainment with regard to the EaP's two overarching goals: acceleration of political association and furthering of economic integration. A complex and sophisticated contractual relationship, as laid out by the AAs with Georgia, Moldova and Ukraine, sharply contrasts with the existence of an outdated contractual framework and so-called 'Partnership Priorities' with Azerbaijan and the complete absence of any institutional and legally binding base with Belarus. The EU-Armenia CEPA, though much less ambitious than the draft AA that was declined by Armenia in September 2013, still represents a case of 'success' when compared to the contractual situation with Azerbaijan and Belarus. Whereas for the latter, the EaP turned out to be the sole platform of engagement with EU officials, for Armenia, the EaP still remains a strategic tool to diversify international cooperation and – after the lost war with Azerbaijan in the fall of 2020 – to strategically hedge vis-à-vis Russia.

By and large, the EaP has sustained and in most cases accelerated political association by harnessing multilateral and bilateral, legal, political or technocratic links. The research also shows that results are equally mixed as far as the goal of furthering economic integration is concerned. They vary both along the associated/non-associated countries dividing line and within each subgroup. Whereas in the case of Ukraine and Moldova the extension and intensification of trade with the EU, along with the gradual eradication of tariff and non-tariff trade barriers, generated a positive effect on countries' macro-economic development, the size of EU trade with Georgia proved to be too small for the DCFTA to produce any significant growth effects. By the same token, the EU has become the largest trading partner for Azerbaijan which lacks a DCFTA, and even for Belarus the EU is the second most important trade partner after Russia. While assumptions can be made about some noted progress in economic integration, convergence or interplay with the EU, little to no progress has been observed in intra-EaP-6 economic integration.

An even more complex picture appears when assessing evolving EaP policy objectives and salient issues of EU–EaP-6 cooperation. The EU's Eastern neighbourhood has evidently not become more stable and secure, and recent developments in Ukraine, Belarus or the South Caucasus underline this. On the other hand, over a little more than just one decade, the EaP has evolved into a framework that nowadays features increased (and increasing) differentiation, that allows for greater ownership and flexibility and that is increasingly guided by an enhanced policy focus. As such, it is bound to allow for more feasible goal setting and more visible goal attainment, and the so-called '20 Deliverables for 2020' and their institutional assessments demonstrate just how the EaP's added-value can be conceived of and pursued. The evaluation of EaP goal attainment across the key four priority areas revealed that in three of them (i.e. 'stronger economy', 'stronger connectivity' and 'stronger society'), the EaP generated positive effects. In contrast, the priority area 'stronger governance', i.e. political reforms and democratic transition at large, registered only some initial and sporadic achievements since 2009.

There is a demand for (democratic) political change across the EU's Eastern neighbourhood, as demonstrated by their civil societies. The lack of political commitment, however, presents a significant challenge even within the EU-associated EaP-3 countries, whose AAs' fine print even legally prescribes the imperative of (anti-corruption, judicial, public administration, legal and economic) reforms. In other cases, such as Belarus or Azerbaijan, the EaP objective of strengthening institutions and good governance remains a matter of distant political rhetoric. As economic and technical issues prevailed in EU-Azerbaijan relations, the political aspects of cooperation have remained low-profiled. In the absence of bilateral channels of strategic political communication and interaction with Belarus, the EaP's added-value to building 'stronger governance' has substantially been limited to desultory technical cooperation and an almost exclusive focus on the strengthening of civil society. In view of the many under-achievements in this deliverables category, as well as some alarming backtracking tendencies in other – more successful – dimensions of EU-EaP-6 interaction, it comes as no surprise that the currently advanced post-2020 EaP strategic objectives include, in one way or another, policy matters that already formed part of the '20 Deliverables for 2020'. Such a partially replicative goal setting approach seems quite indicative of how the EU (and, potentially, EaP countries) assess EaP goal attainment to date. By the same token, it evidently points to the policy framework's continuity and adaptability to new strategic realities, arguably two preconditions to make the EaP more resilient.

Notes

1 The *post-hoc fallacy*, or attribution problem, presents a challenge in assessing tangible effects. It is, in effect, the multiplicity of policy efforts and processes that inhibit cause-effect inferencing, and this is responsible for potential *confounding effects*, or biases, in policy evaluation and assessment. As a result, one is almost inevitably left with assessing EaP achievements and drawbacks against the officially declared objectives.
2 Cf. EaP Summit Joint Declaration 2009: 6, paras. 2–3.; European Parliament Factsheet on the ENP (December 2019), https://www.europarl.europa.eu/factsheets/en/sheet/170/the-european-neighbourhood-policy; See also: https://eeas.europa.eu/diplomatic-network/eastern-partnership/419/eastern-partnership_en.
    No definitive and ordered catalogue of EaP goals existed until the adoption of the 2017 Joint Communication '20 Deliverables by 2020'.
3 The Eastern Partnership Index (EaP Index) charts the progress made by the EaP-6 towards sustainable democratic development and European integration. Two dimensions of European integration are distinguished by the Index: Approximation and Linkage. The linkage dimension encompasses the international links between businesses, civil society, citizens and governments among EaP and EU countries. The approximation dimension captures the multi-dimensional (socio-economic and political) convergence between the EU and EaP countries. For data and methodology, cf.: https://eap-csf.eu/eastern-partnership-index (accessed on 30.06.2020).
4 EEAS, "Eastern Europe," https://eeas.europa.eu/regions/eastern-europe/341/eastern-europe_en
5 European Commission (last updated: 24.11.2020). "EU Trade Policy – Countries and Regions – Ukraine," https://ec.europa.eu/trade/policy/countries-and-regions/countries/ukraine/

6 European Commission (2020). "EU imports of organic agri-food products: Key developments in 2019," *EU Agricultural Market Brief 17*, June 2020, https://ec.europa.eu/info/sites/info/files/food-farming-fisheries/farming/documents/market-brief-organic-imports-june2020_en.pdf

7 European Council (2020). "Eastern Partnership leaders' video conference," 18 June 2020, https://www.consilium.europa.eu/en/meetings/international-summit/2020/06/18/#

8 EEAS (2020) "The Eastern Partnership beyond 2020: Reinforcing resilience – an Eastern Partnership that delivers for all," *EEAS*, 18 March 2020, https://eeas.europa.eu/sites/eeas/files/eap_joint_communication_factsheet_18.03.en_.pdf

References

Ademmer, E., Delcour, L., Hoffmann, K., and Jaroszewicz, M. (2020). Interdependences with external actors and regime persistence in Eastern Partnership countries, *East European Politics*, DOI: 10.1080/21599165.2020.1828871.

Alden, C., and Aran, A. (2017). *Foreign Policy Analysis: New Approaches*, 2nd ed., London and New York: Routledge.

Averre, D. (2009). Competing rationalities: Russia, the EU and the 'shared neighbourhood', *Europe-Asia Studies*, 61(10): 1689–1713.

Axyonova, V., Gerasymchuk, S., Kakachia, K., and Rosca, A. (2018). The European Union as a transformative power, a donor or a security provider? The view from the Eastern Partnership countries, *European Foreign Affairs Review*, 23(Special Issue): 23–40.

Baldwin, D.A. (2000). Success and failure in foreign policy, *Annual Review of Political Science*, 3(1): 167–182.

Beichelt, T. (2014). Die Politik der Östlichen Partnerschaft – inkompatible Grundannahmen und antagonistische Herausforderung, *Integration*, 4: 357–364.

Bolkvadze, K. (2016). Cherry picking EU conditionality: Selective compliance in Georgia's hybrid regime, *Europe-Asia Studies*, 68(3): 409–440.

Bosse, G. (2019). Ten years of the Eastern Partnership: What role for the EU as a promoter of democracy? *European View*, 18(2): 220–232.

Bouchet, N., and Pishchikova, K. (2020). From apathy to action: Attitudes to civic engagement in the Eastern Partnership, *GMF Policy Paper*, 9 (October 2020).

Burlyuk, O., and Shapovalova, N. (2017). "Veni, vidi,... vici?" EU performance and two faces of conditionality towards Ukraine, *East European Politics*, 33(1): 36–55.

Carlsnaes, W. (2002). Foreign policy. In *Handbook of International Relations*, ed. by W. Carlsnaes, T. Risse and B.A. Simmons (London: SAGE), pp. 298–325.

Carlsnaes, W. (2004). Where is the analysis of European foreign policy going? *European Union Politics*, 5(4): 495–508.

Chaban, N., Knodt, M., and Headley, J. (2018). Introduction: The EU and its Eastern neighbours – perceptions and strategic dialogue in the region, *European Foreign Affairs Review*, 23(1): 1–22.

Clark, J.F. (1995). Evaluating the efficacy of foreign policy: An essay on the complexity of foreign policy goals, *Southeastern Political Review*, 23(4): 559–579.

Damen, M. (2019). Diversifying unity: How Eastern Partnership countries develop their economy, governance and identity in a geopolitical context, *DG EXPO Study* EXPO_STU(2019)639307_EN (November 2019).

Delcour, L. (2010). The European Union, a security provider in the Eastern Neighbourhood? *European Security*, 19(4): 535–549.

Delcour, L., and Wolczuk, K. (2015). Spoiler or facilitator of democratization?: Russia's role in Georgia and Ukraine, *Democratization*, 22(3): 459–478.

Delcour, L., and Fernandes, S. (2016). Visa liberalization processes in the EU's Eastern neighbourhood: understanding policy outcomes, *Cambridge Review of International Affairs*, 29(4): 1259–1278.

Dobrescu, M. (2018). The EU, the wider neighbourhood, and foreign and security policy cooperation, *College of Europe in Natolin, AY2018–19 Course materials* (co-taught with A. Tyushka), unpublished (on file with the author).
EaP Summit Joint Declaration (2009). EaP 2009 Prague Summit Declaration, https://www.consilium.europa.eu/uedocs/cms_data/docs/pressdata/en/er/107589.pdf
EaP Summit Joint Declaration (2015). EaP 2015 Riga Summit Declaration, https://www.consilium.europa.eu/en/meetings/international-summit/2015/05/21-22/
EEAS (2019a). Myths about the Eastern Partnership – Factsheet, *EEAS Website*, April 22, 2019, https://eeas.europa.eu/diplomatic-network/eastern-partnership/35712/myths-about-eastern-partnership-factsheet_en.
EEAS (2019b). Association implementation report on Moldova, SWD 325 final, https://eeas.europa.eu/sites/eeas/files/swd_2019_325_f1_joint_staff_working_paper_en_v10_p1_1045191.pdf
EEAS (2020a). Association implementation report on Georgia, SWD 30 final, https://eeas.europa.eu/sites/eeas/files/1_en_document_travail_service_conjoint_part1_v4.pdf
EEAS (2020b). Association implementation report on Ukraine, SWD 329 final, https://eeas.europa.eu/sites/eeas/files/2020_ukraine_association_implementation_report_final.pdf
EU Neighbours East Survey (2019). EU NEIGHBOURS east – Annual Survey Report, 4th Wave (Spring 2019), https://www.euneighbours.eu/en/east/stay-informed/publications/opinion-survey-2019-regional-overview.
European Commission (2017). Eastern Partnership – 20 deliverables for 2020: Focusing on key priorities and tangible results, *Joint Staff Working Document SWD(2017) 300 final, 9.06.2017*, https://ec.europa.eu/transparency/regdoc/rep/10102/2017/EN/SWD-2017-300-F1-EN-MAIN-PART-1.PDF
European Commission (2019). Top 10 achievements of the Eastern Partnership in the last 10 Years, https://ec.europa.eu/neighbourhood-enlargement/sites/near/files/eastern_partnerships_top_10_achievements.pdf
European Commission (2020a). 20 DELIVERABLES FOR 2020 monitoring – state of play in February 2020, *European Commission*, 19.06.2020, https://ec.europa.eu/neighbourhood-enlargement/sites/near/files/monitoring_spring_2020_20_deliverables_for_2020.pdf
European Commission (2020b). Eastern Partnership policy beyond 2020 Reinforcing Resilience – an Eastern Partnership that delivers for all, *Joint Communication to the European Parliament, the European Council, the Council, the European Economic and Social Committee and the Committee of the Regions*, JOIN(2020) 7 final, Brussels, 18.3.2020, https://eeas.europa.eu/sites/eeas/files/1_en_act_part1_v6.pdf
Government Office for Coordination on European and Euro-Atlantic Integration of Ukraine (2020). *Report on Implementation of the Association Agreement between Ukraine and the European Union in 2019* (Kyiv: GOCEEAI Ukraine), https://eu-ua.org/sites/default/files/inline/files/ar_aa_implementation-2019-4_eng.pdf
Graney, K. (2019). *Russia, the Former Soviet Republics, and Europe since 1989: Transformation and Tragedy*, Oxford: OUP.
Gretskiy, I., Treshchenkov, E., and Golubev, K. (2014). Russia's perceptions and misperceptions of the EU eastern partnership, *Communist and Post-Communist Studies*, 47(3–4): 375–383.
Gylfason, T., Martínez-Zarzoso, I., and Wijkman, P.M. (2015). Free trade agreements, institutions and the exports of eastern partnership countries, *Journal of Common Market Studies*, 53(6): 1214–1229.
Haukkala, H. (2008). The European Union as a regional normative hegemon: The case of European Neighbourhood Policy, *Europe-Asia Studies*, 60(9): 1601–1622.
Hill, C. (2003). *The Changing Politics of Foreign Policy*, New York: Palgrave Macmillan.
Hoffmann, N., and Niemann, A. (2018). EU actorness and the European Neighbourhood Policy. In *The Routledge Handbook on the European Neighbourhood Policy*, ed. by T. Schumacher, A. Marchetti and T. Demmelhuber (London and New York: Routledge), pp. 28–38.

Jarábik, B. (2019). Eastern Partnership at 10: Rhetoric, resources and Russia, *New Eastern Europe*, 37(3–4): 44–46.

Kostanyan, H., and Vandecasteele, B. (2013). The socialization potential of the Eastern Partnership Civil Society Forum, *Eastern Journal of European Studies*, 4(2): 95–110.

Kourtikakis, K., and Turkina, E. (2015). Civil society organizations in European Union external relations: A study of interorganizational networks in the Eastern Partnership and the Mediterranean, *Journal of European Integration*, 37(5): 587–609.

Kuzio, T. (2017). Ukraine between a constrained EU and assertive Russia, *Journal of Common Market Studies*, 55(1): 103–120.

Larik, J. (2016). *Foreign Policy Objectives in European Constitutional Law*, Oxford: Oxford University Press.

Lebanidze, B. (2020). *Russia, EU and the Post-Soviet Democratic Failure*, Wiesbaden: Springer.

Lightfoot, S., Szent-Iványi, B., and Wolczuk, K. (2016). Mesmerized by enlargement: The EU's Eastern Neighborhood Policy and new member state transition experience, *East European Politics and Societies*, 30(3): 664–684.

March, J.G., and Olsen, J.P. (1989). *Rediscovering Institutions. The Organizational Basis of Politics*, New York: Free Press.

Mayer, S. (2014). Common foreign and security policy alignment in the Southern Caucasus: Convergence, 'pick and choose' or indifference? *Europe-Asia Studies*, 66(10): 1679–1702.

Merheim-Eyre, I. (2017). Exploring the European Union's rationalities of governing: The case of cross-border mobility in the eastern partnership, *East European Politics*, 33(3): 371–387.

MFA Ukraine (2019). Foreign Ministers of Ukraine, Georgia and Moldova are for differentiation within the framework of the Eastern Partnership, *MFA Ukraine*, 5.12.2019, https://mfa.gov.ua/en/news/76418-ministri-zakordonnih-sprav-ukrajini-gruziji-ta-moldovi-vistupajuty-za-diferencijovanij-pidkhid-u-ramkah-iniciativi-jes-skhidne-partnerstvo.

MFA Ukraine (2021). Association Trio: Memorandum of Understanding between the Ministry of Foreign Affairs of Ukraine, Ministry of Foreign Affairs of Georgia and the Ministry of Foreign Affairs and European Integration of the Republic of Moldova. *MFA Ukraine*, 17 May 2021. https://mfa.gov.ua/en/news/association-trio-memorandum-understanding-between-ministry-foreign-affairs-georgia-ministry-foreign-affairs-and-european-integration-republic-moldova-and-ministry-foreign-affairs-ukraine

NEE (2019). Eastern partnership turns ten, *New Eastern Europe*, 3–4(37), May-August 2019.

Nilsson, M., and Silander, D. (2016). Democracy and security in the EU's eastern neighborhood? Assessing the ENP in Georgia, Moldova, and Ukraine, *Democracy and Security*, 12(1): 44–61.

Nixey, J. (2019). The Eastern Partnership at 10: What is there to celebrate? *New Eastern Europe*, 37(3–4): 33–37.

OECD (2020). *SME Policy Index: Eastern Partner Countries 2020: Assessing the Implementation of the Small Business Act for Europe*. SME Policy Index, European Union, Brussels/OECD Publishing, Paris, https://doi.org/10.1787/8b45614b-en.

Pawlak, P. (2017). Communicating Europe in third countries, *European Parliament Briefing* (March 2017), EPRS_BRI(2017)599340_EN, https://www.europarl.europa.eu/RegData/etudes/BRIE/2017/599340/EPRS_BRI%282017%29599340_EN.pdf

Petrova, I., and Raube, K. (2016). EuroNest: What drives inter-parliamentary cooperation in the Eastern Partnership, *European Foreign Affairs Review*, 21: 35–55.

Raik, K. (2019). The Ukraine crisis as a conflict over Europe's political, economic and security order, *Geopolitics*, 24(1): 51–70.

Rieker, P. (2013). The EU foreign and security policy: High expectations, low capabilities? In *Rethinking Foreign Policy*, ed. by F. Bynander and S. Guzzini (London and New York: Routledge), pp. 150–162.

Roberts, S., and Ziemer, U. (2018). Explaining the pattern of Russian authoritarian diffusion in Armenia, *East European Politics*, 34(2): 152–172.

Saari, S., and Secrieru, S. (2019). Shifting ground: How megatrends are shaping the Eastern Neighbourhood. In *The Eastern Partnership a Decade On: Looking Back, Thinking Ahead*, ed. by S. Secrieru and S. Saari (Paris: EUISS; Chaillot Paper no.153), pp.7–27.

Schilde, K.E. (2014). Who are the Europeans? European identity outside of European integration, *Journal of Common Market Studies*, 52(3): 650–667.

Schunz, S. (2010). How to assess the European Union's influence in international affairs: Addressing a major conceptual challenge for EU foreign policy analysis, *Journal of Contemporary European Research*, 6(1): 22–42.

Seliverstova, O. (2017). Keeping alive the "Imaginary West" in post-Soviet countries, *Journal of Contemporary Central and Eastern Europe*, 25(1): 117–134.

Shyrokykh, K. (2017). Effects and side effects of European Union assistance on the former Soviet republics, *Democratization*, 24(4): 651–669.

Shyrokykh, K., and Rimkutė, D. (2019). EU rules beyond its borders: The policy-specific effects of Transgovernmental Networks and EU Agencies in the European Neighbourhood, *Journal of Common Market Studies*, 57(4): 749–767.

Siljak, D., and Nagy, S.G. (2018). Economic convergence of the Eastern Partnership countries towards the EU-13, *Eastern Journal of European Studies*, 9(2): 169–185.

Slobodchikoff, M.O. (2013). *Strategic Cooperation: Overcoming the Barriers of Global Anarchy*, Lanham, MD: Lexington.

Smith, M.E. (2004). *Europe's Foreign and Security Policy: The Institutionalization of Cooperation*, Cambridge: Cambridge University Press.

Special Eurobarometer 259: 'The European Union and its Neighbours' (October 2006).

Standard Eurobarometer 81: 'Public opinion in the European Union' (Spring 2014).

State Border Guard Service of Ukraine. (2020). Три роки безвізу. Українці здійснили майже 49 мільйонів поїздок в країни ЄС, *SBGS Ukraine*, 11.06.2020, https://dpsu.gov.ua/ua/news/tri-roki-bezvizu-ukrainci-zdiysnili-mayzhe-49-milyoniv-poizdok-v-kraini-s/ (accessed: 05.10.2020).

The Economist Intelligence Unit. (2020). Democracy Index 2019: A year of democratic backsliding and popular protest, *The Economist Intelligence Unit*, 3.09.2020, https://www.eiu.com/n/campaigns/democracy-index-2019.

Tyushka, A. (2017). Association-*Cum*-Integration: The EU-Ukraine association agreement and 'association law' as an institution of Ukraine's European integration, *Croatian Yearbook of European Law and Policy*, 13: 87–132.

Tyushka, A. (2019). Towards a happy 20th anniversary? Future thinking the Eastern Partnership's 3Ds: Dilemmas, design and deliverables, *International Issues & Slovak Foreign Policy Affairs*, 28(1–2): 11–13.

Tyushka, A. (2020). Twists and turns of democratic transition and Europeanisation in East-Central Europe since 1989: Betwixt EU member and neighbour state-building, *Croatian Yearbook of European Law and Policy*, 16: 133–177.

van der Togt, T. (2018). EU's Eastern dilemma: Prioritizing interests over values?, *Clingendael Spectator*, 31.01.2018, https://spectator.clingendael.org/en/publication/eus-eastern-dilemma-prioritising-interests-over-values (accessed on 31.01.2018).

Vieira, A., and Vasilyan, S. (2018). Armenia and Belarus: Caught between the EU's and Russia's conditionalities? *European Politics and Society*, 19(4): 471–489.

Wolczuk, K., and Delcour, L. (2018). Well-meaning but ineffective? Perceptions of the EU's role as a security actor in the South Caucasus, *European Foreign Affairs Review*, 23(Special Issue): 41–60.

Wolfers, A. (1962). *Discord and Collaboration: Essays on International Politics*, Baltimore, MD: The Johns Hopkins Press.

Zarembo, K. (2017). Perceptions of CSDP effectiveness in Ukraine: A host state perspective, *European Security*, 26(2): 190–206.

Zygierewicz, A. (ed.) (2020a). *Association Agreement between the EU and Ukraine: European Implementation Assessment (Update)*. Brussels: EPRS (EPRS_STU(2020)642844_EN), https://www.europarl.europa.eu/RegData/etudes/STUD/2020/642844/EPRS_STU(2020)642844_EN.pdf

Zygierewicz, A. (ed.) (2020b). *Association Agreement between the EU and the Republic of Moldova: European Implementation Assessment (Update)*. Brussels: EPRS (EPRS_STU(2020)642834_EN), https://www.europarl.europa.eu/RegData/etudes/STUD/2020/642834/EPRS_STU(2020)642834_EN.pdf

Zygierewicz, A. (ed.) (2020c). *Association Agreement between the EU and Georgia: European Implementation Assessment (Update)*. Brussels: EPRS (EPRS_STU(2020)642820_EN), https://www.europarl.europa.eu/RegData/etudes/STUD/2020/642820/EPRS_STU(2020)642820_EN.pdf

Conclusion

The EU and its Eastern Neighbourhood – whither 'Eastern Partnership'?

Andriy Tyushka

Throughout the first decade of its existence, the Eastern Partnership (EaP) has unlocked numerous direct and indirect pathways of bilateral and multilateral cooperation between the European Union (EU) and the six EaP countries (EaP-6), offering a rich menu of potential engagement and few, if any, strategic guidelines and well-defined endpoints. Ambivalence, ambiguity, situational dependency, lack of responsiveness and strategic uncertainty are just some of the many challenges the EaP continues to be faced with. For years, EU relations with the EaP-6 have been exposed to internal political changes in both the EU and the Eastern neighbourhood, as well as major regional turbulence. Uncertainties about the future of the EaP are, furthermore, marked by multi-layered uncertainty over the predictability of the trajectories of domestic political transformations and foreign policy orientations of all EaP countries. Undeniably, mass disinformation and a growing post-truth ambience complicate further both strategic relations and daily interactions.

This volume addressed some of these issues as well as manifold dilemmas and opportunities in EU-Eastern neighbours' relations, as manifested through variegated progress and diversity, and it has addressed both enduring and emerging regional challenges. It evaluated EaP deliverables and drawbacks, registering a mixed record of success and underperformance. As this volume sees the light of the day, the EaP is likely to have undergone some revisions. Against this backdrop, this chapter, by way of offering some generic conclusions, discusses some of the main dilemmas and opportunities for EU-Eastern neighbourhood relations in the near future and, based on these, proposes some reflections on the EaP's future design. In what follows, it discusses two major paradigms for the EaP's post-2020 transformation, notably what may turn out to be just an update as opposed to a true upgrade and thus major revisions of the framework. It is nearly axiomatic that, like most policy initiatives, also the EaP periodically needs new impetus. That it even needs some 'fixing' came vividly to the fore as a result of the many ruptures in the EU's Eastern neighbourhood, most of which still resonate today. The poor state of EU-Russia relations at large, due to, though not exclusively, Russia's annexation of Crimea, its aggression in Ukraine's East as well as its generally increased assertiveness in the region (Burlyuk 2017; Krasnodębska 2018; Ikani 2019), represent a significant unintended consequence. That this crisis should not be seen in isolation but regarded as the culmination of a long-term crisis in EU-Russia relations seems to be an agreeable viewpoint among both policymakers and academia alike (Haukkala 2015; Raik 2019). Furthermore, the notion of 'partnership', which is explicitly embedded in the EaP's formula, also necessitates rethinking and resetting of *the* political itself, and endowing the initiative with a new sense of purpose and more clearly defined tasks have rendered the recent revision much overdue. Thus, both policymaking and scholarly communities seem to agree that the EaP is in need of a new vision – and a new version.

The future of the EaP and past research trends

Before this set of Conclusions turns towards the discussion on the future of the EaP, it is important to first turn the perspective backwards and offer a brief reconstruction of the state of the art of the study of the EaP. Annex 2 seeks to do just that by taking stock, in a systematic and comprehensive manner, of the evolution of EaP scholarship over the past decade. The bibliometric and content analysis of the literature on the EaP and EU-Eastern neighbours' relations in 2009–2020 reveals a number of important findings on the disciplinary, methodological and topical positioning of EaP research.

International Relations and Foreign Policy Analysis, together with Public Policy and Political Science in general, are clearly the dominating disciplines in which EaP research is taking place, accounting together for an 82.63% share in the relevant literature, whereas economic, legal and interdisciplinary studies of the EaP and EU-Eastern neighbours' relations are considerably underrepresented. Likewise, theory-informed analysis seems under-represented, as the vast majority of EaP literature – 87.78% – features empirical and conceptual analysis. As far as the latter is concerned, this finding is connected to the fragmented state of the relevant scholarship, as numerous concepts keep proliferating and populating the field. No clear trend of the distribution of empirical analysis across the EaP-6 is identifiable. Single case studies are overwhelmingly at the heart of EaP studies' research design, with comparative case studies accounting just for 15.08%. Moreover, a further 18.16% adopt a so-called 'regionwide comparative outlook' – seemingly comparative analysis that draws on varying sets of EaP countries studied within a single article but that lacks a proper comparative research design. There is also an alarming lack of research that draws on quantitative (4.47%) or mixed (3.63%) research methods, rendering qualitative analysis – accounting for 40.22% of the relevant scholarship – the most popular choice of method. This is accentuated by the fact that more than half of EaP literature (51.68%) does not explicitly specify and rely on any concrete research method at all – a finding that represents an even bigger problem than the unevenness as far as the methods distribution, as discussed above, is concerned.

As regards the academic debate itself, a few important trends and gaps can be identified. First and foremost, as a research object, the EaP is heavily overshadowed by the so-called Russia factor, power politics and geopolitical contestation in the Eastern neighbourhood region. This is also reflected by the fact that EU-Russia competition and regional security are two key areas of enquiry (representing 14.84% of EaP scholarship clustered around a total of 29 topics; see Annex 2 for details). Second, the data-driven analysis confirms the ambiguity as regards the treatment of the EaP as a regional entity: approximately half of the literature corpus (47.84%) remains silent on this matter, whereas the remaining half is disunited in the use of geographical and spatio-political delineations. The most widespread scholarly conventions in designating the 'in-betweenness' of the space located between the EU and Russia, i.e. the area formed by the EaP-6, are 'EU's Eastern Neighbourhood' region (17.30%) and 'post-Soviet' region/space (6.22%). The literature also includes references to 'EaP region' and the EU's 'ENP/neighbourhood region', and less so to 'new (eastern) Europe', the 'EU's near abroad', 'Russia's near abroad (sphere of influence)', or 'wider Europe'. Such a proliferation of competing terms demonstrates the absence of much-needed epistemological consensus and, more importantly, the missing consensus on the existence of a genuinely consolidated and homogeneous region. This poor state is also reflected in the few existing comparative studies that address EaP countries chiefly in their sub-regional – South Caucasian – context or in the framework of the EU's association with the EaP-3.

Third, EaP literature addresses dozens of topics and issue areas. Perhaps, this is unsurprising, given the multi-layered and multi-component nature of the scholarship as a field of EU foreign policy studies and International Relations. Clustered around 29 key topics and issue areas, as done in Annex 2, the decennial EaP scholarship has mainly established itself as an integral part of EU-centred analysis of EU actorness, diplomacy and performance in the Eastern neighbourhood, with a particular focus on external governance, EU norms and rules transfer, EU democracy promotion, EU neighbourhood policy, Europeanization and European integration at large (see Figure A2.28). Less researched are topics related to economic integration and convergence, domestic dynamics in EaP countries or their individual strategies and policies towards both the EU (and, by extension, Russia and other external actors), mutual perceptions and strategic communications, the manifestations and consequences of EU hegemonic power projection, the law and politics of EU association, as well as mobility and migration. Among the least studied subjects are EU-EaP cross-border cooperation and transgovernmental interactions, the impact of Eurasian integration on EU-EaP dynamics and the EaP as such, as well as endogenous and exogenous region-building and regionalization dynamics. This is complemented by rather few studies that revolve around energy security, identity politics and issues in normative convergence, environmental politics, the relations between the EaP-6 and Russia, Russian autocracy promotion in the region and regime persistence in individual EaP countries. This assessment comes against the backdrop of significant variation as far as researchers' preferences for individual EaP countries as objects of study are concerned. While the research on Ukraine and Armenia has established itself in one third of the identified research topics (see Table A2.2), the research on other EaP countries has consolidated in a just couple of domains, with Azerbaijan and Belarus remaining the least grounded objects of analysis in existing EaP scholarship.

The 'EaP *plus*' update of the EaP post-2020

The current debate on whether and how to update the EaP unfolds in the context of already tabled propositions, including those submitted by EU institutions. By and large, these propositions revolve around allowing for further differentiation of relationship formats within the EaP, supposedly creating new opportunities under the EU's differentiated external integration schemes and adding new issue areas onto the EaP agenda, such as, for example, the greening and digitalization of, or resilience-building in, EaP countries. Significantly, such proposals exemplify the update rationale, insofar as the aim of this rationale is to improve matters as they arise, rather than rethink and revise them entirely.

The political climate within the EU and the region as a whole seems to have reduced the political ambitions of EaP participants and generated consensus that the EaP should merely undergo actualization and a pragmatic update (Gherasimov 2020; Korosteleva et al. 2020). At least, actualization and pragmatism are the basic parameters of the EaP, as laid out in the document by the European Commission and the External Action Service (EEAS) of March 2020 (European Commission 2020). However, it is noteworthy that the EaP, while being an integral part of EU foreign policy, is declared to be, at the same time, a 'joint policy initiative' of the EU and EaP partner countries. Thus, it is, in principle, still possible that the EaP may witness new dynamics at least thanks to partners' own impetus, and the joint statement by the governments of Ukraine, Georgia and Moldova (the associated EaP-3), submitted in 2019 on the future of the EaP in the framework of the EU's structural consultation process (*MFA Ukraine* 2019), presents an example of such potential impetus. Importantly, this move by the associated EaP-3 was even explicitly anticipated and endorsed by the European Parliament (Jozwiak 2020). It is thus not surprising that the main discursive framework and, at the same time, basis for additional deliberation is the idea of a broader EaP, or 'EaP *plus*' (Schumacher 2019). Back in June 2020, during the virtual gathering of EaP leaders, the jointly advanced proposal by the associated EaP-3 advocating for enhanced dialogue within the EaP, i.e. 'EU+EaP-3' (Kuleba 2020), essentially echoes the idea of an 'EaP *plus*', as formulated by the European Parliament on 17 November 2017 (EP 2017). In general, the associated EaP-3 foreign ministers' joint statement, presented on 5 December 2019, proposes a partnership of 'enhanced opportunities' just for the three countries, including further gradual sectoral integration (below the level of full EU membership) and differentiation of the process itself (MFA Ukraine 2019). In particular, it:

> call[s] upon the EU/incoming European Commission to engage further in joint discussions on the progress, opportunities and challenges concerning the association-related reforms with the aim of facilitating full implementation of the AA/DCFTAs; invite[s] the EU to consider establishing the EU+ Three Associated Partners dialogue in the areas including, but not limited to, transport, energy, justice and digital economy; [...] and call[s] upon the EU to play a more visible role and further increase its engagement in peaceful conflict resolution in the EaP area, inter alia, by strengthening the EU presence in conflict-affected countries.
> (MFA Ukraine 2019)

The associated EaP-3 also declared, inter alia, their intent to 'consider applying for EU membership in accordance with Article 49 of the Treaty on the European Union' (MFA Ukraine 2019). Quite likely, such a proposal is poised to go beyond of what seems currently feasible on the part of the EU. The low support by EU Member States citizens for further rounds of enlargement – only 37% of EU Member States citizens supported the idea of further enlargement back in 2014 (cf.: Standard EB 81 2014: 143–144) – in conjunction with past discourses by the EU and Member States as regards slow or occasionally even stagnant reform progress in individual EaP countries, demonstrates that the EaP as such has been also suffering from all sorts of 'fatigues', i.e. from the presumably chronic 'enlargement fatigue' to a 'Ukraine fatigue', a 'Moldova fatigue' or even a 'EaP fatigue' more generally. Arguably, these are the outcomes of an ill-suited expectations management. Just like those EaP countries that continue to regard the EaP as a springboard for future EU membership, the EU, in turn, expects from the EaP what it cannot instantly deliver (i.e. stability, security and prosperity), given current realities in the region and individual countries. Therefore, it seems obvious that, first and foremost, better expectations management on both sides is needed. Kobzova (2017), for example, convincingly suggests that the EU should adjust its expectations, and do so by, first, 'expecting the expected' and realistically assess both regionwide and country-specific scope conditions and opportunity structures; second, by minding the neighbours and align to a larger extent with their interests; third, by changing its framing practices and view EaP countries as mere partners rather than friends or even foes; and, fourth, by placing more emphasis on, and then consolidating, credibility of both EU external action and discourse. Yet, the challenge remains as to how not to fatigue membership ambitions of EaP countries, as any such backlash is likely to generate detrimental effects on their commitment to further reforms and the existence of the EaP as such.

Most saliently, the outbreak of the SARS-CoV-2-pandemic in early 2020, as well as the most recent escalation of the conflict between Azerbaijan and Armenia over Nagorno-Karabakh and the seven surrounding areas in autumn 2020, bringing about a new regional order, emerged as unforeseen crash-tests of the EaP's most recently declared resilience track (European Commission 2020), as mentioned in the Introduction to this volume. EU resilience-building towards and beyond the neighbourhood essentially sees reform as resilience, presupposing Eastern neighbours' willingness to engage in EU-style transformation and convergence with EU legislation and practices on a range of issues, and thus as panacea to the existing multitude of problems and challenges the EaP-6 are faced with. Moreover, as the growing body of scholarship argues, the practice of EU resilience-building in the Eastern neighbourhood is strongly affected by path dependency and, therefore, goes hand in hand with deresponsibilization patterns on the part of the EU and a euphemistic discourse which frames these as beneficial for neighbours and an opportunity to obtain greater ownership of EaP policies (cf. e.g.: Joseph and Juncos 2019). This externally engineered resilience-building has attracted significant scholarly critique (Wagner and Anholt 2016; also Juncos 2017; Rouet and Pascariu 2019), not least as it is rooted in the questionable assumption that local communities do possess agency, are aware of both the challenges and weaknesses (and the strengths and capacities) of their respective societies and can actualize their own potential in their own – suitable – way (Korosteleva 2020). The notion that resilience is bound to inform the EaP's post-2020 agenda and even form – in the eyes of the European Commission and the EEAS – an 'overriding policy framework' thus seems to pose more questions than it is likely to respond to.

Current updating dynamics of the EaP are also bound to entail the creation of further opportunities for differentiated – gradual and sectorial – integration among the EU and its Eastern neighbours. As some argue, one can in fact identify, from among the EU's external differentiation menu, some '100 ideas' on how to upgrade the EU's Association Agreements with Georgia, Moldova and Ukraine (Emerson and Blockmans 2020). Albeit an old EU practice in itself, the idea of differentiated – or variegated sectoral – integration has been relatively recently established in, for example, the context of Ukraine's official European integration discourse and represents a much less politicized initiative than any potential EU membership application. Also, as differentiated integration in both its external and internal dimension is gaining more traction within the EU (Schimmelfennig and Winzen 2020), further variegated sector-specific integration steps as part of a post-2020 EaP are likely to materialize. In this regard, the new Vice-Prime Minister for European and Euro-Atlantic Integration of Ukraine, Olga Stefanishyna, formulated a vision of Ukraine's European integration as one that follows the format of the EU's differentiated integration with Norway, i.e. the so-called 'Norwegian track' (Sydorenko and Panchenko 2020).[1] Norway, as a member of the European Economic Area (EEA), benefits from full liberalization of the 'four freedoms' of the EU's common market (except for the fisheries and agriculture sectors).[2] Thus, in the short to medium term, Ukraine is keen on exploiting all opportunities the Association Agreement offers for deepening association and furthering differentiated integration. In this sense, Ukraine's participation in the EaP should be regarded as an 'additional engine of European integration' (Tochytskyi 2020) within the entire framework rather than an act of political symbolism, as it was often portrayed in the recent past. In particular in the EaP's multilateral track, where a 'healthy' climate of good neighbourly relations in the region is supposed to be forged, Ukraine enjoys opportunities to advance its own course of European integration, which, not least due to 'group pressure' dynamics among the associated EaP-3, stands a better chance of gaining shape in the mid- to long run and positively affect also Georgia and Moldova. Whether expanded differentiated integration schemes would then also be offered to – and, most of all, requested by – Armenia, Azerbaijan and an illegitimate Belarusian regime, and whether an answer would be offered as to whether an 'EaP *plus*' would eventually become 'a means towards an end or an end in itself?' (Schumacher 2019: 215), remain highly questionable as the revised EaP is emerging.

The EaP upgrade, or repurposing the EaP post-2020

As much points to the fact that the 'EaP *plus*' logic of the post-2020 EaP essentially revolves around mere face-lifting revisions, some recently published studies, highlighting the need to 'bringing the political back in' (Korosteleva 2017; Simão 2017; Korosteleva et al. 2018) and calling for an upgrade of the EaP, resonate considerably with EaP countries' demands for the framework to become more reflective of their shared concerns rather than narrowly focus on EU-inspired 'joint goals'. As the analysis of official EaP policy discourses conducted elsewhere and in Annex 1 of this volume demonstrates, matters of (hard) security rank as the second-most salient joint policy concern (Tyushka 2019: 11–13; cf. also Annex 1) – a feature that has largely remained unaddressed by the EaP. This is directly related to the second major problem of the framework, notably the illusion of partnership and the missing practice of true partnering. Remedying these two foundational issues – the absence of hard security and true partnering – in the EaP, resurfacing on numerous occasions in the past, might represent a major step towards repurposing the EaP's rationale, design and functions.

The EaP's transition from being an exclusive EU foreign policy framework to becoming a truly 'joint policy framework' is a precondition for 'Partnership' writ-large to be transformed into everyday partnering practice. In turn, such a development would require a change of perception of the subjectivity of Eastern neighbours and, with it, the rectification of the EU's official discourse that continues to revolve around the utilization of an infeasible and rather odd group denomination (i.e. the 'six Eastern Partnership countries'). Also, this would presuppose fully embracing the derivate notion of 'Eastern Partners' or 'Eastern European Partners' – an idea that seems to continue to be pondered through the practice of silence in the EU's institutional discourse. Such revisions, or upgrades, would help to bring the EaP to a new level as far as joint ownership is concerned and bestow upon it the character of strategic partnership, however defined.

It seems obvious that the EaP is unlikely to ever obtain the character of a symmetric partnership among equals, not least in light of the power and capability asymmetries as well as the mounting normative hegemony of the EU in the region and beyond. The reality, though, is that in a world of (strategic) partnerships,[3] such partnerships rarely are symmetrical, and this applies also to the EU's variegated relations with other international actors. Since the adoption of the European Security Strategy of 2003, strategic partnerships have been officially acknowledged as an instrument of EU foreign policy and the corresponding pursuit of EU foreign policy objectives (Renard 2012: 304). Currently, the EU has officially forged strategic partnerships with ten international actors, notably Brazil, Canada, China, India, Japan, Mexico, Russia (suspended in 2016), South Africa, South Korea and the United States. However, even these 10 are neither all strategic, symmetric, identical, equal, nor actually truly strategic – and, as a matter of fact, not all of these actors regard the EU as a 'strategic partner' (Renard 2012: 305–311). Moreover, the notion of strategic partnership serves distinct functions in the EU's foreign policy discourse itself – from being a label and mechanism of differentiation and hierarchization to serving as a normative instrument, destined to advance EU structural foreign policy to encompassing a constitutive speech and positioning act (Blanco 2016).

Existing asymmetries within the EaP stem directly from the character of EU-Eastern neighbourhood relations that, in their own right, suffer from these. The EU-centric external governance literature reveals many aspects of such asymmetries, and in the EaP context it appears far from contested that the (external) governance-partnership nexus is considerably biased towards the governance end, with notions such as partnership and partnering being of a mere rhetorical nature. In the EU's discourse, expressions such as 'joint and common values', 'joint ownership' and 'partnership' ironically seem to be predicates that express asymmetric power relations and, at the same time, conceal the EU's dominant status in relations with its Eastern European neighbours and the neighbourhood at large (Horký-Hlucháň and Kratochvíl 2014: 262–264). Calls for decentring EU relations with its neighbourhood are as old as the EaP itself, and several dichotomies are at the heart of striking such a balance, most notably the dichotomy of hegemony *vs.* partnership, of conditionality *vs.* ownership, of bilateralism *vs.* multilateralism, of differentiation *vs.* homogeneity and of functionality *vs.* geostrategic vision (Bechev and Nicolaïdis 2010: 479–481).

Back in 2015, the revised ENP envisioned a stronger neighbourhood and the ensuing build-up of stronger partnerships. The fifth EaP Summit in Brussels in 2017, too, convened under the motto 'stronger together'. The many crises throughout the neighbourhood and in EU 'partnership diplomacy' itself point to the lamentable '"thinness" of the partnerships' (Smith 2019: 299) that are supposed to underpin EU-Eastern neighbourhood relations, and the consequences this thinness has been having for the EU's credibility as a presumably effective and reliable partner. This is closely related to the acceptance of the EU's 'potential we' among EaP countries. Whereas the EaP-3 accept it, Armenia holds on to it from a distance, and both Belarus and Azerbaijan continue to contest the EU's projection of the 'self'/'potential we', as was shown elsewhere (Vieira 2020; cf. also: Delcour 2019). In such an ambience, and against the broader backdrop of EaP (geo)politicization and growing contestation between the EU and Russia in the region, EaP 'partnership diplomacy' in its current form might soon lead further complications as EaP countries have already begun to assert their own positions more vocally. Being severely affected by, and – quite ironically – even empowered through, this contestation in the 'shared' neighbourhood, EaP countries have started developing their own strategies to defy this marginality, their 'in-betweenness' and the multi-layered asymmetries (Hagemann 2013; Fix et al. 2019; Kakachia et al. 2019). Drawing on these currently unfolding practices of strategic hedging vis-à-vis a resurgent Russia (Meister

2018), the EaP-6 might rather sooner than later also hedge against the EU – a realistic possibility that all the more calls for ambition in the current context of EaP revisions.

Most recently, relations between the EU and the EaP-6 have taken on a new dimension of cooperation and coordination to mitigate the fallouts of the SARS-CoV-2 pandemic, including the provision of EU financial aid to support Eastern European partners and thus even Belarus, the only EaP partner country where the pandemic's existence has been systematically denied by the discredited state authorities (EaP Think Bridge 2020). Following the June 2020 virtual gathering of EaP leaders, the EU's solidarity and support package for EaP countries, approved as part of the EU's global response to the pandemic, includes EUR 58 mln. of financial aid for immediate needs and more than EUR 1 bn. for short- and medium-term support for the social and economic recovery of the region (EEAS 2021; cf. also Table 13.1 in Chapter 13). The EU's extended solidarity with its Eastern neighbourhood had not been obviously anticipated or regulated by relevant EaP documents, issued by the Commission and the EEAS or the Council, respectively. Yet, it does represent proof of the EU's sense of loyalty and commitment, two key parameters that are pivotal for the sustaining of strategic cooperation and partnership at large (Domachowska 2019: 123–133). As far as Ukraine is concerned, the initially earmarked EUR 202 mln. support package was not only increased to a staggering EUR 1.2 bn (Council of the EU 2020) but in May 2020 Ukraine was also invited to join, as an observer, the EU's Health Security Committee, a body that gathers the EU and Member States to coordinate national responses, preparedness and other risk- and crisis-related response activities in pursuit of health security. This invitation has created an important precedent and serves as a valuable example of offering Eastern neighbours more than is merely stipulated by existing Association Agreements.

Another area within the existing EaP framework where significant upgrades are indeed possible is innately connected to the context the initiative was borne into: (hard) security. 'Bringing *the* political back in', and repurposing the EaP, would essentially entail redefining the nature of EU relations with regional actors in Eastern Europe and beyond, including via differentiation and normalization of relations, thus contributing to the establishment of a qualitatively new social order in the region (Korosteleva 2017). An integral element of this should be, according to some, the forging of new sustainable discourses of cohabitation as well as new (and more) inclusive forms of (European) security (Simão 2017). By extension, this would also have to be complemented by the reaching of an agreement between the EU and Russia on bridging their regional cooperation initiatives, thus making the EaP part of both the EU-led European integration project and the Russia-led Eurasian Economic Union (Korosteleva 2016; Nitoiu 2017). Valuable as such propositions may be, they cannot ignore the existence of considerable compatibility issues, let alone questions related to the geostrategic feasibility of such a new social order. Moreover, such *de facto* bridge-building in and over the 'shared neighbourhood', if it ever were to be taken seriously, would inevitably be faced with the normative limits to it, all of which are evident in the seemingly ever-deepening normative divide between the EU and Russia (Kobayashi 2019). Also, as was touched upon by the Introduction to this volume, over the past three decades, post-Soviet/EaP countries have matured, emancipated themselves from Russia's postcolonialism and started moving past 'post-Sovietness', implying that they are no longer prepared to simply accept deals made by regional powers about their future, undermining or even openly contesting their agency. As such, propositions of this sort present a critical juncture, as they submit the limits of partnering between the EU and the EaP-6 to a true litmus test and highlight, arguably more than ever before, the question as to whether EaP revisions will transform the EaP into a true Strategic Partnership or just consolidate past practices of 'muddling through' (Schumacher 2020).

Whither 'Eastern Partnership'? Old and new variables and the future of EU-Eastern neighbours relations

As some of the reprinted articles in this volume show, the dilemmas of making the EaP more viable and effective revolve not only around the choice between updating and upgrading. In fact, any future EaP is confronted with the necessity to address meaningfully both enduring issues and emergent challenges. As exemplified in Chapters 1–5, the emergence and functioning of the EaP have been strongly affected by a set of intertwined, enduring issues, including, first and foremost, the EU's overemphasis of its normative engagement, the projection of the 'ideal' self and an endeavour to build 'ideal neighbours', while ordering, or rather building, the Eastern neighbourhood region itself. Such an approach does not only affect the limits of the EU's attractiveness and its presumptive transformative power. It has been also increasingly contested for more than the past decade, particularly since the outbreak of Russian aggression in Ukraine in 2014. Remarkably, this critical turn of events signifies the scale of 'unintended consequences' that the EU's engagement in the Eastern neighbourhood seems to be fraught with. Likewise, as far as intended consequences are concerned, the balance sheet is a mixed one: significant progress in the EU's relations with some Eastern neighbours and tangible deliverables with all EaP-6 were undeniably registered while, at the same time, countless defaults remain. Reprinted articles in Chapters 7–12 unveil that while there is not only an inherent need for greater within-EaP differentiation, a growing menu of choice has been put in place as regards EU-structured bilateral engagement. The latter evidently range from political association and DCFTA-propelled economic integration, as the most advanced integration-oriented cooperation forms, to other contractual and non-contractual relationship formats that seek to promote EU-EaP countries' convergence outside the integration paradigm.

So far, partners have managed to maintain consensus around these aspects. It is clear, however, that both furthering regional partnership and variegated cooperation will continue to depend on injecting into the EaP at least incremental impulses and incentives, including options for differentiated integration and broader differentiation of relations in general. Currently, for example, major and seemingly irreconcilable frictions are to be observed not only between Armenia and Azerbaijan, following the conclusion of a ceasefire agreement on 10 November 2020, but also between Ukraine and Belarus. These two have traditionally maintained 'neighbourly neutrality' and practised mutual non-interference in their respective domestic affairs but entered on a path of confrontation following Ukraine's non-recognition of the results of presidential election, held in Belarus on 9 August 2020. Ukraine's consistent support for Azerbaijan's territorial integrity, including during the 2020 war in and over Nagorny Karabakh, may be fraught with consequences for Ukraine's relations with Armenia, which, in turn, has been consistently siding with Russia on the whole range of 'Ukrainian issues'. Recently, Ukraine updated its list of strategic partners to include, along with Poland, Lithuania and Turkey, only Azerbaijan and Georgia from among the five remaining EaP countries. This is of significant symbolic importance and demonstrates yet another dimension of the many crossroads the EaP, and with it Eastern partners, is faced with.

As revisions of the EaP are under way, the EU itself is witnessing fundamental change from within, most notably due to Brexit and the departure of the United Kingdom from the EU and arguably in the context of the upcoming Conference on the Future of Europe. As a matter of fact, the EU, as a community of consolidated democracies, has also increasingly become exposed to some of the governance-related challenges Eastern neighbours suffer from. Thus, tendencies of de-democratization and de-Europeanization are observed not only in the EU neighbourhood, but also in the EU itself (cf. e.g.: Szymański 2017; Tyushka 2020), adding another layer of complexity to the updating-upgrading dynamic, as discussed above. Add to this the external factors, including a new wave of significant turbulence in parts of the EU's neighbourhood and the growing presence of 'third' powers, such as Turkey, Iran or China (Popescu and Secrieru 2018). The ever-changing nature of the current geostrategic configuration is complemented by a number of local 'megatrends' that now seem to define the entire Eastern neighbourhood, most prominently embodied in developments such as societies' emancipation from Russian postcolonial hegemony, a growing regional security deficit, fragile and uneven transition to a post-post-Soviet identity, the mobilization of organized civil society and new forms of participation in the management of public affairs, demographic decline, the adaptation to the multi-layered realities of the digital age, etc. (Secrieru and Saari 2019: 7–27). Therefore, any future EaP will require much greater ambition, transparency, determination and commitment of all parties involved, including the EU itself as initiator and main 'stakeholder'. It is difficult to disagree with Gressel and Popescu (2020) that 'the strategic sovereignty of the European Union begins with Eastern Europe', and that, therefore, recent attempts to work towards strategic autonomy will be mainly tested in the context of, but also beyond, the EaP. At the same time, and in spite of ambitious declarations on the part of Commission-President Von der Leyen (2019), according to which the European Commission will pursue a geopolitical agenda, it is quite paradoxical that, substantially, the EaP 'is not an EU geopolitical priority' (Gherasimov 2020: 7) – albeit remaining 'at the heart of EU foreign policy' (Borrell 2020).

Notes

1. For more details on established and emerging models of association in EU-neighbourhood relations, see also: Lippert (2019: 86).
2. At the moment, Ukraine, for example, enjoys significant free trade preferences with the EU, but full liberalization of trade has not yet materialized. Free industrial trade, for example, still requires the conclusion of an agreement on conformity assessment and acceptability of industrial products (ACAA) and free foodstuff trade mechanisms for recognizing food safety certificates and increasing or abolishing tariff quotas. Free trade as far as services are concerned, in particular air transport, is awaiting liberalization through the conclusion of relevant agreements, such as the agreement on a common aviation area (or 'Open Skies' agreements). Ukraine's Vice-Prime Minister Stefanishyna has identified the establishment of these three (industrial, food and aviation) regimes with the EU as the top priority of Ukraine's Office for European and Euro-Atlantic Integration (cf.: Stefanishyna (2020)).
3. There is no consensus within and among scholarly communities as to the nature and definition of strategic partnership, and the inconsistent and varied reference to strategic partnership by international actors has contributed to this lack of agreement. Notwithstanding, analysts tend to agree that strategic partnership represents a formalized (and sometimes institutionalized) form of goal-driven strategic cooperation, quite regardless of accompanying labelling conventions (Tyushka and Czechowska 2019).

References

Bechev, D. and Nicolaïdis, K. (2010). From Policy to Polity: Can the EU's Special Relations with Its 'Neighbourhood' Be Decentred? *JCMS: Journal of Common Market Studies*, *48*(3): 475–500.

Blanco, L.F. (2016). The Functions of 'Strategic Partnership' in European Union Foreign Policy Discourse. *Cambridge Review of International Affairs*, *29*(1): 36–54.

Borrell, J. (2020). The Eastern Partnership Is at the Heart of EU Foreign Policy. *European External Action Service – HR/VP Blog*, 12 June 2020. https://eeas.europa.eu/diplomatic-network/eastern-partnership/80811/eastern-partnership-heart-eu-foreign-policy_en.

Burlyuk, O. (2017). The 'Oops!' of EU Engagement Abroad: Analyzing Unintended Consequences of EU External Action, *JCMS: Journal of Common Market Studies*, *55*(5): 1009–1025.

Council of the EU (2020). COVID-19: Council Adopts €3 Billion Assistance Package to Support Neighbouring Partners, 20 May 2020. https://www.consilium.europa.eu/en/press/press-releases/2020/05/20/covid-19-council-adopts-3-billion-assistance-package-to-support-neighbouring-partners/

Delcour, L. (2019). Armenia's and Georgia's Contrasted Positioning Vis-à- Vis the EU: Between Vocal Centrality and Strategic Marginality. *Journal of Contemporary European Studies*, *27*(4): 439–450.

Domachowska, A. (2019). Strategic Cooperation Sustainability. In *States, International Organizations and Strategic Partnerships*, ed. by L. Czechowska, A. Tyushka, A. Domachowska, K. Gawron-Tabor, and J. Piechowiak-Lamparska. Cheltenham: Edward Elgar Publishing, pp. 123–133.

EaP Think Bridge (2020). Eastern Partnership vs. Coronavirus: Test for Democracy. *EaP Think Bridge*, *16* (January-March 2020): 4–9.

EEAS (2021). The EU's Response to the Coronavirus Pandemic in the Eastern Partnership. *EEAS*, January 2021. https://ec.europa.eu/neighbourhood-enlargement/sites/near/files/coronavirus_support_eap.pdf

Emerson, M., and Blockmans, S. (2020) 100 Ideas for Upgrading the Association Agreements and DCFTAs with Georgia, Moldova and Ukraine. *3DCFTAs*, February 2020. https://3dcftas.eu/publications/100-ideas-for-upgrading-the-association-agreements-and-dcftas-with-georgia-moldova-and-ukraine

European Commission (2020). Eastern Partnership Policy beyond 2020 Reinforcing Resilience – an Eastern Partnership That Delivers for All. *Joint Communication to the European Parliament, the European Council, the Council, the European Economic and Social Committee and the Committee of the Regions*, JOIN(2020) 7 final, Brussels, 18 March 2020. https://data.consilium.europa.eu/doc/document/ST-6930-2020-INIT/en/pdf

European Parliament (2017). European Parliament Recommendation of 15 November 2017 to the Council, the Commission and the EEAS on the Eastern Partnership, in the Run-Up to the November 2017 Summit. (2017/2130(INI)), 15 November 2017, https://op.europa.eu/en/publication-detail/-/publication/27ef2056-c794-11e8-9424-01aa75ed71a1/language-en (accessed: 25.09.2020).

Fix, L., Gawrich, A., Kakachia, K., and Leukavets, A. (2019). Out of the Shadow? Georgia's Emerging Strategies of Engagement in the Eastern Partnership: between External Governance and Partnership Cooperation. *Caucasus Survey*, *7*(1): 1–24.

Gherasimov, C. (2020). An Eastern Policy Update, But No Upgrade. *DGAP Policy Brief, 5* (March 2020).

Gressel, G., and Popescu, N. (2020). EU's Strategic Sovereignty start in Eastern Europe. *EURACTIV*, 11 May 2020. https://www.euractiv.com/section/eastern-europe/opinion/eus-strategic-sovereignty-start-in-eastern-europe/ (accessed: 20.09.2020).

Hagemann, C. (2013). External Governance on the Terms of the Partner? The EU, Russia and the Republic of Moldova in the European Neighbourhood Policy. *Journal of European Integration*, *35*(7): 767–783.

Haukkala, H. (2015). From Cooperative to Contested Europe? The Conflict in Ukraine as a Culmination of a Long-Term Crisis in EU–Russia Relations. *Journal of Contemporary European Studies, 23*(1): 25–40.

Horký-Hlucháň, O., and Kratochvíl, P. (2014). Nothing Is Imposed in This Policy! The Construction and Constriction of the European Neighbourhood. *Alternatives, 39*(4): 252–270.

Ikani, N. (2019). Change and Continuity in the European Neighbourhood Policy: The Ukraine Crisis as a Critical Juncture. *Geopolitics, 24*(1): 20–50.

Joseph, J., and Juncos, A. E. (2019). Resilience as an Emergent European Project? The EU's Place in the Resilience Turn. *JCMS: Journal of Common Market Studies, 57*(5): 995–1011.

Jozwiak, R., (2020). European Parliament Pushes For Eastern Partners' Greater Integration, Slams Russia. *RFE/RFL*, 15 April 2020. https://www.rferl.org/a/european-parliament-pushes-for-eastern-partners-greater-integration-slams-russia/30557682.html (accessed: 25.09.2020).

Juncos, A.E. (2017). Resilience as the New EU Foreign Policy Paradigm: A Pragmatist Turn? *European Security, 26*(1): 1–18.

Kakachia, K., Lebanidze, B., and Dubovyk, V. (2019). Defying Marginality: Explaining Ukraine's and Georgia's Drive Towards Europe. *Journal of Contemporary European Studies, 27*(4): 451–462.

Kobayashi, K. (2019). The Normative Limits of Functional Cooperation: The Case of the European Union and Eurasian Economic Union. *East European Politics, 35*(2): 143–158.

Kobzova, J. (2017). Easing the EU's Eastern Partnership Fatigue. *European Council on Foreign Relations,* 16 November 2017. https://www.ecfr.eu/article/commentary_easing_the_eus_eastern_partnership_fatigue

Korosteleva, E. (2016). Eastern Partnership and the Eurasian Union: Bringing 'The Political' Back in the Eastern Region. *European Politics and Society, 17*(sup1): 67–81.

Korosteleva, E. (2017). Eastern Partnership: Bringing "The Political" Back In. *East European Politics, 33*(3): 321–337.

Korosteleva, E. (2020). Reclaiming Resilience Back: A Local Turn in EU External Governance. *Contemporary Security Policy, 41*(2): 241–262.

Korosteleva, E., Merheim-Eyre, I., and Van Gils, E. (eds.). (2018). *'The Politics' and 'The Political' of the Eastern Partnership Initiative: Reshaping the Agenda*. London and New York: Routledge.

Korosteleva, E., Petrova, I., and Merheim-Eyre, I. (2020). The Eastern Partnership 3.0: Change or Continuity? *Dahrendorf Forum,* 24 April 2020. https://www.dahrendorf-forum.eu/the-eastern-partnership-3-0-change-or-continuity/ (accessed: 25.09.2020).

Krasnodębska, M. (2018). The Ukraine Crisis as an Unintended Consequence of the EU's Public Diplomacy: Reception of the EU's Narratives in Ukraine, *The Hague Journal of Diplomacy, 13*(3): 345–365.

Kuleba, D. (2020). Дмитро Кулеба окреслив пріоритети України в рамках "Східного партнерства" з ЄС. *Міністерство закордонних справ України,* 11 June 2020. https://mfa.gov.ua/news/dmitro-kuleba-okresliv-prioriteti-ukrayini-v-ramkah-shidnogo-partnerstva-z-yes (accessed: 25.09.2020).

Lippert, B. (2019). Die EU und ihre Nachbarschaftsbeziehungen: etablierte Assoziierungsmodelle und neue Grundformen. *Integration, 2*: 83–96.

Meister, S. (2018). Hedging and Wedging: Strategies to Contest Russia's Leadership in Post-Soviet Eurasia. In *Regional Powers and Contested Leadership*, ed. by H. Ebert, D. Flemes. Cham: Palgrave Macmillan, pp. 301–326.

MFA Ukraine. (2019). Foreign Ministers of Ukraine, Georgia and Moldova are for Differentiation within the Framework of the Eastern Partnership. *MFA Ukraine,* 5 December 2019. https://

mfa.gov.ua/en/news/76418-ministri-zakordonnih-sprav-ukrajini-gruziji-ta-moldovi-vistupajuty-za-diferencijovanij-pidkhid-u-ramkah-iniciativi-jes-skhidne-partnerstvo

Nitoiu, C. (2017). European and Eurasian Integration: Competition and Cooperation in the Post-Soviet Space. *Journal of European Integration*, 39(4): 469–475.

Popescu, N., and Secrieru, S. (eds.) (2018). Third Powers in Europe's East. *EUISS Chaillot Paper 144* (March 2018).

Raik, K. (2019). The Ukraine Crisis as a Conflict over Europe's Political, Economic and Security Order. *Geopolitics*, 24(1): 51–70.

Renard, T. (2012). The EU and Its Strategic Partners. In *The Routledge Handbook of European Security*, ed. by S. Biscop and R.G. Whitman. London and New York: Routledge, pp. 302–314.

Rouet, G., and Pascariu, G. (eds.) (2019). *Resilience and The EU's Eastern Neighbourhood Countries: From Theoretical Concepts to a Normative Agenda*. London: Palgrave Macmillan.

Schimmelfennig, F., and Winzen, T. (2020) *Ever Looser Union: Differentiated European Integration*. Oxford: Oxford University Press.

Schumacher, T. (2019). Die Europäische Union, die Östliche Partnerschaft und "Assoziierung Plus": Zur Debatte über die Einbindung assoziierter Nachbarn unterhalb einer EU-Mitgliedschaft. *Integration*, 3: 205–217.

Schumacher, T. (2020). The EU and Its Neighbourhood: The Politics of Muddling Through. *JCMS: Journal of Common Market Studies*, 58: 187–201.

Secrieru, S., and Saari, S. (eds.) (2019). The Eastern Partnership a Decade On: Looking Back, Thinking Ahead. *EUISS Chaillot Paper 153* (July 2019).

Simão, L. (2017). Bringing 'the Political' Back into European Security: Challenges to the EU's Ordering of the Eastern Partnership. *East European Politics*, 33(3): 338–354.

Smith, M. (2019). The Geopolitics of the EU's Partnership Diplomacy: Strategic, Managerial or Reactive? *International Politics*, 56: 288–303.

Standard Eurobarometer 81: 'Public Opinion in the European Union' (Spring 2014).

Stefanishyna, O. (2020). На шляху до членства в Євросоюзі Україна впровадить ще три безвізи. *Інтерв'ю ТСН.иа Більше з Віце-прем'єр-міністеркою Ольгою Стефанішиною*, 23 June 2020. https://tsn.ua/interview/na-shlyahu-do-chlenstva-v-yevrosoyuzi-ukrayina-vprovadit-sche-tri-bezvizi-z-yes-1570975.html (accessed: 22.09.2020).

Sydorenko, S., and Panchenko, Yu. (2020). Перспектива членства в ЄС? Підемо "норвезьким треком": перше інтерв'ю віцепрем'єрки Стефанішиної. *Європейська Правда*, 15 June 2020. https://www.eurointegration.com.ua/interview/2020/06/15/7111086/ (accesssed: 22.09.2020).

Szymański, A. (2017). De-Europeanization and De-Democratization in the EU and Its Eastern Neighbourhood. *Yearbook of the Institute of East-Central Europe*, 15(2): 187–211.

Tochytskyi, M. (2020). Додатковий двигун євроінтеграції. *Дзеркало Тижня*, 19 May 2020, https://zn.ua/ukr/international/dodatkoviy-dvigun-yevrointegraciyi-348192_.html (accessed: 22.09.2020).

Tyushka, A. (2019). Towards a Happy 20th Anniversary? Future Thinking the Eastern Partnership's 3Ds: Dilemmas, Design and Deliverables. *International Issues & Slovak Foreign Policy Affairs*, 28(1–2): 11–13.

Tyushka, A. (2020). Twists and Turns of Democratic Transition and Europeanisation in East-Central Europe since 1989: Betwixt EU Member and Neighbour State-Building. *Croatian Yearbook of European Law and Policy*, 16: 133–177.

Tyushka, A., and Czechowska, L. (2019). Strategic Partnerships, International Politics and IR Theory. In *States, International Organizations and Strategic Partnerships*, ed. by L. Czechowska, A. Tyushka, A. Domachowska, K. Gawron-Tabor, and J. Piechowiak-Lamparska. Cheltenham: Edward Elgar Publishing, pp. 8–43.

Vieira, A. (2020). The European Union's 'Potential We' between Acceptance and Contestation: Assessing the Positioning of Six Eastern Partnership Countries. *Journal of Common Market Studies*, DOI: 10.1111/jcms.13069.

von der Leyen, U. (2019). Speech in the European Parliament Plenary Session Delivered by President-Elect of the European Commission Ursula von der Leyen. *Strasbourg*, 27 November 2019. https://ec.europa.eu/info/sites/info/files/president-elect-speech-original_1.pdf.

Wagner, W., and Anholt, R. (2016). Resilience as the EU Global Strategy's New Leitmotif: Pragmatic, Problematic or Promising? *Contemporary Security Policy, 37*(3): 414–430.

Annexes

Annex 1
Content analysing the Joint Declarations of the Eastern Partnership Summits in 2009–2017

As highlighted by the contributions to this edited volume and the public, political and scholarly debate on the Eastern Partnership (EaP) at large, the 'Eastern Partnership' represents a highly politicized – and mythologized – political undertaking. The many and multilayered official discourses even of EaP participants themselves reveal issues related to the misperception, miscommunication and misunderstanding of the EaP's rationale and practice. In a situation where the discourses and narratives surrounding the EaP become increasingly politicized and contested, corpus analysis of the key official texts on the EaP seems to be timely, promising and, in fact, needed. It helps to uncover temporarily fixed meanings of both the key parameters of the EaP and key facets of the shared discourse by the EU and the six EaP partner countries (EaP-6) about the participants' multilateral and bilateral relations.

In what follows, the five Joint Declarations adopted in the wake of the EaP Summits during 2009–2017 are qualitatively content analysed and presented. The presentation of the findings is preceded by a brief overview of the EaP Summits and other meeting formats in 2009–2020 and a brief methodological note.

The EaP Summits and the Joint Declarations as a corpus: an overview

From 2009 until 2020, five official EaP Summits took place.

The *first* – inaugural – EaP Summit was held on 7 May 2009 in Prague. The EaP Prague Summit Joint Declaration outlined the contours of a 'more ambitious partnership' between the EU and the EaP-6 (Armenia, Azerbaijan, Belarus, Georgia, Moldova and Ukraine) and stipulated the initiative's main goal, notably 'to create the necessary conditions to accelerate political association and further economic integration between the European Union and interested partner countries'.[1]

The *second* EaP Summit was held on 29–30 September 2011 in Warsaw. The EaP Warsaw Summit Joint Declaration positively assessed the progress in implementing the EaP flagship initiatives and called inter alia for 'a deeper bilateral engagement' and the simultaneous 'strengthening of multilateral cooperation'.[2] Since 2011, the (positive) conditionality principle 'more for more' became a new facet of the structured engagement by the EU and the EaP-6.

The *third* EaP Summit took place on 28–29 November 2013 in Vilnius. While surveying potential achievements generated since 2011, the Vilnius EaP Summit also aimed at showing 'the way ahead'.[3] This was of symbolic importance, given the broader background of rising tensions between the EU and Russia and unexpected developments in EU-EaP-6 bilateral relations. Whereas during the EaP Vilnius Summit, Moldova and Georgia initialled their respective Association Agreement with the EU, Ukraine failed to sign its Association Agreement (initialled already in March 2021). In turn, Armenia decided to terminate negotiations over an Association Agreement with the EU as, in September 2013, it began talks to join the Russia-led Eurasian Economic Union.

The *fourth* EaP Summit was held on 21–22 May 2015 in Riga. The Riga EaP Summit Joint Declaration acknowledged the need for further differentiation of the EU's relations with six EaP countries, while recalling that the EaP is founded on 'shared ownership, responsibility, differentiation and mutual accountability'.[4] Notably, in the wake of the unfolding Russian aggression in Ukraine, 'conflict resolution' ranked high on the EaP Riga Summit agenda, and the Joint Declaration reflects the participating partners' commitment to peaceful resolution of unresolved conflicts in the region.

The *fifth* EaP Summit was held on 24 November 2017 in Brussels. Under the motto 'stronger together', the Brussels EaP Summit Joint Declaration called for partners' renewed efforts to promote the peaceful settlement of unresolved conflicts, and support territorial integrity, independence and sovereignty of all partners, and it laid out the paths towards the strengthening of cooperation towards a stronger economy, governance, connectivity and society.[5] Annex 1 to the Brussels EaP Summit Joint Declaration sets out, for the first time, a catalogue of more operationalizable EaP objectives – the so-called '20 Deliverables for 2020' – that revolved around four priority areas of cooperation, as mentioned above. It also bridged partners' commitments towards so-called 'cross-cutting deliverables', including enhanced engagement with civil society organizations, promotion of societal inclusivity and non-discrimination, and strengthening of strategic communications among all partners.

The EaP Summit that was initially planned for 2019 was cancelled due to Brexit, i.e. the United Kingdom's withdrawal from the EU.

On 18 June 2020, a meeting of EU and EaP countries' leaders took place in the format of teleconference and served as platform to review progress made throughout the first ten years of the EaP, and to set priorities for the expected sixth EaP Summit in 2021.

None of the formal and informal meetings of EU and EaP countries' leaders after 2017 resulted in the adoption of joint declarations, as is usually the case at the end of EaP Summit meetings.

The next – *sixth* – EaP Summit is planned to be held in Brussels in December 2021.

On method: corpus linguistics and textual analysis of the EaP Summit Joint Declarations

To offer a structured reflection on the EaP official discourse, as instituted in the respective EaP Summit Joint Declarations, this Annex draws on corpus linguistics and textual analysis methods and techniques within the computer-assisted qualitative content analysis approach.

The sample of documents analysed includes five EaP Summit Declarations, adopted in the period from 2009 until 2017. Both the within-document and multi-document textual analyses of the sampled documents was performed with the use of the *Atlas.ti* software for computer-aided qualitative data analysis.[6]

The analysis built on *corpus linguistic* approaches and several computer-assisted content-analytical methods and techniques.[7] The *wordscores* procedure, a computationally technique of deriving scores for words based on the count of their frequency and/or relative (i.e. rescaled) position vis-à-vis other scored words,[8] was i.a. deployed to map out the frequency of occurrences of EaP-6 country names, or specific EaP policy parameters, such as 'gradual rapprochement' or 'conditionality'.

By taking the textual analysis to the next level – notably 'from words to numbers'[9] – this study, furthermore, built on the *coding* of the textual data and the subsequently applied techniques of *text statistics*. Textual data (quasi-sentences) were coded into several clustered codes, including 'country:', 'year:', 'policy issue:', and 'core:' (the latter stands for essential policy clauses and partnership principles). No aggregate-level grouping of codes was undertaken in order to limit the interpretative bias and, thus, the Annex presents the content and the rhetoric of the sampled documents as explicitly stated. The received structured and quantified textual data was further processed in co-occurrence and salience analyses. A country-policy issue *co-occurrence* (association and correlation) analysis was deployed to reveal the extent and variation of EaP policy issues' association with each of the six EaP countries. An *issue salience* analysis, in turn, helped reveal the weight of policy issues identified in each EaP Summit Joint Declaration and their dynamics throughout the years as well as their overall significance in the period studied.

EaP Summit Joint Declarations 2009–2017: qualitative corpus analysis findings

The content analysis of the five Joint Declarations adopted in the wake of biennial EaP Summits over the eight-year period 2009–2017 reveals a number of regularities and patterns in the official discourse co-shaped by the EU and the EaP-6. First and foremost, the frequency of each *EaP country mentioning* strongly correlates with the status and level of ambitions of partners in so far as the associated EaP-3 feature nearly twice as much as the non-associated EaP countries, with Armenia standing out as being 'in-between' these two groups (see *Figure A1.1*).

The salience attributed to the two foundational principles of bilateral relationship dynamization – *'gradual rapprochement' and 'differentiation'* – is country-wise variegated and inversely proportional: the higher the emphasis on rapprochement, the lesser the emphasis on differentiation (see *Figure A1.2*). Hence, in terms of differentiation, two groups of EaP countries manifest themselves: the associated EaP-3 (lower differentiation) and the non-associated EaP countries (higher emphasis on differentiation). As far as the forging of closer ties and gradual rapprochement clauses are concerned, these vary from very low (Belarus – 3) to moderate (Azerbaijan – 6; Armenia – 7; Georgia – 8) to high (Ukraine – 10; Moldova – 11), as co-occurrence analysis shows (see *Figure A1.2 and Table A1.1*). The reference to *'partnership'* as an underlying form of bilateral engagement has a different pattern, reflective of the state of each EU-EaP bilateralism in question: from the lowest (17 occurrences in the case of Belarus) to two intermediate levels (Azerbaijan – 24, Armenia – 30), up to where partnership features as the most salient mode of engagement (Ukraine – 39; Moldova – 42; Georgia – 44) in discursive terms (see *Table A1.1*). Similar patterns are observable as well as, with regard to the *clauses on the sharedness of norms and values, rules, principles* and the overall attribution of

284   ANNEXES

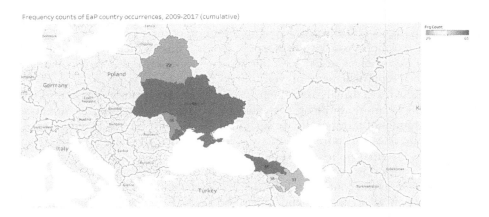

Figure A1.1 Occurrences of countries in EaP Joint Declarations 2009–2017.
Source: Own elaboration based on *Atlas.ti*-powered content analysis data (visualization in *Tableau*).

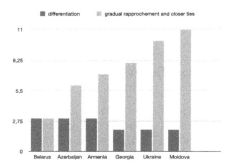

Figure A1.2 Co-occurrences of 'gradual rapprochement' and 'differentiation' clauses vis-à-vis EaP countries in EaP Joint Declarations 2009–2017.
Source: Own elaboration based on *Atlas.ti*-powered content analysis data.

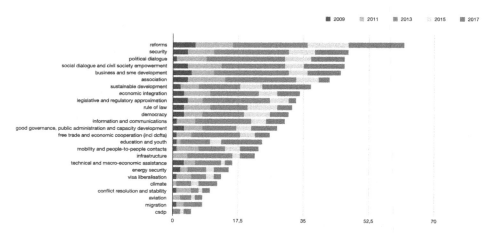

Figure A1.3 Distribution dynamics of policy issues in EaP Joint Declarations throughout 2009–2017 (no. of occurrences).
Source: Own elaboration based on *Atlas.ti*-powered content analysis data.

ANNEX 1 285

strategicness to bilateral relations, save the principle of *conditionality* that co-occurs only vis-à-vis Belarus (see *Table A1.1*).

Across the whole array of policy issues raised in the EaP Joint Declarations 2009–2017, the associated EaP-3 countries appear to be most-connected, with two South Caucasian republics (Armenia and Azerbaijan) forming a separate group of densely *co-occurring EaP*

Table A1.1 Co-occurrences of policy clauses and partnership principles vis-à-vis EaP countries in EaP Joint Declarations 2009–2017

	Armenia	Azerbaijan	Belarus	Georgia	Moldova	Ukraine
core: conditionality			1			
core: differentiation	3	3	3	2	2	2
core: gradual rapprochement and closer ties	7	6	3	8	11	10
core: membership aspirations						
core: partnership	30	24	17	44	42	39
core: principles	1	1		3	2	4
core: rules and norms	4	3	2	6	4	5
core: strategic relations	2	2	2	4	4	4
core: values	2	2	1	3	3	3

Source: Own elaboration based on *Atlas.ti*-powered content analysis data.

Table A1.2 EaP countries co-occurrences in EaP Joint Declarations 2009–2017

	Armenia	Azerbaijan	Belarus	Georgia	Moldova	Ukraine
country: Armenia		24	14	29	28	26
country: Azerbaijan	24		16	23	23	20
country: Belarus	14	16		14	14	14
country: Georgia	29	23	14		40	38
country: Moldova	28	23	14	40		38
country: Ukraine	26	20	14	38	38	

Source: Own elaboration based on *Atlas.ti*-powered content analysis data.

Table A1.3 Co-occurrences of policy issues vis-à-vis EaP countries in EaP Joint Declarations 2009–2017

	Armenia	Azerbaijan	Belarus	Georgia	Moldova	Ukraine
policy issue: association	7	6	3	12	13	11
policy issue: aviation	5	4		6	7	6
policy issue: business and sme development	5	3	3	8	6	7
policy issue: climate	1			1	1	1
policy issue: conflict resolution and stability	1	1		3	1	1
policy issue: csdp				3	3	3
policy issue: democracy			1	2	1	2
policy issue: economic integration	6	4	3	9	10	10
policy issue: education and youth	4	3	4	4	5	4
policy issue: energy security	5	3	2	6	7	7
policy issue: free trade and economic cooperation (incl dcfta)	7	5	3	11	11	10
policy issue: good governance, public administration and ca...	1			3	2	2
policy issue: information and communications	3	2	2	5	4	5
policy issue: infrastructure	6	5	2	8	9	9
policy issue: legislative and regulatory approximation	7	6	5	8	7	8
policy issue: migration	3	3	2	3	3	1
policy issue: mobility and people-to-people contacts	8	7	6	8	9	7
policy issue: political dialogue	10	8	11	13	10	12
policy issue: reforms	8	8	6	12	11	11
policy issue: rule of law	4	4	4	7	5	6
policy issue: security	12	9	6	18	21	20
policy issue: social dialogue and civil society empowerment	6	6	5	11	9	8
policy issue: sustainable development	4	4	2	8	8	8
policy issue: technical and macro-economic assistance	1			3	1	3
policy issue: visa liberalisation	5	5	5	6	7	6

Source: Own elaboration based on *Atlas.ti*-powered content analysis data.

countries and Belarus appearing to be the least-linked country vis-à-vis the remaining partners (see *Table A1.2*).

In terms of specific *policy issues linking to individual EaP countries*, a distinguishable pattern presents itself: the policy issue linkage is considerably higher among the associated EaP-3, whereas the embeddedness of Armenia, Azerbaijan and especially that of Belarus is much more limited (see *Table A1.3*). Security policy and EU association matters as well as reforms, political dialogue and trade and economic integration (including Deep and Comprehensive Free Trade Areas (DCFTA) implementation) highly correlate with references to Georgia, Moldova and Ukraine. Security also looms large in the context of Armenia and Azerbaijan, while it is of marginal relevance in the case of Belarus. The co-occurrence analysis of policy issue and non-EU associated EaP countries' correlations also reveals a number of gaps, i.e. non-correlating or marginally correlating areas, such as democracy and Common Security and Defence Policy (CSDP) cooperation, conflict resolution and stability, cooperation on climate change matters, good governance, public administration and capacity-building as well as technical and macro-economic assistance (see *Table A1.3*, also for further details).

Out of the 25 *policy issues* identified in the EaP Joint Declarations adopted in 2007–2019, seven represent top-salient (discursive) matters of bilateral cooperation (ca. top-30%) and as many fall under the lower-salient policy issues category (ca. bottom-30%), with the remaining 11 policy issues (ca. 40%) enjoying moderate relevance on the agenda for bilateral and multilateral cooperation within the EaP in 2009–2017. Among the *most-salient* bilateral and multilateral engagement matters, the issue of reforms tops the EaP agenda (8.92%) and is closely followed by security (6.76%), political dialogue (6.62%), social dialogue and civil society engagement (6.62%), business and SME development (6.47%), as well as political association with the EU (6.04%) and cooperation on sustainable development (5.32%). The following policy issues exhibit moderate salience (listed in the rank-descending order): economic integration (4.89%); legislative and regulatory approximation (4.75%); enhancement of the rule of law (4.60%) and democracy (4.46%); strengthening of strategic communications (4.32%); capacity-building and development of good governance and public administration (4.03%); enhancement of economic cooperation and free trade, including through the implementation of the DCFTAs (3.74%); stepping up of cooperation in areas of education and youth (3.45%); facilitation of mobility and people-to-people contacts between the EU and the EaP-6 as well as among the latter themselves (3.31%); advancement of connectivity and infrastructure build-up (3.17%); and broadening of the technical and macro-economic assistance (2.30%). Finally, to the policy issues that feature very low on the EaP's overall (i.e. cross-country) cooperation agenda belong cooperation on energy security (2.16%), visa liberalization (1.87%), cooperation on climate change matters (1.73%), matters of conflict resolution and stability (1.44%), cooperation towards the common aviation area (1.15%), migration matters (1.15%) and, lastly, EU-EaP countries' cooperation on CSDP matters (0.72%) (for details on all policy issue occurrences in EaP Joint Declarations, see *Figure A1.3 and Table A1.4*). Importantly, the above-discussed salience analysis data refers to the entire body of EaP Joint Declarations, the EaP in general and the cohort of all six EaP countries. In many cases, this leads to moderation effects as issue salience certainly varies from country to country (see *Table A1.3* for details).[10] Last but not least, the content analysis of the corpus of EaP Joint Declarations adopted at the 2009 and the 2017 EaP Summit reveals a distinguishable discursive shift from focusing on general political and economic matters in

ANNEX 1

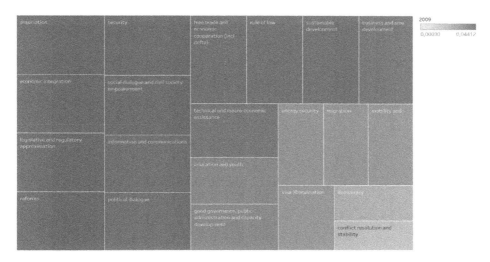

Figure A1.4 Distribution of policy issues in EaP Joint Declaration 2009.
Source: Own elaboration based on *Atlas.ti*-powered content analysis data.

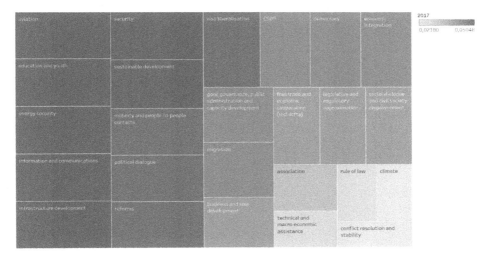

Figure A1.5 Distribution of policy issues in EaP Joint Declaration 2017.
Source: Own elaboration based on *Atlas.ti*-powered content analysis data.

2009 (see *Figure A1.4*) to prioritizing more specific policy issues and areas of bi- and multilateral engagement in 2017 (see *Figure A1.5*), leaving untouched, though, key issues.[11] This combination of flexibility and agility may be emblematic of the dynamic and adaptable nature of the EaP as a goal-driven foreign policy exercise, however, within the fixed strategic parameters.

Table A1.4 Distribution dynamics of policy issues in EaP Joint Declarations throughout 2009–2017 (no. of occurrences and relative shares, %)

Policy issues distribution in EaP Joint Declarations	2009 no. occurrences	2009 share, %	2011 no. occurrences	2011 share, %	2013 no. occurrences	2013 share, %	2015 no. occurrences	2015 share, %	2017 no. occurrences	2017 share, %	TOTALS 2009-2017 total share, %
Reforms	6	11,11%	10	8,26%	20	7,30%	11	10,68%	15	10,49%	8,92%
Security	4	7,41%	7	5,79%	20	7,30%	7	6,80%	9	6,29%	6,76%
Political dialogue	1	1,85%	8	6,61%	21	7,66%	7	6,80%	9	6,29%	6,62%
Social dialogue and civil society empowerment	4	7,41%	9	7,44%	17	6,20%	5	4,85%	11	7,69%	6,62%
Business and sme development	5	9,26%	6	4,96%	20	7,30%	5	4,85%	9	6,29%	6,47%
Association	4	7,41%	10	8,26%	19	6,93%	6	5,83%	3	2,10%	6,04%
Sustainable development	2	3,70%	5	4,13%	11	4,01%	6	5,83%	13	9,09%	5,32%
Economic integration	3	5,56%	7	5,79%	13	4,74%	5	4,85%	6	4,20%	4,89%
Legislative and regulatory approximation	4	7,41%	4	3,31%	18	6,57%	5	4,85%	2	1,40%	4,75%
Rule of law	3	5,56%	7	5,79%	10	3,65%	8	7,77%	4	2,80%	4,60%
Democracy	3	5,56%	5	4,13%	11	4,01%	7	6,80%	5	3,50%	4,48%
Information and communications	1	1,85%	5	4,13%	15	5,47%	4	3,88%	5	3,50%	4,32%
Good governance, public administration and capacity development	3	5,56%	5	4,13%	9	3,28%	4	3,88%	7	4,90%	4,03%
Free trade and economic cooperation (incl dcfta)	1	1,85%	4	3,31%	13	4,74%	4	3,88%	4	2,80%	3,74%
Education and youth	1	1,85%	1	0,83%	8	2,92%	3	2,91%	11	7,69%	3,45%
Mobility and people-to-people contacts	1	1,85%	6	4,96%	7	2,55%	4	3,88%	5	3,50%	3,31%
Infrastructure	0	0,00%	4	3,31%	12	4,38%	2	1,94%	4	2,80%	3,17%
Technical and macro-economic assistance	3	5,56%	3	2,48%	7	2,55%	1	0,97%	2	1,40%	2,30%
Energy security	2	3,70%	2	1,65%	5	1,82%	2	1,94%	4	2,80%	2,16%
Visa liberalisation	1	1,85%	4	3,31%	4	1,46%	2	1,94%	2	1,40%	1,87%
Climate	0	0,00%	1	0,83%	4	1,46%	2	1,94%	5	3,50%	1,73%
Conflict resolution and stability	1	1,85%	4	3,31%	2	0,73%	1	0,97%	2	1,40%	1,44%
Aviation	0	0,00%	2	1,65%	3	1,09%	1	0,97%	2	1,40%	1,15%
Migration	1	1,85%	2	1,65%	3	1,09%	0	0,00%	2	1,40%	1,15%
Csdp	0	0,00%	0	0,00%	2	0,73%	1	0,97%	2	1,40%	0,72%

Source: Own elaboration based on *Atlas.ti*-powered content analysis data.

Notes

1. *Joint Declaration of the Prague Eastern Partnership Summit*, Prague, 7 May 2009, https://www.consilium.europa.eu/media/31797/2009_eap_declaration.pdf
2. *Joint Declaration of the Warsaw Eastern Partnership Summit*, Warsaw, 29–30 September 2011, https://ec.europa.eu/commission/presscorner/api/files/document/print/en/pres_11_341/PRES_11_341_EN.pdf
3. *Joint Declaration of the Vilnius Eastern Partnership Summit*, Vilnius, 28–29 November 2013, https://www.consilium.europa.eu/media/31799/2013_eap-11-28-joint-declaration.pdf
4. *Joint Declaration of the Riga Eastern Partnership Summit, Riga*, 21–22 May 2015, https://www.consilium.europa.eu/media/21526/riga-declaration-220515-final.pdf
5. *Joint Declaration of the Brussels Eastern Partnership Summit*, Brussels, 24 November 2017, https://data.consilium.europa.eu/doc/document/ST-14821-2017-INIT/en/pdf
6. Franzosi, R., Doyle, S., McClelland, L. E., Rankin, C. P., & Vicari, S. (2013). Quantitative narrative analysis software options compared: PC-ACE and CAQDAS (ATLAS. ti, MAXqda, and NVivo). *Quality & Quantity, 47*(6), 3219–3247; Friese, S. (2019). *Qualitative data analysis with ATLAS.ti*, 3rd ed. London: SAGE.
7. Pollach, I. (2012). Taming textual data: The contribution of corpus linguistics to computer-aided text analysis. *Organizational Research Methods, 15*(2), 263–287.
8. Lowe, W. (2008). Understanding wordscores. *Political Analysis, 16*, 356–371.
9. Franzosi, R. (1994). From words to numbers: A set theory framework for the collection, organization, and analysis of narrative data. *Sociological Methodology, 24* 105–136.
10. Note: the data on policy issue salience, as discussed in this section, draws on *code* counting statistics and has not been normalized or weighted according to the code 'weight' (i.e. the word length of the text encapsulated in a code).
11. Note: the data on policy issue salience, as presented in *Figures A1.4* and *A1.5*, draws on *word* counting statistics and has been normalized, that is weighted according to the code 'weight' (i.e. the word length of the text encapsulated in a code).

Annex 2
Studying EU-Eastern Neighbours relations within and beyond the Eastern Partnership in 2009-2020: a bibliometric perspective

As a new, complex and constantly evolving and cross-disciplinary matter, the study of the Eastern Partnership (EaP) shares manifold methodological and theoretical challenges with the study of the European Neighbourhood Policy (ENP), in the framework of which it was conceived and has been operating for already more than one decade. First and foremost, the demarcation of the research object itself presents a substantial challenge; this is followed by the challenge of the ENP's (and EaP's) evolving nature, its broad anchoring in numerous policy areas and fields of study, its lack of ontological and epistemological coherence and proneness to eclecticism, in conjunction with a strong presence of external actors.[1] The foundational question to be asked in this regard is: what do we really study when we study the EaP? By extension, what do we study when we study the EU-Eastern neighbours' relations – both within and beyond the political context of the EaP? Which disciplines, approaches and topics dominate the field? But also: 'Who publishes where?', as a recent study of the geographic diversity of *International Relations* (*IR*) journals sought to reveal.[2] Add to this the question as to what are articles' theoretical lenses and methodological orientations that help identify the epistemic community or communities that have emerged or are still emerging.

This Annex maps the main research traditions and disciplines, areas, topics and objects of study that have produced the major bulk of research on the EaP and EU-Eastern neighbours' relations from 2009 until 2020. Put differently: what is the *'EaP acquis academique'*?

On method: CAQDAS-powered bibliometric and corpus analysis

With the increasing power and functionality of technology, the vastly proliferating academic production increasingly becomes subject of bibliometric analysis – whether to assess the state of the art in the discipline or research area in both national and international contexts.[3] The academic interest in this type of analysis has also emerged in ENP studies and the Europeanization literature in particular.[4] The recent search for epistemic communities as far as the study of the ENP, the EaP and the EU-Russia relations is concerned[5] confirms the rising interest in this traditionally under-represented area of scholarly enquiry.

Bibliometric analysis is essentially about the relational mapping of various attributes of publications within an area of interest, such as volume (quantity and dynamics), authorship, citations, titles, journals, key words or topics. Bibliometric analysis can be used both as a quantitative tool for evaluating scholarly contributions and achievements and as a qualitative tool to reveal research hotspots, patterns and trends as well as more specific features of research design and relationships in general.[6]

Bibliometric research underpinning this Annex has combined both quantitative and qualitative approaches, enhanced by the use of two software tools, notably *VOSviewer* and *Atlas.ti*.

Built on the algorithm for visualizing similarity, *VOSviewer* is an analytical and visualization tool for processing bibliometric network data. It enables the construction of *lexical (semantic), spatial and temporal networks* that reflect patterns of keyword co-occurrence, geographical spread and temporal dynamics of the publications studied.[7] In the *VOSviewer* output graphs, the relatedness of terms is determined on the basis of their co-occurrence in the sampled documents, and the smaller the distance between two terms, the stronger they are related to each other. If there is more than one group of closely related terms, the terms are presented in clusters of related terms, distinctly coloured on the network maps.

Rather than being a mere metaphor, network analysis was used as a method to study relationships and patterns as well as implications of those relationships, such as the strength of association. The *VOSviewer* network analysis tool was used to process (analyze, cluster and visualize) bibliographic data extracted from the output file of the Web of Science database search. Keywords were selected from all the text corpus containing article titles and abstracts. The generated semantic term maps provide clues on major research objects, areas as well as their relationship – in other words: an overview of the state of the art of the research field.

Whilst being a considerable support tool for large-scale and broad-brush quantitative bibliometric review, this semi-automatized approach, however, reaches its limits where topics, ideas and research agendas need to be looked at in a more structured and tailored manner. It is where qualitative approach can deliver, and it was pursued here with the technological support of a CAQDAS tool, notably *Atlas.ti*.

In terms of literature review and bibliometric analysis, *Atlas.ti* provides for a synthesis and thematic analysis, describing the state of the art of knowledge and identifying gaps of the given scholarship.[8] This allows to 'describe the forest, not the trees'. It helps to develop arguments and tell a compelling story about the publications in question.[9] With content analysis and methodological coding at its heart, *qualitative corpus analysis* with *Atlas.ti* allows for further quantification of the content-analytical output and appliance of some crucial data-analytical techniques, like frequency (occurrence) and co-occurrence analysis. *Frequency* often represents the first point of entry into a text corpus. In corpus linguistic terms, frequency is the count of items appearing in a corpus (be those words or codes applied to the text passages). In turn, *co-occurrence* analysis is used in scientometric research to study the strength of association (proximity) between a multitude of relevant data coded, such as authors, journals, publication years, topics, research objects, concepts and methods. Combined, these two techniques enable the detection of salience (of topics, for instance), literature trend analysis or (non-statistical) correlations between select analytical categories. For further statistical correlation analysis of the mined data, other generic software and applications, or specialized statistical analysis tools, such as IBM SPSS, are usually deployed.

The scientific landscape of the EaP *acquis académique* in 2009–2020: a bibliometric analysis

As an area of research, the EaP *acquis académique* can be understood *narrowly* as a record of publications that deal explicitly and exclusively with the 'Eastern Partnership' as a topic or, more *broadly*, as an area of academic enquiry into the EaP as a policy framework

ANNEX 2

in its own right and also as a bulk of bilateral relations between the EU and its Eastern neighbours within and beyond the EaP. The keyword search of articles in the *Web of Science Core Collection* database for 'Eastern Partnership' as a topic returned some 323 records for the period 2009–2020. When the search is limited to journal articles alone, this figure further drops to some 265 publications for over the past ten years; this means roughly 24 articles published annually. When the search is narrowed down even further to include just the titles of the articles, the result is 126 *WoS*-indexed journal article publications. Accepting a narrow understanding of EaP scholarship would thus have substantially (and superficially) limited the scope of analysis and under-represented the broader debate since 2009. This Annex, therefore, draws on a broader understanding of the EaP *acquis academique* that was sourced for bibliometric analysis as follows.

The data gathering occurred in several steps. At first, articles and their bibliographic data were sourced from the *Web of Science Core Collection* database, as recorded in WoS SSCI and ESCI indexes between 2009 and 2020 (inclusive). The WoS *topic search* function used to select relevant publications based on the keyword match in either title, abstract, author-provided keywords or keywords generated via *WoS Keywords Plus* function.[10] The topic-keyword search returned 265 publications for 'Eastern Partner*', 131 publications for 'EU AND Eastern Neighbo*', 978 records for 'EU AND Ukraine', 208 records for 'EU AND Georgia', 199 records for 'EU AND Moldova', 147 records for 'EU AND Belarus', 93 records for 'EU AND Armenia' and 73 records for 'EU AND Azerbaijan'. In total, 2094 publications on the EU-Eastern neighbours' relations within and beyond the EaP framework were retrieved for the period 2009–2019. The filtering of the search results for relevance (with a selection threshold of 60%), discipline (non-social science publications were excluded), and duplications (across the eight search-output files) allowed to bring down the sample to 358 unique journal article publications.

In what follows, this Annex presents the findings of our bibliometric analysis, whereby, in the spirit of methodological triangulation, *VOSviewer* functionality was used to quantitatively process the entire body of EaP scholarship identified, and the *Atlas.ti* was deployed to qualitatively analyze the filtered sample of 358 article publications.

Preliminary examination of the publication record for 'Eastern Partnership' alone reveals a number of characteristics. First, as a research object, the EaP is heavily overshadowed by the so-called Russia factor (see *Figure A2.1*). It is quite emblematic that the most cited article in the field is Richard Sakwa's 2015 publication in *International Affairs* on the 'death of Europe and continental fates after Ukraine'.[11] With 46 citations, this publication tops the cluster of the ten most cited articles (18–46 citations); the block of further 15 publications (or 5%) has been cited between 10 and 17 times; at the same time, 86 publications (32%) have been cited just 1 to 3 times, whereas 118 out of 265 journal articles (45%) have not been cited at all.[12] The average citation of 3.13 per item and the unevenness in citation practices do not only provide evidence of how 'divided we write' but also demonstrate the second main characteristic of EaP scholarship – the absence of dialogue within the epistemic community. Third, even within the narrow sample of EaP scholarship, the sound of it is hardly discernible – due to the multitude of unconnected soundscapes. As regards broader dimensions of EU-Eastern neighbours' relations within and beyond the EaP, existing scholarship looks even more fragmented. Even though distinct trends are in general lacking, the most connected research topics and objects form six identifiable clusters of analysis (*research positioning*) are as follows: EU neighbourhood policy; security and relations with Russia; EU Member States' policies; economic interactions; mobility and migration; Association Agreements and DCFTAs (see clustered networks in *Figure A2.1*). Fourth, in spite of the low and uneven levels of scholarly production, EaP scholarship has experienced accelerated growth after 2013, as three spikes have emerged to date, notably in 2011, 2017 and 2019 (see *Figure A2.2*). Fifth, the volume of journal articles published on the EU relations with each of the six EaP countries is quite unequal.

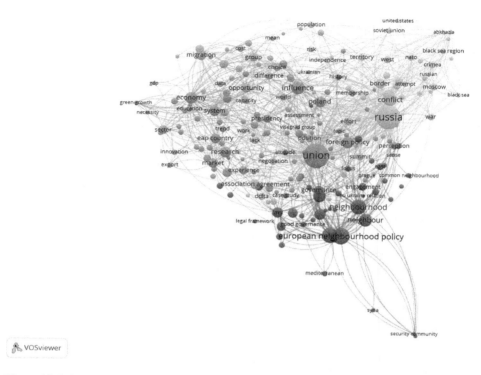

Figure A2.1 Semantic map of the EaP scholarship 2009–2020: a clustered term networks view.
Source: Own elaboration based on WoS Core Collection data processed and visualized with VOSviewer.

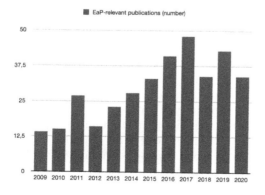

Figure A2.2 The EaP scholarship 2009–2020: publication performance.
Source: Own elaboration based on WoS Core Collection data.

ANNEX 2

The graphs and publication numbers provided above help evaluate how the field of EaP research has grown for more than ten years, and so does the semantic map, presenting networked clusters of co-occurring research topics and objects. Thus, in order to zoom in on hotspots, trends and inherent features of the EaP *acquis academique*, qualitative corpus analysis of the sampled 358 journal articles was further performed.

First, all sampled publications were manually coded with 11 codes each: article author(s) [a:]; publication year [y:]; journal title [j:]; topic [t:]; the Eastern Partnership country concerned [eapc:]; external actors involved [act:]; article's research design [rd:]; research methods [rm:]; theoretically, conceptually or empirically informed research [eot:]; discipline [disc:]; and regional designation or delineation marker [regio:]. The *Atlas.ti*-powered coding and content analysis output contained 805 codes and 5777 links established between codes in total.

Out of 358 articles examined, 32 were published in *East European Politics*, 23 in *Europe-Asia Studies,* 20 in *European Security* and the *Journal of Common Market Studies*, respectively, with the *Eastern Journal of European Studies*, featuring 16 publications on the topic, completing the list of the five outlets where debate on the EaP has taken place most frequently (for more details, see *Figure A2.3*).

As was expected, the *EaP country coverage* in the examined articles exhibits high emphasis on Ukraine (112 mentions); a considerably lower frequency of mentions of Georgia (52), Moldova (33) and Armenia (32); and an even lower occurrence of Azerbaijan (26) and Belarus (18) as main foci of analysis (see *Figure A2.4*).[13] The occurrence of the

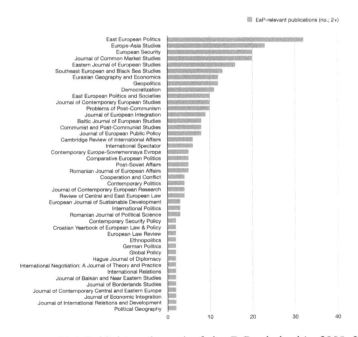

Figure A2.3 Publishing 'homes' of the EaP scholarship 2009–2020: journal outlets and productivity.

Source: Own elaboration based on WoS Core Collection data.

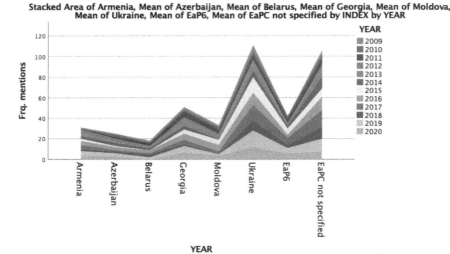

Figure A2.4 Locating the research objects of the EaP scholarship 2009–2020: EaP countries in focus (occurrences).
Source: Own elaboration based on WoS Core Collection data content-analyzed with Atlas.ti.

six EaP countries (EaP-6) as a generic object of study makes up 9.98% (42 mentions) – a number that sharply contrasts with those 25.18% of cases (106 mentions) that do not explicitly specify the EaP in question.[14] The latter indicator loudly speaks about the overly generic and fluid empirical focus of nearly one third of articles examined as well as the methodological flow as regards selecting and specifying the research sample.

The *disciplinary profile* is diverse, judging from the six most productive fields: International Relations & Foreign Policy Analysis (IR&FPA) – 63.27%; Political Science & Public Policy (PolSci&PP) – 19.36%; Economics & International Political Economy (Econ&IPE) – 8.58%; Law – 5.19%; Inter- and Cross-Disciplinary Studies – 3.19% and Comparative Politics – 0.40%. With IR&FPA and PolSci&PP clearly dominating and accounting together for 82.63%, other disciplinary 'pillars' of EaP scholarship, especially Comparative Politics, are all too thinly represented (see *Figure A2.5*).

In terms of *research design* features, the EaP *acquis academique* 2009–2020 exhibits a number of peculiar trends. First and foremost, conceptual and empirical research became consolidated as two main and equally important analytical approaches, with shares of 42.50% and 45.28% of the articles, respectively. Theory-informed studies account for just some 12.22%, and they mainly feature in IR&FPA research on regional security and Econ&IPE studies on economic integration and convergence (see *Figure A2.5*). Importantly, theory-informed analysis, whilst still scarcely present in the field, has experienced steadfast, though limited, growth in EaP scholarship during 2009–2020.

Single case studies dominate the vast majority of EaP research (40.22%), with *comparative case studies* accounting for a considerably lower share (15.08%). Equally low remains the share of broadly scoped and *comparative region-wide enquiries* ('compRegio' – 18.16%) that are not designed as canonical comparative case studies but feature elements of (sporadic and convenient) comparisons. Last but not least, *exploratory research design* accounts for 26.54% and is represented in empirical, conceptual and – albeit less – theoretically informed studies (see *Figure A2.6*).

ANNEX 2

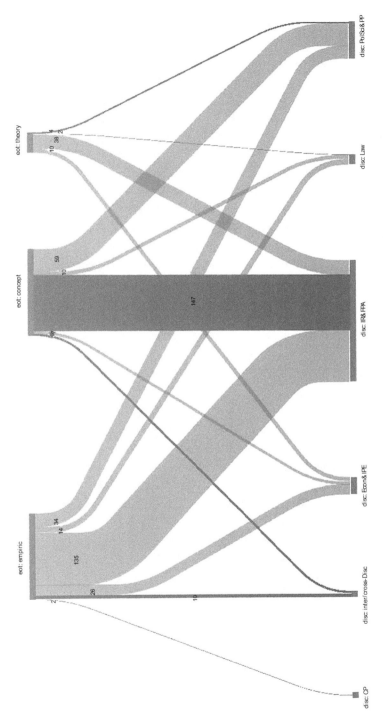

Figure A2.5 The EaP scholarship 2009–2020: disciplinary diversity and main research approaches.

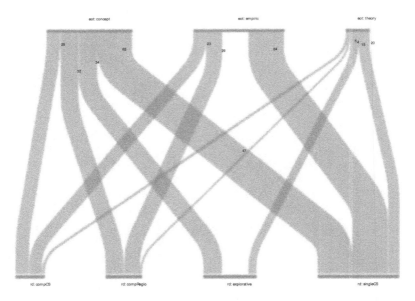

Figure A2.6 The EaP scholarship 2009–2020: main research approaches and research designs.
Source: Own elaboration based on WoS Core Collection data content-analyzed with Atlas.ti (co-occurrence analysis, Sankey diagram visualization).

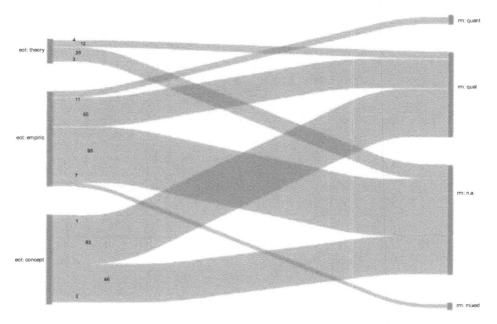

Figure A2.7 The EaP scholarship 2009–2020: main research approaches and research methods.
Source: Own elaboration based on WoS Core Collection data content-analyzed with Atlas.ti (co-occurrence analysis, Sankey diagram visualization).

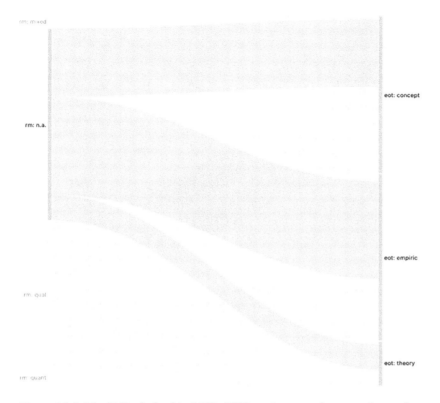

Figure A2.8 The EaP scholarship 2009–2020: main research approaches and research methods (focus on unspecified research methods).

As far as *research methods* are concerned, the EaP *acquis academique* has largely relied on qualitative analysis (40.22%), with quantitative research methods being deployed in just 4.47% of cases and mixed methods accounting for 3.63% (see *Figure A2.7*). More than half of the EaP literature (51.68%) does not explicitly specify and rely on any concrete research methods (see *Figure A2.8*). This is a finding, particularly visible in empirical studies (95 occurrences of articles with non-specified research methods) and concept-based studies (66 occurrences). A diametrically opposite situation can be observed in the case of qualitative research-based studies that clearly dominate conceptual analyses (83 occurrences) and are strongly present in empirical studies (50 occurrences).

The *temporal dynamics* of EaP research production in 2009–2020 reveals a steady trend of a consolidating body of literature that does not rely on explicitly specified research methods (see *Figure A2.9*). Except for qualitative research methods-based studies, experiencing a significant upswing since 2015, research designs featuring quantitative and mixed methods saw a systematic, though negligible as far as volume is concerned, acceleration (see *Figures A2.10–A2.12*).

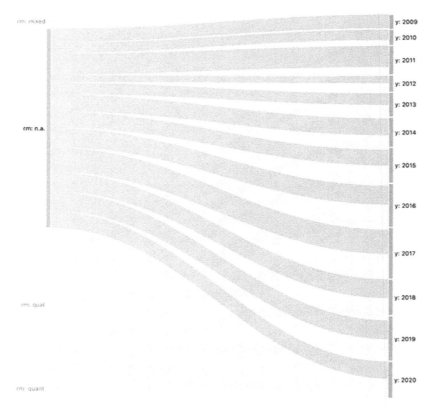

Figure A2.9 The EaP scholarship 2009–2020: research methods development (focus on unspecified research methods).

Data-driven literature review and knowledge mapping: the academic debate on the EaP in 2009–2020

In addition to the detailed bibliometric (meta-)analysis of the sampled publications, the systematic content analysis of the academic debate and discourse along the select parameters helps better map the state of the art in the EaP *acquis academique*. What do we study when we study the EaP, and how we do that are perhaps the two most central questions to ask in this context. Besides key topics and approaches, matters such as geographical delineations and regional designation are equally important areas of enquiry, especially in the context of the EaP's region-building attempts and practices – a truly contested issue area. Finally, as the EaP represents an area of structured bilateral engagement between the EU and the EaP-6, academic curiosity prompts asking questions about the level and density of such bilateral interactions, as well as questions about patterns of intra-EaP engagement and the involvement of external actors in the region more broadly, as represented in the academic debate.

Spatial characteristics of the EaP policy framework

The question of whether the *EaP space* presents, in geographic and political terms, a *regional entity* has long been subject to heated debate both in academia and in politics.

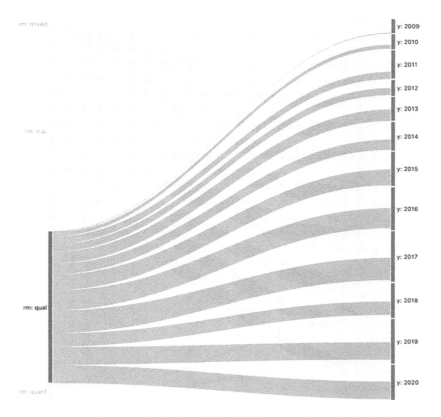

Figure A2.10 The EaP scholarship 2009–2020: research methods development (focus on qualitative research methods).
Source: Own elaboration based on WoS Core Collection data content-analyzed with Atlas.ti (co-occurrence analysis, Sankey diagram visualization).

Critique abounds as regards the intra-regional diversity, or uncommonness, the missing intrinsic intra-regional interactions, and dispersed regional identity facing the (mainly EU-driven) practices of region-building and regionalization from outside. The latter ones include the regularizing of high-level political dialogue, advancing joint policy agendas and thus intensifying contacts between EaP countries' executives, facilitating people-to-people contacts and mobility, as well as putting high stakes on region-bridging infrastructural projects. As the *Atlas.ti*-powered content analysis of the EaP *acquis academique* in 2009–2020 shows, however, approximately half of the literature corpus (47.84%) does not anyhow explicitly delineate the regional identity or belongingness of EaP countries analysed (see *Figure A2.13* for data on region-name occurrences). This finding correlates with the widespread political discourse on the absence of a phenomenon such as the 'EaP region'. The second- and third-most widespread scholarly conventions in designating the space in between the EU and Russia are 'EU's Eastern Neighbourhood' region (17.30%) and 'post-Soviet' region/space (6.22%). Two more regional markers are nearly equally widespread as region-naming conventions, notably 'EaP region' (5.68%) and 'ENP/EU neighbourhood region' (4.05%). The least widespread region-naming conventions with the EU or Russia acting as referent objects

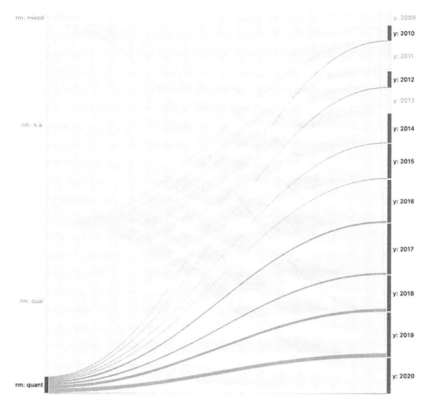

Figure A2.11 The EaP scholarship 2009–2020: research methods development (focus on quantitative research methods).
Source: Own elaboration based on WoS Core Collection data content-analyzed with Atlas.ti (co-occurrence analysis, Sankey diagram visualization).

are: 'new (eastern) Europe' (1.62%), 'EU's near abroad' (0.54%), 'Russia's near abroad (sphere of influence)' (0.54%) and 'wider Europe' (0.27%). The geographic and geostrategic 'in-betweenness' of the countries that form part of the EaP is furthermore encapsulated in non-geographic – but geopolitical – discursive frames that connote EU-Russian great-power competition in the region, such as 'contested neighbourhood' (2.97%), 'shared neighbourhood' (1.89%) and 'common neighbourhood' (0.54%). Finally, the relevant academic discourse also features more neutral *a* geopolitical regional designations such as 'Eastern Europe region' (3.78%), with respective sub-regional components – the 'South Caucasus region' (4.59%) and the 'Black Sea region' (2.16%) (see *Figure A2.13* for all details on occurrences).

Besides this variegated data on region-designation practices (occurrences), EaP scholarship manifests three more foundational characteristics in this regard. First, even the same authors use distinct region-naming conventions, depending on the topic and outlet of their article publication. Second, in a retrospective, the avoidance of region specification has gained ground and became consolidated as a widespread tradition since 2009, and particularly since 2016 – from 6 mentions in 2009 to 28 articles in 2019 that omit explicitly specifying the region studied (see *Figure A2.14*). Similarly, but on a much lower scale, the

ANNEX 2

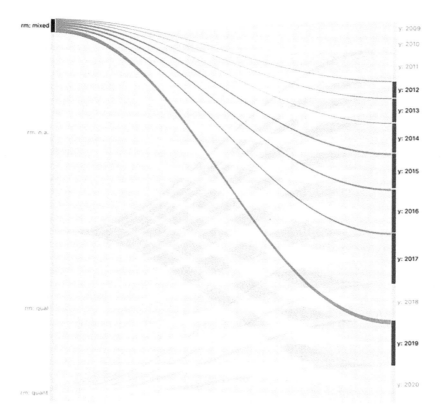

Figure A2.12 The EaP scholarship 2009–2020: research methods development (focus on mixed research methods).
Source: Own elaboration based on WoS Core Collection data content-analyzed with Atlas.ti.

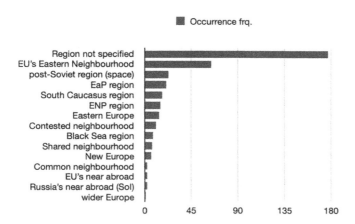

Figure A2.13 The spatial dimension of the EaP: occurrences of space designations in the EaP scholarship 2009–2020.
Source: Own elaboration based on WoS Core Collection data content-analyzed with Atlas.ti.

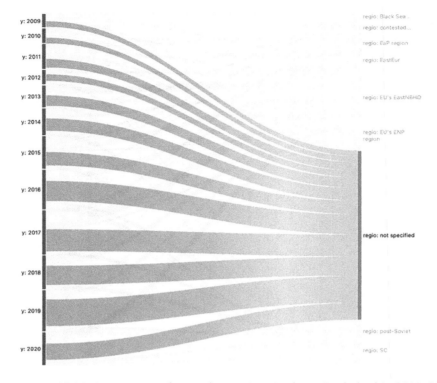

Figure A2.14 Occurrences of space designations in the EaP scholarship 2009–2020 (focus on non-specified regionality of the EaP).

proliferation of the regional marker 'EU's Eastern Neighbourhood' became consolidated for the past decade – from 1 mention in 2009 to 8 in 2020, with a spike of 11 occurrences occurring in the titles of articles published in 2017 (see *Figure A2.15*). Rather surprisingly and paradoxically, the term 'post-Soviet space/region' has not become anachronic for the past decade; it equally became consolidated, though at a truly negligible scale – from 1 occurrence in the titles of articles in 2011 to 4 mentions in 2020 (see *Figure A2.16*). Importantly, the reference to 'post-Soviet space' was oftentimes used for both the designation of the EaP space and a broader regional entity, comprising more than six Eastern European and Central Asian countries that were formerly part of the Soviet Union. Third, there is no clear and coherent pattern of regional designation even when a single EaP country is considered, as the co-occurrence analysis shows. With a precision on the proportional flow between variables (nodes) within a network, the *Sankey* diagram (see *Figure A2.17*) clearly visualizes the variegated and inconsistent discursive practice.

Thus, the data-driven literature review unequivocally confirms high diversity and incoherence of the EaP *acquis academique* 2009–2020 as regards the discourse on the region and space that is encompassed by the EaP.

Intra-EaP connections and comparisons

Somewhat more consistent, though uneven, practices are identifiable in the realm of within-regional comparison between sets of EaP countries, as established in the EaP

ANNEX 2

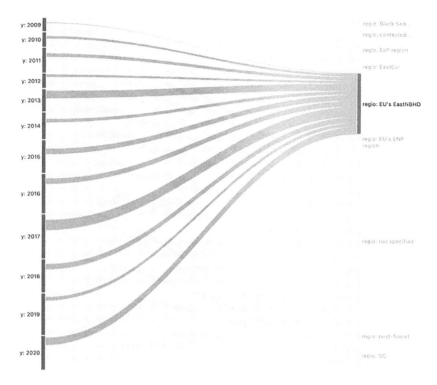

Figure A2.15 Occurrences of space designations in the EaP scholarship 2009–2020 (focus on the EaP space as the 'EU's Eastern neighbourhood region').
Source: Own elaboration based on WoS Core Collection data content-analyzed with Atlas.ti (co-occurrence analysis, Sankey diagram visualization).

acquis académique in 2009–2020 (see *Figure A2.18*). With a total of 58 links, i.e. cases of within-EaP comparison, Georgia tops the list of the most compared EaP countries (see *Figure A2.19*).[15] Georgia is most frequently compared with Azerbaijan (20 co-occurrences) and Armenia (19 co-occurrences), mainly within the South Caucasus sub-regional dimension; a comparative outlook on Georgia-Ukraine dyad profiles the subsequent 11 cases, and the Georgia-Moldova dyad features as an object of comparison in 8 articles. The next best-connected EaP country in terms of comparative analysis is Armenia (40 co-occurring comparisons) chiefly in the sub-regional South Caucasus perspective (19 cases of Armenia-Georgia and 18 cases of Armenia-Azerbaijan constellations and interactions forming the subject of comparison), with negligible analytical bridges made to the cases of Belarus, Moldova and Ukraine (see *Figure A2.20*). A similar situation is to be observed in Azerbaijan's connections as regards intra-EaP comparative outlooks (42 co-occurrences in total) (see *Figure A2.21*). With 30 and 23 co-occurrent cases of comparison, respectively, Ukraine and Moldova are mostly compared with each other (12 cases) as well as with Georgia (11 cases of Ukraine-Georgia and 8 cases of Moldova-Georgia comparison) (see *Figures A2.22 and A2.23*). With just five links EaP-wide, Belarus is the least-studied EaP country in a comparative context, as it features in studies along with Ukraine, Moldova and Armenia but, interestingly, not along Azerbaijan (see *Figure A2.24*).

ANNEXES

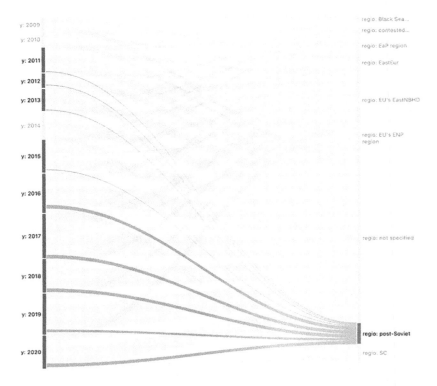

Figure A2.16 Occurrences of space designations in the EaP scholarship 2009–2020 (focus on the EaP space as the 'post-Soviet region/space').
Source: Own elaboration based on WoS Core Collection data content-analyzed with Atlas.ti (co-occurrence analysis, Sankey diagram visualization).

Thus, two trends are identifiable in this respect: the EaP countries are chiefly studied in their sub-regional – South Caucasian – context or in the framework of the EU's association with the EaP-3.

External (f)actors

Since recently, the research programme of EaP scholarship has begun to expand to include also insights into the role of *external actors* in the development of the EaP and EU-Eastern neighbours' relations at large. Equally, comparative analysis beyond the EaP's regional scope have started to emerge. Besides the immense focus on the EU as an actor and cooperation partner in EaP development,[16] the vast share of literature explores the EaP and EU-Eastern neighbours' relations with an eye on Russia (123 co-occurrences); much less attention was paid to the role of EU Member States (31 co-occurrence cases)[17] and EU institutions (23 co-occurrences)[18] (see *Figure A2.25*). Zooming in on other external actors and factors (beyond the EU, its Member States and institutions, or Russia) allows to discern a number of region-adjacent and out-of-area (f)actor analyses (see *Figure A2.26*). In most of the cases, it was Ukraine that was studied

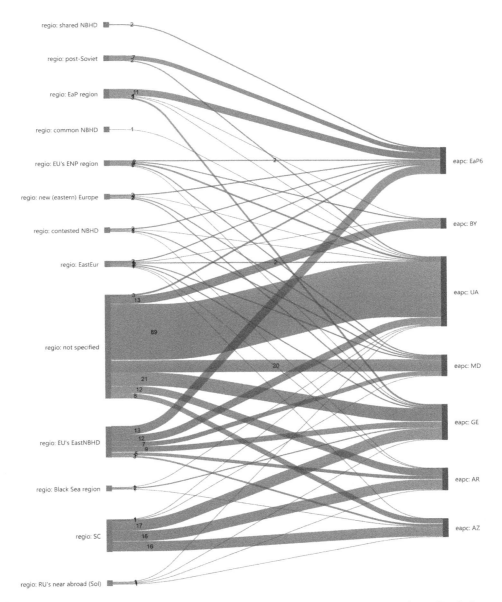

Figure A2.17 Co-occurrences of space designations and EaP countries in the EaP scholarship 2009–2020.
Source: Own elaboration based on WoS Core Collection data content-analyzed with Atlas.ti (co-occurrence analysis, Sankey diagram visualization).

in connection to external actors such as the collective 'West', Israel and Palestine, Serbia and Kosovo, the United Kingdom and the United States, the WTO and other economic agents, including International Financial Institutions. By contrast, the focus on Azerbaijan was extended solely to include Iran as an actor in the region. Furthermore,

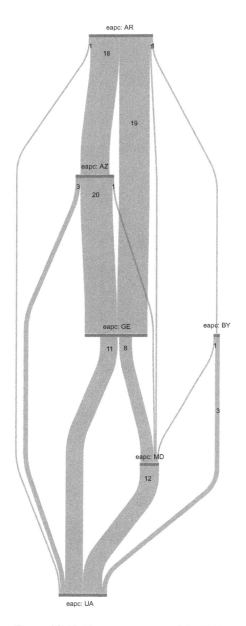

Figure A2.18 Co-occurrences of the EaP countries as objects of comparative analyses in the EaP scholarship 2009–2020.

Source: Own elaboration based on WoS Core Collection data content-analyzed with Atlas.ti (co-occurrence analysis, Alluvial diagram visualization).

comparisons were drawn between the EaP-6/post-Soviet and Western Balkans, Mediterranean as well as Latin American regional dynamics; the roles of NATO, Turkey and Kazakhstan were also examined in the context of EaP development (see *Figure A2.26*).

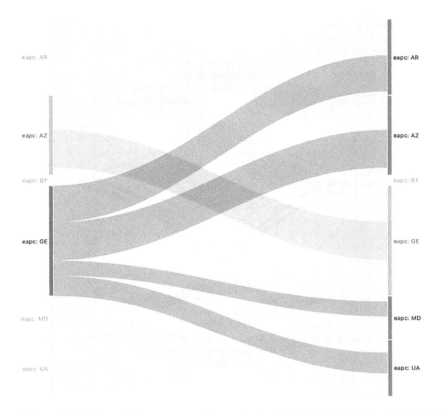

Figure A2.19 Georgia in a comparative outlook of the EaP scholarship 2009–2020.

Salient versus neglected issue areas and topics studied

Detailed bibliometric and content analysis of EaP-relevant publications in 2009–2020 reveals an array of 231 issues, topics and approaches studied for the past decade. Such a number of items makes the sample truly diffuse and unfit for an analysis of basic publication trends, topic-wise. Whereas the most neglected issue areas are showcased in detail 'as they are' in *Figure A2.27* (the smaller the font size, the lesser-researched an issue is), the following discussion is driven by the clustered analysis of aggregated topics (29 topic clusters in total).

The examination of the body of the 2009–2020 EaP literature, broadly scoped, suggests that, along with the three categories of the established, rather well-researched and under-researched topic clusters, there is also an outlier (see *Figure A2.28*).

As the clear *outlier*, EU–Russia competition and regional security matters account for 14.84% in overall topic salience (with 7.93% and 6.91% each, respectively). This is more than double their weight as just 2 categories out of 29 topic clusters: these 2 categories featured in 78 and 68 case analyses, respectively.

Next on the list, 11 topic clusters form the category of *well-researched or established topics* (with 40 to 58 treatments in the literature). Hereto belong, in the descending

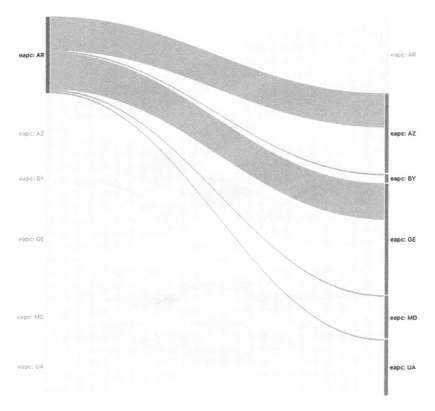

Figure A2.20 Armenia in a comparative outlook of the EaP scholarship 2009–2020.
Source: Own elaboration based on WoS Core Collection data content-analyzed with Atlas.ti (co-occurrence analysis, Sankey diagram visualization).

rank order, the following broad issue areas: state-building and transformation, including revolutions and reforms (5.89%); EU diplomacy and performance (5.69%); EU bilateral relations with the EaP countries (5.59%); the development of the EaP as such (5.39%); EU external governance, diffusion of norms and policies, including rules transfer (5.18%); power politics and regional contestation (5.18%); EU security actorness, including crisis management and conflict mediation (4.88%); EU democracy promotion and EU-induced regime change in the Eastern neighbourhood (4.67%); European integration and Europeanization beyond EU borders (4.67%); national security matters of select EaP countries (4.57%); and EU neighbourhood politics broadly seen (4.07%).

Further seven clustered topics, enjoying treatment in 20 to 38 case studies, make up the category of *moderately well-researched* issue areas and include, in the descending rank order: economic integration and convergence studies (3.86%); internally driven democratization of EaP countries (2.95%); EaP countries' individual strategies and policies of engagement with the EU and other external actors (2.95%); public and political discourses, strategic communications and mutual perceptions (2.74%); EU association

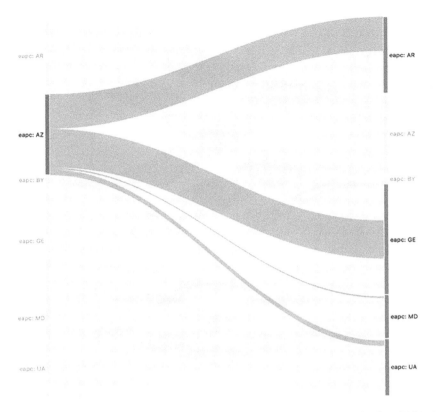

Figure A2.21 Azerbaijan in a comparative outlook of the EaP scholarship 2009–2020.
Source: Own elaboration based on WoS Core Collection data content-analyzed with Atlas.ti (co-occurrence analysis, Sankey diagram visualization).

law and politics (2.54%); EU power projection in the Eastern neighbourhood, including normative, structural and hegemonic/imperial power exercises (2.24%); and mobility and migration matters in EU–EaP countries' relations, including visa liberalization and labour migration dimensions (2.03%).

Finally, the nine remaining topic clusters represent the category of *under-researched* issue areas in the EaP's decadal *acquis academique*. In the rank-descending order, the least researched areas of EU–Eastern neighbours' relations and EaP development are: EU–EaP countries' cross-border cooperation and transgovernmental interactions (1.93%); the impact of Eurasian integration on EU–EaP countries' relations and the EaP in general (1.63%); EaP region-building and regionalization both endogenously and exogenously (1.32%); regional energy security matters and energy geopolitics (1.32%); identity in the context of unfolding processes in the EaP area (1.22%); EU–EaP countries' shared values and norms as well as convergence/divergence dynamics (1.12%); environmental politics and 'green' transition in the region and as a matter of EU–EaP-6 relations (0.71%); the development of EaP countries' relations with Russia in the context of EaP dynamics, and vice versa (0.41%); and, finally, enquiries into

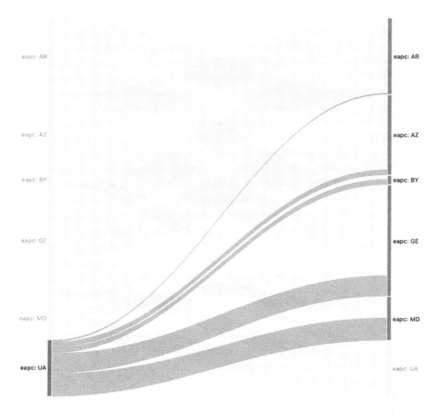

Figure A2.22 Ukraine in a comparative outlook of the EaP scholarship 2009–2020.

matters of regime persistence and autocratization tendencies in select EaP countries (0.41%).

Overall, the salience analysis data suggests that, within EaP scholarship, security looms large in so far as EU-Russia competition in/over the shared region and regional security matters have attracted vast academic attention. Overwhelmingly EU-centric analyses make up the body of literature that is well or moderately well established in the field, whereas a number of issues in EU-EaP bilateral relations are under-represented in the EaP *acquis academique* (see *Figure A2.28*).

Understandably, the above discussion of topic salience generally refers to the EaP-6 as a referent object. As far as established or under-researched topic areas in the case of each of the EaP-6 are concerned, a different – uneven – picture emerges (see *Table A2.1*). According to the findings from the *SPSS*-based statistical correlation analysis, just a few topics have established themselves in country-specific and region-specific contexts (see *Table A2.2*).

EU-Russia competition features as an established topic in general ($r = 0.677$), with reference to all the EaP-6 countries ($r = 0.601$), Ukraine ($r = 0.788$) and Moldova ($r = 0.589$). Regional security analyses highly correlate with the discussion of the EaP

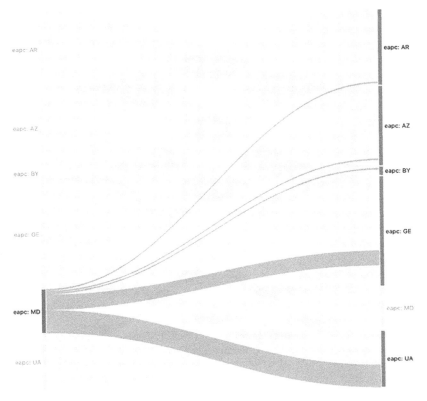

Figure A2.23 Moldova in a comparative outlook of the EaP scholarship 2009–2020.

in general ($r = 0.738$), Ukraine ($r = 0.769$) and Armenia ($r = 0.641$), with similar correlations observed in the case of national security studies and studies of EU security actorness.

Country-wise, research on Moldova has established itself in the field of democratization ($r = 0.851$), EU democracy promotion and EU-induced regime change ($r = 0.658$), EU-Russia competition ($r = 0.589$) and political regime persistence ($r = 0.673$). Research on Georgia highly correlates with identity studies ($r = 0.748$), whereas research on Azerbaijan and Belarus has not yet established itself in any of the identified research areas. Research on Armenia and Ukraine highly correlates with the state of the art in 7 and 11 research fields accordingly, which places these two EaP countries among the most grounded subjects of analysis in a number of issue areas (see *Table A2.2* for more detail).

This data suggests that unevenness permeates existing research output on the EaP and EU-Eastern neighbours relations within and beyond the EaP, and that the apparent state of the art in EaP scholarship as a whole should necessarily be considered as well across the multiple individual dimensions and components it addressed for over the past decade.

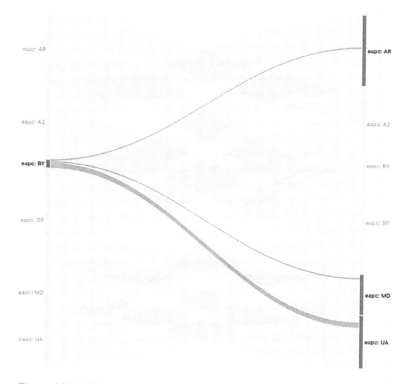

Figure A2.24 Belarus in a comparative outlook of the EaP scholarship 2009–2020.
Source: Own elaboration based on WoS Core Collection data content-analyzed with Atlas.ti (co-occurrence analysis, Sankey diagram visualization).

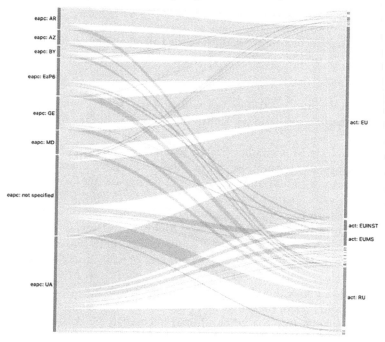

Figure A2.25 Analytical connections: co-occurrences of external actors and EaP countries in the EaP scholarship 2009–2020.
Source: Own elaboration based on WoS Core Collection data content-analyzed with Atlas.ti (co-occurrence analysis, Sankey diagram visualization).

ANNEX 2 315

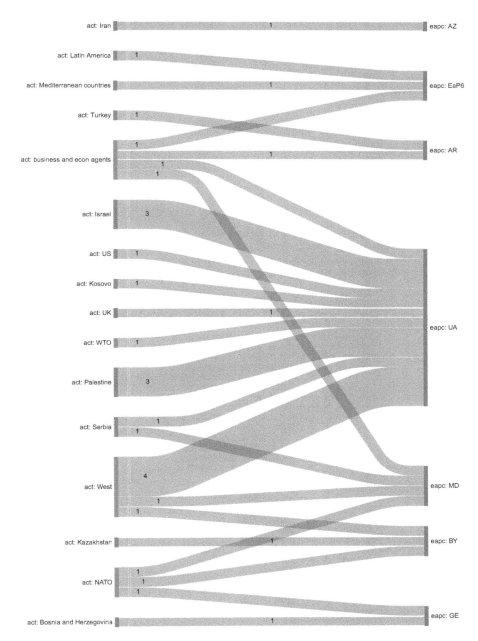

Figure A2.26 Analytical connections: co-occurrences of external actors and EaP countries in the EaP scholarship 2009–2020 (focus on non-EU, EUMS, EUINST and Russia).
Source: Own elaboration based on WoS Core Collection data content-analyzed with Atlas.ti (co-occurrence analysis, Sankey diagram visualization).

Figure A2.27 Issue areas and topical diversity of the EaP scholarship 2009-2020: a comprehensive outlook.

Source: Own elaboration based on WoS Core Collection data content-analyzed with Atlas.ti (salience analysis, Tableau-based world cloud visualization).

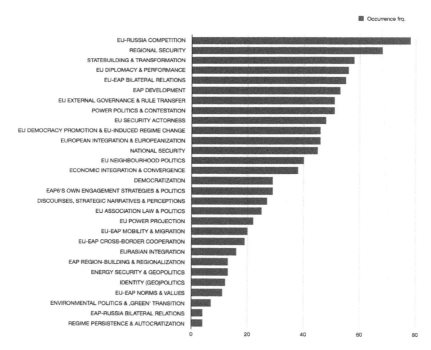

Figure A2.28 Issue areas and topical diversity of the EaP scholarship 2009-2020: a clustered topics outlook.

Source: Own elaboration based on WoS Core Collection data content-analyzed with Atlas.ti (cluster analysis).

Table A2.1 Co-occurrences of clustered topics vis-à-vis EaP countries in the EaP scholarship 2009–2020

	ARMENIA	AZERBAIJAN	BELARUS	GEORGIA	MOLDOVA	UKRANE	EaP6	EaPC NOT SPECIFIED
DEMOCRATIZATION	2	1	4	7	2	8	1	8
DISCOURSES, STRATEGIC NARRATIVES & PERCEPTIONS	5	3	1	5	0	15	2	3
EAP DEVELOPMENT	1	0	0	3	1	13	23	12
EAP REGION-BUILDING & REGIONALIZATION	4	4	1	4	0	2	2	4
EAP-RUSSIA BILATERAL RELATIONS	0	0	1	0	0	0	2	1
EAP6'S OWN ENGAGEMENT STRATEGIES & POLITICS	3	4	5	3	6	5	5	4
ECONOMIC INTEGRATION & CONVERGENCE	3	1	1	4	1	11	4	16
ENERGY SECURITY & GEOPOLITICS	1	4	0	4	0	3	0	5
ENVIRONMENTAL POLITICS & 'GREEN' TRANSITION	0	0	0	1	0	4	0	2
EU ASSOCIATION LAW & POLITICS	0	0	0	7	6	17	2	2
EU DEMOCRACY PROMOTION & EU-INDUCED REGIME CHANGE	6	4	3	5	3	13	4	15
EU DIPLOMACY & PERFORMANCE	7	6	2	11	4	21	7	14
EU EXTERNAL GOVERNANCE & RULE TRANSFER	5	4	3	8	5	15	6	15
EU NEIGHBOURHOOD POLITICS	2	2	3	5	5	10	10	14
EU POWER PROJECTION	4	2	1	3	2	7	1	8
EU SECURITY ACTORNESS	5	4	0	12	8	21	2	7

(Continued)

	ARMENIA	AZERBAIJAN	BELARUS	GEORGIA	MOLDOVA	UKRANE	EaP6	EaPC NOT SPECIFIED
EU-EAP BILATERAL RELATIONS	4	4	6	3	9	27	0	3
EU-EAP CROSS-BORDR COOPERATION	1	1	0	2	2	4	3	8
EU-EAP NORMS & VALUES	3	1	0	3	1	3	1	4
EU-RUSSIA COMPETITION	7	3	3	4	5	21	13	27
EURASIAN INTEGRATION	4	1	3	1	0	3	3	4
EUROPEAN INTEGRATION & EUROPEANIZATION	5	3	1	11	4	21	2	8
IDENTITY	1	1	0	4	1	4	1	2
EU-EAP MOBILITY & MIGRATION	0	0	0	1	4	4	1	13
NATIONAL SECURITY	2	2	1	10	7	22	1	8
POWER POLITICS & CONTESTATION	5	3	4	7	7	12	5	16
REGIME PERSISTENCE & AUTOCRATIZATION	0	0	1	1	1	2	0	1
REGIONAL SECURITY	6	5	2	10	8	28	6	14
STATEBUILDING & TRANSFORMATION	3	3	6	8	8	27	2	13

Source: Own elaboration based on WoS Core Collection data content-analyzed with *Atlas.ti* (co-occurrence analysis).

Table A2.2 Correlations of clustered topics vis-à-vis EaP countries in the EaP scholarship 2009–2020

		Armenia	Azerbaijan	Belarus	Georgia	Moldova	Ukraine	EaP6	EaPC not specified
DEMOCRATIZATION	Pearson Correlation	0,055	−0,034	0,345	0,503	.851**	0,169	0,180	0,210
	Sig. (2-tailed)	0,865	0,917	0,272	0,095	0,000	0,600	0,575	0,512
DISCOURSES, STRATEGIC NARRATIVES & PERCEPTIONS	Pearson Correlation	.659*	0,307	0,158	0,508	−0,154	.808**	.650*	.778**
	Sig. (2-tailed)	0,020	0,332	0,624	0,092	0,632	0,001	0,022	0,003
EAP DEVELOPMENT	Pearson Correlation	0,183	0,094	0,182	0,148	−0,350	0,313	0,563	.696*
	Sig. (2-tailed)	0,569	0,772	0,571	0,646	0,264	0,321	0,056	0,012
EAP REGION-BUILDING & REGIONALIZATION	Pearson Correlation	−0,251	0,215	−0,043	−0,369	−0,411	−0,308	−0,203	−0,216
	Sig. (2-tailed)	0,432	0,502	0,894	0,238	0,184	0,330	0,526	0,500
EAP-RUSSIA BILATERAL RELATIONS	Pearson Correlation	0,064	0,258	0,000	0,000	−0,252	−0,179	−0,125	−0,011
	Sig. (2-tailed)	0,842	0,417	1,000	1,000	0,429	0,577	0,699	0,972
EAP6'S OWN ENGAGEMENT STRATEGIS & POLITICS	Pearson Correlation	0,265	0,111	0,081	0,322	0,313	0,199	0,211	0,333
	Sig. (2-tailed)	0,404	0,732	0,803	0,308	0,321	0,536	0,510	0,290
ECONOMC INTEGRATION & CONVERGENCE	Pearson Correlation	.591*	0,151	−0,041	0,014	−0,072	0,456	0,150	0,514
	Sig. (2-tailed)	0,043	0,640	0,899	0,966	0,824	0,136	0,642	0,087
ENERGY SECURITY & GEOPOLITICS	Pearson Correlation	0,381	0,489	0,047	0,386	−0,299	0,353	0,123	0,187
	Sig. (2-tailed)	0,221	0,107	0,884	0,215	0,346	0,260	0,703	0,561
ENVIRONMENTAL POLITICS & 'GREEN' TRANSITION	Pearson Correlation	0,369	0,214	−0,175	0,496	0,389	0,560	0,395	0,203
	Sig. (2-tailed)	0,238	0,504	0,587	0,101	0,211	0,058	0,203	0,527
EU ASSOCIATION LAW & POLITICS	Pearson Correlation	0,289	0,051	−0,404	0,427	0,396	.751**	.766**	0,326
	Sig. (2-tailed)	0,362	0,876	0,193	0,166	0,202	0,005	0,004	0,300
EU DEMOCRACY PROMOTION & EU-INDUCED REGIME CHANGE	Pearson Correlation	0,331	−0,135	0,110	0,562	.658*	0,435	0,478	0,494
	Sig. (2-tailed)	0,293	0,677	0,734	0,057	0,020	0,158	0,116	0,103
EU DIPLOMACY & PERFORMANCE	Pearson Correlation	0,471	−0,220	−0,420	0,316	0,373	.706*	.611*	0,445
	Sig. (2-tailed)	0,123	0,493	0,174	0,316	0,232	0,010	0,035	0,147
EU EXTERNAL GOVERNANCE & RULE TRANSFER	Pearson Correlation	0,549	0,149	−0,230	0,463	−0,272	0,336	0,447	0,325
	Sig. (2-tailed)	0,065	0,644	0,473	0,130	0,393	0,285	0,145	0,303
EU NEIGHBOURHOOD POLITICS	Pearson Correlation	0,027	−0,086	−0,200	0,443	0,493	−0,012	0,104	−0,132
	Sig. (2-tailed)	0,934	0,789	0,533	0,149	0,103	0,969	0,747	0,683

(Continued)

		Armenia	Azerbaijan	Belarus	Georgia	Moldova	Ukraine	EaP6	EaPC not specified
EU POWER PROJECTION	Pearson Correlation	0,512	−0,253	−0,086	0,068	−0,010	0,446	0,433	.635*
	Sig. (2-tailed)	0,089	0,427	0,791	0,833	0,975	0,146	0,160	0,026
EU SECURITY ACTORNESS	Pearson Correlation	.708**	0,359	0,017	0,403	0,139	.618*	0,527	.763**
	Sig. (2-tailed)	0,010	0,252	0,958	0,194	0,668	0,032	0,078	0,004
EU-EAP BILATERAL RELATIONS	Pearson Correlation	0,060	−0,029	0,482	0,217	0,210	0,561	0,533	0,525
	Sig. (2-tailed)	0,854	0,928	0,113	0,499	0,512	0,058	0,074	0,080
EU-EAP CROSS-BORDR COOPERATION	Pearson Correlation	0,560	0,266	0,116	0,293	−0,564	0,513	0,473	.659*
	Sig. (2-tailed)	0,058	0,403	0,719	0,355	0,056	0,088	0,121	0,020
EU-EAP NORMS & VALUES	Pearson Correlation	0,391	0,121	0,043	0,310	−0,259	.675*	.745**	.632*
	Sig. (2-tailed)	0,209	0,707	0,894	0,327	0,417	0,016	0,005	0,028
EU-RUSSIA COMPETITION	Pearson Correlation	0,490	0,149	0,200	0,476	.589*	.788**	.601*	.677*
	Sig. (2-tailed)	0,105	0,643	0,534	0,118	0,044	0,002	0,039	0,016
EURASIAN INTEGRATION	Pearson Correlation	.617*	0,045	0,052	0,106	−0,366	.662*	0,570	.818**
	Sig. (2-tailed)	0,033	0,890	0,873	0,742	0,242	0,019	0,053	0,001
EUROPEAN INTEGRATION & EUROPEANIZATION	Pearson Correlation	0,425	−0,022	−0,160	0,322	−0,275	.624*	.650*	0,497
	Sig. (2-tailed)	0,169	0,947	0,618	0,308	0,386	0,030	0,022	0,100
IDENTITY	Pearson Correlation	0,366	0,335	−0,065	.748**	0,318	0,500	.640*	0,237
	Sig. (2-tailed)	0,243	0,287	0,842	0,005	0,313	0,098	0,025	0,458
EU-EAP MOBILITY & MIGRATION	Pearson Correlation	0,521	0,172	0,114	0,194	−0,120	0,468	0,326	.632*
	Sig. (2-tailed)	0,083	0,593	0,725	0,546	0,710	0,125	0,301	0,028
NATIONAL SECURITY	Pearson Correlation	.690*	0,374	0,086	0,286	0,042	.720**	0,492	.660*
	Sig. (2-tailed)	0,013	0,232	0,791	0,368	0,896	0,008	0,105	0,020
POWER POLITICS & CONTESTATION	Pearson Correlation	0,228	0,122	0,438	0,380	0,295	0,521	0,530	0,563
	Sig. (2-tailed)	0,476	0,706	0,154	0,223	0,351	0,082	0,076	0,057
REGIME PERSISTENCE & AUTOCRATIZATION	Pearson Correlation	0,355	0,258	−0,359	0,571	.673*	0,418	0,437	0,056
	Sig. (2-tailed)	0,258	0,417	0,252	0,053	0,016	0,176	0,156	0,862
REGIONAL SECURITY	Pearson Correlation	.641*	0,196	0,051	0,351	0,326	.769**	0,537	.738**
	Sig. (2-tailed)	0,025	0,542	0,875	0,264	0,301	0,003	0,072	0,006
STATEBUILDING & TRANSFORMATION	Pearson Correlation	.657*	0,293	−0,037	0,562	0,219	.636*	0,364	0,442
	Sig. (2-tailed)	0,020	0,355	0,910	0,057	0,493	0,026	0,245	0,150

**Correlation is significant at the 0.01 level (2-tailed). NB: Observations $N = 12$ (i.e. years 2009–2020).
*Correlation is significant at the 0.05 level (2-tailed).
Source: Own elaboration based on WoS Core Collection data content-analyzed with Atlas.ti (output table of the SPSS-based statistical correlation analysis).

Notes

1. Exadaktylos, T. (2017). Methodological and theoretical challenges to the study of the European Neighbourhood Policy. In *The Routledge Handbook on the European Neighbourhood Policy*, ed. by T. Schumacher, A. Marchetti and T. Demmelhuber (London and New York: Routledge), pp. 93–104. Here pp. 99–100.
2. Lohaus, M., & Wemheuer-Vogelaar, W. (2020). Who publishes where? Exploring the geographic diversity of global IR journals. *International Studies Review*, doi: 10.1093/isr/viaa062
3. See, for instance: Pehl, M. (2012). The study of politics in Germany: A bibliometric analysis of subfields and methods. *European Political Science*, 11(1), 54–70; Goyal, N. (2017). A "review" of policy sciences: Bibliometric analysis of authors, references, and topics during 1970–2017. *Policy Sciences*, 50(4), 527–537.
4. Exadaktylos, T., & Radaelli, C. M. (2012). Looking for causality in the literature on Europeanization. In *Research Design in European Studies: Establishing Causality in Europeanization*, ed. by T. Exadaktylos & C. M. Radaelli (London: Palgrave Macmillan), pp. 17–43.
5. Romanova, T. (2019). Studying EU-Russian relations: An overview in search for an epistemic community. *Journal of Contemporary European Studies*, 27(2), 135–146.; Izotov, A. (2019). Studying EU–Russia policies in the shared neighbourhood in Russia and in the West. *Journal of Contemporary European Studies*, 27(2), 208–223.; German, T., & Bayramov, A. (2019). The (re)-politicisation of international relations in the post-Soviet space. *East European Politics*, 35(2), 117–121.; Kourtelis, C. (2020). The role of epistemic communities and expert knowledge in the European neighbourhood policy. *Journal of European Integration*, doi: 10.1080/07036337.2020.1739031
6. Glänzel, W. (2000). Science in Scandinavia: A bibliometric approach. *Scientometrics*, 48(2), 121–150.
7. Van Eck, N. J., & Waltman, L. (2010). Software survey: VOSviewer, a computer program for bibliometric mapping. *Scientometrics*, 84: 523–538.; Van Eck, N. J., & Waltman, L. (2014). Visualizing bibliometric networks. In *Measuring Scholarly Impact: Methods and Practice*, ed. by Y. Ding, R. Rousseau and D. Wolfram (Cham: Springer), pp. 285–320.; Van Eck, N., & Waltman, L. (2020). *VOSviewer Manual, v.* 1.6.16 (25 November 2020). Leiden: Leiden University CWTS.
8. Mohamad, A. (2017). Using Atlas.ti 8 Windows in Literature Reviews. *ATLAS.ti*, 9.02.2017, available at: https://atlasti.com/2017/02/09/lit-reviews/
9. Friese, S. (2019). *Qualitative data analysis with ATLAS.ti*, 3rd ed. London: SAGE.
10. "Searching the Topic Field", *Web of Science Core Collection Help*, http://images.webofknowledge.com/WOKRS535R100/help/WOS/hs_topic.html
11. Sakwa, R. (2015). The death of Europe? Continental fates after Ukraine. *International Affairs*, 91(3), 553–579.
12. For this very reason, the citation network analysis, usually performed in bibliometric studies, was not applied here.
13. Many articles treat more than one EaP country as their main object of study. The results in the graph are cumulative.
14. '*EaPC not specified*' stands (a) for theoretical or conceptual studies that do not focus on specific EaP countries, or for (b) what can be named at best a 'convenient' sample, i.e. a sample with only sporadic and unsystematic references to various EaP countries beyond the article's main focus of analysis. In addition to being methodologically slippery, such a non-specification of the sample bears also caveats for extrapolating particularistic facts and findings across the EaP-6 countries, thus forging an ill-suited vision of a coherent and homogeneous set of states within an arguably homogeneous region.
15. Hereto count both the unique dyadic comparisons and overlapping cases of region-wide comparison among all EaP-6.
16. The absolute value of the occurrence of the EU as an 'actor' in *Figure A2.25* should be disregarded, given that the 'EU' has also been one of *the* sampling parameters for journal articles (and, as such, is featured in virtually all articles sampled). Rather, the share of EU should be seen in relative terms vis-à-vis cases that feature other external actors (as shown in greater detail in *Figure A2.26*).
17. Notably, EaP development was mainly discussed in the context of foreign policies of Poland, Bulgaria, Romania, Slovakia, Hungary, Chechia, Estonia, Lithuania, Latvia, Germany and the pre-Brexit United Kingdom.

18 From among the EU institutions and bodies, the role of the European Parliament, the European External Action Service, the High Representative for EU Foreign and Security Policy and Vice-President of the European Commission, and that of EU Agencies were scrutinized in the context of EaP development. The Energy Community, too, featured in EaP analyses.

References

The Eastern Partnership and EU-Eastern neighbours relations: Bibliography (2009–2020)

A. 2009–2019 publications list

Ademmer, E. (2015). Interdependence and EU-demanded policy change in a shared neighbourhood. *Journal of European Public Policy*, 22(5), 671–689.

Ademmer, E., & Börzel, T. A. (2013). Migration, energy and good governance in the EU's Eastern Neighbourhood. *Europe-Asia Studies*, 65(4), 581–608.

Ademmer, E., & Delcour, L. (2016). With a little help from Russia? The European Union and visa liberalization with post-Soviet states. *Eurasian Geography and Economics*, 57(1), 89–112.

Ademmer, E., Delcour, L., & Wolczuk, K. (2016). Beyond geopolitics: Exploring the impact of the EU and Russia in the contested neighborhood. *Eurasian Geography and Economics*, 57(1), 1–18.

Agh, A. (2010). Regionalisation as a driving force of EU widening: Recovering from the EU 'Carrot Crisis' in the 'East'. *Europe-Asia Studies*, 62(8), 1239–1266.

Alexandrova-Arbatova, N. (2015). Security relations in the Black Sea region: Russia and the West after the Ukrainian crisis. *Southeast European and Black Sea Studies*, 15(2), 129–139.

Alexandrova-Arbatova, N. (2016). Geopolitical challenges for the post-bipolar Europe. *Eastern Journal of European Studies*, 7(2), 31–46.

Aliyev, H. (2016). Assessing the European Union's assistance to civil society in its Eastern Neighbourhood: Lessons from the South Caucasus. *Journal of Contemporary European Studies*, 24(1), 42–60.

Axyonova, V., & Gawrich, A. (2018). Regional organizations and secessionist entities: Analysing practices of the EU and the OSCE in post-soviet protracted conflict areas. *Ethnopolitics*, 17(4), 408–425.

Ayvazyan, A. (2016). The EU policy in the South Caucasus and the Neighborhood policy revision. *Contemporary Europe-Sovremennaya Evropa*, 4, 47–56.

Babayan, N. (2012). 'Fear or love thy neighbour'? The EU framework for promoting regional cooperation in the South Caucasus. *Journal of Contemporary European Research*, 8(1), 40–56.

Babayan, N. (2016). A global trend EU-style: Democracy promotion in 'fragile' and conflict-affected South Caucasus. *Global Policy*, 7(2), 217–226.

Baltag, D. (2018). EU external representation post-lisbon: The performance of EU diplomacy in Belarus, Moldova and Ukraine. *Hague Journal of Diplomacy*, 13(1), 75–96.

Barakhvostov, P., & Rusakovich, A. (2017). Eastern partnership countries and Eurasian integration in 2012 similar to 2015. *Journal of Economic Integration*, 32(4), 804–841.

Barbe, E., Costa, O., Herranz, A., & Natorski, M. (2009). Which rules shape EU external governance? Patterns of rule selection in foreign and security policies. *Journal of European Public Policy*, 16(6), 834–852.

Bartlett, W., & Popovski, V. (2015). Institutions and social networks: Explaining barriers to new firm entry and growth in the EU's Eastern Neighbourhood. *International Review of Entrepreneurship*, 13(3), 169–185.

Batora, J., & Rieker, P. (2018). EU-supported reforms in the EU neighbourhood as organized anarchies: The case of post-Maidan Ukraine. *Journal of European Integration*, 40(4), 461–478.

Bayramov, A., & Marusyk, Y. (2019). Ukraine's unfinished natural gas and electricity reforms: One step forward, two steps back. *Eurasian Geography and Economics*, 60(1), 73–96.

Bechev, D. (2015). Understanding the contest between the EU and Russia in their shared neighborhood. *Problems of Post-Communism, 62*(6), 340–349.

Berlinschi, R. (2019). Migration and geopolitical preferences. *Post-Soviet Affairs, 35*(2), 93–121.

Beyer, J., & Wolff, S. (2016). Linkage and leverage effects on Moldova's Transnistria problem. *East European Politics, 32*(3), 335–354.

Bocse, A.-M. (2019). EU energy diplomacy: Searching for new suppliers in Azerbaijan and Iran. *Geopolitics, 24*(1), 145–173.

Börzel, T. A. (2011). When Europe hits… Beyond its borders: Europeanization and the near abroad. *Comparative European Politics, 9*(4–5), 394–413.

Börzel, T. A., & Pamuk, Y. (2012). Pathologies of Europeanisation: Fighting corruption in the Southern Caucasus. *West European Politics, 35*(1), 79–97.

Börzel, T. A., & Lebanidze, B. (2017). 'The transformative power of Europe' beyond enlargement: the EU's performance in promoting democracy in its neighbourhood. *East European Politics, 33*(1), 17–35.

Börzel, T. A., & van Huellen, V. (2014). State-building and the European Union's fight against corruption in the Southern Caucasus: Why legitimacy matters. *Governance-an International Journal of Policy Administration and Institutions, 27*(4), 613–634.

Börzel, T. A., Stahn, A., & Pamuk, Y. (2010). The European Union and the fight against corruption in its near abroad: Can it make a difference? *Global Crime, 11*(2), 122–144.

Bolgova, L. (2019). 'Eastern Partnership' after the Ukrainian crisis: The value of stability or stable values? *Contemporary Europe-Sovremennaya Evropa, 7*, 115–123.

Bolkvadze, K. (2016). Cherry picking EU conditionality: Selective compliance in Georgia's Hybrid Regime. *Europe-Asia Studies, 68*(3), 409–440.

Bosse, G. (2010). The EU's relations with Moldova: Governance, partnership or ignorance? *Europe-Asia Studies, 62*(8), 1291–1309.

Bosse, G. (2012). A partnership with dictatorship: Explaining the paradigm shift in European Union Policy towards Belarus. *JCMS: Journal of Common Market Studies, 50*(3), 367–384.

Bosse, G., & Korosteleva-Polglase, E. (2009). Changing Belarus? The limits of EU governance in Eastern Europe and the promise of partnership. *Cooperation and Conflict, 44*(2), 143–165.

Bossuyt, F., & Panchuk, D. (2017). The participation of CEECs in EU twinning projects: Offering specific added value for EU Transgovernmental Cooperation in the Eastern neighbourhood? *East European Politics and Societies, 31*(2), 334–359.

Browning, C. S. (2018). Geostrategies, geopolitics and ontological security in the Eastern neighbourhood: The European Union and the 'new Cold War'. *Political Geography, 62*, 106–115.

Browning, C. S., & Christou, G. (2010). The constitutive power of outsiders: The European Neighbourhood Policy and the eastern dimension. *Political Geography, 29*(2), 109–118.

Bruns, B. (2019). Homogenous and extra-territorial border regime? Migrations and control efforts across the Eastern EU external border. *Journal of Borderlands Studies, 34*(4), 509–526.

Bruszt, L., & Langbein, J. (2017). Varieties of dis-embedded liberalism. EU integration strategies in the Eastern peripheries of Europe. *Journal of European Public Policy, 24*(2), 297–315.

Bulgari, G. G. (2015). Mapping the EU-Republic of Moldova Trajectory: Roadblocks on the way to economic integration with the EU. *Romanian Journal of European Affairs, 15*(4), 41–60.

Burlyuk, O. (2014). An ambitious failure: Conceptualising the EU approach to rule of law promotion (in Ukraine). *Hague Journal on the Rule of Law, 6*(1), 26–46.

Burlyuk, O. (2017). Same end, different means: The evolution of Poland's support for Ukraine at the European level. *East European Politics and Societies, 31*(2), 311–333.

Burlyuk, O., & Shapovalova, N. (2017). 'Veni, vidi,… Vici?' EU performance and two faces of conditionality towards Ukraine. *East European Politics, 33*(1), 36–55.

Buscaneanu, S. (2015). EU democracy promotion in Eastern ENP countries. *East European Politics and Societies, 29*(1), 248–286.

Buzogany, A. (2013). Selective adoption of EU environmental norms in Ukraine. Convergence a la Carte. *Europe-Asia Studies, 65*(4), 609–630.

Buzogany, A. (2016). EU-Russia regulatory competition and business interests in post-Soviet countries: The case of forestry and chemical security in Ukraine. *Eurasian Geography and Economics, 57*(1), 138–159.

Buzogany, A. (2018). Civil society organisations beyond the European Union: Normative expectations and local realities. *Journal of Contemporary European Research, 14*(2), 187–205.

Buzogany, A. (2019). Europe, Russia, or both? Popular perspectives on overlapping regionalism in the Southern Caucasus. *East European Politics, 35*(1), 93–109.

Cadier, D. (2014). Eastern Partnership vs Eurasian Union? The EU-Russia competition in the shared neighbourhood and the Ukraine Crisis. *Global Policy, 5*, 76–85.

Cadier, D. (2019). The geopoliticisation of the EU's Eastern Partnership. *Geopolitics, 24*(1), 71–99.

Cantir, C., & Kennedy, R. (2015). Balancing on the shoulders of giants: Moldova's Foreign policy toward Russia and the European Union. *Foreign Policy Analysis, 11*(4), 397–416.

Casier, T. (2011). The EU's two-track approach to democracy promotion: The case of Ukraine. *Democratization, 18*(4), 956–977.

Casier, T. (2016). From logic of competition to conflict: Understanding the dynamics of EU-Russia relations. *Contemporary Politics, 22*(3), 376–394.

Casier, T. (2019). The unintended consequences of a European Neighbourhood Policy without Russia. *International Spectator, 54*(1), 76–88.

Celbis, M. G., Wong, P.-H., & Guznajeva, T. (2018). Regional integration and the economic geography of Belarus. *Eurasian Geography and Economics, 59*(3–4), 462–495.

Chaban, N., & Vernygora, V. (2013). The EU in the eyes of Ukrainian general public: Potential for EU public diplomacy? *Baltic Journal of European Studies, 3*(2), 68–95.

Chaban, N., Elgstrom, O., & Knodt, M. (2019). Perceptions of EU mediation and mediation effectiveness: Comparing perspectives from Ukraine and the EU. *Cooperation and Conflict, 54*(4), 506–523.

Chaban, N., Knodt, M., Liekis, S., & Iverson, N. G. (2019). Narrators' perspectives: Communicating the EU in Ukraine, Israel and Palestine in times of conflict. *European Security, 28*(3), 304–322.

Christou, G. (2010). European Union security logics to the east: The European Neighbourhood Policy and the Eastern Partnership. *European Security, 19*(3), 413–430.

Chryssogelos, A.-S. (2017). Transnational European party federations as EU Foreign Policy Actors: The activities of Europarties in Eastern Partnership States. *JCMS: Journal of Common Market Studies, 55*(2), 257–274.

Copsey, N., & Pomorska, K. (2010). Poland's power and influence in the European Union: The case of its eastern policy. *Comparative European Politics, 8*(3), 304–326.

Copsey, N., & Pomorska, K. (2014). The influence of newer member states in the European Union: The case of Poland and the Eastern Partnership. *Europe-Asia Studies, 66*(3), 421–443.

Coroban, C. (2011). Some considerations on the EU Danube Strategy and the Black Sea Region. *Eastern Journal of European Studies, 2*(1), 97–110.

Cross, M. K. D., & Karolewski, I. P. (2017). What type of power has the EU Exercised in the Ukraine-Russia crisis? A framework of analysis. *JCMS: Journal of Common Market Studies, 55*(1), 3–19.

Dahs, A. (2014). Historical regional demographic divergence in Latvia: Lessons of the common past with Eastern Partnership countries. *Baltic Journal of European Studies, 4*(2), 119–133.

Dangerfield, M. (2016). Dilemmas of post-enlargement Europe: Building an 'insecurity zone'? *European Integration Studies, 10*, 8–15.

Danii, O., & Mascauteanu, M. (2011). Moldova under the European Neighbourhood Policy: 'Falling between stools'. *East European Politics, 27*(1), 99–119.

Danzer, A. M., & Dietz, B. (2014). Labour migration from Eastern Europe and the EU's quest for talents. *JCMS: Journal of Common Market Studies, 52*(2), 183–199.

Davies, C. M. (2011). 'Backseat driving': European institutions and crisis management in Moldova. *Romanian Journal of Political Science, 11*(2), 129–153.

Delcour, L. (2010). The European Union, a security provider in the Eastern Neighbourhood? *European Security*, *19*(4), 535–549.

Delcour, L. (2013). Meandering Europeanisation. EU policy instruments and policy convergence in Georgia under the Eastern Partnership. *East European Politics*, *29*(3), 344–357.

Delcour, L. (2015). Between the Eastern Partnership and Eurasian Integration: Explaining post-soviet countries' engagement in (competing) region-building projects. *Problems of Post-Communism*, *62*(6), 316–327.

Delcour, L. (2016). Multiple external influences and domestic change in the contested neighborhood: The case of food safety. *Eurasian Geography and Economics*, *57*(1), 43–65.

Delcour, L. (2018a). Dealing with the elephant in the room: The EU, its 'Eastern neighbourhood' and Russia. *Contemporary Politics*, *24*(1), 14–29.

Delcour, L. (2018b). Regionalism as you like it? Armenia and the Eurasian integration process. *International Spectator*, *53*(3), 55–69.

Delcour, L. (2019). Armenia's and Georgia's contrasted positioning vis-a-vis the EU: Between vocal centrality and strategic marginality. *Journal of Contemporary European Studies*, *27*(4), 439–450.

Delcour, L., & Fernandes, S. (2016). Visa liberalization processes in the EU's Eastern Neighbourhood: Understanding policy outcomes. *Cambridge Review of International Affairs*, *29*(4), 1259–1278.

Delcour, L., & Wolczuk, K. (2015**a**). Spoiler or facilitator of democratization? Russia's role in Georgia and Ukraine. *Democratization*, *22*(3), 459–478.

Delcour, L., & Wolczuk, K. (2015**b**). The EU's unexpected 'ideal neighbour'? The perplexing case of Armenia's Europeanisation. *Journal of European Integration*, *37*(4), 491–507.

Demiryol, T. (2014). The Eastern Partnership and the EU-Turkey energy relations. *Baltic Journal of European Studies*, *4*(2), 50–68.

Di Quirico, R. (2011). The prospects for democratization in the European Union post-Soviet neighbours: An overview. *Comparative European Politics*, *9*(4–5), 432–447.

Dias, V. A. (2013). The EU's post-liberal approach to peace: Framing EUBAM's contribution to the Moldova-Transnistria conflict transformation. *European Security*, *22*(3), 338–354.

Dimitrova, A., & Dragneva, R. (2009). Constraining external governance: Interdependence with Russia and the CIS as limits to the EU's rule transfer in the Ukraine. *Journal of European Public Policy*, *16*(6), 853–872.

Dimitrova, A., & Dragneva, R. (2013). Shaping convergence with the EU in foreign policy and state aid in post-orange Ukraine: Weak external incentives, powerful veto players. *Europe-Asia Studies*, *65*(4), 658–681.

Dogangun, G., & Karadag, Y. (2019). EU's cross-border cooperation and conflict transformation at contested borders in the European Neighbourhood: Lessons from the Turkish-Armenian border. *Geopolitics*, *24*(3), 625–649.

Dragan, G. (2015). Deepening the economic integration in the Eastern Partnership: From a free trade area to a neighbourhood economic community? *Eastern Journal of European Studies*, *6*(2), 9–26.

Dragneva, R., & Wolczuk, K. (2014). The EU-Ukraine association agreement and the challenges of inter-regionalism. *Review of Central and East European Law*, *39*(3–4), 213–244.

Dressler, M. (2018). Decentralising power: Building inclusive peace? The European Union's support to governance reform in Eastern Ukraine. *Peacebuilding*, *6*(3), 201–217.

Eisele, K., & Wiesbrock, A. (2011). Enhancing mobility in the European Neighborhood policy? The cases of Moldova and Georgia. *Review of Central and East European Law*, *36*(2), 127–155.

Elgstrom, O., Chaban, N., Knodt, M., Muller, P., & Pardo, S. (2018). Perceptions of the EU's role in the Ukraine-Russia and the Israel-Palestine conflicts: A biased mediator? *International Negotiation: a Journal of Theory and Practice*, *23*(2), 299–318.

Ferguson, I. (2018). Between new spheres of influence: Ukraine's geopolitical misfortune. *Geopolitics*, *23*(2), 285–306.

Fischer, S. (2009). The European Union and security in the Black Sea region after the Georgia crisis. *Southeast European and Black Sea Studies*, *9*(3), 333–349.

Fix, L. (2018). The different 'shades' of German power: Germany and EU Foreign Policy during the Ukraine Conflict. *German Politics*, *27*(4), 498–515.

Fogel, K. (2015). The multistage nature of labour migration from Eastern and Central Europe (experience of Ukraine, Poland, United Kingdom and Germany during the 2002–2011 period). *Eastern Journal of European Studies*, *6*(2), 55–81.

Franke, A., Gawrich, A., Melnykovska, I., & Schweickert, R. (2010). The European Union's relations with Ukraine and Azerbaijan. *Post-Soviet Affairs*, *26*(2), 149–183.

Freire, M. R. (2019). The quest for status: How the interplay of power, ideas, and regime security shapes Russia's policy in the post-Soviet space. *International Politics*, *56*(6), 795–809.

Freire, M. R., & Simao, L. (2013**a**). 'From words to deeds': European Union democracy promotion in Armenia. *East European Politics*, *29*(2), 175–189.

Freire, M. R., & Simao, L. (2013**b**). The EU's security actorness: The case of EUMM in Georgia. *European Security*, *22*(4), 464–477.

Freyburg, T., Lavenex, S., Schimmelfennig, F., Skripka, T., & Wetzel, A. (2009). EU promotion of democratic governance in the neighbourhood. *Journal of European Public Policy*, *16*(6), 916–934.

Freyburg, T., Lavenex, S., Schimmelfennig, F., Skripka, T., & Wetzel, A. (2011). Democracy promotion through functional cooperation? The case of the European Neighbourhood Policy. *Democratization*, *18*(4), 1026–1054.

Gamkrelidze, T. (2019). The project of Europe: a robust attempt to redefine Georgian identity. *East European Politics, 35*(3), 351–371.

Gawrich, A., Melnykovska, I., & Schweickert, R. (2010). Neighbourhood Europeanization through ENP: The case of Ukraine. *JCMS: Journal of Common Market Studies*, *48*(5), 1209–1235.

Gehring, T., Urbanski, K., & Oberthur, S. (2017). The European Union as an inadvertent great power: EU actorness and the Ukraine Crisis. *JCMS: Journal of Common Market Studies*, *55*(4), 727–743.

Gentile, M. (2015). West oriented in the East-oriented Donbas: A political stratigraphy of geopolitical identity in Luhansk, Ukraine. *Post-Soviet Affairs*, *31*(3), 201–223.

Ghazaryan, N. (2015). A new generation of human rights clauses? The case of association agreements in the Eastern Neighbourhood. *European Law Review*, *40*(3), 391–410.

Glebov, S. (2009). Black Sea security as a regional concern for the Black Sea states and the global powers. *Southeast European and Black Sea Studies*, *9*(3), 351–365.

Gnedina, E. (2015). 'Multi-Vector' Foreign Policies in Europe: Balancing, bandwagoning or bargaining? *Europe-Asia Studies*, *67*(7), 1007–1029.

Gretskiy, I., Treshchenkov, E., & Golubev, K. (2014). Russia's perceptions and misperceptions of the EU Eastern Partnership. *Communist and Post-Communist Studies*, *47*(3–4), 375–383.

Grigoryan, K. (2012). Study of the peculiarities of export developments in EU member countries and in Armenia. *Romanian Journal of European Affairs*, *12*(3), 65–82.

Guschin, A., & Levchenkov, A. (2019). The Western Flank of the post-Soviet space and the 'Eastern Partnership': Experience and prospects of cooperation. *Contemporary Europe-Sovremennaya Evropa*, *7*, 105–114.

Gylfason, T., Martinez-Zarzoso, I., & Wijkman, P. M. (2015). Free trade agreements, institutions and the exports of eastern partnership countries. *JCMS: Journal of Common Market Studies*, *53*(6), 1214–1229.

Hagemann, C. (2013). External governance on the terms of the partner? The EU, russia and the republic of Moldova in the European Neighbourhood Policy. *Journal of European Integration*, *35*(7), 767–783.

Happ, D., & Bruns, B. (2017). The EU and its 'ring of friends' eye-level or top-down relationships? How the EU's external governance is perceived by local experts in Belarus and Ukraine. *Problems of Post-Communism*, *64*(2), 94–105.

Haukkala, H. (2015). From cooperative to contested Europe? The conflict in Ukraine as a culmination of a long-term crisis in EU-Russia relations. *Journal of Contemporary European Studies*, *23*(1), 25–40.

Haukkala, H. (2016). A perfect storm; or what went wrong and what went right for the EU in Ukraine. *Europe-Asia Studies*, *68*(4), 653–664.

Hellquist, E. (2016). Either with us or against us? Third-country alignment with EU sanctions against Russia/Ukraine. *Cambridge Review of International Affairs*, *29*(3), 997–1021.

Hernandez i Sagrera, R. (2014). Exporting EU integrated border management beyond EU borders: Modernization and institutional transformation in exchange for more mobility? *Cambridge Review of International Affairs*, *27*(1), 167–183.

Howorth, J. (2017). 'Stability on the borders': The Ukraine Crisis and the EU's constrained policy towards the Eastern Neighbourhood. *JCMS: Journal of Common Market Studies*, *55*(1), 121–136.

Iglesias, J. D. (2019). Behind closed doors: Discourses and strategies in the European securitized borderlands in Moldova, Serbia and Ukraine. *Journal of Borderlands Studies*, *34*(5), 733–748.

Ikani, N. (2019). Change and continuity in the European Neighbourhood Policy: The Ukraine Crisis as a critical juncture. *Geopolitics*, *24*(1), 20–50.

Ioffe, G. (2011). Belarus and the West: From estrangement to honeymoon. *East European Politics*, *27*(2), 217–240.

Isakova, A., Koczan, Z., & Plekhanov, A. (2016). How much do tariffs matter? Evidence from the customs union of Belarus, Kazakhstan and Russia. *Journal of Economic Policy Reform*, *19*(2), 166–184.

Istomin, I., & Bolgova, I. (2016). Transnistrian strategy in the context of Russian-Ukrainian relations: The rise and failure of 'dual alignment'. *Southeast European and Black Sea Studies*, *16*(1), 169–194.

Izotov, A. (2019). Studying EU-Russia policies in the shared neighbourhood in Russia and in the West. *Journal of Contemporary European Studies*, *27*(2), 208–223.

Jayasundara-Smits, S. (2018). From revolution to reform and back: EU-Security sector reform in Ukraine. *European Security*, *27*(4), 453–468.

Jeandesboz, J. (2015). Intervention and subversion: The EU border assistance mission to Moldova and Ukraine. *Journal of Intervention and Statebuilding*, *9*(4), 442–470.

Kahn-Nisser, S. (2017). Channels of influence: The EU and delta convergence of core labour standards in the Eastern Neighbourhood. *European Journal of Development Research*, *29*(1), 127–143.

Kakachia, K., Lebanidze, B., & Dubovyk, V. (2019). Defying marginality: Explaining Ukraine's and Georgia's drive towards Europe. *Journal of Contemporary European Studies*, *27*(4), 451–462.

Kalinichenko, P., Petrov, R., & Karliuk, M. (2019). International law in Russia, Ukraine, and Belarus: Modern integration projects. *Russian Law Journal*, *7*(3), 107–133.

Karliuk, M. (2017). The Eurasian economic union: An EU-inspired legal order and its limits. *Review of Central and East European Law*, *42*(1), 50–72.

Karolewski, I. P., & Cross, M. K. D. (2017). The EU's power in the Russia-Ukraine crisis: Enabled or constrained? *JCMS: Journal of Common Market Studies*, *55*(1), 137–152.

Kasyanov, R. A. (2019). The EU experience as a model for the development of a single financial market regulation in the Eurasian Economic Union (EAEU). *European Company and Financial Law Review*, *16*(5), 592–621.

Kazharski, A., & Makarychev, A. (2015). Suturing the neighborhood? Russia and the EU in conflictual intersubjectivity. *Problems of Post-Communism*, *62*(6), 328–339.

Kennedy, R. (2016). The limits of soft balancing: The frozen conflict in Transnistria and the challenge to EU and NATO strategy. *Small Wars and Insurgencies*, *27*(3), 512–537.

Khasson, V. (2013). Cross-border cooperation over the Eastern EU border: Between assistance and partnership under the European Neighbourhood and partnership instrument. *East European Politics*, *29*(3), 328–343.

Klatt, M. (2011). Poland and its Eastern Neighbours: Foreign policy principles. *Journal of Contemporary European Research*, 7(1), 61–76.

Kobadze, N. (2018). Black Sea Port in Georgia scrutinised by the Georgian competition authority relying upon EU case law as plans for expansion rejected. *Journal of European Competition Law & Practice*, 9(3), 176–182.

Kobayashi, K. (2019). The normative limits of functional cooperation: The case of the European Union and Eurasian Economic Union. *East European Politics*, 35(2), 143–158.

Kølvraa, C. (2017). Limits of attraction: The EU's Eastern border and the European Neighbourhood Policy. *East European Politics and Societies*, 31(1), 11–25.

Korosteleva, E. (2010). Moldova's European Choice: 'Between two stools'? *Europe-Asia Studies*, 62(8), 1267–1289.

Korosteleva, E. A. (2011**a**). Change or continuity: Is the Eastern Partnership an adequate tool for the European Neighbourhood? *International Relations*, 25(2), 243–262.

Korosteleva, E. A. (2011**b**). The Eastern Partnership initiative: A new opportunity for neighbours? *East European Politics*, 27(1), 1–21.

Korosteleva, E. A. (2013). Evaluating the role of partnership in the European Neighbourhood Policy: The Eastern neighbourhood. *Eastern Journal of European Studies*, 4(2), 11–36.

Korosteleva, E. A. (2016**a**). The European Union and Belarus: Democracy promotion by technocratic means? *Democratization*, 23(4), 678–698.

Korosteleva, E. A. (2016**b**). The European Union, Russia and the Eastern region: The analytics of government for sustainable cohabitation. *Cooperation and Conflict*, 51(3), 365–383.

Korosteleva, E. A. (2017). Eastern Partnership: Bringing "the political" back in. *East European Politics*, 33(3), 321–337.

Korosteleva, E. A., Natorski, M., & Simao, L. (2013). The eastern dimension of the European neighbourhood policy: Practices, instruments and social structures. *East European Politics*, 29(3), 257–272.

Kostanyan, H. (2017). How 'the political' can make the European external action service more effective in the eastern region. *East European Politics*, 33(3), 355–370.

Kostanyan, H., & Orbie, J. (2013). The EEAS' discretionary power within the Eastern Partnership: In search of the highest possible denominator. *Southeast European and Black Sea Studies*, 13(1), 47–65.

Kostanyan, H., & Vandecasteele, B. (2013). The socialization potential of the Eastern Partnership Civil Society Forum. *Eastern Journal of European Studies*, 4(2), 95–110.

Kotulewicz-Wisinska, K. (2016). Visegrad assistance to the eastern partnership countries. *Contemporary Europe-Sovremennaya Evropa*, 6, 72–81.

Kotulewicz-Wisinska, K. (2018). Participation of the Visegrad Group countries in the implementation of the Eastern Partnership programme. *Contemporary Europe-Sovremennaya Evropa*, 7, 96–107.

Kourtikakis, K., & Turkina, E. (2015). Civil society organizations in European Union external relations: A study of interorganizational networks in the Eastern Partnership and the Mediterranean. *Journal of European Integration*, 37(5), 587–609.

Kovalchuk, S., & Kravchuk, A. (2019). The impact of global challenges on 'green' transformations of the agrarian sector of the Eastern Partnership countries. *Baltic Journal of Economic Studies*, 5(1), 87–95.

Krasnodebska, M. (2018). The Ukraine crisis as an unintended consequence of the EU's public diplomacy: Reception of the EU's narratives in Ukraine. *Hague Journal of Diplomacy*, 13(3), 345–365.

Kubicek, P. (2017). Dancing with the devil: Explaining the European Union's engagement with Ukraine under Viktor Yanukovych. *Journal of Contemporary European Studies*, 25(2), 143–162.

Kudelia, S. (2013). When external leverage fails the case of Yulia Tymoshenko's Trial. *Problems of Post-Communism*, 60(1), 29–42.

Kulakevich, T. (2014). Twenty years in the making: Understanding the difficulty for change in Belarus. *East European Politics and Societies*, *28*(4), 887–901.

Kurecic, P. (2017). The 'new cold warriors' and the 'pragmatics': The differences in foreign policy attitudes towards Russia and the Eastern Partnership States among the NATO Member States from Central and South-Eastern Europe. *Croatian International Relations Review*, *23*(80), 61–96.

Kuzio, T. (2010). State-led violence in Ukraine's 2004 elections and orange revolution. *Communist and Post-Communist Studies*, *43*(4), 383–395.

Kuzio, T. (2017). Ukraine between a constrained EU and assertive Russia. *JCMS: Journal of Common Market Studies*, *55*(1), 103–120.

Langbein, J. (2013). Unpacking the Russian and EU impact on policy change in the Eastern Neighbourhood: The case of Ukraine's telecommunications and food safety. *Europe-Asia Studies*, *65*(4), 631–657.

Langbein, J. (2014). European Union governance towards the Eastern Neigbourhood: Transcending or redrawing Europe's East-West divide? *JCMS: Journal of Common Market Studies*, *52*(1), 157–174.

Langbein, J. (2016). (Dis-)integrating Ukraine? Domestic oligarchs, Russia, the EU, and the politics of economic integration. *Eurasian Geography and Economics*, *57*(1), 19–42.

Langbein, J., & Wolczuk, K. (2012). Convergence without membership? The impact of the European Union in the neighbourhood: Evidence from Ukraine. *Journal of European Public Policy*, *19*(6), 863–881.

Larsen, H. B. L. (2012). The Russo-Georgian war and beyond: Towards a European great power concert. *European Security*, *21*(1), 102–121.

Liden, K., Mikhelidze, N., Stavrevska, E. B., & Vogel, B. (2016). EU support to civil society organizations in conflict-ridden countries: A governance perspective from Bosnia and Herzegovina, Cyprus and Georgia. *International Peacekeeping*, *23*(2), 274–301.

Lightfoot, S., Szent-Iványi, B., & Wolczuk, K. (2016). Mesmerized by enlargement: The EU's Eastern Neighborhood Policy and new member state transition experience. *East European Politics and Societies*, *30*(3), 664–684.

Loda, C. (2017). The European Union as a normative power: The case of Armenia. *East European Politics*, *33*(2), 275–290.

Longhurst, K. (2016). Implementing the DCFTA in the context of state capture: Assessing the position of small and medium enterprises. *Eastern Journal of European Studies*, *7*(2), 145–164.

Lussac, S. J. (2010). Ensuring European energy security in Russian 'near abroad': The case of the South Caucasus. *European Security*, *19*(4), 607–625.

Makaryan, S. (2015). Construction of migration policies in the Eastern Neighbourhood of the European Union. *Journal of Contemporary European Studies*, *23*(2), 222–237.

Makarychev, A. (2014). Russia, Ukraine and the Eastern Partnership: From common neighborhood to spheres of influence? *Insight Turkey*, *16*(3), 181–199.

Makarychev, A. (2018). Normative and civilisational regionalisms: The EU, Russia and their common neighbourhoods. *International Spectator*, *53*(3), 1–19.

Manoli, P. (2010). Where is Black Sea regionalism heading? *Southeast European and Black Sea Studies*, *10*(3), 323–339.

Manoli, P. (2012). EU's flexible regional multilateralism towards its Black Sea neighbourhood. *Southeast European and Black Sea Studies*, *12*(3), 431–442.

Manoli, P. (2013). Political Economy aspects of deep and comprehensive free trade agreements. *Eastern Journal of European Studies*, *4*(2), 51–73.

Marcu, S. (2009). The geopolitics of the Eastern border of the European Union: The case of Romania-Moldova-Ukraine. *Geopolitics*, *14*(3), 409–432.

Markowski, S., Brunarska, Z., & Nestorowicz, J. (2014). Migration management in the EU's Eastern Neighbourhood. *Journal of Sociology*, *50*(1), 65–77.

Marples, D. R. (2009). Outpost of tyranny? The failure of democratization in Belarus. *Democratization*, *16*(4), 756–776.

Martinaitis, Z. (2018). European promises: Policy options of Eastern Partnership Policy. *Baltic Journal of European Studies*, *8*(2), 164–181.

Mayer, S. (2014). Common foreign and security policy alignment in the Southern Caucasus: Convergence, 'pick and choose' or indifference? *Europe-Asia Studies*, *66*(10), 1679–1702.

Mayer, S. (2017). The EU and NATO in Georgia: Complementary and overlapping security strategies in a precarious environment. *European Security*, *26*(3), 435–453.

Mendelski, M. (2016). The EU's rule of law promotion in post-Soviet Europe: What explains the divergence between Baltic States and EaP countries? *Eastern Journal of European Studies*, *7*(2), 111–144.

Merheim-Eyre, I. (2017**a**). Exploring the European Union's rationalities of governing: The case of cross-border mobility in the eastern partnership. *East European Politics*, *33*(3), 371–387.

Merheim-Eyre, I. (2017**b**). The visegrad countries and visa liberalisation in the Eastern Neighbourhood a pan tadeusz syndrome? *East European Politics and Societies*, *31*(1), 93–114.

Morozova, O. (2019). Ukraine's journey to Europe: Strategic macronarrative and conceptual metaphors. *European Security*, *28*(3), 323–340.

Mueller, M. (2011). Public opinion toward the European Union in Georgia. *Post-Soviet Affairs*, *27*(1), 64–92.

Natorski, M. (2013). Reforms in the judiciary of Ukraine: Domestic practices and the EU's policy instruments. *East European Politics*, *29*(3), 358–375.

Natorski, M. (2018). EU mediation practices in Ukraine during revolutions: What authority as a peacemaker? *International Negotiation-a Journal of Theory and Practice*, *23*(2), 278–298.

Natorski, M., & Pomorska, K. (2017). Trust and decision-making in times of crisis: The EU's response to the events in Ukraine. *JCMS: Journal of Common Market Studies*, *55*(1), 54–70.

Neuwirth, R. J., & Svetlicinii, A. (2016). The current EU/US-Russia conflict over Ukraine and the WTO: a preliminary note on (trade) restrictive measures. *Post-Soviet Affairs*, *32*(3), 237–271.

Nilsson, M., & Silander, D. (2016). Democracy and security in the EU's Eastern neighborhood? Assessing the ENP in Georgia, Moldova, and Ukraine. *Democracy & Security*, *12*(1), 44–61.

Nitoiu, C. (2016). Towards conflict or cooperation? The Ukraine crisis and EU-Russia relations. *Southeast European and Black Sea Studies*, *16*(3), 375–390.

Nitoiu, C. (2017). European and Eurasian integration: Competition and cooperation in the post-Soviet space. *Journal of European Integration*, *39*(4), 469–475.

Nitoiu, C. (2018). The European Union's 'ideal self' in the post-Soviet space. *Europe-Asia Studies*, *70*(5), 692–710.

Nitoiu, C. (2018). The influence of external actors on foreign policy in the post-Soviet space. *Europe-Asia Studies*, *70*(5), 685–691.

Nitoiu, C., & Sus, M. (2017). The European Parliament's diplomacy—a tool for projecting EU power in times of crisis? The case of the Cox-Kwasniewski Mission. *JCMS: Journal of Common Market Studies*, *55*(1), 71–86.

Nitoiu, C., & Sus, M. (2019). Introduction: the rise of geopolitics in the EU's approach in its Eastern Neighbourhood. *Geopolitics*, *24*(1), 1–19.

Nizhnikau, R. (2015). Institutional change in the Eastern Neighbourhood: Environmental protection and migration policy in Ukraine. *Southeast European and Black Sea Studies*, *15*(4), 495–517.

Nizhnikau, R. (2016). When Goliath meets Goliath: How Russia and the EU created a vicious circle of instability in Moldova. *Global Affairs*, *2*(2): 203–216.

Nizhnikau, R. (2017). Promoting reforms in Moldova. *Problems of Post-Communism*, *64*(2), 106–120.

Noutcheva, G. (2018). Whose legitimacy? The EU and Russia in contest for the Eastern Neighbourhood. *Democratization*, *25*(2), 312–330.

Novaky, N. I. M. (2015). Why so Soft? The European Union in Ukraine. *Contemporary Security Policy*, *36*(2), 244–266.

Nowicka, K., Sagan, I., & Studzińska, D. (2019). Small diplomacy: Cultural cooperation as a factor alleviating societal tensions. The case of Lviv and its Polish partner cities. *Geopolitics*, *24*(3), 565–585.

Olekseyuk, Z., & Schuerenberg-Frosch, H. (2019). Ukraine's unconsidered losses from the annexation of Crimea: What should we account for in the DCFTA forecasts? *Review of Development Economics*, *23*(2), 877–901.

Panchuk, D., Bossuyt, F., & Orbie, J. (2017). The substance of EU democratic governance promotion via transgovernmental cooperation with the Eastern Neighbourhood. *Democratization*, *24*(6), 1044–1065.

Papadimitriou, D., Baltag, D., & Surubaru, N.-C. (2017). Assessing the performance of the European Union in Central and Eastern Europe and in its neighbourhood. *East European Politics*, *33*(1), 1–16.

Pastore, G. (2014). The EU-Ukraine association agreement prior to the Vilnius Eastern Partnership Summit. *Baltic Journal of European Studies*, *4*(2), 5–19.

Patalakh, A. (2017). EU soft power in the Eastern Neighborhood and the Western Balkans in the context of crises. *Baltic Journal of European Studies*, *7*(2), 148–167.

Paul, A. (2015). The EU in the South Caucasus and the impact of the Russia-Ukraine War. *International Spectator*, *50*(3), 30–42.

Pänke, J. (2015). The fallout of the EU's normative imperialism in the Eastern Neighborhood. *Problems of Post-Communism*, *62*(6), 350–363.

Petrov, R. (2012). Energy community as a promoter of the European Union's 'energy acquis' to its neighbourhood. *Legal Issues of Economic Integration*, *39*(3), 331–355.

Petrov, R. (2014). The EU Neighbourhood Policies and the security crises within the Eastern Neighbourhood. *Security and Human Rights*, *25*(3), 298–311.

Petrov, R. (2015). Constitutional challenges for the implementation of association agreements between the EU and Ukraine, Moldova and Georgia. *European Public Law*, *21*(2), 241–253.

Petrov, R. (2018). EU common values in the EU-Ukraine association agreement: Anchor to democracy? *Baltic Journal of European Studies*, *8*(1), 49–62.

Petrov, R., & Kalinichenko, P. (2011). The Europeanization of third country judiciaries through the application of the EU acquis: The cases of Russia and Ukraine. *International & Comparative Law Quarterly*, *60*(2), 325–353.

Pogodda, S., Richmond, O., Tocci, N., Mac Ginty, R., & Vogel, B. (2014). Assessing the impact of EU governmentality in post-conflict countries: Pacification or reconciliation? *European Security*, *23*(3), 227–249.

Polglase, G. (2013). Higher education as soft power in the Eastern Partnership: The case of Belarus. *Eastern Journal of European Studies*, *4*(2), 111–121.

Pop, A. (2016). From cooperation to confrontation: The impact of bilateral perceptions and interactions on the EU-Russia relations in the context of shared neighbourhood. *Eastern Journal of European Studies*, *7*(2), 47–70.

Popescu, G. (2008). The conflicting logics of cross-border reterritorialization: Geopolitics of Euroregions in Eastern Europe. *Political Geography*, *27*(4), 418–438.

Popescu, L. (2011). Challenges at EU's New Eastern frontier twenty years after USSR's Fall. *Romanian Journal of Political Science*, *11*(2), 4–38.

Popescu, N., & Wilson, A. (2009). The 'Sovereign Neighbourhood': Weak statehood strategies in Eastern Europe. *International Spectator*, *44*(1), 7–12.

Portela, C. (2011). The European Union and Belarus: Sanctions and partnership? *Comparative European Politics*, *9*(4–5), 486–505.

Pridham, G. (2011). Ukraine, the European Union and the democracy question. *Romanian Journal of European Affairs*, *11*(4), 18–33.

Pridham, G. (2014). EU/Ukraine relations and the crisis with Russia, 2013–14: A turning point. *International Spectator, 49*(4), 53–61.

Pshenychnykh, A. (2019). Ukrainian perspectives on the Self, the EU and Russia: An intersemiotic analysis of Ukrainian newspapers. *European Security, 28*(3), 341–359.

Rabinovych, M. (2019). EU's development policy vis-a-vis Ukraine after the Euromaidan: Securitisation, state-building and integration. *East European Politics, 35*(3), 332–350.

Radchuk, T. (2011). Contested neighbourhood, or how to reconcile the differences. *East European Politics, 27*(1), 22–49.

Raik, K. (2019). The Ukraine Crisis as a conflict over Europe's political, economic and security order. *Geopolitics, 24*(1), 51–70.

Ratzmann, N. (2012). Securitizing or developing the European Neighbourhood? Migration management in Moldova. *Southeast European and Black Sea Studies, 12*(2), 261–280.

Rieker, P., & Gjerde, K. L. (2016). The EU, Russia and the potential for dialogue—Different readings of the crisis in Ukraine. *European Security, 25*(3), 304–325.

Roch, S. (2017). Between arbitrary outcomes and impeded process: The performance of EU Twinning projects in the EU's Eastern Neighbourhood. *East European Politics, 33*(1), 72–87.

Rommens, T. (2014). The Eastern Partnership: Civil society in between the European and domestic level: The case of Georgia. *East European Politics, 30*(1), 54–70.

Rommens, T. (2017). The Eastern Partnership in Georgia: Europeanizing civil society? *Communist and Post-Communist Studies, 50*(2), 113–123.

Rotman, D., & Veremeeva, N. (2011). Belarus in the context of the neighbourhood policy: Between the EU and Russia. *East European Politics, 27*(1), 73–98.

Sabatovych, I., Heinrichs, P., Hobova, Y., & Velivchenko, V. (2019). The narratives behind the EU's external perceptions: How civil society and elites in Ukraine, Israel and Palestine 'learn' EU norms. *European Security, 28*(3), 284–303.

Sagrera, R. H. I. (2014). Exporting EU integrated border management beyond EU borders: Modernization and institutional transformation in exchange for more mobility? *Cambridge Review of International Affairs, 27*(1), 167–183.

Sakwa, R. (2015). The death of Europe? Continental fates after Ukraine. *International Affairs, 91*(3), 553–579.

Sakwa, R. (2017). The Ukraine syndrome and Europe: Between norms and space. *Soviet and Post-Soviet Review, 44*(1), 9–31.

Samkharadze, I. (2019). Europeanization of energy law and policy beyond the Member States: The case of Georgia. *Energy Policy, 130*, 1–6.

Samokhvalov, V. (2015). Ukraine between Russia and the European Union: Triangle revisited. *Europe-Asia Studies, 67*(9), 1371–1393.

Samokhvalov, V. (2018). Russia and its shared neighbourhoods: A comparative analysis of Russia-EU and Russia-China relations in the EU's Eastern Neighbourhood and Central Asia. *Contemporary Politics, 24*(1), 30–45.

Sasse, G. (2009). The European Neighbourhood Policy and conflict management: A comparison of Moldova and the Caucasus. *Ethnopolitics, 8*(3–4), 369–386.

Sasse, G. (2013). Linkages and the promotion of democracy: The EU's Eastern Neighbourhood. *Democratization, 20*(4), 553–591.

Sauer, T. (2017). The origins of the Ukraine crisis and the need for collective security between Russia and the West. *Global Policy, 8*(1), 82–91.

Scazzieri, L. (2017). Europe, Russia and the Ukraine crisis: The dynamics of coercion. *Journal of Strategic Studies, 40*(3), 392–416.

Schmidtke, O., & Chira-Pascanut, C. (2011). Contested neighbourhood: Toward the 'Europeanization' of Moldova? *Comparative European Politics, 9*(4–5), 467–485.

Sejersen, M. (2019). Democratic sanctions meet black knight support: Revisiting the Belarusian case. *Democratization, 26*(3), 502–520.

Semkou, A., Kolovos, E., Andreadis, I., & Konstantinidou, A. (2019). Integrating energy markets in the wider Europe: The Eastern dimension. *European Journal of Sustainable Development*, *8*(4), 101–113.

Shapovalova, N. (2016). The power of informality: European Union's engagement with non-state actors in Common Security and Defence Policy. *European Security*, *25*(3), 326–345.

Shepotylo, O. (2010). A gravity model of net benefits of EU membership: The case of Ukraine. *Journal of Economic Integration*, *25*(4), 676–702.

Shulga, I., Kurylo, V., Gyrenko, I., & Savych, S. (2019). Legal regulation of energy safety in Ukraine and the European Union: Problems and perspective. *European Journal of Sustainable Development*, *8*(3), 439–447.

Shyrokykh, K. (2017). Effects and side effects of European Union assistance on the former Soviet republics. *Democratization*, *24*(4), 651–669.

Shyrokykh, K. (2018). The evolution of the foreign policy of Ukraine: External actors and domestic factors. *Europe-Asia Studies*, *70*(5), 832–850.

Shyrokykh, K. (2019). Policy-specific effects of Transgovernmental Cooperation: A statistical assessment across the EU's post-Soviet neighbours. *Journal of European Public Policy*, *26*(1), 149–168.

Shyrokykh, K., & Rimkutė, D. (2019). EU rules beyond its borders: The policy-specific effects of Transgovernmental networks and EU agencies in the European Neighbourhood. *JCMS: Journal of Common Market Studies*, *57*(4), 749–767.

Siddi, M. (2016). German foreign policy towards Russia in the aftermath of the Ukraine crisis: A new ostpolitik? *Europe-Asia Studies*, *68*(4), 665–677.

Siddi, M. (2019). The EU's botched geopolitical approach to external energy policy: The case of the Southern Gas Corridor. *Geopolitics*, *24*(1), 124–144.

Sierra, O. P. (2010). A corridor through thorns: EU energy security and the Southern Energy Corridor. *European Security*, *19*(4), 643–660.

Sierra, O. B. P. (2011a). No man's land? A comparative analysis of the EU and Russia's influence in the Southern Caucasus. *Communist and Post-Communist Studies*, *44*(3), 233–243.

Sierra, O. B. P. (2011a). Shaping the neighbourhood? The EU's impact on Georgia. *Europe-Asia Studies*, *63*(8), 1377–1398.

Silander, D., & Nilsson, M. (2013). Democratization without enlargement? The European Neighbourhood Policy on post-communist transitions. *Contemporary Politics*, *19*(4), 441–458.

Siljak, D., & Nagy, S. G. (2018). Economic convergence of the Eastern Partnership countries towards the EU-13. *Eastern Journal of European Studies*, *9*(2), 169–185.

Siljak, D., & Nagy, S. G. (2019). Convergence and transition of the Eastern Partnership countries towards the European Union. *Entrepreneurial Business and Economics Review*, *7*(3), 221–235.

Simão, L. (2012). The problematic role of EU democracy promotion in Armenia, Azerbaijan and Nagorno-Karabakh. *Communist and Post-Communist Studies*, *45*(1–2), 193–200.

Simão, L. (2013). Region-building in the Eastern Neighbourhood: Assessing EU regional policies in the South Caucasus. *East European Politics*, *29*(3), 273–288.

Simão, L. (2014). The EU's conflict resolution policies in the Black Sea Area. *Journal of Balkan and Near Eastern Studies*, *16*(3), 300–313.

Simão, L. (2017). Bringing 'the political' back into European security: Challenges to the EU's ordering of the Eastern Partnership. *East European Politics*, *33*(3), 338–354.

Simons, G. (2012). Security sector reform and Georgia: The European Union's challenge in the Southern Caucasus. *European Security*, *21*(2), 272–293.

Sinkkonen, T. (2011). A security dilemma on the boundary line: An EU perspective to Georgian-Russian confrontation after the 2008 war. *Southeast European and Black Sea Studies*, *11*(3), 265–278.

Sjursen, H., & Rosen, G. (2017). Arguing sanctions. On the EU's response to the crisis in Ukraine. *JCMS: Journal of Common Market Studies*, *55*(1), 20–36.

Smith, N. R. (2015). The EU and Russia's conflicting regime preferences in Ukraine: Assessing regime promotion strategies in the scope of the Ukraine crisis. *European Security, 24*(4), 525–540.

Smith, N. R. (2016). The EU under a realist scope: Employing a neoclassical realist framework for the analysis of the EU's Deep and Comprehensive Free Trade Agreement offer to Ukraine. *International Relations, 30*(1), 29–48.

Solonenko, I. (2009). External democracy promotion in Ukraine: The role of the European Union. *Democratization, 16*(4), 709–731.

Solonenko, I. (2014). The EU's democratization efforts in the Black Sea Region: The challenge of 'domesticating' democracy. *Journal of Balkan and Near Eastern Studies, 16*(3), 343–355.

Steglich, R. (2012). The European Union as a normative power and conflict transformation in Moldova: A 'force for good'? *Journal of Contemporary European Research, 8*(1), 75–89.

Stegniy, O. (2011). Ukraine and the Eastern Partnership: 'Lost in translation'? *East European Politics, 27*(1), 50–72.

Ter-Matevosyan, V., Drnoian, A., Mkrtchyan, N., & Yepremyan, T. (2017). Armenia in the Eurasian Economic Union: Reasons for joining and its consequences. *Eurasian Geography and Economics, 58*(3), 340–360.

Terzyan, A. (2016). The evolution of the European Union's conception in the foreign policy discourse of Armenia: Implications for U-turn and the path beyond the association agreement. *Eastern Journal of European Studies, 7*(2), 165–184.

Terzyan, A. (2017). The EU vs. Russia in the foreign policy discourse of Armenia: The fragility of normative power or the power of Russian coercion? *Eastern Journal of European Studies, 8*(2), 185–203.

Terzyan, A. (2019). Bringing Armenia closer to Europe? Challenges to the EU-Armenia comprehensive and enhanced partnership agreement implementation. *Romanian Journal of European Affairs, 19*(1), 97–110.

Theophylactou, D. A. (2012). Geopolitics, Turkey's EU accession course and Cyprus: Power balances and 'Soft Power' calculations. *Southeast European and Black Sea Studies, 12*(1), 97–114.

Tiede, W., & Rennalls, O. (2012). Recent developments in the Ukrainian judicial system and the impact of international and European Law. *East European Politics and Societies, 26*(1), 93–114.

Timuş, N. (2013). Democracy for export: The Europeanisation of electoral laws in the East European Neighbourhood. *East European Politics, 29*(3), 289–304.

Timuş, N. (2014). Transnational party Europeanization: EPP and Ukrainian parties. *Acta Politica, 49*(1), 51–70.

Toero, C., Butler, E., & Gruber, K. (2014). Visegrad: The evolving pattern of coordination and partnership after EU enlargement. *Europe-Asia Studies, 66*(3), 364–393.

Tomkiewicz, J. (2018). The labour market and income distribution in post-socialist economies—Non-obvious regularities. *Communist and Post-Communist Studies, 51*(4), 315–324.

Trenin, D. (2011). Russia and the New Eastern Europe. *Russian Politics and Law, 49*(6), 38–53.

Trupia, F. (2017). Migranthood and self-governing rights: A new paradigm for the post-communist Eastern Europe. *Eastern Journal of European Studies, 8*(1), 177–195.

Tsuladze, L. (2017). On Europeanisation, national sentiments and confused identities in Georgia. *Communist and Post-Communist Studies, 50*(2), 125–133.

Tudoroiu, T. (2016). Unfreezing failed frozen conflicts: A post-Soviet case study. *Journal of Contemporary European Studies, 24*(3), 375–396.

Turkina, E., & Kourtikakis, K. (2015). Keeping up with the neighbours: Diffusion of norms and practices through networks of employer and employee organizations in the Eastern Partnership and the Mediterranean. *JCMS: Journal of Common Market Studies, 53*(5), 1163–1185.

Turkina, E., & Postnikov, E. (2012). Cross-border inter-firm networks in the European Union's Eastern Neighbourhood: Integration via Organizational Learning. *JCMS: Journal of Common Market Studies, 50*(4), 632–652.

Turkina, E., & Postnikov, E. (2014). From business to politics: Cross-border inter-firm networks and policy spillovers in the EU's Eastern Neighbourhood. *JCMS: Journal of Common Market Studies, 52*(5), 1120–1141.

Tyushka, A. (2015). Association through approximation: Procedural law and politics of legislative and regulatory approximation in the EU-Ukraine association agreement. *Baltic Journal of European Studies, 5*(1), 56–72.

Tyushka, A. (2015). Em*power*ed to deliver: The institutional model and implementation arrangements under the EU-Ukraine association agreement. *Romanian Journal of European Affairs, 15*(1), 5–22.

Tyushka, A. (2017). Association-*cum*-Integration: The EU-Ukraine association agreement and 'association law' as an institution of Ukraine's European Integration. *Croatian Yearbook of European Law & Policy, 13*, 87–132.

Tyushka A. (2017). Building the neighbours: The EU's new association agreements and structural power in the Eastern Neighbourhood, *Journal of Contemporary Central and Eastern Europe, 25*(1), 45–61.

van der Loo, G., & Van Elsuwege, P. (2012). Competing paths of regional economic integration in the post-Soviet space: Legal and political dilemmas for Ukraine. *Review of Central and East European Law, 37*(4), 421–447.

van Elsuwege, P., & Petrov, R. (2011). Article 8 TEU: Towards a new generation of agreements with the neighbouring countries of the European Union? *European Law Review, 36*(5), 688–703.

van Gils, E. (2017). Differentiation through bargaining power in EU-Azerbaijan relations: Baku as a tough negotiator. *East European Politics, 33*(3), 388–405.

van Gils, E. (2018a). Azerbaijan's foreign policy strategies and the European Union: Successful resistance and pursued influence. *Europe-Asia Studies, 70*(5), 738–758.

van Gils, E. (2018b). From 'unilateral' to 'dialogical': Determinants of EU-Azerbaijan negotiations. *Europe-Asia Studies, 70*(10), 1572–1596.

van Middelaar, L. (2016). The return of politics—The European Union after the crises in the Eurozone and Ukraine. *JCMSL: Journal of Common Market Studies, 54*(3), 495–507.

Vankova, Z. (2018). Poland and Bulgaria's bilateral agreements with Eastern Partnership countries in the context of circular migration. *European Journal of Social Security, 20*(2), 188–203.

Vasilyan, S. (2014). 'Moral power' as objectification of the 'civilian'/'normative' 'EUlogy': The European Union as a conflict-dealer in the South Caucasus. *Journal of International Relations and Development, 17*(3), 397–424.

Vasilyan, S. (2017). 'Swinging on a pendulum': Armenia in the Eurasian Economic Union and with the European Union. *Problems of Post-Communism, 64*(1), 32–46.

Veebel, V. (2017). Russia's neo-imperial dependence model: Experiences of former Soviet republics. *Romanian Journal of Political Science, 17*(1), 4–34.

Veebel, V. (2019). European Union as normative power in the Ukrainian-Russian conflict. *International Politics, 56*(5), 697–712.

Verdun, A., & Chira, G. E. (2011). The Eastern Partnership: The burial ground of enlargement hopes? *Comparative European Politics, 9*(4–5), 448–466.

Vieira, A. (2016). Ukraine, Russia and the strategic partnership dynamics in the EU's Eastern Neighbourhood: Recalibrating the EU's 'self', 'we' and 'other'. *Cambridge Review of International Affairs, 29*(1), 128–150.

Vieira, A. V. G. (2014). The politico-military alliance of Russia and Belarus: Re-Examining the role of NATO and the EU in light of the intra-alliance security dilemma. *Europe-Asia Studies, 66*(4), 557–577.

Vieira, A., & Vasilyan, S. (2018). Armenia and Belarus: Caught between the EU's and Russia's conditionalities? *European Politics and Society, 19*(4), 471–489.

Vilson, M. (2015). The foreign policy of the Baltic States and the Ukrainian crisis: A case of Europeanization? *New Perspectives, 23*(2), 49–76.

Weiss, T. (2018). Building leverage at the EU level? Specialisation and coherence in Czech policy on Eastern European transition. *Journal of International Relations and Development, 21*(1), 172–193.

Whitman, R. G., & Wolff, S. (2010). The EU as a conflict manager? The case of Georgia and its implications. *International Affairs, 86*(1), 87–107.

Wilson, A., & Popescu, N. (2009). Russian and European neighbourhood policies compared. *Southeast European and Black Sea Studies, 9*(3), 317–331.

Wolczuk, K. (2009). Implementation without coordination: The impact of EU conditionality on Ukraine under the European Neighbourhood Policy. *Europe-Asia Studies, 61*(2), 187–211.

Wolczuk, K. (2016). Managing the flows of gas and rules: Ukraine between the EU and Russia. *Eurasian Geography and Economics, 57*(1), 113–137.

Wolczuk, K. (2019). State building and European integration in Ukraine. *Eurasian Geography and Economics, 60*(6), 736–754.

Wright, N. (2018). No Longer the Elephant outside the room: Why the Ukraine crisis reflects a deeper shift towards German leadership of European Foreign Policy. *German Politics, 27*(4), 479–497.

Wunderlich, D. (2012). The limits of external governance: Implementing EU external migration policy. *Journal of European Public Policy, 19*(9), 1414–1433.

Yakouchyk, K. (2016). The good, the bad, and the ambitious: Democracy and autocracy promoters competing in Belarus. *European Political Science Review, 8*(2), 195–224.

Yatsyk, A. (2018). "Comprehensive approximation" with the EU: Biopolitical governmentality and its spill-over effects in Georgia. *Journal of Contemporary Central and Eastern Europe, 26*(2–3), 147–163.

Youngs, R. (2009). 'A door neither closed nor open': EU policy towards Ukraine during and since the Orange Revolution. *International Politics, 46*(4), 358–375.

Zarembo, K. (2017). Perceptions of CSDP effectiveness in Ukraine: A host state perspective. *European Security, 26*(2), 190–206.

Zhabotynska, S., & Velivchenko, V. (2019). New media and strategic narratives: The Dutch referendum on Ukraine—EU Association Agreement in Ukrainian and Russian Internet blogs. *European Security, 28*(3), 360–381.

B. 2020 publications list

Ademmer, E., Delcour, L., Hoffmann, K., & Jaroszewicz, M. (2020). Interdependences with external actors and regime persistence in Eastern Partnership countries. *East European Politics*, 1–21. https://doi.org/10.1080/21599165.2020.1828871

Amadio Viceré, M. G. (2020). Looking towards the East: The high representative's role in EU foreign policy on Kosovo and Ukraine. *European Security, 29*(3), 337–358.

Axyonova, V., Cenușa, D., & Gawrich, A. (2020). International negotiations and domestic change in the EU's Eastern Neighborhood: Deconstructing antidiscrimination reforms in Moldova. *East European Politics and Societies*, doi: 10.1177/0888325420968911.

Badalyan, T., & Vasilyan, S. (2020). The perceived rationale, variegated institutional take and impact of the EU's human rights policy in Armenia and Georgia. *Journal of Contemporary European Studies, 28*(4), 514–529.

DeBardeleben, J. (2020). Crisis response, path dependence, and the joint decision trap: The EU's eastern and Russia policies after the Ukraine crisis. *East European Politics, 36*(4), 564–585.

Dekanozishvili, M. (2020). The European Union's credibility–expectations gap in its European Neighbourhood Policy: Perspectives from Georgia and Ukraine. *Southeast European and Black Sea Studies, 20*(2), 289–305.

Delcour, L., & Wolczuk, K. (2020). Mind the gap: Role expectations and perceived performance of the EU in the South Caucasus. *Eurasian Geography and Economics*, 1–22. doi: 10.1080/15387216.2020.1779103

Dobrescu, M., & Schumacher, T. (2020). The politics of flexibility: Exploring the contested statehood–EU actorness Nexus in Georgia. *Geopolitics*, 25(2), 407–427.

Guérin, N., & Rittberger, B. (2020). Are third states pulling the strings? The impact of domestic policy change on EU-third state cooperation. *Journal of European Integration*, 42 (7), 991–1008.

Helwig, N. (2020) Germany in European Diplomacy: Minilateralism as a Tool for Leadership. *German Politics*, 29(1), 25–41.

Klose, S. (2020). Interactionist role theory meets ontological security studies: An exploration of synergies between socio-psychological approaches to the study of International Relations. *European Journal of International Relations*, 26(3), 851–874.

Ladychenko, V., Melnychuk, O., Golovko, L., & Burmak, O. (2020). Waste management at the local level in the EU and Ukraine. *European Journal of Sustainable Development*, 9(1), 329–329.

Langbein, J., Gazizullin, I., & Naumenko, D. (2020). Trade liberalisation and opening in post-Soviet limited access orders. *East European Politics*, doi: 10.1080/21599165.2020.1747440

Libman, A., & Obydenkova, A. V. (2020). Global governance and Eurasian international organisations: Lessons learned and future agenda. *Post-Communist Economies*, doi: 10.1080/14631377.2020.1793587

Luciani, L. (2020). The EU's hegemonic interventions in the South Caucasus: Constructing 'civil' society, depoliticising human rights? *Cooperation and Conflict*. doi: 10.1177/0010836720954478

Lytvyn, H., & A. Tyushka (2020). Rethinking the governance-governmentality- governability nexus at the EU's Eastern frontiers: The Carpathian Euroregion 2.0 and the future of EU-Ukrainian cross-border cooperation, *Eastern Journal of European Studies*, 11(Special Issue): 146–183.

Maass, A. S. (2020). The Actorness of the EU's state-building in Ukraine-before and after Crimea. *Geopolitics*, 25(2), 387–406.

Maksimovtsova, K. (2020). Ukrainian vs. Russian? The securitization of language-related issues in Ukrainian Blogs and on news websites. *East European Politics and Societies*, 34(2), 375–399.

Matiiuk, Y., Poškus, M. S., & Liobikienė, G. (2020). The Implementation of climate change policy in post-Soviet countries achieving long-term targets. *Sustainability*, 12(11), 4558.

Miarka, A. (2020). Transnistria as an instrument of influence of the Russian federation on the security of Moldova in the second decade of the 21st century—selected aspects. *Communist and Post-Communist Studies*, 53(2), 61–75.

Morar, Ş., & Dembińska, M. (2020). Between the West and Russia: Moldova's international brokers in a two-level game. *Eurasian Geography and Economics*, doi: 10.1080/15387216.2020.1836984

Muhhina, K. (2020). Governance stories in the South Caucasus: Narrative policy analysis of the EU's public administration reform assistance to the Eastern Neighbourhood. *Journal of European Integration*, 42(6), 817–835.

Natorski, M. (2020). United we stand in metaphors: EU authority and incomplete politicisation of the crisis in Ukraine. *Journal of European Integration*, 42(5), 733–749.

Nizhnikau, R. (2020). Love the tender: ProZorro and anti- corruption reforms after the Euromaidan revolution. *Problems of Post-Communism*, doi: 10.1080/10758216.2020.1837635

Petrova, I., & Delcour, L. (2020). From principle to practice? The resilience-local ownership nexus in the EU Eastern Partnership policy. *Contemporary Security Policy*, 41(2), 336–360.

Samokhvalov, V., & Strelkov, A. (2020) Cross-dimensional network of democracy promotion: public administration reform in post-Euromaidan Ukraine. *Journal of European Integration*, DOI: 10.1080/07036337.2020.1807537

Schumacher, T. (2020). The EU and its neighbourhood: The politics of muddling through. *JCMS: Journal of Common Market Studies*, 58, 187–201.

Shevtsova, M. (2020). Fighting "Gayropa": Europeanization and instrumentalization of LGBTI rights in Ukrainian Public Debate. *Problems of Post-Communism*, 67(6), 500–510.

Shyrokykh, K. (2020) How effective is EU's human rights persuasion in its post-Soviet neighbourhood? Insights from a statistical assessment. *Journal of Contemporary European Studies*, 28(3), 283–303.

Siddi, M. (2020). Theorising conflict and cooperation in EU-Russia energy relations: Ideas, identities and material factors in the Nord Stream 2 debate. *East European Politics, 36*(4), 544–563.

Silva, P. M., & Selden, Z. (2020). Economic interdependence and economic sanctions: A case study of European Union sanctions on Russia. *Cambridge Review of International Affairs, 33*(2), 229–251.

Tyushka, A. (2020). Twists and turns of democratic transition and Europeanization in East-Central Europe since 1989: Betwixt EU *Member* and *Neighbour State*-Building. *Croatian Yearbook of European Law and Policy, 16*, 133–177.

Vieira, A. (2020). The European Union's 'potential we' between acceptance and contestation: Assessing the positioning of six eastern partnership countries. *JCMS: Journal of Common Market Studies*. doi: 10.1111/jcms.13069.

Weiffen, B., Gawrich, A., & Axyonova, V. (2020). Reorganizing the neighborhood? Power shifts and regional security organizations in the post-Soviet space and Latin America. *Journal of Global Security Studies*, doi: 10.1093/jogss/ogz080.

Index

Note: **Bold** page numbers refer to tables; *italic* page numbers refer to figures and page numbers followed by "n" denote endnotes.

AA-DCFTA 133–134
Ab initio 107
Abkhazia 12, 87, 121, 163–176, 183, 184, 187, 189
Acemoglu, D. 157
acquis academique 292–301, 304, 305, 311, 312
acquis communautaire 3, 41, 49, 85, 103, 107, 119, 133, 134, 140, 170, 188, 190, 193
Action Plan (AP) 41, 43, 48, 65, 183, 184, 220
Administrative Boundary Lines 166, 171, 173
agency: of EaP countries 108–109; and structure 167
Agnew, J. 82, 93n6, 93n7
albeit 8, 77, 84, 180, 189, 198, 217, 225, 269, 274, 296
Aliyev, H. 228
Aliyev, I. 54n40, 54n41, 217, 225–227
Alliance for European Integration (AEI) 45, 149, 157
alternative options 222, 223, 228–231
Anti-corruption National Centre (ANC) 150
anti-corruption reform 140, 150–151, 257, 259
Arab Spring 32n3, 61, 62, 65, 67, 68, 70, 183
Armenia 28, 51, 54n28, 60, 65–67, 109, 180–189, 192–194, 194n3, 216, 252, 256, 258; EaP scholarship *310*; Eurasian integration 47–51; foreign policy 187–188; gas distribution network 186; government 186–188, 195n16, 231; identity 185; modernization process 49; policies 47
Armenian National Security Strategy 185
Armenian Soviet Socialist Republic (ASSR) 185, 195n13
Association Agreements (AAs) 2, 11, 12, 24, 32n8, 39, 43, 45, 46, 48–50, 60, 77, 88–90, 92, 107–109, 110n10, 131, 134–136, 140, 142, 148, 149, 156, 164, 170, 172, 174, 175, 181, 200, 216–219, 224, 226–231, 246, 270, 272, 282, 293
Atlas.ti software 282, 292, 293, 295, 301
Azarov, M. 137
Azerbaijan 4, 12, 26–29, 60, 67, 69, 109, 187, 216–231, 232n1, 232n9, 258, 305, 307; bargaining power 230; EaP scholarship *311*; energy 69, 223; EU and 12, 216–218, 220–222, 224, 228, 229, 232n4, 259, 293; government 60, 67, 216–222, 224–230, 232n1, 232n9; proactive promotion of 225; SMP with 226

Baku 26, 27, 50, 66, 217–220, 222–227, 229–231, 232n1, 232n5
Baldwin, D. A. 242, 254; *Success and Failure in Foreign Policy* 242–243
Baltic Energy Market Interconnection Plan 200
bargaining: chip 26–28, 30, 190; position 26, 28, 223, 224, 229; power 12, 217, 218, 220–223, 225, 226, 229–231; process 43, 116
Barnett, M. 110n7
Barroso, J. M. 138
Bechev, D. 222
Belarus 8, 12, 28, 61, 67, 70, 85, 180–194, 194n9, 195n19, 198–210, 211n15, 232n5, 246, 286, 305; EaP scholarship *314*; engagement 201; EU and 8, 191, 198, 200, 202, 204, 205, 208–210, 293; foreign policy 204, 205; leadership 189, 190; Russia and 180–194, 194n2
Belarusian Ministry of Foreign Affairs 201
Berling, V. 115, 117–118
bibliometric analysis 291–300, 309

bilateral relations 5, 181, 182, 192, 216, 218–221, 228, 232n1, 252, 281–283, 293, 310, 312
Bloom, S. 132
Booth, K. 117, 121
Börzel, T. A. 10, 42
Bosse, G. 207
Bourdieu, P. 113, 115, 116, 124n1, 124n2
Bretherton, C. 167
Brundtland, G. H. 115
Brussels 1, 20, 60, 66, 77, 79, 83, 85, 90, 92, 104, 107, 109, 165, 168–171, 175, 188–191, 193, 195n19, 217, 219–224, 226, 228–230, 252, 254, 271, 282
Brussels EaP Summit Joint Declaration 282
Burlyuk, O. 100, 101, 104, 109
Bush, G. H. 89
Buzan, B. 115

capacity-building 11, 59, 62, 210, 286
capital 11, 13, 41, 79, 114–124, 124n1, 124n2
Carlsnaes, W. 243
Casier, T. 10, 91
Central and Eastern Europe (CEE) 24, 28
Chandler, D. 209, 210
coherence 58, 63, 167, 291, 304
Cold War 22, 41, 79, 80, 88–91, 93n4, 94n26, 113–115, 117, 118, 121, 123
Collective Rapid Reaction Force (CRRF) 54n28
Collective Security Treaty Organization (CSTO) 12, 47, 50, 54n28, 185, 188–190
Color Revolutions 60
colour revolution 67, 120, 157, 186
Common Agricultural Policy 102
Common Foreign and Security Policy (CFSP) 8, 107, 187, 189, 249, 250
Commonwealth of Independent States (CIS) 52n1, 181, 203
communist rule 44, 148
Comprehensive and Enhanced Partnership Agreement (CEPA) 2, 109, 180, 185, 188, 192, 193, 194n3, 246, 258
Comprehensive Institution Building (CIB) 150, 201, 208, 210
computer-assisted qualitative content analysis (CAQDAS) 4, 291–292
conditionality 2, 10, 28, 29, 48, 49, 58–64, **62**, 66, 68–71, 77, 92, 107–109, 118, 120, 132, 133, 137, 140, 141, 153, 180–194, 198–200, 206, 209, 223, 253, 283, 285

conflict management 11, 164, 165, 167–170, 174–176
Connolly, W. 117
constructivism 43, 47
contagion 101
contested statehood 11, 163–172, 174–176, 176n15
co-occurrence 283, *284,* **285,** 286, 292, 304–306, *307, 308, 311, 314, 315,* **317–318**
Copenhagen summit 2009 24
Copsey, N. 85
corpus linguistics 282–283, 292
Council of the European Union 22, 24, 25, 119, 121
cross-cutting deliverables 245, 254–255, 282
Czech Republic 79, 84–91, 94n21

D'Anieri, P. 135
decision-making 24, 92, 104, 114, 201, 202, 209, 210, 217, 219, 221, 223, 243, 249
Deep and Comprehensive Free Trade Areas (DCFTAs) 24, 26, 28, 32n8, 39, 41, 43, 45, 48, 50, 52n1, 61, 62, 107, 131, 133, 148, 177n15, 181, 184, 188, 191, 192, 194n3, 200, 228, 232n4, 246, 252, 253, 258, 268, 273, 286, 293
de facto 6, 10, 39, 42, 46, 104, 163, 164, 166, 168–171, 173–176, 184, 198, 207, 250, 272
Delegation of the European Commission 187, 201
democracy: partial 186; promotion 5, 10, 58, 64–66, 87, 89, 199, 202, 203, 206–211, 213n53, 256, 267, 310, 313; sovereign 121
democratic conditionality 10, 58–63, 69–71; consistency and effectiveness of **62**; golden carrot and consistency 63–64; reform coalitions 66–68; stability 64–66
Deputy Prime Minister for European Affairs 86
Deudney, D. 93n7
dialogical 13, 217, 220, 222, 223, 229, 231
Dillon, M. 10, 113, 116, 117
Directorate-Generals (DGs) 107
disciplinary profile 296
discourse coalition 78–82, 86, 88–92
discourse theory 80
Dodon, I. 46, 152, 155–157, 231
domestic context 40, 92, 222, 226–227, 230
domestic sovereignty 165, 166, 168, 171
Drulák, P. 86, 94n16
Duvall, R. 110n7

INDEX

EaP-3 *see* three Eastern Partnership (EaP-3)
EaP-6 *see* six Eastern Partnership (EaP-6)
'EaPC not specified' 321n14
EaP *plus* 267–270
EaP Prague Summit Joint Declaration 6, 281–282
EaP Summit Joint Declaration 244, 245, 282–287, *284,* **285,** *287,* **288**
EaP Vilnius Summit 282
East-Central European 132, 135, 140
Eastern Neighbourhood Countries (ENC) 64, 85
Eastern Partnership (EaP) 5–8, 77–79, 266–267; achievements 245–254; beyond 2020 257; Civil Society Forum 246; countries 2–5, 7–13, 87, 105, 107–110, 116, 180, 185, 187, 194, 201, 216, 242, 244, 246, 249–257, 259, 265–273, 282, 283, *284,* **285,** 286, 294, 296, *296,* 301, 304–306, *307, 308,* 310–313, *314, 315*; geopoliticisation 80–93; goal 244–245; and Moldova 149–152; and past research 266–267; policy framework 300–304; regional project 41–43; scholarship 4, 266, 267, 293, 294, *294, 295,* 296, *296, 297–315,* 302, 306, 312, 313, **317–319**; structure of 7; Summits 1, 2, 4–6, 90, 224, 244, 245, 254, 257, 271, 281–283, 286; upgrade 270–273
Eastern Partnership Civil Society Forum 168
Eastern Partnership Index (EaP Index) 259n3
Eastern Partnership Integration and Cooperation (EaPIC) programme 13n5
East European policy 103, 106, 109
economic integration 2, 6, 13, 39, 40, 48, 51, 83, 122, 131, 134, 142, 164, 172, 184, 244, 246, 252, 253, 257, 258, 267, 273, 281, 286, 296, 310
economic interdependence 44, 47, 223, 224
Edkins, J. 10, 113, 114, 117, 122
electoral revolutions 59, 62
Electric Networks of Armenia (ENA) 186
Energy Charter Treaty 153, 187
ENP Plus 6
Epstein, R. 141
Essex School 81
EU4Business projects 253
EU Delegation 135–136, 187, 201, 226
EU-EaP-6 cooperation 244, 245, 253, 258, 259, 282, 311
EU-Eastern neighbours relations 5, 13n2, **247–248,** 265, 266, 273–274, 291, 293, 306, 311, 313
EU Grand Strategy 81

EU High Representative Catherine Ashton and the Commissioner for Enlargement Štefan Füle 60
EU integration 25, 29, 43–47, 50, 51, 152
EU Monitoring Mission 167–169
Eurasian Customs Union (ECU) 41, 46, 47, 52n1, 70, 181, 184, 187, 188, 190, 198
Eurasian Economic Commission 41, 188
Eurasian Economic Union (EEU) 12, 28, 39–41, 47, 48, 52n6, 105, 109, 152, 155, 180, 181, 184, 185, 187, 188, 191, 193, 194, 198, 205, 229, 230, 251, 272, 282
Eurasian project 41, 42, 48, 49, 51, 184, 189, 192
Euromaidan 11, 60, 67, 131–133, 136–138, 142, 186
EURONEST 201, 202, 209, 212n36
European Azerbaijan Society (TEAS) 225
European Bank for Reconstruction and Development (EBRD) 137, 141, 253
European Commission 1, 3, 8, 13n1, 25, 29, 118, 119, 136–138, 141, 143n4, 148, 170, 189, 200, 201, 228, 231, 232n1, 252, 254, 268, 274
European Dialogue on Modernisation 189
European Endowment for Democracy (EED) 182, 194n5, 200, 201
European External Action Service (EEAS) 3, 107, 170, 220, 225, 226, 232n1, 249, 251, 256, 257, 269, 272
European integration 11, 23, 28, 29, 31, 42–48, 85, 87, 113, 115, 122, 124, 131–136, 139, 142, 149, 150, 154, 246, 250, 259n3, 267, 269, 270, 272
European Investment Bank (EIB) 137, 200, 201, 253
Europeanization 4, 48, 49, 63, 71, 132, 241, 250, 267, 274, 291, 310
European model of development 49
European Neighbourhood and Partnership Instrument (ENPI) 6, 200
European Neighbourhood Instrument (ENI) 6, 137, 143n2, 143n3, 200
European Neighbourhood Policy (ENP) 1, 3–8, 10, 19, 22, 24, 25, 31, 32n3, 41, 43–45, 48, 58, 59, 62–65, **69,** *69,* 71, 77, 82–85, 91, 100, 102–105, 107, 109, 113, 119–121, 123, 125, 133, 143n2, 151, 164, 180, 181, 183, 187, 198, 216, 220, 228, 291
European Parliament 60, 225, 226, 232n1, 268
European security 10, 113–115, 117–124
European Security Strategy 2003 119, 271

INDEX

European Union (EU): actorness 166–167; beyond enlargement 131–132; bilateral track 6, 8, 11, 200–201, 232n5; conditionality (*see* conditionality); Council Presidency 6, 85, 90; and Eastern neighbours 8–13; failure of 58; financial aid 253–254; ideal self 8, 9, 19–27, **27**, 29–32, 273; identity 19, 20, 25, 30, 31, 117; integration 25, 29, 43–47, 50, 51, 152; legitimacy 2, 21, 23, 25, **27**, 29, 30, 91, 105, 117–120, 123, 203–206, 226, 230, 243; multilateral track 201; norm 29–31, 49, 51, 83, 119, 190, 250, 267; perceptions of 168; policies 5, 11, 12, 20, 25, 48, 78, 79, 84, 87, 102, 104–110, 123, 134, 147–151, 157, 158, 201, 207, 217, 218, 221; policymaking 6, 20, 22, 23, 63, 120, 134, 138, 205, 217, 221, 222, 231, 266; for statebuilding 136–139; and unintended consequences 101–102; *see also* democratic conditionality

Europe Whole and Free 88, 89
EU-Ukrainian Association Agenda 60
external actors 4, 20, 26, 27, 31, 32, 39, 40, 42, 43, 82, 132, 147, 148, 157, 185, 192, 193, 221, 267, 291, 295, 300, 306–308, 310, *314, 315*
externalisation effects 102
external sovereignty 166, 168, 174, 175, 176n15

Filat, V. 53n24, 155, 156
Fisher, F. 93n5
Flockhart, T. 124n6
foreign direct investment (FDI) 186
foreign policy 21, 22, 24, 25, 27, 28, 30, 32n6, 46, 48, 50, 51, 59, 63, 79, 82, 84–86, 91, 93, 101, 102, 116, 183, 188, 208, 228, 242–244, 268, 270, 271
Foreign Policy Analysis (FPA) 13, 242–244, 258, 266, 296
foreign policy goals (FPGs) 242–244
Foucault, M. 122
frequency 209, 283, 292, 295
Friendship Treaty 194
Füle, S. 149

Gagauzia 46, 47, 51, 152, 154, 155
Gazprom 153, 182, 183, 186
Generalised System of Preferences/Generalised System of Preferences+ 172, 173
Geneva International Discussions 167, 169, 174
geopolitical thinking 78, 85, 92, 93
geopoliticisation 78–82, 91, 92; Czech Republic 85–88; pan-European and transatlantic debates 88–90; Poland 84–85

geopolitics 78–82, 88, 91
Georgia 11, 60, 66, 120, 121, 163–176, 252, 256, 305; domestic sovereignty 165; EaP scholarship *309*; EU and 163–165, 170–172, 252, 293; government 174, 175; problematic sovereignty 12, 165, 166, 176; Rose Revolution 59, 66, 163, 183; and Russia 163, 164, 166–171, 173, 175
Germany 6, 26, 92, 94n12, 105, 171, 185
van Gils, E. 116
Global Strategy 2016 19, 32n2, 114, 230
goal-oriented framework (GOF) 242–244, 258
Goldmann, K. 225
good governance 6, 118, 143n3, 201, 209, 210, 220, 245, 254, 256, 257, 259, 286
Gorbachev, M. 89, 115
Grabbe, H. 141
Gurin, C. 157

Hale, J. 183
Hansen, L. 80
Harnisch, S. 21
Haukkala, H. 93n9, 122
hierarchies 113, 115, 116, 121
Hill, C. 243
Horký, O. 87

IBRD 139
identity 19–21, 25, 30, 41, 43, 46, 47, 51, 80, 85, 87, 108, 114–117, 120, 185, 192, 199, 203, 204, 206, 210, 211, 227, 267, 274, 301, 311, 313
immigration 64, 186
Incident Prevention and Response Mechanism 169
integration-oriented agreement 133, 273
interdependence, asymmetrical 102
international relations (IR) 13, 20, 21, 23, 25, 80–82, 101, 114, 117–119, 198, 231, 242, 243, 258, 266, 291, 296
Inter-Parliamentary Assembly (IPA) 246, 249
Inter-State Oil and Gas Transportation to Europe (INOGATE) 182
intra-EaP connections and comparisons 304–306
irreconcilable interests 12, 116, 165, 169, 175, 273
issue salience analysis 283, 286

Jahn, B. 208, 209
joint bilateral institutions 249
Joint Communication 1, 3, 257

INDEX

343

Joint Declarations 244–245, 281–287, *284*, 285, **285**, *285*, 287, **288**
Joint Interim Plan 198
Jordan 62, 65, 68

Kazharski, A. 93n8
Keohane, R. O. 101, 102
Klimpush-Tsintsadze, I. 143n4
Kobzova, J. 268–269
Korosteleva, E. 4, 5, 12, 121
Kosachev, K. 154
Krasner, S. 165, 166, 169
Kratochvíl, P. 87
Kremlin 28, 90, 120, 131, 154
Kuchma, L. 70
Kuus, M. 79, 81, 93n1, 94n27
Kvirikashvili, G. 174

Laundromat scandal 2017 225
Lavenex, S. 102
Law of Georgia on Occupied Territories 171, 173, 176n8
legitimacy 2, 21, 23, 25, **27**, 29, 30, 91, 105, 117–120, 123, 203–206, 226, 230, 243
liberal inter-governmentalism 43, 47
Libya 8, 62, 68
Lindstrom, N. 132
Lukashenko, A. 28, 61, 63, 67, 69, 194n9, 198, 205, 210

Makarychev, A. 93n8
Manners, I. 101
Market Economy Status 200
Mathernova, K. 143n4
Merkel, A. 149
Midterm Plan of Reform Priorities for 2017–2020 139
migration 5, 11, 22–24, 44, 46, 64–66, 69, 122, 164, 165, 170–172, 174–176, 186, 286, 293, 311
Miklos, I. 139
Minister for Reconciliation and Civic Equality 171
Minister of Foreign Affairs 86, 225
Minsk Group 182, 194n6, 194n7, 232n9
mobility 4, 6, 11, 65, 164, 165, 170–172, 174–176, 200, 254, 301
Mobility Partnership 62, 164, 170, 186, 200, 220
Moga, T. L. 31
Moldindconbank 153
Moldova 29, 32n10, 47, 51, 52, 60, 67, 68, 147–158, 249, 313; authorities 45–47, 150, 176n15; communist party in 29; EaP scholarship *313*; Eastern Partnership and EU 149–152; engagement 44–45; EU and 11, 43–47, 148, 150, 156, 252, 293; government 148, 149, 151, 152, 156; politics 149–153, 157; population 47; with Romania 153, 154; Russia and 147–149, 152–158
Moscow 21–22, 28, 29, 46, 50, 51, 77, 78, 85, 87, 90, 92, 93, 104, 105, 109, 120, 152, 153, 155, 156, 169, 180–184, 186–191, 193, 228, 229, 252
Muslim Brotherhood (MB) 62, 68, 70

Nagorno-Karabakh conflict 28, 49–51, 66, 182, 183, 185, 187, 188, 195n18, 218–220, 223–230, 269
NATO 50, 59, 60, 89, 114, 115, 118, 119, 148, 182, 183, 191, 251, 308
negotiation 48, 60, 62, 90, 104, 107, 110n10, 135, 150, 183, 184, 190, 191, 198, 216–218, 229–231; alternative options 228–229; Association Agreement 218–219; bargaining power to 220–223; DCFTA 45; domestic context 226–227; EAEU 191; power base 223–224; self and other 227–228; skill and capacity 224–226; Strategic Modernisation Partnership 219; Strategic Partnership Agreement 219–220
Neumann, I. B. 42
Newly Independent States (NIS) 182
Nicolaidis, C. 222
non-linear approach 202, 209, 211
Non-Recognition and Engagement Policy 164, 165, 168
Northern Dimension Partnership 200
Nye, J. 101, 102

Obama, B. 60
Orange Revolution 67, 183
Orenstein, M. 132
Organization for Economic Cooperation and Development (OECD) 138
Organization for Security and Cooperation in Europe (OSCE) 60, 118, 182
Organized Crime and Corruption Reporting Project (OCCRP) 153
Orthodox Church 152, 154
OSCE Minsk Group 232n9
Ó Tuathail, G. 82, 93n6, 93n7
Our Party 148, 149, 152, 156

Papadimitriou, D. 4
partial democracy 186

Partnership and Cooperation Agreement (PCA) 5, 12, 26, 43, 164, 172, 173, 182, 183, 189, 191, 198, 216, 218, 219, 221, 223, 228–230
partnership diplomacy 271
Party of Socialists (PSRM) 46
Pascariu, G. 4
Penal Code 150–151
Petrova, I. 202, 209
Poland 2, 5, 6, 8, 79, 83–85, 87, 88, 90, 92, 94n12, 108, 201, 273
policy character 82
policy makers 79, 85, 86, 88, 90, 92, 94n16, 115, 118, 165, 183
politics/political 19–23, 25, 29–31, 67, 80–82, 86, 88, 91, 113–118, 120–123, 132, 133, 150–153, 163–176, 199, 202, 210, 267, 310, 311; association 2, 6, 13, 83, 131, 164, 184, 200, 244, 246, 249, 250, 256, 258, 273, 281, 286; boundary 117–120; community 79, 115, 117, 259; conditionality 182, 183, 189, 193, 198, 206, 209; EaP and European security 120–123; economy 93n10, 119, 120; elites 22, 40, 66, 70, 140, 148, 151, 157; irreconcilable process 114–117; leadership 115, 120; liberalisation 66; power 28, 63, 66, 77, 157, 227; process 67, 82, 90, 115, 189, 257; and security 116; stability 65, 66, 147, 150; struggle 80, 122–123; subjectivity 86
Pomorska, K. 85
population 47, 51, 55n45, 67, 147, 155, 157, 169, 171, 174, 186, 195n18, 203–206, 223
post-hoc fallacy/attribution problem 259n1
post-Soviet 8–9, 19–20, 30–32, 39–40, 51–52, 306; Armenia 47–51; ideal self 20–30, **27**; moldova in european integration 43–47; regional project 41–43
power asymmetries 116
power base 223–224
Privileged Partnership 61
Public Administration Reforms (PAR) 137–141, 143n4
Public Administration Reform Strategy (PARS) 138–140
public legitimation 203, 205
Putin, V. 21, 46, 50, 106, 120, 152, 155, 188

qualitative corpus analysis 283–287, *284,* **285,** *287,* **288,** 292, 295

Rada, V. 138
Raube, K. 202, 209

readmission agreement 164, 170, 186, 200, 246, 256
Readmission and Visa Facilitation Agreements 170
Reform Delivery Office (RDO) 139
reform enclaves 132–133, 139–141
Reform Support Teams (RST) 139–140
regional entity 266, 300, 304
regionalism 40–43
regional project 39–43, 51, 52, 205
region-building projects 9, 39, 41, 42, 51, 52, 267, 300, 301, 311
re-politicisation 114, 123, 124
Republic of Moldova 44, 149, 251
Richmond, O. 117
Rieker, P. 243
Riga Summit 219–220, 224–225, 245, 282
Rogers, J. 81
Rogozin, D. 152, 154
rollback policy 67, 86, 87
Rose Revolution 59, 66, 163, 183
Rouet, G. 4
Russia: conditional approaches 189–192; containment of 87; EaP countries 108–109; EU and 12, 23, 39, 40, 46, 77–81, 83, 90–92, 106, 107, 109, 110n10, 117, 120, 122, 147–149, 152, 157, 158, 171, 180–187, 192–194, 205, 265, 271, 272, 282, 291, 301, 302, 309, 312, 313; in European security 118; factor 266, 293; internal and external unintended consequences 105–106; media 154; migration 46; Moldova 149–155; non-decision 104; policies 148–149, 152–155, 181–189; post-election strategy 155–156; unintended consequences 106–108
Russia-Armenia relations 192, 194n2
Russia-Belarus military 194n2
Russian Compatriots Programme 186
Russian Federation 5, 10, 46, 53n12, 54n27, 104, 147, 154, 166

Saienko, O. 143n4
Samokhvalov, V. 141–142
Sargsyan, S. 47, 49, 54n36, 188
Sargsyan, T. 48
SARS-CoV-2 pandemic 1, 249, 256, 269, 272
Saudi Arabia 70
Schimmelfennig, F. 132
Schunz, S. 243
Secretariat of the Cabinet 140
Security Strategy 2003 19, 22, 32n1, 271
Sedelmeier, U. 132, 141

INDEX

Sikorski, R. 85
Simao, L. 120
Sisi, Abdel Fattah el- 70
six Eastern Partnership (EaP-6) 1–4, 9, 11, 13, 244, 245, 249–254, 256–259, 259n3, 265–267, 269, 272, 273, 281–283, 286, 296, 300, 308, 311, 312, 321n14
Six Point Agreement 167
SME Policy Index 2020 253
Smith, M. E. 243
social capital 79, 81, 91, 121, 124n2, 257
social empowerment 199–202, 206–211
Socialist Party (PSM) 148, 149, 152, 155–156
South Caucasus 47, 66, 163–164, 227, 258, 302, 305
South Ossetia 12, 87, 121, 122, 163–169, 171–176, 183, 184, 187, 189
Soviet Union 22, 29, 41, 47, 115, 118, 181, 182, 304
speech act 78, 81
state building 11, 44, 118, 131–132, 136–140, 142, 150, 185, 251, 310
State Building Contract 137, 138
state capacity 134–136, 140, 157, 254
Strange, S. 93n10
Strategic Group of Advisers (SAGSUR) 139
Strategic Modernisation Partnership (SMP) 216–230, 233n42
Strategic Partnership 103–106, 108, 109, 166, 228
Strategic Partnership Agreement (SPA) 216–223, 225–230
Strelets, V. 155
stronger governance 256, 259
Success and Failure in Foreign Policy (Baldwin) 242–243
Sukhumi 166, 168, 169, 171, 173–175, 176n1
Support for Improvement in Governance and Management (SIGMA) 138–139
Support Group for Ukraine (SGUA) 136–137, 140
symbolic power 10, 113, 114, 123, 124n3
Syria 62, 68

Technical Assistance to the Commonwealth of Independent States (TACIS) programme 181–182, 194n4
technocratic engagement 202, 207, 211
temporal dynamics 292, 299
textual analysis 282–283
third country 102, 131, 136, 217, 233n34, 249, 255

three Eastern Partnership (EaP-3) 2, 11, 246, 249–251, 253, 256, 259, 267, 268, 270, 271, 283, 285, 286, 306
three M's (money, market access, and mobility) 65, 83
Ticchi, D. 157
trade 172–174
Transnistria 45–47, 51, 153, 174, 176–177n15
Transport Corridor Europe-Caucasus-Asia (TRACECA) 182
Tricks of the Weak 122
Tskhinvali 166, 168, 169, 171, 172, 175, 176n1
Tuleancev, I. 154
Tunisia 58, 61, 62, 66, 68–71, 104
20 Deliverables for 2020 2, 13, 13n1, 245, 254–259, **255,** 282
Twitter Revolution 63
two-track approach 200
Tymoshenko, Y. 60

Uçarer, E. 102
Ukraine 4, 5, 28–29, 31, 59–60, 67, 77–79, 82, 85, 106, 108, 131–142, 143n4, 185, 246, 250–254, 270, 272, 274n2; crisis 28, 31, 77–79, 82, 84, 88, 89, 91, 105, 106, 109, 191, 252; EaP scholarship *312;* EU and 11, 78, 131, 134, 142, 293; EU Association Agreement 88–90; fatigue 268; Orange Revolution 67, 183; Russia and 131, 133, 142, 185, 190
uncertainty 10, 11, 52, 58, 64, 116, 122, 124, 184, 190, 191, 193, 241, 242, 265
unilateral 12, 19, 23, 25–27, 29, 30, 185, 189, 194n9, 206, 217, 218, 220, 223, 229, 231
unintended consequences 10, 100–101, 103–104, 109, 110n6, 252, 265, 273; EaP countries 108–109; EU and 101–102; internal and external 105–106; managing 102–103, 106–108; non-decision 104
Union Treaty 194n2, 198
Union/Union for the Mediterranean (UfM) 6, 19, 22, 32n5
"Us" 116
Usatii, R. 152, 155, 156

Vachudova, M. 132, 133
values-driven approach 207
vicious circle 148, 156–158
Vihma, A. 82
Vilnius Summit 121, 149, 188, 212n23, 219, 224, 282
Vindigni, A. 157

Visa Facilitation Agreement 170, 186
Visa Liberalisation Action Plan 164, 170–172, 175
Visa Liberalisation Dialogue 170, 171
Visa Liberalization Action Plan (VLAP) 148–150
Vogler, J. 167
Vondra, A. 86
Voronin, V. 155
VOSviewer software 292, 293

Waever, O. 81
Wagner, P. 136, 143n4
Waltz, K. 101
Weber, M. 114
Weldes, J. 80
Western Balkans 133, 140, 186, 251, 308

Wigell, M. 82
Wirminghaus, N. 52n3
Wolfers, A. 102
wordscores procedure 283
World Bank 53n12, 54n27, 60, 61, 150
world politics 19–23, 25, 29–31, 32n1, 32n2, 32n6
World Trade Organization (WTO) 26, 41, 48, 209, 228, 307

Yakunin, V. 153
Yanukovych, V. 28, 31, 60, 67, 70, 77, 92, 131, 135, 137, 205
Yatsenyuk, A. 138

zero-sum approach 77, 105, 108, 189–192
Zhuravlev, A. 154
Žižek, S. 114